# Joe Celko's SQL for Smarties

Fourth Edition

**The Morgan Kaufmann Series in Data Management Systems** (Selected Titles)

*Joe Celko's Data, Measurements and Standards in SQL*
Joe Celko

*Information Modeling and Relational Databases, 2nd Edition*
Terry Halpin, Tony Morgan

*Joe Celko's Thinking in Sets*
Joe Celko

*Business Metadata*
Bill Inmon, Bonnie O'Neil, Lowell Fryman

*Unleashing Web 2.0*
Gottfried Vossen, Stephan Hagemann

*Enterprise Knowledge Management*
David Loshin

*Business Process Change, 2nd Edition*
Paul Harmon

*IT Manager's Handbook, 2nd Edition*
Bill Holtsnider & Brian Jaffe

*Joe Celko's Puzzles and Answers, 2nd Edition*
Joe Celko

*Making Shoes for the Cobbler's Children*
Charles Betz

*Joe Celko's Analytics and OLAP in SQL*
Joe Celko

*Data Preparation for Data Mining Using SAS*
Mamdouh Refaat

*Querying XML: XQuery, XPath, and SQL/XML in Context*
Jim Melton and Stephen Buxton

*Data Mining: Concepts and Techniques, 2nd Edition*
Jiawei Han and Micheline Kamber

*Database Modeling and Design: Logical Design, 4th Edition*
Toby J, Teorey, Sam S. Lightstone, Thomas P. Nadeau

*Foundations of Multidimensional and Metric Data Structures*
Hanan Samet

*Joe Celko's SQL for Smarties: Advanced SQL Programming, 4th Edition*
Joe Celko

*Moving Objects Databases*
Ralf Hartmut Güting and Markus Schneider

*Joe Celko's SQL Programming Style*
Joe Celko

*Data Mining, Second Edition: Concepts and Techniques*
Jiawei Han, Micheline Kamber, Jian pei

*Fuzzy Modeling and Genetic Algorithms for Data Mining and Exploration*
Earl Cox

*Data Modeling Essentials, 3rd Edition*
Graeme C. Simsion and Graham C. Witt

*Location-Based Services*
Jochen Schiller and Agnès Voisard

*Managing Time in Relational Databases: How to Design, Update and Query Temporal Data*
Tom Johnston and Randall Weis

*Database Modeling with Microsoft® Visio for Enterprise Architects*
Terry Halpin, Ken Evans, Patrick Hallock, Bill Maclean

*Designing Data-Intensive Web Applications*
Stephano Ceri, Piero Fraternali, Aldo Bongio, Marco Brambilla, Sara Comai, Maristella Matera

*Mining the Web: Discovering Knowledge from Hypertext Data*
Soumen Chakrabarti

*Advanced SQL: 1999—Understanding Object-Relational and Other Advanced Features*
Jim Melton

*Database Tuning: Principles, Experiments, and Troubleshooting Techniques*
Dennis Shasha, Philippe Bonnet

*SQL:1999—Understanding Relational Language Components*
Jim Melton, Alan R. Simon

*Information Visualization in Data Mining and Knowledge Discovery*
Edited by Usama Fayyad, Georges G. Grinstein, Andreas Wierse

*Transactional Information Systems*
Gerhard Weikum and Gottfried Vossen

*Spatial Databases*
Philippe Rigaux, Michel Scholl, and Agnes Voisard

*Managing Reference Data in Enterprise Database*
Malcolm Chisholm

*Understanding SQL and Java Together*
Jim Melton and Andrew Eisenberg

*Database: Principles, Programming, and Performance, 2nd Edition*
Patrick and Elizabeth O'Neil

*The Object Data Standar*
Edited by R. G. G. Cattell, Douglas Barry

*Data on the Web: From Relations to Semistructured Data and XML*
Serge Abiteboul, Peter Buneman, Dan Suciu

*Data Mining, Third Edition Practical Machine Learning Tools and Techniques with Java Implementations*
Ian Witten, Eibe Frank

*Joe Celko's Data and Databases: Concepts in Practice*
Joe Celko

*Developing Time-Oriented Database Applications in SQL*
Richard T. Snodgrass

*Web Farming for the Data Warehouse*
Richard D. Hackathorn

*Management of Heterogeneous and Autonomous Database Systems*
Edited by Ahmed Elmagarmid, Marek Rusinkiewicz, Amit Sheth

*Object-Relational DBMSs: 2nd Edition*
Michael Stonebraker and Paul Brown, with
Dorothy Moore

*Universal Database Management: A Guide to Object/Relational Technology*
Cynthia Maro Saracco

*Readings in Database Systems, 3rd Edition*
Edited by Michael Stonebraker, Joseph M. Hellerstein

*Understanding SQL's Stored Procedures: A Complete Guide to SQL/PSM*
Jim Melton

*Principles of Multimedia Database Systems*
V. S. Subrahmanian

*Principles of Database Query Processing for Advanced Applications*
Clement T. Yu, Weiyi Meng

*Advanced Database Systems*
Carlo Zaniolo, Stefano Ceri, Christos Faloutsos, Richard T. Snodgrass, V. S. Subrahmanian, Roberto Zicari

*Principles of Transaction Processing, 2nd Edition*
Philip A. Bernstein, Eric Newcomer

*Using the New DB2: IBMs Object-Relational Database System*
Don Chamberlin

*Distributed Algorithms*
Nancy A. Lynch

*Active Database Systems: Triggers and Rules For Advanced Database Processing*
Edited by Jennifer Widom, Stefano Ceri

*Migrating Legacy Systems: Gateways, Interfaces, & the Incremental Approach*
Michael L. Brodie, Michael Stonebraker

*Atomic Transactions*
Nancy Lynch, Michael Merritt, William Weihl, Alan Fekete

*Query Processing for Advanced Database Systems*
Edited by Johann Christoph Freytag, David Maier, Gottfried Vossen

*Transaction Processing*
Jim Gray, Andreas Reuter

*Database Transaction Models for Advanced Applications*
Edited by Ahmed K. Elmagarmid

*A Guide to Developing Client/Server SQL Applications*
Setrag Khoshafian, Arvola Chan, Anna Wong, Harry K. T. Wong

# Joe Celko's SQL for Smarties

## Advanced SQL Programming

Fourth Edition

Joe Celko

AMSTERDAM • BOSTON • HEIDELBERG • LONDON
NEW YORK • OXFORD • PARIS • SAN DIEGO
SAN FRANCISCO • SINGAPORE • SYDNEY • TOKYO
Morgan Kaufmann is an imprint of Elsevier

**Acquiring Editor:** Rick Adams
**Development Editor:** David Bevans
**Project Manager:** Sarah Binns
**Designer:** Joanne Blank

*Morgan Kaufmann* is an imprint of Elsevier
30 Corporate Drive, Suite 400, Burlington, MA 01803, USA



**Library of Congress Cataloging-in-Publication Data**
Application submitted.

**British Library Cataloguing-in-Publication Data**
A catalogue record for this book is available from the British Library.

ISBN: 978-0-12-382022-8

Transferred to Digital Printing in 2012

*Typeset by*: diacriTech, Chennai, India

For information on all MK publications visit our website at *www.mkp.com*.

To Ann and Jackers

# CONTENTS

# About the Author

Joe Celko served 10 years on ANSI/ISO SQL Standards Committee and contributed to the SQL-89 and SQL-92 Standards.

He has written over 900 columns in the computer trade and academic press, mostly dealing with data and databases, and has authored seven other books on SQL for Morgan Kaufmann:

- *SQL for Smarties* (1995, 1999, 2005, 2010)
- *SQL Puzzles and Answers* (1997, 2006)
- *Data and Databases* (1999)
- *Trees and Hierarchies in SQL* (2004)
- *SQL Programming Style* (2005)
- *Analytics and OLAP in SQL* (2005)
- *Thinking in Sets* (2008)

Mr. Celko's past columns include:

- Columns for Simple Talk (Redgate Software)
- "CELKO," *Intelligent Enterprise* magazine (CMP)
- BMC's DBAzine.com e-magazine (BMC Software)
- "SQL Explorer," *DBMS* (Miller Freeman)
- "Celko on SQL," *Database Programming and Design* (Miller Freeman)
- "WATCOM SQL Corner," *Powerbuilder Developers' Journal* (SysCon)
- "SQL Puzzle," *Boxes and Arrows* (Frank Sweet Publishing)
- "DBMS/Report," *Systems Integration* (Cahner Ziff) "Data Desk," *Tech Specialist* (R&D)
- "Data Points," *PC Techniques* (Coriolis Group)
- "Celko on Software," *Computing* (VNC Publications, UK)
- "SELECT * FROM Austin" (Array Publications, The Netherlands)

In addition, Mr. Celko was editor for the "Puzzles & Problems" section of ABACUS (SpringerVerlag) and he ran the CASEFORUM section 18, "Celko on SQL," on CompuServe.

# INTRODUCTION TO THE FOURTH EDITION

This book, like the first, second, and third editions before it, is for the working SQL programmer who wants to pick up some advanced programming tips and techniques. It assumes that the reader is an SQL programmer with a year or more of actual experience. This is not an introductory book, so let's not have any gripes in the amazon.com reviews about that like we did with the prior editions.

The first edition was published 10 years ago, and became a minor classic among working SQL programmers. I have seen copies of this book on the desks of real programmers in real programming shops almost everywhere I have been. The true compliment are the Post-it® notes sticking out of the top. People really use it often enough to put stickies in it! Wow!

## What Changed in Ten Years

Hierarchical and network databases still run vital legacy systems in major corporations. SQL people do not like to admit that IMS and traditional files are still out there in the Fortune 500. But SQL people can be proud of the gains SQL-based systems have made over the decades. We have all the new applications and all the important smaller databases.

OO programming is firmly in place, but may give ground to functional programming in the next decade. Object and object-relational databases found niche markets, but never caught on with the mainstream.

XML is no longer a fad in 2010. Technically, it is syntax for describing and moving data from one platform to another, but its support tools allow searching and reformatting. There is an SQL/XML subcommittee in INCITS H2 (the current name of the original ANSI X3H2 Database Standards Committee) making sure they can work together.

Data warehousing is no longer an exotic luxury only for major corporations. Thanks to the declining prices of hardware and software, medium-sized companies now use the technology. Writing OLAP queries is different from OLTP queries and probably needs its own "Smarties" book now.

Open Source databases are doing quite well and are gaining more and more Standards conformance. The LAMP platform (Linux, Apache, MySQL, and Python/PHP) has most of the web sites. Ingres, Postgres, Firebird, and other products have the ANSI SQL-92 features, most of the SQL-99, and some of the SQL:2003 features.

Columnar databases, parallelism, and Optimistic Concurrency are all showing up in commercial product instead of the laboratory. The SQL Standards have changed over time, but not always for the better. Parts of it have become more relational and set-oriented while other parts put in things that clearly are procedural, deal with nonrelational data, and are based on file system models. To quote David McGoveran, "A committee never met a feature it did not like." And he seems to be quite right.

But with all the turmoil the ANSI/ISO Standard SQL-92 was the common subset that will port across SQL products to do useful work. In fact, years ago, the US government described the SQL-99 standard as "a standard in progress" and required SQL-92 conformance for federal contracts.

We had the FIPS-127 conformance test suite in place during the development of SQL-92, so all the vendors could move in the same direction. Unfortunately, the Clinton administration canceled the program and conformance began to drift. Michael M. Gorman, President of Whitemarsh Information Systems Corporation and secretary of INCITS H2 for over 20 years, has a great essay on this and other political aspects of SQL's history at Wiscorp.com that is worth reading.

Today, the SQL-99 standard is the one to use for portable code on the greatest number of platforms. But vendors are adding SQL:2003 features so rapidly, I do not feel that I have to stick to a minimal standard.

## New in This Edition

In the second edition, I dropped some of the theory from the book and moved it to *Data and Databases* (ISBN 13:978-1558604322). I find no reason to add it back into this edition.

I have moved and greatly expanded techniques for trees and hierarchies into their own book (*Trees and Hierarchies in SQL*, ISBN 13:978-1558609204) because there was enough material to justify it. There is a short mention of some techniques here, but not to the detailed level in the other book.

I put programming tips for newbies into their own book (*SQL Programming Style*, ISBN 13:978-0120887972) because this book is an advanced programmer's book and I assume that the reader is now writing real SQL, not some dialect or his or her native programming language in a thin disguise. I also assume that the reader can translate Standard SQL into his or her local dialect without much effort.

I have tried to provide comments with the solutions, to explain why they work. I hope this will help the reader see underlying principles that can be used in other situations.

A lot of people have contributed material, either directly or via Newsgroups and I cannot thank all of them. But I made a real effort to put names in the text next to the code. In case I missed anyone, I got material or ideas from Aaron Bertrand, Alejandro Mesa, Anith Sen, Craig Mullins (who has done the tech reads on several editions), Daniel A. Morgan, David Portas, David Cressey, Dawn M. Wolthuis, Don Burleson, Erland Sommarskog, Itzak Ben-Gan, John Gilson, Knut Stolze, Ken Henderson, Louis Davidson, Dan Guzman, Hugo Kornelis, Richard Romley, Serge Rielau, Steve Kass, Tom Moreau, Troels Arvin, Vadim Tropashko, Plamen Ratchev, Gert-Jan Strik, and probably a dozen others I am forgetting.

## Corrections and Additions

Please send any corrections, additions, suggestions, improvements, or alternative solutions to me or to the publisher. Especially if you have a better way of doing something.

www.mkp.com

# 1

# DATABASES VERSUS FILE SYSTEMS

*It ain't so much the things we don't know that get us in trouble. It's the things we know that ain't so.*

**Artemus Ward (William Graham Sumner), American Writer and Humorist, 1834–1867**

Databases and RDBMS in particular are nothing like the file systems that came with COBOL, FORTRAN, C, BASIC, PL/I, Java, or any of the procedural and OO programming languages. We used to say that SQL means "Scarcely Qualifies as a Language" because it has no I/O of its own. SQL depends on a host language to get and receive data to and from end users.

Programming languages are usually based on some underlying model; if you understand the model, the language makes much more sense. For example, FORTRAN is based on algebra. This does not mean that FORTRAN is exactly like algebra. But if you know algebra, FORTRAN does not look all that strange to you. You can write an expression in an assignment statement or make a good guess as to the names of library functions you have never seen before.

Programmers are used to working with files in almost every other programming language. The design of files was derived from paper forms; they are very physical and very dependent on the host programming language. A COBOL file could not easily be read by a FORTRAN program and vice versa. In fact, it was hard to share files among programs written in the same programming language!

The most primitive form of a file is a sequence of records that are ordered within the file and referenced by physical position. You open a file then read a first record, followed by a series of next records until you come to the last record to raise

Joe Celko's SQL for Smarties. DOI: 10.1016/B978-0-12-382022-8.00001-6

the end-of-file condition. You navigate among these records and perform actions one record at a time. The actions you take on one file have no effect on other files that are not in the same program. Only programs can change files.

The model for SQL is data kept in sets, not in physical files. The "unit of work" in SQL is the whole schema, not individual tables.

Sets are those mathematical abstractions you studied in school. Sets are not ordered and the members of a set are all of the same type. When you do an operation on a set, the action happens "all at once" to the entire membership. That is, if I ask for the subset of odd numbers from the set of positive integers, I get all of them back as a single set. I do not build the set of odd numbers by sequentially inspecting one element at a time. I define odd numbers with a rule—"If the remainder is 1 when you divide the number by 2, it is odd"—that could test any integer and classify it. Parallel processing is one of many, many advantages of having a set-oriented model.

SQL is not a perfect set language any more than FORTRAN is a perfect algebraic language, as we will see. But when in doubt about something in SQL, ask yourself how you would specify it in terms of sets and you will probably get the right answer.

SQL is much like Gaul—it is divided into three parts, which are three sublanguages:

- DDL: Data Declaration Language
- DML: Data Manipulation Language
- DCL: Data Control Language

The Data Declaration Language (DDL) is what defines the database content and maintains the integrity of that data. Data in files have no integrity constraints, default values, or relationships; if one program scrabbles the data, then the next program is screwed. Talk to an older programmer about reading a COBOL file with a FORTRAN program and getting output instead of errors.

The more effort and care you put into the DDL, the better your RDBMS will work. The DDL works with the DML and the DCL; SQL is an integrated whole and not a bunch of disconnected parts.

The Data Manipulation Language (DML) is where most of my readers will earn a living doing queries, inserts, updates, and deletes. If you have normalized data and build a good schema, then your job is much easier and the results are good. Procedural code will compile the same way every time. SQL does not work that way. Each time a query or other statement is processed, the execution plan can change based on the current state of the database. As quoted by Plato in *Cratylus*, "Everything flows, nothing stands still."

The Data Control Language (DCL) is *not* a data security language, it is an *access control* language. It does not encrypt the data; encryption is not in the SQL Standards, but vendors have such options. It is not generally stressed in most SQL books and I am not going to do much with it.

DCL deserves a small book unto itself. It is the neglected third leg on a three-legged stool. Maybe I will write such a book some day.

Now let's look at fundamental concepts. If you already have a background in data processing with traditional file systems, the first things to unlearn are:

1. Database schemas are not file sets. Files do not have relationships among themselves; everything is done in applications. SQL does not mention anything about the physical storage in the Standard, but files are based on physically contiguous storage. This started with punch cards, was mimicked in magnetic tapes, and then on early disk drives. I made this item first on my list because this is where all the problems start.
2. Tables are not files; they are parts of a schema. The schema is the unit of work. I cannot have tables with the same name in the same schema. A file system assigns a name to a file when it is mounted on a physical drive; a table has a name in the database. A file has a physical existence, but a table can be virtual (VIEW, CTE, query result, etc.).
3. Rows are not records. Records get meaning from the application reading them. Records are sequential, so first, last, next, and prior make sense; rows have no physical ordering (ORDER BY is a clause in a CURSOR). Records have physical locators, such as pointers and record numbers. Rows have relational keys, which are based on uniqueness of a subset of attributes in a data model. The mechanism is not specified and it varies quite a bit from SQL to SQL.
4. Columns are not fields. Fields get meaning from the application reading them, and they may have several meanings depending on the applications. Fields are sequential within a record and do not have data types, constraints, or defaults. This is active versus passive data! Columns are also NULL-able, a concept that does not exist in fields. Fields have to have physical existence, but columns can be computed or virtual. If you want to have a computed column value, you can have it in the application, not the file.

Another conceptual difference is that a file is usually data that deals with a whole business process. A file has to have enough data in itself to support applications for that one business process.

Files tend to be "mixed" data, which can be described by the name of the business process, such as "The Payroll file" or something like that. Tables can be either entities or relationships within a business process. This means that the data held in one file is often put into several tables. Tables tend to be "pure" data that can be described by single words. The payroll would now have separate tables for timecards, employees, projects, and so forth.

## 1.1 Tables as Entities

An entity is a physical or conceptual "thing" that has meaning by itself. A person, a sale, or a product would be an example. In a relational database, an entity is defined by its attributes. Each occurrence of an entity is a single row in the table. Each attribute is a column in the row. The value of the attribute is a scalar.

To remind users that tables are sets of entities, I like to use collective or plural nouns that describe the function of the entities within the system for the names of tables. Thus, "Employee" is a bad name because it is singular; "Employees" is a better name because it is plural; "Personnel" is best because it is collective and does not summon up a mental picture of individual persons. This also follows the ISO 11179 Standards for metadata. I cover this in detail in my book, *SQL Programming Style* (ISBN 978-0120887972).

If you have tables with exactly the same structure, then they are sets of the same kind of elements. But you should have only one set for each kind of data element! Files, on the other hand, were *physically* separate units of storage that could be alike—each tape or disk file represents a step in the PROCEDURE, such as moving from raw data, to edited data, and finally to archived data. In SQL, this should be a status flag in a table.

## 1.2 Tables as Relationships

A relationship is shown in a table by columns that reference one or more entity tables.

Without the entities, the relationship has no meaning, but the relationship can have attributes of its own. For example, a show business contract might have an agent, an employer, and a talent. The method of payment is an attribute of the contract itself, and not of any of the three parties. This means that a column can have REFERENCES to other tables. Files and fields do not do that.

## 1.3 Rows versus Records

Rows are not records. A record is defined in the application program that reads it; a row is defined in the database schema and not by a program at all. The name of the field is in the READ or INPUT statements of the application; a row is named in the database schema. Likewise, the PHYSICAL order of the field names in the READ statement is vital (READ a, b, c is not the same as READ c, a, b; but SELECT a, b, c is the same data as SELECT c, a, b).

All empty files look alike; they are a directory entry in the operating system with a name and a length of zero bytes of storage. Empty tables still have columns, constraints, security privileges, and other structures, even though they have no rows.

This is in keeping with the set theoretical model, in which the empty set is a perfectly good set. The difference between SQL's set model and standard mathematical set theory is that set theory has only one empty set, but in SQL each table has a different structure, so they cannot be used in places where nonempty versions of themselves could not be used.

Another characteristic of rows in a table is that they are all alike in structure and they are all the "same kind of thing" in the model. In a file system, records can vary in size, data types, and structure by having flags in the data stream that tell the program reading the data how to interpret it. The most common examples are Pascal's variant record, C's struct syntax, and COBOL's OCCURS clause.

The OCCURS keyword in COBOL and the VARIANT records in Pascal have a number that tells the program how many times a subrecord structure is to be repeated in the current record.

Unions in C are not variant records, but variant mappings for the same physical memory. For example:

```
union x {int ival; char j[4];} mystuff;
```

defines mystuff to be either an integer (which is 4 bytes on most C compilers, but this code is nonportable) or an array of 4 bytes, depending on whether you say `mystuff.ival` or `mystuff.j[0];`.

But even more than that, files often contained records that were summaries of subsets of the other records—so-called control break reports. There is no requirement that the records in a file be related in any way—they are literally a stream of binary data whose meaning is assigned by the program reading them.

## 1.4 Columns versus Fields

A field within a record is defined by the application program that reads it. A column in a row in a table is defined by the database schema. The data types in a column are always scalar.

The order of the application program variables in the READ or INPUT statements is important because the values are read into the program variables in that order. In SQL, columns are referenced only by their names. Yes, there are shorthands like the SELECT * clause and INSERT INTO <table name> statements, which expand into a list of column names in the physical order in which the column names appear within their table declaration, but these are shorthands that resolve to named lists.

The use of NULLs in SQL is also unique to the language. Fields do not support a missing data marker as part of the field, record, or file itself. Nor do fields have constraints that can be added to them in the record, like the DEFAULT and CHECK() clauses in SQL.

Files are pretty passive creatures and will take whatever an application program throws at them without much objection. Files are also independent of each other simply because they are connected to one application program at a time and therefore have no idea what other files look like.

A database actively seeks to maintain the correctness of all its data. The methods used are triggers, constraints, and declarative referential integrity.

Declarative referential integrity (DRI) says, in effect, that data in one table has a particular relationship with data in a second (possibly the same) table. It is also possible to have the database change itself via referential actions associated with the DRI. For example, a business rule might be that we do not sell products that are not in inventory.

This rule would be enforced by a REFERENCES clause on the Orders table that references the Inventory table, and a referential action of ON DELETE CASCADE. Triggers are a more general way of doing much the same thing as DRI. A trigger is a block of procedural code that is executed before, after, or instead of an INSERT INTO or UPDATE statement. You can do anything with a trigger that you can do with DRI and more.

However, there are problems with TRIGGERs. Although there is a standard syntax for them since the SQL-92 standard, most vendors have not implemented it. What they have is very proprietary syntax instead. Second, a trigger cannot pass information to the optimizer like DRI. In the example in this section, I know that for every product number in the Orders table, I have that same product number in the Inventory table. The optimizer can use that information in setting up EXISTS() predicates and JOINs in the queries. There is no reasonable way to parse procedural trigger code to determine this relationship.

The CREATE ASSERTION statement in SQL-92 will allow the database to enforce conditions on the entire database as a whole. An ASSERTION is not like a CHECK() clause, but the difference is subtle. A CHECK() clause is executed when there are rows in the table to which it is attached.

If the table is empty then all CHECK() clauses are effectively TRUE. Thus, if we wanted to be sure that the Inventory table is never empty, and we wrote:

```
CREATE TABLE Inventory
( ...
CONSTRAINT inventory_not_empty
      CHECK ((SELECT COUNT(*) FROM Inventory) > 0),
... );
```

but it would not work. However, we could write:

```
CREATE ASSERTION Inventory_not_empty
      CHECK ((SELECT COUNT(*) FROM Inventory) > 0);
```

and we would get the desired results. The assertion is checked at the schema level and not at the table level.

## 1.5 Schema Objects

A database is not just a bunch of tables, even though that is where most of the work is done. There are stored procedures, user-defined functions, and cursors that the users create. Then there are indexes and other access methods that the user cannot access directly.

This chapter is a very quick overview of some of the schema objects that a user can create. Standard SQL divides the database users into USER and ADMIN roles. These objects require ADMIN privileges to be created, altered, or dropped. Those with USER privileges can invoke them and access the results.

## 1.6 CREATE SCHEMA Statement

The CREATE SCHEMA statement defined in the standards brings an entire schema into existence all at once. In practice, each product has very different utility programs to allocate physical storage and define a schema. Much of the proprietary syntax is concerned with physical storage allocations.

A schema must have a name and a default character set. Years ago, the default character set would have been ASCII or a local alphabet (8 bits) as defined in the ISO standards. Today, you are more likely to see Unicode (16 bits). There is an optional AUTHORIZATION clause that holds a <schema authorization identifier> for security. After that the schema is a list of schema elements:

```
<schema element> ::=
  <domain definition> | <table definition> | <view definition>
| <grant statement> | <assertion definition>
| <character set definition>
| <collation definition> | <translation definition>
```

A schema is the skeleton of an SQL database; it defines the structures of the schema objects and the rules under which they operate. The data is the meat on that skeleton.

The only data structure in SQL is the table. Tables can be persistent (base tables), used for working storage (temporary tables), or virtual (VIEWs, common table expressions and derived tables). The differences among these types are in implementation, not performance. One advantage of having only one data structure is that the results of all operations are also tables—you never have to convert structures, write special operators, or deal with any irregularity in the language.

The `<grant statement>` has to do with limiting access by users to only certain schema elements. The `<assertion definition>` is still not widely implemented yet, but it is like constraint that applies to the schema as a whole. Finally, the `<character set definition>`, `<collation definition>`, and `<translation definition>` deal with the display of data. We are not really concerned with any of these schema objects; they are usually set in place by the database administrator (DBA) for the users and we mere programmers do not get to change them.

Conceptually, a table is a set of zero or more rows, and a row is a set of one or more columns. This hierarchy is important; actions apply at the schema, table, row, or column level. For example the DELETE FROM statement removes rows, not columns, and leaves the base table in the schema. You cannot delete a column from a row.

Each column has a specific data type and constraints that make up an implementation of an abstract domain. The way a table is physically implemented does not matter, because you access it only with SQL. The database engine handles all the details for you and you never worry about the internals as you would with a physical file. In fact, almost no two SQL products use the same internal structures.

There are two common conceptual errors made by programmers who are accustomed to file systems or PCs. The first is thinking that a table is a file; the second is thinking that a table is a spreadsheet. Tables do not behave like either one of these, and you will get surprises if you do not understand the basic concepts.

It is easy to imagine that a table is a file, a row is a record, and a column is a field. This is familiar and when data moves from SQL to the host language, it has to be converted into host language data types and data structures to be displayed and used. The host languages have file systems built into them.

The big differences between working with a file system and working with SQL are in the way SQL fits into a host program. Using a file system, your programs must open and close files individually. In SQL, the *whole* schema is connected to or disconnected from the program as a single unit. The host program might not be authorized to see or manipulate all the tables and other schema objects, but that is established as part of the connection.

The program defines fields within a file, whereas SQL defines its columns in the schema. FORTRAN uses the FORMAT and READ statements to get data from a file. Likewise, a COBOL program uses a Data Division to define the fields and a READ to fetch it. And so on for every 3GL's programming; the concept is the same, though the syntax and options vary.

A file system lets you reference the same data by a different name in each program. If a file's layout changes, you must rewrite all the programs that use that file. When a file is empty, it looks exactly like all other empty files. When you try to read an empty file, the EOF (end of file) flag pops up and the program takes some action. Column names and data types in a table are defined within the database schema. Within reasonable limits, the tables can be changed without the knowledge of the host program.

The host program only worries about transferring the values to its own variables from the database. Remember the empty set from your high school math class? It is still a valid set. When a table is empty, it still has columns, but has zero rows. There is no EOF flag to signal an exception, because there is no final record.

Another major difference is that tables and columns can have constraints attached to them. A constraint is a rule that defines what must be true about the database after each transaction. In this sense, a database is more like a collection of objects than a traditional passive file system.

A table is not a spreadsheet, even though they look very much alike when you view them on a screen or in a printout. In a spreadsheet you can access a row, a column, a cell, or a collection of cells by navigating with a cursor. A table has no concept of navigation. Cells in a spreadsheet can store instructions and not just data. There is no real difference between a row and column in a spreadsheet; you could flip them around completely and still get valid results. This is not true for an SQL table.

The only underlying commonality is that a spreadsheet is also a declarative programming language. It just happens to be a nonlinear language.

# 2

# TRANSACTIONS AND CONCURRENCY CONTROL

In the old days when we lived in caves and used mainframe computers with batch file systems, transaction processing was easy. You batched up the transactions to be made against the master file into a transaction file. The transaction file was sorted, edited, and ready to go when you ran it against the master file from a tape drive. The output of this process became the new master file and the old master file and the transaction files were logged to magnetic tape in a huge closet in the basement of the company.

When disk drives, multiuser systems, and databases came along, things got complex and SQL made it more so. But mercifully the user does not have to see the details. Well, here is the first layer of the details.

## 2.1 Sessions

The concept of a user session involves the user first connecting to the database. This is like dialing a phone number, but with a password, to get to the database. The Standard SQL syntax for this statement is:

```
CONNECT TO <connection target>

<connection target> ::=
 <SQL-server name>
  [AS <connection name>]
  [USER <user name>]
| DEFAULT
```

However, you will find many differences in vendor SQL products and perhaps operating system level log on procedures that have to be followed.

Once the connection is established, the user has access to all the parts of the database to which he or she has been granted privileges. During this session, the user can execute zero or more

Joe Celko's SQL for Smarties. DOI: 10.1016/B978-0-12-382022-8.00002-8

transactions. As one user inserts, updates, and deletes rows in the database, these changes are not made a permanent part of the database until that user issues a COMMIT WORK command for that transaction.

However, if the user does not want to make the changes permanent, then he or she can issue a ROLLBACK WORK command and the database stays as it was before the transaction.

## 2.2 Transactions and ACID

There is a handy mnemonic for the four characteristics we want in a transaction: the ACID properties. The initials represent four properties we must have in a transaction processing system:

- Atomicity
- Consistency
- Isolation
- Durability

### 2.2.1 Atomicity

Atomicity means that the whole transaction becomes persistent in the database or nothing in the transaction becomes persistent. The data becomes persistent in Standard SQL when a COMMIT statement is successfully executed. A ROLLBACK statement removes the transaction and restores the database to its prior (consistent) state before the transaction began.

The COMMIT or ROLLBACK statement can be explicitly executed by the user or by the database engine when it finds an error. Most SQL engines default to a ROLLBACK unless they are configured to do otherwise.

Atomicity means that if I were to try to insert one million rows into a table and one row of that million violated a referential constraint, then the whole set of one million rows would be rejected and the database would do an automatic ROLLBACK WORK.

Here is the trade-off. If you do one long transaction, then you are in danger of being screwed by just one tiny little error. However, if you do several short transactions in a session, other users can have access to the database between your transactions and they might change things, much to your surprise.

The SQL:2006 Standards have SAVEPOINTs with a chaining option. A SAVEPOINT is like a "bookmarker" in the transaction session. A transaction sets savepoints during its execution and lets the transaction perform a local rollback to the checkpoint. In our example, we might have been doing savepoints every 1000 rows. When the 999,999-th row inserted has an error that would have caused a ROLLBACK, the database engine removes only the work done after the last savepoint was set, and the transaction is restored to the state of uncommitted work (i.e., rows 1–999,000) that existed before the savepoint.

The syntax looks like this:

```
<savepoint statement> ::= SAVEPOINT <savepoint specifer>
<savepoint specifier> ::= <savepoint name>
```

There is an implementation-defined maximum number of savepoints per SQL transaction, and they can be nested inside each other. The level at which you are working is found with:

```
<savepoint level indication> ::=
NEW SAVEPOINT LEVEL | OLD SAVEPOINT LEVEL
```

You can get rid of a savepoint with:

```
<release savepoint statement> ::= RELEASE SAVEPOINT
   <savepoint specifier>
```

The commit statement persists the work done at this level, or all the work in the chain of savepoints.

```
<commit statement> ::= COMMIT [WORK] [AND [NO] CHAIN]
```

Likewise, you can rollback the work for the entire session, up the current chain or back to a specific savepoint.

```
<rollback statement> ::= ROLLBACK [WORK] [AND [NO] CHAIN]
   [<savepoint clause>]
<savepoint clause> ::= TO SAVEPOINT <savepoint specifier>
```

This is all I am going to say about this. You will need to look at your particular product to see if it has something like this. The usual alternatives are to break the work into chunks that are run as transaction with a hot program or to use an ETL tool that scrubs the data completely before loading it into the database.

## 2.2.2 Consistency

When the transaction starts, the database is in a consistent state and when it becomes persistent in the database, the database is in a consistent state. The phrase "consistent state" means that all of the data integrity constraints, relational integrity constraints, and any other constraints are true.

However, this does not mean that the database might go through an inconsistent state during the transaction. Standard SQL has the ability to declare a constraint to be DEFERRABLE or NOT DEFERRABLE for finer control of a transaction. But the rule is that all constraints have to be true at the end of session. This can be tricky when the transaction has multiple statements or fires triggers that affect other tables.

### 2.2.3 Isolation

One transaction is isolated from all other transactions. Isolation is also called serializability because it means that transactions act as if they were executed in isolation from each other. One way to guarantee isolation is to use serial execution like we had in batch systems. In practice, this might not be a good idea, so the system has to decide how to interleave the transactions to get the same effect.

This actually becomes more complicated in practice because one transaction may or may not actually see the data inserted, updated, or deleted by another transaction. This will be dealt with in detail in the section on isolation levels.

### 2.2.4 Durability

The database is stored on a durable media, so that if the database program is destroyed, the database itself persists. Furthermore, the database can be restored to a consistent state when the database system is restored. Log files and back-up procedure figure into this property, as well as disk writes done during processing.

This is all well and good if you have just one user accessing the database at a time. But one of the reasons you have a database system is that you also have multiple users who want to access it at the same time in their own sessions. This leads us to concurrency control.

## 2.3 Concurrency Control

Concurrency control is the part of transaction handling that deals with how multiple users access the shared database without running into each other—sort of like a traffic light system. One way to avoid any problems is to allow only one user in the database at a time. The only problem with that solution is that the other users are going to get slow response time. Can you seriously imagine doing that with a bank teller machine system or an airline reservation system where tens of thousands of users are waiting to get into the system at the same time?

### 2.3.1 The Three Phenomena

If all you do is execute queries against the database, then the ACID properties hold. The trouble occurs when two or more transactions want to change the database at the same time. In the SQL model, there are three ways that one transaction can affect another.

- P0 (Dirty Write): Transaction T1 modifies a data item. Another transaction T2 then further modifies that data item before T1 performs a COMMIT or ROLLBACK. If T1 or T2 then performs a ROLLBACK, it is unclear what the correct data value should be. One reason why Dirty Writes are bad is that they can violate database consistency. Assume there is a constraint between x and y (e.g., x = y), and T1 and T2 each maintain the consistency of the constraint if run alone. However, the constraint can easily be violated if the two transactions write x and y in different orders, which can only happen if there are Dirty Writes.
- P1 (Dirty read): Transaction T1 modifies a row. Transaction T2 then reads that row before T1 performs a COMMIT WORK. If T1 then performs a ROLLBACK WORK, T2 will have read a row that was never committed, and so may be considered to have never existed.
- P2 (Nonrepeatable read): Transaction T1 reads a row. Transaction T2 then modifies or deletes that row and performs a COMMIT WORK. If T1 then attempts to reread the row, it may receive the modified value or discover that the row has been deleted.
- P3 (Phantom): Transaction T1 reads the set of rows N that satisfy some `<search condition>`. Transaction T2 then executes statements that generate one or more rows that satisfy the `<search condition>` used by transaction T1. If transaction T1 then repeats the initial read with the same `<search condition>`, it obtains a different collection of rows.
- P4 (Lost Update): The lost update anomaly occurs when transaction T1 reads a data item and then T2 updates the data item (possibly based on a previous read), then T1 (based on its earlier read value) updates the data item and COMMITs.

These phenomena are not always bad things. If the database is being used only for queries, without any changes being made during the workday, then none of these problems will occur. The database system will run much faster if you do not have to try to protect yourself from them. They are also acceptable when changes are being made under certain circumstances.

Imagine that I have a table of all the cars in the world. I want to execute a query to find the average age of drivers of red sport cars. This query will take some time to run and during that time, cars will be crashed, bought and sold, new cars will be built, and so forth. But I can accept a situation with the three phenomena because the average age will not change that much from the time I start the query to the time it finishes. Changes after the second decimal place really don't matter.

However, you don't want any of these phenomena to occur in a database where the husband makes a deposit to a joint account and his wife makes a withdrawal. This leads us to the transaction isolation levels.

The original ANSI model included only P1, P2, and P3. The other definitions first appeared in Microsoft Research Technical Report: MSR-TR-95-51, "A Critique of ANSI SQL Isolation Levels," by Hal Berenson, Phil Bernstein, Jim Gray, Jim Melton, Elizabeth O'Neil, and Patrick O'Neil (1995).

## 2.3.2 The Isolation Levels

In standard SQL, the user gets to set the isolation level of the transactions in his session. The isolation level avoids some of the phenomena we just talked about and gives other information to the database. The syntax for the `<set transaction statement>` is:

```
SET TRANSACTION < transaction mode list>

<transaction mode> ::=
  <isolation level>
| <transaction access mode>
| <diagnostics size>

<diagnostics size> ::= DIAGNOSTICS SIZE <number of conditions

<transaction access mode> ::= READ ONLY | READ WRITE

<isolation level> ::= ISOLATION LEVEL <level of isolation>

<level of isolation> ::=
  READ UNCOMMITTED
| READ COMMITTED
| REPEATABLE READ
| SERIALIZABLE
```

The optional `<diagnostics size>` clause tells the database to set up a list for error messages of a given size. This is a Standard SQL feature, so you might not have it in your particular product. The reason is that a single statement can have several errors in it and the engine is supposed to find them all and report them in the diagnostics area via a GET DIAGNOSTICS statement in the host program.

The `<transaction access mode>` explains itself. The READ ONLY option means that this is a query and lets the SQL engine know that it can relax a bit. The READ WRITE option lets the SQL engine know that rows might be changed, and that it has to watch out for the three phenomena.

The important clause, which is implemented in most current SQL products, is the `<isolation level>` clause. The isolation level of a transaction defines the degree to which the operations of one transaction are affected by concurrent transactions. The isolation level of a transaction is SERIALIZABLE by default, but the user can explicitly set it in the `<set transaction statement>`.

The isolation levels each guarantee that each transaction will be executed completely or not at all, and that no updates will be lost. The SQL engine, when it detects the inability to guarantee the serializability of two or more concurrent transactions or when it detects unrecoverable errors, may initiate a ROLLBACK WORK statement on its own.

Let's take a look at a table of the isolation levels and the three phenomena (Table 2.1). A Yes means that the phenomena are possible under that isolation level.

The SERIALIZABLE isolation level is guaranteed to produce the same results, as the concurrent transactions would have had if they had been done in some serial order. A serial execution is one in which each transaction executes to completion before the next transaction begins. The users act as if they are standing in a line waiting to get complete access to the database.

A REPEATABLE READ isolation level is guaranteed to maintain the same image of the database to the user during his session.

A READ COMMITTED isolation level will let transactions in this session see rows that other transactions commit while this session is running.

A READ UNCOMMITTED isolation level will let transactions in this session see rows that other transactions create without necessarily committing while this session is running.

Regardless of the isolation level of the transaction, phenomena P1, P2, and P3 shall not occur during the implied reading of schema definitions performed on behalf of executing a statement, the checking of integrity constraints, and the execution of referential actions associated with referential constraints. We do not want the schema itself changing on users.

**Table 2.1 Isolation Levels and the Three Phenomena**

| Isolation Level | P1 | P2 | P3 |
|---|---|---|---|
| SERIALIZABLE | No | No | No |
| REPEATABLE READ | No | No | Yes |
| READ COMMITTED | No | Yes | Yes |
| READ UNCOMMITTED | Yes | Yes | Yes |

### *CURSOR STABILITY Isolation Level*

The CURSOR STABILITY isolation level extends READ COMMITTED locking behavior for SQL cursors by adding a new read action for FETCH from a cursor and requiring that a lock be held on the current item of the cursor. The lock is held until the cursor moves or is closed, possibly by a commit. Naturally, the fetching transaction can update the row, and in that case a write lock will be held on the row until the transaction COMMITs, even after the cursor moves on with a subsequent FETCH. This makes CURSOR STABILITY stronger than READ COMMITTED and weaker than REPEATABLE READ.

CURSOR STABILITY is widely implemented by SQL systems to prevent lost updates for rows read via a cursor. READ COMMITTED, in some systems, is actually the stronger CURSOR STABILITY. The ANSI standard allows this.

The SQL standards do not say *how* you are to achieve these results. However, there are two basic classes of concurrency control methods—optimistic and pessimistic. Within those two classes, each vendor will have its own implementation.

## 2.4 Pessimistic Concurrency Control

Pessimistic concurrency control is based on the idea that transactions are expected to conflict with each other, so we need to design a system to avoid the problems before they start.

All pessimistic concurrency control schemes use locks. A lock is a flag placed in the database that gives exclusive access to a schema object to one user. Imagine an airplane toilet door, with its "occupied" sign.

But again, you will find different kinds of locking schemes. For example, DB2 for z/OS has "latches" that are a little different from traditional locks. The important differences are the level of locking they use; setting those flags on and off costs time and resources. If you lock the whole database, then you have a serial batch processing system, since only one transaction at a time is active. In practice you would do this only for system maintenance work on the whole database. If you lock at the table level, then performance can suffer because users must wait for the most common tables to become available. However, there are transactions that do involve the whole table, and this will use only one flag.

If you lock the table at the row level, then other users can get to the rest of the table and you will have the best possible shared access. You will also have a huge number of flags to process and performance will suffer. This approach is generally not practical.

Page locking is in between table and row locking. This approach puts a lock on subsets of rows within the table, which include the desired values. The name comes from the fact that this is usually implemented with pages of physical disk storage. Performance depends on the statistical distribution of data in physical storage, but it is generally a good compromise.

## 2.5 SNAPSHOT Isolation and Optimistic Concurrency

Optimistic concurrency control is based on the idea that transactions are not very likely to conflict with each other, so we need to design a system to handle the problems as exceptions after they actually occur.

In Snapshot Isolation, each transaction reads data from a snapshot of the (committed) data as of the time the transaction started, called its Start_timestamp or "t-zero." This time may be any time before the transaction's first read. A transaction running in Snapshot Isolation is never blocked attempting a read because it is working on its private copy of the data. But this means that at any time, each data item might have multiple versions, created by active and committed transactions.

When the transaction T1 is ready to commit, it gets a Commit-Timestamp, which is later than any existing `start_timestamp` or `commit_timestamp`. The transaction successfully COMMITs only if no other transaction T2 with a `commit_timestamp` in T1's execution interval `[start_timestamp, commit_timestamp]` wrote data that T1 also wrote. Otherwise, T1 will ROLLBACK. This "first committer wins" strategy prevents lost updates (phenomenon P4). When T1 COMMITs, its changes become visible to all transactions whose `start_timestamps` are larger than T1's `commit-timestamp`.

Snapshot isolation is nonserializable because a transaction's reads come at one instant and the writes at another. We assume we have several transactions working on the same data and a constraint that (x + y) should be positive. Each transaction that writes a new value for x and y is expected to maintain the constraint. Although T1 and T2 both act properly in isolation, the constraint fails to hold when you put them together. The possible problems are:

- A5 (Data Item Constraint Violation): Suppose constraint C is a database constraint between two data items x and y in the database. Here are two anomalies arising from constraint violation.
- A5A Read Skew: Suppose transaction T1 reads x, and then a second transaction 2 updates x and y to new values and

COMMITs. If now T1 reads y, it may see an inconsistent state, and therefore produce an inconsistent state as output.

- A5B Write Skew: Suppose T1 reads x and y, which are consistent with constraint C, and then a T2 reads x and y, writes x, and COMMITs. Then T1 writes y. If there were a constraint between x and y, it might be violated.

Fuzzy Reads (P2) is a degenerate form of Read Skew where x = y. More typically, a transaction reads two different but related items (e.g., referential integrity).

Write Skew (A5B) could arise from a constraint at a bank, where account balances are allowed to go negative as long as the sum of commonly held balances remains nonnegative, with an anomaly arising as in history H5.

Clearly neither A5A nor A5B could arise in histories where P2 is precluded, since both A5A and A5B have T2 write a data item that previously has been read by an uncommitted T1. Thus, phenomena A5A and A5B are useful only for distinguishing isolation levels below REPEATABLE READ in strength.

The ANSI SQL definition of REPEATABLE READ, in its strict interpretation, captures a degenerate form of row constraints, but misses the general concept. To be specific, Locking REPEATABLE READ of Table 2 provides protection from Row Constraint Violations, but the ANSI SQL definition of Table 1, forbidding anomalies A1 and A2, does not.

Returning now to Snapshot Isolation, it is surprisingly strong, even stronger than READ COMMITTED.

This approach predates databases by decades. It was implemented manually in the central records department of companies when they started storing data on microfilm. You do not get the microfilm, but instead they make a timestamped photocopy for you. You take the copy to your desk, mark it up, and return it to the central records department. The Central Records clerk timestamps your updated document, photographs it, and adds it to the end of the roll of microfilm.

But what if user number two also went to the central records department and got a timestamped photocopy of the same document? The Central Records clerk has to look at both timestamps and make a decision. If the first user attempts to put his updates into the database while the second user is still working on his copy, then the clerk has to either hold the first copy or wait for the second copy to show up or to return it to the first user. When both copies are in hand, the clerk stacks the copies on top of each other, holds them up to the light, and looks to see if there are any conflicts. If both updates can be made to the database, he or she does so. If there are conflicts, the clerk must either have rules for resolving the problems or he or she has to reject both transactions. This is a kind of row level locking, done after the fact.

## 2.6 Logical Concurrency Control

Logical concurrency control is based on the idea that the machine can analyze the predicates in the queue of waiting queries and processes on a purely logical level and then determine which of the statements can be allowed to operate on the database at the same time.

Clearly, all SELECT statements can operate at the same time since they do not change the data. After that, it is tricky to determine which statements conflict with the others. For example, one pair of UPDATE statements on two separate tables might be allowed only in a certain order because of PRIMARY KEY and FOREIGN KEY constraints. Another pair of UPDATE statements on the same tables might be disallowed because they modify the same rows and leave different final states in them.

However, a third pair of UPDATE statements on the same tables might be allowed because they modify different rows and have no conflicts with each other.

There is also the problem of having statements waiting in the queue to be executed too long. This is a version of livelock, which we discuss in the next section. The usual solution is to assign a priority number to each waiting transaction and then decrement that priority number when they have been waiting for a certain length of time. Eventually, every transaction will arrive at priority one and be able to go ahead of any other transaction.

This approach also allows you to enter transactions at a higher priority than the transactions in the queue. Although it is possible to create a livelock this way, it is not a problem and it lets you bump less important jobs in favor of more important jobs, such as printing payroll checks versus playing Solitaire.

## 2.7 Deadlock and Livelocks

It is possible for a user to fail to complete a transaction for reasons other than the hardware failing. A deadlock is a situation where two or more users hold resources that the others need and neither party will surrender the objects to which they have locks. To make this more concrete, imagine user A and user B need Tables X and Y. User A gets a lock on Table X, and User B gets a lock on Table Y. They both sit and wait for their missing resource to become available; it never happens. The common solution for a deadlock is for the database administrator (DBA) to kill one or more of the sessions involved and rollback his or her work.

A livelock involves a user who is waiting for a resource, but never gets it because other users keep grabbing it before he or she gets a chance. None of the other users hold onto the resource permanently as in a deadlock, but as a group they never free it. To make this more concrete, imagine user A needs all of Table X. But Table X is always being updated by a hundred other users, so that user A cannot find a page without a lock on it. The user sits and waits for all the pages to become available; it never happens in time.

The database administrator can again kill one or more of the sessions involved and rollback his or her work. In some systems, the DBA can raise the priority of the livelocked session so that it can seize the resources as they become available.

None of this is trivial, and each database system will have its own version of transaction processing and concurrency control. This should not be of great concern to the applications programmer, but should be the responsibility of the database administrator. But it is nice to know what happens under the covers.

# 3

# SCHEMA LEVEL OBJECTS

A database is not just a bunch of tables, even though that is where most of the work is done. There are stored procedures, user-defined functions, and cursors that the users create. Then there are indexes and other access methods that the user cannot access directly.

This chapter is a very quick overview of some of the schema objects that a user can create. Standard SQL divides the database users into USER and ADMIN roles. These objects require ADMIN privileges to be created, altered, or dropped. Those with USER privileges can invoke them and access the results.

## 3.1 CREATE SCHEMA Statement

There is a CREATE SCHEMA statement defined in the standards that brings an entire schema into existence all at once. In practice, each product has very different utility programs to allocate physical storage and define a schema. Much of the proprietary syntax is concerned with physical storage allocations.

A schema must have a name and a default character set, usually ASCII or a simple Latin alphabet as defined in the ISO Standards. There is an optional AUTHORIZATION clause that holds a `<schema authorization identifier>` for access control. After that the schema is a list of schema elements:

```
<schema element> ::=
  <domain definition> | <table definition> | <view definition>
| <grant statement> | <assertion definition>
| <character set definition>
| <collation definition> | <translation definition>
```

A schema is the skeleton of an SQL database; it defines the structures of the schema objects and the rules under which they operate. The data is the meat on that skeleton.

The only data structure in SQL is the table. Tables can be persistent (base tables), used for working storage (temporary tables), virtual (VIEWs, common table expressions, and derived

Joe Celko's SQL for Smarties. DOI: 10.1016/B978-0-12-382022-8.00003-X

tables), or materialized as needed. The differences among these types are in implementation, not performance. One advantage of having only one data structure is that the results of all operations are also tables—you never have to convert structures, write special operators, or deal with any irregularity in the language.

The `<grant statement>` has to do with limiting access by users to only certain schema elements. The `<assertion definition>` is still not widely implemented yet, but it is like a constraint that applies to the schema as a whole. Finally, the `<character set definition>`, `<collation definition>`, and `<translation definition>` deal with the display of data. We are not really concerned with any of these schema objects; they are usually set in place by the DBA (database administrator) for the users and we mere programmers do not get to change them.

### 3.1.1 CREATE TABLE and CREATE VIEW Statements

Since tables and views are the basic unit of work in SQL, they have their own chapters.

## 3.2 CREATE PROCEDURE, CREATE FUNCTION, and CREATE TRIGGER

Procedural construct statements put modules of procedural code written in SQL/PSM or other languages into the database. They can be invoked as needed. These constructs get their own chapters.

## 3.3 CREATE DOMAIN Statement

The DOMAIN is a schema element in Standard SQL that allows you to declare an in-line macro that will allow you to put a commonly used column definition in one place in the schema. The syntax is:

```
<domain definition> ::=
CREATE DOMAIN <domain name> [AS] <data type>
   [<default clause>]
   [<domain constraint>...]
   [<collate clause>]

<domain constraint> ::=
 [<constraint name definition>]
 <check constraint definition> [<constraint attributes>]

<alter domain statement> ::=
 ALTER DOMAIN <domain name> <alter domain action>

<alter domain action> ::=
   <set domain default clause>
```

```
| <drop domain default clause>
| <add domain constraint definition>
| <drop domain constraint definition>
```

It is important to note that a DOMAIN has to be defined with a basic data type and not with other DOMAINs. Once declared, a DOMAIN can be used in place of a data type declaration on a column.

The CHECK() clause is where you can put the code for validating data items with check digits, ranges, lists, and other conditions. Here is a skeleton for US State codes:

```
CREATE DOMAIN StateCode AS CHAR(2)
DEFAULT '??'
CONSTRAINT valid_state_code
CHECK (VALUE IN ('AL', 'AK', 'AZ', ...));
```

Since the DOMAIN is in one place, you do not have to worry about getting the correct data everywhere you define a column from this domain. If you did not have a DOMAIN clause, then you have to replicate the CHECK() clause in multiple tables in the database. The ALTER DOMAIN and DROP DOMAIN statements explain themselves.

## 3.4 CREATE SEQUENCE

Sequences are generators that produce a sequence of values each time they are invoked. You call on them like a function and get the next value in the sequence.

In my earlier books, I used the table "Sequence" for a set of integers from 1 to (n). Since it is now a reserved word, I have switched to "Series" in this book. The syntax looks like this:

```
CREATE SEQUENCE <seq name> AS <data type>
START WITH <value>
INCREMENT BY <value>
[MAXVALUE <value>]
[MINVALUE <value>]
[[NO] CYCLE];
```

To get a value from it, this expression is used wherever it is a legal data type.

```
NEXT VALUE FOR <seq name>
```

If a sequence needs to be reset, you use this statement to change the optional clauses or to restart the cycle.

```
ALTER SEQUENCE <seq name>
RESTART WITH <value>; -- begin over
```

To remove the sequence, use the obvious statement:

```
DROP SEQUENCE <seq name>;
```

Even when this feature becomes widely available, it should be avoided. It is a nonrelational extension that behaves like a sequential file or procedural function rather than in a set-oriented manner. You can currently find it in Oracle, DB2, Postgres, and Mimer products.

## 3.5 CREATE ASSERTION

In Standard SQL, the CREATE ASSERTION allows you to apply a constraint on the tables within a schema but not have the constraint attached to any particular table. The syntax is:

```
<assertion definition> ::=
 CREATE ASSERTION <constraint name> <assertion check>
 [<constraint attributes>]

<assertion check> ::=
 CHECK (<search condition>)
```

As you would expect, there is a DROP ASSERTION statement, but no ALTER ASSERTION statement. An assertion can do things that a CHECK() clause attached to a table cannot do, because it is outside of the tables involved. A CHECK() constraint is always TRUE if the table is empty.

For example, it is very hard to make a rule that the total number of employees in the company must be equal to the total number of employees in all the health plan tables.

```
CREATE ASSERTION Total_Health_Coverage
CHECK (SELECT COUNT(*) FROM Personnel) =
      + (SELECT COUNT(*) FROM HealthPlan_1)
      + (SELECT COUNT(*) FROM HealthPlan_2)
      + (SELECT COUNT(*) FROM HealthPlan_3);
```

Since the CREATE ASSERTION is global to the schema, table check constraint names are also global to the schema and not local to the table where they are declared.

### 3.5.1 Using VIEWs for Schema Level Constraints

Until you can get the CREATE ASSERTION, you have to use procedures and triggers to get the same effects. Consider a schema for a chain of stores that has three tables, thus:

```
CREATE TABLE Stores
(store_nbr INTEGER NOT NULL PRIMARY KEY,
```

```
store_name CHAR(35) NOT NULL,
..);

CREATE TABLE Personnel
(emp_id CHAR(9) NOT NULL PRIMARY KEY,
last_name CHAR(15) NOT NULL,
first_name CHAR(15) NOT NULL,
..);
```

The first two explain themselves. The third table shows the relationship between stores and personnel, namely who is assigned to what job at which store and when this happened. Thus:

```
CREATE TABLE JobAssignments
(store_nbr INTEGER NOT NULL
       REFERENCES Stores (store_nbr)
       ON UPDATE CASCADE
       ON DELETE CASCADE,
emp_id CHAR(9) NOT NULL PRIMARY KEY
       REFERENCES Personnel(emp_id)
       ON UPDATE CASCADE
       ON DELETE CASCADE,
start_date TIMESTAMP DEFAULT CURRENT_TIMESTAMP NOT NULL,
end_date TIMESTAMP,
CHECK (start_date <= end_date),
job_type INTEGER DEFAULT 0 NOT NULL -- unassigned = 0
 CHECK (job_type BETWEEN 0 AND 99),
PRIMARY KEY (store_nbr, emp_id, start_date));
```

Let's invent some job_type codes, such as `0 = 'unassigned'`, `1 = 'stockboy'`, and so on, until we get to `99 = 'Store Manager'`, and we have a rule that each store has at most one manager. In Standard SQL you could write a constraint like this:

```
CREATE ASSERTION ManagerVerification
CHECK (1 <= ALL (SELECT COUNT(*)
        FROM JobAssignments
       WHERE job_type = 99
       GROUP BY store_nbr));
```

This is actually a bit subtler than it looks. If you change the `<=` to `=`, then the stores must have exactly one manager if it has any employees at all.

But as we said, most SQL product still do not allow CHECK() constraints that apply to the table as a whole, nor do they support the scheme level CREATE ASSERTION statement.

So, how to do this? You might use a trigger, which will involve proprietary, procedural code. In spite of the SQL/PSM Standard, most vendors implement very different trigger models and use their proprietary 4GL language in the body of the trigger.

We need a set of TRIGGERs that validates the state of the table after each INSERT and UPDATE operation. If we DELETE an employee, this will not create more than one manager per store. The skeleton for these triggers would be something like this.

```
CREATE TRIGGER CheckManagers
AFTER UPDATE ON JobAssignments -- same for INSERT
IF 1 <= ALL (SELECT COUNT(*)
        FROM JobAssignments
       WHERE job_type = 99
       GROUP BY store_nbr)
THEN ROLLBACK;
ELSE COMMIT;
END IF;
```

But being a fanatic, I want a pure SQL solution that is declarative within the limits of most current SQL products.

Let's create two tables. This first table is a Personnel table for the store managers only and it is keyed on their employee identification numbers. Notice the use of DEFAULT and CHECK() on their job_type to assure that this is really a "managers only" table.

```
CREATE TABLE Job_99_Assignments
(store_nbr INTEGER NOT NULL PRIMARY KEY
       REFERENCES Stores (store_nbr)
       ON UPDATE CASCADE
       ON DELETE CASCADE,
emp_id CHAR(9) NOT NULL
       REFERENCES Personnel (emp_id)
       ON UPDATE CASCADE
       ON DELETE CASCADE,
start_date TIMESTAMP DEFAULT CURRENT_TIMESTAMP NOT NULL,
end_date TIMESTAMP,
CHECK (start_date <= end_date),
job_type INTEGER DEFAULT 99 NOT NULL
       CHECK (job_type = 99));
```

This second table is a Personnel table for employees who are not store manager and it is also keyed on employee identification numbers. Notice the use of DEFAULT for a starting position of unassigned and CHECK() on their job_type to assure that this is really a No managers allowed table.

```
CREATE TABLE Job_not99_Assignments
(store_nbr INTEGER NOT NULL
       REFERENCES Stores (store_nbr)
       ON UPDATE CASCADE
       ON DELETE CASCADE,
emp_id CHAR(9) NOT NULL PRIMARY KEY
       REFERENCES Personnel (emp_id)
```

```
        ON UPDATE CASCADE
        ON DELETE CASCADE,
start_date TIMESTAMP DEFAULT CURRENT_TIMESTAMP NOT NULL,
end_date TIMESTAMP,
CHECK (start_date <= end_date),
job_type INTEGER DEFAULT 0 NOT NULL
        CHECK (job_type BETWEEN 0 AND 98) -- no 99 code
);
```

From these two tables, build this UNION-ed view of all the job assignments in the entire company and show that to users.

```
CREATE VIEW JobAssignments (store_nbr, emp_id, start_date,
   end_date, job_type)
AS
(SELECT store_nbr, emp_id, start_date, end_date, job_type
  FROM Job_not99_Assignments
 UNION ALL
SELECT store_nbr, emp_id, start_date, end_date, job_type
  FROM Job_99_Assignments)
```

The key and job_type constraints in each table working together will guarantee at most one manager per store. The next step is to add INSTEAD OF triggers to the VIEW or write stored procedures, so that the users can insert, update, and delete from it easily. A simple stored procedure, without error handling or input validation, would be:

```
CREATE PROCEDURE InsertJobAssignments
(IN store_nbr INTEGER, IN new_emp_id CHAR(9), IN new_start_
   date DATE, IN new_end_date DATE, IN new_job_type INTEGER)
LANGUAGE SQL
IF new_job_type <> 99
THEN INSERT INTO Job_not99_Assignments
    VALUES (store_nbr, new_emp_id, new_start_date,
       new_end_date, new_job_type);
ELSE INSERT INTO Job_99_Assignments
    VALUES (store_nbr, new_emp_id, new_start_date,
       new_end_date, new_job_type);
END IF;
```

Likewise, a procedure to terminate an employee:

```
CREATE PROCEDURE FireEmployee (IN new_emp_id CHAR(9))
LANGUAGE SQL
IF new_job_type <> 99
THEN DELETE FROM Job_not99_Assignments
     WHERE emp_id = new_emp_id;
ELSE DELETE FROM Job_99_Assignments
     WHERE emp_id = new_emp_id;
END IF;
```

If a developer attempts to change the Job_Assignments VIEW directly with an INSERT, UPDATE, or DELETE, they will get an error message telling them that the VIEW is not updatable because it contains a UNION operation. That is a good thing in one way because we can force them to use only the stored procedures.

Again, this is an exercise in programming a solution within certain limits. The TRIGGER is probably going give better performance than the VIEW.

### 3.5.2 Using PRIMARY KEYs and ASSERTIONs for Constraints

Let's do another version of the "stores and personnel" problem given in a previous section.

```
CREATE TABLE JobAssignments
(emp_id CHAR(9) NOT NULL PRIMARY KEY -- nobody is in two Stores
  REFERENCES Personnel (emp_id)
  ON UPDATE CASCADE
  ON DELETE CASCADE,
store_nbr INTEGER NOT NULL
  REFERENCES Stores (store_nbr)
  ON UPDATE CASCADE
  ON DELETE CASCADE);
```

The key on the SSN will assure that nobody is at two stores and that a store can have many employees assigned to it. Ideally, you would want a constraint to check that each employee does have a branch assignment.

The first attempt is usually something like this:

```
CREATE ASSERTION Nobody_Unassigned
CHECK (NOT EXISTS
      (SELECT *
FROM Personnel AS P
     LEFT OUTER JOIN
     JobAssignments AS J
     ON P.emp_id = J.emp_id
       WHERE J.emp_id IS NULL
AND P.emp_id
    IN (SELECT emp_id FROM JobAssignments
UNION
SELECT emp_id FROM Personnel)));
```

However, that is overkill and does not prevent an employee from being at more than one store. There are probably indexes on the SSN values in both Personnel and JobAssignments, so getting a COUNT() function should be cheap. This assertion will also work.

```
CREATE ASSERTION Everyone_assigned_one_store
CHECK ((SELECT COUNT(emp_id) FROM JobAssignments)
      = (SELECT COUNT(emp_id) FROM Personnel));
```

This is a surprise to people at first because they expect to see a JOIN to do the one-to-one mapping between personnel and job assignments. But the PK-FK requirement provides that for you. Any unassigned employee will make the Personnel table bigger than the JobAssignments table, and an employee in JobAssignments must have a match in personnel. The good optimizers extract things like that as predicates and use them, which is why we want Declarative Referential Integrity (DRI) instead of triggers and application side logic.

You will need to have a stored procedure that inserts into both tables as a single transaction. The updates and deletes will cascade and clean up the job assignments.

Let's change the specs a bit and allow employees to work at more than one store. If we want to have an employee in multiple Stores, we could change the keys on JobAssignments, thus.

```
CREATE TABLE JobAssignments
(emp_id CHAR(9) NOT NULL
   REFERENCES Personnel (emp_id)
   ON UPDATE CASCADE
   ON DELETE CASCADE,
store_nbr INTEGER NOT NULL
   REFERENCES Stores (store_nbr)
   ON UPDATE CASCADE
   ON DELETE CASCADE,
PRIMARY KEY (emp_id, store_nbr));
```

Then use a `COUNT(DISTINCT ..)` in the assertion:

```
CREATE ASSERTION Everyone_assigned_at_least_once
CHECK ((SELECT COUNT(DISTINCT emp_id) FROM JobAssignments)
= (SELECT COUNT(emp_id) FROM Personnel));
```

You must be aware that the uniqueness constraints and assertions work together; a change in one or both of them can also change this rule.

## 3.6 Character Set Related Constructs

There are several schema level constructs for handling characters. You can create a named set of characters for various languages or special purposes, define one or more collation sequences for them, and translate one set into another.

Today, the Unicode Standards and vendor features are commonly used. Most of the characters actually used have Unicode names and collations defined already. For example, SQL text is written in Latin-1, as defined by ISO 8859-1. This is the set used for HTML, consisting of 191 characters from the Latin alphabet. This the most commonly used character set in the Americas, Western Europe, Oceania, Africa, and for standard romanizations of East-Asian languages.

Since 1991, the Unicode Consortium has been working with ISO and IEC to develop the Unicode Standard and ISO/IEC 10646: the Universal Character Set (UCS) in tandem. Unicode and ISO/IEC 10646 currently assign about 100,000 characters to a code space consisting of over a million code points, and they define several standard encodings that are capable of representing every available code point. The standard encodings of Unicode and the UCS use sequences of one to four 8-bit code values (UTF-8), sequences of one or two 16-bit code values (UTF-16), or one 32-bit code value (UTF-32 or UCS-4). There is also an older encoding that uses one 16-bit code value (UCS-2), capable of representing one-seventeenth of the available code points. Of these encoding forms, only UTF-8's byte sequences are in a fixed order; the others are subject to platform-dependent byte ordering issues that may be addressed via special codes or indicated via out-of-band means.

## 3.6.1 CREATE CHARACTER SET

You will not find this syntax in many SQLs. The vendors will default to a system level character set based on the local language settings.

```
<character set definition> ::=
CREATE CHARACTER SET <character set name> [AS]
<character set source> [<collate clause>]

<character set source> ::=
GET <character set specification>
```

The `<collate clause>` usually is defaulted also, but you can use named collations.

## 3.6.2 CREATE COLLATION

```
<collation definition> ::=
CREATE COLLATION <collation name>
  FOR <character set specification>
 FROM <existing collation name> [<pad characteristic>]

<pad characteristic> ::= NO PAD | PAD SPACE
```

The <pad characteristic> option has to do with how strings will be compared to each other. If the collation for the comparison has the NO PAD characteristic and the shorter value is equal to some prefix of the longer value, then the shorter value is considered less than the longer value. If the collation for the comparison has the PAD SPACE characteristic, for the purposes of the comparison, the shorter value is effectively extended to the length of the longer by concatenation of <space>s on the right. SQL normally pads a the shorter string with spaces on the end and then matches them, letter for letter, position by position.

## 3.6.3 CREATE TRANSLATION

This statement defines how one character set can be mapped into another character set. The important part is that it gives this mapping a name.

```
<transliteration definition> ::=
CREATE TRANSLATION <transliteration name>
  FOR <source character set specification>
  TO <target character set specification>
 FROM <transliteration source>

<source character set specification> ::=
<character set specification>

<target character set specification> ::=
<character set specification>

<transliteration source> ::=
<existing transliteration name> | <transliteration routine>

<existing transliteration name> ::= <transliteration name>

<transliteration routine> ::= <specific routine designator>
```

Notice that I can use a simple mapping, which will behave much like a bunch of nested REPLACE() function calls, or use a routine that can do some computations. The reason that having a name for these transliterations is that I can use them in the TRANSLATE() function instead of that bunch of nested REPLACE() function calls. The syntax is simple:

```
TRANSLATE (<character value expression> USING
   <transliteration name>)
```

DB2 and other implementations generalize TRANSLATE() to allow for target and replacement strings, so that you can do a lot of edit work in a single expression. We will get to that when we get to string functions.

4

# LOCATING DATA AND SPECIAL NUMBERS

SQL implementations come with proprietary features to help locate data in physical storage. Some of these features are taken from the hardware and some are independent of it. Sequential numbers, random numbers, and mathematical series with special properties are the most popular.

## 4.1 Exposed Physical Locators

SQL is supposed to use keys. Keys are a logical concept that is divorced completely from physical storage. Unfortunately, bad SQL programmers will use proprietary features to get the hardware to generate exposed physical locators. These numbers represent an event or location in the hardware and have nothing whatsoever to do with the logical model.

Do not confuse exposed physical locators with surrogate keys. In the words of Dr. Codd, "Database users may cause the system to generate or delete a surrogate, but they have no control over its value, *nor is its value ever displayed to them ...*" (ACM TODS, pp 409–410). Think of how an index works in most SQL implementations.

### 4.1.1 ROWID and Physical Disk Addresses

Oracle has the ability to expose the physical address of a row on the hard drive as a special variable called ROWID. This is the fastest way to locate a row in a table since the read-write head is positioned to the row immediately. This exposure of the underlying physical storage at the logical level means that Oracle is committed to using contiguous storage for the rows of a table. This means that they cannot use hashing, distributed databases, dynamic bit vectors, or any of several newer techniques for VLDB

Joe Celko's SQL for Smarties. DOI: 10.1016/B978-0-12-382022-8.00004-1

(very large databases). When the database is moved or reorganized for any reason, the ROWID is changed.

## 4.1.2 IDENTITY Columns

An IDENTITY column provides a way for the SQL engine to automatically generate a unique numeric value for each row that is added to the table. When creating a table where you know that you need to uniquely identify each row that will be added to the table, you can add an IDENTITY column to the table. To guarantee a unique numeric value for each row that is added to a table, you should define a unique index on the IDENTITY column or declare it a primary key. Once created, you cannot alter the table description to include an IDENTITY column.

If rows are inserted into a table with explicit IDENTITY column values specified, the next internally generated value is not updated, and may conflict with existing values in the table. Duplicate values will generate an error message if the uniqueness of the values in the IDENTITY column is being enforced by a PRIMARY KEY or a UNIQUE constraint. Here is the BNF:

```
<column name> INTEGER NOT NULL GENERATED [ALWAYS | BY DEFAULT]
     AS IDENTITY (START WITH <start value>, INCREMENT BY
        <increment value>))
```

The first row entered has the value of `<start value>` placed in the column; every subsequent row added to the table has the associated value increased by `<increment value>`. An IDENTITY column defined as GENERATED ALWAYS is given values that are always generated by the SQL engine. Applications are not allowed to provide an explicit value. An IDENTITY column defined as GENERATED BY DEFAULT gives applications a way to explicitly provide a value for the IDENTITY column. If the application does not provide a value, then the SQL engine will generate one. Since the application controls the value, the SQL engine cannot guarantee the uniqueness of the value. The GENERATED BY DEFAULT clause is meant for use for data propagation where the intent is to copy the contents of an existing table, or for the unload and reloading of a table.

Although there are similarities between IDENTITY columns and sequences, there are also differences. An IDENTITY column has the following characteristics:

1. An IDENTITY column can be defined as part of a table only when the table is created. Once a table is created, you cannot add an IDENTITY column. (However, existing IDENTITY column characteristics may be altered.)

2. A Sybase/Microsoft T-SOL column automatically generates values for a *single* table. When an IDENTITY column is defined as GENERATED ALWAYS, the values used are always generated by the database engine. Applications are not allowed to provide their own values during the modification of the contents of the table. An ANSI SEQUENCE is a free-standing object that can generate values for any use or table.

IDENTITY Columns are based on exposing part of the physical state of the machine during the insertion process, in violation of Dr. Codd's rules for defining a relational database (i.e., Codd's rule #8, Physical Data Independence). Error correction is almost impossible.

The early SQL products were built on existing file systems. The data was kept in physically contiguous disk pages, in physically contiguous rows, made up of physically contiguous columns—in short, just like a deck of punch cards or a magnetic tape. Most of these auto-increment features are an attempt to regain the physical sequence that SQL took out, so we can pretend that we have physically contiguous storage.

But physically contiguous storage is only one way of building a relational database and it is not always the best one. But aside from that, the whole idea of a relational database is that the user is not supposed to know how things are stored at all, much less write code that depends on the particular physical representation in a particular release of a particular product.

The exact method used varies from product to product. But the results of using them are all the same—their behavior is unpredictable and redundant. If you already have proper keys in the tables, these things are at best redundant. At one time, the argument was made that it was "cheaper" to join on simple integers than on longer columns, so let's use IDENTITY for a key. This is simply not true with modern RDBMS products. In fact, many hashing algorithms work better with longer compound keys that make it easier to create a perfect hashing.

Another major disadvantage of auto-incremented numbers as keys is that they have no check digits, so there is no way to determine if they are valid or not (for a discussion of check digits, see *Data & Databases*, Joe Celko, ISBN 978-1-55860-432-2).

So, why do people use them? System-generated values are a fast and easy answer to the problem of obtaining a primary key. It requires no research and no real data modeling. Drug abuse is also a fast and easy answer to problems; I do not recommend either.

The Sybase/SQL Server family allows you to declare an exact numeric pseudo-column with the table property IDENTITY.

This is a count of the attempted physical insertions to the table. Notice the word "attempted"; failures or ROLLBACK will leave a gap in the numbering. This is totally relational but it is often used by incompetent or new SQL programmers to make the tables look like a sequential tape file that is accessed by a record position number or to mimic a pointer in a nonrelational file system or network DBMS.

Let's look at the logical problems in detail. First try to create a table with two columns and try to make them both IDENTITY columns. If you cannot declare more than one column to be of a certain data type, then that thing is not a data type at all, by definition. The SQL Server/Sybase family makes its IDENTITY feature a table characteristic so you can have only one per table.

Next, create a table with one column and make it an IDENTITY column. Now try to insert, update, and delete different numbers from it. If you cannot insert, update, and delete rows from a table, then it is not a table by definition.

Finally create a simple table with one IDENTITY column and a few other columns. Use the statements:

```
BEGIN
INSERT INTO Foobar (a, b, c) VALUES ('a1', 'b1', 'c1');
INSERT INTO Foobar (a, b, c) VALUES ('a2', 'b2', 'c2');
INSERT INTO Foobar (a, b, c) VALUES ('a3', 'b3', 'c3');
END;
```

versus the logically equivalent statement:

```
INSERT INTO Foobar (a, b, c)
VALUES ('a1', 'b1', 'c1'), ('a2', 'b2', 'c2'), ('a3',
   'b3', 'c3');
```

or,

```
INSERT INTO Foobar (a, b, c)
SELECT x, y, z
 FROM Floob; -- assuming Floob has the three rows
```

to put a few rows into the table. Notice that the IDENTITY column sequentially numbered them in the order they were presented in the case of the first code block. If you delete a row, the gap in the sequence is not filled in and the sequence continues from the highest number that has ever been used in that column in that particular table.

The second and third statements are free to order the rows any way they wish. Since a query result is a table, and a table is a set that has no ordering, what should the IDENTITY numbers be? The entire, whole, completed set is presented to Foobar all at once, not a row at a time. There are (n!) ways to number (n) rows. Which one did you pick? The answer has been to use whatever the physical order of the result set happened to be. That nonrelational phrase, "physical order" again!

But it is actually worse than that. If the same query is executed again, but with new statistics or after an index has been dropped or added, the new execution plan could bring the result set back in a different physical order. Can you explain from a logical model why the same rows in the second query get different IDENTITY numbers? In the relational model, they should be treated the same if all the values of all the attributes are identical.

The following statement ought to leave the database the same. You are deleting and reinserting the same data in a single transaction.

```
BEGIN ATOMIC
DELETE FROM Foobar
WHERE identity_col = 41;
INSERT INTO Foobar VALUES (<<values of original row 41>>);
END;
```

But the IDENTITY will be changed. You can do the same sort of thing with an UPDATE that swaps the columns in two different rows since the IDENTITY cannot be changed by the DML statements.

Think about trying to do replication on two databases that differ only by an index or by cache size or something that occasionally gives them different execution plans for the same statements. Want to try to maintain or port such a system?

The CREATE SEQUENCE construct was discussed in Chapter 3. It came in with the SQL-2003 standard and it gets confused with IDENTITY. A sequence object has the following characteristics:

1. A SEQUENCE is a database object that is not tied to any one table.
2. A SEQUENCE generates sequential values that can be used in any SQL statement.

Since a sequence object can be used by any application, there are two expressions used to control the retrieval of the next value in the specified sequence and the value generated previous to the statement being executed. The PREVVAL expression returns the most recently generated value for the specified sequence for a previous statement within the current session. The NEXTVAL expression returns the next value for the specified sequence. The use of these expressions allows the same value to be used across several SQL statements within several tables.

Although these are not all the characteristics of these two items, these characteristics will assist you in determining which to use depending on your database design and the applications using the database.

## 4.2 Generated Identifiers

There are several schemes for generating identifiers, which are unique across any database. The two most popular ones are GUID (Global Unique Identifier) from Microsoft and UUID (Universal Unique Identifier) from the Open Source community.

### 4.2.1 GUIDs

Global Unique Identifiers are unique exposed physical locators generated by a combination of UTC time and the network address of the device creating it. Microsoft says that they should be unique for about a century. According to Wikipedia (http://en.wikipedia.org/wiki/GUID):

> *The algorithm used for generating new GUIDs has been widely criticized. At one point, the user's network card MAC address was used as a base for several GUID digits, which meant that, e.g., a document could be tracked back to the computer that created it. After this was discovered, Microsoft changed the algorithm so that it no longer contains the MAC address. This privacy hole was used when locating the creator of the Melissa worm.*

Besides the usual problems with exposed physical locators, each GUID requires 16 bytes of storage, whereas a simple INTEGER needs only 4 bytes on most machines.

Indexes and PRIMARY KEYs built on GUIDs may have worse performance than shorter key columns. Many newbies justify a GUID key on the grounds that it will improve performance. Besides being false, that level of performance is not a real problem in modern hardware. Hardware built on a 64-bit is becoming common, as are faster and faster disk drives.

The real problem is that GUIDs are difficult to interpret so it becomes difficult to work with them directly and trace them back to their source for validation. In fact, the GUID does not have any sorting sequence, so it is impossible to spot a missing value or use them to order results. All you can do is use a CHECK() with a regular expression for a string of 36 digits and the letters A through F separated by four dashes.

The GUID cannot participate in queries involving aggregate functions; first you would have to cast it as a CHAR(36) and use the string value. Your first thought might have been to make it into a longer INTEGER, but the two data types are not compatible. Other features of this data type are very proprietary and will not port out of a Microsoft environment.

## 4.2.2 UUIDs

The UUID is standardized by the Open Software Foundation (OSF) as part of the Distributed Computing Environment (DCE). The intent of UUIDs is to enable distributed systems to uniquely identify information without significant central coordination.

UUIDs are documented as part of ISO/IEC 11578:1996, "Information technology—Open Systems Interconnection—Remote Procedure Call (RPC)," and more recently in ITU-T Rec. X.667 | ISO/IEC 9834-8:2005. The IETF has published Proposed Standard RFC 4122 that is technically equivalent to ITU-T Rec. X.667 | ISO/IEC 9834-8.

There have been five versions of UUIDs; you can use a UUID to identify something with reasonable confidence that the identifier will never be unintentionally used by anyone for anything else. A UUID is a 16-byte (128-bit) number that consists of 32 hexadecimal digits, displayed in five groups separated by hyphens, in the form 8-4-4-4-12, for a total of 36 characters (32 digits and four hyphens).

The first version of the generation scheme for UUIDs was to use the MAC address of the generating computer, nanosecond clock ticks, and a bit of math. This scheme reveals both the identity of the computer that generated the UUID and the time at which it did so.

The second version UUIDs are similar to version one UUIDs, with local POSIX UID or POSIX GID domain going into the formula.

The third version UUIDs use a scheme deriving a UUID via MD5 from a URL, a fully qualified domain name, an object identifier, and other data elements. MD5 (Message-Digest algorithm 5) is a widely used cryptographic hash function with a 128-bit hash value that became an Internet standard (RFC 1321). Starting in 2004, researchers found more and more problems with MD5. Today, the U.S. Department of Homeland Security said MD5 "should be considered cryptographically broken and unsuitable for further use," and most U.S. government applications will be required to move to the SHA-2 family of hash functions by 2010. Version 3 UUIDs are hexadecimal strings of the form `xxxxxxxx-xxxx-3xxx-xxxx-xxxxxxxxxxxx`.

The fourth version UUIDs use a scheme relying only on random numbers. This algorithm sets the version number as well as two reserved bits. All other bits are set using a random or pseudo-random data source. Version 4 UUIDs have the form `xxxxxxxx-xxxx-4xxx-xxxx-xxxxxxxxxxxx`, with hexadecimal digits x and hexadecimal digits 8, 9, A, or B for y.

The fifth version UUIDs use a scheme with SHA-1 hashing; otherwise it is the same idea as in version 3. RFC 4122 states that version 5 is preferred over version 3 name-based UUIDs. Note that the 160-bit SHA-1 hash is truncated to 128 bits to make the length work out.

To give you an idea about the odds of a duplicate value, you would need to generate one billion UUIDs every second for the next 100 years to get the probability of creating one duplicate close to 50%. The warning here is that we are assuming that the mechanisms for UUID generation are "playing fair" and do not have errors.

## 4.3 Sequence Generator Functions

COUNTER(*), NUMBER(*), IDENTITY, and the like are proprietary features that return a new incremented value each time this function is used in an expression. This is a way to generate unique identifiers. This can be either a function call or a column property, depending on the product. This is also a horrible, nonstandard, nonrelational proprietary extension that should be avoided whenever possible.

We will spend some time later on ways to get sequences and unique numbers inside Standard SQL without proprietary code or using exposed physical locators in the hardware.

### 4.3.1 Unique Value Generators

The most important property of any usable unique value generator is that it will never generate the same value twice. Sequential integers are the first approach vendors implemented in their product as a substitute for a proper key.

In essence, they are a piece of code inside SQL that looks at the last allocated value and adds one to get the next value. Let's start from scratch and build our own version of such a procedure. First create a table called GeneratorValues with one row and two columns:

```
CREATE TABLE GeneratorValues
(lock CHAR(1) DEFAULT 'X' NOT NULL PRIMARY KEY -- only one row
   CHECK (lock = 'X'),
key_val INTEGER DEFAULT 1 NOT NULL -- positive numbers only
   CHECK (key_val > 0));
```

```
-- let everyone use the table
GRANT SELECT, UPDATE(key_val)
ON TABLE GeneratorValues
TO PUBLIC;
```

Now it needs a function to get out a value and do the increment.

```
CREATE FUNCTION Generator()
RETURNS INTEGER
LANGUAGE SQL
DETERMINISTIC
BEGIN
-- SET ISOLATION = SERIALIZABLE;
UPDATE GeneratorValues
 SET key_val = key_val + 1;
RETURN (SELECT key_val FROM GeneratorValues);
COMMIT;
END;
```

This looks pretty good, but if there are multiple users, this code fragment is capable of allocating duplicate values to different users. It is important to isolate the execution of the code to one and only one user at a time by using SET ISOLATION = SERIALIZABLE. Various SQL products will have slightly different ways of achieving this effect based on their concurrency control methods.

More bad news is that in pessimistic locking systems, you can get serious performance problems because of lock contention when a transaction is in serial isolation. The users are put in a single queue for access to the Generator table.

If the application demands gap-free numbering, then we not only have to guarantee that no two sessions ever get the same value, we must also guarantee that no value is ever wasted. Therefore, the lock on the Generator table must be held until the key value is actually used and the entire transaction is committed. Exactly how to handle this is implementation defined, so I am not going to comment on it.

## 4.4 Preallocated Values

In the old days of paper forms, organizations had a forms control officer whose job was to create, issue, and track the forms. A gap in the sequential numbers on a check, bond, stock certificate, or whatever was a serious accounting problem. Paper forms usually were preprinted and issued in blocks of numbers as needed. You can imitate this procedure in a database with a little thought and a few simple stored procedures.

Broadly speaking, there were two types of allocation blocks. In one, the sequence is known. The most common example would be a checkbook. Gaps in the sequence numbers are not allowed, and a destroyed or damaged check has to be explained with a "void" or other notation. The system needs to record which block went to which user, the date and time, and any other information relevant to the auditors.

```
CREATE TABLE FormsControl
(form_nbr CHAR(7) NOT NULL,
seq INTEGER NOT NULL CHECK(seq > 0),
PRIMARY KEY (form_nbr, seq),
recipient CHAR(25) DEFAULT CURRENT_USER NOT NULL,
issue_date TIMESTAMP DEFAULT CURRENT_TIMESTAMP NOT NULL,
..);
```

The tables that use the form numbers need to have constraints verify that the numbers were issued and appear in the Forms Control table. The next sequence number is easy to create, but you probably should restrict access to the base table with a stored procedure designed for one kind of form, along these lines.

```
CREATE FUNCTION NextFlobSeq()
RETURNS INTEGER
LANGUAGE SQL
DETERMINISTIC
BEGIN
INSERT INTO FormsControl (form_nbr, seq, ..
VALUES ('Flob-1/R',
   (SELECT MAX(seq)+1
FROM FormsControl
WHERE form_nbr = 'Flob-1/R'),
   ..);
```

You can also use views on the FormsControl table to limit user access. If you might be dealing with an empty set, then use this scalar expression:

```
(SELECT COALESCE(MAX(seq), 0)+1
  FROM FormsControl
 WHERE form_nbr = 'Flob-1/R'),
```

The COALESCE() will return a zero, thus assuring that the sequence starts with one.

## 4.5 Special Series

Numeric series have special properties that make them useful for identifiers, encryption, and so forth. In this section, we will look at a simple sequence, prime numbers, and random numbers.

## 4.5.1 Series Table

This is a common SQL programming idiom, but different writers will use different table names. In previous editions of this book, I used "Sequence" before it became a reserved word in Standard SQL; I am switching over to "Series" in this edition. You will also see "Numbers" and similar names.

```
CREATE TABLE Series
(seq INTEGER NOT NULL PRIMARY KEY
 CHECK (seq > 0));
```

There are lots of ways of filling this table, but here is one I like:

```
INSERT INTO Series(seq)
WITH Digits(i)
AS (SELECT i
   FROM (VALUES (1), (2), (3), (4), (5), (6), (7), (8),
    (9), (0)) AS X(i))
SELECT (D3.i * 1000 + D2.i * 100 + D1.i * 10 + D0.i + 1)
    AS seq
  FROM Digits AS D0, Digits AS D1, Digits AS D2, Digits AS D3;
```

This template is easy to extend and the `.. + 1` gets rid of the zero.

## 4.5.2 Prime Numbers

I was teaching SQL classes for YAPC-10 ("Yet Another PERL Conference" #10) at Carnegie Mellon University at the end of June 2009. For the record, I have never used PERL and had to Google an overview before I went; it is a very different creature from SQL. One of my students asked if you could write an SQL statement to generate the prime numbers less than 1000 (or any other limit) that scales well. He was bothered by the lack of loops in SQL, and a Prime Number sieve is a common PERL programming exercise. You can Google it and see an animation (http://www.hbmeyer.de/eratosiv.htm) and some PERL code at http://www.perlmonks.org/?node_id=276103.

There are two useful facts from Number Theory:

1. The prime factors of a given number (n) cannot be greater than ceiling ($\sqrt{n}$). Think about it; by definition ($\sqrt{n} * \sqrt{n}$)) = n, and by definition, ceiling ($\sqrt{n}$) >= floor ($\sqrt{n}$), so integer rounding up will be safe. This says that if I look at (a * b = c), where (a < b), then I don't have to look at (b * a = c), so I can start searching for prime factors with small values.
2. All primes are of the form (6 * n ± 1), but not all numbers of that form are primes. For example (n = 1) gives us {5, 7} and

they are both primes. But for (n = 4) we get {23, 25} where (25 = 5 * 5). What this does is remove the multiples of 2 and 3 from consideration.

Let's get all of that into SQL statements. Let's start with a table for the primes:

```
CREATE TABLE Primes
(p INTEGER NOT NULL PRIMARY KEY
 CHECK (p > 1));
```

Now, your puzzle is to fill the table up to some limit, say 1000, just to keep it simple. Let's assume we already have a table named Series with integers from 1 to (n) that we can use.

Method #1

For the first attempt, let's load the Primes table with candidate numbers using math fact #2 from above.

```
INSERT INTO Primes (p)
(SELECT (6 * seq) + 1
 FROM Series
WHERE (6 * seq) + 1 <= 1000
UNION ALL
SELECT (6 * seq) - 1
 FROM Series
WHERE (6 * seq) + 1 <= 1000);
```

An improvement that gets rid of the UNION ALL uses a table constant:

```
INSERT INTO Primes (p)
SELECT (6 * seq) + S.switch
 FROM Series
    CROSS JOIN
    (SELECT switch
     FROM (VALUES (-1), (+1)))
    AS S(switch)
 WHERE (6 * seq) + 1 <= 1000;
```

Now we have too many rows in Primes and need to remove the nonprimes. Now math fact #1 can come into play; test the set of numbers less than the square root to see if there is a factor among them.

```
DELETE FROM Primes
WHERE EXISTS
 (SELECT *
   FROM Primes AS P1
  WHERE P1.p <= CEILING (SQRT (Primes.p))
    AND MOD (Primes.p, P1.p) = 0);
```

Method #2

Another way to load the candidates into Primes is to have the first few known primes hardwired into a query. This is a generalization of the math fact #2, which dealt with multiples of only 2 and 3.

```
INSERT INTO Primes (p)
SELECT seq
 FROM Series
 WHERE 0 NOT IN (MOD(seq, 2), MOD(seq, 3), MOD(seq, 5),
   MOD(seq, 7), ..);
```

The idea is that if we can limit the candidate set for Primes, performance will improve. At the extreme, if the list of MOD (seq, <prime>) expressions goes to a value equal or higher than the upper limit we are looking at, we get the answer immediately.

This is a good trick; many SQL programmers think that an IN() list can only be constants. You might also want to look at how many values it can hold—it is larger than you think.

Method #3

Another candidate pruning trick is based on the math fact that integers with final digits {2, 4, 6, 8, 0} are even numbers; those with final digits {5, 0} are multiples of five. Let's not look at them when we build a candidate table.

```
INSERT INTO Primes (p)
SELECT *
FROM (WITH Digits(i)
        AS (SELECT i
   FROM (VALUES (1), (2), (3), (4), (5), (6), (7), (8),
      (9), (0)) AS X(i),
-- last digit CTE
Units(i)
AS (SELECT i
 FROM (VALUES (1), (3), (7), (9)) AS X(i)

SELECT (D3.i * 1000 + D2.i * 100 + D1.i * 10 + Units.i)
 FROM Units, Digits AS D1, Digits AS D2, Digits AS D3);
```

Method #4

Another approach is to generate all the nonprimes and remove them from the Series table.

```
INSERT INTO Primes (p)
SELECT *
FROM ((SELECT seq FROM Series WHERE seq <= 1000)
      EXCEPT
      (SELECT (F1.seq * F2.seq) AS composite_nbr
```

```
FROM Series AS F1, Series AS F2
WHERE F1.seq BETWEEN 2 AND CEILING (SQRT (1000))
  AND F2.seq BETWEEN 2 AND CEILING (SQRT (1000))
  AND F1.seq <= F2.seq
  AND (F1.seq * F2.seq) <= 1000);
```

Obviously, the Series table in the left-hand clause could be any one of the trimmed candidate tables we previously constructed.

There are faster but more complicated algorithms, like the Sieve of Atkin and the various Wheel Sieves.

### 4.5.3 Random Order Values

In many applications, we do not want to issue the sequence numbers in sequence. This pattern can give information that we do not wish to expose. Instead we want to issue generated values in random order. Do not get mixed up; we want known values that are supplied in random order and not random numbers. Most random number generators can repeat values, which would defeat the purpose of this drill.

Although I usually avoid mentioning physical implementations, one of the advantages of random-order keys is to improve the performance of tree indexes. Tree structured indexes, such as a B-Tree, that have sequential insertions become unbalanced and have to be reorganized frequently. However, if the same set of keys is presented in a random order, the tree tends to stay balanced and you get much better performance.

The generator shown here is an implementation of the additive congruential method of generating values in pseudo-random order, and is due to Roy Hann of Rational Commerce Limited, a CA-Ingres consulting firm. It is based on a shift-register and an XOR-gate, and it has its origins in cryptography. Although there are other ways to do this, this code is nice because:

1. The algorithm can be written in C or another low level language for speed. But math is fairly simple even in base 10.
2. The algorithm tends to generate successive values that are (usually) "far apart," which is handy for improving the performance of tree indexes. You will tend to put data on separate physical data pages in storage.
3. The algorithm does not cycle until it has generated every possible value, so we don't have to worry about duplicates. Just count how many calls have been made to the generator.
4. The algorithm produces uniformly distributed values, which is a nice mathematical property to have. It also does not include zero.

Let's walk through all the iterations of the 4-bit generator illustrated in Figure 4.1.

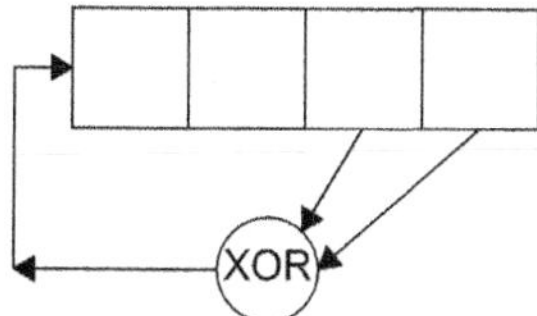


**Figure 4.1** Four Digit Additive Congruency Generator.

Initially the shift register contains the value 0001. The two rightmost bits are XOR-ed together, giving 1, the result is fed into the leftmost bit position, and the previous register contents shift one bit right. The iterations of the register are shown in this table, with their base-10 values:

```
iteration 1: 0001 (1)
iteration 2: 1000 (8)
iteration 3: 0100 (4)
iteration 4: 0010 (2)
iteration 5: 1001 (9)
iteration 6: 1100 (12)
iteration 7: 0110 (6)
iteration 8: 1011 (11)
iteration 9: 0101 (5)
iteration 10: 1010 (10)
iteration 11: 1101 (13)
iteration 12: 1110 (14)
iteration 13: 1111 (15)
iteration 14: 0111 (7)
iteration 15: 0011 (3)
iteration 16: 0001 (1) wrap-around!
```

It might not be obvious that successive values are far apart when we are looking at a tiny 4-bit register. But it is clear that the values are generated in no obvious order, all possible values except 0 are eventually produced, and the termination condition is clear—the generator cycles back to 1.

Generalizing the algorithm to arbitrary binary word sizes, and therefore longer number sequences, is not as easy as you might think. Finding the "tap" positions where bits are extracted for feedback varies according to the word-size in an extremely nonobvious way. Choosing incorrect tap positions results in an incomplete and usually very short cycle that is unusable. If you want the details and tap positions for words of one to 100 bits, see E. J. Watson, "Primitive Polynomials (Mod 2)," *Mathematics of Computation*, v.16, 1962, pp. 368–369.

The following table shows the tap positions 8-, 16-, 31-, 32-, and 64-bit words. That should work with any computer hardware you have. The 31-bit word is the one that is probably the most useful since it gives billions of numbers, uses only two tap positions to make the math easier, and matches most computer hardware. The 32-bit version is not easy to implement on a 32-bit machine because it will usually generate an overflow error.

| Word Length |
|---|
| 8 = {0, 2, 3, 4} |
| 16 = {0, 2, 3, 5} |
| 31 = {0, 3} |
| 32 = {0, 1, 2, 3, 5, 7} |
| 64 = {0, 1, 3, 4} |

Using the preceding table we can see that we need to tap bits 0 and 3 to construct the 31-bit random-order generated value Generator (which is the one most people would want to use in practice):

```
UPDATE Generator31
 SET key_val =
   key_val/2 + MOD(MOD(key_val, 2) + MOD(key_val/8, 2),
      2)*2^30;
```

Or, if you prefer the algorithm in C:

```
int Generator31 ()
{static int n = 1;
n = n >> 1 | ((n^n >> 3) & 1) << 30;
return n;
}
```

## 4.5.4 Other Series

Other series of numbers can be useful and I will take time on the Fibonacci numbers in Chapter 6 because they show up in many places and they are useful for encryption, check digits, and other things in computer science.

You will find that it is easier to download a table of values from the Internet these days than it is to compute them for yourself.

5

# BASE TABLES AND RELATED ELEMENTS

There was only one data structure in SQL; the table. Later standards and vendors added other structures, but they are almost never used and do not port. Tables have different flavors, but they all behave the same way. Conceptually, a table is a set of zero or more rows, and a row is a set of one or more columns. Each column has a specific data type and constraints that make up an implementation of an abstract domain for the values of the attribute modeled by the column. The way a table is physically implemented does not matter, because you access it only with SQL using a key. The database engine handles all the details for you and you never worry about the internals as you would with a physical file. In fact, almost no two SQL products use the same internal structures.

There are two common conceptual errors made by programmers who are accustomed to file systems. The first is thinking that a table is a file; the second is thinking that a table is a spreadsheet. Tables do not behave like either one of these, and you will get surprises if you do not understand the basic concepts.

It is easy to imagine that a table is a file, a row is a record, and a column is a field. This is familiar and when data moves from SQL to the host language, it has to be converted into host language data types and data structures to be displayed and used.

The big differences between working with a file system and working with SQL are in the way SQL fits into a host program. Using a file system, your programs must open and close files individually. In SQL, the whole schema is connected to or disconnected from the program as a single unit. The host program might not be authorized to see or manipulate all the tables and other schema objects, but that is established as part of the connection.

The program defines fields within a file, whereas SQL defines its columns in the schema. `FORTRAN` uses the `FORMAT` and `READ`

Joe Celko's SQL for Smarties. DOI: 10.1016/B978-0-12-382022-8.00005-3

statements to get data from a file. Likewise, a COBOL program uses a DATA DIVISION to define the fields and a READ to fetch it. And so on for every 3GL programming language, the concept is the same, though the syntax and options vary.

A file system lets you reference the same data by a different name in each program. If a file's layout changes, you must rewrite all the programs that use that file. When a file is empty, it looks exactly like all other empty files. When you try to read an empty file, the EOF (end of file) flag pops up and the program takes some action. Column names and data types in a table are defined within the database schema; they are not local to each program like field names. Within reasonable limits, the tables can be changed without the knowledge of the host program.

The host program only worries about transferring the values to its own variables from the database. Remember the empty set from your high school math class? It is still a valid set. When a table is empty, it still has columns and the constraints on it are TRUE, but it has zero rows. There is no EOF flag to signal an exception, because there is no final record.

A constraint is a rule that defines what must be TRUE or UNKNOWN about the database after each transaction. Again, all constraints on an empty table are TRUE. In this sense, a database is more like an active, self-policing collection of objects than a traditional passive file system.

A table is not a spreadsheet, even though they look very much alike when you view them on a screen or in a printout. In a spreadsheet you can access a row, a column, a cell, or a collection of cells by navigating with a cursor. A table has no concept of navigation. Cells in a spreadsheet can store instructions and not just data. There is no real difference between a row and column in a spreadsheet; you could flip them around completely and still get valid results. This is not TRUE for an SQL table.

Tables are made up of rows. The rows have no ordering and are identified by a key (one or more columns whose values are unique in each row). There is no such thing as the first, last, or next row.

Rows are made up of columns. The columns have no ordering and are identified by a name that is unique in each row. The apparent exception is in places in some statements where a default list of row names is created by the engine in the order of the declaration of the table's columns. This is just a nice shorthand.

Columns are made up of scalar values that must have a declared fixed data type. After that, the columns can have constraints, defaults, and other things that the SQL engine uses to assure that the data in them meets the business rules.

## 5.1 CREATE TABLE Statement

The CREATE TABLE statement does all the hard work. The more constraints and effort you put into this statement, the faster and easier your SQL will be. The basic syntax looks like this, but there are actually more options we will discuss later.

```
CREATE TABLE <table name> (<table element list>)

<table element list> ::=
 <table element> | <table element>, <table element list>

<table element> ::=
 <column definition> | <table constraint definition>
```

The table definition includes data in the column definitions and rules for handling that data in the table constraint definitions. This means that a table acts more like an object (with its data and methods) than just a simple, passive file.

### 5.1.1 Column Constraints

Beginning SQL programmers often fail to take full advantage of the options available to them, and they pay for it with errors or extra work in their applications. A column is not like a simple passive field in a file system. It has more than just a data type associated with it. Here is the basic BNF syntax for it.

```
<column definition> ::=
 <column name> <data type>
  [<default clause>]
  [<column constraint>. . .]
  [<constraint attributes>]

<column constraint> ::= NOT NULL
| <check constraint definition>
| <unique specification>
| <references specification>
[<constraint attributes>]
```

The first important thing to notice here is that each column must have a data type, which it keeps unless you ALTER the table. The SQL standard offers many data types, because SQL must work with many different host languages. The data types fall into three major categories: numeric, character, and temporal data types. We will discuss the data types and their rules of operation in other sections; they are fairly obvious, so not knowing the details will not stop you from reading the examples that follow.

Column constraints are rules that are attached to a column; row constraints are attached to multiple columns in the same row; table constraints apply to multiple rows, usually in the aggregate. All the rows in the table are validated against them. File systems have nothing like this, since validation is done in the application programs. They are also one of the most underused features of SQL, so you can look like a real wizard if you can master them.

Constraints can be given a name and some attributes. The constraint name will be used by the SQL engine to alter it and to display an error message.

```
<constraint name definition> ::= CONSTRAINT <constraint name>
<constraint attributes> ::=
<constraint check time> [[NOT] DEFERRABLE]
  |[NOT] DEFERRABLE [<constraint check time>]
<constraint check time> ::= INITIALLY DEFERRED | INITIALLY
   IMMEDIATE
```

A deferrable constraint can be "turned off" during a transaction. The initial state tells you whether to enforce it at the start of the transaction or wait until the end of the transaction before the COMMIT. Only certain combinations of these attributes make sense.

- If INITIALLY DEFERRED is specified, then the constraint has to be DEFERRABLE.
- If INITIALLY IMMEDIATE is specified or implicit and neither DEFERRABLE nor NOT DEFERRABLE is specified, then NOT DEFERRABLE is implicit.

The transaction statement can then use this statement to set the constraints as needed.

```
<set constraints mode statement> ::=
SET CONSTRAINTS <constraint name list> {DEFERRED | IMMEDIATE}
<constraint name list>
 ::= ALL | <constraint name> [{<comma> <constraint
    name>}. . .]
```

This feature was new with Full SQL-92 and it is not widely implemented in the smaller SQL products. In effect, they use NOT DEFERRABLE INITIALLY IMMEDIATE on all the constraints.

### 5.1.2 DEFAULT Clause

The default clause is an underused feature, whose syntax is:

```
<default clause> ::=
 [CONSTRAINT <constraint name>] DEFAULT <default option>

<default option> ::= <literal> | <system value> | NULL

<system value> ::= CURRENT_DATE | CURRENT_TIME |
   CURRENT_TIMESTAMP | SYSTEM_USER | SESSION_USER |
   CURRENT_USER
```

The SQL:2003 Standard also added `CURRENT_PATH` and `<implicitly typed value specification>`. Do not worry about them; they are not very common.

Whenever the SQL engine does not have an explicit value to put into this column during an insertion statement, it will look for a `DEFAULT` clause and insert that value. The default option can be a literal value of the relevant data type, or current timestamp, current date, current user identifier, and so forth. If you do not provide a `DEFAULT` clause and the column is `NULL`-able, the system will provide a `NULL` as the default. If all that fails, you will get an error message about missing data.

This is a good way to make the database do a lot of work that you would otherwise have to code into all the application programs. The most common tricks are to use a zero in numeric columns, a string to encode a missing value (`'{{unknown}}'`) or an explicit default (`'same address'`) in character columns, and the system timestamp to mark transactions.

### 5.1.3 `NOT NULL` Constraint

The most important column constraint is the `NOT NULL`, which forbids the use of `NULL`s in a column. It optionally follows the `DEFAULT`, if any, but most SQLs are more forgiving of the ordering these days. Use `NOT NULL` routinely, then remove it only when you have good reason. It will help you avoid the complications of `NULL` values when you make queries against the data. The other side of the coin is that you should provide a `DEFAULT` value to replace the `NULL` that would have been created.

The `NULL` is a special marker in SQL that belongs to all data types. SQL is the only language that has such a creature; if you can understand how it works, you will have a good grasp of SQL. It is not a value; it is a marker to hold a place where a value might go. But it has to be cast to a data type for physical storage.

A `NULL` means that we have a missing, unknown, miscellaneous, or inapplicable value in the data. It can mean many other things, but just consider those four for now. The problem is that, exactly which of the four possibilities the `NULL` indicates depends on how it is used. To clarify this, imagine that I am looking at a carton of Easter eggs and I want to know their colors. If I see an empty hole, I have a missing egg, which I hope will be provided later. If I see a foil-wrapped egg, I have an unknown color value in my set. If I see a multicolored egg, I have a miscellaneous value in my set. If I see a cue ball, I have an inapplicable value in my set. The way you handle each situation is a little different.

When you use NULLs in math calculations, they propagate in the results so that the answer is another NULL. When you use them in comparisons, they return a logical value of UNKNOWN and give SQL its strange three-valued logic. They can be sorted either always high or always low in the collation sequence with an optional NULLS [FIRST|LAST] subclause in the ORDER BY clause. If no subclauses are given, the vendor is free to set its own default ordering. They group together for some operations but not for others. In short, NULLs cause a lot of irregular features in SQL, which we will discuss later. Your best bet as a new SQL programmer is just to memorize the rules for NULLs until you have enough experience to see the pattern.

### 5.1.4 CHECK( ) Constraints

The check constraint tests the values in the table against a logical expression, which SQL calls a search condition, and rejects rows whose search condition returns FALSE. However, the constraint accepts rows when the search condition returns TRUE or UNKNOWN. This is not the same rule as the WHERE and ON clauses in queries and other data manipulation statements, which reject rows that test UNKNOWN. The reason for this "benefit-of-the-doubt" feature is so that it will be easy to write constraints on NULL-able columns.

A check constraint can be a simple search condition such as CHECK (order_qty >= 0). These simple search conditions are probably the most common cases. The expressions look like the logical tests in virtually every procedural programming language. Because they look familiar, beginning SQL programmers do not use the full power of SQL. This is assuming they use constraints at all!

SQL has several shorthands that make the code much easier to read. For example, CHECK (rating BETWEEN 1 AND 10) replaces two simple comparisons. Likewise, CHECK (sex IN (0, 1, 2, 9)) replaces a chain of OR-ed comparisons with an enumerated list of expressions. Although it is optional, it is a really good idea to use a constraint name. Without it, most SQL products will create a huge, ugly, unreadable random string for the constraint name since they need to have one in the schema tables. If you provide your own, you can find the constraint easily when you want to drop or modify it. The name will also appear in the error messages when the constraint is violated.

For example, you can use a single check clause to enforce the rule that a firm does not hire anyone under 21 years of age for a job that requires a liquor-serving license by checking the birth date and hire date. However, you cannot put the current system date into the CHECK( ) clause logic for obvious reasons—it is always changing.

The real power of the `CHECK()` clause comes from writing complex expressions that verify relationships with other rows, with other tables, or with constants. Before Standard SQL, the `CHECK()` constraint could only reference columns in the table in which it was declared. In Standard SQL, the `CHECK()` constraint can reference any schema object; this is still not widely implemented.

As an example of how complex things can get consider a database of movies. First, let's enforce the rule that no country can export more than 10 titles.

```
CREATE TABLE Exported_Movies
(movie_title CHAR(25) NOT NULL,
country_code CHAR(2) NOT NULL, -- use ISO-3166 codes
sales_amt DECIMAL(12,2) NOT NULL,
PRIMARY KEY (movie_title, country_code),
CONSTRAINT National_Quota
CHECK (-- reference to same table
       10 <= ALL (SELECT COUNT(movie_title)
     FROM Exported_Movies AS E1
   GROUP BY E1.country_code))
);
```

When doing a self-join, you must use the base table name and correlation names. Let's make sure no movies from different countries have the same title.

```
CREATE TABLE ExportMovies
(movie_title CHAR(25) NOT NULL,
country_code CHAR(2) NOT NULL,
sales_amt DECIMAL(12,2) NOT NULL,
PRIMARY KEY (movie_title, country_code),
CONSTRAINT National_Quota
CHECK (NOT EXISTS -- self-join
     (SELECT *
   FROM ExportMovies AS E1
  WHERE ExportMovies.movie_title = E1.movie_title
    AND ExportMovies.country_code <> E1.country_code)
);
```

Here is way to enforce the rule that you cannot export a movie to its own country of origin:

```
CREATE TABLE ExportMovies
(movie_title CHAR(25) NOT NULL,
country_code CHAR(2) NOT NULL,
```

```
sales_amt DECIMAL(12,2) NOT NULL,
PRIMARY KEY (movie_title, country_code),
CONSTRAINT Foreign_film
CHECK (NOT EXISTS  -- reference to second table
 (SELECT *
    FROM Movies AS M1
  WHERE M1.movie_title = ExportMovies.movie_title
    AND M1.country_of_origin = ExportMovies.
      country_code)));
```

These table-level constraints often use a `NOT EXISTS()` predicate. In spite of the fact that you can often do a lot of work in a single constraint, it is a better idea to write a lot of small constraints so that you know exactly what went wrong when one of them is violated.

Constraint names are global to the schema, and not local to the table where they appear. There are two reasons for this. If two different constraints in two different tables had the same name, you would not know which one was violated in an error message. The second reason is that there is schema level declaration, the `CREATE ASSERTION` statement, which we will discuss shortly.

### 5.1.5 `UNIQUE` and `PRIMARY KEY` Constraints

The unique constraint says that no duplicate values are allowed in the column or columns involved.

```
<unique specification> ::= UNIQUE | PRIMARY KEY
```

File system programmers confuse the concept of a `PRIMARY KEY` with the record number they have in a sequential file. The record number is how they navigate in a file, moving a read/write head on a disk or magnetic tape within the file to each record. Obviously, a sequential file can have only one physical ordering. Since the first SQLs were built on top of existing file systems, the `PRIMARY KEY` syntax was designed to mimic the record number. Dr. Codd later realized this was a mistake, but by then it was part of SQL. There is no order in a table, so today the `PRIMARY KEY` in SQL has to do with defaults in referential actions, which we will discuss later.

There are some subtle differences between `UNIQUE` and `PRIMARY KEY`. There can be only one `PRIMARY KEY` per table but many `UNIQUE` constraints in a table. `A PRIMARY KEY` is automatically declared to have a `NOT NULL` constraint on it, but a `UNIQUE` column can have `NULL`s in one or more rows unless you explicitly add a `NOT NULL` constraint. Uniqueness is checked by throwing out the NULLs, then doing an equality test.

Adding the NOT NULL to UNIQUE columns whenever possible is a good idea, as it makes the column into a proper relational key.

There is also a multiple-column form of the <unique specification>, which usually is written at the end of the column declarations. It is a list of columns in parentheses after the proper keyword; it means that the combination of those columns is unique. For example, I might declare PRIMARY KEY (city, department) or UNIQUE (city, department) so I can be sure that though I have offices in many cities and many identical departments in those offices, there is only one personnel department in Chicago.

Consider these variations on the same job assignment table:

```
CREATE TABLE Job_Assignments_1
(emp_name VARCHAR(10) NOT NULL,
city_name VARCHAR(15),
dept_name CHAR(5));
```

Even though it is valid SQL, Job_Assignments_1 has no key. That means that it is not a relational table. The Database Standards Committee debated requiring a PRIMARY KEY in the syntax, but decided to allow this construction so that nonnormalized raw data could be handled inside the database.

```
CREATE TABLE Job_Assignments_2
(emp_name VARCHAR(10) NOT NULL PRIMARY KEY,
city_name VARCHAR(15) UNIQUE,
dept_name CHAR(5));

CREATE TABLE Job_Assignments_3
(emp_name VARCHAR(10) NOT NULL PRIMARY KEY,
city_name VARCHAR(15),
dept_name CHAR(5),
UNIQUE (city_name, dept_name));

CREATE TABLE Job_Assignments_4
(emp_name VARCHAR(10) NOT NULL,
city_name VARCHAR(15) NOT NULL,
dept_name CHAR(5) NOT NULL,
UNIQUE (emp_name, city_name, dept_name)); -- or use
   PRIMARY KEY()
```

Assume the data is inserted in top-to-bottom order in each of the tables, as shown in Table 5.1.

Later in this book, we will discuss overlapping UNIQUE constraints, which can enforce complex table level rules.

**Table 5.1 Constraint Enforcement with NULLs**

| emp_name | city_name | dept_name |
|---|---|---|
| 'Jack' | 'Chicago' | 'Acct' ◀ valid for 1, 2, 3, 4 |
| 'Jack' | 'Chicago' | 'Acct' ◀ invalid for 1, 2, 3, 4 --PK violation |
| 'Jill' | 'Chicago' | NULL ◀ valid for 1, not 2 (Chicago), 3, not 4 |
| 'Hilary' | NULL | 'Acct' ◀ valid for 1, 2, 3, not 4 |
| 'Walt' | NULL | NULL ◀ valid for 1, 2, 3, not 4 |
| 'Fred' | NULL | NULL ◀ valid for 1, 2, 3, not 4 |

## 5.1.6 REFERENCES Clause

The <references specification> is the simplest version of a referential constraint definition, which can be quite tricky. For now, let us just consider the simplest case:

```
<references specification> ::=
[CONSTRAINT <constraint name>]
 REFERENCES <referenced table and columns>
  [MATCH <match type>]
  [<referential triggered action> ]

<match type> ::= FULL | PARTIAL
```

This relates two tables together, so it is different from the other options we have discussed so far. The table where this appears is the referencing table and the table in the REFERENCES clause is the referenced table. They are usually different but they can be the same—a self-reference.

What this says is that the value in this column of the referencing table must appear somewhere in the referenced table's column that is named in the constraint.

Furthermore, the referenced column(s) must be in a UNIQUE constraint. For example, you can set up a rule that the Orders table will have orders only for goods that appear in the Inventory table.

The optional MATCH FULL clause says that the two lists of columns have to be all non-NULL and equal to each other, position for position and value for value. The optional MATCH PARTIAL clause says that the two lists of columns are equal to each other, position for position and value for value, in the non-NULL columns and we will treat the NULLs as if they are equal. This occurs in several places in SQL and has to do with grouping versus equality.

If no reference columns are given, then the PRIMARY KEY column of the referenced table is assumed to be the target. This is one of those places where the PRIMARY KEY is important, but you can always play it safe and explicitly name a column. There is no rule to prevent several columns from referencing the same target column. For example, we might have a table of flight crews that has pilot and copilot columns that both reference a table of certified pilots.

A circular reference is a relationship in which one table references a second table, which optionally references a third, and so forth until the chain comes back to reference the first table. The old gag about "you cannot get a job until you have experience, and you cannot get experience until you have a job!" is the classic version of this.

Notice that the columns in a multicolumn FOREIGN KEY must match to a multicolumn PRIMARY KEY or UNIQUE constraint. The syntax is:

```
[CONSTRAINT <constraint name>]
FOREIGN KEY (<column list>)
 REFERENCES <referenced table name> [(<reference column
    list>)]
```

The REFERENCES clause can have two subclauses that take actions when a database event changes the referenced table. The two database events are updates and deletes and the subclauses look like this:

```
<referential triggered action> ::=
 <update rule> [<delete rule>] | <delete rule> [<update
   rule>]

<update rule> ::= ON UPDATE <referential action>
<delete rule> ::= ON DELETE <referential action>

<referential action> ::= CASCADE | SET NULL | SET DEFAULT
   | NO ACTION
```

When the referenced table is changed, one of the referential actions is set in motion by the SQL engine.

1. The CASCADE option will change the values in the referencing table to the new value in the referenced table. This is a very common method of DDL programming that allows you to set up a single table as the trusted source for an identifier. This way the system can propagate changes automatically. This can save you thousands of lines of application code, improve query optimization, and prevent orphaned data.

Modern SQL products regarded the schema as a whole. The referenced values appeared once in the referenced table, and the referencing tables obtain them by following system-maintained pointer chains or hash tables to that one occurrence in the schema. The results are much faster update cascades, a physically smaller database, faster joins, and faster aggregations.

2. The `SET NULL` option will change the values in the referencing table to a `NULL`. Obviously, the referencing column needs to be `NULL`-able.
3. The `SET DEFAULT` option will change the values in the referencing table to the default value of that column. Obviously, the referencing column needs to have some `DEFAULT` declared for it, but each referencing column can have its own default in its own table.
4. The `NO ACTION` option explains itself. Nothing is changed in the referencing table and an error message about reference violation will be raised. If a referential constraint does not specify any `ON UPDATE` or `ON DELETE` rule, or any update rule, then `NO ACTION` is implicit.

## 5.2 Nested UNIQUE Constraints

One of the basic tricks in SQL is representing a one-to-one or many-to-many relationship with a table that references the two (or more) entity tables involved by their primary keys. This third table has several popular names such as "junction table" or "join table," taken from terms used in prerelational databases, but we know that it is a relationship. This type of table needs to have constraints on to assure that the relationships work properly.

For example, two tables:

```
CREATE TABLE Boys
(boy_name VARCHAR(30) NOT NULL PRIMARY KEY
...);

CREATE TABLE Girls
(girl_name VARCHAR(30) NOT NULL PRIMARY KEY,
...);
```

Yes, I know using names for a key is a bad practice, but it will make my examples easier to read. There are a lot of different relationships that we can make between these two tables. If you don't believe me, just watch the *Jerry Springer Show* sometime. The simplest relationship table looks like this:

```
CREATE TABLE Couples
(boy_name VARCHAR(30) NOT NULL
```

```
     REFERENCES Boys (boy_name)
     ON UPDATE CASCADE
     ON DELETE CASCADE,
girl_name VARCHAR(30) NOT NULL,
     REFERENCES Girls(girl_name)
     ON UPDATE CASCADE
     ON DELETE CASCADE);
```

The Couples table allows us to insert rows like this:

```
('Joe Celko', 'Hilary Duff')
('Joe Celko', 'Lindsay Lohan')
('Tobey Maguire', 'Lindsay Lohan')
('Joe Celko', 'Hilary Duff')
```

Oops! I am shown twice with 'Hilary Duff' because the Couples table does not have its own key. This is an easy mistake to make, but fixing it is not an obvious thing.

```
CREATE TABLE Orgy
(boy_name VARCHAR(30) NOT NULL
     REFERENCES Boys (boy_name)
     ON DELETE CASCADE
     ON UPDATE CASCADE,
girl_name VARCHAR(30) NOT NULL,
     REFERENCES Girls(girl_name)
     ON UPDATE CASCADE
     ON DELETE CASCADE,
PRIMARY KEY (boy_name, girl_name)); —compound key
```

The Orgy table gets rid of the duplicated rows and makes this a proper table. The primary key for the table is made up of two or more columns and is called a compound key. These are valid rows now.

```
('Joe Celko', 'Hilary Duff')
('Joe Celko', 'Lindsay Lohan')
('Tobey Maguire', 'Lindsay Lohan')
```

But the only restriction on the couples is that they appear only once. Every boy can be paired with every girl, much to the dismay of the Moral Majority. I think I want to make a rule that guys can have as many gals as they want, but the gals have to stick to one guy.

The way I do this is to use a `NOT NULL UNIQUE` constraint on the girl_name column, which makes it a key. It is a simple key since it is only one column, but it is also a nested key because it appears as a subset of the compound `PRIMARY KEY`.

```
CREATE TABLE Playboys
(boy_name VARCHAR(30) NOT NULL
     REFERENCES Boys (boy_name)
```

```
      ON UPDATE CASCADE
      ON DELETE CASCADE,
girl_name VARCHAR(30) NOT NULL UNIQUE, -nested key
      REFERENCES Girls(girl_name)
      ON UPDATE CASCADE
      ON DELETE CASCADE,
PRIMARY KEY (boy_name, girl_name)); -compound key
```

The Playboys is a proper table, without duplicates, but it also enforces the condition that I get to play around with one or more ladies, thus:

```
('Joe Celko', 'Hilary Duff')
('Joe Celko', 'Lindsay Lohan')
```

The ladies might want to go the other way and keep company with a series of men.

```
CREATE TABLE Playgirls
(boy_name VARCHAR(30) NOT NULL UNIQUE -nested key
      REFERENCES Boys (boy_name)
      ON UPDATE CASCADE
      ON DELETE CASCADE,
girl_name VARCHAR(30) NOT NULL,
      REFERENCES Girls(girl_name)
      ON UPDATE CASCADE
      ON DELETE CASCADE,
PRIMARY KEY (boy_name, girl_name)); -compound key
```

The Playgirls table would permit these rows from our original set.

```
('Joe Celko', 'Lindsay Lohan')
('Tobey Maguire', 'Lindsay Lohan')
```

Think about all of these possible keys for a minute. The compound `PRIMARY KEY` is now redundant and is called a "super key" in RDBMS terms. If each boy appears only once in the table or each girl appears only once in the table, then each `(boy_name, girl_name)` pair can appear only once. However, the redundancy can be useful in searching the table because it will probably create extra indexes that give us a covering of both names. The query engine then can use just the index and not touch the base tables.

The Moral Majority is pretty upset about this Hollywood scandal and would love for us to stop running around and settle down in nice stable couples.

```
CREATE TABLE Marriages
(boy_name VARCHAR(30) NOT NULL UNIQUE -nested key
      REFERENCES Boys (boy_name)
      ON UPDATE CASCADE
      ON DELETE CASCADE,
```

```
girl_name VARCHAR(30) NOT NULL UNIQUE -nested key
     REFERENCES Girls(girl_name)
     ON UPDATE CASCADE
     ON DELETE CASCADE,
PRIMARY KEY(boy_name, girl_name)); -redundant compound key!!
```

I leave same-sex marriages as an exercise for the reader.

The Couples table allows us to insert these rows from the original set.

```
('Joe Celko', 'Hilary Duff')
('Tobey Maguire', 'Lindsay Lohan')
```

Many products make the assumption that the PRIMARY KEY is in some way special in the data model and will be the way that they should access the table most of the time. In fairness, making special provision for the primary key is not a bad assumption because the REFERENCES clause uses the PRIMARY KEY of the referenced table as the default.

Many new SQL programmers are not aware that a FOREIGN KEY constraint can also reference any UNIQUE constraint in the same table or in another table. The following nightmare code will give you an idea of the possibilities. The multiple column versions follow the same syntax.

```
CREATE TABLE Foo
(foo_key INTEGER NOT NULL PRIMARY KEY,
...
self_ref INTEGER NOT NULL
 REFERENCES Foo(fookey),
outside_ref_1 INTEGER NOT NULL
   REFERENCES Bar(bar_key),
outside_ref_2 INTEGER NOT NULL
 REFERENCES Bar(other_key),
...);

CREATE TABLE Bar
(bar_key INTEGER NOT NULL PRIMARY KEY,
other_key INTEGER NOT NULL UNIQUE,
...);
```

## 5.2.1 Overlapping Keys

But getting back to the nested keys, just how far can we go with them? My favorite example is a teacher's schedule kept in a table like this (I am leaving off reference clauses and CHECK() constraints):

```
CREATE TABLE Class_Schedule
(teacher_name VARCHAR(15) NOT NULL,
```

```
class_name CHAR(15) NOT NULL,
room_nbr INTEGER NOT NULL,
class_period INTEGER NOT NULL,
PRIMARY KEY (teacher_name, class_name, room_nbr,
   class_period));
```

That choice of a primary key is the most obvious one—use all the columns. Typical rows would look like this:

```
('Mr. Celko', 'Database 101', 222, 6)
```

The rules we want to enforce are:

1. A teacher is in only one room each class_period.
2. A teacher teaches only one class each class_period.
3. A room has only one class each class_period.
4. A room has only one teacher in it each class_period.

Stop reading and see what you come up with for an answer. Okay, now consider using one constraint for each rule in the list, thus:

```
CREATE TABLE Class_Schedule_1 –version one, WRONG!
(teacher_name VARCHAR(15) NOT NULL,
class_name CHAR(15) NOT NULL,
room_nbr INTEGER NOT NULL,
class_period INTEGER NOT NULL,
UNIQUE (teacher_name, room_nbr, class_period), –rule #1
UNIQUE (teacher_name, class_name, class_period), –rule #2
UNIQUE (class_name, room_nbr, class_period), –rule #3
UNIQUE (teacher_name, room_nbr, class_period), –rule #4
PRIMARY KEY (teacher_name, class_name, room_nbr,
   class_period));
```

We know that there are four ways to pick three things from a set of four things. Although column order is important in creating an index, we can ignore it for now and then worry about index tuning later.

I could drop the `PRIMARY KEY` as redundant if I have all four of these constraints in place. But what happens if I drop the `PRIMARY KEY` and then one of the constraints?

```
CREATE TABLE Class_Schedule_2 –still wrong
(teacher_name VARCHAR(15) NOT NULL,
class_name CHAR(15) NOT NULL,
room_nbr INTEGER NOT NULL,
class_period INTEGER NOT NULL,
UNIQUE (teacher_name, room_nbr, class_period), –rule #1
UNIQUE (teacher_name, class_name, class_period), –rule #2
UNIQUE (class_name, room_nbr, class_period)); –rule #3
```

I can now insert these rows in the second version of the table:

```
('Mr. Celko', 'Database 101', 222, 6)
('Mr. Celko', 'Database 102', 223, 6)
```

This gives me a very tough sixth period teaching load since I have to be in two different rooms at the same time. Things can get even worse when another teacher is added to the schedule:

```
('Mr. Celko', 'Database 101', 222, 6)
('Mr. Celko', 'Database 102', 223, 6)
('Ms. Shields', 'Database 101', 223, 6)
```

Ms. Shields and I are both in room 223, trying to teach different classes at the same time. Matthew Burr looked at the constraints and the rules came up with this analysis.

```
CREATE TABLE Class_Schedule_3 —corrected version
(teacher_name VARCHAR(15) NOT NULL,
class_name CHAR(15) NOT NULL,
room_nbr INTEGER NOT NULL,
class_period INTEGER NOT NULL,
UNIQUE (teacher_name, class_period), —rules #1 and #2
UNIQUE (room_nbr, class_period)); —rules #3 and #4
```

If a teacher is in only one room each class_period, then given a class_period and a teacher I should be able to determine only one room; that is, room is functionally dependent upon the combination of teacher and class_period. Likewise, if a teacher teaches only one class each class_period, then class is functionally dependent upon the combination of teacher and class_period. The same thinking holds for the last two rules: class is functionally dependent upon the combination of room and class_period, and teacher is functionally dependent upon the combination of room and class_period.

With the constraints that were provided in the first version, you will find that the rules are not enforced. For example, I could enter the following rows:

```
('Mr. Celko', 'Database 101', 222, 6)
('Mr. Celko', 'Database 102', 223, 6)
```

These rows violate rule #1 and rule #2.

However, the unique constraints first provided in Class_Schedule_2 do not capture this violation and will allow the rows to be entered.

The constraint,

```
UNIQUE (teacher_name, room_nbr, class_period)
```

is checking the complete combination of teacher, room, and class_period, and since ('Mr. Celko', 222, 6) is different from ('Mr. Celko', 223, 6), the DDL does not find any problem with both rows being entered, even though that means that Mr. Celko is in more than one room during the same class_period.

```
UNIQUE (teacher_name, class_name, class_period)
```

does not catch its associated rule either since ('Mr. Celko', 'Database 101', 6) is different from ('Mr. Celko', 'Database 102', 6), and so Mr. Celko is able to teach more than one class during the same class_period, thus violating rule #2. It seems that we'd also be able to add the following row:

```
('Ms. Shields', 'Database 103', 222, 6)
```

which violates rules #3 and #4.

### 5.2.2 Single versus Multiple-Column Uniqueness

Lionel Clarke proposed a puzzle on www.simple-talk.com in October 2007, which demonstrates how `UNIQUE` constraints work. You have to move as much of the data as you can from the source tables to the destination tables. There is one restriction though; you can use only one `INSERT INTO` statement.

```
CREATE TABLE Source
(a INTEGER NOT NULL,
b INTEGER NOT NULL,
 PRIMARY KEY (a, b));

INSERT INTO Source (a, b)
VALUES (1, 1), (1, 2), -- a=1 group
  (2, 3), (2, 4), -- a=2 group
  (5, 5), (5, 1), (5, 3), -- a=5 group
  (7, 2), -- a=7 group
  (9, 0), -- a=9 group
  (11, 2); -- a=11 group

CREATE TABLE Destination
(a INTEGER NOT NULL UNIQUE,
b INTEGER NOT NULL UNIQUE,
FOREIGN KEY (a, b)
 REFERENCES Source(a, b));
```

Notice that there are several subsets of Source data that will fit into the Destination table. If I use (1, 1) then I cannot transfer (1, 2) because of the `UNIQUE` constraint on column a; this is looking at the data from the column a viewpoint. Likewise, if I use (5, 5) then I cannot transfer (5, 1) because of the `UNIQUE` constraint on column b. I could have arranged the insertion statement to reflect a column b viewpoint:

```
INSERT INTO Source (b, a) -- flip the columns
VALUES (0, 9), -- b=0 group
  (1, 1), (1, 5), -- b=1 group
  (2, 1), (2, 7), (2, 11), -- b=2 group
  (3, 2), (3, 5), -- b=3 group
  (4, 2), -- b=4 group
  (5, 5); -- b=5 group
```

With a little thought, you can see that you need to pick one pair from each group to get the largest subset. If you are a math major, this is an application of the Axiom of Choice for finite sets.

Here is a first attempt:

```
WITH X (a, b, pair_nbr)
AS
(SELECT a, b, ROW_NUMBER() OVER(ORDER BY a ASC, b DESC)
 FROM Source)

SELECT a, b, pair_nbr
 FROM X AS P1
WHERE NOT EXISTS
  (SELECT *
    FROM X AS P2
   WHERE P2.pair_nbr < P1.pair_nbr
    AND (P1.a = P2.a OR P1.b = P2.b));
```

This should give you *one* valid subset. The idea is to sort and number the rows, then look from the current position P1 at all the previous rows P2 to see if one that repeats a value of a or b exists. That means we reject the current row. This gives me Table 5.2.

Mike Good pointed out that this not my best effort. Another valid solution with five rows instead of four is shown in Table 5.3.

**Table 5.2 Valid Subset with UNIQUE Constraints, Version 1**

| a | b |
|---|---|
| 1 | 2 |
| 2 | 4 |
| 5 | 5 |
| 9 | 0 |

**Table 5.3 Valid Subset with UNIQUE Constraints, Version 2**

| a | b |
|---|---|
| 1 | 1 |
| 2 | 4 |
| 5 | 3 |
| 7 | 2 |
| 9 | 0 |

For other populations, my query does worse. Given any source data population we should be able to rerun the insertion with data in which Source.a and Source.b are swapped, and still get the same number of Destination rows in the answer. My algorithm gets four rows for specified source population, but only three rows when the columns are swapped, which is a sure indication of a logical flaw. By changing the `OVER (ORDER BY ..)` subclause directions and ordering you can get different answers, but there is no guarantee that one of them will be optimal.

Mike Good was right about that not being my best work. My goal was to get the first acceptable answer. When you do NP-complete problems in SQL, you usually get the entire set of candidate answers and the query runs like glue. Here is my "glue query":

```
–create the original source data
CREATE TABLE Source
(pair_nbr INTEGER NOT NULL UNIQUE,
a INTEGER NOT NULL,
b INTEGER NOT NULL,
PRIMARY KEY (a, b));

INSERT INTO Source
VALUES (1, 1, 1), (2, 1, 2), (3, 2, 3), (4, 7, 2),
(5, 2, 4), (6, 5, 5), (7, 5, 1), (8, 5, 3), (9, 9, 0),
   (10, 11, 2);

–CTE to set up all subsets of the 10 sample pairs
WITH Flags (I)
AS (SELECT FROM VALUES ('t'), ('f')),

--CROSS JOIN from Hell to get all subsets and random
   candidate id numbers
Subsets (subset_nbr, f01, f02, f03, f04, f05, f06, f07,
   f08, f09, f10)
```

```
AS
(SELECT ROW_NUMBER() OVER () AS subset_nbr,
       F01.I, F02.I, F03.I, F04.I, F05.I,
       F06.I, F07.I, F08.I, F09.I, F10.I
  FROM Flags AS F01, Flags AS F02, Flags AS F03,
       Flags AS F04, Flags AS F05, Flags AS F06,
       Flags AS F07, Flags AS F08, Flags AS F09, Flags AS F10),

–filter out pairs FROM the permutations
Candidates(subset_nbr, a, b)
AS
(SELECT subset_nbr, S.a, S.b
   FROM Subsets AS P, Source AS S
  WHERE S.pair_nbr = 1 AND P.f01 = 't'
UNION ALL
SELECT subset_nbr, S.a, S.b
 FROM Subsets AS P, Source AS S
WHERE S.pair_nbr = 2 AND P.f02 = 't'
UNION ALL
SELECT subset_nbr, S.a, S.b
 FROM Subsets AS P, Source AS S
WHERE S.pair_nbr =3 AND P.f03 = 't'
UNION ALL
SELECT subset_nbr, S.a, S.b
 FROM Subsets AS P, Source AS S
WHERE S.pair_nbr = 4 AND P.f04= 't'
UNION ALL
SELECT subset_nbr, S.a, S.b
 FROM Subsets AS P, Source AS S
WHERE S.pair_nbr = 5 AND P.f05 = 't'
UNION ALL
SELECT subset_nbr, S.a, S.b
 FROM Subsets AS P, Source AS S
WHERE S.pair_nbr = 6 AND P.f06 = 't'
UNION ALL
SELECT subset_nbr, S.a, S.b
 FROM Subsets AS P, Source AS S
WHERE S.pair_nbr = 7 AND P.f07 = 't'
UNION ALL
SELECT subset_nbr, S.a, S.b
FROM Subsets AS P, Source AS S
WHERE S.pair_nbr = 8 AND P.f08 = 't'
UNION ALL
SELECT subset_nbr, S.a, S.b
FROM Subsets AS P, Source AS S
WHERE S.pair_nbr = 9 AND P.f09 = 't'
UNION ALL
SELECT subset_nbr, S.a, S.b
FROM Subsets AS P, Source AS S
WHERE S.pair_nbr = 10 AND P.f10 = 't')
```

```
SELECT subset_nbr, a, b -- return the winners
 FROM Candidates AS C1
WHERE subset_nbr
IN (SELECT C2.subset_nbr -- find all perms that meet
   uniqueness criteria
     FROM Candidates AS C2
    GROUP BY C2.subset_nbr
   HAVING COUNT(a) = COUNT(DISTINCT a)
      AND COUNT(b) = COUNT(DISTINCT b)
   -- AND COUNT(*) >= 5) —so you don't go nuts looking at
      the output
ORDER BY subset_nbr, a, b;
```

The bad news!

1. This gives duplicate answers under different `subset_nbrs`. Yes, I could do a relational division and remove them, but that would really be messy to read.
2. This is probably going to scale better than you think. Richard Romley wrote an 81-way self-`JOIN` for a Sudoku solver that also returns all possible grids. It is quite fast, even with hundreds of solutions. This is much simpler.

```
CREATE TABLE Source
(a INTEGER NOT NULL,
b INTEGER NOT NULL,
 PRIMARY KEY (a, b));

INSERT INTO Source
VALUES (1, 1), (1, 2),
      (2, 3), (2, 4),
      (5, 5), (5, 1), (5, 3),
      (7, 2),
      (9, 0),
     (11, 2);

CREATE TABLE Destination
(a INTEGER NOT NULL UNIQUE,
b INTEGER NOT NULL UNIQUE,
FOREIGN KEY (a, b) REFERENCES Source(a, b));
```

Let's try another approach. Generate all possible combinations of pairs, then filter out the ones that fail criteria.

```
WITH X (a, b, pair_nbr) AS
(SELECT a, b, ROW_NUMBER () OVER (ORDER BY a ASC, b DESC)
FROM Part1Source)
SELECT a, b, pair_nbr
FROM X AS P1
WHERE NOT EXISTS
(SELECT *
 FROM X AS P2
```

```
WHERE P2.pair_nbr < P1.pair_nbr
AND (P1.a = P2.a OR P1.b = P2.b));
```

This should give you one valid subset. The idea is to sort and number the rows, then look FROM the current position P1 at all the previous rows P2 to see if one that repeats a value of an OR b exists. That means we reject the current row. This gives me Table 5.4.

*MikeGood said:*

*Celko, this not your best effort. Correct Part 1 answer has 5 dest rows for the specified Part1Source population. One valid solution is*

```
1, 1
2, 4
5, 3
7, 2
9, 0
```

*For other populations it does worse. I've been using the following alternate population to help find flaws. The answer should have four dest rows, but the algorithm you just posted finds only two.*

```
1, 1
1, 2
2, 1
2, 2
2, 3
2, 4
3, 3
3, 4
4, 1
```

*One valid solution is*

```
1, 2
2, 3
3, 4
4, 1
```

## Table 5.4 Valid Subset with UNIQUE Constraints, with Pair Numbering

| a | b | pair_nbr |
|---|---|---|
| 1 | 2 | 1 |
| 2 | 4 | 3 |
| 5 | 5 | 5 |
| 9 | 0 | |

*Finally, for any source data population we should be able to rerun test with data in source cols a and b swapped, and still get the same number of dest rows in the answer. Your algorithm gets four rows for specified source population, but only three rows when data in cols is swapped, which is a sure indication of a logical flaw.*

*All that said, I cannot determine if you're onto something here, fundamentally, OR not. Maybe with a little more work?*

*Celko said:*

*Oops! My error; this does not generate duplicates. Here are the answers for the original problem:*

```
172 1 1
172 2 4
172 5 5
172 9 0
172 11 2
=========
186 1 1
186 2 4
186 5 5
186 7 2
186 9 0
=========
427 1 1
427 2 3
427 5 5
427 9 0
427 11 2
=========
441 1 1
441 2 3
441 5 5
441 7 2
441 9 0
=========
652 1 1
652 2 4
652 5 3
652 9 0
652 11 2
=========
666 1 1
666 2 4
666 5 3
666 7 2
666 9 0
```

Mike Good was right about that not being my best work. My goal was to get the first acceptable answer. When you do NP-complete problems in SQL, you usually get the entire set of candidate answers and the query runs like glue. Here is my "glue query":

```
–create the original source data
CREATE TABLE Source
(pair_nbr INTEGER NOT NULL UNIQUE,
a INTEGER NOT NULL,
b INTEGER NOT NULL,
PRIMARY KEY (a, b));

INSERT INTO Source
VALUES (1, 1, 1),(2, 1, 2), (3, 2, 3), (4, 7, 2),
(5, 2, 4), (6, 5, 5), (7, 5, 1),(8, 5, 3),(9, 9, 0),
   (10, 11, 2);

–CTE to set up all subsets of the ten sample pairs
WITH Flags (i)
AS (SELECT FROM VALUES ('t'), ('f')),

–CROSS JOIN FROM Hell to get all subsets and random
   candidate id numbers
Subsets (subset_nbr, f01, f02, f03, f04, f05, f06, f07,
   f08, f09, f10)
AS
(SELECT ROW_NUMBER() OVER () AS subset_nbr,
F01.i, F02.i, F03.i, F04.i, F05.i,
F06.i, F07.i, F08.i, F09.i, F10.i
FROM Flags AS F01, Flags AS F02, Flags AS F03, Flags AS
   F04, Flags AS F05,
Flags AS F06, Flags AS F07, Flags AS F08, Flags AS F09,
   Flags AS F10),

–filter out pairs FROM the permutations
Candidates(subset_nbr, a, b)
AS (
SELECT subset_nbr, S.a, S.b FROM Subsets AS P, Source AS S
   WHERE S.pair_nbr = 1 AND P.f01 = 't'
UNION ALL
SELECT subset_nbr, S.a, S.b FROM Subsets AS P, Source AS S
   WHERE S.pair_nbr = 2 AND P.f02 = 't'
UNION ALL
SELECT subset_nbr, S.a, S.b FROM Subsets AS P, Source AS S
   WHERE S.pair_nbr =3 AND P.f03 = 't'
UNION ALL
SELECT subset_nbr, S.a, S.b FROM Subsets AS P, Source AS S
   WHERE S.pair_nbr = 4 AND P.f04= 't'
UNION ALL
SELECT subset_nbr, S.a, S.b FROM Subsets AS P, Source AS S
   WHERE S.pair_nbr = 5 AND P.f05 = 't'
```

```
UNION ALL
SELECT subset_nbr, S.a, S.b FROM Subsets AS P, Source AS S
   WHERE S.pair_nbr = 6 AND P.f06 = 't'
UNION ALL
SELECT subset_nbr, S.a, S.b FROM Subsets AS P, Source AS S
   WHERE S.pair_nbr = 7 AND P.f07 = 't'
UNION ALL
SELECT subset_nbr, S.a, S.b FROM Subsets AS P, Source AS S
   WHERE S.pair_nbr = 8 AND P.f08 = 't'
UNION ALL
SELECT subset_nbr, S.a, S.b FROM Subsets AS P, Source AS S
   WHERE S.pair_nbr = 9 AND P.f09 = 't'
UNION ALL
SELECT subset_nbr, S.a, S.b FROM Subsets AS P, Source AS S
   WHERE S.pair_nbr = 10 AND P.f10 = 't')

SELECT subset_nbr, a, b —return the winners
FROM Candidates AS C1
WHERE subset_nbr
IN (SELECT C2.subset_nbr —find all perms that meet
   uniqueness criteria
FROM Candidates AS C2
GROUP BY C2.subset_nbr
HAVING COUNT(a) = COUNT(DISTINCT a)
AND COUNT(b) = COUNT(DISTINCT b)
-- AND COUNT(*) >= 5) —so you don't go nuts looking at the
   output
ORDER BY subset_nbr, a, b;
```

## 5.3 CREATE ASSERTION Constraints

In Standard SQL, the CREATE ASSERTION allows you to apply a constraint on the tables within a schema but not have the constraint attached to any particular table. The syntax is:

```
<assertion definition> ::=
 CREATE ASSERTION <constraint name> <assertion check>
 [<constraint attributes>]

<assertion check> ::= CHECK (<search condition>)
```

As you would expect, there is a DROP ASSERTION statement, but no ALTER statement. An assertion can do things that a CHECK() clause attached to a table cannot do, because it is outside of the tables involved. A CHECK() constraint is always TRUE if the table is empty.

For example, it is very hard to make a rule that the total number of employees in the company must be equal to the total number of employees in all the health plan tables.

```
CREATE ASSERTION Total_health_Coverage
CHECK (SELECT COUNT(*) FROM Personnel) =
    + (SELECT COUNT(*) FROM HealthPlan_1)
    + (SELECT COUNT(*) FROM HealthPlan_2)
    + (SELECT COUNT(*) FROM HealthPlan_3);
```

## 5.4 TEMPORARY Tables

In the Standard SQL model, a TEMPORARY table acts very much like a base table. Its structure is persistent in the schema, but it automatically deletes its rows so the users do not have to bother. They can be GLOBAL TEMPORARY tables that are shared among the users. They can be LOCAL TEMPORARY tables whose data is available to one and only one user. These tables have the same user privileges model as a base table.

### 5.4.1 TEMPORARY TABLE Declarations

The idea is that the temporary table can be used with SQL/PSM code to hold intermediate results rather than requerying or recalculating them over and over. The syntax for creating a TEMPORARY TABLE is:

```
CREATE [GLOBAL | LOCAL] TEMP[ORARY] TABLE <table name>
(<table element list>)
ON COMMIT [PRESERVE | DELETE] ROWS;
```

This is just like the usual CREATE TABLE statement with the addition of two pieces of syntax. The <table element>s can be column declarations, constraints, or declarative referential integrity clauses, just as if this were a base table. The differences come from the additional clauses.

The GLOBAL option in the TEMPORARY means that one copy of the table is available to *all* the modules of the application program in which it appears. The GLOBAL TEMPORARY TABLE generally is used to pass shared data between sessions.

The LOCAL option means that one copy of the table is available to *each* module of the application program in which the temporary table appears. The LOCAL TEMPORARY TABLE is generally used as a "scratch table" within a single module. If more than one user accesses the same LOCAL TEMPORARY TABLE, they each get a copy of the table, initially empty, for their session or within the scope of the module that uses it.

If you have trouble imagining multiple tables in the schema with the same name (a violation of a basic rule of SQL about uniqueness of schema objects), then imagine a single table created as declared, but with an extra phantom column that contains a user identifier. What the users are then seeing is an updatable `VIEW` on the `LOCAL TEMPORARY TABLE`, which shows them only the rows where this phantom column is equal to their user identifier, but not the phantom column itself. New rows are added to the `LOCAL TEMPORARY TABLE` with the `DEFAULT` of `CURRENT USER`.

The concept of modules in SQL is discussed in detail in *Understanding SQL's Stored Procedures* by Jim Melton (Morgan-Kaufmann, 1998, ISBN 1-55860-461-8), but you can think of them as programs, procedures, functions, subroutines, or blocks of code, depending on the procedural language that you use.

Since this is a table in the schema, you can get rid of it with a `DROP TABLE <table name>` statement and you can change it with the usual `INSERT INTEGER 0`, `DELETE FROM`, and `UPDATE` statements. The differences are at the start and end of a session or module.

The `ON COMMIT [PRESERVE | DELETE] ROWS` clause describes the action taken when a `COMMIT` statement is executed successfully. The `PRESERVE` option means that the next time this table is used, the rows will still be there and will be deleted only at the end of the session. The `DELETE` option means that the rows will be deleted whenever a `COMMIT` statement is executed during the session. In both cases, the table will be cleared out at the end of the session or module.

## 5.5 Manipulating Tables

The three basic table statements in the SQL DDL are `CREATE TABLE`, `DROP TABLE`, and `ALTER TABLE`. They pretty much do what you would think they do from their names. We will explain them in detail shortly, but they bring a table into existence, remove a table, and change the structure of an existing table in the schema, respectively. Here is a simple list of rules for creating and naming a table.

1. The table name must be unique in the schema, and the column names must be unique within a table. SQL can handle a table and a column with the same name, but it is a good practice to name tables differently from their columns. See items 4 and 6.
2. The names in SQL can consist of letters, underscores, and digits, and vendors commonly allow other printing characters. However, it is a good idea to avoid using anything except letters, underscores, and digits. Special characters are not portable and will not sort the same way in different products.
3. Standard SQL allows you to use spaces, reserved words, and special characters in a name if you enclose them in double quotation marks, but this should be avoided as much as possible.
4. The use of collective, class, or plural names for tables helps you think of them as sets. For example, do not name a table

"Employee" unless there really is only one of them; use something like "Employees," or (better) "Personnel," for the table name.

5. Use the same name for the same attribute everywhere in the schema. That is, do not name a column in one table "sex" and a column in another table "gender" when they refer to the same property. You should have a data dictionary that enforces this on the developers.
6. Use singular attribute names for columns and other scalar schema objects.

I have a separate book on SQL programming style that goes into more detail about this, so I will not mention it again.

A table must have at least one column. Though it is not required, it is also a good idea to place related columns in their conventional order in the table. By default, the columns will print out in the order in which they appear in the table. That is, put name, address, city, state, and ZIP code in that order, so that you can read them easily in a display.

The conventions in this book are that keywords are in uppercase, table names are capitalized, and column names are in lowercase. I also use capital letter(s) followed by digit(s) for correlation names (e.g., the table Personnel would have correlation names P0, P1, . . ., Pn), where the digit shows the occurrence.

### 5.5.1 DROP TABLE <table name>

The DROP TABLE statement removes a table from the database. This is not the same as making the table an empty table. When a schema object is dropped, it is gone forever. The syntax of the statement is:

```
<drop table statement> ::= DROP TABLE <table name> [<drop
   behavior>]
<drop behavior> ::= RESTRICT | CASCADE
```

The <drop behavior> clause has two options. If RESTRICT is specified, the table cannot be referenced in the query expression of any view or the search condition of any constraint. This is supposed to prevent the unpleasant surprise of having other things fail because they depended on this particular table for their own definitions. If CASCADE is specified, then such referencing objects will also be dropped along with the table.

Either the particular SQL product would post an error message, and in effect do a RESTRICT, or you would find out about any dependencies by having your database blow up when it ran into constructs that needed the missing table.

The DROP keyword and <drop behavior> clause are also used in other statements that remove schema objects, such as DROP VIEW, DROP SCHEMA, DROP CONSTRAINT, and so forth.

This is usually a "DBA-only" statement that, for obvious reasons, programmers are not usually allowed to use.

### 5.5.2 ALTER TABLE

The ALTER TABLE statement adds, removes, or changes columns and constraints within a table. This statement is in Standard SQL and it existed in most SQL products before it was standardized. It is still implemented in many different ways, so you should see your product for details. This is also a statement that your DBA will not want you to use without permission. The Standard SQL syntax looks like this:

```
ALTER TABLE <table name> <alter table action>

<alter table action> ::=
| DROP [COLUMN] <column name> <drop behavior>
| ADD [COLUMN] <column definition>
| ALTER [COLUMN] <column name> <alter column action>
| ADD <table constraint definition>
| DROP CONSTRAINT <constraint name> <drop behavior>
```

The DROP COLUMN clause removes the column from the table. Standard SQL gives you the option of setting the drop behavior, which most current products do not. The two options are RESTRICT and CASCADE. RESTRICT will not allow the column to disappear if it is referenced in another schema object. CASCADE will also delete any schema object that references the dropped column.

When this statement is available in your SQL product, I strongly advise that you first use the RESTRICT option to see if there are references before you use the CASCADE option.

As you would expect, the ADD COLUMN clause extends the existing table by putting another column on it. The new column must have a name that is unique within the table and follow the other rules for a valid column declaration. The location of the new column is usually at the end of the list of the existing columns in the table.

The ALTER COLUMN clause can change a column and its definition. Exactly what is allowed will vary from product to product, but usually the data type can be changed to a compatible data type (e.g., you can make a CHAR(n) column longer, but not shorter; change an INTEGER to a REAL; and so forth).

The ADD <table constraint definition> clause lets you put a constraint on a table. But be careful and find out if your SQL product will check the existing data to be sure that it can pass the new constraint. It is possible in some older SQL products to leave bad data in the tables and then have to clean them out with special routines to get to the actual physical storage.

The DROP CONSTRAINT clause requires that the constraint be given a name, so naming constraints is a good habit to get into. If the constraint to be dropped was given no name, you will have to find what name was assigned to it by the SQL engine in the schema information tables and use that name. The standard does not say how such names are to be constructed, only that they are unique within a schema. Actual products will usually pick a long random string of digits and preface it with some letters to make a valid name that is so absurd that no human being would think of it. A constraint name will also appear in warnings and error messages, making debugging much easier. The <drop behavior> option behaves as it did for the DROP COLUMN clause.

## 5.6 Avoiding Attribute Splitting

Attribute splitting takes many forms. It occurs when you have a single attribute, but put its values in more than one place in the schema. The most common form of attribute splitting is to create separate tables for each value. Another form of attribute splitting is to create separate rows in the same table for part of each value. These concepts are probably easier to show with examples.

### 5.6.1 Table Level Attribute Splitting

If I were to create a database with a table for male employees and separate table for female employees, you would immediately see that they should be one table with a column for a sex code. I would have split a table on sex. This is very obvious, but it can also be subtler.

Consider a subscription database that has both organizational and individual subscribers. There are two tables with the same structure and a third table that holds the split attribute, subscription type.

```
CREATE TABLE OrgSubscriptions
(subscr_id INTEGER NOT NULL PRIMARY KEY
   REFERENCES SubscriptionTypes(subscr_id),
org_name CHAR(35),
last_name CHAR(15),
first_name CHAR(15),
address1 CHAR(35) NOT NULL,
 ...);
```

```
CREATE TABLE IndSubscriptions
(subscr_id INTEGER NOT NULL PRIMARY KEY
      REFERENCES SubscriptionTypes(subscr_id),
org_name CHAR(35),
last_name CHAR(15),
first_name CHAR(15),
address1 CHAR(35) NOT NULL,
 ...);

CREATE TABLE SubscriptionTypes
(subscr_id INTEGER NOT NULL PRIMARY KEY,
subscr_type CHAR(1) DEFAULT 'I' NOT NULL
     CHECK (subscr_type IN ('I', 'O'));
```

An organizational subscription can go to just a person (last_name, first_name) or just the organization name (org_name) or both. If an individual subscription has no particular person, it is sent to an organization called '{Current Resident}' instead.

The original specifications enforce a condition that subscr_id be universally unique in the schema.

The first step is to replace the three tables with one for all subscriptions and move the subscription type back into a column of its own, since it is an attribute of a subscription. Next, we need to add constraints to deal with the constraints on each subscription.

```
CREATE TABLE Subscriptions
(subscr_id INTEGER NOT NULL PRIMARY KEY
   REFERENCES SubscriptionTypes(subscr_id),
org_name CHAR(35) DEFAULT '{Current Resident}',
last_name CHAR(15),
first_name CHAR(15),
subscr_type CHAR(1) DEFAULT 'I' NOT NULL
     CHECK (subscr_type IN ('I', 'O'),

CONSTRAINT known_addressee
CHECK (COALESCE (org_name, first_name, last_name) IS NOT NULL);

CONSTRAINT junkmail
CHECK (CASE WHEN subscr_type = 'I'
                 AND org_name = '{Current Resident}'
            THEN 1
            WHEN subscr_type = 'O'
                 AND org_name = '{Current Resident}'
            THEN 0 ELSE 1 END = 1),
address1 CHAR(35) NOT NULL,
..);
```

The known_addressee constraint says that we have to have a line with some addressee for this to be a valid subscription. The junk mail constraint assures that anything not aimed at a known person is classified as an individual subscription.

### 5.6.2 Row Level Attribute Splitting

Consider this table, which directly models a sign-in/sign-out sheet.

```
CREATE TABLE RegisterBook
(emp_name CHAR(35) NOT NULL,
sign_time TIMESTAMP DEFAULT CURRENT_TIMESTAMP NOT NULL,
sign_action CHAR (3) DEFAULT 'IN' NOT NULL
 CHECK (sign_action IN ('IN', 'OUT')),
PRIMARY KEY (emp_name, sign_time));
```

To answer any basic query, you need to use two rows in a self-join to get the sign-in and sign-out pairs for each employee. The correction design would have been:

```
CREATE TABLE RegisterBook
(emp_name CHAR(35) NOT NULL,
sign_in_time TIMESTAMP DEFAULT CURRENT_TIMESTAMP NOT NULL,
sign_out_time TIMESTAMP, -- null means current
PRIMARY KEY (emp_name, sign_in_time));
```

The single attribute, duration, has to be modeled as two columns in Standard SQL, but it was split into rows identified by a code to tell which end of the duration each one represented. If this were longitude and latitude, you would immediately see the problem and put the two parts of the one attribute (geographical location) in the same row.

## 5.7 Modeling Class Hierarchies in DDL

The classic scenario in an OO model calls for a root class with all the common attributes and then specialized subclasses under it. As an example, let me use an example from David Portas, which I like better than my example in the third edition.

```
CREATE TABLE Products
(sku CHAR(17) NOT NULL PRIMARY KEY,
 product_type CHAR(2) NOT NULL
 CHECK (product_type IN ('B', 'C', 'D' /* Book, CD or DVD */)),
 product_title VARCHAR(50) NOT NULL,
 UNIQUE (sku, product_type));

CREATE TABLE Books
(sku CHAR(17) NOT NULL PRIMARY KEY,
 product_type CHAR(2) DEFAULT 'B' NOT NULL
```

```
 CHECK (product_type ='B'),
page_cnt INTEGER NOT NULL,
FOREIGN KEY (sku, product_type)
 REFERENCES Products (sku, product_type)
 ON UPDATE CASCADE
 ON DELETE CASCADE);

CREATE TABLE CDs
(sku CHAR(17) NOT NULL PRIMARY KEY,
 product_type CHAR(2) DEFAULT 'C' NOT NULL
  CHECK (product_type ='C'),
 track_cnt INTEGER NOT NULL,
 FOREIGN KEY (sku, product_type)
  REFERENCES Products (sku, product_type
  ON UPDATE CASCADE
  ON DELETE CASCADE);

CREATE TABLE DVDs
(sku CHAR(17) NOT NULL PRIMARY KEY,
 product_type CHAR(2) DEFAULT 'D' NOT NULL
  CHECK (product_type ='D'),
 play_time INTERVAL HOUR TO SECOND NOT NULL,
 FOREIGN KEY (sku, product_type)
  REFERENCES Products (sku, product_type)
  ON UPDATE CASCADE
  ON DELETE CASCADE);
```

Notice the overlapping candidate keys. I then use a compound candidate key `(sku, product_type)` and a constraint in each subclass table to assure that the `product_type` is locked and agrees with the Vehicles table. Add some DRI actions and you are done.

I can continue to build a hierarchy like this. For example, if I had a Books table that broke down into paperbacks and hardbacks, I could use a schema like this:

```
CREATE TABLE Books
(sku CHAR(17) NOT NULL PRIMARY KEY,
product_type CHAR(2) NOT NULL
   CHECK(product_type IN ('PB', 'HB')),
UNIQUE (sku, product_type),
FOREIGN KEY (sku, product_type)
 REFERENCES Products (sku, product_type)
 ON UPDATE CASCADE
 ON DELETE CASCADE,
..);

CREATE TABLE Paperbacks
(sku CHAR(17) NOT NULL PRIMARY KEY,
product_type CHAR(2) DEFAULT 'PB' NOT NULL
   CHECK(product_type = 'PB'),
```

```
UNIQUE (sku, product_type),
FOREIGN KEY (sku, product_type)
 REFERENCES Books(sku, product_type)
 ON UPDATE CASCADE
 ON DELETE CASCADE,
..);

CREATE TABLE Hardbacks
(sku CHAR(17) NOT NULL PRIMARY KEY,
product_type CHAR(2) DEFAULT 'HB' NOT NULL
   CHECK(product_type = 'HB'),
UNIQUE (sku, product_type),
FOREIGN KEY (sku, product_type)
 REFERENCES Books (sku, product_type)
 ON UPDATE CASCADE
 ON DELETE CASCADE,
..);
```

The idea is to build a chain of identifiers and types in a UNIQUE() constraint that go up the tree when you use a REFERENCES constraint. Obviously, you can do variants of this trick to get different class structures.

Now start hiding all this stuff in VIEWs immediately and add an INSTEAD OF trigger to those VIEWs.

## 5.8 Exposed Physical Locators

SQL is supposed to use keys. Keys are a logical concept that is divorced completely from physical storage. Unfortunately, bad SQL programmers will use proprietary features to get the hardware to generate exposed physical locators. These numbers represent an event or location in the hardware and have nothing whatsoever to do with the logical model.

Do not confuse exposed physical locators with surrogate keys, indexes, hashing, and other physical access methods. In the words of Dr. Codd, "Database users may cause the system to generate or delete a surrogate, but they have no control over its value, *nor is its value ever displayed to them* . . ." (ACM TODS, pp. 409–410)—think of how an index works in most SQL implementations.

## 5.9 Auto-Incrementing Columns

Most SQLs have vendor extensions to create an auto-incrementing column or pseudo-column in their tables. These extensions are nonrelational, highly proprietary, and have major disadvantages. They all are based on exposing part of the physical state of the machine during the insertion process, in violation of Dr. Codd's rules for defining a relational database (i.e., Codd's rule #8, Physical Data Independence; see Chapter 2).

The early SQL products were built on existing file systems. The data was kept in physically contiguous disk pages, in physically contiguous rows, made up of physically contiguous columns. In short, just like a deck of punch cards or a magnetic tape. Most of these auto-increment features are an attempt to regain the physical sequence that SQL took out, so we can pretend that we have physically contiguous storage.

But physically contiguous storage is only one way of building a relational database and it is not always the best one. But aside from that, the whole idea of a relational database is that the user is not supposed to know how things are stored at all, much less write code that depends on the particular physical representation in a particular release of a particular product.

The exact method used varies from product to product. But the results of using them are all the same—their behavior is unpredictable and redundant. If you already have proper keys in the tables, these things are at best redundant. At one time, the argument was made that it was "cheaper" to join on simple integers than on longer columns. This is simply not true with modern RDBMS products.

Another major disadvantage of auto-incremented numbers as keys is that they have no check digits, so there is no way to determine if they are valid or not (for a discussion of check digits, see *Data and Databases*, Joe Celko, ISBN: 978-1-55860-432-2).

So, why do people use them? System-generated values are a fast and easy answer to the problem of obtaining a unique primary key. It requires no research and no real data modeling. Drug abuse is also a fast and easy answer to problems; I do not recommend either.

The Sybase/SQL Server family allows you to declare an exact numeric pseudo-column with the table property `IDENTITY`, so let's call it Microsoft `IDENTITY` to differentiate it from the ANSI Standard feature. Unfortunately, this is now a reserved word in SQL and has different meaning.

This is a count of the attempted physical insertions to the table. Notice the word "attempted"; failures or `ROLLBACK` will leave a gap in the numbering. This is totally unrelational but it is often used by new SQL Programmers to make the tables look like a sequential tape file that is accessed by a record position number or to mimic a pointer in a file system or network DBMS.

Let's look at the logical problems in detail. First try to create a table with two columns and try to make them both `IDENTITY` columns. If you cannot declare more than one column to be of a certain data type, then that thing is not a data type at all, by definition.

Next, create a table with one column and make it an IDENTITY column. Now try to insert, update, and delete different numbers from it. If you cannot insert, update, and delete rows from a table, then it is not a table by definition.

Finally create a simple table with one IDENTITY column and a few other columns. Use the statements:

```
CREATE TABLE Foobar -- not ANSI SQL!
(insertion_attempt_cnt INTEGER IDENTITY(1,1) NOT NULL,
a CHAR(2) NOT NULL,
b CHAR(2) NOT NULL,
c CHAR(2) NOT NULL);

BEGIN
INSERT INTO Foobar (a, b, c) VALUES ('a1', 'b1', 'c1');
INSERT INTO Foobar (a, b, c) VALUES ('a2', 'b2', 'c2');
INSERT INTO Foobar (a, b, c) VALUES ('a3', 'b3', 'c3');
END;
```

versus the logically equivalent statement:

```
INSERT INTO Foobar (a, b, c)
VALUES ('a1', 'b1', 'c1'), ('a2', 'b2', 'c2'), ('a3',
   'b3', 'c3');
```

or,

```
INSERT INTO Foobar (a, b, c)
SELECT x, y, z
 FROM Floob; —assuming Floob has the three rows
```

to put a few rows into the table. Notice that the Microsoft IDENTITY column sequentially numbered them in the order they were presented in the case of the first code block. If you delete a row, the gap in the sequence is not filled in and the sequence continues from the highest number that has ever been used in that column in that particular table.

The second and third statements are free to order the rows any way they wish. Since a query result is a table, and a table is a set that has no ordering, what should the Microsoft IDENTITY numbers be? The entire, whole, completed set is presented to Foobar all at once, not a row at a time. There are (n!) ways to number (n) rows. Which one did you pick? The answer has been to use whatever the physical order of the result set happened to be—that nonrelational phrase, "physical order" again!

But it is actually worse than that. If the same query is executed again, but with new statistics or after an index has been dropped or added, the new execution plan could bring the result set back in a different physical order. Can you explain from a logical model why the same rows in the second query get different Microsoft IDENTITY numbers? In the relational model, they should be treated the same if all the values of all the attributes are identical.

The following statement ought to leave the database the same. You are deleting and reinserting the same data in a single transaction.

```
BEGIN ATOMIC
DELETE FROM Foobar
WHERE id_col = 41;
INSERT INTO Foobar VALUES (<<values of original row 41>>);
END;
```

But the Microsoft IDENTITY will be changed. You can do the same sort of thing with an UPDATE that swaps the columns in two different rows since the Microsoft IDENTITY cannot be changed by the DML statements.

Think about trying to do replication on two databases that differ only by an index or by cache size or something that occasionally gives them different execution plans for the same statements.

Want to try to maintain or port such a system?

### 5.9.1 ROWID and Physical Disk Addresses

Oracle has the ability to expose the physical address of a row on the hard drive as a special variable called ROWID. This is the fastest way to locate a row in a table since the read-write head is positioned to the row immediately. This exposure of the underlying physical storage at the logical level means that Oracle is committed to using contiguous storage for the rows of a table. This means that they cannot use hashing, distributed databases, dynamic bit vectors, or any of several newer techniques for VLDB (Very Large Databases). When the database is moved or reorganized for any reason, the ROWID is changed.

### 5.9.2 IDENTITY Columns

An IDENTITY column provides a way for the SQL engine to automatically generate a unique numeric value for each row that is added to the table. When creating a table where you know that you need to uniquely identify each row that will be added to the table, you can add an identity column to the table. To guarantee a unique numeric value for each row that is added to a table, you should define a unique index on the identity column or declare it a primary key.

*Restrictions*

Once created, you cannot alter the table description to include an identity column.

If rows are inserted into a table with explicit identity column values specified, the next internally generated value is not updated, and may conflict with existing values in the table. Duplicate values will generate an error message if the uniqueness of the values in the identity column is being enforced by a primary key or a unique index that has been defined on the identity column.

It is the AS IDENTITY clause on the CREATE TABLE statement that allows for the specification of the identity column.

The following is an example of defining an identity column on the CREATE TABLE statement:

```
CREATE TABLE table
(<column name> INTEGER NOT NULL GENERATED [ALWAYS | BY
   DEFAULT]
      AS IDENTITY (START WITH <start value>, INCREMENT BY
         <increment value>))
```

In this example the third column is the identity column. You can also specify the value used in the column to uniquely identify each row when added. Here the first row entered has the value of 100 placed in the column; every subsequent row added to the table has the associated value increased by five.

Some additional example uses of an identity column are an order number, an employee number, a stock number, or an incident number. The values for an identity column can be generated by an internal counter attached to the table.

An identity column defined as GENERATED ALWAYS is given values that are always generated by the SQL engine. Applications are not allowed to provide an explicit value. An identity column defined as GENERATED BY DEFAULT gives applications a way to explicitly provide a value for the identity column. If the application does not provide a value, then the SQL engine will generate one. Since the application controls the value, the SQL engine cannot guarantee the uniqueness of the value. The GENERATED BY DEFAULT clause is meant for use for data propagation where the intent is to copy the contents of an existing table; or, for the unloading and reloading of a table.

## 5.9.3 Comparing IDENTITY Columns and Sequences

Although there are similarities between IDENTITY columns and sequences, there are also differences. The characteristics of each can be used when designing your database and applications.

An identity column has the following characteristics:

- An identity column can be defined as part of a table only when the table is created. Once a table is created, you cannot alter it to add an identity column. (However, existing identity column characteristics may be altered.)
- An identity column automatically generates values for a single table.
- When an identity column is defined as `GENERATED ALWAYS`, the values used are always generated by the database manager. Applications are not allowed to provide their own values during the modification of the contents of the table.

## 5.10 Generated Identifiers

There are several schemes for generating Identifiers that are unique across any database. The two most popular ones are GUID (Global Unique Identifier) from Microsoft and UUID (Universal Unique Identifier) from the Open Source Foundation.

### 5.10.1 Industry Standard Unique Identifiers

Validation and Verification are two important concepts in any data element, but they are most important for identifiers. Validation means that the data element's value can be seen to have the correct form. For example, I know that a United States ZIP code is five digits, no more no less. This lets me add a simple constraint to be sure the data have the correct regular express: "CONSTRAINT Valid_Zip_Code CHECK (zip_code SIMILAR TO [:DIGIT:]{5})" in the DDL.

Furthermore, I know that 99950 in Ketchikan, Alaska is the highest code issued and that 00501 in Holtsville, New York (U.S. Internal Revenue Service Center) is the lowest code issued. This lets me do a simple "CONSTRAINT Valid_Zip_Code_Range CHECK (zip_code BETWEEN '00501' AND '99950')" in my DDL. Other valuation methods include checking digits, which I discussed in my book, *Data, Measurements and Standards in SQL* (2009, ISBN 978-0123747228).

Verification is the ability to go to a trusted source and confirm that the identifier actually identifies a real data element. For example, the simple range check on ZIP code tells that 00000 and 99999 are invalid codes, and I can find the subranges that tell me the state to which a ZIP belongs. But I need to go to the US Postal Service to discover 75003 has not been issued as of 2010.

UUIDs, GUIDs, IDENTITY and other auto-incrementing features discussed in Chapter 4 are locally generated via a formula or a counter. Their fixed format allows you to validate them in your own code. But there is no authority that can verify them. You need to see if you can find an Industry Standard Identifier.

### 5.10.2 Department of Defense UIDs

Another related effort is the US Department of Defense (DoD) and NATO program of identifying all physical assets over $5000 in value. This approach to asset identification and management is the UID (Universal Identifier). UID became mandatory in 2004, but was slow in implementation. The parts of bar codes, if they cost more than $5000, are mission-critical or spare/repair parts. These unique identifiers are stored in an enormous database called the UID Registry.

At a UID Forum event in San Diego in February 2007, the DoD announced that more than one million assets had been assigned a UII (unique item identifier) and stored in the UID Registry. The UID Registry will eventually contain more than 100 million entries.

The system builds on existing identification systems as well as having its own rules. Here is a quick list:

- UID Construct 1, composed of Issuing Agency Code, an Enterprise Identifier, and a Serial Number unique within the Enterprise
- UID Construct 2, composed of Issuing Agency Code, an Enterprise Identifier, a Part Number or Batch/Lot Code, and a Serial Number (unique within the Part Number)
- Vehicle Identification Number (VIN)
- Global Returnable Asset Identifier (GRAI)
- Global Individual Asset Identifier (GIAI)
- Electronic Serial Number (ESN), typically assigned to cell phones

The assets that meet the criteria must be identified using the 2D data matrix bar codes (they look like a small checkerboard). Complete UID marking of all legacy assets was to be completed by 2010. You can get details at http://www.acq.osd.mil/dpap/pdi/uid/index.html.

### 5.10.3 Sequence Generator Functions

`COUNTER(*)`, `NUMBER(*)`, `IDENTITY`, and the like are proprietary features that return a new incremented value each time this function is used in an expression. This is a way to generate unique identifiers. This can be either a function call or a column property, depending on the product. This is also a horrible, non-standard, nonrelational proprietary extension that should be avoided whenever possible.

We will spend some time later on ways to get sequences and unique numbers inside Standard SQL without proprietary code or using exposed physical locators in the hardware.

### 5.10.4 Unique Value Generators

The most important property of any usable unique value generator is that it will never generate the same value twice. Sequential integers are the first approach vendors implemented in their product as a substitute for a proper key.

In essence, they are a piece of code inside SQL that looks at the last allocated value and adds one to get the next value. Let's start from scratch and build our own version of such a procedure. First create a table called GeneratorValues with one row and two columns:

```
CREATE TABLE GeneratorValues
(lock CHAR(1) DEFAULT 'X' NOT NULL PRIMARY KEY -- only one row
   CHECK (lock = 'X'),
keyval INTEGER DEFAULT 1 NOT NULL -- positive numbers only
   CHECK (keyval > 0));

-- let everyone use the table
GRANT SELECT, UPDATE(keyval)
ON TABLE GeneratorValues
TO PUBLIC;
```

Now it needs a function to get out a value and do the increment:

```
CREATE FUNCTION Generator()
RETURNS INTEGER
LANGUAGE SQL
DETERMINISTIC
BEGIN
-- SET ISOLATION = SERIALIZABLE;
UPDATE GeneratorValues
 SET keyval = keyval + 1;
RETURN (SELECT keyval FROM GeneratorValues);
COMMIT;
END;
```

This looks pretty good, but if there are multiple users, this code fragment is capable of allocating duplicate values to different users. It is important to isolate the execution of the code to one and only one user at a time by using `SET ISOLATION =`

SERIALIZABLE. Various SQL products will have slightly different ways of achieving this effect based on their concurrency control methods.

More bad news is that in pessimistic locking systems, you can get serious performance problems because of lock contention when a transaction is in serial isolation. The users are put in a single queue for access to the Generator table.

If the application demands gap-free numbering, then we not only have to guarantee that no two sessions ever get the same value, we must also guarantee that no value is ever wasted. Therefore the lock on the Generator table must be held until the key value is actually used and the entire transaction is committed. Exactly how to handle this is implementation defined, so I am not going to comment on it.

### 5.10.5 Verification Sources

Broadly speaking, an identifier can be verified by a single company that controls it, a local agent for the Standards group issuing the identifier, a consortium within the industry, or an appropriate national or international body. Here are some useful examples.

The Data Universal Numbering System (DUNS) is a numeric identifier controlled by Dun & Bradstreet (D&B) for a single business entity. It has been in use since 1965. It started as part of their credit reporting and it is now a common international standard. It is NOT a national tax identifier. For example, DELL Computers requires all of its suppliers, consultants, etc., to bill by using the DUNS. The Office of Management and Budget (OMB) requires a DUNS for all grant applicants for new or renewal. The United Nations also uses it. There are about 160 million DUNS in use in the United States alone.

The DUNS number is a nine-digit random number written without punctuation. Until 2006, it had a MOD 10 check digit, but stopped this feature to increase the range of numbers. There is no charge for a DUNS number and you can apply for it online (http://www.dnb.com/us/duns_update/index.html), but it can take some time. You can also request one and pay an investigation fee to get it is issued immediately.

The Digital Object Identifier (DOI) is a way to identify content objects on the internet. DOI codes are assigned to any entity for use on digital networks. They are used to provide current information, including where they (or information about them) can be found on the Internet. Information about a digital object may change over time, including where to find it, but its DOI name will not change. The International DOI Foundation (http://www.doi.org/), which is an open membership consortium including both commercial and non-commercial partners, is trying to become an ISO Standard. As of this writing, approximately 40 million DOI names have been assigned by DOI System Registration Agencies in the US, Australia, and Europe.

The International Standard Audiovisual Number (ISAN) is a standards identifier for audiovisual works, similar to the International Standard Book Number (ISBN) for books or the International Standard Serial Number (ISSN) for periodicals. The ISAN standard is covered by ISO standard 15706:2002 and ISO 15706-2.

The Global Trade Item Number (GTIN) actually refers to a family of bar codes on retail packaging. For North American companies, the UPC is the most common member of the GTIN. The National Association of Food Chains (NAFC) Parts 1 and 2 of the Universal Grocery Products Identification Code (UGPIC) in 1970. The U.S. Supermarket Ad Hoc Committee on a Uniform Grocery Product Code was formed and in 1973 the Committee had define the UPC system.

An International Securities Identification Number (ISIN) uniquely identifies a security according to ISO 6166. ISINs are issued for bonds, commercial paper, equities and warrants. The ISIN code is a 12-character alpha-numerical string. The ISIN identifies the security, not the exchange (if any) on which it trades; it is not a ticker symbol. Stock traded on several different stock exchanges worldwide (and therefore priced in different currencies) will have the same ISIN on each, though not the same ticker symbol. Stock markets are identified by another identifier, MIC (ISO 10383, "Codes for Exchanges and Market Identification"), a four letter code.

## 5.11 A Remark on Duplicate Rows

Both of Dr. Codd's relational models do not allow duplicate rows and are based on a set theoretical model; SQL has always allowed duplicates rows and been based on a multiset or bag model.

When the question of duplicates came up in SQL committee, we decided to leave it in the standard. The example we used internally, and which Len Gallagher used in a reply letter to *Database Programming & Design* magazine and David Beech used in a letter to *Datamation*, was a cash register receipt with multiple occurrences of cans of cat food on it. That is how this got to be the “cat food problem” in the literature.

The fundamental question is; what are you modeling in a table? Dr. Codd and Chris Date’s position is that a table is a collection of facts. The other position is that a table can represent an entity, a class, or a relationship among entities. With that approach, a duplicate row means more than one occurrence of an entity. This leads to a more object-oriented view of data where I have to deal with different fundamental relationships among “duplicates,” such as:

Identity: “Clark Kent is Superman!” We really have only one entity, but multiple expressions of it. These expression are not substitutable (Clark Kent does not fly until he changes into Superman).

Equality: “Two plus two is four.” We really have only one entity with multiple expressions that are always substitutable.

Equivalency: “You use only half as much Concentrated Sudso as your old detergent to get the same cleaning power!” We have two distinct entities, substitutable both ways under all conditions.

Substitutability: “We are out of gin; would you like a vodka martini?” We have two distinct entities, whose replacement for each other is not always in both directions or under all conditions. You might be willing to accept a glass of vodka when there is no wine, but you can not make a wine sauce with a cup of vodka.

Dr. Codd later added a “degree of duplication” operator to his model as a way of handling duplicates when he realized that there is information in duplication that has to be handled. The degree of duplication is not exactly a `COUNT(*)` or a quantity column in the relation. It does not behave like a numeric column. For example, given table A and let dod mean the “degree of duplication” operator for each row,

**A**

| x | y |
|---|---|
| 1 | a |
| 2 | b |
| 3 | b |

when I do a projection on them, I eliminate duplicates rows in Codd's model, but I can reconstruct the original table from the dod function:

**A**

| y | dod |
|---|---|
| a | 1 |
| b | 2 |

See the difference? It is an operator, not a value.

Haskug said all of this; I try to only use duplicate rows for loading data into an SQL database from legacy sources. It is very frequent when you get data from the real world—like cash register tapes.

Otherwise, I might leave duplicates in results because using a `SELECT DISTINCT` to remove them will: (1) cost too much sorting time and (2) force an ordering in the working table that results in a bad performance hit later.

Dr. Codd mentions this example in his book as "The Supermarket Checkout Problem" (*The Relational Model for Database Management: Version 2,* Addison-Wesley, 1990, Section 23.02.5, pp. 378–379). He critiques the problem and credits it to David Beech in an article entitled "The Need for Duplicate Rows in Tables" (*Datamation,* January 1989).

## 5.12 Other Schema Objects

Let's be picky about definitions. A database is the data that sits under the control of the database management system (DBMS). The DBMS has the schema, rules, and operators that apply to the database. The schema contains the definitions of the objects in the database. But we always just say "the database" as if it had no parts to it.

In the original SQL-89 language, the only data structure the user could access via SQL was the table, which could be permanent (base tables) or virtual (views). Standard SQL also allows the DBA to define other schema objects, but most of these new features are not yet available in SQL products, or the versions of them that are available are proprietary. Let's take a quick look at these new features, but without spending much time on their details.

### 5.12.1 Schema Tables

The usual way an SQL engine keeps the information it needs about the schema is to put it in SQL tables. No two vendors agree on how the schema tables should be named or structured. The Standard SQL standard defines a set of standard schema tables, which no one implements. Though I doubt that anyone will ever implement them, I do feel that vendors will generate schema information in those formats for data exchange.

Every SQL product will allow users to query the schema tables. User groups will have libraries of queries for getting useful information out of the schema tables; you should take the time to get copies of them.

Standard SQL also includes tables for supporting temporal functions, collations, character sets, and so forth, but they might be implemented differently in your actual products.

## 5.13 Temporary Tables

Tables in Standard SQL can be defined as persistent base tables, local temporary tables, or global temporary tables. The complete syntax is:

```
<table definition> ::=
 CREATE [{GLOBAL | LOCAL} TEMPORARY] TABLE <table name>
  <table element list>
  [ON COMMIT {DELETE | PRESERVE} ROWS]
```

A local temporary table belongs to a single user. A global temporary table is shared by more than one user. When a session using a temporary table is over and the work is COMMIT-ed, the table can be either emptied or saved for the next transaction in the user's session. This is a way of giving the users working storage without giving them `CREATE TABLE` (and therefore `DROP TABLE` and `ALTER TABLE`) privileges.

This has been a serious problem in SQL products for some time. When a programmer can create temporary tables on the fly, the design of his or her code quickly becomes a sequential file-processing program with all the temporary working tapes replaced by temporary working tables. Because the temporary tables are actual tables, they take up physical storage space. If a hundred users call the same procedure, it can allocate tables for a hundred copies of the same data and bring performance down to nothing.

## 5.14 CREATE DOMAIN Statement

The DOMAIN is a new schema element in Standard SQL that allows you to declare an in-line macro that will allow you to put a commonly used column definition in one place in the schema. You should expect to see this feature in SQL products shortly, since it is easy to implement. The syntax is:

```
<domain definition> ::=
CREATE DOMAIN <domain name> [AS] <data type>
 [<default clause>]
 [<domain constraint>. . .]
 [<collate clause>]

<domain constraint> ::=
 [<constraint name definition>]
 <check constraint definition> [<constraint attributes>]

<alter domain statement> ::=
 ALTER DOMAIN <domain name> <alter domain action>

<alter domain action> ::=
   <set domain default clause>
 | <drop domain default clause>
 | <add domain constraint definition>
 | <drop domain constraint definition>
```

It is important to note that a DOMAIN has to be defined with a basic data type and not with other DOMAINs. Once declared, a DOMAIN can be used in place of a data type declaration on a column.

The CHECK() clause is where you can put the code for validating data items with check digits, ranges, lists, and other conditions. Since the DOMAIN is in one place, you can make a good argument for writing:

```
CREATE DOMAIN StateCode AS CHAR(2)
  DEFAULT '??'
  CONSTRAINT valid_state_code
  CHECK (VALUE IN ('AL', 'AK', 'AZ', ...));
```

instead of:

```
CREATE DOMAIN StateCode AS CHAR(2)
  DEFAULT '??'
  CONSTRAINT valid_state_code
  CHECK (VALUE IN (SELECT state FROM StateCodeTable));
```

The second method would have been better if you did not have a DOMAIN and had to replicate the CHECK() clause in multiple tables in the database. This would collect the values and their changes in one place instead of many.

## 5.15 CREATE TRIGGER Statement

There is a feature in many versions of SQL, called a TRIGGER, that will execute a block of procedural code against the database when a table event occurs. You can think of a TRIGGER as a generalization of the referential actions.

The procedural code is usually written in a proprietary language, but some products let you attach programs in standard procedural languages. A TRIGGER could be used to automatically handle discontinued merchandise, for example, by creating a credit slip in place of the original order item data.

There is a standard for TRIGGERs using the SQL/PSM. The proposal is fairly complicated and no product has implemented it completely. You should look at what your particular vendor has given you if you want to work with TRIGGERs.

The advantages of TRIGGERs over declarative referential integrity is that you can do everything that declarative referential integrity can and almost anything else, too. The disadvantages are that the optimizer cannot get any data from the procedural code, the TRIGGERs take longer to execute, and they are not portable from product to product.

My advice would be to avoid TRIGGERs when you can use declarative referential integrity instead. If you do use them, check the code very carefully and keep it simple so that you will not hurt performance.

## 5.16 CREATE PROCEDURE Statement

The PROCEDURE is a schema object that allows you to declare and name a body of procedural code using the same proprietary language as the TRIGGERs or to invoke a host language library routine. The two major differences are that a PROCEDURE can accept and return parameters and it is invoked by a call from a user session.

Again, many SQL products have had their own versions of a procedure, so you should look at what your particular vendor has given you, check the code very carefully, and keep it simple so that you will not hurt performance.

The SQL/PSM (see *Understanding SQL's Stored Procedures,* Jim Melton, ISBN 1-55860-461-8) for procedural code is an ISO Standard. Still, even with the move to the ISO Standard, existing implementations will still have their own proprietary syntax in many places.

## 5.17 DECLARE CURSOR Statement

I will not spend much time with cursors in this book, but you should understand them at a high level since you will see them in actual code. In spite of a standard syntax, every product has a proprietary version of cursors. This is because cursors are a low-level construct that works close to the physical implementation in the product.

A CURSOR is a way of converting an SQL result set into a sequential data structure that looks like a simple sequential file that can be handled by the procedural host language that contains the very statement that executes and creates a structure that looks like a sequential file. In fact, the whole cursor process looks like an old-fashioned magnetic tape system!

You might have noticed that in SQL, the keyword CREATE builds persistent schema objects. The keyword DECLARE builds transient objects that disappear with the end of the session in which they were built. This is why you say DECLARE CURSOR and not CREATE CURSOR.

First, you allocate working storage in the host program with a BEGIN DECLARE ... END DECLARE section. This sets up an area where SQL variables can be converted into host language data types and vice versa. NULLs are handled by declaring INDICATOR variables in the host language BEGIN DECLARE section, which are paired with the appropriate host variables. An INDICATOR is an exact numeric data type with a scale of zero—that is, some kind of integer in the host language.

DECLARE CURSOR Statement

The DECLARE CURSOR statement must appear next. The SQL-92 syntax is fairly representative of actual products, but you must read your manual.

```
<declare cursor> ::=
  DECLARE <cursor name> [INSENSITIVE] [SCROLL] CURSOR
   FOR <cursor specification>

<cursor specification> ::=
  <query expression> [<order by clause>]
   [<updatability clause>]

<updatability clause> ::= FOR {READ ONLY | UPDATE [OF
   <column name list>]}

<order by clause> ::= ORDER BY <sort specification list>

<sort specification list> ::=
  <sort specification> [{<comma> <sort specification>}...]

<sort specification> ::= <sort key> [<collate clause>]
 [<ordering specification>]
```

```
<sort key> ::= <column name>
<ordering specification> ::= ASC | DESC
```

A few things need explaining. First of all, the ORDER BY clause is part of a cursor and not part of a SELECT statement. Because some SQL products such as SQL Server and Sybase allow the user to create implicit cursors, many newbies get this wrong. This is easy to implement in products that evolved from sequential file systems and still expose this architecture to the user in violation of Dr. Codd's rules. Oracle is probably the worst offender as of this writing, but some of the "micro-SQLs" are just as bad.

If either INSENSITIVE, SCROLL, or ORDER BY is specified, or if the working table is a read-only, then an <updatability clause> of READ ONLY is implicit. Otherwise, an <updatability clause> of FOR UPDATE without a <column name list> is implicit.

OPEN Statement

The OPEN <cursor name> statement positions an imaginary read/write head before the first record in the cursor. FETCH statements can then move this imaginary read/write head from record to record. When the read/write head moves past the last record, an exception is raised, like an EOF (end of file) flag in a magnetic tape file system.

Watch out for this model! In some file systems, the read/write head starts on the first and the EOF flag is set to TRUE when it reads the last record. Simply copying the algorithms from your procedural code into SQL/PSM might not work.

FETCH Statement

```
<fetch statement> ::= FETCH [[<fetch orientation>]
    FROM] <cursor name> INTO <fetch target list>

<fetch orientation> ::= NEXT | PRIOR | FIRST | LAST
    | {ABSOLUTE | RELATIVE} <simple value specification>
```

The FETCH statement takes one row from the cursor, then converts each SQL data type into a host-language data type and puts the result into the appropriate host variable. If the SQL value was a NULL, the INDICATOR is set to –1; if no indicator was specified, an exception condition is raised.

As you can see, the host program must be sure to check the INDICATORs, because otherwise the value of the parameter will be garbage. If the parameter is passed to the host language without any problems, the INDICATOR is set to zero. If the value being passed to the host program is a non-NULL character string and it has an indicator, the indicator is set to the length of the SQL string and can be used to detect string overflows or to set the length of the parameter.

The <fetch orientation> tells the read/write head which way to move. NEXT and PRIOR read one record forward or backward from the current position. FIRST and LAST put the read/write on the fist or last records, respectively. The ABSOLUTE fetch moves to a given record number. The RELATIVE fetch moves the read/write head forward or backward (n) records from the current position. Again, this is a straight imitation of a sequential file system.

CLOSE Statement

The CLOSE <cursor name> statement resets the cursor read/write head to a position before the first row in the cursor. The cursor still exists, but must be reopened before it can be used. This is similar to the CLOSE FILE operations in FORTRAN or COBOL, but with an important difference! The cursor can be recomputed when it is reopened.

DEALLOCATE Statement

The DEALLOCATE CURSOR statement frees up the working storage in the host program. Think of it as dismounting a tape from the tape drive in a sequential file system.

## 5.17.1 How to Use a CURSOR

The best performance improvement technique for cursors inside the database is not to use them. SQL engines are designed for set processing and work better with sets of data than with individual rows. The times when using CURSOR is unavoidable usually deal with corrections to the database that were caused by an improper design, or when speed of a cursor is faster because of the physical implementation in the product. For example, redundant duplicates can be taken out of a table that does not have a key with a cursor.

The old argument for cursors in the original Sybase SQL Server training course was this example. You own a bookstore and you want to change prices; all books $25 and over are reduced 10%, and all books under $25 are increased 15%.

```
BEGIN ATOMIC
UPDATE Books
 SET price = price * 0.90
WHERE price >= $25.00;
UPDATE Books
 SET price = price * 1.15
WHERE price < $25.00;
END;
```

Oops! Look at a book that was $25.00 ((25.00 * .90) *1.10) = $24.75. So you were told to cursor through the table, and change each row with a cursor.

Today you write:

```
UPDATE Books
 SET price
   = CASE WHEN price < $25.00;
   THEN price * 1.15
   WHEN price >= $25.00
   THEN price * 0.90
   ELSE price END;
```

But Steve Kass pointed out that even back then, it was possible to avoid a cursor:

```
BEGIN ATOMIC
UPDATE Books
 SET price = price * 1.80
WHERE price >= $25.00;
UPDATE Books
 SET price = price * 1.15
WHERE price < $25.00;
UPDATE Books
 SET price = price * 0.50
WHERE price >= $45.00;
END;
```

However, this code makes three passes through the Books table instead of just one. This could be worse than a cursor!

Limit the number of rows and columns in the cursor's `SELECT` statement to only those required by the desired result set. This will avoid unnecessary fetching of data that in turn will require fewer server resources and increase cursor performance.

Use `FOR READ ONLY` instead of `UPDATE` cursors if possible. You will have to watch the transaction isolation level however.

Opening an `INSENSITIVE` cursor can cause its rows to be copied to a working table in many products or locked at the table level in others.

Do a `CLOSE` cursor as soon as you are finished with the result set. This will release any locks on the rows. Always remember to deallocate your cursors when you are finished.

Look for your product options. For example, SQL Server has `FAST_FORWARD` and `FORWARD_ONLY` cursor options when working with unidirectional, read-only result sets. Using `FAST_FORWARD` defines a `FORWARD_ONLY, READ_ONLY` cursor with a number of internal performance optimizations.

Be careful with modifying large numbers of rows via a cursor loop that are contained within a transaction. Depending on the transaction isolation level, those rows may remain locked until the transaction is committed or rolled back, possibly causing resource contention on the server.

In Standard SQL, there is an SQLSTATE code that tells you if the result set of a GROUP BY has members that excluded NULLs from their aggregate computations. This warning can be raised in the DECLARE CURSOR statement, the OPEN statement, or when the row representing such a grouping is FETCH-ed. Know how your product handles this.

The truth is that the host languages have to use cursors because they are designed for sequential file systems.

### 5.17.2 Positioned UPDATE and DELETE Statements

Obviously, the cursor needs an explicit or implicit <updatability clause> of FOR UPDATE for this to work, and it has to be in the same module as the positioned statements. You get an exception when you try to change a READ ONLY cursor or if the cursor is not positioned on a record.

The clause CURRENT OF <cursor name> refers to the record that the imaginary read/write heads is on. This cursor record has to map back to one and only one row in the base table.

UPDATE Statement

```
<update statement: positioned>
 ::= UPDATE <table name>
SET <set clause list>
    WHERE CURRENT OF <cursor name>
```

The cursor remains positioned on its current row, even if an exception condition is raised during the update attempt.

DELETE FROM Statement

```
<delete statement: positioned>
 ::= DELETE FROM <table name>
    WHERE CURRENT OF <cursor name>
```

If, while the cursor is open, another DELETE FROM or UPDATE statement attempts to modify the current cursor record, then a cursor operation conflict warning is raised. The transaction isolation level then determines what happens. If the <delete statement: positioned> deleted the last cursor record, then the position of the cursor is after the last record; otherwise, the position of the cursor is before the next cursor record.

6

# PROCEDURAL, SEMIPROCEDURAL, AND DECLARATIVE PROGRAMMING

This chapter is about programming and your mindset. SQL allows procedural code modules to be kept in the schema and will work inside procedural host languages. Avoid programming SQL as if it is a procedural file system language—SQL is a declarative language and requires a different mindset.

## 6.1 Basics of Software Engineering

The basics of software engineering do not change in SQL. They are realized differently. Most of us (with the exceptions of those rare programmers who started in LISP, APL, FP, Haskell, or other exotic languages) learned a block structured programming language that evolved from Algol-60. The same principles that apply to procedural code still apply to them.

In the late 1970s, we found that we could write better code (i.e., faster, provably correct, easier to maintain, etc.) in languages that had local scoping rules, and code modules with one entry and one exit point. We eliminated the GO TO statement and used a simple set of control structures. This was the structured programming revolution.

## 6.2 Cohesion

Cohesion is how well a module does one and only one thing—that it is logically coherent. The modules should have strong cohesion. You ought to name the module in the format "`<verb><object>`", where the "`<object>`" is a specific logical unit in the data model and "`<verb>`" is a single clear action. There are several types of cohesion. We rank them, going from the worst form of cohesion to the best.

Joe Celko's SQL for Smarties. DOI: 10.1016/B978-0-12-382022-8.00006-5

1. Coincidental cohesion: Coincidental cohesion is when parts of a module are grouped arbitrarily. A Coincidental module is a train wreck of unrelated actions. It is a "Britney Spears, Squids, and Automobiles" module whose description would be a compound or complex sentence. The best example of this in SQL is the OTLT (One True Lookup Table) design flaw. We will get to that later.
2. Logical cohesion: Logical cohesion is when parts of a module are grouped because they logically do the same thing, even if they are different by nature. In SQL the most common example is a general module that does an update, insert, or delete on *any* table—it works on Britney Spears, Squids, or Automobiles. Look for this to be implemented with dynamic SQL.
3. Temporal cohesion: Temporal cohesion is when parts of a module are grouped by when they are processed; for example, a module that does all the initialization for the whole system.
4. Procedural cohesion: Procedural cohesion is when parts of a module are grouped because they always follow a certain sequence of execution. For example, when a user logs onto the database, we check user privileges and log the sign-in.
5. Communicational cohesion: Communicational cohesion is when parts of a module are grouped because they operate on the same data element. Imagine a series of UPDATE statements that affect the same column in one procedure.
6. Sequential cohesion: Sequential cohesion is when parts of a module are grouped because the output from one part is the input to another part, like an assembly line. In SQL, look for the use of temporary tables as a replacement for scratch tapes in a magnetic tape file system.
7. Functional cohesion: Functional cohesion is when a module *always* does a *single well-defined task*, like a mathematical function. This is what we want in a module and it is the basis for functional programming languages.

You can look up the detailed definitions, if you missed them in your introductory classes.

## 6.3 Coupling

Coupling is how dependent modules are on each other. If modules have to be executed in a certain order, then they are strongly coupled. If they can be executed independently of each other and put together like Lego blocks, then they are loosely or weakly coupled. There are several kinds of coupling, which are ranked from worst to best.

1. Content coupling: One module modifies or relies on the internal workings of another module.
2. Common coupling: Two modules share the same global data.
3. External coupling: Two modules share an externally imposed data format, communication protocol, or device interface.
4. Control coupling: One module controls the execution by passing flags. This is one of the reasons that BIT flags are not good SQL programming.
5. Stamp coupling (data-structured coupling): Modules share a composite data structure and use only part of it. This can be done with VIEWs in SQL.
6. Data coupling: Modules share simple data elements. Think about passing parameters; these are the only data that are shared.
7. Message coupling: This is the loosest type of coupling. Modules are not dependent on each other; instead they use a public interface to exchange parameterless messages. This is more of an OO approach, but you see it in triggers, exception handlers, and other SQL features.

This is covered briefly in a chapter on writing stored procedures in my book *SQL Programming Style* (ISBN 978-0120887972). In the meantime, you should read DeMarco, Yourdon, Constantine, Myers, or several other of the pioneers of software engineering.

This is *far* more basic than SQL programming. This is what you are supposed to know before you write any code in *any* language.

## 6.4 The Big Leap

Most programmers discover that it is too big a big leap from a procedural mindset to a declarative mindset, and so they do not quite make the transition all at once. Instead they evolve from a procedural paradigm to a variety of *semiprocedural* programming styles.

This is just the way that we learn; a step at a time, not a leap of insight all at once. The first motion pictures, for example, were shot with a fixed position camera aimed at a stage. That is how people had seen stage plays for several thousand years. W. D. Griffith was to movies as Dr. Codd was to databases. Griffith made the first two-reeler in 1910; nobody had thought about more than one reel before that. Then in 1911 and 1912 he and his cameraman, Billy Bitzer, started moving the camera and lens while filming. He gave us new camera angles such as the close-up and soft focus.

### 6.4.1 A Common Error

Newsgroups are great for finding bad examples. A poster had a skeleton table with integer columns a, b, c, and d and he wanted to know how to write a trigger to assure that d = (a + b + c). Ignoring that he had already decided on the method to use, there are actually several methods for solving this problem:

1. CREATE PROCEDURE: A procedural answer. This means that you put an UPDATE inside the body of a stored procedure and invoke it as needed. If you forget, then your table is wrong.
2. CREATE TRIGGER: A procedural answer. His original answer is an improvement over the stored procedure in that it is always current. Unfortunately, it is going to be firing every time there is an update event on the table, then doing physical disk access.
3. SELECT statement: A declarative answer. He can simply write a SELECT statement with a column "(a + b + c) AS d" so that column d is created only when a particular query needs it.
4. CREATE VIEW: A declarative answer. The VIEW will also create column d only when it is needed, but there is no way to forget to do it and it hides the computation from the users.
5. Computed Column: A declarative answer. A computed column is basically the same as a VIEW, but it is part of the base table that would have been used by the VIEW. In his case, this looked like the best option, but that is not always true.

But the real question is, why did he assume that a trigger was the answer? Because it would *physically materialize* the d value. In a file system there is no such thing as a "virtual field"; fields have physical existence. Any computed value would be in the host program in a local variable. A procedure might not be invoked and the data could get out of control. Another give-away was that the columns for the computation were in left-to-right order, just like fields in a record. This poster had not made even the first step out of his old mindset.

### 6.4.2 An Improvement

In February 2010, I came across an example, in a Newsgroup discussion, of programmers making the steps, but not the leap. The code details are not relevant to the point I'm making so I am going to gloss over them. The thread starts with a posting about a user-defined function that is not working. His opening paragraph was:

> *I have the code below to take a set of INTEGER values and return a VARCHAR based on the combination of inputs. However, I'm getting an error on line 6, which is the first line where the word CASE pops up. Plenty of CASE statements have passed through my hands before, so I'm lost as to why this one is wrong.*

What followed was a CASE expression with BETWEENs and ORs and CASE within CASE constructs. It took pairs of (x, y) and produced an answer from a set of three values, call them {'a', 'b', 'c'}. Again, the coding details are not my point. The body of the function could just as well have been a complicated mathematical expression.

Two replies pointed out that CASE is an expression and not a statement in SQL. They also pointed out that he was returning a VARCHAR(1) instead of a CHAR(1). The CASE expression can be confusing to anyone who has been initially trained with a procedural language that has IF-THEN-ELSE statement constructs.

His code looked like this skeleton:

```
CREATE FUNCTION Find_Foobar (IN x INTEGER, IN y INTEGER)
RETURNS VARCHAR
WITH EXECUTE AS CALLER
AS
BEGIN
<< horrible CASE expression with x and y >>;
END;
```

The clean up and quick fix was:

```
CREATE FUNCTION Find_Foobar (IN in_x INTEGER,
   IN in_y INTEGER)
RETURNS CHAR(1)
WITH EXECUTE AS CALLER
AS
BEGIN
RETURN (<< horrible CASE expression with x and y >>);
END;
```

Someone else then asked if he had considered precalculating the CASE expression results and populating a table with them. This was good advice, since the number of (x, y) pairs involved came to a few thousand cases. There is no point in dismissing this solution when the look-up table is as small as this one. Read-only tables this size tend to be in main storage or cache, so they can be shared among many sessions, and you are not going to save much on memory by choosing a different method.

But the person who made this suggestion went on to add, "You can use the table with your user-defined function or you could use it without the user-defined function," but he did not explain what the differences are. They are important. Putting the data in the read-only tables this size will tend to keep it in main storage or cache. If you are really that tight for primary and/or secondary storage that you cannot fit a ~5K row table in your hardware, buy some chips and disks. They are so cheap today. Now the data can be shared among many sessions. The table and its indexes can be used by the optimizer. In SQL Server you can include the single column foobar in the index to get a covering index and performance improvement.

But if you choose to lock the data inside the procedural code of a user-defined function, can it be shared? Do computations get repeated with each invocation? What about indexes? Ouch! A user-defined function pretty much locks things inside. Standard SQL/PSM has a [NOT] DETERMINISTIC option in its procedure declarations. This tells the compiler whether the procedure or function is always going to return the same answer for the same arguments.

[*Note about Standard SQL terms*: A parameter is the formal place holder in the parameter list of a procedure declaration and an argument is the value passed in the invocation of the procedure.]

A nondeterministic function has to be computed over and over again, every time the user-defined function is called; if the query optimizer does not know for certain whether a procedure or function is deterministic, it has to assume it is not and go the long route.

Here is the skeleton of what was posted.

```
-- Create table
CREATE TABLE Foobar
(x INTEGER NOT NULL,
y INTEGER NOT NULL,
foobar CHAR(1) NOT NULL,
PRIMARY KEY CLUSTERED (x, y));

-- Populate table with recursive CTEs and proprietary SQL
   Server syntax:

INSERT INTO Foobar (x, y, foobar)
WITH
X_CTE(x)
AS
(SELECT * FROM (VALUES (100))
UNION ALL
SELECT x + 1
FROM X_CTE
WHERE x < 300),

Y_CTE(y)
AS
(SELECT * FROM (VALUES (1))
UNION ALL
```

```
SELECT y + 1
 FROM Y_CTE
WHERE y < 100)

SELECT x, y, << horrible CASE expression >> AS foobar
 FROM X_CTE
   CROSS JOIN
   Y_CTE;
```

This is a nice trick, but it is easy enough to rewrite this into portable Standard SQL, using a table of integers called Series (I used to call it Sequence, but that is now a reserved word in Standard SQL; if you have a better name, please tell me). This is the most common SQL auxiliary table; experienced SQL programmers create it and then a Calendar table at the start of almost all new projects.

```
INSERT INTO FooLookup (x, y, foobar)
SELECT X_CTE.x, Y_CTE.y, << horrible CASE expression >> AS
   foobar
FROM (SELECT seq
    FROM Series
   WHERE seq BETWEEN 100 AND 300) AS X_CTE(x)
  CROSS JOIN
  (SELECT seq
    FROM Series
   WHERE seq BETWEEN 1 AND 100) AS Y_CTE(y);
```

Recursion, a procedural tool, is expensive. But that is not my point. The first thought was to use a procedural tool and not a data driven approach to get that CROSS JOIN. See what I mean by a mindset? This is the semiprocedural guy going back to what he knows. He almost got to a declarative mindset.

Now let's go on with the rest of the skeleton code for the function:

```
CREATE FUNCTION Find_Foobar
(IN in_x INTEGER, IN in_y INTEGER)
RETURNS CHAR(1)
WITH EXECUTE AS CALLER
AS
BEGIN
RETURN
COALESCE
((SELECT foobar
  FROM Find_Foobar
 WHERE x = in_x
   AND y = in_y), 'A');
END;
```

The reason for COALESCE() is that 'A' is a default value in the outer CASE expression, but also a valid result in various THEN and ELSE clauses inside inner CASE expressions. The scalar query will return a NULL if it cannot find an (x, y, foobar) row in the table. If we know that the query covers the entire (x, y) universe, then we did not need the COALESCE() and could have avoided a user-defined function completely.

Now, let's think about declarative programming. In SQL that means constraints in the table declaration in the DDL. This skeleton has none except the PRIMARY KEY. Here is a problem that you find with magazine articles and newsgroup postings: It is so easy to skip over the constraints when you provide a skeleton table. You did not need them when you declared a file, did you? What we can forget is that the three SQL sublanguages (DDL, DML, and DCL) work together. In particular, the DDL constraints are used by the DML optimizer to provide a better execution strategy.

The `<< horrible CASE expression >>` implied expectations for x and y. We were given lower limits (100 and 1), but the upper limits were open after a small range of (x, y) pairs. I think we can assume that the original poster expected the vast majority of cases (or all of them) to fall in that small range and wanted to handle anything else as an error. In the real world, there is usually what Jerry Weinberg called "reasonableness checking" in data. The principle is also known as Zipf's Law or the "look for a horse and not a zebra" principle in medicine.

The simple first shot would be to assume we always know the limits and can simply use:

```
CREATE TABLE FooLookup
(x INTEGER NOT NULL
  CHECK (x BETWEEN 100 AND 300),
 y INTEGER NOT NULL
  CHECK (y BETWEEN 1 AND 100),
 foobar CHAR(1) DEFAULT 'A' NOT NULL
  CHECK (foobar) IN ('A', 'B', 'C'),
 PRIMARY KEY (x, y));
```

The DEFAULT 'A' subclause will take care of situations where we did not have an explicit value for foobar. This avoids the COALESCE(). But what if one of the parameters can be anything? That is easy: drop the CHECK() and add a comment. What if one of the parameters is half open or has a huge but sparse space? That is, we know a lower (upper) limit, but not the matching upper (lower) limit. Just use a simple comparison, such as CHECK (y >= 1), instead of a BETWEEN.

A common situation, which was done with nested CASE expression in the original, is that you know a range for a parameter and what the results are for the other parameter within that range. That might be easier to see with code. Here is a CASE expression for some of the possible (x, y) pairs:

```
CASE
WHEN x BETWEEN 100 AND 200
THEN CASE
  WHEN y IN (2, 4, 6, 8) THEN 'B'
  WHEN y IN (1, 3, 5, 7, 9) THEN 'C'
  END

WHEN x BETWEEN 201 AND 300
THEN CASE
  WHEN y IN (2, 4, 6, 8, 99) THEN 'C'
  WHEN y IN (3, 5, 7, 9, 100) THEN 'B'
  END
ELSE 'A'
END
```

This is the DML version of a constraint. It lives only in the UPDATE, INSERT, or SELECT statement where it appears. What we really want are constraints in the DDL so that all statements, present and future, use it. The trick is to create the table with low and high values for each parameter range; a single value is shown with the low and high values equal to each other.

```
CREATE TABLE FooLookup
(low_x INTEGER NOT NULL,
high_x INTEGER NOT NULL,
 CHECK (low_x <= high_x),
low_y INTEGER NOT NULL,
high_y INTEGER NOT NULL,
 CHECK (low_y <= high_y),
foobar CHAR(1) NOT NULL
 CHECK (foobar) IN ('A', 'B', 'C'),
PRIMARY KEY (x, y));
```

CASE expression now becomes Table 6.1.

As a safety device, put the default 'A' in ranges outside the rest of the table. I used −9999 and 9999 for the least and greatest limits, but you get the idea.

The query has to use BETWEENs on the high and low limits:

```
SELECT F.foobar, ..
FROM FooLookup AS F, ..
WHERE my_x BETWEEN F.low_x AND F.high_x
 AND my_y BETWEEN F.low_y AND F.high_y
 AND ..;
```

Is this always going to be the best way to do something? Who knows. Test it.

**Table 6.1 Function Look Up Table**

| low_x | high_x | low_y | high_y | foobar |
|---|---|---|---|---|
| 100 | 200 | 2 | 2 | 'B' |
| 100 | 200 | 6 | 6 | 'B' |
| 100 | 200 | 8 | 8 | 'B' |
| 100 | 200 | 1 | 1 | 'C' |
| 100 | 200 | 3 | 3 | 'C' |
| 100 | 200 | 5 | 5 | 'C' |
| 100 | 200 | 7 | 7 | 'C' |
| 100 | 200 | 9 | 9 | 'C' |
| 201 | 300 | 2 | 2 | 'C' |
| 201 | 300 | 4 | 4 | 'C' |
| 201 | 300 | 6 | 6 | 'C' |
| 201 | 300 | 8 | 8 | 'C' |
| 201 | 300 | 99 | 99 | 'C' |
| 201 | 300 | 3 | 3 | 'B' |
| 201 | 300 | 5 | 5 | 'B' |
| 201 | 300 | 7 | 7 | 'B' |
| 201 | 300 | 9 | 9 | 'B' |
| 201 | 300 | 100 | 00 | 'B' |
| 301 | 9999 | 101 | 9999 | 'A' |
| −9999 | 99 | −9999 | 0 | 'A' |

## 6.5 Rewriting Tricks

There is a big leap from a procedural mindset to a declarative one for most programmers. Most of them do not quite make that leap all at once, but make a gradual step-wise transition from procedural to semiprocedural programming styles.

Procedural code can appear in procedures, but is this necessarily always true? Procedures can be no more than a BEGIN-END block with a sequence of SQL statements without any IF-THEN-ELSE or WHILE-DO loop logic in it. Is such a block procedural or declarative when all it has is one declarative statement in it? I would say it was declarative. Is a block procedural or declarative when it has IF-THEN-ELSE or WHILE-DO loop control logic? I would say procedural.

You can get rid of a lot of IF-THEN-ELSE control logic with CASE expressions. Before the CASE expression, there were unexpected pitfalls in trying to apply procedural logic to SQL. The classic example is an UPDATE statement that was part of Sybase/SQL Server classes for decades. You have a bookstore and want to change the prices of the books. Any book over $25 will be discounted by 10% (we will advertise that) and books under $25 will be increased by 15% (we will not advertise that). The immediate solution is to write this:

```
BEGIN
UPDATE Books
 SET price = price * 1.10
WHERE price < 25.00;
UPDATE Books
 SET price = price * 0.85
WHERE price >= 25.00;
END;
```

But it does not work! Look at a book that sells for $24.95 currently. Its price jumps to $27.45 when the first UPDATE is done. But when we do the second UPDATE, the price goes down to $23.33. That is not what we meant to do. Flipping the updates does not help.

This was the classic argument for cursors. Hang in a loop and use an IF-THEN-ELSE statement to do the update of the current row in the cursor, just like a magnetic tape file. But this is not required today. We have the CASE expression, which is declarative.

```
UPDATE Books
 SET price
  = CASE
   WHEN price < 25.00
   THEN price * 1.10
   ELSE price * 0.85
   END;
```

Loops can be replaced with various constructs, most of which apply set-oriented operations to the table involved, instead of doing RBAR (pronounced "re-bar," like the steel rods used in concrete construction; RBAR is an acronym for Row By Agonizing Row, coined by Jeff Moden). But another common change is to use the ROW_NUMBER() and other ordinal functions to replace a counting loop in procedural code.

## 6.5.1 Data Tables versus Generator Code

You will often see recursion being used to create a table of sequential numbers. This is the procedural mindset in action; it is better replaced with a declarative look-up table. But let's take a similar problem, the calculation of the Fibonacci series, and look at the procedural, semiprocedural, and declarative approaches to it. I'm not trying to suggest that this is a practical problem: If you really needed this data, then you'd download it into a table. The problem is to build a table of Fibonacci numbers with n and the n-th Fibonacci number. I do not want to talk about the Fibonacci series. No, that is a lie. I would love to write a whole book on it, but a lot of other people beat me to it (see the References section). Darn! The usual definition for the series is recursive:

```
CREATE FUNCTION fib(IN n INTEGER)
RETURNS INTEGER
IF n = 0
THEN RETURN 0;
ELSE IF n = 1
 THEN RETURN 1;
 ELSE IF n > 1
  THEN RETURN (fib(n-2) + fib(n-1));
  END IF;
 END IF;
END IF;
```

### 6.5.2 Using Computation to Replace a Look-up

The most extreme example I can remember of using computation to replace a look-up was decades ago at Georgia Tech when we had CDC Cyber series computers. The hardware had the best floating point hardware and speed in its days. To give you an idea of what I mean, CDC had a COBOL compiler that converted COBOL picture data to floating point numbers, did the math, and converted back to COBOL picture formats. It outperformed the IBM machines on campus.

Rather than do table look-up in FORTRAN, one of our sales team members had just had a course on Chebyshev polynomials and fitting data to curves, and had a software package to create these polynomials. The formula was impossible for a human being to understand, but it was faster than reading a disk and the data had a pattern that worked well with polynomials. Do not do this on anything but a supercomputer. I will now avoid the issue of performance versus maintenance.

### 6.5.3 Fibonacci Series

This series is a good example of changing your mindset. There is a little debate about whether to start at (n = 0) or at (n = 1), but the idea is that fib(n) = (fib(n − 2) + fib(n − 1)), so the series is

0, 1, 1, 2, 3, 5, 8, etc. Here is a completely procedural loop to compute a table of Fibonacci numbers:

```
BEGIN
DECLARE a INTEGER;
DECLARE b INTEGER;
DECLARE fib INTEGER;
SET a = 0;
SET b = 1;
SET fib = 0;
WHILE fib < 1000
DO
 SET fib = a + b;
 SET a = b;
 SET b = fib;
 INSERT INTO Fibonacci VALUES (a);
END WHILE;
END;
```

But when the programmers discover recursive CTEs, they produce this code:

```
WITH Fib(a, b) AS
(SELECT a, b FROM (VALUES (0, 1))
UNION ALL
SELECT b, a+b
  FROM Fib
 WHERE b < 100)
SELECT a FROM Fib;
```

This is still thinking like a programmer and not like a mathematician. These series often have what is called a closed form. That means the values can be computed without iteration or recursion. In the case of the Fibonacci series there is a simple formula that uses the constant phi (also known as the Golden ratio).

```
CREATE FUNCTION Fibonacci(IN n INTEGER)
RETURNS INTEGER
BEGIN DECLARE phi DECIMAL (35, 25);
  1. SET phi = 1.6180339887498948482045868

RETURN
ROUND (((POWER (phi, n)
    - POWER (1.0 - phi, n))
  / SQRT (5.0)), 0);
END;
```

You can get phi to one million decimal places at this web site: http://goldennumber.net/phi20000.htm.

*References*

http://msdn.microsoft.com/en-us/library/ms175521.asp
http://goldennumber.net/
*The Golden Ratio: The Story of PHI, the World's Most Astonishing Number*, Mario Livio
*The Golden Section: Nature's Greatest Secret*, Scott Olsen
*The Divine Proportion*, Herbert Edwin Huntley
*The Fabulous Fibonacci Numbers*, Alfred S. Posamentier
*A Mathematical History of the Golden Number*, Roger Herz-Fischler
*The Golden Section (Spectrum)*, Hans Walser

## 6.6 Functions for Predicates

One of the strangest examples of a semiprocedural mindset is among SQL Server programmers. They create UDFs (user-defined functions) to use in constraints. Here is part of a posting for a puzzle to pack eggs from a basket into cartons that hold a dozen or fewer eggs.

```
CREATE TABLE Eggs
(basket_id INTEGER NOT NULL
REFERENCES Baskets(basket_id),
carton_id INTEGER NOT NULL
REFERENCES Cartons(carton_id));

CREATE FUNCTION CartonCount
(in_carton_id INTEGER) RETURNS INTEGER
RETURN
(SELECT COUNT(*) FROM Eggs
WHERE carton_id = in_carton_id);

ALTER TABLE Eggs
ADD CONSTRAINT carton_limit
CHECK (CartonCount(carton_id) BETWEEN 1 AND 12);
```

There was no key in the original Eggs table so the optimizer has nothing to use. The UDFs make the code more complex and proprietary. A declarative DDL might be: CREATE TABLE Eggs `(basket_nbr INTEGER NOT NULL, carton_nbr INTEGER NOT NULL, PRIMARY KEY (basket_nbr, carton_nbr), egg_cnt INTEGER DEFAULT 1 NOT NULL CONSTRAINT carton_limit CHECK (egg_cnt BETWEEN 1 AND 12));`

This assumes that the egg cartons use the basket number as part of the key, then have a carton number for the final part of the key. The predicate in the carton_limit constraint can be used by an optimizer.

## 6.7 Procedural versus Logical Decomposition

SQL programmers not used to thinking in sets will misuse decomposition as their problem-solving method. It is a good heuristic; break the problem into disjoint subproblems, solve each special case and put them back together. But all too often, the consolidation is done with UNION ALL or a series of insertions to a scratch table.

This is a *procedural* decomposition/consolidation and we want a *logical* one instead. Again, this is easier to explain with an example. Let's start with a simple table of company offices.

```
CREATE TABLE Offices
(duns CHAR(9) NOT NULL
  CHECK (duns SIMILAR TO '[:DIGITS:]{9}'),
office_id INTEGER NOT NULL
  CHECK (office_id > 0),
PRIMARY KEY (duns, office_id)
office_type CHAR(1) DEFAULT 'N' NOT NULL
  CHECK (office_type IN ('C', 'N', ..)),
dba_name VARCHAR(15) NOT NULL
);
```

The DUNS is an industry standard identifier for companies and the office id is an integer that we made up for the various office locations in a company. The only office types we care about are corporate ('C') and noncorporate ('N'), but there might be others. We want a query that will return rows that meet the following criteria:

1. We have only one office on file for the company and it is a noncorporate office.
2. We have one or more offices on file for the company and at least one of them is a corporate office.
3. We have many offices on file for the company and none of them is a corporate office. We skip this company.

Given this sample data, I have marked the desired rows in Table 6.2.

### 6.7.1 Procedural Decomposition Solution

This is a rewrite of an answer from Tom Cooper that uses decomposition into special cases for a solution.

```
SELECT O.duns,
   MAX(O.office_id) AS office_id,
   MAX(O.office_type) AS office_type,
   MAX(O.dba_name) AS dba_name
 FROM Offices AS O
```

**Table 6.2 Offices & DBAs**

| Duns | office_id | office_type | dba_name |
|---|---|---|---|
| 132345678 | 1302 | 'N' | 'Fred' |
| 132345678 | 1303 | 'N' | 'Sam' |
| 132345678 | 1306 | 'N' | 'Mary' |
| 132400000 | 304 | 'C' | 'Bill' ◄ criteria #2 |
| 132400000 | 305 | 'N' | 'Melvin' ◄ criteria #2 |
| 132456885 | 9907 | 'N' | 'Ned' ◄ criteria #1 |
| 139824328 | 2001 | 'C' | 'Irving' |

```
GROUP BY O.duns
HAVING COUNT(*) = 1
 AND MAX(O.office_type) = 'N'
UNION ALL
SELECT O1.duns, O1.office_id, O1.office_type, O1.dba_name
 FROM Offices AS O1
WHERE EXISTS
  (SELECT
    FROM Offices AS O2
    WHERE O1.duns = O2.duns
    GROUP BY O2.duns
   HAVING MAX(O2.office_type)
     <> MIN(O2.office_type);
```

The query has two parts. The first part,

```
SELECT O.duns, MAX(O.office_id) AS office_id,
  MAX(O.office_type) AS office_type,
  MAX(O.dba_name) AS dba_name
 FROM Offices AS O
GROUP BY O.duns
HAVING COUNT(*) = 1
 AND MAX(O.office_type) = 'N'
```

gets the row for companies that meet criteria #1. The GROUP BY and HAVING COUNT(*) = 1 clauses enforce the single row part of the criteria. Since we are grouping by duns, we can't select the other columns directly; we have to do some dummy aggregate function; since there is only one row, `MAX(office_id)` is the same as `office_id`. The same logic applies to the `office_type` and `dba_name` columns.

So we have the rows for companies that have only one row. But we only want those rows that have `(office_type = 'N')`, so that is the other part of the HAVING clause. `(AND MAX(O.office_type) = 'N')`.

To that we UNION ALL the query for criteria #2:

```
SELECT O1.duns, O1.office_id, O1.office_type, O1.dba_name
  FROM Offices AS O1
WHERE EXISTS (SELECT O2.duns
        FROM Offices AS O2
        WHERE O1.duns = O2.duns
        GROUP BY O2.duns
        HAVING MAX(O2.office_type) <> MIN(O2.office_type));
```

The second part gets all rows where the company has at least two rows in the table and those rows have different values in office_type (that is, the max value is not equal to the min value). Notice the user of the self-join here.

## 6.7.2 Logical Decomposition Solution

The most important part of this query is getting the DUNS for the qualified companies, since we can find everything else from that. The skeleton query is:

```
SELECT O1.duns, O1.office_id, O1.office_type, O1.dba_name
  FROM Offices AS O1
WHERE O1.duns IN (<qualified duns>);
```

We are using a nested top-down approach instead of special cases at the same level of abstraction. The problem of finding the qualified DUNS is not split into two parts and then consolidated. It is also a smaller problem to solve. We know we are working with a grouping problem, so we can expect to use a GROUP BY or a PARTITION BY somewhere in the subproblems. Going with the GROUP BY, this skeleton becomes:

```
<qualified duns> ::=
SELECT O2.duns
  FROM Offices AS O2
GROUP BY duns
HAVING (<criteria #1>)
   OR (<criteria #2>)
```

Let's look at `<criteria #1>`. The count has to be one and then the office type has to be 'N'; since we have only one row, we know that the minimum is the same as the maximum, so we can use either of them for the second part of criteria #1. The skeleton gets more flesh:

```
<criteria #1> ::=
SELECT O2.duns
```

```
 FROM Offices AS O2
GROUP BY duns
HAVING (COUNT(*) = 1 AND MIN(O2.office_type)= 'N')
  OR (<criteria #2>)
```

Let's look at `<criteria #2>`. The count has to be greater than one, which is easy. The office type of 'C' is the minimum value in this domain and we want to have at least one of them. We use the MIN() in this case, but if the desired value was not the minimum, we could have used `MIN(CASE WHEN office_type = <target value> THEN 0 ELSE 1 END)` to get the same effect. The skeleton gets enough flesh to walk:

```
SELECT O1.duns, O1.office_id, O1.office_type, O1.dba_name
 FROM Offices AS O1
WHERE O1.duns
  IN (SELECT O2.duns
     FROM Offices AS O2
     GROUP BY duns
    HAVING (COUNT(*) = 1 AND MIN(O2.office_type)= 'N')
      OR (COUNT(*) > 1 AND MIN(O2.office_type)= 'C'));
```

# PROCEDURAL CONSTRUCTS

Although SQL is a declarative language, it does have procedural features: stored procedures, triggers, and cursors. Stored procedures, or more properly, Persistent Stored Modules (SQL/PSM), give SQL its own 4GL programming language. Triggers are stored procedures attached to one table and controlled by database events such as inserts, updates, and deletes on it. Cursors convert a query, update, or delete statement into a sequential file structure that can be accessed one row at a time.

We will now discuss each one in more detail, but you will find that stored procedures are by far the most useful of the three. Triggers exist because the early SQL Standards did not have declarative referential integrity (DRI) actions. Later SQL products such as DB2 for z/OS supported declarative referential integrity (RI) long before they supported triggers. You should write only a few triggers in a schema, *if any*, and then only for functionality that cannot be supported by DRI. Cursors exist because SQL has to interface to application programming languages that use a sequential file model of data. Today, there are other mechanisms for these interfaces and there is no need to use a cursor inside a properly designed schema. The few cursors that you will see today are embedded in COBOL programs.

## 7.1 CREATE PROCEDURE

The ANSI/ISO Standard 4GL programming language in SQL is the SQL/PSM (Persistent Stored Modules). The defining document is ISO/IEC 9075-4:2003, Information technology—Database languages—SQL—Part 4: Persistent Stored Modules (SQL/PSM).

However, many SQL products have had their own procedure languages, so you should look at what your particular vendor has given you. Oracle has a proprietary language called PL/SQL, which is very close to SQL/PSM. IBM now supports both PL/SQL and SQL/PSM.

**Joe Celko's SQL for Smarties. DOI: 10.1016/B978-0-12-382022-8.00007-7**

T-SQL is the proprietary 4GL language with Microsoft and Sybase SQL Server. It is a simple one-pass compiler not intended for application development work. It has its roots in 16-bit UNIX C compilers that first implemented SQL Server.

Informix 4GL is the proprietary application language for Informix. It is based on Algol and is "under the hood" in many mainframe software packages.

The SQL/PSM was based on the ADA programming language, but looks a lot like other modern block structured programming languages. Each module starts with a header that tells the SQL/PSM compiler as much as it can about the code; the body is a block and can be exited with a return statement. Blocks are nested inside each other.

The blocks declare local variables at the start of the block, has code in the middle, and error handlers at the end of the block. The local variables are the usual SQL data types, but schema objects cannot be created in the SQL/PSM. The control of flow structures are the usual nested blocks (BEGIN-END and BEGIN ATOMIC-END for transactions), selection of control flow (IF-THEN-ELSE, CASE), and iterations (WHILE, etc.) mixed with SQL statements.

The error handler is an interrupt-driven model. When an exception is raised, control jumps to the appropriate error handler no matter where it happens in the block.

This book uses simple SQL/PSM for procedures, but does not attempt to teach the language. It needs a book of its own.

## 7.2 CREATE TRIGGER

A trigger is attached to a single base table. It is a procedure that is executed when a "database event" happens in the schema. The trigger event is either deletion, insertion, or replacement of a collection of rows in the table.

The triggered action is specified to take place either immediately before the triggering event or immediately after it, according to its specified trigger action time, BEFORE or AFTER. A trigger is either a delete trigger, an insert trigger, or an update trigger, according to its trigger event.

The event can be a direct statement like INSERT INTO, UPDATE, DELETE FROM, or MERGE. But referential actions like CASCADE, SET NULL, or SET DEFAULT can also fire a trigger. There is an option to prevent cascading, if you don't want it.

A collection of rows being deleted, inserted, or replaced is known as a transition table. For a delete trigger there is just one transition table, known as the OLD transition table. For an insert trigger there is just one transition table, known as a NEW transition table. For an update trigger there is both an OLD transition table (the rows being replaced) and a NEW transition table (the replacement rows), these two tables having the same cardinality. The conceptual model is that the OLD rows are removed as a set; the NEW rows are inserted as a set. You can give these transition tables aliases in a special REFERENCING clause.

If this is an AFTER trigger, it is executed after the event that fired it.

If this is a BEFORE trigger, it is executed before the event that fired it. There is a special kind of BEFORE trigger called the INSTEAD OF trigger. This trigger is used with VIEWs. Since there is no single base table for the event to change, this trigger holds code that works on the base tables from which the VIEW is built. This lets you make the VIEW behave as if it were a base table when seen by the users. Here is a simple example, where we have a nonupdatable VIEW based on a JOIN on a table of countries and one of cities.

```
CREATE VIEW Geography (country_name, city_name)
AS
SELECT country_name, city_name
 FROM Countries, Cities
WHERE Countries.country_code = Cities.country_code;
```

This trigger will let you insert a new row into the two underlying tables by accessing the Geography VIEW.

```
CREATE TRIGGER Add_New_Town
INSTEAD OF INSERT
ON Geography
REFERENCING NEW AS CP -- Current_Places
BEGIN
INSERT INTO Countries (country_name)
SELECT DISTINCT CP.country_name
 FROM CP
      LEFT OUTER JOIN
      Countries AS C
      ON CP.country_name = C.country_name
WHERE C.country_name IS NULL; -- Exclude countries already
   in the table

INSERT INTO Cities (city_name, country_code)
SELECT DISTINCT CP.city_name, Countries.country_code
FROM CP
     INNER JOIN
     Countries AS C
     ON CP.country_name = C.country_name
       LEFT OUTER JOIN
```

```
        Cities
        ON CP.city_name = Cities.city_name
    WHERE Cities.city_name IS NULL; -- Exclude cities
      already in the table
END;
```

A trigger can be at the row or statement level. For a statement level trigger, we perform an action on the table as a whole. For a row level trigger, only the rows involved in the action are affected.

Since I will not be discussing TRIGGERs in this book, let me give you an example so that you can see most of the syntax in a trigger declaration. When the `quote_price` column of a table of stock quotations is updated, the new quote should be copied, with a timestamp, to the `QuoteHistory` table. Also, the `price_trend` column of quotations should be updated to reflect whether the stock is:

1. Rising in value
2. At a new high for the year
3. Dropping in value
4. At a new low for the year
5. Steady in value

CREATE TRIGGER statements that accomplish this are as follows.

```
CREATE TRIGGER Stock_Trends
NO CASCADE
BEFORE UPDATE OF quote_price -- column in base table
ON Quotations
REFERENCING NEW AS NQP -- New Quote Prices
     OLD AS OQP -- Old Quote Prices
FOR EACH ROW -- only look at changed rows
BEGIN ATOMIC
SET
NQP.price_trend
= CASE
  WHEN NQP.quote_price
      >= (SELECT MAX(quote_price)
           FROM QuoteHistory
          WHERE ticker_symbol = NQP.ticker_symbol
           AND EXTRACT (YEAR FROM quote_price_timestamp)
             = EXTRACT(YEAR FROM CURRENT DATE))
  THEN 'High'
  WHEN NQP.quote_price
     <= SELECT MIN(quote_price)
         FROM QuoteHistory
        WHERE ticker_symbol = NQP.ticker_symbol
         AND EXTRACT (YEAR FROM quote_price_timestamp)
            = EXTRACT(YEAR FROM CURRENT DATE))
```

```
    THEN 'Low'
    WHEN NQP.quote_price > OQP.quote_price
    THEN 'Rising'
    WHEN NQP.quote_price < OQP.quote_price
    THEN 'Dropping'
    WHEN NQP.quote_price = OQP.quote_price
    THEN 'Steady' END;
  END;
```

You should also have a TRIGGER to handle the quotation history table.

```
CREATE TRIGGER Record_History
AFTER UPDATE OF quote_price
ON Quotations
 REFERENCING NEW AS NQP -- New Quote Prices
FOR EACH ROW
BEGIN ATOMIC
INSERT INTO QuoteHistory
VALUES (NQP.ticker_symbol, NQP.quote_price, CURRENT_TIMESTAMP);
END;
```

The advantage of TRIGGERs over declarative referential integrity (DRI) is that you can do everything that DRI can and almost anything else, too. The disadvantages are that the optimizer cannot get any data from the procedural code, the TRIGGERs take longer to execute, and they are not portable from product to product. They also force sequential execution, instead of allowing parallelism.

My advice would be to avoid TRIGGERs when you can use DRI instead. If you do use them, check the code very carefully and keep it simple so that you will not hurt performance.

## 7.3 CURSORs

I will not spend much time with cursors in this book, but you should understand them at a high level since you will see them in actual code. In spite of a standard syntax, every product has a proprietary version of cursors. This is because cursors are a low-level construct that work close to the physical implementation in the product.

A CURSOR is a way of converting an SQL result set into a sequential data structure that looks like a simple sequential file that can be handled by the procedural host language, and contains the very statement that executes and creates a structure that looks like a sequential file. In fact, the cursor model in SQL is based on an old-fashioned magnetic tape system!

You might have noticed that in SQL, the keyword CREATE builds persistent schema objects. The keyword DECLARE builds transient objects that disappear with the end of the session in which they were built. This is why you say DECLARE CURSOR and not CREATE CURSOR.

First, you allocate working storage in the host program with a BEGIN DECLARE . . . END DECLARE section. This sets up an area where SQL variables can be converted into host language data types and vice versa. NULLs are handled by declaring INDICATOR variables in the host language BEGIN DECLARE section, which are paired with the appropriate host variables. An INDICATOR is an exact numeric data type with a scale of zero—that is, some kind of integer in the host language.

## 7.3.1 DECLARE CURSOR Statement

The DECLARE CURSOR statement must appear next. The SQL-92 syntax is fairly representative of actual products, but you must read your manual.

```
<declare cursor> ::=
    DECLARE <cursor name> [INSENSITIVE] [SCROLL] CURSOR
      FOR <cursor specification>

<cursor specification> ::=
    <query expression> [<order by clause>]
      [<updatability clause>]

<updatability clause> ::= FOR {READ ONLY | UPDATE [OF
   <column name list>]}

<order by clause> ::= ORDER BY <sort specification list>

<sort specification list> ::=
    <sort specification> [{<comma> <sort specification>}. . .]

<sort specification> ::= <sort key> [<collate clause>]
 [<ordering specification>]

<sort key> ::= <column name>
<ordering specification> ::= ASC | DESC
```

A few things need explaining. First of all, the ORDER BY clause is part of a cursor and not part of a SELECT statement. Because some SQL products, such as SQL Server and Sybase, allow the user to create implicit cursors, many newbies get this wrong. This is easy to implement in products that evolved from sequential file systems and still expose this architecture to the user in violation of Dr. Codd's rules. Oracle is probably the worst offender as of this writing, but some of the "micro-SQLs" are just as bad.

If either INSENSITIVE, SCROLL, or ORDER BY is specified, or if the working table is a read-only, then an <updatability clause> of READ ONLY is implicit. Otherwise, an <updatability clause> of FOR UPDATE without a <column name list> is implicit.

## 7.3.2 The ORDER BY clause

Contrary to popular belief, the ORDER BY clause is not part of the SELECT statement; it is part of a CURSOR declaration. The reason that people think it is part of the SELECT statement is that the only way you can get to the result set of a query in a host language is via a cursor. When a vendor tool builds a cursor under the covers for you, they usually allow you to include an ORDER BY clause on the query.

Most optimizers will look at the result set and see from the query if it is already in sorted order as a result of fetches done with an index, thus avoiding a redundant sorting operation. The bad news is that many programmers have written code that depended on the way that their particular release of a particular brand of SQL product presented the result. When an index is dropped or changed, when the database is upgraded to a new release or has to be ported to another product, this automatic ordering can disappear.

As part of a cursor, the ORDER BY clause has some properties that you probably did not know existed. Here is the Standard syntax.

```
<order by clause> ::=
   ORDER BY <sort specification list>

<sort specification list> ::=
   <sort specification> [{ <comma> <sort specification> }. . . ]

<sort specification> ::=
   <sort key> [<collate clause >] [<ordering specification>]

<sort key> ::= <column name> | <scalar expression>

<ordering specification> ::= [ASC | DESC] {NULLS FIRST |
   NULLS LAST}
```

The first things to note is that the sort keys are column names that must appear in the SELECT clause. The use of the positional number of a column is a depreciated feature in Standard SQL. Deprecation is a term in the standards world that means this feature will be removed from the next release of the standard, and therefore should not be used, so your old code needs to be updated.

These are illegal sorts:

```
SELECT a, (b+c) AS d
  FROM Foobar
 ORDER BY a, b, c; -- illegal!!
```

The columns b and c simply do not exist in the result set of the cursor, so there is no way to sort on them. However, after the SQL-99 Standard you were allowed to use a computation in the ORDER BY.

```
SELECT a, b, c -- illegal!!
  FROM Foobar
 ORDER BY a, b, (b+c)
```

The correct way to do this is to put the function calls or expressions in the SELECT list, name that column, and use the name in the ORDER BY clause. This lets the user see on what values the sorting is done. Think about it—what good is a report or display when you have no idea how it was sorted?

Furthermore, the sorting columns pass information to middle-tier machines that can resort the data before distributing it to other front-end clients.

The sort order is based on the collation sequence of the column to which it is attached. The collation can be defined in the schema on character columns, but in most SQL products today collation is either ASCII or Unicode. You can expect Unicode to become more popular.

### *The ORDER BY and NULLs*

Whether a sort key value that is NULL is considered greater or less than a non-NULL value is implementation-defined. There are SQL products that do it either way; here is a quick list:

1. PostgreSQL—Higher
2. DB2—Higher
3. MS SQL Server—Lower
4. MySQL—Lower
5. Oracle—Higher

The SQL-99 Standard added the optional `{NULLS FIRST | NULLS LAST}` subclause to the `<ordering specification>` that has been implemented in DB2 and Oracle, among others. There is a story here.

In March 1999, Chris Farrar brought up a question from one of their developers, which caused him to examine a part of the ANSI/ISO Standard that I thought I understood. Chris found some differences between the general understanding and the actual wording of the specification. The situation can be described as follows: A table, Sortable, with two integer columns, a and b, containing two rows that happen to be in this physical order:

Sortable

| alpha | beta |
|---|---|
| NULL | 8 |
| NULL | 4 |

Given the pseudo-query:

```
SELECT alpha, beta
  FROM Sortable
 ORDER BY alpha, beta;
```

The first question is whether it is legal SQL for the cursor to produce the result sequence shown in Table 7.1.

The problem is that although the standard set up a rule to make the NULLs group together either before or after the known values, we never said that they have to act as if they were equal to each other. What is missing is a statement that when comparing NULL to NULL, the result in the context of ORDER BY is that NULL is equal to NULL, just as it is in a GROUP BY. This was the intent of the committee, so the expected result should have been those shown in Table 7.2.

**Table 7.1 Cursor Result Sequence Version 1**

| alpha | beta |
|---|---|
| NULL | 8 |
| NULL | 4 |

**Table 7.2 Cursor Result Sequence Version 2**

| alpha | beta |
|---|---|
| NULL | 4 |
| NULL | 8 |

Phil Shaw, former IBM representative and one of the smartest and oldest members of the committee, dug up the section of the SQL-89 Standard that answered this problem. In SQL-89, the last General Rule of `<comparison predicate>` specified this:

> *Although "x = y" is unknown if both x and y are NULL values, in the context of GROUP BY, ORDER BY, and DISTINCT, a NULL value is identical to or is a duplicate of another NULL value.*

This is the grouping versus equality issue that causes all NULLs to go into the same group, rather than each in its own group. Apply that rule, and then apply the rules for ORDER BY, the NULL values of column alpha of the two rows are equal, so you have to order the rows by the columns to the right in the ORDER BY.

The sort keys are applied from left to right and a column name can appear only once in the list. But there is no obligation on the part of SQL to use a stable `(sequence preserving)` sort. A stable sort on cities, followed by a stable order on states, would result in a list with cities sorted within each state, and the states sorted. Although stability is a nice property, the nonstable sorts are generally much faster.

You can use computed columns to get specialized sorting orders. For example, construct a table with a character column and an integer column. The goal is to order the results so that it first sorts the integer column descending, but then groups the related character column within the integers. This is much easier with an example:

```
CREATE TABLE Fruit_Test
(fruit_name CHAR(10) NOT NULL,
taste_score INTEGER NOT NULL,
PRIMARY KEY (fruit_name, taste_score));

INSERT INTO Fruit_Test
VALUES ('Apples', 2), ('Apples', 1), ('Oranges', 5),
     ('Apples', 5), ('Banana', 2);
```

I'm looking to order the results as the following:

```
('Apples', 5)
('Apples', 2)
('Apples', 1)
('Oranges', 5)
('Banana', 2)
```

In the preceding, the first pass of the sort would have produced this by sorting on the integer column:

```
SELECT F1.fruit_name, F1.taste_score,
 FROM Fruit_Test AS F1
ORDER BY F1.taste_score DESC;
```

One outcome might have been any of these:

```
Result #1
('Apples', 5)
('Oranges', 5)
('Apples', 2)
('Banana', 2)
('Apples', 1)

Result #2
('Oranges', 5)
('Apples', 5)
('Apples', 2)
('Banana', 2)
('Apples', 1)

Result #3
('Oranges', 5)
('Apples', 5)
('Banana', 2)
('Apples', 2)
('Apples', 1)

Result #4
('Apples', 5)
('Oranges', 5)
('Banana', 2)
('Apples', 2)
('Apples', 1)
```

If you use:

```
SELECT F1.fruit_name, F1.taste_score,
 FROM Fruit_Test AS F1
ORDER BY F1.taste_score DESC, F1.fruit_name ASC;

Result
('Apples', 5)
('Oranges', 5)
('Apples', 2)
('Banana', 2)
('Apples', 1)
```

But this is not what we wanted—the order within fruits has been destroyed. Likewise:

```
SELECT F1.fruit_name, F1.taste_score
 FROM Fruit_Test AS F1
ORDER BY F1.fruit_name ASC, F1.taste_score DESC;

Results
('Apples', 5)
('Apples', 2)
```

```
('Apples', 1)
('Banana', 2)
('Oranges', 5)
```

But this is still not what we wanted—the order within scores has been destroyed. We need a dummy column to preserve the ordering, thus:

```
SELECT F1.fruit_name, F1.taste_score,
     (SELECT MAX(taste_score)
        FROM Fruit_Test AS F2
       WHERE F1.fruit_name = F2.fruit_name)
     AS taste_score_preserver
  FROM Fruit_Test AS F1
ORDER BY taste_score_preserver DESC,
       F1.fruit_name ASC, F1.taste_score DESC;
```

Cursors include an `<updatability clause>`, which tells you if the cursor is FOR READ ONLY or for UPDATE [OF `<column name list>`], but this clause in optional. If ORDER BY is specified or if the result table is a read-only table, then the `<updatability clause>` defaults to FOR READ ONLY.

### *The ORDER BY and CASE Expressions*

SQL-99 allows you to use a function in an ORDER BY clause. Although it is now legal, it is still not a good programming practice. Users should see the fields that are used for the sort so they can use them to read and locate lines of data in reports. The sorting values are usually on the left side of each line since we read left to right. The most portable method is to use a CASE expression, which takes an external parameter of the form:

```
SELECT first_name, last_name, dept_name,
     CASE :flag
     WHEN 'f' THEN first_name
     WHEN 'l' THEN last_name
     WHEN 'd' THEN dept_name
     ELSE NULL END AS sort_col
  FROM Personnel
ORDER BY sort_col;
```

Obviously, the expression in the THEN clauses must be of the same data type or CAST into the same data type. Controlling the direction of the sort is a little trickier and requires two columns, one of which is always set to all NULLs.

```
SELECT last_name,
      CASE :flag
      WHEN 'la' THEN last_name ELSE NULL END AS sort_col1,
      CASE :flag
```

```
     WHEN 'ld' THEN last_name ELSE NULL END AS sort_col2
 FROM Personnel
ORDER BY sort_col1, sort_col2 DESC;
```

You can get a bit fancy with this basic idea:

```
SELECT . . .
     CASE :flag_1
        WHEN 'a' THEN CAST (a AS CHAR(n))
        WHEN 'b' THEN CAST (b AS CHAR(n))
        WHEN 'c' THEN CAST (c AS CHAR(n))
        ELSE NULL END AS sort_1,
     CASE :flag_2
        WHEN 'x' THEN CAST (x AS CHAR(n))
        WHEN 'y' THEN CAST (y AS CHAR(n))
        WHEN 'z' THEN CAST (z AS CHAR(n))
        ELSE NULL END AS sort_2,
          . . .
     CASE :flag_n
        WHEN 'n1' THEN CAST (n1 AS CHAR(n))
        WHEN 'n2' THEN CAST (n2 AS CHAR(n))
        WHEN 'n3' THEN CAST (n3 AS CHAR(n))
        ELSE NULL END AS sort_2,
 FROM MyTable
WHERE . . .
ORDER BY sort_1, sort_2, . . .;
```

If you have more than one sort column and only a limited set of combinations then use concatenation.

```
CASE :flag_1
     WHEN 'ab'
     THEN CAST(a AS CHAR(n)) ||' ' || CAST(b AS CHAR(n))
     WHEN 'ba'
     THEN CAST(b AS CHAR(n)) ||' ' || CAST(a AS CHAR(n))
     ELSE NULL END AS sort_1,
```

If you need ASC and DESC options, then use a combination of CASE and ORDER BY:

```
CASE :flag_1
WHEN :flag_1 = 'a' AND :flag_1_ad = 'ASC'
THEN CAST (a AS CHAR(n))
WHEN :flag_1 = 'b' AND :flag_1_ad = 'ASC'
THEN CAST (b AS CHAR(n))
WHEN :flag_1 = 'c' AND :flag_1_ad = 'ASC'
THEN CAST (c AS CHAR(n))
ELSE NULL END AS sort_1_a,

CASE :flag_1
WHEN :flag_1 = 'a' AND :flag_1_ad = 'DESC'
THEN CAST (a AS CHAR(n))
```

```
WHEN :flag_1 = 'b' AND :flag_1_ad = 'DESC'
THEN CAST (b AS CHAR(n))
WHEN :flag_1 = 'c' AND :flag_1_ad = 'DESC'
THEN CAST (c AS CHAR(n))
ELSE NULL END AS sort_1_d
..
ORDER BY sort_1_a ASC, sort_1_d DESC
```

I have shown explicit CAST(<exp> AS CHAR(n)), but if the data types of the THEN clause expressions were already the same, there would be no reason to force the conversions. You change the ELSE NULL clause to any constant of the appropriate data type, but it should be something useful to the reader. A neater way of doing this is to use one column for each sorting option.

```
SELECT MyTable.*,
    CASE WHEN :flag = 'a' THEN a ELSE NULL END AS sort1,
    CASE WHEN :flag = 'b' THEN b ELSE NULL END AS sort2,
    CASE WHEN :flag = 'c' THEN c ELSE NULL END AS sort3
  FROM Personnel
 WHERE . . .
 ORDER BY sort1, sort2, sort3;
```

This code is easy to read and you do not have worry about CAST() operations. The trade-off is a larger result set being sent to the cursor.

### 7.3.3 OPEN Statement

The OPEN <cursor name> statement positions an imaginary read/write head before the first record in the cursor. FETCH statements can then move this imaginary read/write head from record to record. When the read/write head moves past the last record, an exception is raised, like an EOF (end of file) flag in a magnetic tape file system.

Watch out for this model! In some file systems, the read/write head starts on the first and the EOF flag is set to TRUE when it reads the last record. Simply copying the algorithms from your procedural code into SQL/PSM might not work.

### 7.3.4 FETCH Statement

```
<fetch statement> ::= FETCH [[<fetch orientation>]
     FROM] <cursor name> INTO <fetch target list>

<fetch orientation> ::= NEXT | PRIOR | FIRST | LAST
     | {ABSOLUTE | RELATIVE} <simple value specification>
```

The FETCH statement takes one row from the cursor, then converts each SQL data type into a host-language data type and puts the result into the appropriate host variable. If the SQL value was a NULL, the INDICATOR is set to –1; if no indicator was specified, an exception condition is raised.

As you can see, the host program must be sure to check the INDICATORs, because otherwise the value of the parameter will be garbage. If the parameter is passed to the host language without any problems, the INDICATOR is set to zero. If the value being passed to the host program is a non-NULL character string and it has an indicator, the indicator is set to the length of the SQL string and can be used to detect string overflows or to set the length of the parameter.

The `<fetch orientation>` tells the read/write head which way to move. NEXT and PRIOR read one record forward or backward from the current position. FIRST and LAST put the read/write on the first or last records, respectively. The ABSOLUTE fetch moves to a given record number. The RELATIVE fetch moves the read/write head forward or backward (n) records from the current position. Again, this is a straight imitation of a sequential file system.

## 7.3.5 CLOSE Statement

The CLOSE <cursor name> statement resets the cursor read/write head to a position before the first row in the cursor. The cursor still exists, but must be reopened before it can be used. This is similar to the CLOSE FILE operations in FORTRAN or COBOL, but with an important difference! The cursor can be recomputed when it is reopened.

## 7.3.6 DEALLOCATE Statement

The DEALLOCATE CURSOR statement frees the working storage in the host program. Think of it as dismounting a tape from the tape drive in a sequential file system.

## 7.3.7 How to Use a CURSOR

The best performance improvement technique for cursors inside the database is not to use them. SQL engines are designed for set processing and not with individual rows. The times when using a cursor is unavoidable usually deal with corrections to the database that were caused by an improper design. In rare cases the speed of a cursor is faster because of the physical implementation in the product.

For example, redundant duplicate rows can be taken out of a table that does not have a key with a cursor. Since SQL is set-oriented, a query tends to try to return the entire set of answers. If you are dealing with an NP-Complete problem (Traveling Salesman, huge combinatorial problems, etc.—things that run longer than you can afford to wait) then you are often happy to find the first "good enough for us" answer that comes up. These are actually a job for procedural algorithms with backtracking and other techniques.

The old argument for cursors in the original Sybase SQL Server training course was this example, which we discussed in chapter 6. You own a bookstore and you want to change prices; all books $25 and over are reduced 10%, and all books under $25 are increased 15%.

```
BEGIN ATOMIC
UPDATE Books
  SET price = price * 0.90
WHERE price >= $25.00;
UPDATE Books
  SET price = price * 1.15
WHERE price < $25.00;
END;
```

Oops! Look at a book that was $25.00 ((25.00 * .90) * 1.10) = $24.75. So you were told to cursor through the table, and change each row with a cursor.

Today you write:

```
UPDATE Books
  SET price
     = CASE WHEN price < $25.00;
     THEN price * 1.15
     WHEN price >= $25.00
     THEN price * 0.90
     ELSE price END;
```

But Steve Kass pointed out that even back then, it was possible to avoid a cursor:

```
BEGIN ATOMIC
UPDATE Books
  SET price = price * 1.80
WHERE price >= $25.00;
UPDATE Books
  SET price = price * 1.15
WHERE price < $25.00;
UPDATE Books
  SET price = price * 0.50
WHERE price >= $45.00;
END;
```

However, this code makes three passes through the Books table instead of just one. This could be worse than a cursor!

Limit the number of rows and columns in the cursor's SELECT statement to only those required in the desired result set. This will avoid unnecessary fetching of data that in turn will require fewer server resources and increase cursor performance.

Use FOR READ ONLY instead of UPDATE cursors if possible. You will have to watch the transaction isolation level however.

Opening an INSENSITIVE cursor can cause its rows to be copied to a working table in many products or locked at the table level in others.

Do a CLOSE cursor as soon as you are finished with the result set. This will release any locks on the rows. Always remember to deallocate your cursors when you are finished.

Look for your product options. For example, SQL Server has FAST_FORWARD and FORWARD_ONLY cursor options when working with unidirectional, read-only result sets. Using FAST_FORWARD defines a FORWARD_ONLY, READ_ONLY cursor with a number of internal performance optimizations.

Be careful with modifying large numbers of rows via a cursor loop that are contained within a transaction. Depending on the transaction isolation level, those rows may remain locked until the transaction is committed or rolled back, possibly causing resource contention on the server.

In Standard SQL, there is an SQLSTATE code that tells you if the rows of a GROUP BY query have members that excluded NULLs from their aggregate computations. This warning can be raised in the DECLARE CURSOR statement, the OPEN statement, or when the row representing such a grouping is FETCH-ed. Its implementation is defined in the Standards, so know how your product handles this.

When an SQL statement executes, an error status code is automatically generated. This code represents success, failure, warning, or no data found. This error status code is stored in a built-in variable called SQLSTATE.

The SQLSTATE status code is a five-character string that can contain only digits and uppercase letters.

The first two characters of the SQLSTATE status code indicate a class. The last three characters of the SQLSTATE code indicate a subclass. The following tables show the structure of the SQLSTATE code. This example uses the value 08001, where 08 is the class code and 001 is the subclass code. The value 08001 represents the error unable to connect with the database environment.

| SQLSTATE | Class Codes |
|---|---|
| 00 | Success |
| 01 | Success with warning |
| 02 | No data found |
| 03 and over | Error or warning |

In particular,
21000 = a cardinality violation. You can execute a GET DIAGNOSTICS statement to obtain additional error information.
But the warnings that can be raised are:
01I09 = Cardinalities of the projection list and of the INTO list are not equal
01I06 = Vendor extension to ANSI-compliant syntax
SQLSTATE Classes predefined by SQL92.

| Class | Condition |
|---|---|
| 00 | success completion |
| 01 | warning |
| 02 | no data |
| 07 | dynamic SQL error |
| 08 | connection exception |
| 0A | feature not supported |
| 21 | cardinality violation |
| 22 | data exception |
| 23 | integrity constraint violation |
| 24 | invalid cursor state |
| 25 | invalid transaction state |
| 26 | invalid SQL statement name |
| 27 | triggered data change violation |
| 28 | invalid authorization specification |
| 2A | direct SQL syntax error or access rule violation |
| 2B | dependent privilege descriptors still exist |
| 2C | invalid character set name |
| 2D | invalid transaction termination |
| 2E | invalid connection name |
| 33 | invalid SQL descriptor name |
| 34 | invalid cursor name |
| 35 | invalid condition number |
| 37 | dynamic SQL syntax error or access rule violation |
| 3C | ambiguous cursor name |
| 3D | invalid catalog name |
| 3F | invalid schema name |
| 40 | transaction rollback |
| 42 | syntax error or access rule violation |
| 44 | with check option violation |
| HZ | remote database access. The class code HZ is reserved for conditions defined in International Standard ISO/IEC DIS 9579-2, Remote Database Access. |

### 7.3.8 Positioned UPDATE and DELETE Statements

Obviously, the cursor needs an explicit or implicit `<updatability clause>` of FOR UPDATE for this to work and has to be in the same module as the positioned statements. You get an exception when you try to change a READ ONLY cursor or if the cursor is not positioned on a row.

The clause CURRENT OF `<cursor name>` refers to the row that the imaginary read/write heads is on. This cursor has to map back to one and only one row in the base table.

UPDATE Statement

```
<update statement: positioned>
 ::= UPDATE <table name>
SET <set clause list>
      WHERE CURRENT OF <cursor name>
```

The cursor remains positioned on its current row, even if an exception condition is raised during the update attempt.

DELETE FROM Statement

```
<delete statement: positioned>
 ::= DELETE FROM <table name>
      WHERE CURRENT OF <cursor name>
```

If, while the cursor is open, another DELETE FROM or UPDATE statement attempts to modify the current cursor record, then a cursor operation conflict warning is raised. The transaction isolation level then determines what happens. If the `<delete statement: positioned>` deleted the last cursor record, then the position of the cursor is after the last record; otherwise, the position of the cursor is before the next cursor record.

## 7.4 SEQUENCEs

The CREATE SEQUENCE declaration acts like a function that returns a different value each time it is invoked. The starting value, increment size, and upper and lower limits are part of the declaration. These can be pretty much any supported exact numeric values that make sense. The clause is whether to restart the process when the upper (or lower) limit is reached. For example, to generate sequential part numbers, we could write:

```
CREATE SEQUENCE part_num AS INTEGER
START WITH 1
INCREMENT BY 1
MAXVALUE 100000
MINVALUE 1
CYCLE;
```

Other options are NO MAXVALUE, NO MINVALUE, and NO CYCLE for the last three parameters. ORDER or NO ORDER are options in the DB2 implementation. This tells you if the numbers have been generated in sequential order as requested or not; the default is NO ORDER.

This example will reuse numbers when 100,000 is reached. Yes, it is possible to get duplicate values if you exceed the cycle size.

To use a SEQUENCE, the syntax is either NEXT VALUE FOR `<sequence name>` or PREVIOUS VALUE FOR `<sequence name>` instead of a conventional function call. If NEXT VALUE is invoked in the same statement as the PREVIOUS VALUE, then regardless of their order in the statement, PREVIOUS VALUE returns the previous (i.e., unincremented) value and NEXT VALUE returns the next value. For example:

```
INSERT INTO Orders (order_nbr, ..)
VALUES (NEXT VALUE FOR Order_Seq, ..);
```

The same basic declaration can be used in a table to describe the behavior of a column. Again, an example is easier to see than a long explanation.

```
CREATE TABLE Personnel
(emp_id INTEGER
  GENERATED [ALWAYS | BY DEFAULT] AS IDENTITY
  START WITH 100
  INCREMENT 1
  MINVALUE 100
  NO MAXVALUE
  NO CYCLE,
salary_amt DECIMAL(7,2),
..);
```

The GENERATED [ALWAYS | BY DEFAULT] AS IDENTITY parameter tells us if the column is always assigned a SEQUENCE number, or if we can override it with an explicit value and use the SEQUENCE number as the column's default value.

A SEQUENCE is available globally, and this form of generated column is local to its table.

## 7.5 Generated Columns

Generated columns are also called computed or derived columns. They are declared in a base table much like they would be in a VIEW. Each generated column is defined by a scalar expression. All column references in such expressions must be to columns of the base table containing that generated column. Values for generated columns are computed and assigned automatically every time a row is inserted. Again, an example is easier to see than an explanation.

```
CREATE TABLE Personnel
(emp_id INTEGER NOT NULL,
salary_amt DECIMAL(7,2) NOT NULL,
bonus_amt DECIMAL(7,2) NOT NULL,
total_comp_amt GENERATED ALWAYS AS (salary_amt + bonus_amt),
hr_clerk_user_id GENERATED ALWAYS AS (CURRENT_USER));
```

Notice that you cannot use an expression as a generated default value.

## 7.6 Table Functions

Table functions return a table (one or more rows) based on a statement expressed in a specific language, such as SQL, C, or Java. You can use a table function anywhere a table could be used, but it takes zero or more input parameters. If the table function has no input parameters, you get the whole table back, as if it were a VIEW or base table.

A table function that uses an SQL statement to return its table is really a different syntax for simple VIEW. The real purpose of this construct is to get external data into SQL.

For example, the following syntax defines a table function that selects aggregated sales figures from the Sales table:

```
CREATE FUNCTION SalesSummary
(fiscal_period INTEGER, store_id INTEGER)
RETURNS
TABLE (fiscal_period INTEGER,
store_id INTEGER,
sales_amt DECIMAL (7,2))
LANGUAGE SQL
READS SQL DATA
DETERMINISTIC
RETURN
(SELECT fiscal_period, store_id, SUM(sales)
 FROM Sales
GROUP BY fiscal_period, store_id);
```

This table function has two input parameters: fiscal_period and store_id. Since a function has only IN parameters, there are no INOUT and OUT options on the parameters.

```
SELECT T1.fiscal_period, T1.store_id, T1.sales_amt
 FROM Calendar AS C,
    Stores AS S,
```

```
    TABLE (SalesSummary(C.fiscal_period, S.store_id)) AS T1
WHERE C.fiscal_period = T1.fiscal_period
  AND S.store_id = T1.store_id;
```

The Calendar and Stores tables are joined to each row that the table function returns, based on matching fiscal_period and store_id values. This is a correlated subquery with a different syntax.

This is not a good example of how to use this feature. You find that inexperienced SQL programmers will use functions rather than derived tables or VIEWs simply because the syntax looks more like their procedural language. All this does is make the code harder for experienced SQL programmers to read and maintain.

The real strengths of table functions are in calling programs in a procedural language. This can be done to transfer data from a non-SQL data source. If you have a large volume of external data, you should look at ETL tools instead, but this is handy for smaller volumes of data. The procedural language can also create data that SQL would have problems building. For example, statistical calculations involve floating point corrections that most SQL engines do not have. Likewise, SQL was not meant for string manipulations, GIS applications, and many other specialized applications that other languages were.

# 8

# AUXILIARY TABLES

Auxiliary tables are a way of building functions and look-up tables that would be difficult if not impossible to do with the limited computational power of SQL. What SQL is good at is working with tables. Auxiliary tables are not really a part of the data model, but serve as adjuncts to do queries via joins rather than computations.

They are usually very static and constructed from an outside data source. Thus they do not require the same constraint for safety; however since the optimizer can use the constraints for queries, you should include them. As a general statement, they need to have a primary key declared so that it will create a fast access method for searching and joining the auxiliary table to other tables in the schema, not to protect the data from redundancy.

The most important auxiliary table is a Calendar because the Common Era calendar is too irregular for easy computations. Holidays fall on lunar and solar cycles; there are hundreds of fiscal calendars, and so forth. The discussion of Calendar tables will be given in the section on temporal queries. This section will look at various kinds of numeric auxiliary tables.

## 8.1 The Series Table

The Series table is a simple list of integers from 1 to (n) that is used in place of looping constructs in a procedural language. Rather than incrementing a counter value, we try to work in parallel with a complete set of values.

I used to use the name "Sequence" for this table. Unfortunately, SEQUENCE is now a reserved word for a construct in Standard SQL that builds a sequence of numbers, but values are dispensed one at a time as if it were a function call, with local storage to retain the last used value and to maintain certain rules about the numbering. Other people use the name "Numbers" for the table,

Joe Celko's SQL for Smarties. DOI: 10.1016/B978-0-12-382022-8.00008-9

**Table 8.1 List of Integers**

| Seq | cardinal | ordinal. . . |
|---|---|---|
| 1 | 'one' | 'first' |
| 2 | 'two' | 'second' |
| 3 | 'three' | 'third' |
| ... | ... | ... |
| 101 | 'One hundred and one' | 'One hundred and first' |
| ... | ... | ... |

but it is more than some random collection of integers. This table has the general declaration:

```
CREATE TABLE Series
(seq INTEGER NOT NULL PRIMARY KEY
   CONSTRAINT non_negative_nbr
   CHECK (seq > 0)
-- cardinal_name VARCHAR(25) NOT NULL,
-- ordinal_name VARCHAR(25) NOT NULL,
. . .
CONSTRAINT numbers_are_complete
CHECK ((SELECT COUNT(*) FROM Series) =
   (SELECT MAX(seq) FROM Series));
```

with data like that shown in Table 8.1.

This table is a list of all the integers from 1 to some value (n). The ordinal and cardinal columns are simply examples of handy things that you might want to do with an integer, such as turn it into English words, which would be difficult in a procedural language or with the limitations of SQL.

I have found that is it a bad idea to start with zero, though that seems more natural to computer programmers. The reason for omitting zero is that this auxiliary table is often used to provide row numbering by being CROSS JOIN-ed to another table, and the zero would throw off the one-to-one mapping.

### 8.1.1 Enumerating a List

Given a table in a data warehouse for a report that uses the monthly sales data shown as an attribute (the monthly amounts have to be NULL-able to hold missing values for the future), thus:

```
CREATE TABLE AnnualSales1
(salesman CHAR(15) NOT NULL PRIMARY KEY,
```

```
jan DECIMAL(5,2),
feb DECIMAL(5,2),
mar DECIMAL(5,2),
apr DECIMAL(5,2),
may DECIMAL(5,2),
jun DECIMAL(5,2),
jul DECIMAL(5,2),
aug DECIMAL(5,2),
sep DECIMAL(5,2),
oct DECIMAL(5,2),
nov DECIMAL(5,2),
"dec" DECIMAL(5,2)); -- DEC is a reserved word
```

The goal is to “flatten” it out so that it looks like this:

```
CREATE TABLE AnnualSales2
(salesman_name CHAR(15) NOT NULL PRIMARY KEY,
sales_month CHAR(3) NOT NULL
    CONSTRAINT valid_month_code
    CHECK (sales_month
      IN ('Jan', 'Feb', 'Mar', 'Apr',
         'May', 'Jun', 'Jul', 'Aug',
         'Sep', 'Oct', 'Nov', 'Dec'),
sales_amt DECIMAL(5,2) NOT NULL,
PRIMARY KEY(salesman, sales_month));
```

The trick is to build a VIEW of the original table with a number beside each month:

```
CREATE VIEW NumberedSales
AS SELECT salesman,
      1 AS M01, jan,
      2 AS M02, feb,
      3 AS M03, mar,
      4 AS M04, apr,
      5 AS M05, may,
      6 AS M06, jun,
      7 AS M07, jul,
      8 AS M08, aug,
      9 AS M09, sep,
     10 AS M10, oct,
     11 AS M11, nov,
     12 AS M12, "dec" -- reserved word
 FROM AnnualSales1;
```

Now you can use the Series table or you can use a VALUES table constructor to build one. The flatten VIEW is:

```
CREATE VIEW AnnualSales2 (salesman, sales_month,
   sales_amt)
AS SELECT S1.salesman_name,
```

```
  (CASE WHEN A.nbr = M01 THEN 'Jan'
     WHEN A.nbr = M02 THEN 'Feb'
     WHEN A.nbr = M03 THEN 'Mar'
     WHEN A.nbr = M04 THEN 'Apr'
     WHEN A.nbr = M05 THEN 'May'
     WHEN A.nbr = M06 THEN 'Jun'
     WHEN A.nbr = M07 THEN 'Jul'
     WHEN A.nbr = M08 THEN 'Aug'
     WHEN A.nbr = M09 THEN 'Sep'
     WHEN A.nbr = M10 THEN 'Oct'
     WHEN A.nbr = M11 THEN 'Nov'
     WHEN A.nbr = M12 THEN 'Dec'
     ELSE NULL END),
  (CASE WHEN A.nbr = M01 THEN jan
     WHEN A.nbr = M02 THEN feb
     WHEN A.nbr = M03 THEN mar
     WHEN A.nbr = M04 THEN apr
     WHEN A.nbr = M05 THEN may
     WHEN A.nbr = M06 THEN jun
     WHEN A.nbr = M07 THEN jul
     WHEN A.nbr = M08 THEN aug
     WHEN A.nbr = M09 THEN sep
     WHEN A.nbr = M10 THEN oct
     WHEN A.nbr = M11 THEN nov
     WHEN A.nbr = M12 THEN "dec" -- reserved word
     ELSE NULL END)
FROM NumberedSales AS S1
   CROSS JOIN
   (SELECT seq FROM Series WHERE seq <= 12) AS
      A(month_nbr);
```

If your SQL product has derived tables, this can be written as a single VIEW query.

### 8.1.2 Mapping a Series into a Cycle

It is sometimes handy to map a sequence of numbers to a cycle. The general formula is:

```
SELECT seq, MOD (((seq + (:n-1))/ :n), :n)
FROM Series;
```

As an example, consider the following problem in which we want to display an output with what is called "snaking" in a report. Each id has several descriptions and we want to see them in cycles of four (n = 4); when a department has more than four job descriptions, we want to start a new row with an incremented position each subset of four or fewer job descriptions.

```
CREATE TABLE Companies
(dept_nbr INTEGER NOT NULL,
job_nbr INTEGER NOT NULL, -- sequence within department
company_descr CHAR(6) NOT NULL,
PRIMARY KEY (dept_nbr, job_nbr));

INSERT INTO Companies
VALUES (1, 1, 'desc01'), (1, 2, 'desc02'), (1, 3,
   'desc03'),
  (2, 1, 'desc04'), (2, 2, 'desc05'), (2, 3, 'desc06'),
  (2, 4, 'desc07'), (2, 5, 'desc08'), (2, 6, 'desc09'),
  (3, 1, 'desc10'), (3, 2, 'desc11'), (3, 3, 'desc12');
```

I am going to use a VIEW rather than a derived table to make the logic in the intermediate step easier to see.

```
CREATE VIEW Foo2 (dept_nbr, row_grp, d1, d2, d3, d4)
AS
SELECT dept_nbr, (MOD((job_nbr + 3)/4), 4),
  MAX(CASE WHEN MOD(job_nbr, 4) = 1
      THEN company_descr ELSE '   ' END) AS d1,
  MAX(CASE WHEN MOD(job_nbr, 4) = 2
      THEN company_descr ELSE '   ' END) AS d2,
  MAX(CASE WHEN MOD(job_nbr, 4) = 3
      THEN company_descr ELSE '   ' END) AS d3,
  MAX(CASE WHEN MOD(job_nbr, 4) = 0
      THEN company_descr ELSE '   ' END) AS d4
FROM Companies AS F1
GROUP BY dept_nbr, job_nbr;

SELECT dept_nbr, row_grp,
  MAX(d1) AS d1, MAX(d2) AS d2, MAX(d3) AS d3, MAX(d4) AS d4
FROM Foo2
GROUP BY dept_nbr, row_grp
ORDER BY dept_nbr, row_grp;
```

| Results | | | | | |
|---|---|---|---|---|---|
| dept_nbr | row_grp | d1 | d2 | d3 | d4 |
| 1 | 1 | desc1 | desc2 | desc3 | |
| 2 | 1 | desc4 | desc5 | desc6 | desc7 |
| 2 | 2 | desc8 | desc9 | | |
| 3 | 1 | desc10 | desc11 | desc12 | |

This is a bad coding practice. Display is a function of the front end and should not be done in the database.

### 8.1.3 Replacing an Iterative Loop

Although is not recommended as a technique, and it will vary from SQL dialect to dialect, it is a good exercise in learning to think in sets. You are given a quoted string that is made up of integers separated by commas and your goal is to break each of integers out as a row in a table.

The obvious approach is to write procedural code that will loop over the input string and cut off all characters from the start up to, but not including, the first comma, cast the substring as an integer, and then iterate through the rest of the string.

```
CREATE PROCEDURE ParseList (IN inputstring VARCHAR(1000))
LANGUAGE SQL
BEGIN DECLARE i INTEGER;
SET i = 1; -- iteration control variable
-- add sentinel comma to end of input string
SET inputstring = TRIM (BOTH '' FROM inputstring || ', ');
WHILE i < CHAR_LENGTH(inputstring)
 DO WHILE SUBSTRING(inputstring, i, 1) <> ', '
  DO SET i = i + 1;
  END WHILE;
SET outputstring = SUBSTRING(inputstring, 1, i-1);
INSERT INTO Outputs VALUES (CAST (outputstring AS
   INTEGER));
SET inputstring = SUBSTRING(inputstring, i+1);
END WHILE;
END;
```

Another way to do this is with a Series table and this strange-looking query:

```
CREATE PROCEDURE ParseList (IN inputstring VARCHAR(1000))
LANGUAGE SQL
INSERT INTO ParmList (parameter_position, param)
SELECT S1.i,
   CAST (SUBSTRING ((', ' || inputstring ||', ')
         FROM (S1.i + 1)
         FOR (S2.i - S1.i - 1))
      AS INTEGER)
 FROM Series AS S1,
   Series AS S2
WHERE SUBSTRING((', ' || inputstring ||', ') FROM S1.i
   FOR 1) = ', '
 AND SUBSTRING((', ' || inputstring ||', ') FROM S2.i
   FOR 1) = ', '
 AND S2.i
 = (SELECT MIN(S3.i)
     FROM Series AS S3
     WHERE S1.i < S3.i
```

```
    AND SUBSTRING((', ' || inputstring ||', ')
        FROM S3.i
        FOR 1) = ', ')
AND S1.i < CHAR_LENGTH (inputstring+ 1)
AND S2.i < CHAR_LENGTH (inputstring+ 2);
```

The trick here is to concatenate commas on the left and right sides of the input string. To be honest, you would probably want to trim blanks and perhaps do other tests on the string, such as seeing that `LOWER(:instring) = UPPER(:instring)` to avoid alphabetic characters, and so forth. That edited result string would be kept in a local variable and used in the INSERT INTO statement.

The integer substrings are located between the `i-th` and `((i+1)-th` comma pairs. In effect, the Sequence table replaces the loop counter. The Series table has to have enough numbers to cover the entire string, but unless you really like to type a long parameter list, this should not be a problem. The last two predicates are to avoid a Cartesian product with the Series table.

## 8.2 Lookup Auxiliary Tables

In the old days, when engineers used slide rulers, other people went to the back of their math and financial books to use printed tables of functions. Here you could find trigonometry, or compound interest, or statistical functions. Today, you would more likely calculate the function because computing power is so cheap. Pocket calculators that sold for hundreds of dollars in the 1960s are now on spikes next to chewing gum in the check-out line at office supply stores.

In the days of keypunch data entry, there would be loose-leaf notebooks of which encoding schemes to use sitting next to the incoming paper forms. Today, you will more likely see a WIMP (Windows, Icons, Menus, and Pulldowns or Pop-ups) interface.

Although the physical mechanisms have changed, the idea of building a table (in the nonrelational sense) is still valid. An auxiliary table holds a static or relatively static set of data. The users do not change the data. Updating one of these tables is a job for the database administrator or the data repository administrator, if your shop is that sophisticated. One of the problems with even a simple look-up table change is that the existing data often has to be changed to the new encoding scheme, and this required administrative privileges.

The primary key of an auxiliary table is never an identifier; an identifier is unique in the schema and refers to one entity anywhere it appears. These are values, not entities. Look-up tables that work with values are not entities by definition. Monstrosities likes `value_id` and `<something>_code_id` are absurd on the face of them.

This is a short list of postfixes that can be used as the name of the key column in auxiliary tables. There is a more complete list of postfixes in my book, *SQL Programming Style* (2005, ISBN 978-0-12-088797-2):

- `_nbr` or `num: Tag number`; a string of digits that names something. Do not use _no since it looks like the Boolean yes/no value. I prefer `nbr` to `num` since it is used as a common abbreviation in several European languages.
- `_name` or `nm`: An alphabetic name that explains itself. It is also called a nominal scale.
- `_code` or `_cd`: A code is a standard maintained by a trusted source, usually outside of the enterprise. For example the ZIP code is maintained by the United States Postal Service. A code is well understood in its context, so you might not have to translate it for humans.
- `_cat`: Category, an encoding that has an external source that has very distinct groups of entities. There should be strong formal criteria for establishing the category. The classification of Kingdom in biology is an example.
- `_class`: An internal encoding that does not have an external source that reflects a subclassification of the entity. There should be strong formal criteria for the classification. The classification of plants in biology is an example.
- `_type`: An encoding that has a common meaning both internally and externally. Types are usually less formal than a class and might overlap. For example a driver's license might be motorcycle, automobile, taxi, truck, and so forth.

The differences among type, class, and category are an increasing strength of the algorithm for assigning the type, class, or category. A category is very distinct; you will not often have to guess if something is "animal, vegetable, or mineral" to put it in one of those categories.

A class is a set of things that have some commonality; you have rules for classifying an animal as a mammal or a reptile. You may have some cases where it is harder to apply the rules, such as the egg-laying mammal in Australia, but the exceptions tend to become their own classification—monotremes in this example.

A type is the weakest of the three, and it might call for a judgment. For example, in some states a three-wheeled motorcycle is licensed as a motorcycle. In other states, it is licensed as an automobile. And in some states, it is licensed as an automobile only if it has a reverse gear.

The three terms are often mixed in actual usage. Stick with the industry standard, even if violates the definitions just given.

- _status: An internal encoding that reflects a state of being that can be the result of many factors. For example, credit_status might be computed from several sources.
- _addr or _loc: An address or location for an entity. There can be a subtle difference between an address and location.
- _date or dt: Date, temporal dimension. It is the date of something—employment, birth, termination, and so forth; there is no such column name as just a date by itself.

## 8.2.1 Simple Translation Auxiliary Tables

The most common form of look-up has two columns, one for the value to be looked up and one for the translation of that value into something the user needs. A simple example would be the two-letter ISO 3166 country codes in a table like this:

```
CREATE TABLE CountryCodes
(country_code CHAR(2) NOT NULL PRIMARY KEY, -- iso-3166
country_name VARCHAR(20) NOT NULL);
```

You can add a unique constraint on the descriptive column, but most programmers do not bother since these tables do not change much and when they do change, it is done with data provided by a trusted source. This makes OLTP database programmers a bit uneasy, but Data Warehouse database programmers understand it.

## 8.2.2 Multiple Translation Auxiliary Tables

Although we want the encoding value to stay the same, we often need to have multiple translations. There can be a short description, a long description, or just a different one depending on who was looking at the data. For example, consider displaying error messages in various languages in a single table:

```
CREATE TABLE ErrorMessages
(err_msg_code CHAR(5) NOT NULL PRIMARY KEY,
english_err_msg CHAR(25) NOT NULL ...
french_err_msg NCHAR(25) NOT NULL ..
...
esperanto NCHAR (25) NOT NULL);
```

Yes, this does require a structure change to add a new language. However, since the data is static the convenience of having all the related translations in one place is probably worth it. This inherently forces you to have all the languages for each error code, whereas a strict First Normal Form (1NF) table does not.

Your first thought is that an application using this table would be full of code, like:

```
SELECT CASE :my_language
  WHEN 'English' THEN english_err
  WHEN 'French' THEN french_err
  ... END AS err_msg
FROM ErrorMessages
WHERE err_msg_code = '42';
```

This is not usually the case. You have another table that finds the language preferences of the CURRENT_USER and presents a VIEW to him or her in the language he or she desires.

You don't invent or add languages very often—though I do know of one product that was adding Klingon to its error messages. Seriously, it was for a demo at a trade show to show off the internationalization features. ("Unknown error = Die in ignorance!!" Sort of a user-surly interface instead of user-friendly.)

### 8.2.3 Multiple Parameter Auxiliary Tables

This type of auxiliary table has two or more parameters that it uses to seek a value. The classic example from college freshman statistics courses is the Student's t-distribution for small samples (Table 8.2). The value of (r) is the size of the sample minus one and the percentages are the confidence intervals. Loosely speaking, the Student's t-distribution is the best guess at the population distribution that we can make without knowing the standard deviation with a certain level of confidence.

**Table 8.2 Student's T-Distribution**

| r | 90% | 95% | 97.5% | 99.5% |
|---|---|---|---|---|
| 1 | 3.07766 | 6.31371 | 12.7062 | 63.65600 |
| 2 | 1.88562 | 2.91999 | 4.30265 | 9.92482 |
| 3 | 1.63774 | 2.35336 | 3.18243 | 5.84089 |
| 4 | 1.53321 | 2.13185 | 2.77644 | 4.60393 |
| 5 | 1.47588 | 2.01505 | 2.57058 | 4.03212 |
| 10 | 1.37218 | 1.81246 | 2.22814 | 3.16922 |
| 30 | 1.31042 | 1.69726 | 2.04227 | 2.74999 |
| 100 | 1.29007 | 1.66023 | 1.98397 | 2.62589 |
| | 1.28156 | 1.64487 | 1.95999 | 2.57584 |

William Gosset created this statistic in 1908. His employer, Guinness Breweries, required him to publish under a pseudonym, so he chose "Student" and that name stuck.

### 8.2.4 Range Auxiliary Tables

In a range auxiliary table, there is one parameter, but it must fall inside a range of values. The most common example would be reporting periods or ranges. There is no rule that prevents these ranges from overlapping. For example, Swimsuit Season and BBQ Grill Sale might have a large number of days in common at a department store. However, it is usually a good idea not to have disjoint ranges.

```
CREATE TABLE ReportPeriods
(period_name CHAR(15) NOT NULL,
period_start_date DATE NOT NULL,
period_end_date DATE NOT NULL,
CHECK(period_start_date < period_end_date),
PRIMARY KEY (period_start_date, period_end_date));
```

The searching is done with a `BETWEEN` predicate. A `NULL` can be useful as a marker for an open-ended range. Consider a table for grades in a school. The `CHECK()` constraint is not needed because of the static nature of the data, but it gives the optimizer extra information about the two columns and might help improve performance.

```
CREATE TABLE LetterGrades
(letter_grade CHAR(1) NOT NULL PRIMARY KEY,
low_score DECIMAL(6,3) NOT NULL,
high_score DECIMAL(6,3));

INSERT INTO LetterGrades
VALUES ('F',0.000, 60.000),
  ('D', 60.999, 70.000),
  ('C', 70.999, 80.000),
  ('B', 80.999, 90.000),
  ('A', 90.999, NULL);
```

If we had made the last range `('A', 90.999, 100.000)`, then a student who did extra work and got a total score over 100.000 would not have gotten a grade. The alternatives are to use a dummy value, such as `('A', 90.999, 999.999)` or to use a `NULL` and add the predicate.

```
SELECT ..
FROM ..
WHERE Exams.score
  BETWEEN LetterGrades.low_score
    AND COALESCE (LetterGrades.high_score, Exams.score);
```

The choice of using a dummy value or a NULL will depend on the nature of the data.

### 8.2.5 Hierarchical Auxiliary Tables

In a hierarchical auxiliary table, there is one parameter, but it must fall inside one or more ranges of values and those ranges must be nested inside each other. We want to get an entire path of categories back as a result.

A common example would be the Dewey Decimal Classification system, which we might encode as:

```
CREATE TABLE DeweyDecimalClassification
(category_name CHAR(35) NOT NULL,
low_ddc INTEGER NOT NULL
   CHECK (low_ddc BETWEEN 000 AND 999),
high_ddc INTEGER NOT NULL
   CHECK (high_ddc BETWEEN 000 AND 999),
CHECK (low_ddc <= high_ddc),
PRIMARY KEY (low_ddc, high_ddc));

INSERT INTO DeweyDecimalClassification
VALUES ('Natural Sciences & Mathematics', 500, 599),
   ('Mathematics', 510, 519),
   ('General Topics', 511, 511),
   ('Algebra & Number Theory', 512, 512),
   ...,
   ('Probabilities & Applied Mathematics', 519, 519);
```

Thus a search on 511 returns three rows in the look-up table. The leaf nodes of the hierarchy always have `(low_ddc = high_ddc)` and the relative nesting level can be determined by `(high_ddc - low_ddc)` or by the range values themselves.

Again, you can have a constraint on the table that prevents overlapping ranges, but this is not usually placed on the table since it is checked when the table is loaded. However, the `CHECK (low_ddc <= high_ddc)` can pass along information to the optimizer and the `PRIMARY KEY (low_ddc, high_ddc)` will create a useful index for the joins.

### 8.2.6 One True Look-up Table

I think that Paul Keister was the first person to coin the phrase OTLT (One True Look-up Table) for a common SQL programming technique that is popular with newbies. Later D. C. Peterson called it a MUCK (Massively Unified Code-Key) table. The technique crops up time and time again, but I'll give him credit as the first guy to give it a name. Simply put, the idea is to have one table do all of the code look-ups in the schema. It usually looks like this:

```
CREATE TABLE MagicalUniversalLookups
(code_type CHAR(10) NOT NULL,
code_value VARCHAR(255) NOT NULL,
code_description VARCHAR(255) NOT NULL,
PRIMARY KEY (code_value, code_type));
```

So if we have Dewey Decimal Classification (library codes), ICD (International Classification of Diseases), and two-letter ISO 3166 country codes in the schema, we have them all in one honking big table.

Let's start with the problems in the DDL and then look at the awful queries you have to write (or hide in VIEWs). So we need to go back to the original DDL and add a CHECK() constraint on the code_type column. (Otherwise, we might "invent" a new encoding system by typographical error.)

The Dewey Decimal and ICD codes are numeric, and the ISO 3166 is alphabetic. Oops, we need another CHECK constraint that will look at the code_type and make sure that the string is in the right format. Now the table looks something like this, if anyone attempted to do it right, which is not usually the case:

```
CREATE TABLE MagicalUniversalLookups
(code_type CHAR(10) NOT NULL
   CHECK(code_type IN ('DDC', 'ICD', 'ISO3166', ..),
code_value VARCHAR(255) NOT NULL,
   CHECK
   (CASE WHEN code_type = 'DDC'
          AND code_value
            SIMILAR TO '[0-9][0-9][0-9].[0-9][0-9][0-9]'
        THEN 1
        WHEN code_type = 'ICD'
          AND code_value
            SIMILAR TO '[0-9][0-9][0-9].[0-9][0-9][0-9]'
        THEN 1
        WHEN code_type = 'ISO3166'
          AND code_value
            SIMILAR TO '[A-Z][A-Z]'
        THEN 1 ELSE 0 END = 1),
code_description VARCHAR(255) NOT NULL,
PRIMARY KEY (code_value, code_type));
```

Since the typical application database can have dozens and dozens of codes in it, just keep extending this pattern for as long as required. Not very pretty is it? That is why most OTLT programmers do not bother with it and thus destroy data integrity.

The next thing you notice about this table is that the columns are pretty wide VARCHAR(n), or even worse, that they NVARCHAR(n). The size of the string is most often the largest one allowed in that particular SQL product.

Since you have no idea what is going to be shoved into the table, there is no way to predict and design with a safe, reasonable maximum size. The size constraint has to be put into the WHEN clause of that second `CHECK()` constraint between `code_type` and `code_value`.

These large sizes tend to invite bad data. You give someone a `VARCHAR(n)` column, and you eventually get a string with a lot of white space and a small odd character sitting at the end of it. You give someone an `NVARCHAR(255)` column and eventually it will get a Buddhist sutra in Chinese Unicode. I am sure of this because I load the Heart Sutra when I get called to evaluate a database.

If you make an error in the `code_type` or `code_description` among codes with the same structure, it might not be detected. You can turn 500.000 from "Natural Sciences and Mathematics" in Dewey Decimal codes into "Coal Workers Pneumoconiosis" in ICD and vice versa. This can be really hard to find when one of the similarly structured schemes had unused codes in it.

Now let's consider the problems with actually using the OTLT in the DML. It is always necessary to add the `code_type` as well as the value that you are trying to look up.

```
SELECT P1.ssn, P1.last_name, ..., L1.code_description
FROM MagicalUniversalLookups AS L1, Personnel AS P1
WHERE L1.code_type = 'ICD'
 AND L1.code_value = P1.icd
 AND ..;
```

In this sample query, I need to know the `code_type` of the Personnel table sickness column and of every other encoded column in the table. If you got a `code_type` wrong, you can still get a result.

I also need to allow for some overhead for type conversions. It would be much more natural to use DECIMAL (6,3) for Dewey Decimal codes instead of `VARCHAR(n)`, so that is probably how it appears in the Personnel table. But why not use `CHAR(7)` for the code? If I had a separate table for each encoding scheme, then I would have used a `FOREIGN KEY` and matched the data types in the referenced and referencing tables. There is no definitive guide for data type choices in the OTLT approach.

When I go to execute a query, I have to pull in the entire OTLT table, even if I only use one code. If one code is at the start of the physical storage, and another is at the end of physical storage, I can do a lot of paging. When I update the OTLT table, I have to lock out everyone until I am finished. It is like having to carry an encyclopedia set with you when all you needed is a magazine article.

I am going to venture a guess that this idea came from OO programmers who think of it as some kind of polymorphism done in SQL. They say to themselves that a table is a class, which it is not, and therefore it ought to have polymorphic behaviors, which it does not.

Maybe there are good reasons for the data modeling principle that a well-designed table is a set of things of the same kind instead of a pile of unrelated items.

## 8.3 Auxiliary Function Tables

SQL is not a computational language like FORTRAN and the specialized math packages. It typically does not have the numerical analysis routines to compensate for floating point rounding errors, or algebraic reductions in the optimizer. But it is good at joins.

Most auxiliary look-up tables are for simple decoding, but they can be used for more complex functions. Let's consider two financial calculations that you cannot do easily: the Net Present Value (NPV) and its related Internal Rate of Return (IRR). Let me stop and ask how would you program the NPV and IRR in SQL? The answer posted on most Newsgroups replies was to write a procedure directly from the equation in the vendor-specific 4GL language and then call it.

As a quick review, let's start with the net present value (NPV) calculation. Imagine that you just won the lottery. You can get the money in a lump sum or have it in monthly payouts over 20 years. What is the best deal? The lottery will pay you more total money over time than in a single payment. But if you can invest the single lump sum at a given interest rate yourself, you might do better. The Net Present Value tells you what a series of payouts is worth as a lump sum at a given interest rate.

To make this more concrete, let's show a little code and data for your two investments options.

```
CREATE TABLE CashFlows
(project_id CHAR(15) NOT NULL,
time_period INTEGER NOT NULL,
 CHECK (time_period > = 0),
payment_amt DECIMAL(12,4) NOT NULL,
PRIMARY KEY (project_id, time_period));

INSERT INTO CashFlows
VALUES ('Acme', 0, -1000.0000),('Acme', 1, 500.0000),
    ('Acme', 2,400.0000),
   ('Acme', 3, 200.0000), ('Acme', 4, 200.0000),
   ('Beta', 0, -1000.0000), ('Beta', 1, 100.0000),
      ('Beta', 2, 200.0000),
   ('Beta', 3, 200.0000), ('Beta', 4, 700.0000);
```

To begin, I invest $1,000 at the start of each project; the time period is zero and the amount is always negative. Every year I get a different amount back on my investment so that at the end of the fourth year, I've received a total of $13,000 on the Acme project less my initial $1,000 for a profit of $12,000. Likewise the Beta project returns $15,000 at the end.

Beta looks like a better investment. Let's assume we can get 10% return on an investment and that we put our cash flows into that investment. The net present value function in pseudo-code is:

```
FOR t FROM 0 TO n
DO SUM(a[t]/ POWER(1.00 + r), t)))
END FOR;
```

where a[i] is the cash flow for time period (i), time period (t = 0) is the initial investment (it is always negative), and r is the interest rate.

When we run them through the equation, we find that Acme has an NPV of $71.9896 and Beta is worth −$115.4293, so Acme is really the better project. We can get more out of the Acme cash flow than the Beta cash flow.

## 8.3.1 Inverse Functions with Auxiliary Tables

The Internal Rate of Return (IRR) depends on the NPV. It finds the interest rate at which your investment would break even if you invested back into the same project. Thus if you can get a better rate, this is a good investment.

Let's build another table.

```
CREATE TABLE Rates
(rate DECIMAL(6,4) NOT NULL PRIMARY KEY);
```

Now let's populate it with some values. One trick to fill the Rates table with values is to use a `CROSS JOIN` and keep values inside a reasonable range.

```
CREATE TABLE Digits(digit DECIMAL (6,4) PRIMARY KEY);
INSERT INTO Digits
VALUES (0.0000), (0.0001), (0.0002), (0.0003), (0.0004),
  (0.0005), (0.0006), (0.0007), (0.0008), (0.0009);

INSERT INTO Rates (rate)
SELECT DISTINCT (D1.digit *1000) + (D2.digit *100) +
   (D3.digit *10) + D4.digit
FROM Digits AS D1, Digits AS D2, Digits AS D3, Digits
   AS D4
WHERE ((D1.digit *1000) + (D2.digit *100) + (D3.digit *10)
   + D4.digit)
 BETWEEN {{lower limit}} AND {{upper limit}};
    -- pseudo-code
DROP TABLE Digits;
```

We now have two choices. We can build a VIEW or CTE that uses the cash flow table, thus:

```
CREATE VIEW NPV_by_Rate(project_id, rate, npv)
AS
SELECT CF.project_id, R1.rate,
 SUM(amount / POWER((1.00 + R1.rate), time_period))
FROM CashFlows AS CF, Rates AS R1
GROUP BY R1.rate, CF.project_id;
```

or we can set the amount in the formula to 1 and store the multiplier for the (rate, time_period) pair in another table:

```
INSERT INTO NPV_Mulipliers (time_period, rate,
   npv_multiplier)
SELECT S.seq, R1.rate,
 SUM(1.00/(POWER((1.00 + R1.rate), seq)))
FROM Series AS S, Rates AS R1
WHERE S.seq <= {{ upper limit }} --pseudo-code
GROUP BY S.seq, R1.rate;
```

The Series table contains integers 1 to (n) and it is a standard auxiliary table used to avoid iteration.

Assuming we use the VIEW, the IRR is now the single query:

```
SELECT 'Acme', rate AS irr, npv
FROM NPV_by_Rate
WHERE ABS(npv)
= (SELECT MIN(ABS(npv))
   FROM NPV_by_Rate)
AND project_id = 'Acme';
```

In my sample data, I get an IRR of 13.99% at an NPV of −0.04965 for the Acme project. Assume you have hundreds of projects to consider; would you rather write one query or hundreds of procedure calls?

This web site has a set of slides that deal with the use of interpolation to find the IRR: www.yorku.ca/adms3530/Interpolation.pdf. Using the method described on the web site, we can write the interpolation for the Acme example as:

```
SELECT R1.rate + (R1.rate * (R1.npv/(R1.npv - R2.npv)))
   AS irr
FROM NPV_by_Rate AS R1, NPV_by_Rate AS R2
WHERE R1.project_id = 'Acme'
 AND R2.project_id = 'Acme'
 AND R1.rate = 0.1000
 AND R2.rate = 0.2100
 AND R1.npv > 0
 AND R2.npv < 0;
```

The important points are that the NPVs from R1 and R2 have to be on both sides of the zero point, so that you can do a linear interpolation between the two rates with which they are associated.

The trade-off is speed for accuracy. The IRR function is slightly concave and not linear; that means that if you graph it, the shape of the curve buckles toward the origin. Picking good (R1.rate, R2.rate) pairs is important, but if you want to round off to the nearest whole percentage, you probably have a larger range than you might think. The answer, 0.1399 from the original table look-up method, rounds to 14%, as do all the interpolations in Table 8.3.

The advantages of using an auxiliary function table are:

1. All host programs will be using the same calculations.
2. The formula can be applied to hundreds or thousands of projects at one time instead doing one project, as you would with a spreadsheet or financial calculator.

Robert J. Hamilton (bobha@seanet.com) posted proprietary T-SQL functions for the NPV and IRR functions. The NPV function was straightforward, but he pointed out several problems with finding the IRR.

By definition IRR is the rate at which the NPV of the cash flows equals zero. When IRR is well behaved the graph of NPV as a function of rate is a curve that crosses the x-axis once and only once. When IRR is not well behaved, the graph crosses the x-axis many times, which means the IRR is either multivalued or is undefined.

At this point, we need to ask what the appropriate domain is for IRR. As it turns out NPV is defined for all possible rates, both positive and negative, except where NPV approaches an asymptote at rate of −100% and the power function blows up. What does a negative rate mean when calculating NPV? What does it mean to have a negative IRR? Well it depends on how you look at it.

**Table 8.3 Interpolations**

| RI | R2 | IRR |
|---|---|---|
| 0.1000 | 0.2100 | 0.140135 |
| 0.1000 | 0.2000 | 0.143537 |
| 0.0999 | 0.2000 | 0.143457 |
| 0.0999 | 0.1999 | 0.143492 |
| 0.0800 | 0.1700 | 0.135658 |

If you take a mathematical approach, a negative IRR is just another solution to the equation. If you take an economic approach, a negative IRR means you are losing money on the project. Perhaps if you live in a deflationary economy, then a negative cash flow might be profitable in terms of real money, but that is a very unusual situation and we can dismiss negative IRRs as unreasonable.

This means that a table look-up approach to the IRR has to have a very fine granularity and enough of a scope to cover a lot of situations for the general case. It also means that it is probably not the way to go. Expressing rates to 5 or 6 decimal places is common in home mortgage finance (i.e., APR 5.6725%), and this degree of precision using the set-based approach does not scale well. Moreover, this is exacerbated by the requirements of using IRR in hyperinflationary economies where solutions of 200%, 300%, and higher are meaningful.

Here are Mr. Hamilton's functions written in SQL/PSM; one uses a straight-line algorithm as you find in Excel and other spreadsheets, and a bounding box algorithm. The bounding box algorithm has better domain integrity but can inadvertently "skip over" a solution when widening its search.

```
CREATE TABLE CashFlows
(t INTEGER NOT NULL CHECK (t >= 0),
amount DECIMAL(12,4) NOT NULL);

CREATE TABLE Rates
(rate DECIMAL(7,5) NOT NULL);

CREATE TABLE Digits
(digit DECIMAL(6,4));
INSERT INTO Digits
VALUES (0.0000), (0.0001), (0.0002), (0.0003), (0.0004),
  (0.0005), (0.0006), (0.0007), (0.0008), (0.0009);

INSERT INTO Rates
SELECT D1.digit * 1000 + D2.digit * 100 + D3.digit * 10 +
   D4.digit FROM Digits AS D1, Digits AS D2, Digits AS D3,
   Digits AS D4;

INSERT INTO Rates
SELECT rate-1 FROM Rates WHERE rate >= 0;

INSERT INTO Rates
SELECT rate-2 FROM Rates WHERE rate >= 0;

DROP TABLE Digits;

CREATE FUNCTION NPV (IN my_rate FLOAT)
RETURNS FLOAT
DETERMINISTIC
CONTAINS SQL
RETURN (CASE WHEN -- prevent divide by zero at rate = -100%
```

```
    ABS (1.0 + my_rate) >= 1.0e-5
    THEN (SELECT SUM (amount * POWER ((1.0 + my_rate), -t))
         FROM CashFlows)
    ELSE NULL END);

CREATE FUNCTION irr_bb (IN guess FLOAT)
RETURNS FLOAT
DETERMINISTIC
CONTAINS SQL

BEGIN
 DECLARE maxtry INTEGER;
 DECLARE x1 FLOAT;
 DECLARE x2 FLOAT;
 DECLARE f1 FLOAT;
 DECLARE f2 FLOAT;
 DECLARE x FLOAT;
 DECLARE dx FLOAT;
 DECLARE x_mid FLOAT;
 DECLARE f_mid FLOAT;
```

—initial bounding box around guess

```
 SET x1 = guess - 0.005;
 SET f1 = NPV (x1);
 IF f1 IS NULL THEN RETURN (f1); END IF;

 SET x2 = guess + 0.005;
 SET f2 = NPV (x2);
 IF f2 IS NULL THEN RETURN (f2); END IF;
```

—expand bounding box to include a solution

```
 SET maxtry = 50;
 WHILE maxtry > 0 -- try until solution is bounded
   AND (SIGN(f1) * SIGN(f2)) <> -1
 DO IF ABS (f1) < ABS (f2)
  THEN -- move lower bound
    SET x1 = x1 + 1.6 * (x1 - x2);
    SET f1 = NPV (x1);
    IF f1 IS NULL -- no irr
    THEN RETURN (f1);
    END IF;
  ELSE -- move upper bound
    SET x2 = x2 + 1.6 * (x2 - x1);
    SET f2 = NPV (x2);
    IF f2 IS NULL -- no irr
    THEN RETURN (f2);
    END IF;
  END IF;
  SET maxtry = maxtry - 1;
  END WHILE;
```

```
IF (SIGN(f1) * SIGN(f2)) <> -1
THEN RETURN (CAST (NULL AS FLOAT));
END IF;
END;
```

—now find solution with binary search

```
SET x = CASE WHEN f1 < 0
        THEN x1
        ELSE x2 END;
SET dx = CASE WHEN f1 < 0
        THEN (x2 - x1)
        ELSE (x1 - x2) END;
SET maxtry = 50;
WHILE maxtry > 0
DO SET dx = dx / 2.0; -- reduce steps by half
 SET x_mid = x + dx;
 SET f_mid = NPV (x_mid);
 IF f_mid IS NULL -- no irr
 THEN RETURN (f_mid);
 ELSE IF ABS (f_mid) < 1.0e-5 -- epsilon for problem
   THEN RETURN (x_mid); -- irr found
   END IF;
 END IF;
 IF f_mid < 0
 THEN SET x = x_mid;
 END IF;
 SET maxtry = maxtry - 1;
END WHILE;
RETURN (CAST (NULL AS FLOAT));
END;
```

If you prefer to compute the IRR as a straight line, you can use this function.

```
CREATE FUNCTION irr_sl (IN guess FLOAT)
RETURNS FLOAT
DETERMINISTIC
CONTAINS SQL
BEGIN
DECLARE maxtry INTEGER;
DECLARE x1 FLOAT; DECLARE x2 FLOAT;
DECLARE f1 FLOAT; DECLARE f2 FLOAT;

SET maxtry = 50; -- iterations
WHILE maxtry > 0
 DO SET x1 = guess;
   SET f1 = NPV (x1);
   IF f1 IS NULL -- no irr
   THEN RETURN (f1);
   ELSE IF ABS (f1) < 1.0e-5 -- irr within epsilon range
```

```
  THEN RETURN (x1);
  END IF;
END IF;
```

—try again with new guess using two-point formula

```
SET x2 = x1 + 1.0e-5;
SET f2 = NPV (x2);
IF f2 IS NULL -- no irr
THEN RETURN (f2);
END IF;
IF ABS (f2 - f1) < 1.0e-5
THEN RETURN (CAST (NULL AS FLOAT)); -- check for divide
   by zero
END IF;
SET guess = x1 - f1 * (x2 - x1)/ (f2 - f1);
SET maxtry = maxtry - 1;
END WHILE;
END;
```

—Test table, holds results of straight line algorithm

```
CREATE TABLE Test_StraightLine
(rate DECIMAL(7,5) NOT NULL,
npv FLOAT,
irr DECIMAL(7,5));

CREATE TABLE Test_BoundedBox
(rate DECIMAL(7,5) NOT NULL,
npv FLOAT,
irr DECIMAL(7,5));
```

—original scenario
—try t = 0 cashflow of: –391, irr undefined;
—try t = 0 cashflow of: –350, irr multivalued;
—0, irr single-valued (well-behaved)

```
DELETE FROM CashFlows
INSERT INTO CashFlows
VALUES (0, -350), (1, 100), (2, 100), (3, 100),
   (4, 100), (5, 100), (6, 100), (7, 100), (8, 100),
   (9, 100), (10, 100), (11, 100), (12, 100), (13, 100),
   (14, 100), (15, -1500);
```

—scenario 1a: single valued irr

```
DELETE FROM CashFlows
INSERT INTO CashFlows
VALUES (0, -800), (1, 100), (2, 100), (3, 100), (4, 100),
  (5, 100), (6, 100), (7, 100), (8, 100), (9, 100),
  (10, 100);
```

—scenario 1b: single valued irr, signs reversed

```
DELETE FROM CashFlows;
INSERT INTO CashFlows
VALUES (0, 800), (1, -100), (2, -100), (3, -100), (4, -100),
  (5, -100), (6, -100), (7, -100), (8, -100), (9, -100),
  (10, -100);
```

—scenario 2: double valued irr

```
DELETE FROM CashFlows;
INSERT INTO CashFlows
VALUES (0, -300), (1, 100), (2, 100), (3, 100), (4, 100),
  (5, 100), (6, 100),(7, 100), (8, 100), (9, 100),
  (10, -690);
```

—scenario 3: double valued irr with solutions very close together

```
DELETE FROM CashFlows;
INSERT INTO CashFlows
VALUES (0, -310), (1, 100), (2, 100), (3, 100), (4, 100),
  (5, 100), (6, 100), (7, 100), (8, 100), (9, 100),
  (10, -690);
```

—scenario 4: undefined irr

```
DELETE FROM CashFlows;
INSERT INTO CashFlows
VALUES (0, -320), (1, 100), (2, 100), (3, 100), (4, 100),
  (5, 100), (6, 100), (7, 100), (8, 100), (9, 100),
  (10, -690);
```

—run the test

```
DELETE FROM Test_StraightLine;
INSERT INTO Test_StraightLine (rate, npv, irr)
SELECT rate, NPV (rate), irr_sl(rate)
FROM Rates;

DELETE FROM Test_BoundedBox ;
INSERT INTO Test_BoundedBox (rate, npv, irr)
SELECT rate, NPV (rate), irr_bb(rate)
FROM Rates;
```

—View results of the test

```
SELECT SL.rate, SL.npv AS npv_sl, SL.irr AS irr_sl,
   BB.npv AS npv_bb,
   BB.irr AS irr_bb
FROM Test_StraightLine AS SL, Test_BoundedBox
WHERE BB.rate = SL.rate;
```

A computational version of the IRR due to Richard Romley returns approximations that become more and more accurate as you feed estimates back into the formula.

```
CREATE FUNCTION IRR(IN project_id CHAR(15), IN my_i
   DECIMAL(12,8))
RETURNS DECIMAL(12,8)
LANGUAGE SQL
DETERMINISTIC
RETURN (SELECT CASE WHEN ROUND(my_i, 4) = ROUND(T.i, 4)
        THEN 100 * (my_I - 1)
        ELSE IRR(project_id, T.i) END
   FROM (SELECT SUM((amount * (time_period + 1))
          /(POWER(my_i, time_period)))
          / SUM((amount * (time_period))
          /(POWER(my_i, time_period + 1)))
      FROM CashFlows WHERE project_id = my_project_id));
```

## 8.3.2 Interpolation with Auxiliary Function Tables

SQL is not a functional programming language, so you often have to depend on vendor extensions providing a good library or on being able to write the functions with the limited power in standard SQL.

However, SQL is good at handling tables and you can often set up auxiliary tables of the general form:

```
CREATE TABLE SomeFunction
(parameter <data type> NOT NULL PRIMARY KEY,
result <data type> NOT NULL);
```

when the range of the function is relatively small. Thus, the pseudo-code expression:

```
SELECT SomeFunction(T1.x), . . .
 FROM TableOne AS T1
WHERE etc
```

is replaced by

```
SELECT F1.result,
 FROM TableOne AS T1, SomeFunction AS F1
WHERE T1.x = F1.parameter
 AND etc
```

However, if the function has a large range, the SomeFunction table can become huge or completely impractical.

A technique that has fallen out of favor since the advent of cheap, fast computers is interpolation. It consists of using two known functional values, a and b, and their results in the function, f(a) and f(b), to find the result of a value, x, between them.

Linear interpolation is the easiest method and if the table has a high precision, it will work quite well for most applications. It is based on the idea that a straight line drawn between two function values f(a) and f(b) will approximate the function well enough that you can take a proportional increment of x relative to (a, b) and get a usable answer for f(x).

The algebra looks like this:

$$f(x) = f(a) + (x - a)*((f(b) - f(a))/(b - a))$$

where (a <= x <= b) and x is not in the table. This can be translated into SQL like this, where x is: myparameter, F1 is related to the variable a, and F2 is related to the variable b:

```
SELECT :myparameter AS my_input,
  (F1.answer + (:myparameter - F1.param)
  * ((F2.answer - F1.answer)
   / (CASE WHEN F1.param = F2.param
        THEN 1.00
        ELSE F2.param - F1.param END)))
  AS answer
FROM SomeFunction AS F1, SomeFunction AS F2
WHERE F1.param --establish a and f(a)
 = (SELECT MAX(param)
      FROM SomeFunction
      WHERE param  <=:myparameter)
 AND F2.param --establish b and f(b)
 = (SELECT MIN(param)
      FROM SomeFunction
      WHERE param >= :myparameter);
```

The CASE expression in the divisor is to avoid division by zero errors when f(x) is in the table.

The rules for interpolation methods are always expressible in four-function arithmetic, which is good for standard SQL. In the old days, the function tables gave an extra value with each parameter and result pair, called delta squared, which was based on finite differences. Delta squared was like a second derivative and could be used in a formula to improve the accuracy of the approximation.

This is not a book on numerical analysis, so you will have to go to a library to find details—or ask an old engineer.

## 8.4 Global Constants Tables

When you configure a system, you might want to have a way to set and keep constants in the schema. One method for doing this is to have a one-row table that can be set with default values at the start, and then updated only by someone with administrative privileges.

```
CREATE TABLE Constants
(lock CHAR(1) DEFAULT 'X'
   NOT NULL PRIMARY KEY
   CHECK (lock = 'X'),
```

```
pi FLOAT DEFAULT 3.142592653 NOT NULL,
 e FLOAT DEFAULT 2.71828182 NOT NULL,
phi FLOAT DEFAULT 1.6180339887 NOT NULL,
...);
```

To initialize the row, execute this statement.

```
INSERT INTO Constants VALUES DEFAULTS;
```

The lock column assures there is only one row and the default values load the initial values. These defaults can include the current user and current timestamp, as well as numeric and character values.

Another version of this idea that does not allow for any updates is a VIEW defined with a table constructor.

```
CREATE VIEW Constants (pi, e, phi, ..)
AS VALUES (3.141592653), (2.71828182), (1.6180339887), ..;
```

The next step is to put in a formula for the constants so that they will be computed on any platform to which this DDL is moved, using the local math library and hardware precision.

## 8.4.1 Preallocated Values

As we discussed in chapter 4, in the old days of paper forms, organizations had a forms control officer whose job was to created, issue, and track the forms. A gap in the sequential numbers on a check, bond, stock certificate, or whatever was a serious accounting problem. Paper forms were usually preprinted and issued in blocks of numbers as needed. You can imitate this procedure in a database with a little thought and a few simple stored procedures.

Broadly speaking, there were two types of allocation blocks. In one, the sequence is known. The most common example would be a checkbook. Gaps in the sequence numbers are not allowed, and a destroyed or damaged check has to be explained with a "void" or other notation. The system needs to record which block went to which user, the date and time, and any other information relevant to the auditors.

```
CREATE TABLE FormsControl
(form_nbr CHAR(7) NOT NULL,
seq INTEGER NOT NULL CHECK(seq > 0),
PRIMARY KEY (form_nbr, seq),
recipient CHAR(25) DEFAULT CURRENT_USER NOT NULL,
issue_date TIMESTAMP DEFAULT CURRENT_TIMESTAMP NOT NULL,
..);
```

The tables that use the form numbers need to have constraints verify the numbers were issued and appear in the Forms Control table. The next sequence number is easy to create, but you probably should restrict access to the base table with a stored procedure designed for one kind of form, along these lines.

```
CREATE FUNCTION NextFlobSeq()
RETURNS INTEGER
LANGUAGE SQL
DETERMINISTIC
BEGIN
INSERT INTO FormsControl (form_nbr, seq, ..
VALUES ('Flob-1/R',
  (SELECT MAX(seq)+1
FROM FormsControl
WHERE form_nbr = 'Flob-1/R'),
  ..);
```

You can also use views on the FormsControl table to limit user access. If you might be dealing with an empty, then use this scalar expression:

```
(SELECT COALESCE(MAX(seq), 0)+1
 FROM FormsControl
 WHERE form_nbr = 'Flob-1/R'),
```

The COALESCE() will return a zero, thus assuring that the sequence starts with one.

## 8.4.2 Prime Numbers

We discussed methods for finding prime numbers in Chapter 4. We can use a flag in the Series table beside the Primes, based on the methods given there.

## 8.4.3 Fibonacci Numbers

Fibonacci numbers are defined recursively (as are many other mathematical series) so there is a temptation to use a recursive CTE.

If you are not familiar with Fibonacci series, it is defined by the formula

$$F(0) = 0$$
$$F(1) = 1$$
$$F(2) = 1$$
$$F(n) = F(n - 1) + F(n - 2)$$

In English, you start with a pair of numbers, (0,1), as the first two Fibonacci numbers, and after that any Fibonacci number (greater than 2) is the sum of the two previous numbers. That gives us 0, 1, 1, 2, 3, 5, 8, 13, 21, 34, 55, 89, and so on.

This series occurs so often in nature and mathematical functions that you will find whole books devoted to it.

We can solve this using a recursive CTE, thus:

```
WWITH RECURSIVE Fibonacci(n, f, f1)
AS(
(VALUES CAST(1 AS BIGINT), CAST(0 AS BIGINT),
   CAST(1 AS BIGINT))
UNION ALL
SELECT(n + 1),(f + f1), f
FROM Fibonacci
WHERE n < 100) - or other limit for BIGINT

SELECT n, f AS f_nbr
FROM Fibonacci;
```

It looks nice and clever. But many such series have a closed form that is easy and faster than a recursive query; for example, the constant phi and the formula,

```
ROUND (((POWER (phi, :n)- POWER (1.0 - phi, :n))/
SQRT (5.0)), 0);
```

where phi = `FLOOR(POWER(1.61803398874989, n)/SQRT(5) +.5)`

You can load the table in one update statement. You can use more decimal places for phi, if you want more numbers.

## 8.4.4 Random Order Values

In many applications, we do not want to issue the sequence numbers in sequence. This pattern can give information that we do not wish to expose. Instead we want to issue generated values in random order. Do not get mixed up; we want known values that are supplied in random order and not random numbers. Most random number generators can repeat values, which would defeat the purpose of this drill.

Although I usually avoid mentioning physical implementations, one of the advantages of random-order keys is to improve the performance of tree indexes. Tree structured indexes, such as a B-Tree, that have sequential insertions become unbalanced and have to be reorganized frequently. However, if the same set of keys is presented in a random order, the tree tends to stay balanced and you get much better performance.

The generator shown here is an implementation of the additive congruential method of generating values in pseudo-random order and is due to Roy Hann of Rational Commerce Limited, a CA-Ingres consulting firm. It is based on a shift-register and an XOR-gate, and it has its origins in cryptography. Although there are other ways to do this, this code is nice because:

1. The algorithm can be written in C or another low level language for speed. But math is fairly simple even in base 10.
2. The algorithm tends to generate successive values that are (usually) "far apart," which is handy for improving the performance of tree indexes. You will tend to put data on separate physical data pages in storage.
3. The algorithm does not cycle until it has generated every possible value, so we don't have to worry about duplicates. Just count how many calls have been made to the generator.
4. The algorithm produces uniformly distributed values, which is a nice mathematical property to have. It also does not include zero.

Let's walk through all the iterations of the 4-bit Generator illustrated in Figure 8.1.

Initially the shift register contains the value 0001. The two rightmost bits are XOR-ed together, giving 1, and the result is fed into the leftmost bit position and the previous register contents shift one bit right. The iterations of the register are shown in Table 8.4., with their base-10 values.

It might not be obvious that successive values are far apart when we are looking at a tiny 4-bit register. But it is clear that the values are generated in no obvious order, all possible values except 0 are eventually produced, and the termination condition is clear—the Generator cycles back to 1.

Generalizing the algorithm to arbitrary binary word sizes, and therefore longer number sequences, is not as easy as you might think. Finding the "tap" positions where bits are extracted for feedback varies according to the word-size in an extremely nonobvious way. Choosing incorrect tap positions results in an incomplete and usually very short cycle that is unusable. If you want the details and tap positions for words of one to 100 bits, see E. J. Watson, "Primitive Polynomials (Mod 2)," *Mathematics of Computation*, v.16, 1962, pp.368–369.

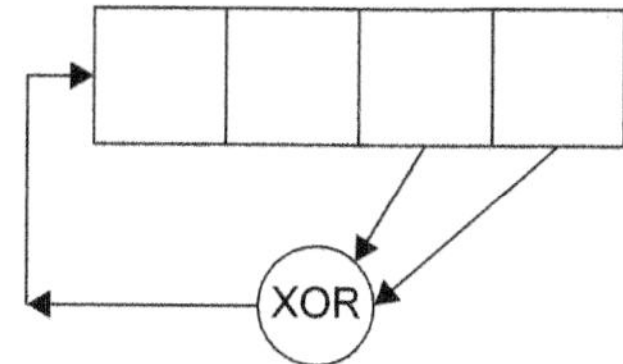


**Figure 8.1** 4-bit Generator

## Table 8.4 Iterations with Base-10 Values

```
iteration 1: 0001 (1)
iteration 2: 1000 (8)
iteration 3: 0100 (4)
iteration 4: 0010 (2)
iteration 5: 1001 (9)
iteration 6: 1100 (12)
iteration 7: 0110 (6)
iteration 8: 1011 (11)
iteration 9: 0101 (5)
iteration 10: 1010 (10)
iteration 11: 1101 (13)
iteration 12: 1110 (14)
iteration 13: 1111 (15)
iteration 14: 0111 (7)
iteration 15: 0011 (3)
iteration 16: 0001 (1) wrap-around!
```

Table 8.5 shows the tap positions 8, 16, 31, 32, and 64-bit words. That should work with any computer hardware you have. The 31-bit word is the one that is probably the most useful since it gives billions of numbers, uses only two tap positions to make the math easier, and matches most computer hardware. The 32-bit version is not easy to implement on a 32-bit machine because it will usually generate an overflow error.

Using Table 8.5, we can see that we need to tap bits 0 and 3 to construct the 31-bit random-order generated value Generator (which is the one most people would want to use in practice):

```
UPDATE Generator31
 SET keyval =
   keyval/2 + MOD(MOD(keyval, 2) + MOD(keyval/8, 2),
     2)*2^30;
```

Or, if you prefer the algorithm in C:

```
int Generator31 ()
{static int n = 1;
n = n >> 1 | ((n^n >> 3) & 1) << 30;
return n;
}
```

**Table 8.5 Tap Positions**

| Word Length |
| --- |
| 8 = {0, 2, 3, 4} |
| 16 = {0, 2, 3, 5} |
| 31 = {0, 3} |
| 32 = {0, 1, 2, 3, 5, 7} |
| 64 = {0 1, 3, 4} |

## 8.5 A Note on Converting Procedural Code to Tables

Sometimes an idea is easier to see with an example. In February 2010, a newsgroup poster asked for help with a user-defined function they had written. What followed was a CASE expression with BETWEENs and ORs and CASE within CASE constructs. It took pairs of (x, y) and produced an answer from a set of three values, call them {'A', 'B', 'C'}. Again, the coding details are not my point. The body of the function could have been a complicated mathematical expression. The quick fix was in the CASE expression syntax for his immediate problem. His code looked like this skeleton:

```
CREATE FUNCTION FindFoobar (IN in_x INTEGER, IN in_y
   INTEGER)
RETURNS CHAR(1)
LANGUAGE SQL
DETERMINISTIC
BEGIN
<< horrible CASE expression with x and y >>;
END;
```

Now a second poster asked of the original posters if he had considered precalculating the CASE expression results and populating a table with them? This was a good piece of advice, since the number of (x, y) pairs involved came to a few thousand cases. Worrying about minimizing storage when the look-up table is this small is silly. Read-only tables this size tend to be in main storage or cache, so they can be shared among many sessions.

But the poster went on to say, "You can use the table with your function or you could use it without the function," but he did not explain what the differences are. They are important. Putting the data in the read-only tables this size will tend to keep it in main storage or cache. If you are really that tight for primary and/or secondary storage that you cannot fit a ~5K row table in your hardware, buy some chips and disks. It is cheap today. Now the data can be shared among many sessions. The table and its indexes can be used by the optimizer. In SQL Server you can include the single column Foobar in the index to get a covering index and performance improvement.

But when the data is locked inside the procedural code of a function, can it be shared or do computations get repeated with each invocation? What about indexes? Ouch! A function pretty much locks things inside. Standard SQL/PSM has a `[NOT] DETERMINISTIC` option in its procedure declarations. This tells the compiler if the procedure or function is going to always return the same answer for the same arguments (note about Standard SQL terms: a parameter is the formal place holder in the parameter list of a declaration and an argument is the value passed in the invocation of the procedure). A nondeterministic function has to be computed over and over; if you don't know about a procedure or function, this is what you have to assume.

Here is the skeleton of what was posted.

—Create table

```
CREATE TABLE Foobar
(x INTEGER NOT NULL,
y INTEGER NOT NULL,
foobar CHAR(1) NOT NULL,
PRIMARY KEY (x, y));
```

—Populate table with data

```
INSERT INTO FooLookup (x, y, foobar)
SELECT X_CTE.x, Y_CTE.y, << horrible CASE expression >> AS
   foobar
FROM (SELECT seq
   FROM Series
  WHERE seq BETWEEN 100 AND 300) AS X_Range (x)
  CROSS JOIN
  (SELECT seq
   FROM Series
  WHERE seq BETWEEN 1 AND 100) AS Y_Range (y);
```

Now let's go on with the rest of the skeleton code for the function:

```
CREATE FUNCTION Find_Foobar
(IN in_x INTEGER, IN in_y INTEGER)
RETURNS CHAR(1)
```

```
LANGUAGE SQL
DETERMINISTIC
BEGIN
RETURN
COALESCE
((SELECT foobar
  FROM FooLookup
  WHERE x = in_x
  AND y = in_y), 'A');
END;
```

The reason for COALESCE() is that 'A' is a default value in the outer CASE expression, but also a valid result in various THEN and ELSE clauses inside inner CASE expressions. The scalar query will return a NULL if it cannot find an (x, y, foobar) row in the table. If we know that the query covers the entire (x, y) universe, then we did not need the COALESCE() and could have avoided a function completely.

Now, let's think about declarative programming. In SQL that means constraints in the table declaration in the DDL. This skeleton has none except the PRIMARY KEY. Ouch! Here is a problem with magazine articles and newsgroup postings; you often skip over the constraints when you post a skeleton table. You did not need them when you declared a file, do you? What is forgotten is that the three SQL sublanguages (DDL, DML, and DCL) work together. In particular, the DDL constraints are used by the DML optimizer.

The << horrible CASE expression >> implied expectations for x and y. We were given lower limits (100 and 1), but the upper limits were open after a small range of (x, y) pairs. I think we can assume that the original poster expected the vast majority of cases (or all of them) to fall in that small range and wanted to handle anything else as an error. In the real world, there is usually what Jerry Weinberg called "reasonableness checking" in data. The principle is also known as Zipf's Law or the "look for a horse and not a zebra" principle in medicine.

The simple first shot would be to assume we always know the limits and can simply use:

```
CREATE TABLE FooLookup
(x INTEGER NOT NULL
 CHECK (x BETWEEN 100 AND 300),
y INTEGER NOT NULL
 CHECK (y BETWEEN 1 AND 100),
foobar CHAR(1)
 DEFAULT 'A'
 NOT NULL
 CHECK (foobar) IN ('A', 'B', 'C'),
PRIMARY KEY (x, y));
```

The DEFAULT 'A' subclause will take care of situations where we did not have an explicit value for foobar. This avoids the COALESCE(). But what if one of the parameters can be anything? That is easy; drop the CHECK() and add a comment. What if one of the parameters is half open or has a huge but sparse space? That is, we know a lower (upper) limit, but not the matching upper (lower) limit. Just use a simple comparison, such as CHECK (y >= 1), instead of a BETWEEN.

A common situation, which was done with nested CASE expression in the original, is that you know a range for a parameter and what the results for the other parameter within that range are. That might be easier to see with code. Here is a CASE expression for some of the possible (x,y) pairs:

```
CASE
WHEN x BETWEEN 100 AND 200
THEN CASE
 WHEN y IN (2, 4, 6, 8) THEN 'B'
 WHEN y IN (1, 3, 5, 7, 9) THEN 'C'
 END
WHEN x BETWEEN 201 AND 300
THEN CASE
 WHEN y IN (2, 4, 6, 8, 99) THEN 'C'
 WHEN y IN (3, 5, 7, 9, 100) THEN 'B'
 END
ELSE 'A'
END
```

This is the DML version of a constraint. It lives only in the INSERT, UPDATE, or SELECT statement where it appears. What we really want is constraints in the DDL so that all statements, present and future, use it. The trick is to create the table with low and high values for each parameter range; a single value is shown with the low and high values equal to each other.

```
CREATE TABLE FooLookup
(low_x INTEGER NOT NULL,
high_x INTEGER NOT NULL,
 CHECK (low_x <= high_x),
low_y INTEGER NOT NULL,
high_y INTEGER NOT NULL,
CHECK (low_y <= high_y),
foobar CHAR(1) NOT NULL
 CHECK (foobar) IN ('A', 'B', 'C'),
PRIMARY KEY (x, y));
```

CASE expression now becomes Table 8.6.

## Table 8.6 CASE Expression

| low_x | high_x | low_y | high_y | foobar |
|---|---|---|---|---|
| 100 | 200 | 2 | 2 | 'B' |
| 100 | 200 | 6 | 6 | 'B' |
| 100 | 200 | 8 | 8 | 'B' |
| 100 | 200 | 1 | 1 | 'C' |
| 100 | 200 | 3 | 3 | 'C' |
| 100 | 200 | 5 | 5 | 'C' |
| 100 | 200 | 7 | 7 | 'C' |
| 100 | 200 | 9 | 9 | 'C' |
| 201 | 300 | 2 | 2 | 'C' |
| 201 | 300 | 4 | 4 | 'C' |
| 201 | 300 | 6 | 6 | 'C' |
| 201 | 300 | 8 | 8 | 'C' |
| 201 | 300 | 99 | 99 | 'C' |
| 201 | 300 | 3 | 3 | 'B' |
| 201 | 300 | 5 | 5 | 'B' |
| 201 | 300 | 7 | 7 | 'B' |
| 201 | 300 | 9 | 9 | 'B' |
| 201 | 300 | 100 | 100 | 'B' |
| 301 | 9999 | 101 | 9999 | 'A' |
| -9999 | 99 | -9999 | 0 | 'A' |

As a safety device, put the default 'A' in ranges outside the rest of the table. I used –9999 and 9999 for the least and greatest limits, but you get the idea.

The query has to use BETWEENs on the high and low limits:

```
SELECT F.foobar, ..
 FROM FooLookup AS F, ..
WHERE my_x BETWEEN F.low_x AND F.high_x
 AND my_y BETWEEN F.low_y AND F.high_y
 AND ..;
```

Is this always going to be the best way to do something? Who knows? Test it.

9

# NORMALIZATION

The Relational Model and the Normal Forms of the Relational Model were first defined by Dr. E. F. Codd (Codd 1970), then extended by other writers after him. He invented the term "normalized relations" by borrowing from the political jargon of the day. A branch of mathematics called relations deals with mappings among sets defined by predicate calculus from formal logic. Just as in an algebraic equation, there are many forms of the same relational statement, but the "normal forms" of relations are certain formally defined desirable constructions. The goal of normal forms is to avoid certain data anomalies that can occur in unnormalized tables.

Data anomalies are easier to explain with an example, but first please be patient while I define some terms. A predicate is a statement of the form A(x), which means that x has the property A. For example, "John is from Indiana" is a predicate statement; here, "John" is the subject and "is from Indiana" is the predicate. A relation is a predicate with two or more subjects. "John and Bob are brothers" is an example of a relation. The common way of visualizing a set of relational statements is as a table, where the columns are attributes of the relation and each row is a specific relational statement.

When Dr. Codd defined the relational model, he gave 0 to 12 rules for the visualization of the relation as a table:

0. Yes, there is a rule zero. For a system to qualify as a relational database management system, that system must use its relational facilities (exclusively) to manage the database. SQL is not so pure on this rule, since you can often do procedural things to the data. But after a few decades with SQL, I can say that with each release of the Standards and of actual SQL products, we get closer to this goal.
1. The Information Rule: This simply requires all information in the database to be represented in one and only one way, namely by scalar values in columns within rows of tables. SQL is good here, but columns are found by their names and not by their

Joe Celko's SQL for Smarties. DOI: 10.1016/B978-0-12-382022-8.00009-0

positions in a row in a strict RDBMS model. SQL allows the use of a * as shorthand for a list of column names, and makes default assumptions about the ordering of columns within a row.

2. The Guaranteed Access Rule: This rule is essentially a restatement of the fundamental requirement for Keys. It states that every individual scalar value in the database must be logically addressable by specifying the name of the containing table, the name of the containing column, and a key value of the containing row. SQL follows this rule for tables that have a key, but SQL does not require a table to have a key at all.
3. Systematic Treatment of `NULL` Values: The DBMS is required to support a representation of missing information and inapplicable information that is systematic, distinct from all regular values, and independent of data type. It is also implied that such representations must be manipulated by the DBMS in a systematic way. SQL has a `NULL` that is used for both missing information and inapplicable information, rather than having two separate tokens as Dr. Codd wished in his second version of the Relational Model.
4. Active Online Catalog Based on the Relational Model: The system is required to support an online, in-line, relational catalog that is accessible to authorized users by means of their regular query language. SQL does this.
5. The Comprehensive Data Sublanguage Rule: The system must support at least one relational language that (a) has a linear syntax, (b) can be used both interactively and within application programs, and (c) supports data definition operations (including view definitions), data manipulation operations (update as well as retrieval), security and integrity constraints, and transaction management operations (begin, commit, and rollback).

   SQL is pretty good on this point, since all of the operations Codd defined can be written in the Data Manipulation Language (DML).
6. The `VIEW` Updating Rule: All views that are theoretically updatable must be updatable by the system. SQL is weak here, and has elected to standardize on the safest case. View updatability is now known to be NP-complete and therefore impossible to enforce in general. `INSTEAD OF` triggers in SQL allow solutions for particular schemas.
7. High-Level Insert, Update, and Delete: The system must support set-at-a-time `INSERT`, `UPDATE`, and `DELETE` operators. SQL does this.
8. Physical Data Independence: This is self-explanatory; users are never aware of the physical implementation and deal only with a logical model. Any real `product_name` is going to have some physical dependence, but SQL is better than most programming languages on this point. In particular, indexing and access methods are assigned to a *physical* DBA rather than a *logical* DBA and are kept away from the users.

9. Logical Data Independence: This is self-explanatory. Logical data independence is the ability to modify the conceptual schema without having to also modify the application programs. SQL is quite good about this point if you write good, portable code.
10. Integrity Independence: Integrity constraints must be specified separately from application programs and stored in the catalog. It must be possible to change such constraints as and when appropriate without unnecessarily affecting existing applications. Standard SQL has this.
11. Distribution Independence: Existing applications should continue to operate successfully (a) when a distributed version of the DBMS is first introduced and (b) when existing distributed data is redistributed around the system.
12. The Nonsubversion Rule: If the system provides a low-level (record-at-a-time, bit level) interface, that interface cannot be used to subvert the system (e.g., bypassing a relational security or integrity constraint). SQL is good about this one.

Codd also specified nine structural features, three integrity features, and 18 manipulative features, all of which are required as well. He later extended the list from 12 rules to 333 in the second version of the relational model (*The Relational Model for Database Management: Version 2*, 1990, ISBN 978-0201141924). You can look them up for yourself.

Normal forms are an attempt to make sure that you do not destroy true data or create false data in your database. One of the ways of avoiding errors is to represent a fact only once in the database, since if a fact appears more than once, one of the instances of it is likely to be in error—a man with two wristwatches can never be sure what time it is. This is why we synchronize clocks from an atomic clock, making them into `VIEW`s on one data source.

This process of table design is called normalization. It is not mysterious, but it can get complex. You can buy CASE (Computer Assisted Software Engineering) tools to help you do it, but you should know a bit about the theory before you use such a tool.

## 9.1 Functional and Multivalued Dependencies

A normal form is a way of classifying a table based on the functional dependencies (FDs for short) in it. A functional dependency means that if I know the value of one attribute, I can always determine the value of another. The notation used in relational theory is an arrow between the two attributes, for example A → B, which can be read in English as "A determines B." If I know your employee number, I can determine your name; if I know a part number, I can determine the weight and color of the part; and so forth.

A multivalued dependency (MVD) means that if I know the value of one attribute, I can always determine the values of a set of another attribute. The notation used in relational theory is a double-headed arrow between the two attributes, for instance `A ↠ B`, which can be read in English as "A determines many Bs." If I know a teacher's name, I can determine a list of her students; if I know a part number, I can determine the part numbers of its components; and so forth.

## 9.2 First Normal Form (1NF)

Consider a requirement to maintain data about class schedules at a school. We are required to keep the course_name, class_section, dept_name, time, room_nbr, professor, student, student_major, and student_grade. Suppose that we initially set up a Pascal file with records that look like this:

```
Classes = RECORD
  course_name: ARRAY [1:7] OF CHAR;
 class_section: CHAR;
  time_period: INTEGER;
    room_nbr: INTEGER;
   room_size: INTEGER;
   professor: ARRAY [1:25] OF CHAR;
   dept_name: ARRAY [1:10] OF CHAR;
    students: ARRAY [1:class_size]
          OF RECORD
           student_name ARRAY [1:25] OF CHAR;
           student_major ARRAY [1:10] OF CHAR;
           student_grade CHAR;
           END;
      END;
```

I picked Pascal because it is easy to read and the data type names look a bit like SQL. This table is not in the most basic normal form of relational databases. First Normal Form (1NF) means that the table has no repeating groups. That is, every column is a scalar value, not an array or a list or anything with its own structure. It also means that it has one and only one meaning; it can be hat size, or shoe size, but never both and never either.

In SQL, it is impossible not to be in 1NF unless the vendor has added array or other extensions to the language. The Pascal RECORD could be "flattened out" in SQL and the field names changed to data element names to look like this:

```
CREATE TABLE Classes
(course_name CHAR(7) NOT NULL,
class_section CHAR(1) NOT NULL,
time_period INTEGER NOT NULL,
room_nbr INTEGER NOT NULL,
room_size INTEGER NOT NULL,
professor_name CHAR(25) NOT NULL,
dept_name CHAR(10) NOT NULL,
student_name CHAR (25) NOT NULL,
student_major CHAR(10) NOT NULL,
student_grade CHAR(1) NOT NULL);
```

This table is acceptable to SQL. In fact, we can locate a row in the table with a combination of (course_name, class_section, student_name), so we have a key. But what we are doing is hiding the Students record array, which has not changed its nature by being flattened.

There are problems.

If Professor 'Jones' of the math department dies, we delete all his rows from the Classes table. This also deletes the information that all his students were taking a math class and maybe not all of them wanted to drop out of school just yet. I am deleting more than one fact from the database. This is called a deletion anomaly.

If student 'Wilson' decides to change one of his math classes, formerly taught by Professor 'Jones,' to English, we will show Professor 'Jones' as an instructor in both the math and the English departments. I could not change a simple fact by itself. This creates false information, and is called an update anomaly.

If the school decides to start a new department, which has no students yet, we cannot put in the data about the professor we just hired until we have classroom and student data to fill out a row. I cannot insert a simple fact by itself. This is called an insertion anomaly.

There are more problems in this table, but you see the point. Yes, there are some ways to get around these problems without changing the tables. We could permit NULLs in the table. We could write TRIGGERs to check the table for false data. These are tricks that will only get worse as the data and the relationships become more complex. The solution is to break the table up into other tables, each of which represents one relationship or simple set of facts.

### 9.2.1 Note on Repeated Groups

The definition of 1NF is that the table has no repeating groups and that all columns are scalar values. This means a column cannot have arrays, linked lists, tables within tables, or record structures, like those you find in other programming languages. This was very easy to avoid in Standard SQL, since the language had no support for them. This is no longer true after SQL-99, which introduces several very nonrelational "features" and since several vendors added their own support for arrays, nested tables, and variant data types.

Aside from relational purity, there are good reasons to avoid these features. They are not widely implemented and the vendor-specific extensions will not port. Furthermore, the optimizers cannot easily use them, so they degrade performance.

Old habits are hard to change, so new SQL programmers often try to force their old model of the world into Standard SQL in several ways.

#### *Repeating Columns*

One way you "fake it" in SQL is to use a group of columns where all the members of the group have the same semantic value; that is, they represent the same attribute in the table. Consider the table of an employee and his children:

```
CREATE TABLE Employees
(emp_nbr INTEGER NOT NULL,
emp_name VARCHAR(30) NOT NULL,
...
child1 CHAR(30), birthday1 DATE, sex1 CHAR(1),
child2 CHAR(30), birthday2 DATE, sex2 CHAR(1),
child3 CHAR(30), birthday3 DATE, sex3 CHAR(1),
child4 CHAR(30), birthday4 DATE, sex4 CHAR(1));
```

This looks like the layouts of many existing file system records in COBOL and other 3GL languages. The birthday and sex information for each child is part of a repeated group and therefore violates 1NF. This is faking a four-element array in SQL; the subscript just happens to be part of the column name!

Suppose I have a table with the quantity of a product_name sold in each month of a particular year, and I originally built the table to look like this:

```
CREATE TABLE Abnormal
(product_name CHAR(10) NOT NULL PRIMARY KEY,
 month_01 INTEGER, -- null means no data yet
 month_02 INTEGER,
 ...
 month_12 INTEGER);
```

and I wanted to flatten it out into a more normalized form, like this:

```
CREATE TABLE Normal
(product_name CHAR(10) NOT NULL,
 month_nbr INTEGER NOT NULL,
 product_qty INTEGER NOT NULL,
 PRIMARY KEY (product_name, month_nbr));
```

I can use the statement:

```
INSERT INTO Normal (product_name, month_nbr, product_qty)
SELECT product_name, 1, month_01
 FROM Abnormal
WHERE month_01 IS NOT NULL
UNION ALL
SELECT product_name, 2, month_02
 FROM Abnormal
WHERE month_02 IS NOT NULL
...

UNION ALL
SELECT product_name, 12, month_12
 FROM Abnormal
WHERE bin_12 IS NOT NULL;
```

Although a `UNION ALL` expression is usually slow, this has to be run only once to load the normalized table and then the original table can be dropped.

### *Parsing a List in a String*

Another popular method is to use a string and fill it with a comma-separated list. The result is a lot of string handling procedures to work around this kludge. Consider this example:

```
CREATE TABLE InputStrings
(key_col CHAR(10) NOT NULL PRIMARY KEY,
input_string VARCHAR(255) NOT NULL);

INSERT INTO InputStrings VALUES ('first', '12, 34, 567, 896');
INSERT INTO InputStrings VALUES ('second',
   '312, 534, 997, 896'); ...
```

This will be the table that gets the outputs, in the form of the original key column and one parameter per row.

```
CREATE TABLE Parmlist
(key_col CHAR(5) NOT NULL PRIMARY KEY,
parm INTEGER NOT NULL);
```

It makes life easier if the lists in the input strings start and end with a comma. You will also need a table called Series, which is a set of integers from 1 to (n).

```
SELECT key_col,
   CAST (SUBSTRING (',' || I1.input_string || ',',
      MAX(S1.seq || 1),
            (S2.seq - MAX(S1.seq || 1)))
     AS INTEGER),
   COUNT(S2.seq) AS place
 FROM InputStrings AS I1, Series AS S1, Series AS S2
WHERE SUBSTRING (',' || I1.input_string || ',', S1.seq, 1)
   = ','
  AND SUBSTRING (',' || I1.input_string || ',', S2.seq, 1)
    = ','
  AND S1.seq < S2.seq
  AND S2.seq <= DATALENGTH(I1.input_string) + 1
GROUP BY I1.key_col, I1.input_string, S2.seq;
```

The S1 and S2 copies of Series are used to locate bracketing pairs of commas, and the entire set of substrings located between them is extracts and cast as integers in one nonprocedural step.

The trick is to be sure that the left-hand comma of the bracketing pair is the closest one to the second comma. The place column tells you the relative position of the value in the input string.

A very fast version of this trick is due to Ken Henderson. Instead of using a comma to separate the fields within the list, put each value into a fixed length substring and extract them by using a simple multiplication of the length by the desired array index number. This is a direct imitation of how many compilers handle arrays at the hardware level.

Having said all this, the right way would be to put the list into a single column in a table. This can be done in languages that allow you to pass array elements into SQL parameters, like this:

```
INSERT INTO Parmlist
VALUES (:a[1]), (:a[2]), (:a[3]), ..., (:a[n]);
```

Or if you want to remove NULLs and duplicates,

```
INSERT INTO Parmlist
SELECT DISTINCT x
 FROM VALUES (:a[1]), (:a[2]), (:a[3]), ..., (:a[n]) AS
   List(x)
WHERE x IS NOT NULL;
```

## 9.3 Second Normal Form (2NF)

A table is in Second Normal Form (2NF) if it is in 1NF and has no partial key dependencies. That is, if X and Y are columns and X is a key, then for any Z that is a proper subset of X, it cannot be the case that $Z \rightarrow Y$. Informally, the table is in 1NF and it has a key that determines all nonkey attributes in the table.

In the Pascal example, our users tell us that knowing the student and course_name is sufficient to determine the class_section (since students cannot sign up for more than one class_section of the same course_name) and the student_grade. This is the same as saying that (student_name, course_name) → (class_section, student_grade).

After more analysis, we also discover from our users that (student_name → student_major) — students have only one student_major. Since student is part of the (student_name, course_name) key, we have a partial key dependency! This leads us to the following decomposition:

```
CREATE TABLE Classes
(course_name CHAR(7) NOT NULL,
class_section CHAR(1) NOT NULL,
time_period INTEGER NOT NULL,
room_nbr INTEGER NOT NULL,
room_size INTEGER NOT NULL,
professor_name CHAR(25) NOT NULL,
PRIMARY KEY (course_name, class_section));

CREATE TABLE Enrollment
(student_name CHAR (25) NOT NULL,
course_name CHAR(7) NOT NULL,
class_section CHAR(1) NOT NULL,
student_grade CHAR(1) NOT NULL,
PRIMARY KEY (student_name, course_name));

CREATE TABLE Students
(student_name CHAR (25) NOT NULL PRIMARY KEY,
student_major CHAR(10) NOT NULL);
```

At this point, we are in 2NF. Every attribute depends on the entire key in its table. Now if a student changes majors, it can be done in one place. Furthermore, a student cannot sign up for different sections of the same class, because we have changed the key of Enrollment. Unfortunately, we still have problems.

Notice that while room_size depends on the entire key of Classes, it also depends on room_nbr. If the room_nbr is changed for a course_name and class_section, we may also have to change the room_size, and if the room_nbr is modified (we knock down a wall), we may have to change room_size in several rows in Classes for that room_nbr.

## 9.4 Third Normal Form (3NF)

Another normal form can address these problems. A table is in Third Normal Form (3NF) if it is in 2NF and for all X → Y, where X and Y are columns of a table, X is a key or Y is part of a candidate key. (A candidate key is a unique set of columns that identify each row in a table; you cannot remove a column from the candidate key without destroying its uniqueness.) This implies that the table is in 2NF, since a partial key dependency is a type of transitive dependency. Informally, all the nonkey columns are determined by the key, the whole key, and nothing but the key.

The usual way that 3NF is explained is that there are no transitive dependencies, but this is not quite right. A transitive dependency is a situation where we have a table with columns (A, B, C) and (A → B) and (B → C), so we know that (A → C). In our case, the situation is that (course_name, class_section) → room_nbr and room_nbr → room_size. This is not a simple transitive dependency, since only part of a key is involved, but the principle still holds. To get our example into 3NF and fix the problem with the room_size column, we make the following decomposition:

```
CREATE TABLE Rooms
(room_nbr INTEGER NOT NULL PRIMARY KEY,
room_size INTEGER NOT NULL);

CREATE TABLE Classes
(course_name CHAR(7) NOT NULL,
class_section CHAR(1) NOT NULL,
PRIMARY KEY (course_name, class_section),
time_period INTEGER NOT NULL,
room_nbr INTEGER NOT NULL);

CREATE TABLE Enrollment
(student_name CHAR (25) NOT NULL,
course_name CHAR(7) NOT NULL,
PRIMARY KEY (student_name, course_name),
class_section CHAR(1) NOT NULL,
student_grade CHAR(1) NOT NULL);

CREATE TABLE Students
(student_name CHAR (25) NOT NULL PRIMARY KEY,
student_major CHAR(10) NOT NULL);
```

A common misunderstanding about relational theory is that 3NF tables have no transitive dependencies. As indicated earlier, if X→Y, X does not have to be a key if Y is part of a candidate key. We still have a transitive dependency in the example—(room_nbr, time_period) → (course_name, class_section)—but since the right side of the dependency is a key, it is technically in 3NF. The unreasonable behavior that this table structure still has is that several course_names can be assigned to the same room_nbr at the same time.

Another form of transitive dependency is a computed column. For example:

```
CREATE TABLE Stuff
(width INTEGER NOT NULL,
```

```
length INTEGER NOT NULL,
height INTEGER NOT NULL,
volume INTEGER NOT NULL
    CHECK (width * length * height = volume),
PRIMARY KEY (width, length, height));
```

The volume column is determined by the other three columns, so any change to one of the three columns will require a change to the volume column.

As an aside, a better way to do this is with a computed column:

```
CREATE TABLE Stuff
(width INTEGER NOT NULL,
length INTEGER NOT NULL,
height INTEGER NOT NULL,
(width * length * height) AS volume)
PRIMARY KEY (width, length, height));
```

The `CHECK()` constraint will throw an error, while the computed column will keep running.

## 9.5 Elementary Key Normal Form (EKNF)

Elementary Key Normal Form (EKNF) is a subtle enhancement on 3NF. By definition, EKNF tables are also in 3NF. This happens when there is more than one unique composite key and they overlap. Such cases can cause redundant information in the overlapping column(s). For example, in the following table, let's assume that a course code number is also a unique identifier for a given subject:

```
CREATE TABLE Enrollment
(student_idINTEGER NOT NULL,
course_code CHAR(6) NOT NULL,
course_name VARCHAR(15) NOT NULL,
PRIMARY KEY (student_id, course_name)
-- , UNIQUE (student_id, course_code) alternative key
);
```

Enrollment

| student_id | course_code | course_name |
|---|---|---|
| 1 | 'CS-100' | 'ER Diagrams' |
| 1 | 'CS-114' | 'Database Design' |
| 2 | 'CS-114' | 'Database Design' |

This table, although it is in 3NF, violates EKNF. The primary key of the table is the combination of (student_id, course_name). However, we can also see an alternate key (student_id, course_code) as well. This schema could result in update and deletion anomalies because values of both course_name and course_code tend to be repeated for a given subject.

The following schema is a decomposition of the previous table in order to satisfy EKNF:

```
CREATE TABLE Subjects
(course_code CHAR(6) NOT NULL PRIMARY KEY,
course_name VARCHAR(15) NOT NULL);

CREATE TABLE Enrollment
(student_id INTEGER NOT NULL,
course_code CHAR(6) NOT NULL,
PRIMARY KEY (student_id, course_code));
```

For reasons that will become obvious in the following class_section, ensuring a table is in EKNF is usually skipped, as most designers will move directly on to Boyce-Codd Normal Form after ensuring that a schema is in 3NF. Thus, EKNF is included here only for reasons of historical accuracy and completeness.

## 9.6 Boyce-Codd Normal Form (BCNF)

A table is in BCNF when for all nontrivial FDs (X → A), X is a superkey for the whole schema. A superkey is a unique set of columns that identify each row in a table, but you can remove some columns from it and it will still be a key. Informally, a superkey is carrying extra weight.

BCNF is the normal form that actually removes all transitive dependencies. A table is in BCNF if for all (X→Y), X is a key—period. We can go to this normal form just by adding another key with UNIQUE (room_nbr, time_period) constraint clause to the table Classes.

There are some other interesting and useful "higher" normal forms, but they are outside of the scope of this discussion. In our example, we have removed all the important anomalies with BCNF.

Third Normal Form was concerned with the relationship between key and nonkey columns. However, a column can often play both roles. Consider a table for computing each salesman's bonus gifts that has for each salesman his base salary, the number of sales points he has won in a contest, and the bonus gift awarded for that combination of salary range and points. For example, we might give a fountain pen to a beginning salesman with a base pay rate somewhere between $15,000 and $20,000 and 100 sales points, but give a car to a master salesman, whose salary is between $30,000 and $60,000 and who has 200 points. The functional dependencies are, therefore,

```
(pay_step, points) → gift
gift → points
```

Let's start with a table that has all the data in it and normalize it.

Gifts

| salary_amt | points | gift |
|---|---|---|
| 15000 | 100 | 'Pencil' |
| 17000 | 100 | 'Pen' |
| 30000 | 200 | 'Car' |
| 31000 | 200 | 'Car' |
| 32000 | 200 | 'Car' |

This schema is in 3NF, but it has problems. You cannot insert a new gift into our offerings and points unless we have a salary to go with it. If you remove any sales points, you lose information about the gifts and salaries (e.g., only people in the $30,000 range can win a car). And, finally, a change in the gifts for a particular point score would have to affect all the rows within the same pay step. This table needs to be broken apart into two tables:

PayGifts

| Salary_amt | gift |
|---|---|
| 15000 | 'Pencil' |
| 17000 | 'Pen' |
| 30000 | 'Car' |
| 31000 | 'Car' |
| 32000 | 'Car' |

GiftsPoints

| gift | points |
|---|---|
| 'Pencil' | 100 |
| 'Pen' | 100 |
| 'Car' | 200 |

## 9.7 Fourth Normal Form (4NF)

Fourth Normal Form (4NF) makes use of multivalued dependencies. The problem it solves is that the table has too many of them. For example, consider a table of departments, their projects, and the parts they stock. The MVDs in the table would be:

```
dept_name →→ jobs
dept_name →→ parts
```

Assume that dept_name 'd1' works on jobs 'j1', and 'j2' with parts 'p1' and 'p2'; that dept_name 'd2' works on jobs 'j3', 'j4', and 'j5' with parts 'p2' and 'p4'; and that dept_name 'd3' works on job 'j2' only with parts 'p5' and 'p6'. The table would look like this:

| dept | job | part |
|---|---|---|
| 'd1' | 'j1' | 'p1' |
| 'd1' | 'j1' | 'p2' |
| 'd1' | 'j2' | 'p1' |
| 'd1' | 'j2' | 'p2' |
| 'd2' | 'j3' | 'p2' |
| 'd2' | 'j3' | 'p4' |
| 'd2' | 'j4' | 'p2' |
| 'd2' | 'j4' | 'p4' |
| 'd2' | 'j5' | 'p2' |
| 'd2' | 'j5' | 'p4' |
| 'd3' | 'j2' | 'p5' |
| 'd3' | 'j2' | 'p6' |

If you want to add a part to a `dept_name`, you must create more than one new row.

Likewise, to remove a part or a job from a row can destroy information. Updating a part or job name will also require multiple rows to be changed.

The solution is to split this table into two tables, one with `(dept_name, jobs)` in it and one with `(dept_name, parts)` in it. The definition of 4NF is that we have no more than one MVD in a table. If a table is in 4NF, it is also in BCNF.

## 9.8 Fifth Normal Form (5NF)

Fifth Normal Form (5NF), also called the Join-Projection Normal Form or the Projection-Join Normal Form, is based on the idea of a lossless JOIN or the lack of a join-projection anomaly. This problem occurs when you have an n-way relationship, where (n > 2). A quick check for 5NF is to see if the table is in 3NF and all the candidate keys are single columns.

As an example of the problems solved by 5NF, consider a table of mortgages that records the `buyer_name`, the `seller_name`, and the `lender_name`:

Mortgages

| buyer_name | seller_name | lender_name |
|---|---|---|
| 'Smith' | 'Jones' | 'National Bank' |
| 'Smith' | 'Wilson' | 'Home Bank' |
| 'Nelson' | 'Jones' | 'Home Bank' |

This table is a three-way relationship, but because older CASE tools allow only binary relationships it might have to be expressed in an E-R diagram as three binary relationships, which would generate `CREATE TABLE` statements leading to these tables:

BuyersLenders

| buyer_name | lender_name |
|---|---|
| 'Smith' | 'National Bank' |
| 'Smith' | 'Home Bank' |
| 'Nelson' | 'Home Bank' |

SellersLenders

| seller_name | lender_name |
|---|---|
| 'Jones' | 'National Bank' |
| 'Wilson' | 'Home Bank' |
| 'Jones' | 'Home Bank' |

BuyersSellers

| buyer_name | seller_name |
|---|---|
| 'Smith' | 'Jones' |
| 'Smith' | 'Wilson' |
| 'Nelson' | 'Jones' |

The trouble is that when you try to assemble the original information by joining pairs of these three tables together, thus:

```
SELECT BS.buyer_name, SL.seller_name, BL.lender_name
 FROM BuyersLenders AS BL,
    SellersLenders AS SL,
    BuyersSellers AS BS
WHERE BL.buyer_name = BS.buyer_name
  AND BL.lender_name = SL.lender_name
  AND SL.seller_name = BS.seller_name;
```

you will recreate all the valid rows in the original table, such as ('Smith', 'Jones', 'National Bank'), but there will also be false rows, such as ('Smith', 'Jones', 'Home Bank'), which were not part of the original table. This is called a join-projection anomaly.

There are also strong JPNF and overstrong JPNF, which make use of JOIN dependencies (JD for short). Unfortunately, there is no systematic way to find a JPNF or 4NF schema, because the problem is known to be NP complete. This is a mathematical term that means as the number of elements in a problem increase, the effort to solve it increases so fast and requires so many resources that you cannot find a general answer.

As an aside, Third Normal Form is very popular with CASE tools and most of them can generate a schema where all the tables are in 3NF. They obtain the FDs from an E-R (entity-relationship) diagram or from a statistical analysis of the existing data, then put them together into tables and check for normal forms.

The bad news is that it is often possible to derive more than one 3NF schema from a set of FDs. Most of CASE tools that produce an E-R diagram will find only one of them, and go no further. However, if you use an ORM (Object Role Model) tool properly, the schema will be in 5NF. I suggest strongly that you read any of the books by Terry Halpin on this technique.

## 9.9 Domain-Key Normal Form (DKNF)

Ronald Fagin defined Domain/Key Normal Form (DKNF) in 1981 as a schema having all the domain constraints and functional dependencies enforced. There is not yet a general algorithm that will always generate the DKNF solution given a set of constraints. We can, however, determine DKNF in many special cases and it is a good guide to writing DDL in the real world.

Let's back up a bit and look at the mathematical model under normalization. A functional dependency has axioms that can be used in normalization problems. These six axioms, known as Armstrong's axioms, are as follows.

*Reflexive*: X → X
*Augmentation*: if X → Y then XZ → Y
*Union*: if (X → Y and X → Z) then X → YZ
*Decomposition*: if X → Y and Z a subset of Y, then X → Z
*Transitivity*: if (X → Y and Y → Z) then X → Z
*Pseudo-transitivity*: if (X → Y and YZ → W) then XZ → W

They make good sense if you just look at them, which is something we like in a set of axioms. In the real world, the FDs are the business rules we are trying to model.

In the normalization algorithm for 3NF (developed by P. A. Berstein, 1976) we use the axioms to get rid of redundant FDs. For example, if we are given:

```
A → B
A → C
B → C
DB → E
DAF → E
```

A → C is redundant because it can be derived from A → B and B → C with transitivity. Also DAF → E is redundant because it can be derived from DB → E and A → B with transitivity (which gives us DA → E) and augmentation (which then allows DAF → E). What we would like to find is the smallest set of FDs from which we can generate all the given rules. This is called a nonredundant cover. For the preceding FDs, one cover would be:

```
A → B
B → C
DB → E
```

Once we do this Berstein shows that we can just create a table for each of the FDs where A, B, and DB are the respective keys. We have taken it easy so far but now it's time for a challenge.

As an example of a schema with multiple 3NF tables, here is a problem that was used in a demonstration by DBStar Corporation (now Evoke Software). The company used it as an example in a demonstration that comes with their CASE tool.

We are given an imaginary and simplified airline that has a database for scheduling flights and pilots. Most of the relationships are obvious things. Flights have only one departure time and one destination. They can get a different pilot and can be assigned to a different gate each day of the week. The functional dependencies for the database are:

```
 1. flight → destination
 2. flight → hour
 3. (day, flight) → gate
 4. (day, flight) → pilot
 5. (day, hour, pilot) → gate
 6. (day, hour, pilot) → flight
 7. (day, hour, pilot) → destination
 8. (day, hour, gate) → pilot
 9. (day, hour, gate) → flight
10. (day, hour, gate) → destination
```

A purist will look at this collection of FDs and can be bothered by the redundancies in this list. But in the real world, when you interview people, they do not speak to you in a minimal set of requirements. People repeat facts and see only the data in terms of their situation. In fact, they very often leave out relationships that they considered to be too obvious to mention.

Your problem is to find 3NF or stronger database schemas in these FDs. You have to be careful! You have to have all the columns, obviously, but your answer could be in 3NF and still ignore some of the FDs. For example, this will not work:

```
CREATE TABLE PlannedSchedule
(flight, destination, hour, PRIMARY KEY (flight));

CREATE TABLE ActualSchedule
(day, flight, gate, pilot, PRIMARY KEY (day, flight));
```

If we apply the Union axiom to some of the FDs, we get:

```
(day, hour, gate) → (destination, flight, pilot)
(day, hour, pilot) → (destination, flight, gate)
```

This says that the user has required that if we are given a day, an hour, and a gate we should be able to determine a unique flight for that day, hour, and gate. We should also be able to determine a unique flight given a day, hour, and pilot.

Given the PlannedSchedule and ActualSchedule tables, you cannot produce views where either of the two constraints we just mentioned is enforced. If the query "What flight does pilot X have on day Y and hour Z?" gives you more than one answer, it violates the FDs and common sense. Here is an example of a schema that is allowable in this proposed schema, which is undesirable given our constraints:

PlannedSchedule

| flight | hour | destination |
|---|---|---|
| 118 | 17:00 | Dallas |
| 123 | 13:00 | Omaha |
| 155 | 17:00 | Los Angeles |
| 171 | 13:00 | New York |
| 666 | 13:00 | Atlanta |

ActualSchedule

| day | flight | pilot | gate |
|---|---|---|---|
| Wed | 118 | Tom | 12A |
| Wed | 155 | Tom | 13B |
| Wed | 171 | Tom | 12A |
| Thu | 123 | John | 12A |
| Thu | 155 | John | 12A |
| Thu | 171 | John | 13B |

The constraints mean that we should be able to find a unique answer to each the following questions and not lose any information when inserting and deleting data.

1. Which flight is leaving from gate 12A on Thursdays at 13:00 hrs? This looks fine until you realize that you don't know about flight 666, which was not required to have anything about its day or pilot in the ActualSchedule table. And likewise, I can add a flight to the ActualSchedule table that has no information in the PlannedSchedule table.
2. Which pilot is assigned to the flight that leaves gate 12A on Thursdays at 13:00 hrs? This has the same problem as before.
3. What is the destination of the flight in queries 1 and 2? This has the same problem as before.
4. What gate is John leaving from on Thursdays at 13:00 hrs?
5. Where is Tom flying to on Wednesdays at 17:00 hrs?
6. What flight is assigned to Tom on Wednesdays at 17:00 hrs?

It might help if we gave an example of how one of the FDs in the problem can be derived using the axioms of FD calculus, just like you would do a geometry proof:

```
Given:
1) (day, hour, gate) → pilot
2) (day, hour, pilot) → flight
```

```
prove that:
(day, hour, gate) → flight.

3) (day, hour) → (day, hour);      Reflexive
4) (day, hour, gate) → (day, hour); Augmentation on 3
5) (day, hour, gate) → (day, hour, pilot); Union 1 & 4
6) (day, hour, gate) → flight; Transitive 2 and 5
Q.E.D
```

The answer is to start by attempting to derive each of the functional dependencies from the rest of the set. What we get are several short proofs, each requiring different "given" functional dependencies in order to get to the derived FD.

Here is a list of each of the proofs used to derive the 10 fragmented FDs in the problem. With each derivation we include every derivation step and the legal FD calculus operation that allows me to make that step. An additional operation that we include here that was not included in the axioms we listed earlier is left reduction. Left reduction says that if XX → Y then X → Y. The reason it was not included is that this is actually a theorem and not one of the basic axioms (side problem: can you derive left reduction?).

```
Prove: (day, hour, pilot) → gate
a) day → day;           Reflexive
b) (day, hour, pilot) → day;    Augmentation (a)
c) (day, hour, pilot) → (day, flight); Union (6, b)
d) (day, hour, pilot) → gate;    Transitive (c, 3)
Q.E.D.

Prove: (day, hour, gate) → pilot
a) day → day;           Reflexive
b) day, hour, gate → day;    Augmentation (a)
c) day, hour, gate → (day, flight); Union (9, b)
d) day, hour, gate → pilot;    Transitive (c, 4)
Q.E.D.

Prove: (day, flight) → gate
a) (day, flight, pilot) → gate; Pseudotransitivity (2, 5)
b) (day, flight, day, flight) → gate; Pseudotransitivity (a, 4)
c) (day, flight) → gate;    Left reduction (b)
Q.E.D.

Prove: (day, flight) → pilot
a) (day, flight, gate) → pilot; Pseudotransitivity (2, 8)
b) (day, flight, day, flight) → pilot; Pseudotransitivity
   (a, 3)
c) (day, flight) → pilot;    Left reduction (b)
Q.E.D.

Prove: (day, hour, gate) → flight
a) (day, hour) → (day, hour);    Reflexivity
```

```
b) (day, hour, gate) → (day, hour);     Augmentation (a)
c) (day, hour, gate) → (day, hour, pilot);  Union (b, 8)
d) (day, hour, gate) → flight;      Transitivity (c, 6)
Q.E.D.

Prove: (day, hour, pilot) → flight
a) (day, hour) → (day, hour);  Reflexivity
b) (day, hour, pilot) → (day, hour); Augmentation (a)
c) (day, hour, pilot) → day, hour, gate; Union (b, 5)
d) (day, hour, pilot) → flight;     Transitivity (c, 9)
Q.E.D.

Prove: (day, hour, gate) → destination
a) (day, hour, gate) → destination; Transitivity (9, 1)
Q.E.D.

Prove: (day, hour, pilot) → destination
a) (day, hour, pilot) → destination;    Transitivity (6, 1)
Q.E.D.
```

Now that we've shown you how to derive eight of the 10 FDs from other FDs, you can try mixing and matching the FDs into sets so that each set meets the following criteria:

1. Each attribute must be represented on either the left or right side of at least one FD in the set.
2. If a given FD is included in the set then all the FDs needed to derive it cannot also be included.
3. If a given FD is excluded from the set then the FDs used to derive it must be included.

This produces a set of "nonredundant covers," which can be found with trial, error, and common sense. For example, if we excluded (day, hour, gate) → flight we must then include (day, hour, gate) → pilot and vice versa+ because each are used in the other's derivation. If you want to be sure your search was exhaustive, however, you may want to apply a more mechanical method, which is what the CASE tools do for you.

The algorithm for accomplishing this task is basically to generate all the combinations of sets of the FDs. (flight → destination) and (flight → hour) are excluded in the combination generation because they cannot be derived. This gives us (2^8) or 256 combinations of FDs. Each combination is then tested against the criteria.

Fortunately, a simple spreadsheet does all the tedious work. In this problem the criteria #1 eliminates only 15 sets. Then a criterion #2 eliminates 152 sets and a criterion #3 drops another 67. This leaves us with 22 possible covers, five of which are the answers we are looking for (we will explain the other 17 later).

These five nonredundant covers are:

```
Set I:
flight → destination
flight → hour
(day, hour, gate) → flight
(day, hour, gate) → pilot
(day, hour, pilot) → gate

Set II:
flight → destination
flight → hour
(day, hour, gate) → pilot
(day, hour, pilot) → flight
(day, hour, pilot) → gate

Set III:
flight → destination
flight → hour
(day, flight) → gate
(day, flight) → pilot
(day, hour, gate) → flight

Set IV:
flight → destination
flight → hour
(day, flight) → gate
(day, hour, gate) → pilot
(day, hour, pilot) → flight

Set V:
flight → destination
flight → hour
(day, flight) → pilot
(day, hour, gate) → flight
(day, hour, pilot) → gate
(day, hour, pilot) → flight
```

At this point we perform unions on FDs with the same left-hand side and make tables for each grouping with the left-hand side as a key. We can also eliminate symmetrical FDs (defined as $X \rightarrow Y$ and $Y \rightarrow X$, and written with a two headed arrow, $X \leftrightarrow Y$) by collapsing them into the same table.

These possible schemas are in at least 3NF. They are given in shorthand SQL DDL (Data Declaration Language) without data type declarations.

```
Solution 1:
CREATE TABLE R1 (flight, destination, hour,
PRIMARY KEY (flight));
CREATE TABLE R2 (day, hour, gate, flight, pilot,
```

```
  PRIMARY KEY (day, hour, gate),
  UNIQUE (day, hour, pilot),
  UNIQUE (day, flight),
  UNIQUE (flight, hour));

Solution 2:
CREATE TABLE R1 (flight, destination, hour, PRIMARY KEY
(flight));
CREATE TABLE R2 (day, flight, gate, pilot,
 PRIMARY KEY (day, flight));
CREATE TABLE R3 (day, hour, gate, flight,
 PRIMARY KEY (day, hour, gate),
 UNIQUE (day, flight),
 UNIQUE (flights, hour));
CREATE TABLE R4 (day, hour, pilot, flight,
 PRIMARY KEY (day, hour, pilot));

Solution 3:
CREATE TABLE R1 (flight, destination, hour, flight
 PRIMARY KEY (flight));
CREATE TABLE R2 (day, flight, gate, PRIMARY KEY (day,
   flight));
CREATE TABLE R3 (day, hour, gate, pilot,
 PRIMARY KEY (day, hour, gate),
 UNIQUE (day, hour, pilot),
 UNIQUE (day, hour, gate));
CREATE TABLE R4 (day, hour, pilot, flight
 PRIMARY KEY (day, hour, pilot),
 UNIQUE(day, flight),
 UNIQUE (flight, hour));

Solution 4:
CREATE TABLE R1 (flight, destination, hour, PRIMARY KEY
   (flight));
CREATE TABLE R2 (day, flight, pilot, PRIMARY KEY (day,
   flight));
CREATE TABLE R3 (day, hour, gate, flight,
 PRIMARY KEY (day, hour, gate),
 UNIQUE (flight, hour));
CREATE TABLE R4 (day, hour, pilot, gate,
 PRIMARY KEY (day, hour, pilot));
```

Once you look at these solutions, they are a mess, but they are a 3NF mess! Is there a better answer? Here is one in BCNF and only two tables, proposed by Chris Date (*Relational Database Writings*, 1991–1994, ISBN 0-201-82459-0, p. 224).

```
CREATE TABLE DailySchedules (flight, destination, hour
   PRIMARY KEY (flight));
CREATE TABLE PilotSchedules (day, flight, gate, pilot,
   PRIMARY KEY (day, flight));
```

This is a workable schema. But we could expand the constraints to give us better performance and more precise error messages, since schedules are not likely to change:

```
CREATE TABLE DailySchedules
(flight, hour, destination,
UNIQUE (flight, hour, destination),
UNIQUE (flight, hour),
UNIQUE (flight));

CREATE TABLE PilotSchedules
(day, flight, day, hour, gate, pilot,
UNIQUE (day, flight, gate),
UNIQUE (day, flight, pilot),
UNIQUE (day, flight),
FOREIGN KEY (flight, hour) REFERENCES R1(flight, hour));
```

## 9.10 Practical Hints for Normalization

CASE tools implement formal methods for doing normalization. In particular, E-R (Entity-Relationship) diagrams are very useful for this. However, a few informal hints can help speed up the process and give you a good start.

Broadly speaking, tables represent either entities, relationships or they are auxiliary tables. This is why E-R diagrams work so well as a design tool. The auxiliary tables do not show up on the diagrams, since they are functions, translations, and look-ups that support a declarative computational model.

The tables that represent entities should have a simple, immediate name suggested by their contents—a table named Students has student data in it, not student data and their bowling scores. It is also a good idea to use plural or collective nouns as the names of such tables to remind you that a table is a *set* of entities; the rows are the single instances of them.

Tables that represent one, many-to-one, or many relationships should be named by their contents and should be as minimal as possible. For example, Students are related to Classes by a third (relationship) table for their attendance. These tables might represent a pure relationship or they might contain attributes that exist within the relationship, such as a `student_grade` for the class attended. Since the only way to get a `student_grade` is to attend the class, the relationship is going to have a compound key made up of references to the entity keys. We will probably name it `ReportCards`, `Grades`, or something similar. Avoid naming entities based on `M:M` relationships by combining the two table names; for example, `Students_Courses` is an easy but really bad name for the Enrollment entity.

Avoid NULLs whenever possible. If a table has too many NULL-able columns, it is probably not normalized properly. Try to use a NULL only for a value that is missing now, but will be resolved later. Even better, put missing values into the encoding schemes for that column. I have a whole book on this topic, *SQL Programming Style* (2005, ISBN 978-0120887972), and mention it in other books.

As a gross generalization, normalized databases will tend to have a lot of tables with a small number of columns per table. Don't panic when you see that happen. People who first worked with file systems (particularly on computers that used magnetic tape) tend to design one monster file for an application and do all the work against its records. This made sense in the old days, since there was no reasonable way to JOIN a number of small files together without having the computer operator mount and dismount lots of different magnetic tapes. The habit of designing this way carried over to disk systems, since the procedural programming languages were still the same for the databases as they had been for the sequential file systems.

The same nonkey attribute in more than one table is probably a normalization problem. This is not a certainty, just a guideline. The key that determines that attribute should be in only one table, and therefore its attributes should be with it. The key attributes will be referenced by related tables.

As a practical matter, you are apt to see the same attribute under different names and need to make the names uniform in the entire database. The columns date_of_birth, birthdate, birthday, and dob are very likely the same attribute of an employee. You now have the ISO 11179 for naming guidelines, as discussed in *SQL Programming Style.*

# 9.11 Key Types

The keys, logical and physical, for a table can be classified by their behavior and their source. Table 9.1 is a quick table of my classification system.

Now let's define terms in detail.

## 9.11.1 Natural Keys

A natural key is a subset of attributes that occur in a table and act as a unique identifier. The user sees them. You can go to the external reality and verify them. An example is UPC codes on consumer goods (read the package bar code), coordinates (get a GPS).

**Table 9.1 Classification System**

| | Natural key | Artificial key | Exposed physical locator | Surrogate key |
|---|---|---|---|---|
| Constructed from real attributes | Y | N | N | Y |
| Verifiable in reality | Y | N | N | N |
| Verifiable in itself | Y | Y | N | N |
| Visible to the user | Y | Y | Y | N |

Newbies worry about a natural compound key becoming very long. My answer is, so what? This is the twenty-first century and we have much better computers than we did in the 1950s when key size was a real physical issue. To replace a natural two- or three-integer compound key with a huge GUID that no human being or other system can possibly understand because they think it will be faster only cripples the system and makes it more error prone. I know how to verify the (longitude, latitude) pair of a location; how do you verify the GUID assigned to it?

A long key is not always a bad thing for performance. For example, if I use (city, state) as my key, I get a free index on just (city) in many systems. I can also add extra columns to the key to make it a superkey when such a superkey gives me a covering index (i.e., an index that contains all the columns required for a query, so that the base table does not have to be accessed at all).

## 9.11.2 Artificial Keys

An artificial key is an extra attribute added to the table that is seen by the user. It does not exist in the external reality, but can be verified for syntax or check digits inside itself. An example is the open codes in the UPC/EAN scheme that a user can assign to his or her own stuff. The check digits still work, but you have to verify them inside your own enterprise.

Experienced database designers tend toward keys they find in industry standard codes, such as UPC/EAN, VIN, GTIN, ISBN, and so on. They know that they need to verify the data against the reality they are modeling. A trusted external source is a good thing to have. I know why this VIN is associated with this car, but why is an auto-number value of 42 associated with this car? Try to verify the relationship in the reality you are modeling. It makes as much sense as locating a car by its parking space number.

### 9.11.3 Exposed Physical Locators

An exposed physical locator is not based on attributes in the data model and is exposed to the user. There is no way to predict it or verify it. The system obtains a value through some physical process totally unrelated to the logical data model. The user cannot change them without destroying the relationships among the data elements.

Examples would be physical row locations encoded as a number, string, or proprietary data type. If hashing tables were accessible in an SQL product, then they would qualify, but they are usually hidden from the user.

Many programmers object to putting auto-numbering features into this category. To convert the number into a physical location requires a search rather than a hashing table look-up or positioning a read/writer head on a disk drive, but the concept is the same. The hardware gives you a way to go to a *physical location* that has nothing to do with the *logical* data model, and that cannot be changed in the physical database, or verified externally.

Most of the time, exposed physical locators are used for faking a sequential file's positional record number, so I can reference the physical storage location—a 1960s ISAM file in SQL. You lose all the advantages of an abstract data model, SQL set oriented programming; carry extra data; and destroy the portability of code.

The early SQLs were based on preexisting file systems. The data was kept in physically contiguous disk pages, in physically contiguous rows, made up of physically contiguous columns—in short, just like a deck of punch cards or a magnetic tape. Most programmers still carry that mental model, which is why I keep ranting about file versus table, row versus record, and column versus field.

But physically contiguous storage is only one way of building a relational database and it is not the best one. The basic idea of a relational database is that user is not supposed to know how or where things are stored at all, much less write code that depends on the particular physical representation in a particular release of a particular product on particular hardware at a particular time. This is discussed in the section on `IDENTITY` columns.

Finally, an appeal to authority, with a quote from Dr. Codd: "Database users may cause the system to generate or delete a surrogate, but they have no control over its value, nor is its value ever displayed to them."

This means that a surrogate ought to act like an index; created by the user, managed by the system, and NEVER seen by a user. That means never used in code, DRI, or anything else that a user writes.

Codd also wrote the following:

> *There are three difficulties in employing user-controlled keys as permanent surrogates for entities.*

1. *The actual values of user-controlled keys are determined by users and must therefore be subject to change by them (e.g., if two companies merge, the two employee databases might be combined with the result that some or all of the serial numbers might be changed).*
2. *Two relations may have user-controlled keys defined on distinct domains (e.g., one uses social security numbers, while the other uses employee serial numbers) and yet the entities denoted are the same.*
3. *It may be necessary to carry information about an entity either before it has been assigned a user-controlled key value or after it has ceased to have one (e.g., an applicant for a job and a retiree).*

*These difficulties have the important consequence that an equi-join on common key values may not yield the same result as a join on common entities. A solution—proposed in part [4] and more fully in [14]—is to introduce entity domains which contain system-assigned surrogates. Database users may cause the system to generate or delete a surrogate, but they have no control over its value, nor is its value ever displayed to them.*

*Codd, E., "Extending the Database Relational Model to Capture More Meaning,"* ACM Transactions on Database Systems, *4(4), pp. 397–434, 1979.*

## 9.12 Practical Hints for Denormalization

The subject of denormalization is a great way to get into religious wars. At one extreme, you will find relational purists who think that the idea of not carrying a database design to at least 5NF is a crime against nature. At the other extreme, you will find people who simply add and move columns all over the database with ALTER statements, never keeping the schema stable.

The reason given for denormalization is performance. A fully normalized database requires a lot of JOINs to construct common VIEWs of data from its components. JOINs used to be very costly in terms of time and computer resources, so "preconstructing" the JOIN in a denormalized table can save quite a bit. Today, we have better hardware and software. The VIEWs can be materialized and indexed if they are used frequently by the sessions. Today, only data warehouses should be denormalized, and never a production OLTP system. The extra procedural code needed to maintain the data integrity of a denormalized schema is just not worth it.

Consider this actual problem, which appeared on CompuServe's ORACLE forum some years ago. A pharmaceutical company has an inventory table and a price changes table that look like this. The drugs are identified by their National Drug Code (NDC) from the US Food & Drug Administration.

```
CREATE TABLE Drugs
(ndc CHAR(11) NOT NULL PRIMARY KEY,
drug_name VARCHAR(30) NOT NULL,
drug_qty INTEGER NOT NULL
     CONSTRAINT positive_quantity
     CHECK(drug_qty >= 0),
...);

CREATE TABLE Prices
(ndc CHAR(11) NOT NULL,
start_date DATE NOT NULL,
end_date DATE NOT NULL
     CONSTRAINT started_before_endded
     CHECK(start_date <= end_date),
drug_price DECIMAL(8,2) NOT NULL,
PRIMARY KEY (drug_nbr, start_date));
```

Every order has to use the order date to find what the selling price was when the order was placed. The current price will have a value of "eternity" (a dummy date set so high that it will not be reached like '9999-12-31' or a NULL). The (end_date + INTERVAL '1' DAY) of one price will be equal to the start_date of the next price for the same drug.

While this is normalized, performance was bad. Every report, invoice, or query will have a JOIN between Drugs and Prices. The trick might be to add more columns to the Drugs, like this:

```
CREATE TABLE Drugs
(ndc CHAR(11) PRIMARY KEY,
drug_name VARCHAR(30) NOT NULL,
drug_qty INTEGER NOT NULL
     CONSTRAINT positive_quantity
     CHECK(drug_qty >= 0),
current_start_date DATE NOT NULL,
current_end_date DATE NOT NULL,
CONSTRAINT current_start_before_ended
 CHECK(current_start_date <= current_end_date),
current_drug_price DECIMAL(8,2) NOT NULL,
prior_start_date DATE NOT NULL,
prior_end_date DATE NOT NULL,
CONSTRAINT prior_start_before_ended
 CHECK(prior_start_date <= prior_end_date),
    AND (current_start_date = prior_end_date + INTERVAL
       '1' DAY
prior_drug_price DECIMAL(8,2) NOT NULL,
...);
```

This covered over 95% of the orders in the actual company because very few orders have more than two price changes before they are taken out of stock. The odd exception was trapped by a procedural routine.

The other method is to add `CHECK()` constraints that will enforce the rules that were destroyed by denormalization. We will discuss this later, but the overhead for inserting, updating, and deleting to the table are huge. In fact, in many cases denormalized tables cannot be changed until a complete set of columns is built outside the table. Furthermore, although one set of queries is improved, all others are damaged.

Today, however, only data warehouses should be denormalized. `JOIN`s are far cheaper than they were and the overhead of handling exceptions with procedural code is far greater than any extra database overhead.

### 9.12.1 Row Sorting

On May 27, 2001, Fred Block posted a problem on the SQL Server Newsgroup. I will change the problem slightly, but the idea was that he had a table with five character string columns that had to be sorted alphabetically within each row. This "flattened table" is a very common denormalization, which might involve months of the year as columns, or other things that are acting as repeating groups in violation of 1NF.

Let's declare the table to look like this and dive into the problem.

```
CREATE TABLE Foobar
(key_col INTEGER NOT NULL PRIMARY KEY,
c1 VARCHAR(20) NOT NULL,
c2 VARCHAR(20) NOT NULL,
c3 VARCHAR(20) NOT NULL,
c4 VARCHAR(20) NOT NULL,
c5 VARCHAR(20) NOT NULL);
```

This means that we want this condition to hold:

```
CHECK ((c1 <= c2) AND (c2 <= c3)
   AND (c3 <= c4) AND (c4 <= c5))
```

Obviously, if he had added this constraint to the table in the first place, we would be fine. Of course, that would have pushed the problem to the front end and I would not have a topic for this section.

What was interesting was how everyone who read this Newsgroup posting immediately envisioned a stored procedure that would take the five values, sort them, and return them to their original row in the table. The only way to make this approach work for the whole table was to write an update cursor and loop through all the rows of the table. Itzik Ben-Gan posted a simple procedure that loaded the values into a temporary table, then pulled them out in sorted order, starting with the minimum value, using a loop.

Another trick is the Bose-Nelson sort ("A Sorting Problem," R. C. Bose and R. J. Nelson, *Journal of the ACM*, vol. 9, pp. 282–296), which I had written about in *Dr. Dobb's Journal* back in 1985. This is a recursive procedure that takes an integer and then generates swap pairs for a vector of that size. A swap pair is a pair of position numbers from 1 to (n) in the vector that need to be exchanged if their contents are out of order. These swap pairs are also related to Sorting Networks in the literature (see *The Art of Computer Programming*, Donald Knuth, vol 3, ISBN 978-0201896855).

You are probably thinking that this method is a bit weak because the results are good only for sorting a fixed number of items. But a table only has a fixed number of columns, so that is not such a problem in denormalized SQL.

You can set up a sorting network that will sort five items (I was thinking of a Poker hand), with the minimal number of exchanges, nine swaps, like this:

```
Swap(c1, c2);
Swap(c4, c5);
Swap(c3, c5);
Swap(c3, c4);
Swap(c1, c4);
Swap(c1, c3);
Swap(c2, c5);
Swap(c2, c4);
Swap(c2, c3);
```

You might want to deal yourself a hand of five playing cards in one suit to see how it works. Put the cards face down in a line on the table and pick up the pairs, swapping them if required, then turn over the row to see that it is in sorted order when you are done.

In theory, the minimum number of swaps needed to sort (n) items is CEILING (log2 (n!)) and as (n) increases, this approaches O(n*log2(n)). The computer science majors will remember that Big O expression as the expected performance of the best sorting algorithms, such as Quicksort. The Bose-Nelson method is very good for small values of (n). If (n < 9) then it is perfect, actually. But as things get bigger, Bose-Nelson approaches O(n ^ 1.585). In English, this method is good for a fixed size list of 16 or fewer items and goes to hell after that.

You can write a version of the Bose-Nelson procedure that will output the SQL code for a given value of (n). The obvious direct way to do a Swap() is to write a chain of UPDATE statements. Remember that in SQL, the SET clause assignments happen in parallel, so you can easily write a SET clause that exchanges the two items when they are out of order. Using the previous swap chain, we get this block of code:

```
BEGIN ATOMIC
-- Swap(c1, c2);
UPDATE Foobar
 SET c1 = c2, c2 = c1
WHERE c1 > c2;

-- Swap(c4, c5);
UPDATE Foobar
 SET c4 = c5, c5 = c4
WHERE c4 > c5;

-- Swap(c3, c5);
UPDATE Foobar
 SET c3 = c5, c5 = c3
WHERE c3 > c5;

-- Swap(c3, c4);
UPDATE Foobar
 SET c3 = c4, c4 = c3
WHERE c3 > c4;

-- Swap(c1, c4);
UPDATE Foobar
 SET c1 = c4, c4 = c1
WHERE c1 > c4;

-- Swap(c1, c3);
UPDATE Foobar
 SET c1 = c3, c3 = c1
WHERE c1 > c3;

-- Swap(c2, c5);
UPDATE Foobar
 SET c2 = c5, c5 = c2
WHERE c2 > c5;

-- Swap(c2, c4);
UPDATE Foobar
 SET c2 = c4, c4 = c2
WHERE c2 > c4;

-- Swap(c2, c3);
UPDATE Foobar
 SET c2 = c3, c3 = c2
WHERE c2 > c3;

END;
```

This is fully portable, standard SQL code and it can be machine generated. But that parallelism is useful. It is worthwhile to combine some of the UPDATE statements. But you have to be careful not to change the effective sequence of the swap operations.

If you look at the first two UPDATE statements, you can see that they do not overlap. This means you could roll them into one statement like this:

```
-- Swap(c1, c2) AND Swap(c4, c5);
UPDATE Foobar
 SET c1 = CASE WHEN c1 <= c2 THEN c1 ELSE c2 END,
   c2 = CASE WHEN c1 <= c2 THEN c2 ELSE c1 END,
   c4 = CASE WHEN c4 <= c5 THEN c4 ELSE c5 END,
   c5 = CASE WHEN c4 <= c5 THEN c5 ELSE c4 END
WHERE c4 > c5 OR c1 > c2;
```

The advantage of doing this is that you have to execute only one UPDATE statement and not two. Updating a table, even on nonkey columns, usually locks the table and prevents other users from getting to the data. If you could roll the statements into one single UPDATE, you would have the best of all possible worlds, but I doubt that the code would be easy to read.

We can see this same pattern in the pair of statements.

```
Swap(c1, c3);
Swap(c2, c5);
```

But there are other patterns, so you can write general templates for them. Consider this one:

```
Swap(x, y);
Swap(x, z);
```

If you write out all possible triplets and apply these two operations on them, thus:

```
(x, y, z) => (x, y, z)
(x, z, y) => (x, z, y)
(y, x, z) => (x, y, z)
(y, z, x) => (x, z, y)
(z, x, y) => (x, y, z)
(z, y, x) => (x, y, z)
```

The result of this pattern is that x is the lowest of the three values, and y and z either stay in the same relative position to each other or get sorted properly. Getting them properly sorted would have the advantage of saving exchanges later and also reducing the set of the subset being operated upon by each UPDATE statement. With a little thought, we can write this symmetric piece of code.

```
-- Swap(x, y) AND Swap(x, z);
UPDATE Foobar
 SET x = CASE WHEN x BETWEEN y AND z THEN y
```

```
            WHEN z BETWEEN y AND x THEN y
            WHEN y BETWEEN z AND x THEN z
            WHEN x BETWEEN z AND y THEN z
            ELSE x END,
    y = CASE WHEN x BETWEEN y AND z THEN x
            WHEN x BETWEEN z AND y THEN x
            WHEN z BETWEEN x AND y THEN z
            WHEN z BETWEEN y AND x THEN z
            ELSE y END,
    z = CASE WHEN x BETWEEN z AND y THEN y
            WHEN z BETWEEN x AND y THEN y
            WHEN y BETWEEN z AND x THEN x
            WHEN z BETWEEN y AND x THEN x
            ELSE z END
WHERE x > z OR x > y;
```

While it is very tempting to write more and more of these pattern templates, it might be more trouble than it is worth because of increased maintenance and readability.

Here is an SQL/PSM program for the Bose-Nelson sort, based on the version given in *The C/C++ User's Journal* (February 1993 issue, "Sorting Networks," Frederick Hegeman). It assumes that you have a procedure called `PRINT()` for output to a text file. You can translate it into the programming language of your choice easily, as long as it supports recursion.

```
BEGIN
DECLARE i_mid INTEGER;
DECLARE j_mid INTEGER;
IF i2 = i1 AND j2 = j1
THEN CALL PRINT('swap (', i1, ', ', j1, ');');
ELSE IF i2 = i1+1 AND j2 = j1
  THEN CALL PRINT('swap(', i1, ', ', j1, ');');
     CALL PRINT('swap(', i2, ', ', j1, ');');
  ELSE IF i2 = i1+1 AND j2 = j1+1
     THEN CALL PRINT('swap (', i1, ', ', j2, ');');
        CALL PRINT('swap (', i1, ', ', j1, ');');
     ELSE SET i_mid = i1 + (i2-i1+1)/2 - 1;
        IF MOD((i2-i1+1),2) = 0 AND i2-i1 <> j2 -j1
        THEN SET j_mid = (j1 + j2-j1)/2 -1;
         CALL BoseMerge(i1, i_mid, j1, j_mid);
         CALL BoseMerge(ii_mid+1, i2, j_mid+1, j2);
         CALL BoseMerge(ii_mid+1, i2, j1, j_mid);
        END IF;
     END IF;
  END IF;
END IF;
END;
```

# NUMERIC DATA TYPES

SQL is not a computational language; the arithmetic capability of SQL is weaker than that of any other high-level programming language you have ever used. But there are some tricks that you need to know working with numbers in SQL and when passing them to a host program. Much of the arithmetic and the functions are implementation-defined, so you should experiment with your particular product and make notes on the defaults, precision, and tools in the math library of your database.

This section deals with the arithmetic that you would use across a row instead of down a column; they are not quite the same.

## 10.1 Numeric Types

The SQL standard has a very wide range of numeric types. The idea is that any host language can find an SQL numeric type that matches one of its own.

You will also find some vendor extensions in the numeric data types, the most common of which is MONEY in the Sybase/SQL Server family. This is really a `DECIMAL` or `NUMERIC` data type, which also accepts and displays currency symbols in input and output. This not only violates the principle of not formatting data, but SQL Server version has problems with its math. You may find vendors who allow leading zeroes, commas, decimal points, and other formatting in the database, but these "features" should not be used.

Numbers in SQL are classified as either exact or approximate. An exact numeric value has a precision, P, and a scale, S. The precision is a positive integer that determines the number of significant digits in a particular radix. The standard says the radix can be either binary or decimal, so you need to know what your implementation does. The scale is a nonnegative integer that tells you how many radix places the number has.

Joe Celko's SQL for Smarties. DOI: 10.1016/B978-0-12-382022-8.00010-7

Today, there are not that many base-10 platforms so you probably have a binary machine. However, a number can have one of many binary representations—twos-complement, ones-complement, high end or low end, and various word sizes. The proper mental model of numbers in SQL is not to worry about the "bits and bytes" level of the physical representation, but to think in abstract terms.

The data types `NUMERIC`, `DECIMAL`, `INTEGER`, `BIGINT`, and `SMALLINT` are exact numeric types. An integer has a scale of zero but the syntax simply uses the word `INTEGER` or the abbreviation `INT`, but hardcore SQL programmers do not use this abbreviation.

`SMALLINT` has a scale of zero, but the range of values it can hold are less than or equal to the range that `INTEGER` can hold in the implementation. Likewise, `BIGINT` has a scale of zero, but the range of values it can hold are greater than or equal to the range that `INTEGER` can hold in the implementation. `BIGINT` was added in SQL-99, but had been common in products before then.

Your SQL may also have a `TINYINT` exact numeric type with a range of 0 to 255; it is not standard. For every numeric type, the least value is less than zero and the greatest value is greater than zero and should be replaced with

```
CREATE DOMAIN TinyInt
AS
SMALLINT CHECK (VALUE BETWEEN 0 AND 255);
```

`DECIMAL(p,s)` can also be written `DEC(p,s)`, but it is not used by SQL programmers. For example, `DECIMAL(8,2)` could be used to hold the number 123456.78, which has eight significant digits and two decimal places.

The difference between `NUMERIC` and `DECIMAL` is subtle. `NUMERIC` specifies the exact precision and scale to be used. `DECIMAL` specifies the exact scale, but the precision is implementation-defined to be equal to or greater than the specified value. That means `DECIMAL` can have some room for rounding and `NUMERIC` does not. Mainframe COBOL programmers can think of NUMERIC as a PICTURE numeric type, whereas `DECIMAL` is like a BCD. Personal-computer programmers these days probably have not seen anything like this.

An approximate numeric value consists of a mantissa and an exponent. The mantissa is a signed numeric value; the exponent is a signed integer that specifies the magnitude of the mantissa. An approximate numeric value has a precision. The precision is a positive integer that specifies the number of significant binary digits in the mantissa. The value of an approximate numeric value is the mantissa multiplied by 10 to the exponent. `FLOAT(P)`,

REAL, and DOUBLE PRECISION are the approximate numeric types. There is a subtle difference between FLOAT(P), which has a binary precision equal to or greater than the value given, and REAL, which has an implementation-defined precision.

In the real world REAL and DOUBLE PRECISION are the IEEE Standard 754 for floating point numbers; FLOAT(P) is almost never used and will probably be deprecated in the Standards. IEEE math functions are built into processor chips so they will run faster than a software implementation. IEEE Standard 754 is binary and uses 32 bits for single precision and 64 bits for double precision, which is just right for personal computers and most Unix and Linux platforms.

The range for single precision numbers is approximately ± 10^–44.85 to 10^38.53, and for double precision, approximately ± 10^–323.3 to 10^308.3. However, there are some special values in the IEEE standard that are not part of SQL.

Zero cannot be directly represented in this format, so it is modeled as a special value denoted with an exponent field of zero and a fraction field of zero. The sign field can make this either –0 and +0, which are distinct values that compare as equal.

If the exponent is all zeroes, but the fraction is nonzero (else it would be interpreted as zero), then the value is a "denormalized" number (same term we use for tables, different meaning), which is not assumed to have a leading 1 before the binary point. Thus, this represents a number (–s * 0.f * 2 – 126), where s is the sign bit and f is the fraction. For double precision, denormalized numbers are of the form (–s * 0.f * 2 –1022). You can interpret zero as a special type of denormalized number.

The two values "+infinity" and "–infinity" are denoted with an exponent of all ones and a fraction of all zeroes. The sign bit distinguishes between negative infinity and positive infinity. Being able to denote infinity as a specific value is useful because it allows operations to continue past overflow situations. Operations with infinite values are well defined in IEEE floating point. We have nothing like it in SQL.

The value NaN (Not a Number) is used to represent a bit configuration that does not represent number. NaNs are represented by a bit pattern with an exponent of all ones and a nonzero fraction. There are two categories of NaN: QNaN (Quiet NaN) and SNaN (Signaling NaN).

A QNaN is a NaN with the most significant fraction bit set. QNaNs propagate freely through most arithmetic operations. These values pop out of an operation when the result is not mathematically defined, like division by zero.

An SNaN is a NaN with the most significant fraction bit clear. It is used to signal an exception when used in operations. SNaNs can be handy to assign to uninitialized variables to trap premature usage.

Semantically, QNaNs denote indeterminate operations, whereas SNaNs denote invalid operations.

SQL has not accepted the IEEE model for mathematics for several reasons. Much of the SQL standard allows implementation-defined rounding, truncation, and precision so as to avoid limiting the language to particular hardware platforms. If the IEEE rules for math were allowed in SQL, then we need type conversion rules for infinite and a way to represent an infinite exact numeric value after the conversion. People have enough trouble with NULLs, so let's not go there.

### 10.1.1 `BIT`, `BYTE`, and `BOOLEAN` Data Types

The ANSI Standards provide for `BOOLEAN`, `BINARY`, and `BINARY VARYING` data types and operations. Machine-level things like a bit or byte data type have no place in SQL and are almost never used. SQL has a three-valued logic and it does not naturally accommodate Boolean algebra. The value `TRUE` is greater than the value `FALSE`, and any comparison involving `NULL` or an `UNKNOWN` truth value will return an `UNKNOWN` result. But what does ((x = 1) >= (y = 42)) mean conceptually? And aren't there better ways to express the intent?

SQL is a high-level language; it is abstract and defined without regard to `PHYSICAL` implementation. This basic principle of data modeling is called data abstraction. Bits and bytes are the lowest units of hardware-specific, physical implementation you can get. Are you on a high-end or low-end machine? Does the machine have 8, 16, 32, 64, or 128 bit words? Twos complement or ones complement math? Hey, the SQL Standards allow decimal machines, so bits do not have to exist at all!

What about `NULL`s in this data type? To be an SQL data type, you have to have `NULL`s, so what is a `NULL` bit? By definition, a bit is in one of two states, on or off, and has no `NULL`. If your vendor adds `NULL`s to bits, how are the bit-wise operations defined? Oh what a tangled web we weave when first we mix logical and physical models.

What about the host languages? Did you know that +1, +0, −0, and −1 are all used for `BOOLEAN`s, but not consistently? In C#, Boolean values are 0/1 for `FALSE/TRUE`, whereas VB.NET has Boolean values of 0/–1 for `FALSE/TRUE` and they are proprietary languages from the same vendor. That means all the host languages—present, future, and not-yet-defined—can be different.

For standard programming languages C and COBOL, BOOLEAN values are mapped to integer variables in the host language. For standard programming languages Ada, Fortran, Pascal, and PL/I, BOOLEAN variables are directly supported. All data types in SQL have to be NULLable, so the SQL Standard requires that a NULL Boolean is UNKNOWN; unfortunately, this makes the behavior of the data type inconsistent. The rule for NULLs has always been that they propagate. Consider the expressions:

```
(1 = 1) OR NULL yields NULL which is UNKNOWN
(1 = 1) OR UNKNOWN yields TRUE
(1 = 1) AND UNKNOWN yields UNKNOWN
(1 = 1) AND NULL yields NULL which is UNKNOWN
```

Using assembly language style bit flags has its own problems.

There are usually two situations for using bits in practice. Either the bits are individual attributes or they are used as a vector to represent a single attribute. In the case of a single attribute, the encoding is limited to two values, which do not port to host languages or other SQLs, cannot be easily understood by an end user, and cannot be expanded.

In the second case what some newbies do, who are still thinking in terms of second- and third-generation programming languages or even punch cards, is build a vector for a series of yes/no status codes, failing to see the status vector as a single attribute. Did you ever play the children's game "20 Questions" when you were young?

Imagine you have six components for a loan approval, so you allocate bits in your second-generation model of the world. You have 64 possible vectors, but only five of them are valid (i.e., you cannot be rejected for bankruptcy and still have good credit). For your data integrity, you can:

1. Ignore the problem. This is actually what most newbies do. I have spent three decades cleaning up bad SQL and I see it all the time.
2. Write elaborate CHECK() constraints with user-defined functions or proprietary bit-level library functions that cannot port and that run like cold glue.

Now we add a seventh condition to the vector—which end does it go on? Why? How did you get it in the right place on all the possible hardware that it will ever use? Did all the code that references a bit in a word by its position do it right after the change?

You need to sit down and think about how to design an encoding of the data that is high level, general enough to expand, abstract, and portable. For example, is that loan approval a hierarchical code? Concatenation code? Vector code? Did you provide codes for unknown, missing, and N/A values? It is not easy to design such things!

`BINARY` and `BINARY VARYING` data types were meant to provide a standard term for storing data in various formats that are not part of the SQL data types, such as images, video, audio, and so forth.

## 10.2 Numeric Type Conversion

There are a few surprises in converting from one numeric type to another. The SQL standard left it up to the implementation to answer a lot of basic questions, so the programmer has to know his or her package.

### 10.2.1 Rounding and Truncating

When an exact or approximate numeric value is assigned to an exact numeric column, it may not fit. SQL says that the database engine will use an approximation that preserves leading significant digits of the original number after rounding or truncating. The choice of whether to truncate or round is implementation-defined, however. This can lead to some surprises when you have to shift data among SQL implementations, or storage values from a host language program into an SQL table. It is probably a good idea to create the columns with more decimal places than you think you need.

Truncation is defined as truncation toward zero; this means that 1.5 would truncate to 1, and −1.5 would truncate to −1. This is not true for all programming languages; everyone agrees on truncation toward zero for the positive numbers, but you will find that negative numbers may truncate away from zero (i.e., −1.5 would truncate to −2).

SQL is also indecisive about rounding, leaving the implementation free to determine its method. There are two major types of rounding in programming, the scientific method and the commercial method.

The scientific method looks at the digit to be removed. If this digit is 0, 1, 2, 3, or 4, you drop it and leave the higher-order digit to its left unchanged. If the digit is 5, 6, 7, 8, or 9, you drop it and increment the digit to its left. This method works with a small set of numbers and was popular with FORTRAN programmers because it is what engineers use.

The commercial method looks at the digit to be removed. If this digit is 0, 1, 2, 3, or 4, you drop it and leave the digit to its left unchanged. If the digit is 6, 7, 8, or 9, you drop it and increment the digit to its left. However, when the digit is 5, you want to have a rule that will round up about half the time.

One rule is to look at the digit to the left: If it is odd, then leave it unchanged; if it is even, increment it. There are other versions of the decision rule, but they all try to make the rounding error as small as possible. This method works with a large set of numbers and is popular with bankers because it reduces the total rounding error in the system.

Another convention is to round to the nearest even number, so that both 1.5 and 2.5 round to 2, and 3.5 and 4.5 both round to 4. This rule keeps commercial rounding symmetric. The following expression uses the `MOD()` function to determine if you have an even number or not.

```
ROUND (CAST (amount - .0005 AS DECIMAL (14,4)) -
 (CAST (MOD (CAST (amount * 100.0 + .99 AS INTEGER), 2) AS
DECIMAL (14,4))/1000.0), 2);
```

In commercial transactions, you carry money amounts to four or more decimal places, but round them to two decimal places for display. This is a GAAP (Generally Accepted Accounting Practice) in the United States for US dollars and a law in the European Union for working with euros.

Here is your first programming exercise for the notes you are making on your SQL.

Generate a table of 5000 random numbers, both positive and negative, with four or more decimal places. Round the test data to two decimal places and total them using both methods. Notice the difference and save those results. Now load those same numbers into a table in your SQL, like this:

```
CREATE TABLE RoundTest
(original DECIMAL(10,4) NOT NULL,
 rounded DECIMAL(10,2) NOT NULL);

-- insert the test data
INSERT INTO RoundTest (original)
VALUES (2134.5678. 0.00),
 etc.

UPDATE RoundTest SET rounded = original;

-- write a program to use both rounding methods
-- compare those results to this query

SELECT SUM(original), SUM(rounded)
  FROM RoundTest;
```

Compare these results to those from the other two tests. Now you know what your particular SQL is doing. Or if you got a third answer, there might be other things going on, which we will deal with in Chapter 29 on aggregate functions. We will postpone discussion here, but the order of the rows in a SUM() function can make a difference in accumulated floating-point rounding error.

Scientific software has special routines to correct such rounding problems, but most SQL databases do not. Floating math is rare in commercial applications and most commercial computers do not have floating point processors.

### 10.2.2 CAST() Function

Standard SQL defined the general CAST(`<cast operand> AS <data type>`) function for all data type conversions. The `<cast operand>` can be either a `<column name>`, a `<value expression>`, or a `NULL`.

For numeric-to-numeric conversion, you can do anything you wish, but you have to watch for the rounding errors. The comparison predicates can hide automatic type conversions, so be careful. SQL implementations might have formatting options in their conversion functions that are not part of the standard. These functions either use a picture string, like COBOL or some versions of BASIC, or return their results in a format set in an environment variable. This is very implementation-dependent. It also violates the principle of a tiered architecture that formatting is done in the front end and not the database.

## 10.3 Four Function Arithmetic

SQL was originally weaker than a pocket calculator. Today, the Standards include most of the basic math functions. The dyadic arithmetic operators +, −, *, and / stand for addition, subtraction, multiplication, and division, respectively. The multiplication and division operators are of equal precedence and are performed before the dyadic plus and minus operators.

In algebra and in some programming languages, the precedence of arithmetic operators is more restricted. They use the "My Dear Aunt Sally" rule; that is, multiplication is done before division, which is done before addition, which is done before subtraction. This can lead to subtle errors.

For example, consider `(largenum + largenum - largenum)`, where `largenum` is the maximum value that can be represented in its numeric data type. If you group the expression from left to right, you get `((largenum + largenum) - largenum) = overflow error!` However, if you group the expression from right to left, you get `(largenum + (largenum - largenum)) = largenum`.

Because of these differences, an expression that worked one way in the host language may get different results in SQL and vice versa. SQL could reorder the expressions to optimize them, but in practice, you will find that many implementations will simply parse the expressions from left to right. The best way to be safe is always to make extensive use of parentheses in complicated expressions, whether they are in the host language or in your SQL.

The monadic plus and minus signs are allowed and you can string as many of them in front of a numeric value of variables as you like. The bad news about this decision is that SQL also uses Ada-style comments, which put the text of a comment line between a double dash and a newline character. This means that the parser has to figure out whether "--" is two minus signs or the start of a comment. Standard SQL also support C-style comment brackets (i.e., /* comment text */). Such brackets can be used in international data transmission standards that do not recognize a newline in a transmission, so the double-dash convention will not work.

If both operands are exact numeric, the data type of the result is exact numeric, as you would expect. Likewise, an approximate numeric in a calculation will cast the results to approximate numeric. The kicker is in how the results are assigned in precision and scale.

Let S1 and S2 be the scale of the first and second operands, respectively. The precision of the result of addition and subtraction is implementation-defined, and the scale is the maximum of S1 and S2. The precision of the result of multiplication is implementation-defined, and the scale is (S1 + S2). The precision and scale of the result of division are implementation-defined, and so are some decisions about rounding or truncating results.

The ANSI X3H2 INCITS (nee ANSI X3H2) Database Standards Committee debated about requiring precision and scales in the standard in the early days of SQL and finally gave up. This means I can start losing high-order digits, especially with a division operation, where it is perfectly legal to make all results single-digit integers.

Nobody does anything that stupid in practice. In the real world, some vendors allow you to adjust the number of decimal places as a system parameter, some default to a known number of decimal places, and some display as many decimal places as they can so that you can round off to what you want. You will simply have to learn what your implementation does by experimenting with it.

The ANSI/ISO Standards now require the following basic math functions. There are other functions that produce numeric results; they are involved with aggregations and table-level operations.

1. MOD (<numeric dividend expression>, <numeric divisor expression>) = modulus function
2. ABS(<numeric expression>) = absolute value function
3. LN (<numeric expression>) = natural logarithm function
4. EXP (<numeric expression>) = exponential function
5. POWER (<numeric expression>, <numeric power expression>) = expression to a power
6. SQRT (<numeric expression>) = square root
7. FLOOR (<numeric expression>) = greatest integer value less than or equal to the argument
8. {CEIL | CEILING} (<numeric expression>) = least integer value greater than or equal to the argument

Precision and scale are implementation-defined for these functions, of course, but they tend to follow the same design decisions as the arithmetic did. The reason is obvious: They are using the same library routines under the covers as the math package in the database engine.

## 10.4 Arithmetic and NULLs

NULLs are probably one of the most formidable database concepts for the beginner. This book has a detailed study of how NULLs work in SQL, but this section is concerned with how they act in arithmetic expressions.

The NULL in SQL is only one way of handling missing values. The usual description of NULLs is that they represent currently unknown values that might be replaced later with real values when we know something. Missing values actually cover a lot of territory. The Interim Report 75-02-08 to the ANSI X3 (SPARC Study Group 1975) showed 14 different kinds of incomplete data that could appear as the result of operations or as attribute values. They included such things as arithmetic underflow and overflow, division by zero, string truncation, raising zero to the zero-th power, and other computational errors, as well as missing or unknown values.

The NULL is a global creature, not belonging to any particular data type, but able to replace any of their values. This makes arithmetic a bit easier to define. You have to specifically forbid NULLs in a column by declaring the column with a NOT NULL constraint. But in Standard SQL you can use the CAST function to declare a specific data type for a NULL, such as CAST (NULL AS INTEGER). One reason for this convention is completeness; another is to let you pass information about how to create a column to the database engine.

The basic rule for math with NULLs is that they propagate. An arithmetic operation with a NULL will return a NULL. That makes sense; if a NULL is a missing value, then you cannot determine the results of a calculation with it. However, the expression (NULL/0) looks strange to people. The first thought is that a division by zero should return an error; if NULL is a true missing value to be determined later, there is no value to which it can resolve and make that expression valid. However, SQL propagates the NULL, while a non-NULL divided by zero will cause a runtime error.

## 10.5 Converting Values to and from NULL

Since host languages do not support NULLs, the programmer can elect either to replace them with another value that is expressible in the host language or to use INDICATOR variables to signal the host program to take special actions for them.

An indicator parameter is an integer host parameter that is specified immediately following another host parameter. When the first host parameter gets a NULL, the indicator is set to a negative value. Indicators also show positive numbers to show string data truncation occurred during a transfer between a host program and SQL. A zero means there were no problems with the conversion.

### 10.5.1 NULLIF( ) Function

Standard SQL specifies two functions, NULLIF() and the related COALESCE(), that can be used to replace expressions with NULL and vice versa. They are part of the CASE expression family.

The NULLIF(V1, V2) function has two parameters. It is equivalent to the following CASE expression:

```
NULLIF(V1, V2) := CASE
          WHEN (V1 = V2)
          THEN NULL
          ELSE V1 END;
```

That is, when the first parameter is equal to the second, the function returns a NULL; otherwise, it returns the first parameter's value. The properties of this function allow you to use it for many purposes. The important properties are these:

1. NULLIF(x, x) will return NULL for all values of x. This includes NULL, since (NULL = NULL) is UNKNOWN, not TRUE.
2. NULLIF(0, (x - x)) will convert all non-NULLs of x into NULL. But it will convert x NULL into x zero, since (NULL - NULL) is NULL, and the equality test will fail.
3. NULLIF(1, (x - x + 1)) will convert all non-NULLs of x into NULL. But it will convert a NULL into a 1. This can be generalized for all numeric data types and values.

### 10.5.2 COALESCE( ) Function

The COALESCE(<value expression>, ..., <value expression>) function scans the list of <value expression>s from left to right, determines the highest data type in the list, and returns the first non-NULL in the list, casting it to the highest data type. If all the <value expression>s are NULL, the result is NULL.

The most common use of this function in math expressions is in a SELECT list where there are columns that have to be added, but one can be a NULL. For example, to create a report of the total pay for each employee, you might write this query:

```
SELECT emp_nbr, emp_name, (salary_amt + commission_amt)
   AS pay_tot
 FROM Personnel;
```

But salesmen may work on commission_amt only or on a mix of salary_amt and commission_amt. The office staff is on salary_amt only. This means an employee could have NULLs in his salary_amt or commission_amt column, which would propagate in the addition and produce a NULL result. A better solution would be:

```
SELECT emp_nbr, emp_name
      (COALESCE(salary_amt, 0.00) + COALESCE(commission_amt, 0.00))
       AS paycheck_amt
 FROM Personnel;
```

A more elaborate use for this function is with aggregate functions. Consider a table of customers' purchases with a category code and the amount of each purchase. You are to construct a query that will have one row, with one column for each category and one column for the grand total of all customer purchases. The table is declared like this:

```
CREATE TABLE Customers
(cust_nbr INTEGER NOT NULL,
 purchase_nbr INTEGER NOT NULL,
 cust_category CHAR(1)
    CONSTRAINT proper_category
    CHECK (cust_category IN ('A', 'B', 'C'),
purchase_amt DECIMAL(8, 2) NOT NULL,
. . . PRIMARY KEY (cust_nbr, purchase_nbr));
```

As an example of the use of COALESCE(), create a table of payments made for each month of a single year. (Yes, this could be done with a column for the months, but bear with me.)

```
CREATE TABLE Payments
(cust_nbr INTEGER NOT NULL,
 jan DECIMAL(8,2),
```

```
feb DECIMAL(8,2),
mar DECIMAL(8,2),
apr DECIMAL(8,2),
may DECIMAL(8,2),
jun DECIMAL(8,2),
jul DECIMAL(8,2),
aug DECIMAL(8,2),
sep DECIMAL(8,2),
oct DECIMAL(8,2),
nov DECIMAL(8,2),
"dec" DECIMAL(8,2), -- DEC is a reserved word
PRIMARY KEY cust_nbr);
```

The problem is to write a query that returns the customer and the amount of the last payment he made. Unpaid months are shown with a NULL in them. We could use a COALESCE function like this:

```
SELECT cust_nbr,
    COALESCE ("dec", nov, oct, sep,
       aug, jul, jun, may, apr, mar, feb, jan)
  FROM Customers;
```

Of course this query is a bit incomplete, since it does not tell you in what month this last payment was made. This can be done with the rather ugly-looking expression that will turn a month's non-NULL payment into a character string with the name of the month. The general case for a column called "mon", which holds the number of a month within the year, is NULLIF (COALESCE (NULLIF (0, mon-mon), 'Month'), 0) where 'Month' is replaced by the string for the actual name of the particular month. A list of these statements in month order in a COALESCE will give us the name of the last month with a payment. The way this expression works is worth working out in detail.

```
Case 1: mon is a numeric value

NULLIF(COALESCE(NULLIF(0, mon - mon), 'Month'), 0)
NULLIF(COALESCE(NULLIF(0, 0), 'Month'), 0)
NULLIF(COALESCE(NULL, 'Month'), 0)
NULLIF('Month', 0)
('Month')

Case 2: mon is NULL

NULLIF(COALESCE(NULLIF(0, mon-mon), 'Month'), 0)
NULLIF(COALESCE(NULLIF(0, NULL-NULL), 'Month'), 0)
NULLIF(COALESCE(NULLIF(0, NULL), 'Month'), 0)
NULLIF(COALESCE(0, 'Month'), 0)
NULLIF(0, 0)
(NULL)
```

You can do a lot of work by nesting SQL functions. LISP programmers are used to thinking this way, but most procedural programmers are not. It just takes a little practice and time.

## 10.6 Mathematical Functions

The SQL:2003 Standard extended the original four-function math to include a small library of functions. Most of them have been in actual products for decades.

SQL is not a computational language, so it should not have a math function library like, say, FORTRAN, nor a string function library like ICON. Geographical information is not part of the language but might be an extension.

### 10.6.1 Number Theory Operators

`MOD(n, m)` is the function that performs modulo or remainder arithmetic. If either n or m is `NULL`, then the result is `NULL`. If m is zero, then we get a division by zero exception. Otherwise, the result is the unique nonnegative exact numeric value r with scale zero such that:

1. r has the same sign as n.
2. The absolute value of r is less than the absolute value of m.
3. n = m * k + r for some exact numeric value k with scale zero.

This is tricky when the values of n and m are not cardinals (i.e., positive, nonzero integers). Experiment and find out how your package handles negative numbers and decimal places. In particular, many other procedural languages have slightly different definitions. If you are foolish enough to use "features" that allow other programming languages to be embedded in the DDL, then you cannot have consistent data. This was a major issue for Pascal, among others.

In September 1996, Len Gallagher proposed an amendment for the `MOD` function in SQL3. Originally, the working draft defined `MOD(n, m)` only for positive values of both m and n, and leaves the result to be implementation-dependent when either m or n is negative.

Negative values of n have no required mathematical meaning, and many implementations of MOD either don't define it at all, or give some result that is the easiest to calculate on a given hardware platform.

However, negative values for m do have a very nice mathematical interpretation that we wanted to see preserved in the SQL definition of `MOD()`. Let's propose the following:

1. If n is positive, then the result is the unique nonnegative exact numeric quantity r with scale zero such that r is less than

m and n = (m * k) + r for some exact numeric quantity k with scale zero.

2. Otherwise, the result is an implementation-defined exact numeric quantity r with scale zero, which satisfies the requirements that r is strictly between m and (–m), and that n = (m * k) + r for some exact numeric quantity k with scale zero, and a completion condition is raised: Warning—implementation-defined result.

This definition guarantees that the `MOD()` function, for a given positive value of n, will be a homomorphism under addition from the mathematical group of all integers, under integer addition, to the modular group of integers `{0, 1..., m-1}` under modular addition. This mapping then preserves the following group properties:

1. The additive identity is preserved: `MOD(0, m) = 0`
2. Additive inverse is preserved in the modular group defined by `MOD(-MOD(n, m), m) = m - MOD(n, m):`

```
MOD(-n, m) = - MOD(n, m)
```

3. The addition property is preserved where "{{circled plus sign}}" is modular addition defined by `MOD((MOD(m, m) + MOD(n, m)),m)`

```
MOD((m + n), m) = MOD(m, m){{circledplussign}}MOD(n,m)
```

4. Subtraction is preserved under modular subtraction, which is defined as `MOD((MOD(m, m) {{ circled minus sign }} MOD(n, m)), m)`

```
MOD(m - n,m) = MOD(m,m){{circled minus sign}}MOD(n,m)
```

From this definition, we would get the following:

```
MOD(12, 5) = 2
MOD(-12, 5) = 3
```

There are some applications where the "best" result to `MOD`(–12, 5) might be "–2" or "–3" rather than "3"; and that is probably why various implementations of the `MOD` function differ. But the advantages of being able to rely on the preceding mathematical properties outweigh any other considerations. If a user knows what the SQL result will be, then it is easy to modify the expressions of a particular application to get the desired application result. Table 10.1 is a chart of the differences in SQL implementations.

```
Type A:
 Oracle 7.0 and Oracle 8.0

Type B:
 DataFlex - ODBC:
```

**Table 10.1 SQL Implementation Differences**

| test | m | n | Type A | Type B | Type C | Proposal |
|---|---|---|---|---|---|---|
| a | 12 | 5 | 2 | 2 | 2 | 2 |
| b | –12 | 5 | –2 | –2 | –2 | 3 |
| c | –12 | –5 | –2 | –2 | (–2,3) | (2,–3) |
| d | –12 | –5 | 2 | 2 | 2 | –2 |
| e | NULL | 5 | NULL | NULL | NULL | NULL |
| f | NULL | NULL | NULL | NULL | NULL | NULL |
| g | 12 | NULL | NULL | NULL | NULL | NULL |
| h | 12 | 0 | 12 | NULL | error | 12 |
| i | –12 | 0 | –12 | NULL | error | –12 |
| j | 0 | 5 | 0 | 0 | 0 | 0 |
| k | 0 | –5 | 0 | 0 | 0 | 0 |

```
SQL Server 6.5, SP2
SQLBase Version 6.1 PTF level 4
Xbase
```

```
Type C:
 DB2/400, V3r2:
 DB2/6000 V2.01.1
 Sybase SQL Anywhere 5.5
 Sybase System 11
```

`ABS(n)` = Returns the absolute value of n. If (n) is `NULL`, then the result is `NULL`.

`SIGN(n)` = Returns −1 if n is negative, 0 if n is zero, and +1 if n is positive. If (n) is `NULL`, then the result is NULL. This function is the "signum" in mathematical terminology.

## 10.6.2 Exponential Functions

`POWER(x, n)` = Raise the number x to the n-th power. If either parameter is `NULL`, then the result is NULL. If x is zero and n is negative, then an exception condition is raised: data exception—invalid. A nonnegative number to the zero power is always one, and if VE is positive, then the result is zero.

`SQRT(x)` = Return the square root of x. It is defined as a shorthand for `POWER` (x, 0.5).

`LN(x)` = Natural logarithm of x. If x is zero or negative, then an exception condition is raised: data exception — invalid argument for natural logarithm.

`EXP(x)` = Returns the constant e (~ 2.71828182845904523536 .. ) to the x power; the inverse of a natural logarithm. If x is `NULL` then the result is `NULL`. If the result is not representable in the declared type of the result, then an exception is raised.

## 10.6.3 Scaling Functions

`FLOOR(x)` = The largest integer less than or equal to x. If x is `NULL` then the result is `NULL`.

`CEILING(x)` = The smallest integer greater than or equal to x. If x is `NULL` then the result is `NULL`.

Although not part of the Standards, these are very common in actual products. They can be written with multiplication and division, which would be subject to the local truncation and rounding rules of their product.

`ROUND(x, p)` = Round the number x to p decimal places. If either parameter is `NULL`, the result is `NULL`.

TRUNCATE(x, p) = Truncate the number x to p decimal places. If either parameter is `NULL`, the result is `NULL`.

The following two functions are in MySQL, Oracle, Mimer, and SQL-2003, but are often mimicked with CASE expressions in actual code.

`LEAST (<expression list>)` = The expressions have to be of the same data type. This function returns the lowest value, whether numeric, temporal, or character.

`GREATEST(<expression list>)` = As the preceding, but it returns the highest value.

## 10.6.4 Converting Numbers to Words

A common function in report writers converts numbers into words so that they can be used to print checks, legal documents, and other reports. This is not a common function in SQL products, nor is it part of the standards.

A method for converting numbers into words using only standard SQL by Stu Bloom follows. This was posted on January 2,2002, on the SQL Server Programming newsgroup. First, create a table:

```
CREATE TABLE NbrWords
(number INTEGER PRIMARY KEY,
 word VARCHAR(30) NOT NULL);
```

Then populate it with the literal strings of NbrWords from 0 to 999. Assuming that your range is 1 – 999,999,999 use the following query. It should be obvious how to extend it for larger numbers and fractional parts.

```
CASE WHEN :num < 1000
  THEN (SELECT word FROM NbrWords
      WHERE number = :num)
  WHEN :num < 1000000
  THEN (SELECT word FROM NbrWords
      WHERE number = :num / 1000)
     || ' thousand '
     || (SELECT word FROM NbrWords
        WHERE MOD (number = :num, 1000))
  WHEN :num < 1000000000
  THEN (SELECT word FROM NbrWords
      WHERE number = :num / 1000000)
     || ' million '
     || (SELECT word FROM NbrWords
      WHERE number = MOD((:num / 1000), 1000))
     || CASE WHEN MOD((:num / 1000), 1000) > 0
         THEN ' thousand '
         ELSE '' END
     || (SELECT word FROM NbrWords
      WHERE number = MOD(:num, 1000))
END;
```

Whether 2500 is "twenty-five hundred" or "two thousand, five hundred" is a matter of taste and not science. This can be done with a shorter list of words and a different query, but this is probably the best compromise between code and the size of the table.

## 10.7 Unique Value Generators

The most important property of any usable unique value generator is that it will never generate the same value twice. Sequential integers are the first approach vendors implemented in their products as a substitute for a proper key.

In essence, they are a piece of code inside SQL that looks at the last allocated value and adds one to get the next value. Let's start from scratch and build our own version of such a procedure. First create a table called GeneratorValues with one row and two columns:

```
CREATE TABLE GeneratorValues
(lock CHAR(1) DEFAULT 'X' NOT NULL PRIMARY KEY -- only one row
   CHECK (lock = 'X'),
keyval INTEGER DEFAULT 1 NOT NULL -- positive numbers only
  CHECK (keyval > 0));

 -- let everyone use the table
GRANT SELECT, UPDATE(keyval)
ON TABLE GeneratorValues
TO PUBLIC;
```

Now it needs a function to get out a value and do the increment.

```
CREATE FUNCTION Generator()
RETURNS INTEGER
LANGUAGE SQL
DETERMINISTIC
BEGIN
 -- SET ISOLATION = SERIALIZABLE;
UPDATE GeneratorValues
  SET keyval = keyval + 1;
RETURN (SELECT keyval FROM GeneratorValues);
COMMIT;
END;
```

This looks pretty good, but if there are multiple users, this code fragment is capable of allocating duplicate values to different users. It is important to isolate the execution of the code to one and only one user at a time by using `SET ISOLATION = SERIALIZABLE`. Various SQL products will have slightly different ways of achieving this effect based on their concurrency control methods.

More bad news is that in pessimistic locking systems, you can get serious performance problems because of lock contention when a transaction is in serial isolation. The users are queued for access to the Generator table.

If the application demands gap-free numbering, then we not only have to guarantee that no two sessions ever get the same value, we must also guarantee that no value is ever wasted. Therefore, the lock on the Generator table must be held until the key value is actually used and the entire transaction is committed. Exactly how this is handled is implementation-defined, so I am not going to comment on it.

## 10.7.1 Sequences with Gaps

Very often an application does not really need a gap-free number sequence. If the purpose of the generated value is only to provide a unique identifier, then there is no reason to insist on a gap-free numbering sequence (in fact, there may be excellent reasons to insist that values be nonsequential—more about that later). Similarly, if the generated value is only a sort key, there is no reason to insist that the sequence be gap-free, only that it be strictly increasing.

Once this requirement is eliminated we can design the application to allocate a generated value and then immediately `COMMIT`, before beginning the "real" transaction. If the "real" transaction is subsequently rolled back or never even begun, and the generated value is wasted, we don't care. Because the `COMMIT` is done immediately the lock on the Generator table is held only long enough to process the update and log the transaction. But we can still do even better than this.

### 10.7.2 Preallocated Values

In the old days of paper forms, the company had a forms control officer whose job was to track the forms. A gap in the sequential numbers on a check, bond, stock certificate, or whatever was a serious accounting problem. Paper forms were usually preprinted and issued in blocks of numbers as needed. You can imitate this procedure in a database with a little thought and a few simple stored procedures.

Broadly speaking, there were two types of allocation blocks. In one, the sequence is known. The most common example would be a checkbook. Gaps in the sequence numbers are not allowed, and a destroyed or damaged check has to be explained with a "void" or other notation. The system needs to record which block went to which user, the date and time, and any other information relevant to the auditors.

```
CREATE TABLE FormsControl
(form_nbr CHAR(7) NOT NULL,
 seq INTEGER NOT NULL CHECK(seq > 0),
 PRIMARY KEY (form_nbr, seq),
 recipient CHAR(25) DEFAULT CURRENT_USER NOT NULL,
 issue_date TIMESTAMP DEFAULT CURRENT_TIMESTAMP NOT NULL,
 ..
);
```

The tables that use the form numbers need to have constraints that verify the numbers were issued and appear in the Forms Control table. The next sequence number is easy to create, but you probably should restrict access to the base table with a stored procedure designed for one kind of form, along these lines:

```
CREATE FUNCTION NextFlobSeq( )
RETURNS INTEGER
LANGUAGE SQL
BEGIN
INSERT INTO FormsControl (form_nbr, seq, ..
VALUES ('Flob-1/R',
    (SELECT MAX(seq)+1
       FROM FormsControl
      WHERE form_nbr = 'Flob-1/R'),
     .. );
 ..
END;
```

You can also use views on the FormsControl table to limit user access. If you might be dealing with an empty, then use this scalar expression:

```
(SELECT COALESCE(MAX(seq), 0) + 1
   FROM FormsControl
  WHERE form_nbr = 'Flob-1/R'),
```

The COALESCE()will return a zero, thus assuring that the sequence starts with one.

## 10.8 IP Addresses

Internet Protocol version 6 (IPv6) replaces Internet Protocol version 4 (IPv4), which was made up of four integers each in the range 0 to 255, separated by dots. The problem is that we will run out of IP space by 2010 or 2011 at the latest. Version 6 requires eight sets of four hexadecimal digits separated by colons.

Although technically a numeric data type, IP addresses are stored as binary and displayed with digital strings. IPv6 was defined in December 1998 by the Internet Engineering Task Force (IETF) with the publication of an Internet standard specification, RFC 2460. There was no version 5; it was an experimental flow-oriented streaming protocol (Internet Stream Protocol) intended to support video and audio.

The new standard uses a 128-bit address, whereas IPv4 uses only 32 bits. There are a lot of details and new things in the standards, but they aren't relevant to this discussion; this is only about data representation.

### 10.8.1 CHAR(39) Storage

You could keep the IP address as a CHAR (39) that is (8 * 4 digits + 7 colons) and an easy regular expression in the DDL. The main advantage is that this is human-readable and binary is not. But it is legal to drop leading zeroes in each group for readability. Although that is a good goal, it makes comparisons a bit harder.

### 10.8.2 Binary Storage

Most current hardware supports 64 bit integers, but not 128 bits. Thankfully, the IPv6 standard uses a host identifier portion of 64 bits to facilitate an automatic mechanism for forming the host identifier from Link Layer media addressing information (MAC address). It is possible to use two BIGINTs for the data.

### 10.8.3 Separate SMALLINTs

The IP address is displayed as groups that each have meaning in the system, so we can model an IP address in separate columns. Notice that the IP address is still an atomic data element, but it is being modeled as scalar values. Check that you have such a data type in your product; if not, you can define it as:

```
CREATE DOMAIN SmallInt
AS INTEGER DEFAULT 0 CHECK (VALUE BETWEEN 0 AND 65535);
```

Then use that data type to declare a nonscalar atomic data element, thus:

```
ip1 SMALLINT NOT NULL,
ip2 SMALLINT NOT NULL,
 ..
ip8 SMALLINT NOT NULL
```

The trick here is to index the octets in reverse order, since the final grouping is the most selective.

11

# TEMPORAL DATA TYPES

Clifford Simak wrote a science fiction novel entitled, *Time Is the Simplest Thing*, in 1977. He was wrong. And the problems did not start with the Y2K problems we had in 2000, either. The calendar is irregular and the only ISO Standard unit of time is the second; years, months, weeks, hours, minutes, and so forth are not part of the SI system, but are mentioned in the ISO standards as conventions.

SQL-92 added temporal data to the language, acknowledging what was already in most SQL products by that time. The problem is that each vendor made a trade-off internally. We will get into SQL code later, but it is better to start with foundations.

## 11.1 Notes on Calendar Standards

Leap years did not exist in the Roman or Egyptian solar calendars prior to the year 708 AUC (*ab urbe condita*, Latin for "from the founding of the City [Rome]").

Unfortunately, the solar year is not an even number of days; there are 365.2422 days in a year and the fraction adds up over time. The civil and religious solar calendars had drifted with respect to the solar year by approximately one day every four years. For example, the Egyptian calendar drifted completely around approximately every 1,461 years. As a result, it was useless for agriculture, so the Egyptians relied on the stars to predict the flooding of the Nile. Sosigenes of Alexandria knew that the calendar had drifted completely around more than twice since it was first introduced.

To realign the calendar with the seasons, Julius Caesar decreed that the year 708 (that is the year 46 BCE to us) would have 445 days. Caesar, on the advice of Sosigenes, also introduced leap years (known as bissextile years) at this time. Many Romans simply referred to 708 AUC as the "year of confusion" and thus began the Julian calendar, which became the standard for the world from that point forward.

Joe Celko's SQL for Smarties. DOI: 10.1016/B978-0-12-382022-8.00011-9

The Julian calendar had a leap year day every four years and was reasonably accurate in the short or medium range, but it drifted by approximately three days every 400 years. This is a result of the 0.0022 fraction of a day adding up.

It had gotten 10 days out of step with the seasons by 1582. (A calendar without a leap year would have drifted completely around slightly more than once between 708 AUC and 2335 AUC—that is, 1582 CE to us.) The Summer Solstice, so important to planting crops, had no relationship to June 21. Scientists finally convinced Pope Gregory to realign the calendar by dropping almost two weeks from the month of October in 1582 CE. The years 800 CE and 1200 CE were leap years anywhere in the Christian world. But whether 1600 CE was a leap year depended on where you lived. European countries did not move to the new calendar at the same time or follow the same pattern of adoption.

**Note**: The abbreviations AD (*Anno Domini*, Latin for "in the year of Our Lord") and BC (Before Christ) have been replaced by CE for "Common Era" and BCE for "Before Common Era" in ISO Standard to avoid religious references.

The calendar corrections had economic and social ramifications. In Great Britain and its colonies, September 2, 1752 was followed by September 14, 1752. The calendar reform bill of 1751 was entitled, "An Act for Regulating the Commencement of the Year and For Correcting the Calendar Now in Use." The bill included provisions to adjust the amount of money owed or collected from rents, leases, mortgages, and similar legal arrangements, so that rents and so forth were prorated by the number of actual elapsed days in the time period affected by the calendar change. Nobody had to pay the full monthly rate for the short month of September in 1752 and nobody had to pay the full yearly rate for the short year.

The serious, widespread, and persistent rioting was not due to the commercial problems that resulted, but to the common belief that each person's days were "numbered" and that everyone was preordained to be born and die at a divinely ordained time that no human agency could alter in any way.

Thus the removal of 11 days from the month of September shortened the lives of everyone on Earth by 11 days. And there was also the matter of the missing 83 days due to the change of the New Year's Day from March 25 to January 1, which was believed to have a similar effect.

If you think this behavior is insane, consider the number of people today who get upset about the yearly one-hour clock adjustments for Daylight Saving Time.

To complicate matters, the beginning of the year also varied from country to country. Great Britain preferred to begin the year on March 25, whereas other countries began at Easter, December 25, or perhaps March 1 and January 1—all important details for historians to keep in mind.

In Great Britain and its colonies, the calendar year 1750 began on March 25 and ended on March 25—that is, the day after March 24, 1750 was March 25, 1751. The leap year day was added to the end of the last full month in the year, which was then February. The extra leap year day comes at the end of February, since this part of the calendar structure was not changed.

In Latin, *septem* means seventh, from which we derived September. Likewise, *octem* means eighth, *novem* means ninth, and *decem* means tenth. Thus, September should be the seventh month, October should be the eighth, November should be the ninth, and December should be the tenth.

So, how come September is the ninth month? September was the seventh month until 1752 when the New Year was changed from March 25 to January 1.

Until fairly recently, nobody agreed on the proper display format for dates. Every nation seems to have its own commercial conventions. Most of us know that Americans put the month before the day and the British do the reverse, but do you know any other national conventions? National date formats may be confusing when used in an international environment. When it was 12/16/95 in Boston, it was 16/12/95 in London, 16.12.95 in Berlin and 95-12-16 in Stockholm. Then there are conventions within industries within each country that complicate matters further.

Faced with all the possibilities, software vendors came up with various general ways of formatting dates for display. The usual ones are some mixtures of a two- or four-digit year, a three-letter or two-digit month, and a two-digit day within the month. Slashes, dashes, or spaces can separate the three fields.

At one time, NATO tried to use Roman numerals for the month to avoid language problems among treaty members. The United States Army did a study and found that the four-digit year, three-letter month and two-digit day format was the least likely to be missorted, misread, or miswritten by English speakers. That is also the reason for "24-hour" or "military" time.

Today, you want to set up a program to convert your data to conform to ISO 8601 "Data Elements and Interchange Formats – Information Interchange – Representation of Dates and Times" as a corporate standard and EDIFACT for EDI messages. This is the yyyy-mm-dd format that is part of Standard SQL and will become part of other standard programming languages as they add temporal data types.

The full ISO 8601 timestamp can be either a local time or UTC time. UTC is the code for Universal Coordinated Time, which replaced the older GMT, which was the code for Greenwich Mean Time, which is still improperly used in popular media.

In 1970 the Coordinated Universal Time system was devised by an international advisory group of technical experts within the International Telecommunication Union (ITU). The ITU felt it was best to designate a single abbreviation for use in all languages in order to minimize confusion. The two alternative original abbreviation proposals for the Universal Coordinated Time were CUT (English: Coordinated Universal Time) and TUC (French: *Temps Universel Coordinne*). UTC was selected both as a compromise between the French and English proposals and because the C at the end looks more like an index in UT0, UT1, UT2, and a mathematical-style notation is always the most international approach.

Universal Coordinated Time is not quite the same thing as astronomical time. The Earth wobbles a bit and the UTC had to be adjusted to the solar year with a leap second added or removed once a year to keep them in synch. As of this writing, UTC will be based on an atomic clock without a leap second adjustment.

Another problem in the United States is that besides having four time zones, we also have "lawful time" to worry about. This is the technical term for time required by law for commerce. Usually, this means whether or not you use Daylight Saving Time (DST) and how it is defined locally.

The need for UTC time in the database and lawful time for display and input has not been generally handled yet. EDI and replicated databases must use UTC time to compare timestamps. A date without a time zone is ambiguous in a distributed system. A transaction created DATE '1995-12-17' in London may be younger than a transaction created DATE '1995-12-16' in Boston. With a time zone, both are adjusted to UTC internally.

## 11.2 SQL Temporal Data Types

SQL-86 and SQL-89 have no notion of time. SQL-92 added datetime and interval data types. Although Standard SQL supports time-varying data through the temporal data types, the language really has no notion of a time-varying table. SQL also has no concept of current or sequenced constraints, queries, modifications or views, nor of the critical distinction between valid time (modeling the behavior of the enterprise in reality) and transaction time (capturing the evolution of the stored data).

SQL only supports what are called nonsequenced operations. Standard SQL has a very complete description of its temporal data types. There are rules for converting from numeric and character strings into these data types and there is a schema table for global time-zone information that is used to make sure that temporal data types are synchronized. It is so complete and elaborate that smaller SQLs have not implemented it yet. As an international standard, Standard SQL has to handle time for the whole world, and most of us work with only local time. If you have ever tried to figure out the time in a foreign city to place a telephone call, you have some idea of what is involved.

The common terms and conventions related to time are also confusing. We talk about "an hour" and use the term to mean a particular point within the cycle of a day ("The train arrives at 13:00 hrs") or to mean an interval of time not connected to another unit of measurement ("The train takes three hours to get there"). The number of days in a month is not uniform; the number of days in a year is not uniform; weeks are not easily related to months; and so on.

Standard SQL has two basic kinds of temporal data types. The datetimes (`DATE`, `TIME`, and `TIMESTAMP`) represent points in the time line, and the interval data types and `INTERVAL`s (`DAY`, `HOUR`, `MINUTE`, and `SECOND` with decimal fraction) are durations of time. Standard SQL also has a full set of operators for these data types. But you will still find vendor-specific syntax in most existing SQL implementations today.

### 11.2.1 Internal Representations

The syntax and power of date, timestamp, and time features vary so much from product to product that it is impossible to give anything but general advice. This chapter will assume that you have simple date arithmetic in your SQL, but you might find that some library functions would let you do a better job than what you see here. Please continue to check your manuals until the Standard SQL standards are implemented.

As a general statement, there are two ways of representing temporal data internally. The UNIX representation is based on keeping a single binary string of 64 or more bits that counts the computer clock ticks from a base starting date and time. The other representation I will call the COBOL method, since it uses separate fields for the year, month, day, hours, minutes, and seconds. These fields can be characters, BCD, or other another internal format.

The UNIX method is very good for calculations, but the engine must convert from the external ISO 8601 format to the internal format and vice versa. The COBOL format is the opposite; good for display purposes, but weaker on calculations.

### 11.2.2 Display Format Standards

The ANSI date formats are described in ANSI X3.30. Their formats include the ISO standard, but add a four-digit year, followed by the two-digit month (01–12), followed by the two-digit day within month (01–31). This option is called the calendar date format. Standard SQL uses this all-numeric yyyy-mm-dd hh:mm:ss[ss..] format to conform to ISO 8601, which had to avoid language-dependent abbreviations.

Many programs still use a year-in-century date format of some kind. This was supposed to save space in the old days when that sort of thing mattered (i.e., when punch cards had only 80 columns). Programmers assumed that they would not need to tell the difference between the years 1900 and 2000 because they were too far apart. Old COBOL programs that did date arithmetic on these formats returned erroneous negative results. If COBOL had a DATE data type, instead of making the programmers write their own routines, this would not have happened. Relational database users and some 4GL programmers can gloat over this, since they have DATE data types built into their languages.

### 11.2.3 Handling Timestamps

`TIMESTAMP(n)` is defined as a timestamp to (n) decimal places (e.g., `TIMESTAMP(9)` is nanosecond precision), where the precision is hardware-dependent. The FIPS-127 standard requires at least five decimal places after the second and modern products typically go to seven decimal places.

`TIMESTAMP`s usually serve two purposes. They can be used as a true timestamp to mark an event connected to the row in which they appear. Or they can be used as a sequential number for building a unique key that is not temporal in nature. Some DB2 programs use the microseconds component of a timestamp and invert the numbers to create a "random" number for keys; of course, this method of generation does not preclude duplicates being generated, but it is a quick and dirty way to create a somewhat random number. It helps to use such a method when using the timestamp itself would generate data "hot spots" in the table space. For example, the date and time when a payment is made on an account are important and a true timestamp is required for legal reasons. The account number just has to be different from all other account numbers, so we need a unique number, and `TIMESTAMP` is a quick way of getting one.

Remember that a `TIMESTAMP` will read the system clock once and use that same time on all the items involved in a transaction. It does not matter if the actual time it took to complete the transaction was days; a transaction in SQL is done as a whole unit or is not done at all. This is not usually a problem for small transactions, but it can be in large batched ones where very complex updates have to be done.

`TIMESTAMP` as a source of unique identifiers is fine in most single-user systems, since all transactions are serialized and of short enough duration that the clock will change between transactions; peripherals are slower than CPUs. But in a client/server system, two transactions can occur at the same time on different local workstations. Using the local client machine clock can create duplicates and adds the problem of coordinating all the clients. The coordination problem has two parts:

1. How do you get the clocks to start at the same time? I do not mean just the technical problem of synchronizing multiple machines to the microsecond but also the one or two clients who forgot about Daylight Saving Time.
2. How do you make sure the clocks stay the same? Using the server clock to send a timestamp back to the client increases network traffic yet does not always solve the problem.

The modern solution is to use the NIST time signal to set and synchronize all clocks, not just those in computers. Official US government time, as provided by NIST and USNO (United States Naval Observatory), is available on the Internet at http://www.time.gov. NIST also offers an Internet Time Service (ITS) and an Automated Computer Time Service (ACTS) that allow setting of computer and other clocks through the Internet or over standard commercial telephone lines. Free software for using these services on several types of popular computers can be downloaded there. The NIST web site at http://tf.nist.gov has information on time and frequency standards and research.

Many operating systems that represent the system time as a long binary string based on a count of machine cycles since a starting date. One trick is to pull off the least significant digits of this number and use them as a key. But this will not work as transaction volume increases. Adding more decimal places to the timestamp is not a solution either. The real problem lies in statistics.

Open a telephone book (white pages) at random. Mark the last two digits of any 13 consecutive numbers, which will give you a sample of numbers between 00 and 99, which we will assume is uniformly distributed. What are the odds that you will have a pair of identical numbers? It is not 1 in 100, as you might first think. Start with one number and add a second number to the set; the odds that the second number does not match the first are 99/100. Add a third number to the set; the odds that it matches neither the first nor the second number are 98/100. Continue this line of reasoning and compute (0.99 * 0.98 * ... * 0.88) = 0.4427 as the odds of not finding a pair. Therefore, the odds that you will find a pair are 0.5572, a bit better than even. By the time you get to 20 numbers, the odds of a match are about 87%; at 30 numbers, the odds exceed a 99% probability of one match. You might want to carry out this model for finding a pair in three-digit numbers and see when you pass the 50% mark.

A good key generator needs to eliminate (or at least minimize) identical keys and give a statistical distribution that is fairly uniform to avoid excessive index reorganization problems. Most key-generator algorithms that use the system clock depend on one or more "near key" values, such as employee name, to create a unique identifier.

The mathematics of such algorithms is much like that of a hashing algorithm. Hashing algorithms also try to obtain a uniform distribution of unique values. The difference is that a hashing algorithm must ensure that a hash result is both unique (after collision resolution) and repeatable, so that it can find the stored data. A key generator needs only to ensure that the resulting key is unique in the database, which is why it can use the system clock and a hashing algorithm cannot.

You can often use a random-number generator in the host language to create pseudo-random numbers to insert into the database for these purposes. Most pseudo-random number generators will start with an initial value, called a seed, then use it to create a sequence of numbers. Each call will return the next value in the sequence to the calling program. The sequence will have some of the statistical properties of a real random sequence, but the same seed will produce the same sequence each time, which is why the numbers are called pseudo-random numbers. This also means that if the sequence ever repeats a number, it will begin to cycle. (This is not usually a problem, since the size of the cycle can be hundreds of thousands or even millions of numbers.)

## 11.2.4 Handling Times

Older, smaller databases live and work in one time zone. If you have a database that covers more than one time zone, you might consider storing time in UTC and adding a numeric column to hold the local time-zone offset. The time zones start at UTC, which has an offset of zero. This is how the system-level time-zone table in Standard SQL is defined. There are also ISO standard three-letter codes for the time zones of the world, such as EST, for Eastern Standard Time, in the United States. The offset is usually a positive or negative number of hours, but there are still a few odd zones that differ by 15 minutes from the expected pattern.

Now you have to factor in Daylight Saving Time on top of that to get what is call "lawful time," which it is the basis for legal agreements. The US government uses Daylight Saving Time (DST) on federal lands inside of states that do not use DST. If the hardware clock in the computer in which the database resides is the source of the timestamps, you can get a mix of gaps and duplicate times over a year. This is why Standard SQL uses UTC internally.

You should use a 24-hour time format, which is less prone to errors than 12-hour (AM/PM) time, since it is less likely to be misread or miswritten. This format can be manually sorted more easily and is less prone to computational errors. Americans use the ISO Standard colon as a field separator between hours, minutes, and seconds; Europeans still use a period in some countries. This is not a problem for them, since they also use a comma for a decimal point. Most databases give you these display options.

One of the major problems with time is that there are three kinds: fixed events ("He arrives at 13:00 hrs"), durations ("The trip takes three hours"), and intervals ("The train leaves at 10:00 hrs and arrives at 13:00 hrs"), which are all interrelated. SQL-92 introduced an INTERVAL data type. An INTERVAL is a unit of duration of time rather than a fixed point in time; its units are years, months, days, hours, minutes, and seconds.

There are two classes of intervals. One class, called year-month intervals, has an express or implied precision that includes no fields other than YEAR and MONTH, though it is not necessary to use both. The other class, called day-time intervals, has an express or implied interval precision that can include any fields other than `YEAR` or `MONTH`—that is, `DAY`, `HOUR`, `MINUTE`, and `SECOND` (with decimal places).

## 11.2.5 Time Zones and DST

The British Railroads were the first agency to get legally established time zones in the 1880s. Canada, then the United States followed, thanks to the work of a Canadian civil and railway engineer, Sandford Fleming. He was instrumental in convening the 1884 International Prime Meridian Conference in Washington, which gave us the current system of international standard time. Standard time in time zones became law in the United States with the Standard Time Act of 1918. The Department of Transportation has had responsibility for the time laws since 1966. Time zone boundaries have changed greatly since their original introduction, and changes still occasionally occur.

Daylight Saving Time has been used in the United States and in many European countries since World War I. It was introduced as a war time measure to save energy and it outlasted both World Wars. Those conventions have also changed over the years. You simply need to find out what the current situation is and make changes to your database's schema information tables.

On top of all this, there are a few places on Earth that have time zone offsets that are not in whole hours. This is why Stanford SQL has syntax for time zone in hours and minutes. Hopefully, this will disappear with nondecimal currencies and nonmetric units of measurement in my lifetime.

Time zones with fractional hour displacements are shown here:

http://www.timeanddate.com/worldclock/city.html?n=5
http://www.timeanddate.com/worldclock/city.html?n=54
http://www.timeanddate.com/worldclock/city.html?n=176
http://www.timeanddate.com/worldclock/city.html?n=246

but the strange ones are:

http://www.timeanddate.com/worldclock/city.html?n=5
http://www.timeanddate.com/worldclock/city.html?n=63

The TIMEZONE_HOUR value can be between –14 and 14, but when the value of TIMEZONE_HOUR is either –14 or 14, the value of TIMEZONE_MINUTE is restricted to be 00 (zeros). Likewise, TIMEZONE_MINUTE values are between –59 and 59.

The declaration of a time zone has to be on a TIME or TIMESTAMP column, with this syntax:

```
[WITH | WITHOUT] TIME ZONE
```

for example:

```
CREATE TABLE Foobar
(start_date TIME WITH TIME ZONE NOT NULL,
end_time TIMESTAMP WITHOUT TIME ZONE);
```

## 11.3 INTERVAL Data Types

INTERVAL data types are either year–month interval or a day–time interval. They can be either single words, such as DAY or HOUR, or a range such as HOUR TO SECOND. This is why strings are used rather than integers—you have to put in punctuation to separate the fields. Table 11.1 gives you a quick list of the keywords for the INTERVAL data types. Here are the formal BNF definitions.

```
<interval literal> ::=
INTERVAL [+ | -] <interval string> <interval qualifier>

<interval string> ::=
 <date value string>
  | <time value string> [<time zone interval string>]
  | <timestamp string>

<interval qualifier> ::=

<interval string> ::= [+ | - ] { <year-month literal>
   | <day-time literal> }

<year-month literal> ::= <years value> [<minus sign>
   <months value>]
| <months value>

<day-time literal> ::= <day-time interval> | <time interval>

<day-time interval> ::=
<days value> [<space> <hours value> [<colon> <minutes value>
[<colon> <seconds value>]]]

<time interval> ::=
<hours value> [<colon> <minutes value> [<colon>
   <seconds value>]]
| <minutes value> [<colon> <seconds value>]
   | <seconds value>

<years value> ::= <datetime value>

<months value> ::= <datetime value>

<days value> ::= <datetime value>

<hours value> ::= <datetime value>

<minutes value> ::= <datetime value>

<seconds value> ::= <seconds integer value>
   [<period> [<seconds fraction>]]

<seconds integer value> ::= <unsigned integer>

<seconds fraction> ::= <unsigned integer>

<datetime value> ::= <unsigned integer>
```

The `<interval qualifier>` describes the precision of the interval data type. A value described by an interval data type descriptor is always signed.

Values in interval fields other than `SECOND` are integers and have precision 2 when not the first field. `SECOND`, however, can be

## Table 11.1 ANSI/ISO Standard Interval Data Types

| Interval Field and Description | Keyword |
|---|---|
| Years, constrained by implementation leading field precision | YEAR |
| Months within years constrained to 0–11 | MONTH |
| Days, constrained by implementation leading field precision | DAY |
| Hours within days, constrained to 0–23 | HOUR |
| Minutes within hours, constrained to 0–59 | MINUTE |
| Seconds within minutes, constrained to 0–59.999. | SECOND |

defined to have an `<interval fractional seconds precision>` that indicates the number of decimal digits in the seconds value. When not the first field, `SECOND` has a precision of two places before the decimal point. Fields comprising an item of type interval are also constrained by the definition of the Common Era calendar.

`YEAR`, `MONTH`, and `YEAR TO MONTH` intervals are comparable only with other year-month intervals. If two year–month intervals have different interval precisions, they are, for the purpose of any operations between them, effectively converted to the same precision by appending new `<primary datetime field>`s to either the most significant end of one interval, the least significant end of one interval, or both. New least significant `<primary datetime field>`s are assigned a value of 0 (zero). When it is necessary to add new most significant datetime fields, the associated value is effectively converted to the new precision in a manner obeying the natural rules for dates and times associated with the Common Era calendar.

`DAY`, `HOUR`, `MINUTE`, `SECOND`, `DAY TO HOUR`, `DAY TO MINUTE`, `DAY TO SECOND`, `HOUR TO MINUTE`, `HOUR TO SECOND`, and `MINUTE TO SECOND` intervals are comparable only with other day–time intervals. If two day–time intervals have different interval precisions, they are, for the purpose of any operations between them, effectively converted to the same precision by appending new `<primary datetime field>`s to either the most significant end of one interval or the least significant end of one interval, or both. New least significant `<primary datetime field>`s are assigned a value of 0 (zero). When it is necessary to add new most significant datetime fields, the associated value is effectively converted to the new precision in a manner obeying the natural rules for dates and times associated with the Common Era calendar.

In Standard SQL, the interval values are given by strings and not by integers or decimals. However, you can write things like this, assuming it makes sense, to an integer out of them:

```
CAST (CAST (<string expression> AS INTERVAL <interval
   type>) AS <exact numeric data type>)
```

Within an `<interval literal>` that contains a `<year-month literal>`, the `<interval qualifier>` shall not specify `DAY`, `HOUR`, `MINUTE`, or `SECOND`. Within the definition of an `<interval literal>` that contains a `<day-time literal>`, the `<interval qualifier>` shall not specify `YEAR` or `MONTH`. Within the definition of a `<datetime literal>`, the value of the `<time zone interval>` shall be in the range −12:59 to +14:00. Informally, this says that you need to use sensible values.

## 11.4 Temporal Arithmetic

Almost every SQL implementation has a `DATE` data type, but the functions available for them vary quite a bit. The most common ones are a constructor that builds a date from integers or strings; extractors to pull out the month, day, or year; and some display options to format output.

You can assume that your SQL implementation has simple date arithmetic functions, although with different syntax from product to product, such as

1. A date plus or minus a number of days yields a new date.
2. A date minus a second date yields an integer number of days between the dates.

Table 11.2 displays the valid combinations of `<datetime>` and `<interval>` data types in the Standard SQL standard.

There are other rules, which deal with time zones and the relative precision of the two operands, that are intuitively obvious.

**Table 11.2 Valid `<datetime>` and `<interval>` Combinations**

```
<datetime> - <datetime> = <interval>
<datetime> + <interval> = <datetime>
<interval> (* or/) <numeric> = <interval>
<interval> + <datetime> = <datetime>
<interval> + <interval> = <interval>
<numeric> * <interval> = <interval>
```

There is the Standard CURRENT_DATE function that returns the current date from the system clock. However, you will still find vendor dialect named for the function, such as TODAY, SYSDATE, Now(), and getdate(). There may also be a function to return the day of the week from a date, which is sometimes called DOW() or WEEKDAY(). Standard SQL provides for CURRENT_DATE, CURRENT_TIME [(<time precision>)], and CURRENT_TIMESTAMP [(<timestamp precision>)] functions, which are self-explanatory.

## 11.5 The Nature of Temporal Data Models

Richard T. Snodgrass at the University of Arizona is the world's leading expert on temporal databases. His out-of-print book, *Developing Time-Oriented Database Applications in SQL* (ISBN 10 1-55860-436-7) is available at the university web site as a PDF file (http://www.cs.arizona.edu/~rts/tdbbook.pdf). He also wrote a series of articles in *Database Programming and Design* (volume 11, issues 6–10) in 1998, which are readable for the working programmer.

Currently, the Morgan-Kaufmann database series has a book on this topic in the series, *How to Design, Update and Query Temporal Data,* by Tom Johnston and Randall Weis (ISBN 978-0-12-375041-9).

I am not going to try to summarize two excellent books on a complex topic in a general SQL book.

Temporal data is pervasive. It has been estimated that one of every 50 lines of database application code involves a date or time value. Data warehouses are by definition time-varying: Ralph Kimball states that every data warehouse has a time dimension. Often the time-oriented nature of the data is what lends it value.

### 11.5.1 Modeling Durations

Time is a continuum, which means that there is an infinite number of points between any two points. The particular model that we use in ISO Standards is a half-open interval, which includes the starting point but goes up to the ending point in time, but does not include it. This is usually shown as a line with a closed dot at the start and an open dot on the other end. For most commercial purposes, a granularity of a day is fine.

Let me use a history table for price changes. A price has duration and we can model it with a pair of dates. In particular, we can use a NULL for the current status. Here is a skeleton price history table.

```
CREATE TABLE PriceHistory
(upc CHAR(13) NOT NULL -- industry standard
```

```
 REFERENCES Inventory(upc),
price_prev_date DATE NOT NULL,
price_start_date DATE DEFAULT CURRENT_DATE NOT NULL,
price_end_date DATE, -- null means current price
 CHECK(price_start_date < price_end_date),
 CHECK (price_start_date = price_prev_date + INTERVAL '1'
   DAY), -- prevents gaps
PRIMARY KEY (upc, price_start_date),
item_price DECIMAL (12,2) NOT NULL
 CHECK (item_price > 0.00),
etc.);
```

You use a BETWEEN predicate to get the appropriate price. You can enforce the "one null per item" with a trigger but technically this should work in full Standard SQL:

```
CHECK (COUNT(*) OVER (PARTITION BY upc)
  = COUNT(price_end_date) OVER (PARTITION BY upc) +1)

SELECT ..
 FROM PriceHistory AS H, Orders AS O
WHERE O.sales_date BETWEEN H.price_start_date
    AND COALESCE (price_end_date, CURRENT_DATE);
```

It is also a good idea to have a VIEW with the current data:

```
CREATE VIEW CurrentPrices (..)
AS
SELECT ..
 FROM PriceHistory
WHERE price_end_date IS NULL;
```

Now your only problem is to write a stored procedure that will update the table and insert a new row. You can do this with a single MERGE statement, or with a short block of SQL/PSM code:

```
CREATE PROCEDURE UpdateItemPrice
(IN in_upc CHAR(13), IN new_item_price DECIMAL (12,4))
LANGUAGE SQL
BEGIN ATOMIC
UPDATE PriceHistory
  SET price_end_date = CURRENT_DATE
WHERE upc = in_upc;
INSERT INTO PriceHistory (upc, price_prev_date, price_
   start_date, price_end_date, item_price)
VALUES (in_upc, CURRENT_DATE, CURRENT_DATE + INTERVAL '1'
   DAY, NULL, new_item_price);
END;
```

This will make the price change go into effect tomorrow.

There is a common kludge to repair a failure to design a history table properly that you can put in a VIEW if you are not able to set things right. Assume that every day we take a short inventory and put it in a journal. The journal is a clipboard paper form that has one line per item per day, perhaps with gaps in the data. We want to get this into the proper format, namely periods shown with a (start_date, end_date) pair for durations where each item had the same quantity on hand. This is due to Alejandro Mesa.

```
CREATE TABLE InventoryJournal
(journal_date DATETIME NOT NULL,
item_id CHAR(2) NOT NULL,
 PRIMARY KEY (journal_date, item_id),
onhand_qty INTEGER NOT NULL);

WITH ItemGroups
AS
(SELECT journal_date, item_id, onhand_qty,
   ROW_NUMBER() OVER(ORDER BY item_id, journal_date,
     onhand_qty)
   - ROW_NUMBER() OVER(PARTITION BY item_id, onhand_qty
        ORDER BY journal_date) AS item_grp_nbr
  FROM Journal),

QtyByDateRanges
AS
(SELECT MIN(journal_date) AS start_date,
    MAX(journal_date) AS end_date,
    item_id, onhand_qty
  FROM ItemGroups
 GROUP BY item_id, onhand_qty, item_grp_nbr)

SELECT start_date, end_date, item_id, onhand_qty
 FROM QtyByDateRanges;
```

This might be easier to see with some data and intermediate steps:

```
INSERT INTO InventoryJournal
VALUES('2015-01-01', 'AA', 100),('2015-01-01', 'BB', 200),
   ('2015-01-02', 'AA', 100),('2015-01-02', 'BB', 200),
   ('2015-01-03', 'AA', 100),('2015-01-03', 'BB', 300);

start_date     end_date item_id   onhand_qty
==========================================
'2015-01-01'  '2015-01-03'        'AA'100
'2015-01-01'  '2015-01-02'        'BB'1200
'2015-01-03'  '2015-01-03'        'BB'1300
```

## 11.5.2 Relationships among Durations

These (start_time, end_time) pairs can have several relationships, which are easy to see if you draw time lines. Let's assume we have T1 and T2 pairs.

T1 and T2 do not overlap (Figure 11.1) means that the two durations do not share any points in time, or in code: ((T1.start_time < T2.end_time) OR (T1.start_time > T2.end_time)).

T1 occurs during T2 (Figure 11.2) means that ((T2.start_time <= T1.start_time) AND (T1.end_time <= T2.end_time)).

Two durations abut (Figure 11.3) when (T1.end_time = T2.start_time) and they can often be concatenated into a single (T1.start_time, T2.end_time) pair.

T1 overlaps T2 (Figure 11.4) can be found with the OVERLAPS predicate. That is defined in detail in another chapter. It is a good exercise to write it for yourself.

If you need these relationships frequently, it might be worth considering writing functions to make code easier to write and read. The general format would be <function name> (IN start_time_1 DATE, IN end_time_1 DATE, IN start_time_2 DATE, IN end_time_2 DATE).

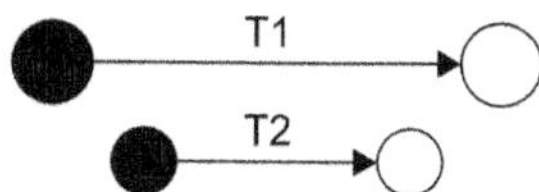


**Figure 11.1**
T1 and T2 Do Not Overlap

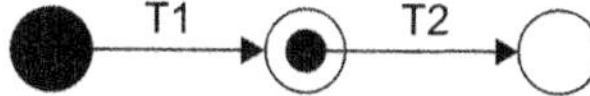


**Figure 11.2**
T1 Occurs during T2

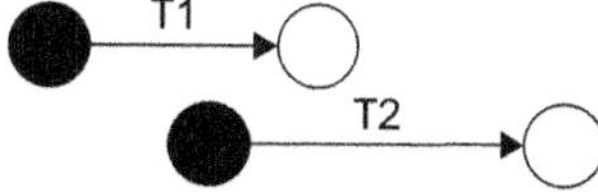


**Figure 11.3**
Two Durations Abut

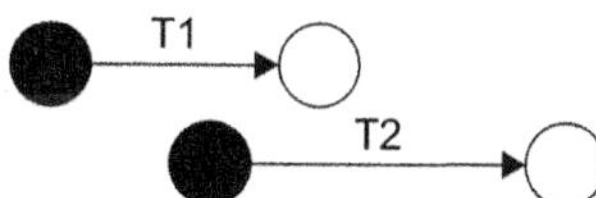


**Figure 11.4**
T1 Overlaps T2

# CHARACTER DATA TYPES

SQL-89 defined a `CHARACTER(n)` or `CHAR(n)` data type, which represents a fixed-length string of (n) printable characters, where (n) is always greater than zero. Some implementations allow the string to contain control characters, but this is not the usual case. The allowable characters were usually drawn from ASCII or Unicode character sets and most often uses those collation sequences for sorting.

SQL-92 added the `VARYING CHARACTER(n)` or `VARCHAR(n)`, which was already present in many implementations. A `VARCHAR(n)` represents a string that varies in length from 1 to (n) printable characters. This is important; SQL does not allow a string column of zero length, but you may find vendors who do, so that you can store an empty string.

SQL-92 also added `NATIONAL CHARACTER(n)` and `NATIONAL VARYING CHARACTER(n)` data types (or `NCHAR(n)` and `NVARCHAR(n)`, respectively), which are made up of printable characters drawn from ISO-defined UNICODE character sets. The literal values use the syntax `N'<string>'` in these data types.

SQL-92 also allows the database administrator to define collation sequences and do other things with the character sets. A Consortium (http://www.unicode.org/) maintains the Unicode standards and makes them available in book form (*Unicode Standard Version 5.2*, ISBN 978-1-936213-00-9 or at http://www.unicode.org/versions/Unicode5.2.0/).

When the Standards got to SQL:2006, we had added a lot of things to handle Unicode and XML data, but kept the basic string manipulations pretty simple compared to what vendors have. I am not going to deal with the Unicode and XML data in any detail because most working SQL programmers are using ASCII or a national character set exclusively in their databases.

## 12.1 Problems with SQL Strings

Different programming languages handle strings differently. You simply have to do some unlearning when you get to SQL. Here are the major problem areas for programmers.

Joe Celko's SQL for Smarties. DOI: 10.1016/B978-0-12-382022-8.00012-0

In SQL, character strings are printable characters enclosed in single quotation marks. Many older SQL implementations and several programming languages use double quotation marks or make it an option so that the single quotation mark can be used as an apostrophe. SQL uses two apostrophes together to represent a single apostrophe in a string literal. Double quote marks have a special meaning in SQL; they allow you to create a name that would otherwise be illegal.

Character sets fall into three categories: those defined by national or international standards, those provided by implementations, and those defined by applications. All character sets, however defined, always contain the `<space>` character by default. Character sets defined by applications can be defined to "reside" in any schema chosen by the application. Character sets defined by standards or by implementations reside in the Information Schema (named `INFORMATION_SCHEMA`) in each catalog, as do collations defined by standards and collations and form-of-use conversions defined by implementations. There is a default collating sequence for each character repertoire, but additional collating sequences can be defined for any character repertoire. This can be important in languages that have more than one collating sequence in use. For example, in German dictionaries, "öf" would come before "of," but in German telephone it is the opposite ordering. It is a good idea to look at http://userguide.icu-project.org/collation for a guide to the current Unicode rules.

### 12.1.1 Problems of String Equality

No two languages agree on how to compare character strings as equal unless they are identical in length and match position for position, exactly character for character.

The first problem is whether uppercase and lowercase versions of a letter compare as equal to each other. Only Latin, Greek, Cyrillic, and Arabic have cases; the first three have upper- and lowercases, and Arabic is a connected script that has initial, middle, terminal, and stand-alone forms of its letters. Most programming languages, including SQL, ignore case in the program text, but not always in the data. Some SQL implementations allow the DBA to set uppercase and lowercase matching as a system configuration parameter.

The Standard SQL has two functions that change the case of a string:

- `LOWER(<string expression>)` shifts all letters in the parameter string to corresponding lowercase letters.
- `UPPER(<string expression>)` shifts all letters in the string to uppercase.

Most implementations have had these functions (perhaps with different names) as vendor library functions.

Equality between strings of unequal length is calculated by first padding out the shorter string with blanks on the right-hand side until the strings are of the same length. Then they are matched, position for position, for identical values. If one position fails to match, the equality fails.

In contrast, the Xbase languages (FoxPro, dBase, and so on) truncate the longer string to the length of the shorter string and then match them position for position. Other programming languages ignore upper- and lowercase differences.

### 12.1.2 Problems of String Ordering

SQL-89 was silent on the collating sequence to be used. In practice, almost all SQL implementations used either ASCII or Unicode, which are both Roman I character sets in ISO terminology. A few implementations have a Dictionary or Library order option (uppercase and lowercase letters mixed together in alphabetic order: A, a, B, b, C, c, ...), and many vendors offer a national-language option that is based on the appropriate ISO standard.

National language options can be very complicated. The Nordic languages all share a common ISO character set, but they do not sort the same letters in the same position. German was sorted differently in Germany and in Austria. Spain decided to quit sorting ch and ll as if they were single characters. You really need to look at the ISO Unicode implementation for your particular product.

The Standard SQL allows the DBA to define a collating sequence that is used for comparisons. The feature is becoming more common as we become more globalized, but you have to see what the vendor of your SQL product actually supports.

### 12.1.3 Problems of String Grouping

Because the SQL equality test has to pad out the shorter of the two strings with spaces, you may find doing a `GROUP BY` on a `VARCHAR(n)` has unpredictable results:

```
CREATE TABLE Foobar (x VARCHAR(5) NOT NULL);
INSERT INTO Foobar VALUES ('a'), ('a '), ('a '), ('a ');
```

Now, execute the query:

```
SELECT x, CHAR_LENGTH(x)
FROM Foobar
GROUP BY x;
```

The value for CHAR_LENGTH(x) will vary for different products. The most common answers are 1, 4, and 5 in this example. A length of 1 is returned because it is the length of the shortest string or because it is the length of the first string physically in the table. A length of 4 is returned because it is the length of the longest string in the table. A length of 5 is returned because it is the greatest possible length of a string in the table.

You might want to add a constraint that makes sure to trim the trailing blanks to avoid problems.

## 12.2 Standard String Functions

SQL-92 defines a set of string functions that appear in most products, but with vendor-specific syntax. You will probably find that products will continue to support their own syntax, but will also add the Standard SQL syntax in new releases. Let's look at the basic operations.

String concatenation is shown with the || operator, taken from PL/I. However, you can also find the plus sign being overloaded in the Sybase/SQL Server family and some products using a function call like CONCAT(s1, s2) instead.

The SUBSTRING(<string> FROM <start> FOR <length>) function uses three arguments: the source string, the starting position of the substring, and the length of the substring to be extracted. Truncation occurs when the implied starting and ending positions are not both within the given string. The SQL:2006 Standard extends this to binary strings and allows you to define the length of substrings in bits. Don't worry about it until you have a special situation.

DB2 and other products have a LEFT and a RIGHT function. The LEFT function returns a string consisting of the specified number of leftmost characters of the string expression, and RIGHT, well, that is kind of obvious.

The fold functions are a pair of functions for converting all the lowercase characters in a given string to uppercase, UPPER(string>), or all the uppercase ones to lowercase LOWER(<string>).

The TRIM([[<trim specification>] [<trim character>] FROM] <trim source>) produces a result string that is the source string with an unwanted character removed. The <trim source> is the original character value expression. The <trim specification> is either LEADING or TRAILING or BOTH and the <trim character> is the single character that is to be removed. If you don't provide a <trim character>, then space is assumed. Most products still do not have the <trim character> option and work with only space.

The `TRIM()` function removes the leading and/or trailing occurrences of a character from a string. The default character if one is not given is a space. The SQL-92 version is a very general function, but you will find that most SQL implementations have a version that works only with spaces. Many early SQLs had two functions: `LTRIM` for left-most (leading) blanks and `RTRIM` for right-most (trailing) blanks.

A character translation is a function for changing each character of a given string according to some many-to-one or one-to-one mapping between two not necessarily distinct character sets.

The syntax `TRANSLATE(<string expression> USING <translation>)` assumes that a special schema object, called a translation, has already been created to hold the rules for doing all this.

`CHAR_LENGTH(<string>)`, also written `CHARACTER_LENGTH(<string>)`, determines the length of a given character string, as an integer, in characters. In most current products, this function is usually expressed as `LENGTH()` and the next two functions do not exist at all; they assume that the database will only hold ASCII or Unicode characters.

`BIT_LENGTH(<string>)` determines the length of a given character string, as an integer, in bits.

`OCTET_LENGTH(<string>)` determines the length of a given character string, as an integer, in octets. Octets are units of 8 bits that are used by the one and two (Unicode) octet characters sets. This is the same as `TRUNCATE (BIT_LENGTH (<string>)/8)`.

The `POSITION(<search string> IN <source string>)` determines the first position, if any, at which the `<search string>` occurs within the `<source string>`. If the `<search string>` is of length zero, then it occurs at position 1 for any value of the `<source string>`. If the `<search string>` does not occur in the `<source string>`, zero is returned. You will also see `LOCATE()` in DB2 and `CHAR_INDEX()` in SQL Server.

## 12.3 Common Vendor Extensions

The original SQL-89 Standard did not define any functions for `CHAR(n)` data types. The Standard SQL added the basic functions that have been common to implementations for years. However, there are other common or useful functions and it is worth knowing how to implement them outside of SQL.

Many vendors also have functions that will format dates for display by converting the internal format to a text string.

A vendor whose SQL is tied to a 4GL is much more likely to have these extensions simply because the 4GL can use them.

These functions generally use either a COBOL-style picture parameter or a globally set default format. Some of this conversion work is done with the CAST() function in Standard SQL, but since SQL does not have any output statements, such things will be vendor extensions for some time to come.

Vendor extensions are varied, but there are some that are worth mentioning. The names will be different in different products, but the functionality will be the same.

SPACE(n) produces a string of (n) spaces for (n > 0).

LPAD(n) and RPAD(n) pad a string on the left and right side with spaces.

REPLICATE (<string expression>, n) produces a string of (n) repetitions of the <string expression>. DB2 calls this one REPEAT() and you will see other local names for it.

REPLACE (<target string>, <old string>, <new string>) replaces the occurrences of the <old string> with the <new string> in the <target string>.

As an aside, here's a nice trick to reduce several contiguous spaces in a string to a single space to format text:

```
CREATE FUNCTION BigSqueeze
(IN original_str VARCHAR(100000))
RETURNS VARCHAR(100000)
DETERMINISTIC
READS SQL DATA
BEGIN
DECLARE marker_char CHAR(1);
SET marker_char = '$'; -- this never appears in string

RETURN
(CASE WHEN POSITION (SPACE(2) IN original_str) = 0
  THEN TRIM(BOTH SPACE(1) FROM original_str)
  ELSE REPLACE (
     REPLACE (
     REPLACE (TRIM(BOTH SPACE(1) FROM original_str),
           SPACE(2), SPACE(1)|| marker_char),
           marker_char || SPACE(1), SPACE(0)),
           marker_char, SPACE(0)) -- remove marker
  END);
END;
```

The SPACE(n) function returns a string of (n) blanks; this is easier to read and write than constant strings. If the input string has no multiple spaces inside it, then just trim off the leading and trailing blanks; this is faster than extra code to check for them.

If we do have multiple spaces inside the string, then do the trim and use three nested REPLACE() calls. Pairs of <space><space>

become `<space><marker>`, then `<marker><space>` pairs become an empty string.

The marker has to be a character that does not appear in the original string, so it could set as a constant rather than a local value.

REVERSE(<string expression>) reverses the order of the characters in a string to make it easier to search.

FLIP(<string expression>, <pivot>) will locate the pivot character in the string, then concatenate all the letters to the left of the pivot onto the end of the string and finally erase the pivot character. This is used to change the order of names from "military format" to "civilian format"; for example, FLIP('smith, John', ',') yields John Smith. This function can be written with the standard string functions, however.

NUMTOWORDS(<numeric expression>) will write out the numeric value as a set of English words to be used on checks or other documents that require both numeric and text versions of the same value.

## 12.3.1 Phonetic Matching

People's names are a problem for designers of databases. Names are variable-length, can have strange spellings, and are not unique. American names have a diversity of ethnic origins, which give us names pronounced the same way but spelled differently and vice versa.

Ignoring this diversity of names, errors in reading or hearing a name lead to mutations. Anyone who gets junk mail is aware of this; I get mail addressed to "Selco," "Selko," "Celco," as well as "Celko," which are phonetic errors, and also some that result from typing errors, such as "Cellro," "Chelco," and "Chelko" in my mail stack. Such errors result in the mailing of multiple copies of the same item to the same address. To solve this problem, we need phonetic algorithms that can find similar sounding names.

### *Soundex Functions*

The Soundex family of algorithms is named after the original algorithm. A Soundex algorithm takes a person's name as input and produces a character string that identifies a set of names that are (roughly) phonetically alike.

SQL products often have a Soundex algorithm in their library functions. It is also possible to compute a Soundex in SQL, using string functions and the CASE expression in the Standard SQL. Names that sound alike do not always have the same Soundex code. For example, "Lee" and "Leigh" are pronounced alike, but have different Soundex codes because the silent g in "Leigh" is given a code.

Names that sound alike but start with a different first letter will always have a different Soundex; for example, "Carr" and "Karr" will be separate codes.

Finally, Soundex is based on English pronunciation so European and Asian names may not encode correctly. Just looking at French surnames like "Beaux" with a silent x and "Beau" without it, we will create two different Soundex codes.

Sometimes names that don't sound alike have the same Soundex code. Consider the relatively common names "Powers," "Pierce," "Price," "Perez," and "Park," which all have the same Soundex code. Yet "Power," a common way to spell Powers 100 years ago, has a different Soundex code.

### *The Original Soundex*

Margaret O'Dell and Robert C. Russell patented the original Soundex algorithm in 1918. The method is based on the phonetic classification of sounds by how they are made.

In case you wanted to know, the six groups are bilabial, labiodental, dental, alveolar, velar, and glottal. The algorithm is fairly straightforward to code and requires no backtracking or multiple passes over the input word. This should not be too surprising, since it was in use before computers and had to be done by hand by clerks. Here is the algorithm:

**1.0** Capitalize all letters in the word. Pad the word with rightmost blanks as needed during each procedure step.

**2.0** Retain the first letter of the word.

**3.0** Drop all occurrences of the following letters after the first position: A, E, H, I, O, U, W, Y.

**4.0** Change letters from the following sets into the corresponding digits given:

```
1 = B, F, P, V
2 = C, G, J, K, Q, S, X, Z
3 = D, T
4 = L
5 = M, N
6 = R
```

**5.0** Retain only one occurrence of consecutive duplicate digits from the string that resulted after step 4.0.

**6.0** Pad the string that resulted from step 5.0 with trailing zeros and return only the first four positions, which will be of the form `<uppercase letter><digit><digit><digit>`.

An alternative version of the algorithm, due to Russell, changes the letters in step 3.0 to 9s, retaining them. Then step 5.0 is replaced by two steps:

**5.1** which removes redundant duplicates as before, followed by
**5.2** which removes all 9s and closes up the spaces.

This allows pairs of duplicate digits to appear in the result string. This version has more granularity and will work better for a larger sample of names.

The problem with the Soundex is that it was a manual operation used by the Census Bureau long before computers. The algorithm used was not always applied uniformly from place to place. Surname prefixes, such as "La," "De," von," or "van" are generally dropped from the last name for Soundex, but not always.

If you are searching for surnames such as "DiCaprio" or "LaBianca," you should try the Soundex for both with and without the prefix. Likewise leading syllables like "Mc," "Mac," and "O" were also dropped.

Then there was a question about dropping H and W along with the vowels. The United States Census Soundex did it both ways, so a name like "Ashcraft" could be converted to "Ascrft" in the first pass, and finally Soundexed to "A261," as it is in the 1920 New York Census. The Soundex code for the 1880, 1900, and 1910 censuses followed both rules. In this case Ashcraft would be A226 in some places. The reliability of Soundex is 95.99% with selectivity factor of 0.213% for a name inquiry.

This version is easy to translate into various dialects. The `WHILE` loop would be better done with a `REPEAT` loop, but not all products have that construct. The `TRANSLATE`s could be one statement but this is easier to read. Likewise, the `REPLACE` functions could be nested.

```
CREATE FUNCTION Soundex(IN in_name VARCHAR(50))
RETURNS CHAR(4)
DETERMINISTIC
LANGUAGE SQL
BEGIN ATOMIC
DECLARE header_char CHAR(1);
DECLARE prior_name_size INTEGER;
```

— split the name into a head and a tail

```
SET header_char = UPPER (SUBSTRING (in_name FROM 1 FOR 1));
SET in_name = UPPER (SUBSTRING (in_name FROM 2 FOR
   CHAR_LENGTH(in_name)));
```

— clean out vowels

```
SET in_name = TRANSLATE (in_name, '        ', 'AEHIOUWY');
```

—clean out spaces and add zeros

```
SET in_name = REPLACE (in_name, ' ', '') || '0000';
```

—consonant changes

```
SET in_name = TRANSLATE(in_name, '1111', 'BFPV');
SET in_name = TRANSLATE(in_name, '22222222', 'CGJKQSXZ');
SET in_name = TRANSLATE(in_name, '33', 'DT');
SET in_name = TRANSLATE(in_name, '4', 'L');
SET in_name = TRANSLATE(in_name, '55', 'MN');
SET in_name = TRANSLATE(in_name, '6', 'R');
```

—loop to clean out duplicate digits

```
WHILE 1 = 1
DO
 SET prior_name_size = CHAR_LENGTH (in_name);
 SET in_name = REPLACE(in_name, '11', '1');
 SET in_name = REPLACE(in_name, '22', '2');
 SET in_name = REPLACE(in_name, '33', '3');
 SET in_name = REPLACE(in_name, '44', '4');
 SET in_name = REPLACE(in_name, '55', '5');
 SET in_name = REPLACE(in_name, '66', '6');
```

—no size change means no more duplicate digits, time to output the answer

```
  IF prior_name_size = CHAR_LENGTH(in_name)
  THEN RETURN header_char || SUBSTRING (in_name FROM 1 FOR 3);
  END IF;
 END WHILE;
 END;
```

### *Metaphone*

Metaphone is another improved Soundex that first appeared in *Computer Language* magazine (Philips, 1990). A Pascal version written by Terry Smithwick (Smithwick, 1991), based on the original C version by Lawrence Philips, is reproduced with permission here:

```
FUNCTION Metaphone (p: STRING): STRING;
CONST
VowelSet = ['A', 'E', 'I', 'O', 'U'];
FrontVSet = ['E', 'I', 'Y'];
VarSonSet = ['C', 'S', 'T', 'G'];
 { variable sound - modified by following 'h' }
FUNCTION SubStr (A : STRING;
Start, Len : INTEGER) : STRING;
BEGIN
SubStr := Copy (A, Start, Len);
END;
```

```
FUNCTION Metaphone (p: STRING): STRING;
VAR
 i, l, n: BYTE;
 silent, new: BOOLEAN;
 last, this, next, nnext: CHAR;
 m, d: STRING;
BEGIN {Metaphone}
IF (p = ")
THEN BEGIN
 Metaphone:= ";
 EXIT;
 END;
{Remove leading spaces}
FOR i:= 1 TO Length (p)
DO p[i]:= UpCase (p[i]);
{Assume all alphas}
{initial preparation of string}
d:= SubStr (p, 1, 2);
IF d IN ('KN', 'GN', 'PN', 'AE', 'WR')
THEN p:= SubStr (p, 2, Length (p) - 1);
IF (p[1] = 'X')
THEN p:= 's' + SubStr (p, 2, Length (p) - 1);
IF (d = 'WH')
THEN p:= 'W' + SubStr (p, 2, Length (p) - 1);
{Set up for Case statement}
l:= Length (p);
m:= ";
  {Initialize the main variable}
new:= TRUE;
  {this variable only used next 10 lines!!!}
n:= 1;
  {Position counter}
WHILE ((Length (m) < 6) AND (n <> l))
DO BEGIN { Set up the 'pointers' for this loop-around}
 IF (n > 1)
 THEN last:= p[n-1]
 ELSE last:= #0;
 { use a nul terminated string}
 this:= p[n];
 IF (n < l)
 THEN next:= p[n+1]
 ELSE next:= #0;
 IF ((n+1) < l)
 THEN nnext:= p[n+2]
 ELSE nnext:= #0;
 new:= (this = 'C') AND (n > 1) AND (last = 'C');
 {'CC' inside word}
 IF (new)
 THEN BEGIN
```

```
  IF ((this IN VowelSet) AND (n = 1))
  THEN m:= this;
 CASE this OF
 'B': IF NOT ((n = 1) AND (last = 'M'))
  THEN m:= m + 'B';
 {-mb is silent}
'C': BEGIN {-sce, i, y = silent}
 IF NOT ((last = 's') AND (next IN FrontVSet))
 THEN BEGIN
   IF (next = 'i') AND (nnext = 'A')
   THEN m:= m + 'X'{ -cia- }
   ELSE IF (next IN FrontVSet)
    THEN m:= m + 's' { -ce, i, y = 's' }
    ELSE IF (next = 'H') AND (last = 's')
      THEN m:= m + 'K' { -sch- = 'K' }
      ELSE IF (next = 'H')
        THEN IF (n = 1) AND ((n+2) < = 1)
          AND NOT (nnext IN VowelSet)
          THEN m:= m + 'K'
          ELSE m:= m + 'X';
  END {Else silent}
 END;
{Case C}
'D': IF (next = 'G') AND (nnext IN FrontVSet)
  THEN m:= m + 'J'
  ELSE m:= m + 'T';
'G': BEGIN
 silent:= (next = 'H') AND (nnext IN VowelSet);

 IF (n > 1) AND (((n+1) = 1) OR ((next = 'n') AND
  (nnext = 'E') AND (p[n+3] = 'D') AND ((n+3) = 1))
{Terminal -gned}
 AND (last = 'i') AND (next = 'n'))
 THEN silent:= TRUE;
{if not start and near -end or -gned.)}
 IF (n > 1) AND (last = 'D'gnuw) AND (next IN FrontVSet)
 THEN {-dge, i, y}
 silent:= TRUE;
 IF NOT silent
 THEN IF (next IN FrontVSet)
  THEN m:= m + 'J'
  ELSE m:= m + 'K';
 END;
'H': IF NOT ((n = 1) OR (last IN VarSonSet)) AND (next IN
VowelSet)
  THEN m:= m + 'H';
 {else silent (vowel follows)}
'F', 'J', 'L', 'M', 'N', 'R': m:= m + this;
'K': IF (last <> 'C')
  THEN m:= m + 'K';
```

```
'P': IF (next = 'H')
   THEN BEGIN
    m:= m + 'F';
    INC (n);

    END {Skip the 'H'}
   ELSE m:= m + 'P';
'Q': m:= m + 'K';
's': IF (next = 'H')
   OR ((n > 1) AND (next = 'i') AND (nnext IN ['O', 'A']))
 THEN m:= m + 'X'
 ELSE m:= m + 's';
'T': IF (n = 1) AND (next = 'H') AND (nnext = 'O')
 THEN m:= m + 'T' { Initial Tho- }
 ELSE IF (n > 1) AND (next = 'i') AND (nnext IN ['O', 'A'])
  THEN m:= m + 'X'
  ELSE IF (next = 'H')
   THEN m:= m + '0'
   ELSE IF NOT ((next = 'C') AND (nnext = 'H'))
    THEN m:= m + 'T';
{-tch = silent}
'V': m:= m + 'F';
'W', 'Y': IF (next IN VowelSet)
  THEN m:= m + this;
 {else silent}
'X': m:= m + 'KS';
'Z': m:= m + 's';
END;
{Case}
INC (n);
END; {While}
END; {Metaphone}
Metaphone:= m
END;
```

### NYSIIS Algorithm

The New York State Identification and Intelligence System (NYSIIS) algorithm is more reliable and selective than Soundex, especially for grouped phonetic sounds. It does not perform well with ‘Y’ groups because ‘Y’ is not translated. NYSIIS yields an alphabetic string key that is filled or rounded to 10 characters.

```
(1) Translate first characters of name:
  MAC => MCC
  KN => NN
  K => C
  PH => FF
  PF => FF
  SCH => SSS
```

```
(2) Translate last characters of name:
  EE => Y
  IE => Y
  DT,RT,RD,NT,ND => D
(3) The first character of key = first character of name.
(4) Translate remaining characters by following rules,
   scanning one character at a time
  a. EV => AF else A,E,I,O,U => A
  b. Q => G Z => S M => N
  c. KN => N else K => C
  d. SCH => SSS PH => FF
  e. H => If previous or next character is a consonant
      use the previous character.
  f. W => If previous character is a vowel, use the
      previous character.
  Add the current character to result if the current
      character is to equal to the last key character.
(5) If last character is S, remove it
(6) If last characters are AY, replace them with Y
(7) If last character is A, remove it
```

The stated reliability of NYSIIS is 98.72% with a selectivity factor of 0.164% for a name inquiry. This was taken from Robert L. Taft, "Name Search Techniques," New York State Identification and Intelligence System.

## 12.4 Cutter Tables

Another encoding scheme for names has been used for libraries for over 100 years. The catalog number of a book often needs to reduce an author's name to a simple fixed-length code. Although the results of a Cutter table look much like those of a Soundex, their goal is different. They attempt to preserve the original alphabetical order of the names in the encodings.

But the librarian cannot just attach the author's name to the classification code. Names are not the same length, nor are they unique within their first letters. For example, "Smith, John A." and "Smith, John B." are not unique until the last letter.

What librarians have done about this problem is to use Cutter tables. These tables map authors' full names into letter-and-digit codes. There are several versions of the Cutter tables. The older tables tended to use a mix of letters (both upper- and lowercase) followed by digits. The three-figure single letter is followed by three digits. For example, using that table:

```
"Adams, J" becomes "A214"
"Adams, M" becomes "A215"
"Arnold" becomes "A752"
```

```
"Dana" becomes "D168"
"Sherman" becomes "S553"
"Scanlon" becomes "S283"
```

The distribution of these numbers is based on the actual distribution of names of authors in English-speaking countries. You simply scan down the table until you find the place where your name would fall and use that code.

Cutter tables have two important properties. They preserve the alphabetical ordering of the original name list, which means that you can do a rough sort on them. The second property is that each grouping tends to be of approximately the same size as the set of names gets larger. These properties can be handy for building indexes in a database.

If you would like copies of the Cutter tables, you can find some of them on the Internet. Princeton University Library has posted their rules for names, locations, regions, and other things (http://infoshare1.princeton.edu/katmandu/class/cutter.html).

You can also get hardcopies from this publisher:
Hargrave House
7312 Firethorn
Littleton, CO 80125
Web site: http://www.cuttertables.com

## 12.5 Nested Replacement

Another trick with `REPLACE()` is to nest it. Most implementations can go to 32 levels deep, so you can write things like:

```
REPLACE(
 REPLACE(
  ..
   REPLACE(foobar, 'Z', 'z'),
  ..
 'B', 'b'),
'A', 'a')
```

This is obviously a bad way to implement `LOWER()`, but you can use it to remove dashes, commas, embedded blanks, and other punctuation in a string. The advantage is that function calls avoid loops and recursion, so they should run quite fast.

# NULLs: MISSING DATA IN SQL

A discussion of how to handle missing data enters a sensitive area in relational database circles. Dr. E. F. Codd, creator of the relational model, favored two types of missing-value tokens in his book on the second version of the relational model, one for "unknown" (the eye color of a man wearing sunglasses) and one for "not applicable" (the eye color of an automobile). Chris Date, leading author on relational databases, advocates not using any general-purpose tokens for missing values at all. Standard SQL uses one token, based on Dr. Codd's original relational model.

Perhaps Dr. Codd was right—again. In Standard SQL, adding ROLLUP and CUBE created a need for a function to test NULLs to see if they were, in fact, "real NULLs" (i.e., present in the data and therefore assumed to model a missing value) or "created NULLs" (i.e., created as place holders for summary rows in the result set).

In their book, *A Guide to Sysbase and SQL Server* (ISBN 978-0201557107, 1992), David McGoveran and C. J. Date said, "It is this writer's opinion that NULLs, at least as currently defined and implemented in SQL, are far more trouble than they are worth and should be avoided; they display very strange and inconsistent behavior and can be a rich source of error and confusion." (Please note that these comments and criticisms apply to any system that supports SQL-style NULLs, not just to SQL Server specifically.)

SQL takes the middle ground and has a single general-purpose NULL for missing values. Rules for NULLs, in particular statements, appear in the appropriate sections of this book. This section will discuss NULLs and missing values in general.

People have trouble with things that "are not there" in some sense. There is no concept of zero in Egyptian, Mayan, Chinese, Roman numerals, and virtually all other traditional numeral systems. It was centuries before Hindu-Arabic numerals became popular in Europe. In fact, many early Renaissance accounting firms advertised that they did *not* use the fancy, newfangled notation and kept records in well-understood Roman numerals instead.

**Joe Celko's SQL for Smarties. DOI: 10.1016/B978-0-12-382022-8.00013-2**

Many of the conceptual problems with zero arose from not knowing the difference between ordinal and cardinal numbers. Ordinal numbers measure position (an ordering); cardinal numbers measure quantity or magnitude. The argument against the zero was this: If there is no quantity or magnitude there, how can you count or measure it? What does it mean to multiply or divide a number by zero? There was considerable linguistic confusion over words that deal with the lack of something.

There is a Greek paradox that goes like this:

1. No cat has 12 tails.
2. A cat has one more tail than no cat.
3. Therefore, a cat has 13 tails.

Likewise, it was a long time before the idea of an empty set found its way into mathematics. The argument was that if there are no elements, how could you have a set of them? Is the empty set a subset of itself? Is the empty set a subset of all other sets? Is there only one universal empty set or one empty set for each type of set?

Computer science now has its own problem with missing data. The Interim Report 75-02-08 to the ANSI X3 (SPARC Study Group 1975) had 14 different kinds of incomplete data that could appear as the result of queries or as attribute values. These types included overflows, underflows, errors, and other problems in trying to represent the real world within the limits of a computer.

Instead of discussing the theory for the different models and approaches to missing data, I would rather explain why and how to use NULLs in SQL. In the rest of this book, I will be urging you not to use them, which may seem contradictory, but it is not. Think of a NULL as a drug; use it properly and it works for you, but abuse it and it can ruin everything. Your best policy is to avoid them when you can and use them properly when you must.

## 13.1 Empty and Missing Tables

An empty table or view is a different concept from a missing table. An empty table is one that is defined with columns and constraints, but that has zero rows in it. This can happen when a table or view is created for the first time, or when all the rows are deleted from the table. It is a perfectly good table. By definition, all of its constraints are `TRUE`.

A missing table has been removed from the database schema with a `DROP TABLE` statement, or it never existed at all (you probably typed the name wrong). A missing view is a bit different. It can be absent because of a DROP VIEW statement or a typing error, too. But it can also be absent because a table or view from which it was built has been removed. This means that the view cannot be constructed at run time and the database reports a failure. If you used CASCADE behavior when you dropped a table, the view would also be gone; but more on that later.

The behavior of an empty TABLE or VIEW will vary with the way it is used. Look at sections of this book that deal with predicates that use a subquery. In general, an empty table can be treated either as a NULL or as an empty set, depending on context.

## 13.2 Missing Values in Columns

The usual description of NULLs is that they represent currently unknown values that may be replaced later with real values when we know something. Actually, the NULL covers a lot more territory, since it is the only way of showing any missing values. Going back to basics for a minute, we can define a row in a database as an entity, which has one or more attributes (columns), each of which is drawn from some domain. Let us use the notation E(A) = V to represent the idea that an entity, E, has an attribute, A, which has a value, V. For example, I could write "John(hair) = black" to say that John has black hair.

SQL's general-purpose NULLs do not quite fit this model. If you have defined a domain for hair color and one for car color, then a hair color should not be comparable to a car color, because they are drawn from two different domains. You would need to make their domains comparable with an implicit or explicit casting function. This is done in Standard SQL, which has a CREATE DOMAIN statement, but most implementations still do not have this feature yet. Trying to find out which employees drive cars that match their hair is a bit weird outside of Los Angeles, but in the case of NULLs, do we have a hit when a bald-headed man walks to work? Are no hair and no car somehow equal in color? In SQL-89 and higher, we would get an UNKNOWN result, rather than an error, if we compared these two NULLs directly. The domain-specific NULLs are conceptually different from the general NULL because we know what kind of thing is UNKNOWN. This could be shown in our notation as E(A) = NULL to mean that we know the entity, we know the attribute, but we do not know the value.

Another flavor of NULL is "Not Applicable," shown as N/A on forms and spreadsheets and called "I-marks" by Dr. E. F. Codd in his second version of the Relational Model. To pick an example near to my heart, a bald man's hair-color attribute is a missing-value NULL drawn from the hair-color domain, but his feather-color attribute is a "Not Applicable" NULL. The attribute itself is missing, not just the value. This missing-attribute NULL could be written as E(NULL) = NULL in the formula notation.

How could an attribute not belonging to an entity show up in a table? Consolidate medical records and put everyone together for statistical purposes. You should not find any male pregnancies in the result table (let us just ignore strange medical advances at http://www.malepregnancy.com/). The programmer has a choice as to how to handle pregnancies. He or she can have a column in the consolidated table for "number of pregnancies" and put a zero or a NULL in the rows where sex_code = 1 ('male' in the ISO Standards) and then add some CHECK() clauses to make sure that this integrity rule is enforced.

The other way is to have a column for "medical condition" and one for "number of occurrences" beside it. Another CHECK() clause would make sure male pregnancies do not appear. But what happens when the sex is known to be a person rather than a lawful entity like a corporation, and all we have is a name like 'Alex Morgan', who could be either sex? Can we use the presence of one or more pregnancies to determine that Alex is a woman? What if Alex is a woman who never had children? The case where we have NULL(A) = V is a bit strange. It means that we do not know the entity, but we are looking for a known attribute, A, which has a value of V. This is like asking "What things are colored red?," which is a perfectly good, though insanely vague, question that is very hard to ask in an SQL database.

If you want to try writing such a query in SQL, you have to get to the system tables to get the table and column names, then JOIN them to the rows in the tables and come back with the PRIMARY KEY of that row.

For completeness, we could play with all eight possible combinations of known and unknown values in the basic E(A) = V formula. But such combinations are of little use or meaning. The "total ignorance" NULL, shown as NULL(NULL) = NULL, means that we have no information about the entity, even about its existence, its attributes, or their values. But NULL(NULL) = V would mean that we know a value, but not the entity or the attribute. This is like the running joke from Douglas Adam's *Hitchhiker's Guide to the Galaxy*, in which the answer to the question, "What is the meaning of life, the universe, and everything?" is 42. (I found that interesting since I also teach a domino game named Forty-two, which is played in Texas.)

## 13.3 Context and Missing Values

Create a domain called Tricolor that is limited to the values 'Red', 'White', and 'Blue' and a column in a table drawn from that domain with a UNIQUE constraint on it. If my table has a 'Red' and two NULL values in that column, I have some information about the two NULLs. I know they will be either ('White', 'Blue') or ('Blue', 'White') when their rows are resolved. This is what Chris Date calls a "distinguished NULL," which means we have some information in it.

If my table has a 'Red', a 'White', and a NULL value in that column, can I change the last NULL to 'Blue' because it can only be 'Blue' under the rule? Or do I have to wait until I see an actual value for that row? There is no clear way to handle this situation. Multiple values cannot be put in a column, nor can the database automatically change values as part of the column declaration.

This idea can be carried farther with marked NULL values. For example, we are given a table of hotel rooms that has columns for check-in date and check-out date. We know the check-in date for each visitor, but we do not know his or her check-out dates. Instead we know relationships among the NULLs. We can put them into groups—Mr. and Mrs. X will check out on the same day, members of tour group Y will check out on the same day, and so forth. We can also add conditions on them: Nobody checks out before his check-in date, tour group Y will leave after Jan 7, 2015, and so forth. Such rules can be put into SQL database schemas, but it is very hard to do. The usual method is to use procedural code in a host language to handle such things.

Another context is statistical and probabilistic. Using my previous example of "Alex Morgan" as an ambiguous sex_code, I can take the birth date and make a guess. In the 1940–1950 time period, Alex was almost exclusively a male first name; in the 1990–2000 time period, Alex was more than half female. This gets into fuzzy logic and probabilistic data; I do not want to deal with it in this book.

David McGoveran has proposed that each column that can have missing data should be paired with a column that encodes the reason for the absence of a value (McGoveran 1993, 1994a,b,c). The cost is a bit of extra logic, but the extra column makes it easy to write queries that include or exclude values based on the semantics of the situation.

You might want to look at solutions statisticians have used for missing data. In many kinds of computations, the missing values are replaced by an average, median, or other value constructed from the data set.

## 13.4 Comparing NULLs

A NULL cannot be compared to another NULL (equal, not equal, less than, greater than, and so forth all return UNKNOWN). This is where we get SQL's three-valued logic instead of two-valued logic. Most programmers do not easily think in three values. But think about it for a minute. Imagine that you are looking at brown paper bags and are asked to compare them without seeing inside of either of them. What can you say about the predicate, "Bag A has more tuna fish than Bag B"—TRUE or FALSE? You cannot say one way or the other, so you use a third logical value, UNKNOWN.

If I execute "SELECT * FROM SomeTable WHERE SomeColumn = 2;" and then execute "SELECT * FROM SomeTable WHERE SomeColumn <> 2;" I expect to see all the rows of SomeTable between these two queries in a world of two valued logic. However, I also need to execute "SELECT * FROM SomeTable WHERE SomeColumn IS NULL;" to do that. The IS [NOT] NULL predicate will return only TRUE or FALSE.

A special predicate was introduced in the SQL:2003 Standard with the syntax,

```
<expression 1> IS DISTINCT FROM <expression 2>
```

which is logically equivalent to:

```
((<expression 1> = <expression 2> OR (<expression 1>IS NULL
   AND <expression 2> IS NULL))
```

Likewise the infixed comparison operator,

```
<expression 1> IS NOT DISTINCT FROM <expression 2>
NOT (<expression 1> IS DISTINCT FROM <expression 2>)
```

is equivalent to:

```
(<expression 1> <> <expression 2>
OR (<expression 1>IS NULL AND <expression 2> IS NOT NULL)
OR (<expression 1>IS NOT NULL AND <expression 2> IS NULL))
```

Besides being simpler and lending itself to better optimization, the IS [NOT] DISTINCT FROM operator gives you traditional two valued-logic. It is based on another concept in SQL—the difference between equality and grouping. Grouping, the equivalence relation used in the GROUP BY clause and other places in the language, treats all NULLs as one equivalence class.

## 13.5 NULLs and Logic

George Boole developed two-valued logic and attached his name to Boolean algebra forever (*An Investigation of the Laws of Thought*, ISBN 978-0486600284). This is not the only possible logical system. Do a Google search on "Multivalued logics" and you will come up with lots of material. SQL's search conditions look a lot like a proposal from Jan Łukasiewicz, the inventor of Polish Notation, for a three-valued logic.

Two-valued logic is the one that works best with a binary (two-state) computer and with a lot of mathematics. But SQL has three-valued logic: TRUE, FALSE, and UNKNOWN. The UNKNOWN value results from using NULLs in comparisons and other predicates, but UNKNOWN is a logical value and not the same as a NULL, which is a data value marker. That is why you have to say (x IS [NOT] NULL) in SQL and not use (x = NULL) instead.

Table 13.1 contains the three logical operators that come with SQL.

All other predicates in SQL resolve themselves to chains of these three operators. But that resolution is not immediately clear in all cases, since it is done at runtime in the case of predicates that use subqueries.

**Table 13.1 SQL's Three Operators**

| | NOT |
|---|---|
| TRUE | FALSE |
| UNKNOWN | UNKNOWN |
| FALSE | TRUE |

| AND | TRUE | UNKNOWN | FALSE |
|---|---|---|---|
| TRUE | TRUE | UNKNOWN | FALSE |
| UNKNOWN | UNKNOWN | UNKNOWN | FALSE |
| FALSE | FALSE | FALSE | FALSE |

| OR | TRUE | UNKNOWN | FALSE |
|---|---|---|---|
| TRUE | TRUE | TRUE | TRUE |
| UNKNOWN | TRUE | UNKNOWN | UNKNOWN |
| FALSE | TRUE | UNKNOWN | FALSE |

If you are into mathematical logic, then you noticed that we have no implication operator. In fact, it is not possible to map 2-Valued Logic implication into SQL's 3-Valued Logic. Therefore, we have no inference rules. David McGoveran pointed out that this means we have no inference rules in SQL, so it is not a predicate logic. That is why we say "search condition" and not "predicate" in the formal definition of SQL.

Implication is usually shown with a two-tailed arrow and a two-valued truth table, as in Table 13.2.

This is traditionally read as "a true premise (a) cannot imply a false conclusion (b)" but it does not work as well when you try to map it into 3-Valued Logic. We can write the usual implication as ¬(a∧¬b) in 2-Valued Logic, which is the English phrase I just gave in symbols, and we get the truth table in Table 13.3.

But implication ("Smisteru rule") can also be written (¬a∨b) in 2-Valued Logic and we get the truth table in Table 13.4 when we map it to 3-Valued Logic:

**Table 13.2 Implication (Traditional 2-Valued Logic)**

| a ⇒ b | TRUE | FALSE |
|---|---|---|
| TRUE | TRUE | FALSE |
| FALSE | TRUE | TRUE |

**Table 13.3 Implication (3-Valued, Version 1)**

| a imp b | TRUE | UNKNOWN | FALSE |
|---|---|---|---|
| TRUE | TRUE | **FALSE** | FALSE |
| UNKNOWN | TRUE | UNKNOWN | UNKNOWN |
| FALSE | TRUE | TRUE | TRUE |

**Table 13.4 Implication (3-Valued, Version 2)**

| a imp b | TRUE | UNKNOWN | FALSE |
|---|---|---|---|
| TRUE | TRUE | **UNKNOWN** | FALSE |
| UNKNOWN | TRUE | UNKNOWN | UNKNOWN |
| FALSE | TRUE | TRUE | TRUE |

Oops! When the premise is UNKNOWN in the first version of implication, we get this expansion:

```
¬(UNKNOWN ∧¬ FALSE)
¬(UNKNOWN ∧ TRUE)
¬(TRUE)
(FALSE)
```

but with the second implication we get:

```
(UNKNOWN ∨¬FALSE)
(UNKNOWN ∨ TRUE)
(TRUE)
```

If you are *not* into mathematical logic, then ignore the last paragraphs and keep thinking that a search condition is a predicate. And learn the differences in the DDL and DML logic rules.

### 13.5.1 NULLs in Subquery Predicates

People forget that a subquery often hides a comparison with a NULL. Consider these two tables:

```
CREATE TABLE Table1 (col1 INTEGER);
INSERT INTO Table1 (col1) VALUES (1), (2);

CREATE TABLE Table2 (col1 INTEGER);
INSERT INTO Table2 (col1) VALUES (1), (2), (3), (4), (5);
```

Notice that the columns are NULL-able. Execute this query:

```
SELECT col1
FROM Table2
WHERE col1 NOT IN (SELECT col1 FROM Table1);

Result
col1
======
3
4
5
```

Now insert a NULL and reexecute the same query:

```
INSERT INTO Table1 (col1) VALUES (NULL);
SELECT col1
FROM Table2
WHERE col1 NOT IN (SELECT col1 FROM Table1);
```

The result will be empty. This is counter intuitive, but correct. The `NOT IN` predicate is defined as:

```
SELECT col1
FROM Table2
WHERE NOT (col1 IN (SELECT col1 FROM Table1));
```

The `IN` predicate is defined as:

```
SELECT col1
FROM Table2
WHERE NOT (col1 = ANY (SELECT col1 FROM Table1));
```

which becomes:

```
SELECT col1
FROM Table2
WHERE NOT ((col1 = 1)
 OR (col1 = 2)
 OR (col1 = 3)
 OR (col1 = 4)
 OR (col1 = 5)
 OR (col1 = NULL));
```

The last expression is always `UNKNOWN`, so applying DeMorgan's laws the query is really:

```
SELECT col1
FROM Table2
WHERE ((col1 <> 1)
  AND (col1 <> 2)
  AND (col1 <> 3)
  AND (col1 <> 4)
  AND (col1 <> 5)
  AND UNKNOWN);
```

Look at the truth tables and you will see this always reduces to `UNKNOWN` and an `UNKNOWN` is always rejected in a search condition in a `WHERE` clause.

## 13.5.2 Logical Value Predicate

Standard SQL solved some of the 3-Valued Logic (3VL) problems by adding a new predicate of the form:

```
<search condition> IS [NOT] TRUE | FALSE | UNKNOWN
```

which will let you map any combination of 3VL to two values. For example, `((credit_score < 750) OR (eye_color = 'Blue')) IS NOT FALSE` will return `TRUE` if `(credit_score IS NULL)` or `(eye_color IS NULL)` and the remaining condition does not matter.

This is not widely implemented yet.

## 13.6 Math and NULLs

NULLs propagate when they appear in arithmetic expressions (+, −, *, /) and return NULL results. NULL propagation is so strong that even NULL/0 returns a NULL. See Chapter 10, Numeric Data Types, for more details.

## 13.7 Functions and NULLs

All standard computational functions propagate NULLs; that means a NULL argument gives NULL result of the appropriate data type. Most vendors propagate NULLs in the functions they offer as extensions of the standard ones required in SQL. For example, the cosine of a NULL will be NULL. There are two functions that convert NULLs into values.

1. NULLIF (V1, V2) returns a NULL when the first parameter equals the second parameter. The function is equivalent to the following case specification:

```
CASE WHEN (V1 = V2)
 THEN NULL
ELSE V1 END
```

2. COALESCE (V1, V2, V3, ..., Vn) processes the list from left to right and returns the first parameter that is not NULL. If all the values are NULL, it returns a NULL.

## 13.8 NULLs and Host Languages

This book does not discuss using SQL statements embedded in any particular host language. You will need to pick up a book for your particular language. However, you should know how NULLs are handled when they have to be passed to a host program. No standard host language for which an embedding is defined supports NULLs, which is another good reason to avoid using NULLs in your database schema.

Roughly speaking, the programmer mixes SQL statements bracketed by EXEC SQL and a language-specific terminator (the semicolon in Pascal and C, END-EXEC in COBOL, and so on) into the host program. This mixed-language program is run through an SQL preprocessor that converts the SQL into procedure calls the host language can compile; then the host program is compiled in the usual way.

There is an EXEC SQL BEGIN DECLARE SECTION, EXEC SQL END DECLARE SECTION pair that brackets declarations for the host parameter variables that will get values from the database via CURSORs.

This is the "neutral territory" where the host and the database pass information. SQL knows that it is dealing with a host variable because these have a colon prefix added to them when they appear in an SQL statement. A CURSOR is an SQL query statement that executes and creates a structure that looks like a sequential file. The records in the CURSOR are returned, one at a time, to the host program in the BEGIN DECLARE section with the FETCH statement. This avoids the impedance mismatch between record processing in the host language and SQL's set orientation.

NULLs are handled by declaring INDICATOR variables in the host language BEGIN DECLARE section, which are paired with the host variables. An INDICATOR is an exact numeric data type with a scale of zero—that is, some kind of integer in the host language.

The FETCH statement takes one row from the cursor, then converts each SQL data type into a host-language data type and puts that result into the appropriate host variable. If the SQL value was a NULL, the INDICATOR is set to minus one; if no indicator was specified, an exception condition is raised. As you can see, the host program must be sure to check the INDICATORs, because otherwise the value of the parameter will be garbage. If the parameter is passed to the host language without any problems, the INDICATOR is set to zero. If the value being passed to the host program is a non-NULL character string and it has an indicator, the indicator is set to the length of the SQL string and can be used to detect string overflows or to set the length of the parameter.

Other SQL interfaces such as ODBC, JDBC, and so on have similar mechanisms for telling the host program about NULLs even though they might not use cursors.

## 13.9 Design Advice for NULLs

*If you're that concerned with NULLs, than use the ISNULL function, that's what it's there for.*

**Jay, 2009-12-20 in a posting on the Microsoft SQL Server Programming Newsgroup**

I wish this quotation was a fake. First of all, Jay did not know that MS SQL Server has had COALESCE() for years, so he was writing SQL in a hillbilly dialect with the proprietary ISNULL() syntax. And then the content of the sentence is just wrong. Yet, I fear that he is not alone. A competent SQL programmer has a simple process for handling NULLs in his DDL.

First, declare all your base tables with NOT NULL constraints on all columns and then justify using NULLs in them. NULLs still confuse people who do not know SQL and NULLs are expensive. NULLs are usually implemented with an extra bit somewhere in the row where the column appears, rather than in the column itself. They adversely affect storage requirements, indexing, and searching.

NULLs are not permitted in PRIMARY KEY columns. Think about what a PRIMARY KEY that was NULL (or even partially NULL) would mean. A NULL in a key means that the data model does not know what makes the entities in that table unique from each other. That in turn says that the RDBMS cannot decide whether the PRIMARY KEY does or does not duplicate a key that is already in the table.

NULLs should be avoided in FOREIGN KEYs. SQL allows this "benefit of the doubt" relationship, but it can cause a loss of information in queries that involve joins. For example, given a part number code in Inventory that is referenced as a FOREIGN KEY by an Orders table, you will have problems getting a listing of the parts that have a NULL. This is a mandatory relationship; you cannot order a part that does not exist.

An example of an optional foreign key is a relationship between a Personnel table, a Jobs table, and a Job_Assignments table. The new hire has all of his personnel information and we have a bunch of open jobs, but we have not assigned him a job yet. We might want to show his job as a NULL in Job_Assignments.

NULLs should not be allowed in encoding schemes that are known to be complete. For example, employees are people and people are either male or female. On the other hand, if you are recording the sex of lawful persons (humans, corporations, and other legal entities), you need the ISO sex codes, which use 0 = unknown, 1 = male, 2 = female, and 9 = legal persons, such as corporations.

The use of all zeros and all nines for Unknown and N/A is quite common in numeric encoding schemes. This convention is a leftover from the old punch card days, when a missing value was left as a field of blanks that could be punched into the card later. FORTRAN read blanks in numeric fields as zeroes.

Likewise, a field of all nines would sort to the end of the file and it was easy to hold down the 9 key when the keypunch machine was in numeric shift.

However, you have to use NULLs in date columns when a DEFAULT date does not make sense. For example, if you do not know someone's birth date, a default date does not make sense; if a warranty has no expiration date, then a NULL can act as an "eternity" symbol. Unfortunately, you often know relative times, but it is difficult to express them in a database. For example, a pay raise occurs some time after you have been hired, not before.

A convict serving on death row should expect a release date resolved by an event: his termination by execution or by natural causes. This leads to extra columns to hold the status and to control the transition constraints.

There is a proprietary extension to date values in MySQL. If you know the year but not the month, you may enter '1949-00-00'. If you know the year and month but not the day, you may enter '1949-09-00'. You cannot reliably use date arithmetic on these values, but they do help in some instances, such as sorting people's birth dates or calculating their (approximate) age.

For people's names, you are probably better off using a special dummy string for unknown values rather than the general `NULL`. In particular, you can build a list of `'John Doe #1'`, `'John Doe #2'`, and so forth to differentiate them; and you cannot do that with a `NULL`. Quantities have to use a `NULL` in some cases. There is a difference between an unknown quantity and a zero quantity; it is the difference between an empty gas tank and not having a car at all. Using negative numbers to represent missing quantities does not work because it makes accurate calculations too complex.

When the host programming languages had no DATE data type, this could have been handled with a character string of '9999-99-99' for 'eternity' or 'the end of time'; it is actually the last date in the ISO 9601 Standard. When 4GL products with a DATE data type came onto the market, programmers usually inserted the maximum possible date for 'eternity'. But again, this will show up in calculations and in summary statistics. The best trick was to use two columns, one for the date and one for a flag. But this made for fairly complex code in the 4GL.

### 13.9.1 Avoiding NULLs from the Host Programs

You can avoid putting `NULL`s into the database from the host programs with some programming discipline.

1. Initialization in the host program: Initialize all the data elements and displays on the input screen of a client program before inserting data into the database. Exactly how you can make sure that all the programs use the same default values is another problem.
2. Automatic defaults: The database is the final authority on the default values.
3. Deducing values: Infer the missing data from the given values. For example, patients reporting a pregnancy are female; patients reporting prostate cancer are male. This technique can also be used to limit choices to valid values for the user.

4. Tracking missing data: Data is tagged as missing, unknown, in error, out of date, or whatever other condition makes it missing. This will involve a companion column with special codes. Most commercial applications do not need this, but a data quality audit could use this kind of detail.
5. Determining impact of missing data on programming and reporting: Numeric columns with NULLs are a problem because queries using aggregate functions can provide misleading results. Aggregate functions drop out the NULLs before doing the math and the programmer has to trap the SQLSTATE 01003 for this to make corrections. It is a Warning and will not create a ROLLBACK.
6. Preventing missing data: Use batch process to scan and validate data elements before it goes into the database. In the early 2000s, there was a sudden concern for data quality when CEOs started going to jail for failing audits. This has led to a niche in the software trade for data quality tools.
7. The data types and their NULL-ability constraints have to be consistent across databases (e.g., the chart of account should be defined the same way in both the desktop spreadsheets and enterprise level databases).

## 13.10 A Note on Multiple NULL Values

In a discussion on CompuServe in 1996 July, Carl C. Federl came up with an interesting idea for multiple missing value tokens in a database.

If you program in embedded SQL, you are used to having to work with an INDICATOR column. This is used to pass information to the host program, mostly about the NULL or NOT NULL status of the SQL column in the database. What the host program does with the information is up to the programmer. So why not extend this concept a bit and provide an indicator column? Let's work out a simple example.

```
CREATE TABLE Bob
(keycol INTEGER NOT NULL PRIMARY KEY,
valcol INTEGER NOT NULL,
multi_indicator INTEGER NOT NULL
CHECK (multi_indicator IN (0, -- Known value
    1, -- Not applicable value
    2, -- Missing value
    3 -- Approximate value));
```

Let's set up the rules: When all values are known, we do a regular total. If a value is "not applicable," then the whole total is "not applicable." If we have no "not applicable" values, then "missing value" dominates the total; if we have no "not applicable" and no "missing" values, then we give a warning about approximate values. The general form of the queries will be:

```
SELECT SUM (valcol),
 (CASE WHEN NOT EXISTS (SELECT multi_indicator
        FROM Bob
        WHERE multi_indicator > 0)
   THEN 0
   WHEN EXISTS (SELECT *
        FROM Bob
        WHERE multi_indicator = 1)
   THEN 1
   WHEN EXISTS (SELECT *
        FROM Bob
        WHERE multi_indicator = 2)
   THEN 2
   WHEN EXISTS (SELECT *
        FROM Bob
        WHERE multi_indicator = 3)
   THEN 3
   ELSE NULL END) AS totals_multi_indicator
FROM Bob;
```

Why would I muck with the valcol total at all? The status is over in the `multi_indicator` column, just like it was in the original table. Here is an exercise for you:

1. Make up a set of rules for multiple missing values and write a query for the `SUM()`, `AVG()`, `MAX()`, `MIN()`, and `COUNT()` functions.
2. Set degrees of approximation (±5, ±10, etc.) in the `multi_indicator`. Assume the valcol is always in the middle. Make the `multi_indicator` handle the fuzziness of the situation.

```
CREATE TABLE MultiNull
(groupcol INTEGER NOT NULL,
keycol INTEGER NOT NULL,
valcol INTEGER NOT NULL CHECK (valcol >= 0),
valcol_null INTEGER NOT NULL DEFAULT 0,
CHECK(valcol_null IN
(0, -- Known Value
1, -- Not applicable
2, -- Missing but applicable
3, -- Approximate within 1%
4, -- Approximate within 5%
5, -- Approximate within 25%
6, -- Approximate over 25% range)),
PRIMARY KEY (groupcol, keycol),
CHECK (valcol = 0 OR valcol_null NOT IN (1,2));
```

```
CREATE VIEW Group_MultiNull
(groupcol, valcol_sum, valcol_avg, valcol_max, valcol_min,
row_cnt, notnull_cnt, na_cnt, missing_cnt, approximate_cnt,
appr_1_cnt, approx_5_cnt, approx_25_cnt, approx_big_cnt)
AS
SELECT groupcol, SUM(valcol), AVG(valcol), MAX(valcol),
 MIN(valcol), COUNT(*),
 SUM (CASE WHEN valcol_null = 0 THEN 1 ELSE 0 END)
  AS notnull_cnt,
 SUM (CASE WHEN valcol_null = 1 THEN 1 ELSE 0 END)
  AS na_cnt,
 SUM (CASE WHEN valcol_null = 2 THEN 1 ELSE 0 END)
  AS missing_cnt,
 SUM (CASE WHEN valcol_null IN (3, 4, 5, 6) THEN 1 ELSE 0
   END)
  AS approximate_cnt,
 SUM (CASE WHEN valcol_null = 3 THEN 1 ELSE 0 END)
  AS appr_1_cnt,
 SUM (CASE WHEN valcol_null = 4 THEN 1 ELSE 0 END)
  AS approx_5_cnt,
 SUM (CASE WHEN valcol_null = 5 THEN 1 ELSE 0 END)
  AS approx_25_cnt,
 SUM (CASE WHEN valcol_null = 6 THEN 1 ELSE 0 END)
  AS approx_big_cnt
FROM MultiNull
GROUP BY groupcol;

SELECT groupcol, valcol_sum, valcol_avg, valcol_max,
   valcol_min,
   (CASE WHEN row_cnt = notnull_cnt
      THEN 'All are known'
     ELSE 'Not all are known' END) AS warning_message,
    row_cnt, notnull_cnt, na_cnt, missing_cnt,
     approximate_cnt,
    appr_1_cnt, approx_5_cnt, approx_25_cnt, approx_big_cnt
FROM Group_MultiNull;
```

Although this is a bit complex for the typical application, it is not a bad idea for a "staging area" database that attempts to scrub the data before it goes to a data warehouse.

# 14

# MULTIPLE COLUMN DATA ELEMENTS

The concept of a data element being atomic or scalar is usually taken to mean that it is represented with a single column in a table. This is not always true. A data element is atomic when it cannot be decomposed into independent, meaningful parts. Doing so would result in attribute splitting, a very serious design flaw we discussed in other parts of this book.

Consider an (x, y) coordinate system. A single x or y value identifies a continuum of points, while the pair has to be taken together to give you a single location on the plane. It would be inconvenient to put both coordinates into one column, so we model them in two columns. This is notation and not the abstract data element.

## 14.1 Distance Functions

Since geographical data is important, you might find it handy to locate places by their longitude and latitude, then calculate the distances between two points on the globe. This is not a standard function in most SQL products, but it is handy to know.

Assume that we have the values Latitude1, Longitude1, Latitude2, and Longitude2, which locate the two points, and that they are in radians, and we have trig functions.

To convert decimal degrees to radians, multiply the number of degrees by pi/180 = 0.017453293 radians/degree, where pi is approximately 3.14159265358979. If you can get more decimals, do it.

```
CREATE FUNCTION Distance
(IN latitude1 FLOAT, IN longitude1 FLOAT,
IN latitude2 FLOAT, IN longitude2 FLOAT)
RETURNS FLOAT
LANGUAGE SQL
DETERMINISTIC
BEGIN
```

Joe Celko's SQL for Smarties. DOI: 10.1016/B978-0-12-382022-8.00014-4

```
DECLARE r FLOAT;
DECLARE lat FLOAT;
DECLARE lon FLOAT;
DECLARE a FLOAT;
DECLARE c FLOAT;
SET r = 6367.00 * 0.6214;
```

— calculate the Deltas …

```
SET lon = longitude2 - longitude1;
SET lat = latitude2 - latitude1;
```

—Intermediate values …

```
SET a = SIN(lat / 2) + COS(latitude1)
    * COS(latitude2) * SIN(lon / 2);
```

—Intermediate result c is the great circle distance in radians …

```
SET c = 2 * ARCSIN(LEAST(1.00, SQRT(a)));
```

—Multiply the radians by the radius to get the distance

```
 RETURN (r * c);
END;
```

LEAST() function protects against possible round off errors that could sabotage computation of the ARCSIN() if the two points are very nearly antipodal. It exists as a vendor extension in Oracle and MySQL, but can be written with a CASE expression in Standard SQL.

Scott Coleman pointed out that the calculation of distance between two points using standard spherical geometry can be inaccurate for short distances (10 miles or less) because the sine function of very small angles approaches zero. The haversine approach (http://en.wikipedia.org/wiki/Haversine_formula) turns this around, so it is very accurate at small distances but has larger errors (about 10 miles) for points on opposite sides of the earth.

```
CREATE FUNCTION HaversineDistance
   (rlat1 FLOAT, rlon1 FLOAT, rlat2 FLOAT, rlon2 FLOAT)
RETURNS FLOAT
LANGUAGE SQL
DETERMINISTIC
BEGIN
```

—parameters are in radians

```
DECLARE c FLOAT;
SET c = POWER(SIN((rlat2 - rlat1) / 2.0)), 2)
  + COS(rlat1) * COS(rlat2) * POWER (SIN((rlon2 - rlon1) /
   2.0), 2);
```

```
RETURN (3956.088331329 * (2.0 * ATN2(SQRT(c),
   SQRT(1.0 - c))));
END;
```

Notice there is an assumption of trig functions in your SQL. If you need to convert from degrees, use:

```
SET DegToRad = CAST (180.0 / PI AS DOUBLE PRECISION)
```

And use it as a divisor. The atan2(x, y) function is used to convert from Cartesian(x, y) to polar (theta, radius) coordinates.

## 14.2 Storing an IPv4 Address in SQL

Although not exactly a data type, IP addresses are being used as unique identifiers for people or companies. If you need to verify them, you can send an e-mail or ping them. There are three popular ways to store an IP address: a string, an integer, and a set of four octets.

In a test conducted in SQL Server, all three methods required about the same amount of time, work, and I/O to return data as a string. The latter two have some additional computations, but the overhead was not enough to affect performance very much.

The conclusion was that the octet model with four `TINYINT` columns had three advantages: simpler programming, indexes on individual octets, and human readability. But you should look at what happens in your own environment. `TINYINT` is a one bit integer data type found in SQL Server and other products; `SMALLINT` is the closest to it in Standard SQL.

### 14.2.1 A Single `VARCHAR(15)` Column

The most obvious way to store IP addresses in a `VARCHAR(15)` column, like this '63.246.173.210', with a `CHECK()` constraint that uses a `SIMILAR TO` predicate to be sure that it has the "dots and digits" in the right positions. You have to decide the meaning of leading zeros in an octet and trim them to do string comparisons.

The good points are that programming is reasonably simple and it is immediately human-readable. The bad points are that this has a higher storage costs and it needs pattern matching string functions in searches. It also is harder to pass to some host programs that expect to see the octets to make their IP connections.

To convert the string into octets, you need to use a string procedure. You can write one based on the code given for parsing a comma-separated string into individual integers.

### 14.2.2 One INTEGER Column

This has the lowest storage requirements of all the methods and it keeps the address in one column. Searching and indexing are also minimal.

The bad side is more that programming; it is much more complex and you need to write user functions to break it apart into octets. It is also not very human-readable. Given an INTEGER value like 2130706433, can you tell me it represents '127.0.0.1' on sight?

```
CREATE FUNCTION IPIntegerToString (IN ip INTEGER)
RETURNS VARCHAR(15)
LANGUAGE SQL
DETERMINISTIC
BEGIN
DECLARE o1 INTEGER;
DECLARE o2 INTEGER;
DECLARE o3 INTEGER;
DECLARE o4 INTEGER;

IF ABS(ip) > 2147483647
THEN RETURN '255.255.255.255';
END IF;

SET o1 = ip / 16777216;
IF o1 = 0
THEN SET o1 = 255;
   SET ip = ip + 16777216;
ELSE IF o1 < 0
   THEN IF MOD(ip, 16777216) = 0
 THEN SET o1 = o1 + 256;
 ELSE SET o1 = o1 + 255;
    IF o1 = 128
    THEN SET ip = ip + 2147483648;
    ELSE SET ip = ip + (16777216 * (256 - o1));
    END IF;
 END IF;
   ELSE SET ip = ip - (16777216 * o1);
   END IF;
END IF;

SET ip = MOD(ip, 16777216);
SET o2 = ip / 65536;
SET ip = MOD(ip, 65536);
SET o3 = ip / 256;
SET ip = MOD(ip, 256);
SET o4 = ip;
```

— return the string

```
RETURN
CAST(o1 AS VARCHAR(3)) || '.' ||
```

```
CAST(o2 AS VARCHAR(3)) || '.' ||
CAST(o3 AS VARCHAR(3)) || '.' ||
CAST(o4 AS VARCHAR(3));
END;
```

### 14.2.3 Four SMALLINT Columns

The good points are that this has a lower storage cost than VARCHAR(15), searching is easy and relatively fast, and you can index on each octet of the address. If you have an SQL with a TINYINT (usually one byte) data type, then you can save even more space.

The bad point is that programming is slightly more complex.

```
CREATE TABLE FourColumnIP
(octet1 SMALLINT NOT NULL
    CHECK (octet1 BETWEEN 0 AND 255),
octet2 SMALLINT NOT NULL
    CHECK (octet2 BETWEEN 0 AND 255),
octet3 SMALLINT NOT NULL
    CHECK (octet3 BETWEEN 0 AND 255),
octet4 SMALLINT NOT NULL
    CHECK (octet4 BETWEEN 0 AND 255),
..);
```

You will need a view for display, but that is straightforward.

```
CREATE VIEW DisplayIP (IP_address_display)
AS
SELECT (CAST(octet1 AS VARCHAR(3))||'.'||
   CAST(octet2 AS VARCHAR(3))||'.'||
   CAST(octet3 AS VARCHAR(3))||'.'||
   CAST(octet4 AS VARCHAR(3))
FROM FourColumnIP;
```

## 14.3 Storing an IPv6 Address in SQL

The original designers of TCP/IP defined an IP address as a 32-bit number. The Internet Assigned Numbers Authority (IANA) manages the IP address space allocations globally. IANA works in cooperation with five Regional Internet Registries (RIRs) to allocate IP address blocks to Local Internet Registries (Internet service providers) and other entities.

The IP version 6 addresses are huge compared to IPv4 and are not likely to run out anytime soon. The problem is that it is a redesign of the Internet Protocol and not a simple extension. The address size was increased from 32 to 128 bits (16 bytes). The new design is so large that that subnet routing prefixes are easy to construct without any kludges. Large blocks can be assigned for efficient routing. Windows Vista, Apple Computer's Mac OS X, Linux distributions, and most other operating systems include native support for the IPv6 protocol.

### 14.3.1 A Single CHAR(32) Column

The most obvious way to store IPv6 addresses is in a CHAR(32) column without the colons or a CHAR(40) column with colons. The hexadecimal display format is a simple fixed format. The letters for 10 (a) through 15 (d) are usually done in lowercase to avoid confusion with digits. Use a CHECK() constraint that uses a SIMILAR TO predicate to be sure that it has the "colons and digits" in the right positions.

```
ipv6 CHAR(40) NOT NULL
 CHECK (ipv6 SIMILAR TO '([0-9a-d]:){7}[0-9a-d]')
```

Since the string is fixed length, it is easy to slice it up into substrings. The trick with searching for the substrings is to use underscores in a LIKE predicate instead of an ampersand wildcard or a regular expression. The simple LIKE predicate will match character for character rather than create a finite automaton under the covers.

## 14.4 Currency and Other Unit Conversions

Currency has to be expressed in both an amount and a unit of currency. The ISO 4217 currency code gives you a standard way of identifying the unit. Today, only Mauritania and Madagascar have nondecimal currencies. The value of the main unit is so low that the subunit is too small to be of any practical use and coins of the subunit are no longer used.

You will need to talk to the accounting department about the number of decimal places to use in computations. The rules for euros are established by the European Union and those for dollars are part of the GAAP (Generally Accepted Accounting Practices).

```
CREATE TABLE InternationalMoney
( ..
currency_code CHAR(3) NOT NULL,
currency_amt DECIMAL (12,4) NOT NULL,
..);
```

This mixed table is not easy to work with, so it is best to create VIEWs with a single currency for each group of users. This will entail maintaining an exchange rate table to use in the VIEWs.

```
CREATE VIEW EuroMoney (.. euro_amt, ..)
AS
SELECT .. (M1.currency_amt * E1.conversion_factor), ..
 FROM InternationalMoney AS M1,
    ExchangeRate AS E1
WHERE E1.to_currency_code = 'EUR'
  AND E1.from_currency_code = M1.curency_code;
```

But there is a gimmick. There are specific rules about precision and rounding that are mandatory in currency conversion to, from, and through the euro. Conversion between two national currencies must be "triangulated"; this means that you first convert currency #1 to euros, then convert the euros to currency #2. Six-figure conversion rates are mandatory, but you should check the status of "Article 235 Regulation" to be sure that nothing has changed since this writing.

## 14.5 Social Security Numbers

The closest thing the United States has to a Universal identification number is the Social Security Number (SSN). You are supposed to validate the SSN when you hire a new employee, but a lot of programmers have no idea how to do it. I am not going to go into the privacy issues, recent laws, or anything to do with legal aspects. This is a column for working programmers and all we care about is how to use these numbers in our code.

The SSN is composed of three parts, all digits and separated by dashes in the format "XXX-XX-XXXX." These parts are called the Area, Group, and Serial. For the most part (there are a few exceptions), the Area is determined by where the individual applied for the Social Security Number (before 1972) or resided at the time of application (after 1972). Table 14.1 shows the Area numbers used in the United States and its possessions.

If an Area number is shown more than once it means that certain numbers have been transferred from one State to another, or that an Area has been divided for use among certain geographic locations. The actual assignment is done based on the ZIP code given on the application. You can blame population shifts for this. You do not have to have a SSN to work in the United States. Since 1996, the IRS issued over eight million tax payer identification numbers to foreign workers without an SSN. In 2004 alone there were 900,000 such numbers issued.

The Group portion of the Social Security Number has no meaning other than to determine whether or not a number has been assigned. There was an urban myth that the ethnicity of the card holder was coded in the Group number and I have no

## Table 14.1 Area Numbers Used in the United States and Its Possessions

| | | | |
|---|---|---|---|
| 000-000 | Invalid code | 676-679 | |
| 001-003 | New Hampshire | 433-439 | Louisiana |
| 004-007 | Maine | 659-665 | |
| 008-009 | Vermont | 440-448 | Oklahoma |
| 010-034 | Massachusetts | 449-467 | Texas |
| 035-039 | Rhode Island | 627-645 | |
| 040-049 | Connecticut | 468-477 | Minnesota |
| 050-134 | New York | 478-485 | Iowa |
| 135-158 | New Jersey | 486-500 | Missouri |
| 159-211 | Pennsylvania | 501-502 | North Dakota |
| 212-220 | Maryland | 503-504 | South Dakota |
| 221-222 | Delaware | 505-508 | Nebraska |
| 223-231 | Virginia | 509-515 | Kansas |
| 691-699 | | 516-517 | Montana |
| 232-236 | West Virginia | 518-519 | Idaho |
| 232 | North Carolina | 520 | Wyoming |
| 237-246 | | 521-524 | Colorado |
| 681-690 | | 650-653 | |
| 247-251 | South Carolina | 525,585 | New Mexico |
| 654-658 | | 648-649 | |
| 252-260 | Georgia | 526-527 | Arizona |
| 667-675 | | 600-601 | |
| 261-267 | Florida | 764-765 | |
| 589-595 | | 528-529 | Utah |
| 766-772 | | 646-647 | |
| 268-302 | Ohio | 530 | Nevada |
| 303-317 | Indiana | 680 | |
| 318-361 | Illinois | 531-539 | Washington |
| 362-386 | Michigan | 540-544 | Oregon |
| 387-399 | Wisconsin | 545-573 | California |
| 400-407 | Kentucky | 602-626 | |
| 408-415 | Tennessee | 574 | Alaska |
| 756-763 | | 575-576 | Hawaii |
| 416-424 | Alabama | 750-751 | |
| 425-428 | Mississippi | 577-579 | District of Columbia |
| 587-588 | | 580 | Virgin Islands |
| 752-755 | allocated, but not issued yet | 580-584 | Puerto Rico |
| | | 596-599 | |
| 429-432 | Arkansas | 586 | Guam |

| | | | |
|---|---|---|---|
| 586 | American Samoa | 729-733 | Enumeration at Entry* |
| 586 | Philippine Islands | | |
| 666 | permanently unassigned | 734-899 | unassigned, for future use |
| 700-728 | Railroad Board - discontinued in 1963 | 900-999 | Invalid code** |

*No SSNs with an Area number above 728 have been assigned in the 700 series, except for 729 through 733 and 764 through 772.

**Although 900–999 are not valid Area numbers, they were used for program purposes when state aid to the aged, blind, and disabled was converted to a federal program administered by the Social Security Administration. You might also see this range of Area numbers used to construct student id numbers for foreign students in the days when schools used SSN as the student id number.

idea how that one got started. The Social Security Administration publishes a list of the highest group assigned for each Area once a month. You can download this data at http://www.ssa.gov/employer/highgroup.txt.

The only validation check on SSN is the way the Group numbers are issued. The first numbers issued are the odd numbers from 1 through 9, followed by the even numbers from 10 through 98, within each Area number. After all numbers in Group 98 of a particular area have been issued, then even Groups 2 through 8 are issued, followed by odd Groups 11 through 99.

For example, if the highest group assigned for area XXX is 72, then we know that the number XXX-04-XXXX is an invalid Group number because even Groups under 9 have not yet been assigned.

Fifty or 60 years ago, wallets came with fake Social Security cards already in them to make them look good when they were on display—much like the photos of a family in a dime store picture frame that looks better than your real family. Many people simply used these fake cards. The numbers look valid, but the IRS and other government agencies have a list of them.

The Serial portion of the Social Security Number has no meaning. The Serial number ranges from 0001 to 9999, but it is not assigned in strictly numerical order. The Serial number 0000 is never assigned.

There are commercial firms and nonprofit web sites that will verify SSNs for living and deceased persons. They usually tell you if the person holding that number is alive or dead, along with the year and place of issue. Some of these sites are set up by government agencies or universities to help employers, hospitals, or other concerned parties validate SSNs. The commercial sites can do bulk validations from files that you submit to them, at a cost of about one cent per SSN.

Here is a small sample to get you started. I am not recommending one source over another in this listing.

http://www.veris-ssn.com

http://www.searchbug.com/peoplefinder/ssn.aspx

http://privacy.cs.cmu.edu/dataprivacy/projects/ssnwatch/

http://info.dhhs.state.nc.us/olm/manuals/dma/eis/man/Eis1103.htm

http://www.comserv-inc.com/products/ssndtect.htm

## 14.6 Rational Numbers

A rational number is defined as a fraction (a/b) where a and b are both integers. Likewise, an irrational number cannot be defined that way. The classic example of an irrational number is the square root of two. Technical, a binary computer can only represent a subset of the rational numbers. But for some purposes, it is handy to actually model them as (numerator, denominator) pairs. For example, Vadim Tropashko uses rational numbers in the nested interval model for hierarchies in SQL (see my book, *Trees and Hierarchies in SQL for Smarties*, Morgan-Kaufmann, 2004; ISBN 978-1-55860-920-4). This means that you need a set of user-defined functions to do basic four-function math and to reduce the fractions.

Elementary school students, when questioned what the sum of 1/2 and 1/4 is will add the denominators and numerators like this: 1/2 + 1/4 = (1 + 1)/(2 + 4) = 2/6 = 1/3. This operation is called the mediant, and it returns the simplest number between the two fractions, if we use smallness of denominator as a measure of simplicity. Indeed, the average of 1/4 and 1/2 has denominator 8 and the mediant has 3.

# TABLE OPERATIONS

There are only four things you can do with a set of rows in an SQL table: insert them into a table, delete them from a table, update the values in their columns, or query them. The unit of work is a set of whole rows inside a base table.

When you worked with file systems, access was one record at a time, then one field within a record. Since you had repeated groups and other forms of variant records, you could change the structure of each record in the file.

The mental mode in SQL is that you grab a subset, as a unit, all at once in a base table and insert, update, or delete, as a unit, all at once. Imagine that you have enough computer power that you can allocate one processor to every row in a table. When you blow your whistle, all the processors do their work in parallel.

## 15.1 DELETE FROM Statement

The `DELETE FROM` statement in SQL removes zero or more rows of one table. Interactive SQL tools will tell the user how many rows were affected by an update operation and Standard SQL requires the database engine to raise a completion condition of "no data" if there were zero rows. There are two forms of `DELETE FROM` in SQL: positioned and searched. The positioned deletion is done with cursors; the searched deletion uses a `WHERE` clause like the search condition in a `SELECT` statement.

### 15.1.1 The `DELETE FROM` Clause

The syntax for a searched deletion statement is:

```
<delete statement: searched> ::=
DELETE FROM <target table> [[AS] <correlation name>]
[WHERE <search condition>]
```

The `DELETE FROM` clause simply gives the name of the updatable table or view to be changed. Notice that a correlation name is allowed in the `DELETE FROM` clause, as of the SQL:2003 Standard.

Joe Celko's SQL for Smarties. DOI: 10.1016/B978-0-12-382022-8.00015-6

The SQL model for an alias table name has always been that the engine effectively creates a new table with that new name and populates it with rows identical to the base table or updatable view from which it was built. If you had a correlation name, you would be deleting from this system-created temporary table and it would vanish at the end of the statement. The base table would never have been touched.

The new model is that an updatable VIEW is constructed. This leads to some problems when the same data is used as a VIEW and a base table at the same time.

For this discussion, we will assume the user doing the deletion has applicable DELETE privileges for the table. The positioned deletion removes the row in the base table that is the source of the current cursor row. The syntax is:

```
<delete statement: positioned> ::=
DELETE FROM <target table> [[AS] <correlation name>]
WHERE CURRENT OF <cursor name>
```

Cursors in SQL are generally more expensive than nonprocedural code and, in spite of the existence of standards, they vary widely in current implementations. If you have a properly designed table with a key, you should be able to avoid them in a DELETE FROM statement.

### 15.1.2 The WHERE Clause

The most important thing to remember about the WHERE clause is that it is optional. If there is no WHERE clause, all rows in the table are deleted. The table structure still exists, but there are no rows.

Most, but not all, interactive SQL tools will give you a warning when you are about to do this, and will ask for confirmation. Unless you wanted to clear out the table, immediately do a ROLLBACK to restore the table; if you COMMIT or have set the tool to automatically commit the work, then the data is pretty much gone. The DBA will have to do something to save you. And don't feel bad about doing it at least once while you are learning SQL.

Because we wish to remove a subset of rows all at once, we cannot simply scan the table one row at a time and remove each qualifying row as it is encountered; we need to have the whole subset all at once. The way most SQL implementations do a deletion is with two passes on the table. The first pass marks all the candidate rows that meet the WHERE clause condition. This is also when most products check to see if the deletion will violate any constraints. The most common violations involve trying to remove a value that is referenced by a foreign key ("Hey, we still have orders for those Pink Lawn Flamingos; you cannot drop them from inventory yet!"). But other constraints in CREATE ASSERTION statements, CHECK() constraints, or TRIGGERs can also cause a ROLLBACK.

After the subset is validated, the second pass removes it, either immediately or by marking them so that a housekeeping routine can later reclaim the storage space. Then any further housekeeping, such as updating indexes, is done last.

The important point is that while the rows are being marked, the entire table is still available for the WHERE condition to use. In many, if not most cases, this two-pass method does not make any difference in the results. The WHERE clause is usually a fairly simple predicate that references constants or relationships among the columns of a row. For example, we could clear out some Personnel with this deletion:

```
DELETE FROM Personnel
WHERE iq <= 100; -- constant in simple predicate
```

or,

```
DELETE FROM Personnel
WHERE hat_size = iq; -- uses columns in the same row
```

A good optimizer could recognize that these predicates do not depend on the table as a whole, and would use a single scan for them. The two passes make a difference when the table references itself. Let's fire employees whose IQs are below average for their departments.

```
DELETE FROM Personnel
WHERE iq < (SELECT AVG(P1.iq)
        FROM Personnel AS P1 -- must have correlation name
      WHERE Personnel.dept_nbr = P1.dept_nbr);
```

We have the following data:

Personnel

| emp_nbr | dept_nbr | iq |
|---|---|---|
| 'Able' | 'Acct' | 101 |
| 'Baker' | 'Acct' | 105 |
| 'Charles' | 'Acct' | 106 |
| 'Henry' | 'Mkt' | 101 |
| 'Celko' | 'Mkt' | 170 |
| 'Popkin' | 'HR' | 120 |
| .. | | |

If this were done one row at a time, we would first go to Accounting and find the average IQ, (101 + 105 + 106)/3.0 = 104, and fire Able. Then we would move sequentially down the table, and again find the average IQ, (105 + 106)/2.0 = 105.5 and fire Baker. Only Charles would escape the downsizing.

Now sort the table a little differently, so that the rows are visited in reverse alphabetic order. We first read Charles's IQ and compute the average for Accounting (101 + 105 + 106)/3.0 = 104, and retain Charles. Then we would move sequentially down the table, with the average IQ unchanged, so we also retain Baker. Able, however, is downsized when that row comes up.

It might be worth noting that early versions of DB2 would delete rows in the sequential order in which they appear in physical storage. Sybase's SQL Anywhere (nee WATCOM SQL) had an optional `ORDER BY` clause that sorted the table, then did a sequential deletion on the table. This feature was used to force a sequential deletion in cases where order does not matter, thus optimizing the statement by saving a second pass over the table. But it also can give the desired results in situations where you would otherwise have to use a cursor and a host language.

Anders Altberg, Johannes Becher, and I tested different versions of a `DELETE` statement whose goal was to remove all but one row of a group. The column dup_cnt is a count of the duplicates of that row in the original table. The three statements tested were:

```
D1:
DELETE FROM Test
 WHERE EXISTS (SELECT *
        FROM Test AS T1
       WHERE T1.dup_id = Test.dup_id
        AND T1.dup_cnt < dup_cnt)
D2:
DELETE FROM Test
 WHERE dup_cnt > (SELECT MIN(T1.dup_cnt)
          FROM Test AS T1
         WHERE T1.dup_id = Test.dup_id);
D3:
BEGIN ATOMIC
INSERT INTO WorkingTable(dup_id, min_dup_cnt)
SELECT dup_id, MIN(dup_cnt)
  FROM Test
 GROUP BY dup_id;
DELETE FROM Test
 WHERE dup_cnt > (SELECT min_dup_cnt
          FROM WorkingTable
         WHERE Working.dup_id = Test.dup_id);
END;
```

Their relative execution speeds in one SQL desktop product were:

```
D1: 3.20 seconds
D2: 31.22 seconds
D3: 0.17 seconds
```

Without seeing the execution plans, I would guess that statement D1 went to an index for the EXISTS() test and returned TRUE on the first item it found. On the other hand D2 scanned each subset in the partitioning of Test by dup_id to find the MIN() over and over. Finally, the D3 version simply does a JOIN on simple scalar columns. With Standard SQL, you could write D3 as:

```
D3-2:
DELETE FROM Test
 WHERE dup_cnt >
   (SELECT min_dup_cnt
     FROM (SELECT dup_id, MIN(dup_cnt)
          FROM Test
         GROUP BY dup_id)
        AS WorkingTable(dup_id, min_dup_cnt)
     WHERE Working.dup_id = Test.dup_id);
```

Having said all this, the faster way to remove redundant duplicates is most often with a CURSOR that does a full table scan.

### 15.1.3 Deleting Based on Data in a Second Table

The WHERE clause can be as complex as you wish. This means you can have subqueries that use other tables. For example, to remove customers who have paid their bills from the Deadbeats table, you can use a correlated EXISTS predicate, thus:

```
DELETE FROM Deadbeats
WHERE EXISTS (SELECT *
        FROM Payments AS P1
       WHERE Deadbeats.cust_nbr = P1.cust_nbr
        AND P1.paid_amt > = Deadbeats.due_amt);
```

The scope rules from SELECT statements also apply to the WHERE clause of a DELETE FROM statement, but it is a good idea to qualify all the column names.

### 15.1.4 Deleting within the Same Table

SQL allows a DELETE FROM statement to use columns, constants, and aggregate functions drawn from the table itself. For example, it is perfectly all right to remove everyone who is below average in a class with this statement:

```
DELETE FROM Students
 WHERE grade < (SELECT AVG(grade) FROM Students);
```

But the DELETE FROM clause does not allow for correlation names on the table in the DELETE FROM clause, so not all WHERE clauses that could be written as part of a SELECT statement will work in a DELETE FROM statement. For example, a self-join on the working table in a subquery is impossible.

```
DELETE FROM Personnel AS B1 --correlation name is INVALID SQL
 WHERE Personnel.boss_nbr = B1.emp_nbr
  AND Personnel.salary > B1.salary);
```

There are ways to work around this. One trick is to build a VIEW of the table and use the VIEW instead of a correlation name. Consider the problem of finding all employees who are now earning more than their boss and deleting them. The employee table being used has a column for the employee's identification number, emp_nbr, and another column for the boss's employee identification number, boss_nbr.

```
CREATE VIEW Bosses
AS SELECT emp_nbr, salary FROM Personnel;

DELETE FROM Personnel
WHERE EXISTS (SELECT *
      FROM Bosses AS B1
      WHERE Personnel.boss_nbr = B1.emp_nbr
       AND Personnel.salary > B1.salary);
```

Simply using the Personnel table in the subquery will not work. We need an outer reference in the WHERE clause to the Personnel table in the subquery, and we cannot get that if the Personnel table were in the subquery. Such views should be as small as possible so that the SQL engine can materialize them in main storage.

### *Redundant Duplicates in a Table*

Redundant duplicates are unneeded copies of a row in a table. You most often get them because you did not put a UNIQUE constraint on the table and then you inserted the same data twice. Removing the extra copies from a table in SQL is much harder than you would think. In fact, if the rows are exact duplicates, you cannot do it with a simple DELETE FROM statement. Removing redundant duplicates involves saving one of them while deleting the other(s). But if SQL has no way to tell them apart, it will delete all rows that were qualified by the WHERE clause. Another problem is that the deletion of a row from a base table can trigger referential actions, which can have unwanted side effects.

For example, if there is a referential integrity constraint that says a deletion in Table1 will cascade and delete matching rows in Table2, removing redundant duplicates from T1 can leave me with no matching rows in T2. Yet I still have a referential integrity rule that says there must be at least one match in T2 for the single row I preserved in T1. SQL allows constraints to be deferrable or nondeferrable, so you might be able to suspend the referential actions that the transaction below would cause:

```
BEGIN
INSERT INTO WorkingTable --use DISTINCT to kill
   duplicates
SELECT DISTINCT * FROM MessedUpTable;

DELETE FROM MessedUpTable; --clean out messed-up table
INSERT INTO MessedUpTable --put working table into it
SELECT * FROM WorkingTable;

DROP TABLE WorkingTable; --get rid of working table
END;
```

### *Redundant Duplicates Removal with ROWID*

Leonard C. Medel came up with several interesting ways to delete redundant duplicate rows from a table in an Oracle database.

Let's assume that we have a table:

```
CREATE TABLE Personnel
(emp_id INTEGER NOT NULL,
name CHAR(30) NOT NULL,
..);
```

The classic Oracle "delete dups" solution is the statement:

```
DELETE FROM Personnel
WHERE ROWID < (SELECT MAX(P1.ROWID)
      FROM Personnel AS P1
      WHERE P1.dup_id = Personnel.dup_id
       AND P1.name = Personnel.name);
       AND ..);
```

The column, or more properly pseudo-column, ROWID is based on the physical location of a row in storage. It can change after a user session but not during the session. It is the fastest possible physical access method into an Oracle table because it goes directly to the physical disk address of the data. It is also a complete violation of Dr. Codd's rules that require that the physical representation of the data be hidden from the users.

Doing a quick test on a 100,000 row table, Mr. Medel achieved about a tenfold improvement with these two alternatives. In English, the first alternative is find the highest ROWID for each group of one or more duplicate rows, and then delete every row, except the one with highest ROWID.

```
DELETE FROM Personnel
WHERE ROWID
  IN (SELECT P2.ROWID
      FROM Personnel AS P2,
        (SELECT P3.dup_id, P3.name, ..
             MAX(P3.ROWID) AS max_rowid
          FROM Personnel AS P3
          GROUP BY P3.dup_id, P3.name, ..)
        AS P4
          WHERE P2.ROWID <> P4.max_rowid
           AND P2.dup_id = P4.dup_id
           AND P2.name = P4.name);
```

Notice that the `GROUP BY` clause needs all the columns in the table.

The second approach is to notice that the set of all rows in the table minus the set of rows we want to keep defines the set of rows to delete. This gives us the following statement:

```
DELETE FROM Personnel
WHERE ROWID
  IN (SELECT P2.ROWID
      FROM Personnel AS P2
      EXCEPT
      SELECT MAX(P3.ROWID)
       FROM Personnel AS P3
       GROUP BY P3.dup_id, P3.name, ..);
```

The reason that both of these approaches are faster than the short classic version is that they avoid a correlated subquery expression in the `WHERE` clause.

A modern version uses the `ROW_NUMBER()` functions to get an equivalent of the Oracle `ROWID` in an updatable `VIEW`:

```
CREATE VIEW OrderedPersonnel
AS
SELECT *, ROW_NUMBER() OVER (PARTITION BY <<all columns>>)
   AS r
 FROM Personnel;

DELETE FROM OrderedPersonnel
WHERE r > 1;
```

### 15.1.5 Deleting in Multiple Tables without DRI Actions

There is no way to directly delete rows from more than one table in a single DELETE FROM statement. There are three approaches to removing related rows from multiple tables. One is to use a temporary table of the deletion values; another is to use referential integrity actions; the third is to use INSTEAD OF triggers on a view or base table. For the purposes of this section, let us assume that we have a database with an Orders table and an Inventory table. Our business rule is that when something is out of stock, we delete it from all the orders.

Assume that no referential integrity constraints have been declared at all. First create a temporary table of the products to be deleted based on your search criteria, then use that table in a correlated subquery to remove rows from each table involved.

```
CREATE MODULE Foobar
CREATE LOCAL TEMPORARY TABLE Discontinue
(part_nbr INTEGER NOT NULL UNIQUE)
ON COMMIT DELETE ROWS;
..
PROCEDURE CleanInventory(..)
BEGIN ATOMIC
INSERT INTO Discontinue
SELECT DISTINCT part_nbr --pick out the items to be removed
 FROM ..
WHERE .. ;--using whatever criteria you require
DELETE FROM Orders
WHERE part_nbr IN (SELECT part_nbr FROM Discontinue);
DELETE FROM Inventory
WHERE part_nbr IN (SELECT part_nbr FROM Discontinue);
COMMIT WORK;
END;
..
END MODULE;
```

In the Standard SQL model, the temporary table is persistent in the schema, but its content is not. TEMPORARY tables are always empty at the start of a session and they always appear to belong to only the user of the session. The GLOBAL option means that each application gets one copy of the table for all the modules, whereas LOCAL would limit the scope to the module in which it is declared.

## 15.2 INSERT INTO Statement

The INSERT INTO statement is the only way to get new data into a base table. In practice, there are always other tools for loading large amounts of data into a table, but they are very vendor dependent.

## 15.2.1 INSERT INTO Clause

The syntax for INSERT INTO is:

```
<insert statement> ::= INSERT INTO <insertion target>
   <insert columns and source>
<insertion target> ::= <table name>
```

Notice that the target is a table name and not an alias.

```
<insert columns and source> ::=
<from subquery> | <from constructor> | <from default>

<from subquery> ::=
[<left paren> <insert column list> <right paren>]
[<override clause>] <query expression>

<from constructor> ::=
[<left paren> <insert column list> <right paren>]
[<override clause>]
<contextually typed table value constructor>

<override clause> ::=
OVERRIDING USER VALUE | OVERRIDING SYSTEM VALUE

<from default> ::= DEFAULT VALUES

<insert column list> ::= <column name list>
```

The two basic forms of an INSERT INTO are a table constant (usually a single row) insertion and a query insertion. The table constant insertion is done with a VALUES() clause. The list of insert values usually consists of constants or explicit NULLs, but in theory they could be almost any expression, including scalar SELECT subqueries.

The DEFAULT VALUES clause is a shorthand for VALUES (DEFAULT, DEFAULT,..., DEFAULT), so it is just shorthand for a particular single row insertion.

The tabular constant insertion is a simple tool, mostly used in interactive sessions to put in small amounts of data. A query insertion executes the query and produces a working table, which is inserted into the target table all at once. In both cases, the optional list of columns in the target table has to be union-compatible with the columns in the query or with the values in the VALUES clause. Any column not in the list will be assigned NULL or its explicit DEFAULT value.

The <override clause> is part of SQL:2006 and needs a little explanation, even though it is not widely available. It has to do with how the insertion will handle an IDENTITY column whose values are generated by default. It is actually a more complicated mess that I do not wish to discuss.

## 15.2.2 The Nature of Inserts

In theory, an insert using a query will place the rows from the query in the target table all at once. The set-oriented nature of an insertion means that a statement like

```
INSERT INTO SomeTable (somekey, transaction_time)
SELECT millions, CURRENT_TIMESTAMP
FROM HugeTable;
```

will have one value for `transaction_time` in all the rows of the result, no matter how long it takes to load them into SomeTable. Keeping things straight requires a lot of checking behind the scenes. The insertion can fail if just one row violates a constraint on the target table. The usual physical implementation is to put the rows into the target table, but to mark the work as uncommitted until the whole transaction has been validated. Once the system knows that the insertion is to be committed, it must rebuild all the indexes. Rebuilding indexes will lock out other users and might require sorting the table if the table had a clustered index. If you have had experience with a file system, your first thought might be to drop the indexes, insert the new data, sort the table, and re-index it. The utility programs for index creation can actually benefit from having a known ordering. Unfortunately, this trick does not always work in SQL. The indexes maintain the uniqueness and referential integrity constraints and cannot be easily dropped and restored. Files stand independently of each other; tables are part of a whole database.

## 15.2.3 Bulk Load and Unload Utilities

All versions of SQL have a language extension or utility program that will let you read data from an external file directly into a table. There is no standard for this tool, so they are all different. Most of these utilities require the name of the file and the format in which it is written. The simpler versions of the utility just read the file and put it into a single target table. At the other extreme, Oracle uses a miniature language that can do simple editing as each record is read. If you use a simpler tool, it is a good idea to build a working table in which you stage the data for cleanup before loading it into the actual target table. You can apply edit routines, look for duplicates, and put the bad data into another working table for inspection. Some of these utilities will also build the table if it does not already exist. This, of course, requires the metadata for the table definition, which is usually stored with the data as a result of a previous bulk unload (or export).

The corresponding output utility, which converts a table into a file, usually offers a choice of format options; any computations and selection can be done in SQL. Some of these programs will accept a SELECT statement or a VIEW; some will only convert a base table. Most tools now have an option to output INSERT INTO statements along with the appropriate CREATE TABLE and CREATE INDEX statements.

## 15.3 The UPDATE Statement

The function of the UPDATE statement in SQL is to change the values in zero or more columns of zero or more rows of one table. SQL implementations will tell you how many rows were affected by an update operation or as a minimum return the SQLSTATE value for zero rows affected. There are two forms of UPDATE statements: positioned and searched. The positioned UPDATE is done with cursors; the searched UPDATE uses a WHERE that resembles the search condition in a SELECT statement.

Cursors allow the updating of the CURRENT OF <cursor name> row; that is covered in the chapter on CURSORs.

### 15.3.1 The UPDATE Clause

The syntax for a searched update statement is

```
<update statement> :: =
 UPDATE <table name> [[AS] <correlation name>]
   SET <set clause list>
 [WHERE <search condition>]

<set clause list> :: =
 <set clause> [{, <set clause>}..]

<set clause> :: = <object column> = <update source>

<update source> :: = <value expression> | NULL | DEFAULT

<object column> :: = <column name>
```

The UPDATE clause simply gives the name of the base table or updatable view to be changed. Originally, no correlation name is allowed in the UPDATE clause. The SQL model for an alias table name was that the engine effectively creates a new table with that new name and populates it with rows identical to the base table or updatable view from which it was built. If you had a correlation name, you would be deleting from this system-created temporary table and it would vanish at the end of the statement. The base table would never have been touched. Having said this, the SQL:2003 Standard allows for a correlation name and the fiction is that an updatable VIEW is created on the base table or original view.

The SET clause is a list of columns to be changed or made; the WHERE clause tells the statement which rows to use. For this discussion, we will assume the user doing the update has applicable UPDATE privileges for each <object column>.

Standard SQL:2003 allows a row constructor in the SET clause. The syntax looks like this.

```
UPDATE Foobar
 SET (a, b, c) = (1, 2, 3)
WHERE x < 12;
```

This is shorthand for the usual syntax, where the row constructor values are matched position for position with the SET clause column list.

## 15.3.2 The WHERE Clause

As mentioned, the most important thing to remember about the WHERE clause is that it is optional. If there is no WHERE clause, all rows in the table are changed. This is a common error; if you make it, immediately execute a ROLLBACK statement or call the Database Administrator for help.

All rows that test TRUE for the <search condition> are marked as a subset and not as individual rows. It is also possible that this subset will be empty. This subset is used to construct a new set of rows that will be inserted into the table when the subset is deleted from the table. Note that the empty subset is a valid update that will fire declarative referential actions and triggers.

## 15.3.3 The SET Clause

Each assignment in the <set clause list> is executed in parallel and each SET clause changes all the qualified rows at once. Or at least that is the theoretical model. In practice, implementations will first mark all the qualified rows in the table in one pass, using the WHERE clause. If there were no problems, then the SQL engine makes a copy of each marked row in working storage. Each SET clause is executed based on the old row image and the results are put in the new row image. Finally, the old rows are deleted and the new rows are inserted. If an error occurs during all this, then the system does a ROLLBACK, the table is left unchanged, and the errors are reported. This parallelism is not like what you find in a traditional third-generation programming language, so it may be hard to learn.

For example, this statement is illegal:

```
UPDATE MyTable
SET a = b, a = c;
```

In a traditional programming language, the second SET clause would take effect as the statement is executed left to right. In SQL, this leads to the error of trying to put two values, b and c, in column a.

This feature lets you write a statement that will swap the values in two columns, thus:

```
UPDATE MyTable
SET a = b, b = a;
```

This is not the same thing as:

```
BEGIN ATOMIC
UPDATE MyTable
SET a = b;
UPDATE MyTable
SET b = a;
END;
```

In the first UPDATE, columns a and b will swap values in each row. In the second pair of UPDATEs, column a will get all the values of column b in each row. In the second UPDATE of the pair, a, which now has the same value as the original value of b, will be written back into column b—no change at all. There are some limits as to what the value expression can be. The same column cannot appear more than once in a <set clause list>—which makes sense, given the parallel nature of the statement. Since both go into effect at the same time, you would not know which SET clause to use.

## 15.3.4 Updating with a Second Table

The right way to do this today is to use the MERGE statement. But you will see old code that uses some of these tricks.

Most updating is done with simple expressions of the form SET <column name> = <constant value>, because UPDATEs are done via data entry programs. It is also possible to have the <column name> on both sides of the equal sign! This will not change any values in the table, but can be used as a way to trigger referential actions that have an ON UPDATE condition. However, the <set clause list> does not have to contain only simple expressions. It is possible to use one table to post summary data to another. The scope of the <table name> is the entire <update statement>, so it can be referenced in the WHERE clause. This is easier to explain with an example. Assume we have the following tables:

```
CREATE TABLE Customers
(cust_nbr INTEGER NOT NULL PRIMARY KEY,
acct_amt DECIMAL(8,2) NOT NULL);

CREATE TABLE Payments
(trans_nbr INTEGER NOT NULL PRIMARY KEY,
cust_nbr INTEGER NOT NULL,
trans_amt DECIMAL(8,2) NOT NULL);
```

The problem is to post all the payment amounts to the balance in the Customers table, overwriting the old balance. Such a posting is usually a batch operation, so a searched UPDATE statement seems the logical approach.

```
UPDATE Customers
 SET acct_amt
   = acct_amt
     - (SELECT SUM(amt)
         FROM Payments AS P1
         WHERE Customers.cust_nbr = P1.cust_nbr)
WHERE EXISTS
  (SELECT *
    FROM Payments AS P2
    WHERE Customers.cust_nbr = P2.cust_nbr);
```

When there is no payment, the scalar query will return an empty set. The SUM() of an empty set is always NULL. One of the most common programming errors made when using this trick is to write a query that may return more than one row. If you did not think about it, you might have written the last example as:

```
UPDATE Customers
 SET acct_amt
   = acct_amt
     - (SELECT payment_amt
         FROM Payments AS P1
         WHERE Customers.cust_nbr = P1.cust_nbr)
WHERE EXISTS
  (SELECT *
    FROM Payments AS P2
    WHERE Customers.cust_nbr = P2.cust_nbr);
```

But consider the case where a customer has made more than one payment and we have both of them in the Payments table; the whole transaction will fail. The UPDATE statement should return an error message about cardinality violations and ROLLBACK the entire UPDATE statement. In the first example, however, we know that we will get a scalar result because there is only one SUM(amt).

Here is a way to update only the nonambiguous rows in a table from another table.

```
WITH NP(gtin, price, new_price, cardinality_cnt)
AS
(SELECT X.*
 FROM (SELECT P.gtin, P.price, N.price,
        COUNT(*)OVER(PARTITION BY P.gtin)
      FROM PriceList AS P,
        NewPriceList AS N
      WHERE P.gtin = N.gtin)
    AS X (gtin, price, new_price, cardinality_cnt)
 WHERE X.cardinality_cnt = 1),

UPDATE PriceList
 SET price
    = (SELECT NP.new_price
        FROM NP
       WHERE PriceList.gtin = NP.gtin)
WHERE EXISTS
    (SELECT *
       FROM NP
      WHERE PriceList.gtin = NP.gtin);
```

The second common programming error that is made with this kind of UPDATE is to use an aggregate function that does not return zero when it is applied to an empty table, such as the AVG(). Suppose we wanted to post the average payment amount made by the Customers; we could not just replace SUM() with AVG() and acct_amt with average balance in the previous UPDATE. Instead, we would have to add a WHERE clause to the UPDATE that gives us only those customers who made a payment, thus:

```
UPDATE Customers
 SET payment = (SELECT AVG(P1.amt)
         FROM Payments AS P1
        WHERE Customers.cust_nbr = P1.cust_nbr)
WHERE EXISTS (SELECT *
         FROM Payments AS P1
        WHERE Customers.cust_nbr = P1.cust_nbr);
```

You can use the WHERE clause to avoid NULLs in cases where a NULL would propagate in a calculation.

Another solution is to use a COALESCE() function to take care of the empty subquery result problem. The general form of this statement is:

```
UPDATE T1
 SET c1 = COALESCE ((SELECT c1
             FROM T2
             WHERE T1.keycol = T2.keycol), T1.c1),
   c2 = COALESCE ((SELECT c2
             FROM T2
             WHERE T1.keycol = T2.keycol), T1.c2),
   ..
WHERE .. ;
```

This will also leave the unmatched rows alone, but it will do a table scan on T1. Jeremy Rickard improved this by putting the `COALESCE()` inside the subquery `SELECT` list. This assumes that you have row constructors in your SQL product. For example:

```
UPDATE T2
 SET (c1, c2, ..)
  = (SELECT COALESCE (T1.c1, T2.c1),
         COALESCE (T1.c2, T2.c2),
         ..
       FROM T1
       WHERE T1.keycol = T2.keycol)
 WHERE .. ;
```

### 15.3.5 Using the CASE Expression in UPDATEs

The CASE expression is very handy for updating a table. The first trick is to realize that you can write `SET a = a` to do nothing. The statement given earlier can be rewritten as:

```
UPDATE Customers
 SET payment
  = CASE WHEN EXISTS
        (SELECT *
         FROM Payments AS P1
         WHERE Customers.cust_nbr = P1.cust_nbr)
       THEN (SELECT AVG(P1.amt)
         FROM Payments AS P1
         WHERE Customers.cust_nbr = P1.cust_nbr)
       ELSE payment END; -- do nothing
```

This statement will scan the entire table since there is no `WHERE` clause. That might be a bad thing in this example—I would guess that only a small number of customers make a payment on any given day. But very often you were going to do table scans anyway and this version can be faster.

But the real advantage of the CASE expression is the ability to combine several `UPDATE` statements into one statement. The execution time will be greatly improved and will save you a lot of procedural code or really ugly SQL. Consider this example. We have an inventory of books and we want to (1) reduce the books priced $25.00 and over by 10% and (2) increase the price of the books under $25.00 by 15% to make up the difference. The immediate thought is to write:

```
BEGIN ATOMIC -- wrong!
UPDATE Books
 SET price = price * 0.90
WHERE price > = 25.00;
UPDATE Books
 SET price = price * 1.15
WHERE price < 25.00;
END;
```

But this does not work. Consider a book priced at $25.00; it goes through the first `UPDATE` and it is repriced at $22.50; it then goes through the second `UPDATE` and is repriced at $25.88, which is not what we wanted. Flipping the two statements will produce the desired results for this book, but given a book priced at $24.95, we will get $28.69 and then $25.82 as a final price.

```
UPDATE Books
 SET price = CASE WHEN price < 25.00
           THEN price = price * 1.15
           ELSE price = price * 0.90 END;
```

This is not only faster, but it is correct. However, you have to be careful and be sure that you did not really want a series of functions applied to the same columns in a particular order. If that is the case, then you need to try to make each assignment expression within the SET clause stand by itself as a complete function instead of one step in a process. Consider this example:

```
BEGIN ATOMIC
UPDATE Foobar
 SET a = x
WHERE r = 1;
UPDATE Foobar
 SET b = y
WHERE s = 2;
UPDATE Foobar
 SET c = z
WHERE t = 3;
UPDATE Foobar
 SET c = z + 1
WHERE t = 4;
END;
```

This can be replaced by:

```
UPDATE Foobar
 SET a = CASE WHEN r = 1 THEN x ELSE a END,
   b = CASE WHEN s = 2 THEN y ELSE b END,
   c = CASE WHEN t = 3 THEN z
          WHEN t = 4 THEN z + 1
          ELSE c END
WHERE r = 1
   OR s = 2
   OR t IN (3, 4);
```

The WHERE clause is optional, but might improve performance if the index is right and the candidate set is small. Notice that this approach is driven by the destination of the UPDATE—the columns appear only once in the SET clause. The traditional approach is driven by the source of the changes—you first make updates from one data source, then the next, and so forth. Think about how you would do this with a set of magnetic tapes applied against a master file.

## 15.4 A Note on Flaws in a Common Vendor Extension

Although I do not like to spend much time discussing nonstandard SQL-like languages, the T-SQL language from Sybase and Microsoft has a horrible flaw in it that users need to be warned about. Several of the "power users" have wanted to deprecate it and teach people to use the MERGE statement.

They have a proprietary syntax that allows a FROM clause in the UPDATE statement. If the base table being updated is represented more than once in the FROM clause, then its rows can be operated on multiple times, in a total violation of relational principles. The correct answer is that when you try to put more than one value into a column, you get a cardinality violation and the UPDATE fails. Here is a quick example:

```
CREATE TABLE T1 (x INTEGER NOT NULL);
INSERT INTO T1 VALUES (1), (2), (3), (4);

CREATE TABLE T2 (x INTEGER NOT NULL);
INSERT INTO T2 VALUES (1), (1), (1), (1);
```

Now try to update T1 by doubling all the rows that have a match in T2. The FROM clause in the original Sybase version gave you a CROSS JOIN.

```
UPDATE T1
 SET T1.x = 2 * T1.x
 FROM T2
WHERE T1.x = T2.x;

T1
 x
====
16
 2
 3
 4
```

This is a very simple example, as you can see, but you get the idea. Some of this problem has been fixed in the current version of Sybase, but the syntax is still not standard or portable.

The Microsoft version solved the cardinality problem by simply grabbing one of the values based on the current physical arrangement of the rows in the table. This is a simple example from Adam Machanic:

```
CREATE TABLE Foo
(col_a CHAR(1) NOT NULL,
col_b INTEGER NOT NULL);

INSERT INTO Foo VALUES ('A', 0), ('B', 0), ('C', 0);

CREATE TABLE Bar
(col_a CHAR(1) NOT NULL,
col_b INTEGER NOT NULL);

INSERT INTO Bar
VALUES ('A', 1), ('A', 2), ('B', 1), ('C', 1);
```

You run this proprietary UPDATE with a FROM clause:

```
UPDATE Foo
 SET Foo.col_b = Bar.col_b
 FROM Foo INNER JOIN Bar
  ON Foo.col_a = Bar.col_a;
```

The result of the UPDATE cannot be determined. The value of the column will depend upon either order of insertion, (if there are no clustered indexes present), or on order of clustering (but only if the cluster is not fragmented).

A trick due to Alex Kuznetsov is to use a COUNT() to be sure there is no cardinality violation.

```
UPDATE Foo
   SET Foo.col_b = Bar.col_b
  FROM Foo, Bar
WHERE Foo.col_a = Bar.col_a
   AND (SELECT COUNT(*)
```

```
FROM Bar
WHERE Foo.col_a = Bar.col_a) = 1;
```

## 15.5 MERGE Statement

SQL-99 added a single statement to mimic a common magnetic tape file system "merge and insert" procedure, but in a relational way. This is also called an "upsert" in the literature. The simplest business logic, in a pseudo-code, is like this:

```
FOR EACH row IN the Transactions table
DO IF working row NOT IN Master table
 THEN INSERT working row INTO the Master table;
 ELSE UPDATE Master table
    SET Master table columns to the Transactions table values
    WHERE they meet a matching criteria;
 END IF;
END FOR;
```

In the 1950s, we would sort the transaction tape(s) and Master tape on the same key, read each one looking for a match, then perform whatever logic is needed. In its simplest form, the MERGE statement looks like this:

```
MERGE INTO <table name> [AS [<correlation name>]]
USING <table reference> ON <search condition>
{WHEN [NOT] MATCHED [AND <search condition>]
THEN <modification operation>} ..
[ELSE IGNORE];
```

You will notice that use of a correlation name in the MERGE INTO clause is in complete violation of the principle that a correlation name effectively creates a temporary table. There are several other places where SQL:2003 destroyed the original SQL language model, but you do not have to write irregular syntax in all cases.

After a row is MATCHED (or not) to the target table, you can add more <search condition>s in the WHEN clauses in the Standards. Some of the lesser SQLs do not allow extra <search condition>s, so be careful. You can often work around this limitation with logic in the ON, WHERE clauses, and CASE expressions.

The <modification operation> clause can include insertion, update, or delete operations that follow the same rules as those single statements. This can hide complex programming logic in a single statement. But the NOT MATCHED indicates the operation to be performed on the rows where the ON search condition is FALSE or UNKNOWN. Only INSERT or a signal-statement to raise an exception can be specified after THEN.

Let's assume that that we have a table of Personnel salary changes at the branch office in a table called PersonnelChanges. Here is a MERGE statement, which will take the contents of the PersonnelChanges table and merge them with the Personnel table. Both of them use the emp_nbr as the key. Here is a typical, but very simple use of MERGE INTO.

```
MERGE INTO Personnel
USING (SELECT emp_nbr, salary, bonus, comm
   FROM PersonnelChanges) AS C
ON Personnel.emp_nbr = C.emp_nbr
WHEN MATCHED
THEN UPDATE
   SET (Personnel.salary, Personnel.bonus, Personnel.comm)
     = (C.salary, C.bonus, C.comm)
WHEN NOT MATCHED
THEN INSERT
  (Personnel.emp_nbr, Personnel.salary, Personnel.bonus,
     Personnel.comm)
  VALUES (C.emp_nbr, C.salary, C.bonus, C.comm);
```

If you think about it for a minute, if there is a match, then all you can do is UPDATE the row. If there is no match, then all you can do is INSERT the new row.

Consider a fancier version of the second clause, and an employee type that determines the compensation pattern:

```
WHEN MATCHED AND c.emp_type = 'sales'
THEN UPDATE
   SET (Personnel.salary, Personnel.bonus, Personnel.comm)
     = (C.salary, C.bonus, C.comm)
WHEN MATCHED AND c.emp_type = 'executive'
THEN UPDATE
   SET (Personnel.salary, Personnel.bonus, Personnel.comm)
     = (C.salary, C.bonus, 0.00)
WHEN MATCHED AND c.emp_type = 'office'
THEN UPDATE
   SET (Personnel.salary, Personnel.bonus, Personnel.comm)
     = (C.salary, 0.00, 0.00)
```

There are proprietary versions of this statement in particular; look for the term "upsert" in the literature. These statements are most often used for adding data to a data warehouse in their product.

Your first thought might be that MERGE is a shorthand for this code skeleton:

```
BEGIN ATOMIC
UPDATE T1
```

```
 SET (a, b, c, ..
   = (SELECT a, b, c, ..
       FROM T2
       WHERE T1.somekey = T2.somekey),
WHERE EXISTS
  (SELECT *
   FROM T2
   WHERE T1.somekey = T2.somekey);

INSERT INTO T1
SELECT *
FROM T2
WHERE NOT EXISTS
  (SELECT *
   FROM T2
   WHERE T1.somekey = T2.somekey);
END;
```

But there are some subtle differences. The MERGE is a single statement so it can be optimized as a whole. The two separate UPDATE and INSERT statements can be optimized as a single statement, and will probably be executed in the order written.

The WHEN [NOT] MATCHED clauses with additional search conditions can be executed in parallel or rearranged based on new statistics.

# COMPARISON OR THETA OPERATORS

Dr. Codd introduced the term "theta operators" in his early papers, for what a programmer would have called a comparison predicate operator. The large number of data types in SQL makes doing comparisons a little harder than in other programming languages. Values of one data type have to be promoted to values of the other data type before the comparison can be done. SQL is a strongly typed language, which means a lot of type castings are not possible—you cannot turn Christmas into a number and find its square root.

The comparison operators are overloaded and will work for `<numeric>`, `<character>`, and `<datetime>` data types. The symbols and meanings for comparison operators are shown in Table 16.1.

You will also see != or ¬= for "not equal to" in some older SQL implementations. These symbols are borrowed from the C and PL/I programming languages, respectively, and have never been part of Standard SQL. It is a bad habit to use them since it destroys portability of your code and makes it harder to read.

The comparison operators will return a logical value of `TRUE`, `FALSE` or `UNKNOWN`. The values `TRUE` and `FALSE` follow the usual rules and `UNKNOWN` is always returned when one or both of the operands is a `NULL`. Please pay attention to the new `IS [NOT] DISTINCT FROM` operator and look at functions that work with `NULL`s.

## 16.1 Converting Data Types

Numeric data types are all mutually comparable and mutually assignable. If an assignment would result in a loss of the most significant digits, an exception condition is raised. If least significant digits are lost, the implementation defines what rounding or truncating occurs and does not report an exception condition. Most often, one value is converted to the same data type as the other and then the comparison is done in the usual way. The

Joe Celko's SQL for Smarties. DOI: 10.1016/B978-0-12-382022-8.00016-8

**Table 16.1 Symbols and Meanings for Comparison Operators**

| OPERATOR | NUMERIC | CHARACTER | DATETIME |
|---|---|---|---|
| < | less than | collates before | earlier than |
| = | equal to | collates equal to | same time as |
| > | greater than | collates after | later than |
| <= | at most | collates before or equal | no earlier than |
| <> | not equal | not the same as | not the same time as |
| >= | at least | collates after or equal | no later than |

chosen data type is the "higher" of the two, using the following ordering: SMALLINT, INTEGER, BIGINT, DECIMAL, NUMERIC, REAL, FLOAT, DOUBLEPRECISION.

Floating-point hardware will often affect comparisons for REAL, FLOAT, and DOUBLEPRECISION numbers. There is no good way to avoid this, since it is not always reasonable to use DECIMAL or NUMERIC in their place. A host language will probably use the same floating-point hardware, so at least any errors will be consistent across the application.

CHARACTER and CHARACTER VARYING data types are comparable if and only if they are taken from the same character repertoire. That means that ASCII characters cannot be compared to graphics characters, English cannot be compared to Arabic, and so on. In most implementations this is not a problem, because the database has only one repertoire.

The comparison takes the shorter of the two strings and pads it with spaces. The strings are compared position by position from left to right, using the collating sequence for the repertoire—ASCII or EBCDIC in most cases.

Temporal (or <datetime>, as they are called in the standard) data types are mutually assignable only if the source and target of the assignment have the same <datetime> fields. That is, you cannot compare a date and a time. The CAST() operator can do explicit type conversions before you do a comparison.

Table 16.2 contains valid combinations of source (rows in the table) and target (columns) data types in Standard SQL. Y ("yes") means that the combination is syntactically valid without restriction; M ("maybe") indicates that the combination is valid subject

## Table 16.2 Valid Combinations of Source and Target Data Types in Standard SQL

| | EN | AN | VC | FC | VB | FB | D | T | TS | YM | DT |
|---|---|---|---|---|---|---|---|---|---|---|---|
| EN | Y | Y | Y | Y | N | N | N | N | N | N | M |
| AN | Y | Y | Y | Y | N | N | N | N | N | N | N |
| C | Y | Y | M | M | Y | Y | Y | Y | Y | Y | Y |
| B | N | N | Y | Y | Y | Y | N | N | N | N | N |
| D | N | N | Y | Y | N | N | Y | N | Y | N | N |
| T | N | N | Y | Y | N | N | N | Y | Y | N | N |
| TS | N | N | Y | Y | N | N | Y | Y | Y | N | N |
| YM | M | N | Y | Y | N | N | N | N | N | Y | N |
| DT | M | N | Y | Y | N | N | N | N | N | N | Y |

EN = Exact Numeric; AN = Approximate Numeric; C = Character (Fixed- or Variable-length); FC = Fixed-length Character; VC = Variable-length Character; B = Bit String (Fixed- or Variable-length); FB = Fixed-length Bit String; VB = Variable-length Bit String; D = Date; T = Time; TS = Timestamp; YM = Year–Month Interval; DT = Day–Time Interval

to other syntax rules; and N ("no") indicates that the combination is not valid.

### 16.1.1 Date Display Formats

SQL is silent about formatting data for display, as it should be. Dates have many different national formats and you will find many vendor extensions that allow the user to format temporal data into strings and to input dates in various display formats. Only a subset of the ISO 8601 formats are used in Standard SQL for temporal data. SQL has only the yyyy-mm-dd for dates, and 24-hour or "military" time.

### 16.1.2 Other Display Formats

Character and exact numeric data types are usually displayed as you would expect. Approximate numeric data might be shown in decimal or exponential formats. This is implementation-defined. However, the Standard defines an approximate numeric literal as:

```
<approximate numeric literal>::= <mantissa> E <exponent>
<mantissa>::= <exact numeric literal>
<exponent>::= <signed integer>
```

But some host languages do not require a <mantissa> and some allow a lowercase 'e' for the separator. SQL requires a leading zero where other languages might not.

## 16.2 Row Comparisons in SQL

Standard SQL generalized the theta operators so they would work on row expressions and not just on scalars. This is not a popular feature yet, but it is very handy for situations where a key is made from more than one column, and so forth. This makes SQL more orthogonal and it has an intuitive feel to it. Take three row constants:

```
A = (10, 20, 30, 40);

B = (10, NULL, 30, 40);

C = (10, NULL, 30, 100);
```

It seems reasonable to define a row comparison as valid only when the data types of each corresponding column in the rows are union-compatible. If not, the operation is an error and should report a warning. It also seems reasonable to define the results of the comparison to the AND-ed results of each corresponding column using the same operator. That is, (A = B) becomes:

```
((10, 20, 30, 40) = (10, NULL, 30, 40));
```

which becomes:

```
((10 = 10) AND (20 = NULL) AND (30 = 30) AND (40 = 40))
```

which becomes:

```
(TRUE AND UNKNOWN AND TRUE AND TRUE);
```

which becomes:

```
(UNKNOWN);
```

This seems to be reasonable and conforms to the idea that a NULL is a missing value that we expect to resolve at a future date, so we cannot draw a conclusion about this comparison just yet. Now consider the comparison (A = C), which becomes:

```
((10, 20, 30, 40) = (10, NULL, 30, 100));
```

which becomes:

```
((10 = 10) AND (20 = NULL) AND (30 = 30) AND (40 = 100));
```

which becomes:

```
(TRUE AND UNKNOWN AND TRUE AND FALSE);
```

which becomes:

```
(FALSE);
```

There is no way to pick a value for column 2 of row C such that the UNKNOWN result will change to TRUE because the fourth column is always FALSE. This leaves you with a situation that is not very intuitive. The first case can resolve to TRUE or FALSE, but the second case can only go to FALSE.

Standard SQL decided that the theta operators would work as shown in the following rules. The expression RX <comp op> RY is shorthand for a row RX compared to a row RY; likewise, RXi means the i-th column in the row RX. The results are still TRUE, FALSE, or UNKNOWN, if there is no error in type matching. The rules favor solid tests for TRUE or FALSE, using UNKNOWN as a last resort.

The idea of these rules is that as you read the rows from left to right, the values in one row are always greater than or less than those in the other row after some column. This is how it would work if you were alphabetizing words.

The rules are:

1. RX = RY is TRUE if and only if RXi = RYi for all i.
2. RX <> RY is TRUE if and only if RXi <> RYi for some i.
3. RX < RY is TRUE if and only if RXi = RYi for all i < n and RXn < RYn for some n.
4. RX > RY is TRUE if and only if RXi = RYi for all i < n and RXn > RYn for some n.
5. RX <= RY is TRUE if and only if Rx = Ry or Rx < Ry.
6. RX >= RY is TRUE if and only if Rx = Ry or Rx > Ry.
7. RX = RY is FALSE if and only if RX <> RY is TRUE.
8. RX <> RY is FALSE if and only if RX = RY is TRUE.
9. RX < RY is FALSE if and only if RX >= RY is TRUE.
10. RX > RY is FALSE if and only if RX <= RY is TRUE.
11. RX <= RY is FALSE if and only if RX > RY is TRUE.
12. RX >= RY is FALSE if and only if RX < RY is TRUE.
13. RX <comp op> RY is UNKNOWN if and only if RX <comp op> RY is neither TRUE nor FALSE.

The negations are defined so that the NOT operator will still have its usual properties. Notice that a NULL in a row will give an UNKNOWN result in a comparison. Consider this expression:

```
(a, b, c) < (x, y, z)
```

which becomes

```
((a < x)
OR ((a = x) AND (b < y))
OR ((a = x) AND (b = y) AND (c < z)))
```

The standard allows a single-row expression of any sort, including a single-row subquery, on either side of a comparison. Likewise, the BETWEEN predicate can use row expressions in any position in Standard SQL.

## 16.3 IS [NOT] DISTINCT FROM Operator

The SQL 2003 Standards added a verbose but useful theta operator. SQL has two kinds of comparisons, or equivalence classes: equality and grouping.

Equality treats NULLs as incomparable and gets us into the three-valued logic that returns {TRUE, FALSE, UNKNOWN}.

Grouping treats NULLs as equal values and gets us into the usual two-valued logic that returns {TRUE, FALSE}. This is why a GROUP BY puts all the NULLs in one group and you get that behavior in other places.

The theta operators we have discussed so far are based on the equality model, so if you wanted a comparison that grouped NULLs you had to write elaborate CASE expressions. Now you can do it in one infix operator for either rows or scalars.

```
<expression 1> IS NOT DISTINCT FROM <expression 2>
```

is logically equivalent to

```
(<expression 1> IS NOT NULL
 AND <expression 2> IS NOT NULL
 AND <expression 1> = <expression 2>)
OR (<expression 1> IS NULL AND <expression 2> IS NULL)
```

The following usual pattern for adding NOT into SQL constructs,

```
<expression 1> IS DISTINCT FROM <expression 2>
```

is a shorthand for

```
NOT (<expression 1> IS NOT DISTINCT FROM <expression 2>)
```

This double negative was because the IS NOT DISTINCT FROM was defined first.

You will see an attempt to get this functionality with search conditions like:

```
COALESCE (x, <absurd value>) = COALESCE (y, <absurd value>)
```

The idea is that when x and y are both NULL, the absurd values will test equal and return TRUE. Some optimizers look for this construct and generate better code. However, it is always safer to use the proper constructs in the language.

# 17

# VALUED PREDICATES

Valued predicates is my term for a set of related unary Boolean predicates that return TRUE or FALSE based on a property of their argument.

## 17.1 IS NULL

```
<null predicate> ::= <row value constructor> IS [NOT] NULL
```

It is the only way to test to see if an expression is NULL or not, and it has been in SQL-86 and all later versions of the standard. The SQL-92 Standard extended it to accept <row value constructor> instead of a single column or scalar expression.

This extended version will start showing up in implementations when other row expressions are allowed. If all the values in the row R are the NULL value, then R IS NULL is TRUE; otherwise, it is FALSE. If none of the values in R are NULL value, R IS NOT NULL is TRUE; otherwise, it is FALSE. The case where the row is a mix of NULL and non-NULL values is defined by Table 17.1, where Degree means the number of columns in the row expression.

Note that R IS NOT NULL has the same result as NOT R IS NULL if and only if R is of degree one. This is a break in the usual pattern of predicates with a NOT option in them. Here are some examples:

```
(1, 2, 3) IS NULL = FALSE
(1, NULL, 3) IS NULL = FALSE
(1, NULL, 3) IS NOT NULL = FALSE
(NULL, NULL, NULL) IS NULL = TRUE
(NULL, NULL, NULL) IS NOT NULL = FALSE
NOT (1, 2, 3) IS NULL = TRUE
NOT (1, NULL, 3) IS NULL = TRUE
NOT (1, NULL, 3) IS NOT NULL = TRUE
NOT (NULL, NULL, NULL) IS NULL = FALSE
NOT (NULL, NULL, NULL) IS NOT NULL = TRUE
```

Joe Celko's SQL for Smarties. DOI: 10.1016/B978-0-12-382022-8.00017-X

**Table 17.1 Cases Where a Row Is a Mix of NULL and Non-NULL Values**

| Degree of R | R IS NULL | R IS NOT NULL | NOT (R IS NULL) | NOT (R IS NOT NULL) |
|---|---|---|---|---|
| Degree = 1 | | | | |
| NULL | TRUE | FALSE | FALSE | TRUE |
| Not NULL | FALSE | TRUE | TRUE | FALSE |
| Degree > 1 | | | | |
| All NULLs | TRUE | FALSE | FALSE | TRUE |
| Some NULLs | FALSE | FALSE | TRUE | TRUE |
| No NULLs | FALSE | TRUE | TRUE | FALSE |

### 17.1.1 Sources of NULLs

It is important to remember where NULLs can occur. They are more than just a possible value in a column. Aggregate functions on empty sets, OUTER JOINs, arithmetic expressions with NULLs, and so forth all return NULLs. These constructs often show up as columns in VIEWs.

## 17.2 IS [NOT]{TRUE | FALSE | UNKNOWN} Predicate

This predicate tests a condition that has the truth-value TRUE, FALSE, or UNKNOWN, and returns TRUE or FALSE. The syntax is:

```
<Boolean test> ::=
  <Boolean primary> [IS [NOT] <truth value>]

<truth value> ::= TRUE | FALSE | UNKNOWN

<Boolean primary> ::=
  <predicate> | <left paren> <search condition> <right paren>
```

As you would expect, the expression IS NOT <logical value> is the same as NOT (x IS <logical value>), so the predicate can be defined by Table 17.2.

If you are familiar with some of Chris Date's writings, his MAYBE(x) predicate is not the same as the ANSI (x) IS NOT FALSE predicate, but it is equivalent to the (x) IS UNKNOWN predicate.

## Table 17.2 Defining the Predicate, TRUE, FALSE, or UNKNOWN

| IS <logical value> | TRUE | FALSE | UNKNOWN |
|---|---|---|---|
| TRUE | TRUE | FALSE | FALSE |
| FALSE | FALSE | TRUE | FALSE |
| UNKNOWN | FALSE | FALSE | TRUE |

Date's predicate excludes the case where all conditions in the predicate are TRUE.

Date points out that it is difficult to ask a conditional question in English. To borrow one of Chris Date's examples (Date 1990), consider the problem of finding employees who might be programmers born before January 18, 1975 with a salary less than $50,000. The statement of the problem is a bit unclear as to what the "might be" covers—just being a programmer, or all three conditions. Let's assume that we want some doubt on any of the three conditions. With this predicate, the answer is fairly easy to write:

```
SELECT *
 FROM Personnel
WHERE (job_title = 'Programmer'
  AND birth_date < DATE '1975-01-18')
  AND (salary_amt < 50000.00) IS UNKNOWN;
```

could be expanded in the old SQLs as:

```
SELECT *
 FROM Personnel
WHERE (job_title = 'Programmer'
  AND birth_date < CAST (1975-01-18' AS DATE)
  AND salary_amt < 50000.00.00)
 OR (job_title IS NULL
  AND birth_date < CAST (1975-01-18' AS DATE)
  AND salary_amt < 50000.00.00)
 OR (job_title = 'Programmer'
  AND birth_date IS NULL
  AND salary_amt < 50000.00.00)
 OR (job_title = 'Programmer'
  AND birth_date < CAST (1975-01-18' AS DATE)
  AND salary_amt IS NULL)
```

```
OR (job_title IS NULL
 AND birth_date IS NULL
 AND salary_amt < 50000.00.00)
OR (job_title IS NULL
 AND birth_date < CAST (1975-01-18' AS DATE)
 AND salary_amt IS NULL)
OR (job_title = 'Programmer'
 AND birth_date IS NULL
 AND salary_amt IS NULL)
OR (job_title IS NULL
 AND birth_date IS NULL
 AND salary_amt IS NULL);
```

The problem is that every possible combination of NULLs and non-NULLs has to be tested. Since there are three predicates involved, this gives us (3^2) = 8 combinations to check out. The IS NOT UNKNOWN predicate does not have to bother with the combinations, only the final logical value.

## 17.3 IS [NOT] NORMALIZED Predicate

<string> IS [NOT] NORMALIZED determines if a Unicode string is one of the four normal forms (D, C, KD, and KC). The use of the words "normal form" here are not the same as in a relational context. In the Unicode model, a single character can be built from several other characters. Accent marks can be put on basic Latin letters. Certain combinations of letters can be displayed as ligatures ('ae' becomes 'æ'). Some languages, such as Hangul (Korean) and Vietnamese, build glyphs from concatenating symbols in two dimensions. Some languages have special forms of one letter that are determined by context, such as the terminal lowercase sigma in Greek or accented 'u' in Czech. In short, writing is more complex than putting one letter after another.

The Unicode standard defines the order of such constructions in their normal forms. You can still produce the same results with different orderings and sometimes with different combinations of symbols. But it is very handy when you are searching such text to know that it is normalized rather than trying to parse each glyph on the fly. You can find details about normalization and links to free software at www.unicode.org.

18

# CASE EXPRESSIONS

The CASE expression is probably the most useful addition in SQL-92. This is a quick overview of how to use the expression, but you will find other tricks spread throughout the book.

- The reason it is so important is that it works with any data type.
- It allows the programmer to avoid procedural code by replacing IF-THEN-ELSE control flow with CASE expression inside the query. This helps the optimizer.
- It makes SQL statements equivalent to primitive recursive functions. Only a math major cares about this, but it is important.

You can look up what that means in a book on the theory of computation, but it is a nice mathematical property that guarantees certain kinds of problems can be solved.

## 18.1 The CASE Expression

It allows the programmer to pick a value based on a logical expression in his code. ANSI stole the idea and the syntax from the now-defunct ADA programming language (ADA was born in 1987 with a US Department of Defense mandate and died in 1997 when the mandate was removed. Technically, there is a 2005 Standard). Here is the syntax for a <case specification>:

```
<case specification> ::= <simple case> | <searched case>

<simple case> ::=
  CASE <case operand>
   <simple when clause>...
   [<else clause>]
  END

<searched case> ::=
  CASE
   <searched when clause>...
   [<else clause>]
  END
```

Joe Celko's SQL for Smarties. DOI: 10.1016/B978-0-12-382022-8.00018-1

```
<simple when clause> ::= WHEN <when operand> THEN <result>

<searched when clause> ::= WHEN <search condition> THEN
   <result>

<else clause> ::= ELSE <result>

<case operand> ::= <value expression>

<when operand> ::= <value expression>

<result> ::= <result expression> | NULL

<result expression> ::= <value expression>
```

The searched CASE expression is probably the most used version of the expression. First the expression is given a data type by seeing what the highest data type in its THEN clauses is. The WHEN ... THEN ... clauses are executed in left-to-right order. The first WHEN clause that tests TRUE returns the value given in its THEN clause.

And, yes, you can nest CASE expressions inside each other. If no explicit ELSE clause is given for the CASE expression, then the database will insert an implicit ELSE NULL clause before the END keyword. If you wish to return a NULL from a THEN, however, you should use a CAST (NULL AS <data type>) expression to establish the data type for the compiler.

—this works

```
CASE WHEN 1 = 1
  THEN NULL
  ELSE CAST(NULL AS INTEGER) END
```

—this works

```
CASE WHEN 1 = 1
  THEN CAST(NULL AS INTEGER)
  ELSE NULL END
```

—this does not work; no <result> to establish a data type

```
CASE WHEN 1 = 1
  THEN NULL
  ELSE NULL END
```

—might or might not work in your SQL

```
CAST (CASE WHEN 1 = 1
  THEN NULL
  ELSE NULL END AS INTEGER)
```

I recommend always writing an explicit ELSE clause, so that you can change it later when you find a value to return. I would also recommend that you explicitly cast a NULL in the CASE expression THEN clauses to the desired data type.

If the THEN clauses have results of different data types, the compiler will find the most general one and CAST() the others to it. But again, actual implementations might have slightly different ideas about how and when this casting should be done.

The <simple case expression> is defined as a searched CASE expression in which all the WHEN clauses are made into equality comparisons against the <case operand>. For example,

```
CASE iso_sex_code
WHEN 0 THEN 'Unknown'
WHEN 1 THEN 'Male'
WHEN 2 THEN 'Female'
WHEN 9 THEN 'N/A'
ELSE NULL END
```

could also be written as:

```
CASE
WHEN iso_sex_code = 0 THEN 'Unknown'
WHEN iso_sex_code = 1 THEN 'Male'
WHEN iso_sex_code = 2 THEN 'Female'
WHEN iso_sex_code = 9 THEN 'N/A'
ELSE NULL END
```

There is a gimmick in this definition, however. The expression,

```
CASE foo
WHEN 1 THEN 'bar'
WHEN NULL THEN 'no bar'
END
```

becomes

```
CASE WHEN foo = 1 THEN 'bar'
  WHEN foo = NULL THEN 'no_bar' -- problem!
  ELSE NULL END
```

The "WHEN foo = NULL" clause is always UNKNOWN. This definition can get really weird with a random number generator in the expression. Let's assume that RANDOM() uses a seed value and returns a uniformly distributed random floating point number between 0.0000 and 0.99 .. 9 whenever it is called.

This expression will spend most of its time in the ELSE clause instead of returning a number word between one and five.

```
SET pick_one = CASE CAST((5.0 * RANDOM()) + 1 AS INTEGER)
        WHEN 1 THEN 'one'
        WHEN 2 THEN 'two'
        WHEN 3 THEN 'three'
```

```
WHEN 4 THEN 'four'
WHEN 5 THEN 'five'
ELSE 'This should not happen' END;
```

The expansion will reproduce the CAST() expression for each WHEN clause and the RANDOM() function will be reevaluated each time. You need to be sure that it is evaluated only once.

```
BEGIN
DECLARE pick_a_number INTEGER;
SET pick_a_number = CAST((5.0 * RANDOM()) + 1 AS INTEGER);
SET pick_one = CASE pick_a_number
        WHEN 1 THEN 'one'
        WHEN 2 THEN 'two'
        WHEN 3 THEN 'three'
        WHEN 4 THEN 'four'
        WHEN 5 THEN 'five'
        ELSE 'This should not happen' END;
END;
```

The variable pick_a_number is also expanded in the WHEN clause, but because it is not a function call, it is not evaluated over and over.

### 18.1.1 The COALESCE() and NULLIF() Functions

The SQL-92 Standard defines other functions in terms of the CASE expression, which makes the language a bit more compact and easier to implement. For example, the COALESCE() function can be defined for one or two expressions by

1. COALESCE (<value exp #1>) is equivalent to (<value exp #1>)
2. COALESCE (<value exp #1>, <value exp #2>) is equivalent to

```
CASE WHEN <value exp #1> IS NOT NULL
  THEN <value exp #1>
  ELSE <value exp #2> END
```

then we can recursively define it for (n) expressions, where (n >= 3), in the list by

```
COALESCE (<value exp #1>, <value exp #2>, . . ., n),
```

as equivalent to:

```
CASE WHEN <value exp #1> IS NOT NULL
  THEN <value exp #1>
  ELSE COALESCE (<value exp #2>, . . ., n)
END
```

Likewise, NULLIF (<value exp #1>, <value exp #2>) is equivalent to:

```
CASE WHEN <value exp #1> = <value exp #2>
  THEN NULL
  ELSE <value exp #1> END
```

## 18.1.2 CASE Expressions with GROUP BY

A CASE expression is very useful with a GROUP BY query. For example, to determine how many employees of each sex_code by department you have in your personnel table you can write:

```
SELECT dept_nbr,
   SUM(CASE WHEN sex_code = 1 THEN 1 ELSE 0) AS males,
   SUM(CASE WHEN sex_code = 2 THEN 1 ELSE 0) AS females
 FROM Personnel
GROUP BY dept_nbr;
```

or

```
SELECT dept_nbr,
   COUNT(CASE WHEN sex_code = 1 THEN 1 ELSE NULL) AS males,
   COUNT(CASE WHEN sex_code = 2' THEN 1 ELSE NULL) AS females
 FROM Personnel
GROUP BY dept_nbr;
```

I am not sure if there is any general rule as to which form will run faster. Aggregate functions remove NULLs before they perform their operations, so the order of execution might be different in the ELSE 0 and the ELSE NULL versions.

The previous example shows the CASE expression inside the aggregate function; it is possible to put aggregate functions inside a CASE expression. For example, assume you are given a table of employee's skills:

```
CREATE TABLE PersonnelSkills
(emp_id CHAR(11) NOT NULL,
skill_code CHAR(11) NOT NULL,
primary_skill_flg CHAR(1) NOT NULL
          CONSTRAINT primary_skill_given
          CHECK (primary_skill_flg IN ('Y', 'N'),
PRIMARY KEY (emp_id, skill_code));
```

Each employee has a row in the table for each of his skills. If the employee has multiple skills they will have multiple rows in the table and the primary skill indicator will be a 'Y' for the main skill. If the employee has only one skill (which means one row in the table), the value of primary_skill_flg is indeterminate. The problem is to list each employee once along with:

1. His or her only skill if he or she has only one row in the table; or
2. His or her primary skill if he or she has multiple rows in the table.

```
SELECT emp_id,
  CASE WHEN COUNT(*) = 1
    THEN MAX(skill_code)
    ELSE MAX(CASE WHEN primary_skill_flg = 'Y'
```

```
            THEN skill_code END)
            ELSE NULL END)
   END AS main_skill
  FROM PersonnelSkills
 GROUP BY emp_id;
```

This solution looks at first like a violation of the rule in SQL that prohibits nested aggregate functions, but if you look closely, it is not. The outermost CASE expression resolves to an aggregate function, namely MAX(). The ELSE clause simply has to return an expression inside its MAX() that can be resolved to a single value.

### 18.1.3 CASE, CHECK( ) Clauses and Logical Implication

Complicated logical predicates can be put into a CASE expression that returns either 'T'(TRUE) or 'F'(FALSE).

```
CONSTRAINT implication_example
CHECK (CASE WHEN dept_nbr = 'D1'
    THEN CASE WHEN salary < 44000.00
        THEN 'T' ELSE 'F' END
    ELSE 'T' END = 'T')
```

This is a logical implication operator we mentioned briefly in the chapter on NULLs and 3-Valued Logic. It is usually written as an arrow with two stems (⇒) and its definition is usually stated as "a true premise cannot imply a false conclusion" or as "if a then b" in English.

In English, this condition says "if an employee is in department 'D1', then his salary is less than $44,000.00," which is not the same as saying (dept_nbr = 'D1' AND salary < 44000.00) in the constraint. In standard Boolean logic, there is a simple transformation called the "Smisteru rule," after the engineer who discovered it, which says that $(a \Rightarrow b)$ is equivalent to $(\neg a \vee b)$.

But in SQL, the rule is that a CHECK() constraint succeeds when the answer is TRUE or UNKNOWN whereas an ON or WHERE clause fails when the answer is FALSE or UNKNOWN. This leads to all kinds of problems with implication in 3-Valued Logic with two sets of rules—one for DDL and one for DML!

Let's try the Smisteru transform first:

```
CREATE TABLE Foobar_DDL_1
(a CHAR(1) CHECK (a IN ('T', 'F')),
b CHAR(1) CHECK (b IN ('T', 'F')),
CONSTRAINT implication_example
CHECK (NOT (A = 'T') OR (B = 'T')));
INSERT INTO Foobar_DDL_1
```

```
VALUES ('T', 'T'),
  ('T', 'F'), -- fails
  ('T', NULL),
  ('F', 'T'),
  ('F', 'F'),
  ('F', NULL),
  (NULL, 'T'),
  (NULL, 'F'),
  (NULL, NULL);

SELECT * FROM Foobar_DDL_1;
```

Results

```
a       b
===========
T       T
T       NULL
F       T
F       F
F       NULL
NULL    T
NULL    F
NULL    NULL
```

Now my original version:

```
CREATE TABLE Foobar_DDL
(a CHAR(1) CHECK (a IN ('T', 'F')),
b CHAR(1) CHECK (b IN ('T', 'F')),
CONSTRAINT implication_example_2
CHECK(CASE WHEN A = 'T'
    THEN CASE WHEN B = 'T'
      THEN 1 ELSE 0 END
    ELSE 1 END = 1));

INSERT INTO Foobar_DDL
VALUES ('T', 'T')
  ('T', 'F'), -- fails
  ('T', NULL),
  ('F', 'T'), ('F', 'F'), ('F', NULL),
  (NULL, 'T'), (NULL, 'F'), (NULL, NULL);

SELECT * FROM Foobar_DDL;
```

Results

```
a       b
============
T       T
F       T
F       F
F       NULL
```

```
NULL    T
NULL    F
NULL    NULL
```

Both agree that a TRUE premise cannot lead to a FALSE conclusion, but Smisteru allows ('T', NULL). Not quite the same implication operators!

Let's now look at the query side of the house:

```
CREATE TABLE Foobar_DML
(a CHAR(1) CHECK (a IN ('T', 'F')),
b CHAR(1) CHECK (b IN ('T', 'F')));

INSERT INTO Foobar_DML
VALUES ('T', 'T'),
  ('T', 'F'),
  ('T', NULL),
  ('F', 'T'),
  ('F', 'F'),
  ('F', NULL),
  (NULL, 'T'),
  (NULL, 'F'),
  (NULL, NULL);
```

Using the Smisteru rule as the search condition:

```
SELECT * FROM Foobar_DML WHERE (NOT (A ='T') OR (B = 'T'));
```

Results

```
a       b
==========
T       T
F       T
F       F
F       NULL
NULL    T
```

Using the original predicate:

```
SELECT * FROM Foobar_DML
WHERE CASE WHEN A = 'T'
    THEN CASE WHEN B = 'T'
      THEN 1 ELSE 0 END
    ELSE 1 END = 1;
```

Results

```
a       b
==========
T       T
F       T
```

```
F       F
F       NULL
NULL    T
NULL    F
NULL    NULL
```

This is why I used the CASE expression; it works the same way in both the DDL and DML.

## 18.2 Subquery Expressions and Constants

Subquery expressions are SELECT statements inside of parentheses. Well, there is more to it than that.

The four flavors of subquery expressions are tabular, columnar, row, and scalar subquery expressions. As you might guess from the names, the tabular or table subquery returns a table as a result, so it has to appear any place that a table is used in SQL-92, which usually means it is in the FROM clause.

The columnar subquery returns a table with a single column in it. This was the important one in the original SQL-86 and SQL-89 standards because the IN, <comp op> ALL, and <comp op> {ANY|SOME} predicates were based on the ability of the language to convert the single column into a list of comparisons connected by ANDs or ORs.

The row subquery returns a single row. It can be used anywhere a row can be used. This sort of query is the basis for the singleton SELECT statement used in the embedded SQL. It is not used too much right now, but with the extension of theta operators to handle row comparisons, it might become more popular.

The scalar subquery returns a single scalar value. It can be used anywhere a scalar value can be used, which usually means it is in the SELECT or WHERE clauses. If a scalar subquery returns an empty result, it is converted to a NULL. If a scalar subquery returns more than one row, you get a cardinality violation.

I will make the general statement now that the performance of scalar subqueries depends a lot on the architecture of the hardware upon which your SQL is implemented. A massively parallel machine can allocate a processor to each scalar subquery and get drastic performance improvement.

A table constant of any shape can be constructed using the VALUES() expression. New SQL programmers think that this is only an option in the INSERT INTO statement. However, Standard SQL allows you to use it to build a row as a comma-separated list of scalar expressions, and then build a table as a comma-separated list of those row constructors. Consider this look-up table of ZIP code ranges by state:

```
CREATE VIEW ZIP_Codes (state_code, low_zip, high_zip)
AS VALUES ('AK', 99500, 99998),
     ...
     ('GA', 30000, 30399),
     ...
     ('WY', 82000, 83100);
```

This table cannot be changed without dropping the VIEW and rebuilding it. It has no named base table.

## 18.3 Rozenshtein Characteristic Functions

A characteristic function converts a logical expression into a one if it is TRUE and to a zero if it is FALSE. This is what we have been doing with some of the CASE expressions shown here, but not under that name. The literature uses a lowercase delta (δ) or an uppercase Chi (χ) as the symbol for this operator. Programmers first saw this in Ken Iverson's APL programming language and then later in Donald Knuth's books on programming theory.

The name comes from the fact that it is used to define a set by giving a rule for membership in the set.

David Rozenshtein found ways of implementing characteristic functions with algebraic expression on numeric columns in the Sybase T-SQL language (see *Optimizing Transact SQL*, SQL Forum Press, 1995, ISBN 10: 0-9649812-0-3) before they had a CASE expression in their product. Without going into the details, I will borrow Dr. Rozenshtein's notation and give the major formulas for putting converted numeric comparisons into a computed characteristic function:

```
(a = b) becomes (1 - ABS(SIGN(a - b)))
(a <> b) becomes (ABS(SIGN(a - b)))
(a < b) becomes (1 - SIGN(1 + SIGN(a - b)))
(a <= b) becomes (SIGN(1 - SIGN(a - b)))
(a > b) becomes (1 - SIGN(1 - SIGN(a - b)))
(a >= b) becomes (SIGN(1 + SIGN(a - b)))
```

The basic logical operators can also be put into computed characteristic functions. If we ignore NULLs and use standard Boolean logic, we can write these expressions,

```
NOT (a) becomes (1 - a)
(a AND b) becomes SIGN(a * b)
(a OR b) becomes SIGN(a + b)
```

If you remember George Boole's original notation for Boolean Algebra, this will look very familiar. But be aware that if a or b is a NULL, then the results will be a NULL and not a one or zero—something that Mr. Boole never thought about.

Character strings can be handled with the POSITION function, if you are careful:

```
(a = s) becomes POSITION (a IN s)
(a <> s) becomes SIGN (1 - POSITION (a IN s))
```

His book gives more tricks, but many of them depend on Sybase's T-SQL functions and they are not portable. Another problem is that the code can become very hard to read and what is happening is not obvious to the next programmer to read the code.

Use the CASE expression instead, since the optimizers will do an equal or better job. I told you about this technique so you can replace legacy code.

# 19

# LIKE AND SIMILAR TO PREDICATES

The LIKE predicate is a simple string pattern-matching test with the syntax:

```
<like predicate> ::=
   <match value> [NOT] LIKE <pattern>
     [ESCAPE <escape character>]

<match value> ::= <character value expression>
<pattern> ::= <character value expression>
<escape character> ::= <character value expression>
```

The expression M NOT LIKE P is equivalent to NOT (M LIKE P), which follows the usual syntax pattern in SQL. There are two wildcards allowed in the <pattern> string. They are the '%' and '_' characters. The '_' character represents a single arbitrary character; the '%' character represents an arbitrary substring, possibly of length zero. Notice that there is no way to represent zero or one arbitrary character. This is not the case in many text-search languages, and can lead to problems or very complex predicates.

Any other character in the <pattern> represents that character itself. This means that SQL patterns are case-sensitive, but many vendors allow you to set case sensitivity on or off at the database system level.

The <escape character> is used in the <pattern> to specify that the character that follows it is to be interpreted as a literal rather than a wildcard. This means that the escape character is followed by the escape character itself, an '_', or a '%'. Old C programmers are used to this convention, where the language defines the escape character as '\', so this is a good choice for SQL programmers too.

Joe Celko's SQL for Smarties. DOI: 10.1016/B978-0-12-382022-8.00019-3

## 19.1 Tricks with Patterns

The '_' character tests much faster than the '%' character. The reason is obvious: the parser that compares a string to the pattern needs only one operation to match an underscore before it can move to the next character, but has to do some look-ahead parsing to resolve a percentage sign. The wildcards can be inserted in the middle or beginning of a pattern. Thus, 'B%K' will match 'BOOK', 'BLOCK', and 'BK', but it will not match 'BLOCKS'.

The parser would scan each letter and classify it as a wildcard match or an exact match. In the case of 'BLOCKS', the initial 'B' would be an exact match and the parser would continue; 'L', 'O', and 'C' have to be wildcard matches, since they don't appear in the pattern string; 'K' cannot be classified until we read the last letter. The last letter is 'S', so the match fails.

For example, given a column declared to be seven characters long, and a LIKE predicate looking for names that start with 'Mac', you would usually write:

```
SELECT *
 FROM People
WHERE last_name LIKE 'Mac%';
```

but this might actually run faster:

```
SELECT *
 FROM People
WHERE last_name LIKE 'Mac_'
 OR last_name LIKE 'Mac__'
 OR last_name LIKE 'Mac___ '
 OR last_name LIKE 'Mac____';
```

The trailing blanks are also characters that can be matched exactly.

Putting a '%' at the front of a pattern is very time-consuming. The reason is simple; SQL products that use tree-structured indexes build them from left to right, so the index cannot be used by the optimizer and the table must be scanned. For example, you might try to find all names that end in 'son' with the query

```
SELECT *
 FROM People
WHERE last_name LIKE '%son';
```

The use of underscores instead will make a real difference in most SQL implementations for this query, because most of them always parse from left to right.

```
SELECT *
  FROM People
 WHERE last_name LIKE '_son'
   OR last_name LIKE '__son '
   OR last_name LIKE '___son '
   OR last_name LIKE '____son';
```

Remember that the '_' character requires a matching character and the '%' character does not. Thus, the query

```
SELECT *
  FROM People
 WHERE last_name LIKE 'John_%';
```

and the query

```
SELECT *
  FROM People
 WHERE last_name LIKE 'John%';
```

are subtly different. Both will match to 'Johnson' and 'Johns', but the first will not accept 'John' as a match. This is how you get a "one-or-more-characters" pattern match in SQL.

Remember that the <pattern> as well as the <match value> can be constructed with concatenation operators, SUBSTRING(), and other string functions. For example, let's find people whose first names are part of their last names with the query

```
SELECT *
  FROM People
 WHERE last_name LIKE '%' || first_name || '%';
```

which will show us people like 'John Johnson', 'Anders Andersen', and 'Bob McBoblin'. This query will also run very slowly. However, this is case sensitive and would not work for names such as 'Jon Anjon', so you might want to modify the statement to:

```
SELECT *
  FROM People
 WHERE UPPER (last_name) LIKE '%' || UPPER(first_name) || '%';
```

## 19.2 Results with NULL Values and Empty Strings

As you would expect, a NULL in the predicate returns an UNKNOWN result. The NULL can be the escape character, pattern, or match value.

If M and P are both character strings of length zero, `M LIKE P` defaults to `TRUE`. If one or both are longer than zero characters, you use the regular rules to test the predicate.

## 19.3 LIKE Is Not Equality

A very important point that is often missed is that two strings can be equal but not `LIKE` in SQL. The test of equality first pads the shorter of the two strings with rightmost blanks, then matches the characters in each, one for one. Thus 'Smith' and 'Smith   ' (with three trailing blanks) are equal. However, the `LIKE` predicate does no padding, so 'Smith' `LIKE` 'Smith   ' tests `FALSE` because there is nothing to match to the blanks.

A good trick to get around these problems is to use the `TRIM()` function to remove unwanted blanks from the strings within either or both of the two arguments.

## 19.4 Avoiding the LIKE Predicate with a Join

Beginners often want to write something similar to "`<string> IN LIKE (<pattern list>)`" rather than a string of `OR`-ed `LIKE` predicates. That syntax is illegal, but you can get the same results with a table of patterns and a join.

```
CREATE TABLE Patterns
(template VARCHAR(10) NOT NULL PRIMARY KEY);

INSERT INTO Patterns
VALUES ('Celko%'),
  ('Chelko%'),
  ('Cilko%'),
  ('Selko%),
  ('Silko%');

SELECT A1.last_name
  FROM Patterns AS P1, Authors AS A1
WHERE A1.last_name LIKE P1.template;
```

This idea can be generalized to find strings that differ from a pattern by one position and without actually using a LIKE predicate. First, assume that we have a table of sequential numbers and these following tables with sample data.

— the match patterns

```
CREATE TABLE MatchList (pattern CHAR(9) NOT NULL PRIMARY KEY);
INSERT INTO MatchList
VALUES ('_========'), ('=_======='), ('==_======'),
  ('===_====='), ('====_===='), ('=====_==='),
  ('======_=='), ('=======_='), ('========_');
```

— the strings to be matched or near-matched

```
CREATE TABLE Target (nbr CHAR(9) NOT NULL PRIMARY KEY);
INSERT INTO Target VALUES ('123456089'), ('543434344');
```

— the strings to be searched for those matches

```
CREATE TABLE Source (nbr CHAR(9) NOT NULL PRIMARY KEY);
INSERT INTO Source
VALUES ('123456089'), ('123056789'), ('123456780'),
  ('123456789'), ('023456789'), ('023456780');
```

We are using an equal sign in the match patterns as a signal to replace it with the appropriate character in the source string and see if they match, but to skip over the underscore.

```
SELECT DISTINCT TR1.nbr
 FROM Series AS SE1, Source AS SR1,
   MatchList AS ML1, Target AS TR1
WHERE NOT EXISTS
 (SELECT *
   FROM Series AS SE1, Source AS SR2,
     MatchList AS ML2, Target AS TR2
   WHERE SUBSTRING (ML2.pattern FROM seq FOR 1) = '='
    AND SUBSTRING (SR2.nbr FROM seq FOR 1)
      <> SUBSTRING (TR2.nbr FROM seq FOR 1)
    AND SR2.nbr = SR1.nbr
    AND TR2.nbr = TR1.nbr
    AND ML2.pattern = ML1.pattern
    AND SE1.seq BETWEEN 1 AND (CHARLENGTH (TR2.nbr) -1));
```

This code is due to Jonathan Blitz. Today, you might want to consider a Regular expression, but this is still quite simple and will use the LIKE parser rather than a full-blown SIMILAR TO.

## 19.5 CASE Expressions and LIKE Search Conditions

The CASE expression in Standard SQL lets the programmer use the LIKE predicate in some interesting ways. The simplest example is counting the number of times a particular string appears inside another string. Assume that text_col is CHAR(25) and we want the count of a particular string, 'term', within it.

```
SELECT text_col,
  CASE
  WHEN text_col LIKE '%term%term%term%term%term%term%'
  THEN 6
  WHEN text_col LIKE '%term%term%term%term%term%'
  THEN 5
  WHEN text_col LIKE '%term%term%term%term%'
  THEN 4
  WHEN text_col LIKE '%term%term%term%'
  THEN 3
  WHEN text_col LIKE '%term%term%'
  THEN 2
  WHEN text_col LIKE '%term%'
  THEN 1
  ELSE 0 END AS term_tally
 FROM Foobar
WHERE text_col LIKE '%term%';
```

This depends on the fact that a CASE expression executes the WHEN clauses in order of their appearance. We know that the most substring can appear is six times because of the length of text_col.

Another use of the CASE is to adjust the pattern within the LIKE predicate.

```
name LIKE CASE
      WHEN language = 'English'
      THEN 'Red%'
      WHEN language = 'French'
      THEN 'Rouge%'
      ELSE 'R%' END
```

## 19.6 SIMILAR TO Predicates

As you can see, the LIKE predicate is pretty weak, especially if you have used a version of grep(), a utility program from the UNIX operating system. The name is short for "general regular expression parser" and before you ask, a regular expression is a class of formal languages. If you are a computer science major, you have seen them; otherwise, don't worry about it. The bad news is that there are several versions of grep() in the UNIX community, such as egrep(), fgrep(), xgrep(), and a dozen or so others.

## Table 19.1 Special Pattern Symbols

| | |
|---|---|
| \| | Alternation (either of two alternatives) |
| * | Repetition of the previous item zero or more times |
| + | Repetition of the previous item one or more times |
| {<low value> [, <high value>]} | Repeat the construct at least <low.value> times and no more than <high value> times |
| () | May be used to group items into a single unit |
| [...] | A bracket expression specifies a match to any of the characters inside the brackets |

## Table 19.2 Abbreviations of Commonly Used Character Subsets

| | |
|---|---|
| [:ALPHA:] | Match any alphabetic character, regardless of case. |
| [:UPPER:] | Match any uppercase alphabetic character |
| [:LOWER:] | Match any lowercase alphabetic character |
| [:DIGIT:] | Match any numeric digit |
| [:ALNUM:] | Match any numeric digit or alphabetic character |

The SQL-99 standard added a regular expression predicate of the form [<string expression> SIMILAR TO <pattern> ESCAPE <character>], which is based on the POSIX version of grep() found in ISO/IEC 9945.

The special symbols in a pattern are shown in Table 19.1.

Table 19.2 contains abbreviations for lists of commonly used character subsets, taken from POSIX.

Some examples are as follows.

1. The letters 'foo' or 'bar' followed by any string:

```
Foobar SIMILAR TO '(foo|bar)%'
```

2. The 'SER #' followed by one or more digits:

```
serial_nbr SIMILAR TO ' SER #[:DIGIT:]+'
serial_nbr SIMILAR TO ' SER [:DIGIT:]+'
```

**Table 19.3 Basic Tokens**

| | |
|---|---|
| . | Any character (same as the SQL underscore) |
| ^ | Start of line (not used in an SQL string) |
| $ | End of line (not used in an SQL string) |
| \ | The next character is a literal and not a special symbol; this is called an ESCAPE in SQL and the expression can have an optional ESCAPE clause on the end |
| [^] | Match anything but the characters inside the brackets, after the caret |

You should still read your product manual for details, but most grep() functions accept other special symbols for more general searching that the SIMILAR TO predicate. And they do not have rules about propagating NULLs. The basic tokens are given in Table 19.3.

Regular expressions have a lot of nice properties, especially for validating strings. You can find web sites with regular expressions for such things as URLs, VIN, and other standard encoding schemes.

## 19.7 Tricks with Strings

This is a list of miscellaneous tricks that you might not think about when using strings.

### 19.7.1 String Character Content

A weird way of providing an edit mask for a varying character column to see if it has only digits in it was proposed by Ken Sheridan on the ACCESS forum of CompuServe in October 1999. If the first character is not a zero, then you can check that the VARCHAR(n) string is all digits with:

```
CAST (LOG10 (CAST (test_column AS INTEGER) AS INTEGER) = n
```

If the first (n) characters are not all digits then it will not return (n). If they are all digits, but the (n+1) character is also a digit it will return (n+1), and so forth. If there are nondigit characters in the string, then the innermost CAST() function will fail to convert the test_column into a number. If you do have to worry about leading zeros or blanks then concatenate '1' to the front of the string.

Another trick is to think in terms of whole strings and not in a "character at a time" mind set. So how can I tell if a string is all alphabetic, partly alphabetic, or completely nonalphabetic without scanning each character? The answer from the folks at Ocelot software is surprisingly easy:

```
CREATE TABLE Foobar
(no_alpha VARCHAR(6) NOT NULL
       CHECK (UPPER(no_alpha) = LOWER(no_alpha)),
some_alpha VARCHAR(6) NOT NULL
       CHECK (UPPER(some_alpha) <> LOWER(some_alpha)),
all_alpha VARCHAR(6) NOT NULL
       CHECK (UPPER(all_alpha) <> LOWER(all_alpha)
         AND LOWER (all_alpha)
           BETWEEN 'aaaaaa' AND 'zzzzzz'),
...);
```

Letters have different upper- and lowercase values, but other characters do not. This lets us edit a column for no alphabetic characters, some alphabetic characters, and all alphabetic characters.

## 19.7.2 Searching versus Declaring a String

You need to be very accurate when you declare a string column in your DDL, but thanks to doing that, you can slack off a bit when you search on those columns in your DML. For example, most credit card numbers are made up of four groups of four digits, and each group has some validation rule, thus:

```
CREATE TABLE CreditCards
(card_nbr CHAR(17) NOT NULL PRIMARY KEY
CONSTRAINT valid_card_nbr_format
 CHECK (card_nbr SIMILAR TO
    '[:DIGIT:]{4}-[:DIGIT:]{4}-[:DIGIT:]{4}-[:DIGIT:]{4}'
CONSTRAINT valid_bank_nbr
 CHECK (SUBSTRING (card_nbr FROM 1 FOR 4)
    IN ('2349', '2345', ..),
..);
```

Since we are sure that the credit card number is stored correctly, we can search for it with a simple `LIKE` predicate. For example to find all the cards that contain 1234 in the third group, you can use this:

```
SELECT card_nbr
 FROM CreditCards
WHERE card_nbr LIKE '____-____-1234-____';
```

or even,

```
SELECT card_nbr
 FROM CreditCards
WHERE card_nbr LIKE '__________1234_____';
```

The SIMILAR TO predicate will build an internal finite state machine to parse the pattern, and the underscores in the LIKE can be optimized so that it can run in parallel down the whole column.

### 19.7.3 Creating an Index on a String

Many string encoding techniques have the same prefix because we read from left to right and tend to put the codes for the largest category to the left. For example, the first group of digits in the credit card numbers is the issuing bank. The syntax might look like this:

```
CREATE INDEX acct_searching
  ON CreditCards
 WITH REVERSE(card_nbr); -- not Standard SQL
```

If your SQL has the ability to define a function in an index, you can reverse or rearrange the string to give faster access. This is very vendor dependent, but often the query must explicitly use the same function as the index.

An alternative is to store the rearranged value in the base table and show the actual value in a view. When the view is invoked, the rearranged value will be used for the query without the users knowing it.

20

# BETWEEN AND OVERLAPS PREDICATES

The BETWEEN and OVERLAPS predicates both offer a shorthand way of showing that one value lies within a range defined by two other values. BETWEEN works with scalar range limits of all types; the OVERLAPS predicate looks at two time periods (defined either by start and end points or by a starting time and an INTERVAL) to see if they overlap in time.

## 20.1 The BETWEEN Predicate

The BETWEEN predicate is a feature of SQL that is used enough to deserve special attention. It is also just tricky enough to fool beginning programmers.

```
<between predicate>
 ::= <row value predicand> <between predicate part 2>

<between predicate part 2> ::=
[NOT] BETWEEN [ASYMMETRIC | SYMMETRIC]
<row value predicand> AND <row value predicand>
```

If neither SYMMETRIC nor ASYMMETRIC is specified, then ASYMMETRIC is implicit. This is the original definition of the shorthand that only worked with single valued predicands. This is most likely what you will see in your product.

ASYMMETRIC is the original version of BETWEEN; the first parameter is the ordered lower limit and the second parameter is the ordered upper limit. ASYMMETRIC is a version of BETWEEN that was implemented in Microsoft "semi-SQL" ACCESS language that allowed the upper and lower limited to flip. ANSI X3H2 approved this change for ONE meeting that Microsoft attended and X3H2 reversed itself the next. Microsoft went home and did it wrong.

Let x, y, and z be the first, second, and third row value predicands, respectively, so we can start defining this predicate.

**Joe Celko's SQL for Smarties. DOI: 10.1016/B978-0-12-382022-8.00020-X**

```
1. x NOT BETWEEN SYMMETRIC y AND z
means
NOT (x BETWEEN SYMMETRIC y AND z)
```

No surprises here, since that is how SQL has handled optional NOT in all constructs.

```
2. X BETWEEN SYMMETRIC y AND z
means
((x BETWEEN ASYMMETRIC y AND z)
OR (x BETWEEN ASYMMETRIC z AND y))
```

There is a historical note about the early days of ANSI X3H2. We voted to make this the definition of "x BETWEEN y AND z" at one meeting. This was revoked at the next committee meeting, but Microsoft had gone ahead and changed it in their ACCESS database product. They failed to read the follow up papers.

```
3. x NOT BETWEEN ASYMMETRIC y AND z
means
NOT (x BETWEEN ASYMMETRIC y AND z)
```

No surprises here, since that is how SQL has handled optional NOT in all constructs.

```
4. x BETWEEN ASYMMETRIC y AND z
means
x >= y AND x <= z
```

Please note that the endpoints are included in this definition. This predicate works with any data types that can be compared. Most programmers miss this fact and use it only for numeric values. It can be used for character strings and temporal data as well. The <row value> predicands can be expressions or constants, but again, programmers tend to use just constants or column names.

Many optimizers will take special steps for the BETWEEN because SQL implementations often use B+ and other tree indexes that have ranges in their nodes. It is easier for optimizers to produce an efficient `(<column name> BETWEEN :var1 AND :var2)` than it is to optimize `(:var BETWEEN <column name 1> AND <column name 2>)` where :var is either a host variable or a literal because of indexing.

It is also more human-readable than its definition and shows a higher level of abstraction.

### 20.1.1 Results with NULL Values

The results of this predicate with NULLs for the <row value predicand>s follow directly from the definition. If both <row value predicand>s are NULL, the result is UNKNOWN for any value of

<value expression>. If one <row value predicand> is NULL, but not both of them, the result is determined by the value of the first <row value predicand> and its comparison with the remaining non-NULL term. If the first <row value predicand> is NULL, the results are UNKNOWN for any values of <row value predicand>s.

### 20.1.2 Results with Empty Sets

Notice that if first second <row value predicand> is less than the third <row value predicand>, the ASYMMETRIC expression will always be FALSE unless the value is NULL; then it is UNKNOWN. That is a bit confusing, since there is no value to which <value expression> could resolve itself that would produce a TRUE result. But this follows directly from expanding the definition.

```
x BETWEEN ASYMMETRIC 12 AND 15 -- depends on the value of x
x BETWEEN ASYMMETRIC 15 AND 12 -- always FALSE
x BETWEEN ASYMMETRIC NULL AND 15 -- always UNKNOWN
NULL BETWEEN ASYMMETRIC 12 AND 15 -- always UNKNOWN
x BETWEEN ASYMMETRIC 12 AND NULL -- always UNKNOWN
x BETWEEN ASYMMETRIC x AND x -- always TRUE

x BETWEEN SYMMETRIC 12 AND 15 -- depends on the value of x
x BETWEEN SYMMETRIC 15 AND 12 -- depends on the value of x
x BETWEEN SYMMETRIC NULL AND 15 -- always UNKNOWN
NULL BETWEEN SYMMETRIC 12 AND 15 -- always UNKNOWN
x BETWEEN SYMMETRIC 12 AND NULL -- always UNKNOWN
x BETWEEN SYMMETRIC x AND x -- always TRUE
```

### 20.1.3 Programming Tips

The BETWEEN range includes the endpoints, so you have to be careful. For example, changing a percent range on a test into a letter grade:

**Grades**

| low_score | high_score | grade |
|---|---|---|
| 90 | 100 | 'A' |
| 80 | 90 | 'B' |
| 70 | 80 | 'C' |
| 60 | 70 | 'D' |
| 00 | 60 | 'F' |

will not work when a student gets a grade on the borderlines (90, 80, 70, or 60). One way to solve the problem is to change the table by adding 1 to the low scores. Of course, the student who got 90.1 will argue that he should have gotten an 'A' and not a 'B'. If you add 0.01 to the low scores, the student who got 90.001 will argue that he should have gotten an 'A' and not a 'B' and so forth. This is a problem with a continuous variable. A better solution might be to change the predicate to `(score BETWEEN low_score AND high_score) AND (score > low_score)` or simply to `((low_score < score) AND (score <= high_score))`. Neither approach will be much different in this example, since few values will fall on the borders between grades and this table is very, very small.

As a sidebar, you might want to look up an introductory book to Fuzzy Logic (*Fuzzy Thinking: The New Science of Fuzzy Logic*, Bart Kosko, ISBN: 978-0006547136). In that model, an entity can have a degree of membership in a set rather than being strictly in or out of the set. There are some experimental databases that use Fuzzy Logic.

However, some indexing schemes might make the BETWEEN predicate the better choice for larger tables of this sort. They will keep index values in trees whose nodes hold a range of values (look up a description of the B tree family in a computer science book). An optimizer can compare the range of values in the BETWEEN predicate to the range of values in the index nodes as a single action. If the BETWEEN predicate were presented as two comparisons, it might execute them as separate actions against the database, which would be slower.

## 20.2 OVERLAPS Predicate

The OVERLAPS predicate is a feature still not available in most SQL implementations because it requires more of the Standard SQL temporal data features than most implementations have. Many programmers have been "faking" the functionality of the INTERVAL data type with the existing date and time features of their products.

### 20.2.1 Time Periods and OVERLAPS Predicate

Temporal data types and functions are the most irregular features in SQL products. By the time the ANSI/ISO Standards were written, each dialect had its own dialect. But let's start with the concept of an INTERVAL, which is a measure of temporal duration, expressed in units such as days, hours, minutes, and so forth. This is how you add or subtract days to or from a date, hours and minutes to or from a time, and so forth. A time period is defined as having start and stop points in time.

The OVERLAPS predicate compares two time periods. These time periods are defined as row values with two columns. The first column (the starting time) of the pair is always a <datetime> data type and the second column (the termination time) is a <datetime> data type that can be used to compute a <datetime> value. If the starting and termination times are the same, this is an instantaneous event.

The BNF for this predicate is:

```
<overlaps predicate>
 ::= <overlaps predicate part 1> <overlaps predicate part 2>
<overlaps predicate part 1> ::= <row value predicand 1>
<overlaps predicate part 2> ::= OVERLAPS <row value
   predicand 2>
<row value predicand 1> ::= <row value predicand>
<row value predicand 2> ::= <row value predicand>
```

The result of the <overlaps predicate> is formally defined as the result of the following expression:

```
(S1 > S2 AND NOT (S1 >= T2 AND T1 >= T2))
OR (S2 > S1 AND NOT (S2 >= T1 AND T2 >= T1))
OR (S1 = S2 AND (T1 <> T2 OR T1 = T2))
```

where S1 and S2 are the starting times of the two time periods and T1 and T2 are their termination times.

The rules for the OVERLAPS predicate should be intuitive, but they are not. The principles that we wanted in the Standard were the following.

1. A time period includes its starting point, but does not include its end point. The reason for this model is that it follows the ISO convention that there is no 24:00 hrs today; it is 00:00 hrs tomorrow. Half-open durations have closure properties that are useful. The concatenation of two half-open durations is an half-open duration.
2. If the time periods are not instantaneous, they overlap when they share a common time period.
3. If the first term of the predicate is an INTERVAL and the second term is an instantaneous event (a <datetime> data type), they overlap when the second term is in the time period (but is not the end point of the time period).
4. If the first and second terms are both instantaneous events, they overlap only when they are equal.
5. If the starting time is NULL and the finishing time is a known <datetime> value, the finishing time becomes the starting time and we have an event. If the starting time is NULL and the finishing time is an INTERVAL value, then both the finishing and starting times are NULL.

Please consider how your intuition reacts to these results, when the granularity is at the YEAR-MONTH-DAY level. Remember that a day begins at 00:00 hrs.

(today, today) OVERLAPS (today, today) is TRUE
(today, tomorrow) OVERLAPS (today, today) is TRUE
(today, tomorrow) OVERLAPS (tomorrow, tomorrow) is FALSE
(yesterday, today) OVERLAPS (today, tomorrow) is FALSE

This is still not very intuitive, so let's draw pictures. Consider a table of hotel guests with the days of their stays and a table of special events being held at the hotel. The tables might look like this:

```
CREATE TABLE Guests
(guest_name CHARACTER(30) NOT NULL PRIMARY KEY,
arrival_date DATE NOT NULL,
departure_date DATE NOT NULL,
...);

Guests
guest_name          arrival_date      departure_date
=====================================================
'Dorothy Gale'      '2015-02-01'      '2015-11-01'
'Indiana Jones'     '2015-02-01'      '2015-02-01'
'Don Quixote'       '2015-01-01'      '2015-10-01'
'James T. Kirk'     '2015-02-01'      '2015-02-28'
'Santa Claus'       '2015-12-01'      '2015-12-25'

CREATE TABLE Celebrations
(celeb_name CHARACTER(30) PRIMARY KEY,
 celeb_start_date DATE NOT NULL,
 celeb_end_date DATE NOT NULL,
 ...);

Celebrations
celeb_name              celeb_start_date celeb_end_date
=======================================================
'Apple Month'           '2015-02-01'     '2015-02-28'
'Christmas Season'      '2015-12-01'     '2015-12-25'
'Garlic Festival'       '2015-01-15'     '2015-02-15'
'National Pear Week'    '2015-01-01'     '2015-01-07'
'New Year's Day'        '2015-01-01'     '2015-01-01'
'St. Fred's Day'        '2015-02-24'     '2015-02-24'
'Year of the Prune'     '2015-01-01'     '2015-12-31'
```

The BETWEEN operator will work just fine with single dates that fall between the starting and finishing dates of these celebrations, but please remember that the BETWEEN predicate will include the endpoint of an interval and that the OVERLAPS predicate will not. To find out if a particular date occurs during an event, you can simply write queries like

```
SELECT guest_name, celeb_name
 FROM Guests, Celebrations
WHERE arrival_date BETWEEN celeb_start_date AND
   celeb_end_date
  AND arrival_date <> celeb_end_date;
```

which will find the guests who arrived at the hotel during each event. The final predicate can be kept, if you want to conform to the ANSI convention, or dropped if that makes more sense in your situation. From now on, we will keep both endpoints to make the queries easier to read.

```
SELECT guest_name, celeb_name
 FROM Guests, Celebrations
WHERE arrival_date BETWEEN celeb_start_date AND
   celeb_end_date;

Results
guest_name              celeb_name
=========================================
'Dorothy Gale'          'Apple Month'
'Dorothy Gale'          'Garlic Festival'
'Dorothy Gale'          'Year of the Prune'
'Indiana Jones'         'Apple Month'
'Indiana Jones'         'Garlic Festival'
'Indiana Jones'         'Year of the Prune'
'Don Quixote'           'National Pear Week'
'Don Quixote'           'New Year's Day'
'Don Quixote'           'Year of the Prune'
'James T. Kirk'         'Apple Month'
'James T. Kirk'         'Garlic Festival'
'James T. Kirk'         'Year of the Prune'
'Santa Claus'           'Christmas Season'
'Santa Claus'           'Year of the Prune'
```

The obvious question is which guests were at the hotel during each event. A common programming error when trying to find out if two intervals overlap is to write the query with the BETWEEN predicate, thus:

```
SELECT guest_name, celeb_name
 FROM Guests, Celebrations
WHERE arrival_date BETWEEN celeb_start_date AND
   celeb_end_date
  OR departure_date BETWEEN celeb_start_date AND
   celeb_end_date;
```

This is wrong, because it does not cover the case where the event began and finished during the guest's visit. Seeing this error, the programmer will sit down and draw a timeline diagram of all four possible overlapping cases, as shown in Figure 20.1.

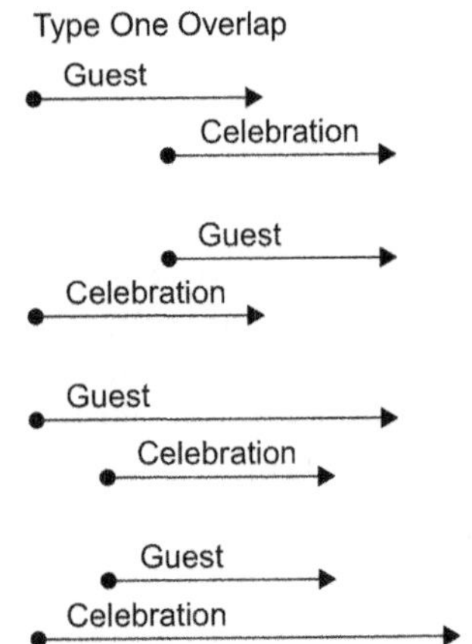


**Figure 20.1 Timeline Diagram of All Possible Overlapping Cases**

So the programmer adds more predicates, thus:

```
SELECT guest_name, celeb_name
 FROM Guests, Celebrations
WHERE arrival_date BETWEEN celeb_start_date AND
    celeb_end_date
   OR departure_date BETWEEN celeb_start_date AND
    celeb_end_date
   OR celeb_start_date BETWEEN arrival_date AND
    departure_date
   OR celeb_end_date BETWEEN arrival_date AND
    departure_date;
```

A thoughtful programmer will notice that the last predicate is not needed and might drop it, but either way, this is a correct query. But it is not the best answer. In the case of the overlapping intervals, there are two cases where a guest's stay at the hotel and an event do not both fall within the same time frame: Either the guest checked out before the event started or the event ended before the guest arrived. If you want to do the logic, that is what the first predicate will work out to be when you also add the conditions that `arrival_date <= departure_date and celeb_start_date <= celeb_end_date`. But it is easier to see in a timeline diagram, as Figure 20.2 shows.

Both cases can be represented in one SQL statement as

```
SELECT guest_name, celeb_name
 FROM Guests, Celebrations
WHERE NOT ((departure_date < celeb_start_date) OR
   (arrival_date > celeb_end_date));
```

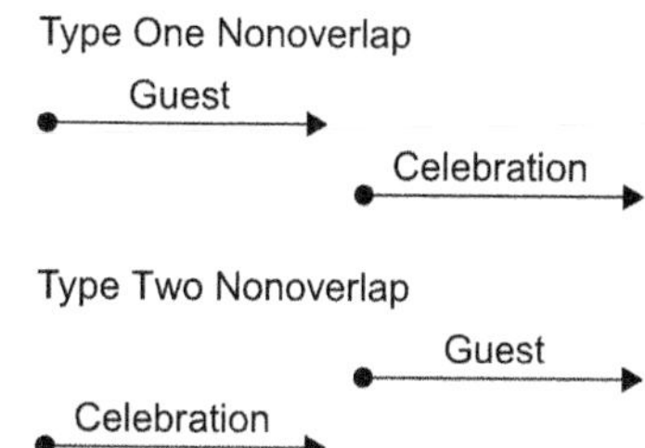


**Figure 20.2 Timeline Diagram**

```
VIEW GuestsEvents
guest_name           celeb_name
=====================================
'Dorothy Gale'       'Apple Month'
'Dorothy Gale'       'Garlic Festival'
'Dorothy Gale'       'St. Fred's Day'
'Dorothy Gale'       'Year of the Prune'
'Indiana Jones'      'Apple Month'
'Indiana Jones'      'Garlic Festival'
'Indiana Jones'      'Year of the Prune'
'Don Quixote'        'Apple Month'
'Don Quixote'        'Garlic Festival'
'Don Quixote'        'National Pear Week'
'Don Quixote'        'New Year's Day'
'Don Quixote'        'St. Fred's Day'
'Don Quixote'        'Year of the Prune'
'James T. Kirk'      'Apple Month'
'James T. Kirk'      'Garlic Festival'
'James T. Kirk'      'St. Fred's Day'
'James T. Kirk'      'Year of the Prune'
'Santa Claus'        'Christmas Season'
'Santa Claus'        'Year of the Prune'
```

This VIEW is handy for other queries. The reason for using the NOT in the WHERE clause is so that you can add or remove it to reverse the sense of the query. For example, to find out how many celebrations each guest could have seen, you would write

```
CREATE VIEW GuestCelebrations (guest_name, celeb_name)
AS SELECT guest_name, celeb_name
   FROM Guests, Celebrations
  WHERE NOT ((departure_date < celeb_start_date) OR
     (arrival_date > celeb_end_date));

SELECT guest_name, COUNT(*) AS celebcount
 FROM GuestCelebrations
GROUP BY guest_name;
```

```
Results
guest_name          celebcount
==============================
'Dorothy Gale'      4
'Indiana Jones'     3
'Don Quixote'       6
'James T. Kirk'     4
'Santa Claus'       2
```

and then to find out how many guests were at the hotel during each celebration, you would write

```
SELECT celeb_name, COUNT(*) AS guest_cnt
 FROM GuestCelebrations
GROUP BY celeb_name;

Result
celeb_name                 guest_cnt
====================================
'Apple Month'              4
'Christmas Season'         1
'Garlic Festival'          4
'National Pear Week'       1
'New Year's Day'           1
'St. Fred's Day'           3
'Year of the Prune'        5
```

This last query is only part of the story. What the hotel management really wants to know is how many room nights were sold for a celebration. A little algebra tells you that the length of an event is `(celeb_end_date - celeb_start_date + INTERVAL '1' DAY)` and that the length of a guest's stay is `(Guest.departure_date - Guest.arrival_date + INTERVAL '1' DAY)`. Let's do one of those timeline charts again, in Figure 20.3.

What we want is the part of the Guests interval that is inside the Celebrations interval.

Guests 1 and 2 spent only part of their time at the celebration; Guest 3 spent all of his time at the celebration and Guest 4 stayed even longer than the celebration. That interval is defined by the two points `(CASE WHEN arrival_date > celeb_start_date`

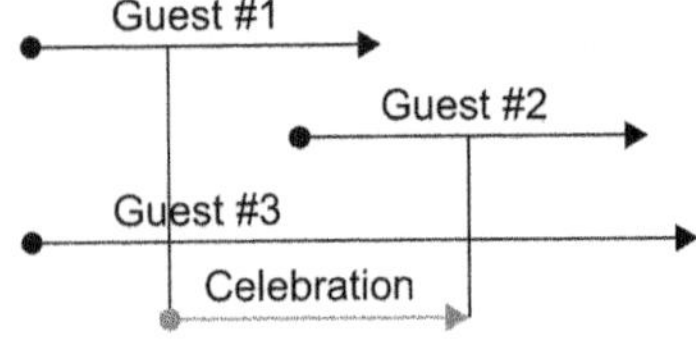


**Figure 20.3 Timeline Diagram**

THEN arrival_date ELSE celeb_start_date END) and (CASE WHEN departure_date < celeb_end_date THEN departure_date ELSE celeb_end_date END).

Instead, you can use the aggregate functions in SQL to build a VIEW on a VIEW, like this:

```
CREATE VIEW Working (guest_name, celeb_name, entry_date,
   exit_date)
AS
SELECT GE.guest_name, GE.celeb_name, celeb_start_date,
   celeb_end_date
 FROM GuestCelebrations AS GE, Celebrations AS E1
WHERE E1.celeb_name = GE.celeb_name
UNION
SELECT GE.guest_name, GE.celeb_name, arrival_date,
   departure_date
 FROM GuestCelebrations AS GE, Guests AS G1
WHERE G1.guest_name = GE.guest_name;
```

```
VIEW Working
guest_name          celeb_name              entry_date     exit_date
===================================================================
'Dorothy Gale'     'Apple Month'           '2015-02-01'   '2015-02-28'
'Dorothy Gale'     'Apple Month'           '2015-02-01'   '2015-11-01'
'Dorothy Gale'     'Garlic Festival'       '2015-02-01'   '2015-11-01'
'Dorothy Gale'     'Garlic Festival'       '2015-01-15'   '2015-02-15'
'Dorothy Gale'     'St. Fred's Day'        '2015-02-01'   '2015-11-01'
'Dorothy Gale'     'St. Fred's Day'        '2015-02-24'   '2015-02-24'
'Dorothy Gale'     'Year of the Prune'     '2015-02-01'   '2015-11-01'
'Dorothy Gale'     'Year of the Prune'     '2015-01-01'   '2015-12-31'
'Indiana Jones'    'Apple Month'           '2015-02-01'   '2015-02-01'
'Indiana Jones'    'Apple Month'           '2015-02-01'   '2015-02-28'
'Indiana Jones'    'Garlic Festival'       '2015-02-01'   '2015-02-01'
'Indiana Jones'    'Garlic Festival'       '2015-01-15'   '2015-02-15'
'Indiana Jones'    'Year of the Prune'     '2015-02-01'   '2015-02-01'
'Indiana Jones'    'Year of the Prune'     '2015-01-01'   '2015-12-31'
'Don Quixote'      'Apple Month'           '2015-02-01'   '2015-02-28'
'Don Quixote'      'Apple Month'           '2015-01-01'   '2015-10-01'
'Don Quixote'      'Garlic Festival'       '2015-01-01'   '2015-10-01'
'Don Quixote'      'Garlic Festival'       '2015-01-15'   '2015-02-15'
'Don Quixote'      'National Pear Week'    '2015-01-01'   '2015-01-07'
'Don Quixote'      'National Pear Week'    '2015-01-01'   '2015-10-01'
'Don Quixote'      'New Year's Day'        '2015-01-01'   '2015-01-01'
'Don Quixote'      'New Year's Day'        '2015-01-01'   '2015-10-01'
'Don Quixote'      'St. Fred's Day'        '2015-02-24'   '2015-02-24'
'Don Quixote'      'St. Fred's Day'        '2015-01-01'   '2015-10-01'
'Don Quixote'      'Year of the Prune'     '2015-01-01'   '2015-12-31'
'Don Quixote'      'Year of the Prune'     '2015-01-01'   '2015-10-01'
```

```
'James T. Kirk'     'Apple Month'          '2015-02-01'    '2015-02-28'
'James T. Kirk'     'Garlic Festival'      '2015-02-01'    '2015-02-28'
'James T. Kirk'     'Garlic Festival'      '2015-01-15'    '2015-02-15'
'James T. Kirk'     'St.Fred's Day'        '2015-02-01'    '2015-02-28'
'James T. Kirk'     'St. Fred's Day'       '2015-02-24'    '2015-02-24'
'James T. Kirk'     'Year of the Prune'    '2015-02-01'    '2015-02-28'
'James T. Kirk'     'Year of the Prune'    '2015-01-01'    '2015-12-31'
'Santa Claus'       'Christmas Season'     '2015-12-01'    '2015-12-25'
'Santa Claus'       'Year of the Prune'    '2015-12-01'    '2015-12-25'
'Santa Claus'       'Year of the Prune'    '2015-01-01'    '2015-12-31'
```

This will put the earliest and latest points in both intervals into one column. Now we can construct a VIEW like this:

```
CREATE VIEW Attendees (guest_name, celeb_name, entry_date,
   exit_date)
AS
SELECT guest_name, celeb_name, MAX(entry_date),
   MIN(exit_date)
 FROM Working
GROUP BY guest_name, celeb_name;
```

```
VIEW Attendees
guest_name          celeb_name              entry_date   exit_date
=====================================================================
'Dorothy Gale'      'Apple Month'           '2015-02-01' '2015-02-28'
'Dorothy Gale'      'Garlic Festival'       '2015-02-01' '2015-02-15'
'Dorothy Gale'      'St. Fred's Day'        '2015-02-24' '2015-02-24'
'Dorothy Gale'      'Year of the Prune'     '2015-02-01' '2015-11-01'
'Indiana Jones'     'Apple Month'           '2015-02-01' '2015-02-01'
'Indiana Jones'     'Garlic Festival'       '2015-02-01' '2015-02-01'
'Indiana Jones'     'Year of the Prune'     '2015-02-01' '2015-02-01'
'Don Quixote'       'Apple Month'           '2015-02-01' '2015-02-28'
'Don Quixote'       'Garlic Festival'       '2015-01-15' '2015-02-15'
'Don Quixote'       'National Pear Week'    '2015-01-01' '2015-01-07'
'Don Quixote'       'New Year's Day'        '2015-01-01' '2015-01-01'
'Don Quixote'       'St. Fred's Day'        '2015-02-24' '2015-02-24'
'Don Quixote'       'Year of the Prune'     '2015-01-01' '2015-10-01'
'James T. Kirk'     'Apple Month'           '2015-02-01' '2015-02-28'
'James T. Kirk'     'Garlic Festival'       '2015-02-01' '2015-02-15'
'James T. Kirk'     'St. Fred's Day'        '2015-02-24' '2015-02-24'
'James T. Kirk'     'Year of the Prune'     '2015-02-01' '2015-02-28'
'Santa Claus'       'Christmas Season'      '2015-12-01' '2015-12-25'
'Santa Claus'       'Year of the Prune'     '2015-12-01' '2015-12-25'
```

The Attendees VIEW can be used to compute the total number of room days for each celebration. Assume that the difference of two dates will return an integer that is the number of days between them:

```
SELECT celeb_name,
    SUM(exit_date - entry_date + INTERVAL '1' DAY)
    AS room_days
 FROM Attendees
GROUP BY celeb_name;

Result
celeb_name              room_days
=================================
'Apple Month'           85
'Christmas Season'      25
'Garlic Festival'       63
'National Pear Week'    7
'New Year's Day'        1
'St. Fred's Day'        3
'Year of the Prune'     602
```

If you would like to get a count of the room days sold in the month of January, you could use this query, which avoids a BETWEEN or OVERLAPS predicate completely.

```
SELECT SUM(CASE WHEN depart > DATE '2015-01-31'
         THEN DATE '2015-01-31'
         ELSE depart END
     - CASE WHEN arrival_date < DATE '2015-01-01'
          THEN DATE '2015-01-01'
          ELSE arrival_date END + INTERVAL '1' DAY)
    AS room_days
 FROM Guests
WHERE depart > DATE '2015-01-01'
  AND arrival_date <= DATE '2015-01-31';
```

# THE [NOT] IN() PREDICATE

The IN() predicate is one of the "abbreviations" that is allowed in SQL. It can be expanded into the usual AND, OR, and NOT logical operators, but it is easier to see the intent of the programmer with this syntax. New SQL programmers stick to the more familiar "nonabbreviated" logic for two reasons: (1) it looks like their procedural language and (2) they think the optimizer will do better with nonabbreviated logic. This is not true at all.

The IN() syntax is very natural and was borrowed and generalized from the Pascal language. It takes a value on the left side and sees if it is in a list of comparable values on the right side. Standard SQL allows value expressions in the list or for you to use a query to construct the list. The syntax is:

```
<in predicate> ::=
<row value predicand> = [NOT] IN <in predicate value>

<in predicate value> ::= <table subquery> | <left paren>
   <in value list> <right paren>

<in value list> ::= <row value expression> [{<comma>
   <row value expression>}..]
```

The expression

```
<row value constructor> NOT IN <in predicate value>
```

means

```
NOT (<row value constructor> IN <in predicate value>)
```

This pattern for the use of the keyword NOT is found in most of the other SQL predicates.

The SQL:2006 Standards say that if the <in value list> consists of a single <row value expression>, then that <row value expression> shall not be a <scalar subquery>. This syntax rule resolves an ambiguity in which <in predicate value> might be interpreted either as a <table subquery> or as a <scalar subquery>. This means that:

```
(<in predicate value>)
```

**Joe Celko's SQL for Smarties. DOI: 10.1016/B978-0-12-382022-8.00021-1**

is equivalent to the <table value constructor>:

```
(VALUES <in predicate value>)
```

Using DB2 version 9.7, the following will not work:

```
SELECT *
 FROM Foobar
WHERE (x, y) IN (( 'x1', y1));
```

It returns an error SQL0104N. An unexpected token "," was found following ", y) in (('x1'". Expected tokens may include: "+". SQLSTATE=42601. However, this does work:

```
SELECT *
 FROM Foobar
WHERE (x, y) IN (VALUES ('x1', 1));
```

The `<row value constructor> IN <in predicate value>` has the same effect as `<row value constructor> = ANY <in predicate value>` by definition. Most optimizers will recognize this and execute the same code for both. This means that if the `<in predicate value>` is empty, such as one you would get from a subquery that returns no rows, the results will be equivalent to `(<row value constructor> = (NULL, .., NULL))`, which is always evaluated to UNKNOWN. Likewise, if the `<in predicate value>` is an explicit list of NULLs, the results will be UNKNOWN. However, please remember that there is a difference between an empty table and a table with rows of all NULLs.

IN() predicates with a subquery and can sometimes be converted into EXISTS predicates, but there are some problems and differences in the predicates. The conversion to an EXISTS predicate might be a good way to improve performance, but it will not be as easy to read as the original IN() predicate. An EXISTS predicate can use indexes to find (or fail to find) a single value that confirms (or denies) the predicate, whereas the IN() predicate often has to build the results of the subquery in a working table. Know your SQL product.

## 21.1 Optimizing the IN() Predicate

Many database engines have no statistics about the relative frequency of the values in a list of constants, so they will scan that list in the order in which they appear. People like to order lists alphabetically or in numeric order, but it might be better to order the list from most frequently occurring values to least frequent. It is also pointless to have duplicate values in the constant list, since the predicate will return TRUE if it matches the first duplicate it finds and never get to the second occurrence. Likewise, if the predicate is FALSE for that value, it wastes computer time to traverse a needlessly long list.

Many SQL engines perform an IN() predicate with a subquery by building the result set of the subquery first as a temporary working table, then scanning that result table from left to right. This can be expensive in many cases; for example, in a query to find employees in a city with a major sports team (we want them to get tickets for us), we could write:

```
SELECT emp_name
 FROM Personnel AS P
WHERE P.city_name
   IN (SELECT S.city_name
       FROM SportTeams AS S);
```

assuming that city names are unique. But let us further assume that our personnel are located in (n) cities and the sports teams are in (m) cities, where (m) is much greater than (n). If the matching cities appear near the front of the list generated by the subquery expression, it will perform much faster than if they appear at the end of the list. In the case of a subquery expression you have no control over how the subquery is presented back in the containing query.

However, you can order the expressions in a list in the most likely to occur order, such as

```
SELECT emp_name
 FROM Personnel
WHERE city_name
   IN ('New York', 'Chicago', 'Atlanta', ..., 'Austin');
```

Standard SQL allows row expression comparisons, so if you have a Standard SQL implementation with separate columns for the city and state, you could write:

```
SELECT *
 FROM Personnel
WHERE (city_name, state_code)
   IN (SELECT city_name, state_code
       FROM SportTeams);
```

Today, all major versions of SQL remove duplicates in the result table of the subquery, so you do not have to use an explicit SELECT DISTINCT in the subquery. You might see this in legacy code.

The major SQL products also kick in optimizations where the list gets to a certain size. This can lead to weird behavior from a human viewpoint; a list of (n) values below the threshold (k) items takes longer to search a list with (n >= k) items.

Some of the tricks are:

1. Construct a working table with an index.
2. Construct a working table with a hidden column of the frequency of each value and sort on it. The initial frequency values can come from the statistics on the left-side table.
3. Organize the list as a heap in an array. A heap is an array such that for each element in position (n) in the list, the (n + 1) element is lower and the (2n + 1) element is greater. It is a quick way to do a binary search.

Another trick is to replace the IN() predicate with a JOIN operation. For example, you have a table of restaurant telephone numbers and a guidebook and you want to pick out the four-star places, so you write this query:

```
SELECT R.restaurant_name, R.phone_nbr
 FROM Restaurants AS R
WHERE E.restaurant_name
  IN (SELECT Q.restaurant_name
       FROM QualityGuide AS Q
      WHERE Q.michelin_stars = 4);
```

If there is an index on QualityGuide.michelin_stars, the SQL engine will probably build a temporary table of the four-star places and pass it on to the outer query. The outer query will then handle it as if it were a list of constants.

However, this is not the sort of column that you would normally index. Without an index on Michelin stars, the engine will simply do a sequential search of the QualityGuide table. This query can be replaced with a JOIN query, thus:

```
SELECT R.restaurant_name, R.phone_nbr
 FROM Restaurants AS R, QualityGuide AS Q
WHERE michelin_stars = 4
  AND R.restaurant_name = Q.restaurant_name;
```

This query should run faster, since restaurant_name is a key for both tables and will be indexed to ensure uniqueness. However, this can return duplicate rows in the result table that you can handle with a SELECT DISTINCT. Consider a more budget-minded query, where we want places with a meal under $10 and the menu guidebook lists all the meals. The query looks about the same:

```
SELECT R.restaurant_name, R.phone_nbr
 FROM Restaurants AS R
WHERE R.restaurant_name
  IN (SELECT M.restaurant_name
       FROM MenuGuide AS M
      WHERE M.meal_price <= 10.00);
```

and you would expect to be able to replace it with

```
SELECT R.restaurant_name, R.phone_nbr
 FROM Restaurants AS R, MenuGuide AS M
WHERE M.meal_price <= 10.00
  AND R.restaurant_name = M.restaurant_name;
```

Every item in Murphy's Two-Dollar Hash House will get a line in the results of the JOIN-ed version, however. This can be fixed by changing SELECT restaurant_name, phone_nbr to SELECT DISTINCT restaurant_name, phone_nbr, but it will cost more time to remove the duplicates. There is no good general advice, except to experiment with your particular product.

The NOT IN() predicate is probably better replaced with a NOT EXISTS predicate. Using the restaurant example again, our friend John has a list of eateries and we want to see those that are not in the guidebook. The natural formation of the query is:

```
SELECT J.*
 FROM JohnsBook AS J
WHERE J.restaurant_name
  NOT IN (SELECT Q.restaurant_name
        FROM QualityGuide AS Q);
```

But you can write the same query with a NOT EXISTS predicate and it will probably run faster:

```
SELECT J.*
 FROM JohnsBook AS J
WHERE NOT EXISTS
 (SELECT *
    FROM QualityGuide AS Q
   WHERE Q.restaurant_name = J.restaurant_name);
```

The reason the second version will probably run faster is that it can test for existence using the indexes on both tables. The NOT IN() version has to test all the values in the subquery table for inequality. Many SQL implementations will construct a temporary table from the IN() predicate subquery if it has a WHERE clause, but the temporary table will not have any indexes. The temporary table can also have duplicates and a random ordering of its rows, so that the SQL engine has to do a full-table scan.

## 21.2 Replacing ORs with the IN( ) Predicate

A simple trick that beginning SQL programmers often miss is that an IN() predicate can often replace a set of OR-ed predicates. For example:

```
SELECT *
 FROM QualityControlReport
```

```
WHERE test_1 = 'passed'
 OR test_2 = 'passed'
 OR test_3 = 'passed'
 OR test_4 = 'passed';
```

can be rewritten as:

```
SELECT *
 FROM QualityControlReport
WHERE 'passed' IN (test_1, test_2, test_3, test_4);
```

The reason this is hard to see is that programmers get used to thinking of either a subquery or a simple list of constants; they miss the fact that the IN() predicate list can be a list of expressions. The optimizer would have handled each of the original predicates separately in the WHERE clause, but it has to handle the IN() predicate as a single item, which can change the order of evaluation. This might or might not be faster than the list of OR-ed predicates for a particular query. This formulation might cause the predicate to become non-indexable, you should check the indexability rules of your particular DBMS.

## 21.3 NULLs and the IN() Predicate

NULLs make some special problems in a NOT IN() predicate with a subquery. Consider these two tables:

```
CREATE TABLE Table1 (x INTEGER);
INSERT INTO Table1 VALUES (1), (2), (3), (4);

CREATE TABLE Table2 (x INTEGER);
INSERT INTO Table2 VALUES (1), (NULL), (2);
```

Now execute the query:

```
SELECT *
FROM Table1
WHERE x NOT IN (SELECT x FROM Table2)
```

Let's work it out step by painful step:

1. Do the subquery:

```
SELECT *
  FROM Table1
 WHERE x NOT IN (1, NULL, 2);
```

2. Convert the NOT IN() to its definition:

```
SELECT *
  FROM Table1
 WHERE NOT (x IN (1, NULL, 2));
```

3. Expand `IN()` predicate:

```
SELECT *
  FROM Table1
 WHERE NOT ((x = 1) OR (x = NULL) OR (x = 2));
```

4. Apply DeMorgan's law:

```
SELECT *
  FROM Table1
 WHERE ((x <> 1) AND (x <> NULL) AND (x <> 2));
```

5. Constant logical expression:

```
SELECT *
  FROM Table1
 WHERE ((x <> 1) AND UNKNOWN AND (x <> 2));
```

6. Reduction of `OR` to constant:

```
SELECT *
 FROM Table1
WHERE UNKNOWN;
```

7. Results are always empty.
   Now try this with another set of tables:

```
CREATE TABLE Table3 (x INTEGER);
INSERT INTO Table3 VALUES (1), (2), (NULL), (4);

CREATE TABLE Table4 (x INTEGER);
INSERT INTO Table3 VALUES (1), (3), (2);
```

Let's work out the same query step by painful step again.

1. Do the subquery:

```
SELECT *
  FROM Table3
 WHERE x NOT IN (1, 3, 2);
```

2. Convert the `NOT IN()` to Boolean expression:

```
SELECT *
  FROM Table3
 WHERE NOT (x IN (1, 3, 2));
```

3. Expand `IN()` predicate:

```
SELECT *
  FROM Table3
 WHERE NOT ((x = 1) OR (x = 3) OR (x = 2));
```

4. DeMorgan's law:

```
SELECT *
  FROM Table3
 WHERE ((x <> 1) AND (x <> 3) AND (x <> 2));
```

5. Computed result set; I will show it as a UNION with substitutions:

```
SELECT *
  FROM Table3
 WHERE ((1 <> 1) AND (1 <> 3) AND (1 <> 2)) -- FALSE
UNION ALL
SELECT *
  FROM Table3
 WHERE ((2 <> 1) AND (2 <> 3) AND (2 <> 2)) -- FALSE
UNION ALL
SELECT * FROM Table3
 WHERE ((CAST(NULL AS INTEGER) <> 1)
    AND (CAST(NULL AS INTEGER) <> 3)
    AND (CAST(NULL AS INTEGER) <> 2)) -- UNKNOWN
UNION ALL
SELECT *
  FROM Table3
 WHERE ((4 <> 1) AND (4 <> 3) AND (4 <> 2)); -- TRUE
```

6. Result is one row = (4).

## 21.4 IN() Predicate and Referential Constraints

One of the most popular uses for the IN() predicate is in a CHECK() clause on a table. The usual form is a list of values that are legal for a column, such as

```
CREATE TABLE Addresses
(addressee_name CHAR(25) NOT NULL PRIMARY KEY,
 street_loc CHAR(25) NOT NULL,
 city_name CHAR(20) NOT NULL,
 state_code CHAR(2) NOT NULL
      CONSTRAINT valid_state_code
      CHECK (state_code IN ('AL', 'AK', ..)),
 ..);
```

This method works fine with a short list of values, but it has problems with a longer list. Please note that "short" and "long" are very relative as storage gets bigger, cheaper, and faster.

It might be important to arrange the values in the order that they are most likely to match to the two-letter state_code to speed up the search. Even though DML could have optimizations, the DDL might not! You also have to remember that DML and DDL treat NULLs differently. An UNKNOWN is treated as TRUE in the DDL and as FALSE in the DML.

In Standard SQL a constraint can reference other tables, so you could write the same constraint as:

```
CREATE TABLE Addresses
(addressee_name CHAR(25) NOT NULL PRIMARY KEY,
 street_loc CHAR(25) NOT NULL,
 city_name CHAR(20) NOT NULL,
 state_code CHAR(2) NOT NULL,
 CONSTRAINT valid_state_code
 CHECK (state_code
   IN (SELECT state_code
        FROM ZipCodes AS Z
       WHERE Z.state_code = Addresses.state_code)),
 );
```

The advantage of this is that you can change the ZipCodes table and thereby change the effect of the constraint on the Addresses table. This is fine for adding more data in the outer reference (i.e., Puerto Rico joins the Union and gets the code 'QB'), but it has a bad effect when you try to delete data in the outer reference (i.e., California secedes from the Union and every row with 'CA' for a state code is now invalid, or Texas splits into five new states with new ZIP codes and state codes).

As a rule of thumb, use the `IN(<list>)` predicate in a `CHECK()` constraint when the list is short, static, and unique to one table. When the list is long, dynamic, or global to many tables then put the `IN(<select statement>)` predicate in a `CHECK()` constraint on the domain.

Use a `REFERENCES` clause to a look-up table when the list is long and dynamic, or when several other schema objects (`VIEW`s, stored procedures, etc.) reference the values. A separate table can have an index and that makes a big difference in searching and doing joins.

## 21.5 IN( ) Predicate and Scalar Queries

As mentioned before, the list of an `IN()` predicate can be any scalar expression. This includes scalar subqueries, but most people do not seem to know that this is possible. For example, given tables that model warehouses, trucking centers, and so forth, we can find out whether we have a product, identified by its UPC code, somewhere in the enterprise.

```
SELECT P.upc
 FROM Picklist AS P
WHERE P.upc
  IN ((SELECT upc FROM Warehouse AS W WHERE W.upc = P.upc),
```

```
  (SELECT upc FROM Stores AS S WHERE S.upc = P.upc),
  (SELECT upc FROM Garbage AS G WHERE G.upc = P.upc));
```

The empty result sets will become NULLs in the list. The alternative to this is usually a chain of OUTER JOINs or an OR-ed list of EXISTS() predicates.

This is a strange construction at the time I am writing this chapter and might not work very well. But check it out when you are reading this book. The trend in SQL is toward parallel query processing so each of the scalar expressions could be done at the same time.

A more useful version is in stored procedures with a long parameter list of related values. The simplest version is to use a list of constants like this:

```
SELECT *
 FROM Parameter_List
WHERE Parameter_List.i
   IN (SELECT X.i
       FROM (VALUES (1), (2), (3)) AS X(i));
```

This can be generalized to row constructors:

```
SELECT Parameter_List.*
 FROM Parameter_List
WHERE (Parameter_List.i, Parameter_List.j)
   IN (SELECT X.i, X.j
        FROM (VALUES (1, 'a'), (2, 'b'), (3, 'c'))
       AS X(i, j));
```

But the real power comes from taking an input list of parameters and converting it into a table with the VALUES() construct. For example, given a variable list of GTIN (Global Trade Item Number) item identifiers, you can construct a procedure to return a result based on that list. If not, all parameters are given in the CALL and then NULLs will be passed instead.

```
CREATE PROCEDURE Foobar
(IN in_gtin_1 CHAR(15), .. IN in_gtin_n CHAR(15))
LANGUAGE SQL
SQL DATA
..
BEGIN
..
SELECT << something here >>
 FROM Products AS P
WHERE gtin
```

```
    IN (SELECT Picklist.item
        FROM (VALUES (in_gtin_1),
              ..., (in_gtin_n)) AS Picklist(item)
        WHERE Picklist.item IS NOT NULL);
..
END;
```

Alternatively, the VALUES() list elements can be expressions such as COALESCE (in_gtin_n, '123456789012345') or anything that returns an appropriate scalar value.

# EXISTS( ) PREDICATE

The EXISTS predicate is very natural. It is a test for a nonempty set (read: table). If there are any rows in its subquery, it is TRUE; otherwise, it is FALSE. This predicate does not give an UNKNOWN result. The syntax is:

```
<exists predicate> ::= [NOT] EXISTS <table subquery>
```

It is worth mentioning that a <table subquery> is always inside parentheses to avoid problems in the grammar during parsing.

In SQL-89, the rules stated that the subquery had to have a SELECT clause with one column or an asterisk (*). If the SELECT * option was used, the database engine would (in theory) pick one column and use it. This fiction was needed because SQL-89 defined subqueries as having only one column. Things are better today.

Some early SQL implementations would work better with EXISTS(SELECT <column> ..), EXISTS(SELECT <constant> ..), or EXISTS(SELECT * ..) versions of the predicate. Today, there is no difference in the three forms in any SQL I know. The EXISTS(SELECT * ..) is now the preferred form since it shows that we are working at the table level, without regard to columns.

Indexes are very useful for EXISTS() predicates because they can be searched while the base table is left *completely alone.* For example, we want to find all the employees who were born on the same day as *any* famous person. The query could be

```
SELECT P.emp_name AS famous_person_birth_date_guy
  FROM Personnel AS P
 WHERE EXISTS
  (SELECT *
    FROM Celebrities AS C
    WHERE P.birth_date = C.birth_date);
```

If the table Celebrities has an index on its birth_date column, the optimizer will get the current employee's birth_date P.birth_date and look up that value in the index. If the value is in the index, the predicate is TRUE and we do not need to look at the Celebrities table at all.

Joe Celko's SQL for Smarties. DOI: 10.1016/B978-0-12-382022-8.00022-3

If it is not in the index, the predicate is FALSE and there is still no need to look at the Celebrities table. This should be fast, since indexes are smaller than their tables and are structured for very fast searching.

However, if Celebrities has no index on its birth_date column, the query may have to look at every row to see if there is a birth_date that matches the current employee's birth_date. There are some tricks that a good optimizer can use to speed things up in this situation.

## 22.1 EXISTS and NULLs

A NULL might not be a value, but it does exist in SQL. This is often a problem for a new SQL programmer who is having trouble with the concept of NULLs and how they behave.

Think of them as being like a brown paper bag—you know that something is inside because you lifted it up and felt a weight, but you do not know exactly what that something is. If you felt an empty bag, you know to stop looking. For example, we want to find all the Personnel who were not born on the same day as a famous person. This can be answered with the negation of the original query, like this:

```
SELECT P.emp_name AS famous_birth_date_person
 FROM Personnel AS P
WHERE NOT EXISTS
   (SELECT *
     FROM Celebrities AS C
     WHERE P.birth_date = C.birth_date);
```

But assume that among the Celebrities, we have a movie star who will not admit her age, shown in the row ('Gloria Glamor', NULL). A new SQL programmer might expect that Ms. Glamor would not match to anyone, since we do not know her birth_date yet. Actually, she will match to everyone, since there is a chance that they may match when some tabloid newspaper finally gets a copy of her birth certificate. But work out the subquery in the usual way to convince yourself:

```
..
WHERE NOT EXISTS
   (SELECT *
     FROM Celebrities
     WHERE P.birth_date = NULL);
```

becomes

```
..
WHERE NOT EXISTS
  (SELECT *
    FROM Celebrities
    WHERE UNKNOWN);
```

which then becomes

```
..
WHERE TRUE;
```

and you will see that the predicate tests to UNKNOWN because of the NULL comparison, and therefore fails whenever we look at Ms. Glamor.

Another problem with NULLs is found when you attempt to convert IN predicates to EXISTS predicates. Using our example of matching our Personnel to famous people, the query can be rewritten as:

```
SELECT P.emp_name AS famous_birth_date_person
 FROM Personnel AS P
WHERE P.birth_date
  NOT IN
  (SELECT C.birth_date
    FROM Celebrities AS C);
```

However, consider a more complex version of the same query, where the celebrity has to have been born in New York City. The IN predicate would be:

```
SELECT P.emp_name, 'was born on a day without a famous New
   Yorker!'
 FROM Personnel AS P
WHERE P.birth_date
  NOT IN
  (SELECT C.birth_date
    FROM Celebrities AS C
    WHERE C.birth_city_name = 'New York');
```

and you would think that the EXISTS version would be:

```
SELECT P.emp_name, 'was born on a day without a famous New
   Yorker!'
 FROM Personnel AS P
WHERE NOT EXISTS
  (SELECT *
   FROM Celebrities AS C
   WHERE C.birth_city_name = 'New York'
    AND C.birth_date = P.birth_date);
```

Assume that Gloria Glamor is our only New Yorker and we still do not know her birth_date. The subquery will be empty for every employee in the NOT EXISTS predicate version, because her NULL birth_date will not test equal to the known employee birthdays.

That means that the NOT EXISTS predicate will return TRUE and we will get every employee to match to Ms. Glamor. But now look at the IN predicate version, which will have a single NULL in the subquery result. This predicate will be equivalent to (Personnel.birth_date = NULL), which is always UNKNOWN, and we will get no Personnel back.

Likewise, you cannot, in general, transform the quantified comparison predicates into EXISTS predicates, because of the possibility of NULL values. Remember that x <> ALL <subquery> is shorthand for x NOT IN <subquery> and x = ANY <subquery> is shorthand for x IN <subquery>, and it will not surprise you.

In general, the EXISTS predicates will run faster than the IN predicates. The problem is in deciding whether to build the query or the subquery first; the optimal approach depends on the size and distribution of values in each, and that cannot usually be known until runtime.

## 22.2 EXISTS and INNER JOINs

The [NOT] EXISTS predicate is almost always used with a correlated subquery. Very often the subquery can be "flattened" into a JOIN, which will often run faster than the original query. Our sample query can be converted into:

```
SELECT P.emp_name AS famous_birth_date_person
 FROM Personnel AS P, Celebrities AS C
WHERE P.birth_date = C.birth_date;
```

The advantage of the JOIN version is that it allows us to show columns from both tables. We should make the query more informative by rewriting the query:

```
SELECT P.emp_name, C.emp_name
 FROM Personnel AS P, Celebrities AS C
WHERE P.birth_date = C.birth_date;
```

This new query could be written with an EXISTS() predicate, but that is a waste of resources.

```
SELECT P.emp_name, 'has the same birth_date as ',
   C.emp_name
 FROM Personnel AS P, Celebrities AS C
WHERE EXISTS
  (SELECT *
    FROM Celebrities AS C2
    WHERE P.birth_date = C2.birth_date
    AND C.emp_name = C2.emp_name);
```

## 22.3 NOT EXISTS and OUTER JOINs

The NOT EXISTS version of this predicate is almost always used with a correlated subquery. Very often the subquery can be "flattened" into an OUTER JOIN, which will often run faster than the original query. Our other sample query was:

```
SELECT P.emp_name AS Non_famous_New_Yorker_birth_date
 FROM Personnel AS P
WHERE NOT EXISTS
   (SELECT *
     FROM Celebrities AS C
     WHERE C.birth_city_name = 'New York'
      AND C.birth_date = P.birth_date);
```

which we can replace with:

```
SELECT P.emp_name AS famous_New_Yorker_birth_date
 FROM Personnel AS P
     LEFT OUTER JOIN
     Celebrities AS C
     ON C.birth_city_name = 'New York'
      AND C.birth_date = E2.birth_date
WHERE C.emp_name IS NULL;
```

This is assuming that we know each and every celebrity name in the Celebrities table. If the column in the WHERE clause could have NULLs in its base table, then we could not prune out the generated NULLs. The test for NULL should always be on (a column of) the primary key, which cannot be NULL. Relating this back to the example, how could a celebrity be a celebrity with an unknown name? Even The Unknown Comic had a name ("The Unknown Comic").

## 22.4 EXISTS( ) and Quantifiers

Formal logic makes use of quantifiers that can be applied to propositions. The two forms are "For all x, P(x)" and "For some x, P(x)". If you want to look up formulas in a textbook, the traditional symbol for the universal quantifier is ∀, an inverted letter A, and the symbol for the existential quantifier is ∃, a rotated letter E.

The big question over 100 years ago was that of existential import in formal logic. Everyone agreed that saying "All men are mortal" implies that "No men are not mortal," but does it also imply that "Some men are mortal"—that we have to have at least one man who is mortal?

Existential import lost the battle and the modern convention is that "All men are mortal" has the same meaning as "There are no men who are immortal," but does not imply that any men exist at all. This is the convention followed in the design of SQL. Consider the statement "Some salesmen are liars" and the way we would write it with the EXISTS() predicate in SQL:

```
..
EXISTS(SELECT *
    FROM Personnel AS P, Liars AS L
    WHERE P.job = 'Salesman'
     AND P.emp_name = L.emp_name);
```

If we are more cynical about salesmen, we might want to formulate the predicate, "All salesmen are liars" with the EXISTS predicate in SQL, using the transform rule just discussed:

```
..
NOT EXISTS(SELECT *
     FROM Personnel AS P
     WHERE P.job = 'Salesman'
      AND P.emp_name
       NOT IN
       (SELECT L.emp_name
         FROM Liars AS L));
```

which, informally, says, "There are no salesmen who are not liars" in English. In this case, the IN predicate can be changed into a JOIN, which should improve performance and be a bit easier to read.

## 22.5 EXISTS() and Referential Constraints

Standard SQL was designed so that the declarative referential constraints could be expressed as EXISTS() predicates in a CHECK() clause. For example:

```
CREATE TABLE Addresses
(addressee_name CHAR(25) NOT NULL PRIMARY KEY,
 street_addr CHAR(25) NOT NULL,
 city_name CHAR(20) NOT NULL,
 state_code CHAR(2) NOT NULL
   REFERENCES ZipCodes(state_code),
..);
```

could be written as:

```
CREATE TABLE Addresses
(addressee_name CHAR(25) NOT NULL PRIMARY KEY,
street_addr CHAR(25) NOT NULL,
```

```
city_name CHAR(20) NOT NULL,
state_code CHAR(2) NOT NULL,
CONSTRAINT valid_state_code
 CHECK (EXISTS(SELECT *
        FROM ZipCodes AS Z1
        WHERE Z1.state_code = Addresses.state_code)),
..);
```

There is no advantage to this expression for the Database Administrator, since you cannot attach referential actions with the CHECK() constraint. However, an SQL database can use the same mechanisms in the SQL compiler for both constructions.

## 22.6 EXISTS and Three-Valued Logic

This example is due to an article by Lee Fesperman at FirstSQL (http://www.firstsql.com/) using Chris Date's "Suppliers_Parts" table with three rows. FirstSQL is a product based on the two NULLs Codd proposed in his *Second Relational Model.* It asks questions about the three-valued logic and whether an UNKNOWN exists in the same sense as a known value.

```
CREATE TABLE Suppliers_Parts
(sup_nbr CHAR(2) NOT NULL PRIMARY KEY,
part_nbr CHAR(2) NOT NULL,
onhand_qty INTEGER CHECK (onhand_qty > 0));

sup_nbr part_nbr onhand_qty
==============================
'S1'    'P'      NULL
'S2'    'P'      200
'S3'    'P'      1000
```

The row ('S1', 'P', NULL) means that supplier 'S1' supplies part 'P' but we do not know what quantity he has. The query we wish to answer is, "Find suppliers of part 'P', but not with a quantity of 1000 on hand"; the correct answer is 'S2' based on an on-hand quantity of 200 units. All suppliers in the table supply 'P', and we disqualify 'S3', who has a quantity of 1000 units, but we do not know what quantity 'S1' has. The only supplier we select for certain is 'S2'.

An SQL query to retrieve this result would be:

```
SELECT SPX.sup_nbr
 FROM SupplierParts AS SPX
WHERE px.part_nbr = 'P'
  AND 1000
```

```
NOT IN (SELECT SPY.onhand_qty
     FROM SupplierParts AS SPY
     WHERE SPY.sup_nbr = SPX.sup_nbr
      AND SPY.part_nbr = 'P');
```

According to Standard SQL, this query should return only 'S2', but when we transform the query into what *looks like* an equivalent version, using NOT EXISTS instead, we obtain:

```
SELECT SPX.sup_nbr
 FROM SupplierParts AS SPX
WHERE SPX.part_nbr = 'P'
  AND NOT EXISTS
   (SELECT *
     FROM SupplierParts AS SPY
     WHERE SPY.sup_nbr = SPX.sup_nbr
      AND SPY.part_nbr = 'P'
      AND SPY.onhand_qty = 1000);
```

which will return ('S1', 'S2'). You can argue that this is the wrong answer because we do not definitely know whether or not 'S1' supplies 'P' in quantity 1000 or less or more. The EXISTS() predicate will return TRUE or FALSE, even in situations where a subquery predicate returns an UNKNOWN (i.e., NULL = 1000).

The solution is to modify the predicate that deals with the quantity in the subquery to explicitly say that you do or not want to give the "benefit of the doubt" to the NULL. You have several alternatives:

1. (SPY.onhand_qty = 1000) IS NOT FALSE
   This uses the valued predicates in Standard SQL for testing logical values. Frankly, this is confusing to read and worse to maintain.
2. (SPY.onhand_qty = 1000 OR SPY.onhand_qty IS NULL)
   This uses another test predicate, but the optimizer can probably use any index on the "onhand_qty" column.
3. (COALESCE(SPY.onhand_qty, 1000) = 1000)
   This is portable and easy to maintain. The only disadvantage is that some SQL products might not be able to use an index on the "onhand_qty" column because it is in an expression.

The real problem is that the query was formed with a double negative in the form of a NOT EXISTS and an implicit IS NOT FALSE condition. The problem stems from the fact that the EXISTS() predicate is one of the few two-value predicates in SQL and that (NOT (NOT UNKNOWN)) = UNKNOWN.

23

# QUANTIFIED SUBQUERY PREDICATES

A quantifier is a logical operator that states the quantity of objects for which a statement is TRUE. This is a logical quantity, not a numeric measurement or count; it relates a statement to the whole set of possible objects. In everyday life, you see statements like, "There is only one mouthwash that stops dinosaur breath," "All doctors drive Mercedes," "Some people got rich investing in cattle futures," or "Nobody eats Grandmother's fruitcake," which are quantified.

The first statement, about the mouthwash, is a uniqueness quantifier. If there were two or more products that could save us from dinosaur breath, it would be FALSE. The second statement has what is called a universal quantifier, since it deals with all doctors—find one exception and the statement is FALSE. If you can find anyone who has eaten Grandmother's fruitcake, the third statement is FALSE. The last statement has an existential quantifier, since it asserts that one or more people exist who got rich on cattle futures—find one example, such as Hillary Clinton, and the statement is TRUE.

SQL has forms of these quantifiers that are not quite like those in formal logic. They are based on extending the use of comparison predicates to allow result sets to be quantified and they use SQL's three-valued logic, so they do not return just TRUE or FALSE. They can be expressed as ANDs, ORs, and NOTs built from the rows in the subquery they use.

## 23.1 Scalar Subquery Comparisons

Standard SQL allows both scalar and row comparisons, but most queries use only scalar expressions. If a subquery returns a single-row, single-column result table, it is treated as a scalar value in Standard SQL in virtually any place a scalar could appear.

Joe Celko's SQL for Smarties. DOI: 10.1016/B978-0-12-382022-8.00023-5

For example, to find out if we have any teachers who are more than one year older than the students, I could write:

```
SELECT T1.teacher_name
 FROM Teachers AS T1
WHERE T1.birth_date
  >(SELECT MAX(S1.birth_date) - INTERVAL '365' DAY
       FROM Students AS S1);
```

In this case, the scalar subquery will be run only once and reduced to a constant value by the optimizer before scanning the Teachers table.

A correlated subquery is more complex, because it will have to be executed for each value from the containing query. For example, to find which suppliers have sent us fewer than 100 parts, we would use this query. Notice how the `SUM(onhand_qty)` has to be computed for each supplier number, `sup_nbr`.

```
SELECT sup_nbr, sup_name
 FROM Suppliers
WHERE 100 > (SELECT SUM(onhand_qty)
       FROM Shipments
       WHERE Shipments.sup_nbr = Suppliers.sup_nbr);
```

If a scalar subquery returns a `NULL`, we have rules for handling comparison with `NULL`s. But what if it returns an empty result—a supplier that has not shipped us anything? In Standard SQL, the empty result table is converted to a `NULL` of the appropriate data type.

In Standard SQL, you can place scalar or row subqueries on either side of a comparison predicate as long as they return comparable results. But you must be aware of the rules for row comparisons. For example, the following query will find the product manager who has more of his product at the stores than in the warehouse:

```
SELECT manager_name, product_nbr
 FROM Stores AS S1
WHERE (SELECT SUM(onhand_qty)
         FROM Warehouses AS W1
        WHERE S1.product_nbr = W1.product_nbr)
      < (SELECT SUM(shelf_qty)
           FROM RetailStores AS R1
          WHERE S1.product_nbr = R1.product_nbr);
```

Here is a programming tip: The main problem with writing these queries is getting a result with more than one row in it. You can guarantee uniqueness in several ways. An aggregate function on an ungrouped table will always be a single value. A `JOIN` with the containing query based on a key will always be a single value.

## 23.2 Quantifiers and Missing Data

The quantified predicates are used with subquery expressions to compare a single value to those of the subquery, and take the general form <value expression> <comp op> <quantifier> <subquery>. The predicate <value expression> <comp op> [ANY|SOME] <table expression> is equivalent to taking each row, s, (assume that they are numbered from 1 to n) of <table expression> and testing <value expression> <comp op> s with ORs between the expanded expressions:

```
((<value expression> <comp op> s1)
OR (<value expression> <comp op> s2)
 ..
OR (<value expression> <comp op> sn))
```

When you get a single TRUE result, the whole predicate is TRUE.

As long as <table expression> has cardinality greater than zero and one non-NULL value, you will get a result of TRUE or FALSE. The keyword SOME is the same as ANY, and the choice is just a matter of style and readability. Likewise, <value expression> <comp op> ALL <table expression> takes each row, s, of <table expression> and tests <value expression> <comp op> s with ANDs between the expanded expressions:

```
((<value expression> <comp op> s1)
AND (<value expression> <comp op> s2)
 ..
AND (<value expression> <comp op> sn))
```

When you get a single FALSE result, the whole predicate is FALSE. As long as <table expression> has cardinality greater than zero and all non-NULL values, you will get a result of TRUE or FALSE.

That sounds reasonable so far. Now let EmptyTable be an empty table (no rows, cardinality zero) and NullTable be a table with only NULLs in its rows and a cardinality greater than zero. The rules for SQL say that <value expression> <comp op> ALL NullTable always returns UNKNOWN, and likewise <value expression> <comp op> ANY NullTable always returns UNKNOWN. This makes sense, because every row comparison test in the expansion would return UNKNOWN, so the series of OR and AND operators would behave in the usual way.

However, <value expression> <comp op> ALL EmptyTable always returns TRUE and <value expression> <comp op> ANY EmptyTable always returns FALSE. Most people have no trouble seeing why the ANY predicate works that way; you cannot find a match, so the result is FALSE. But most people have lots of trouble seeing why the

ALL predicate is TRUE. This convention is called existential import, and I have just discussed it in the chapter about the EXISTS predicate. It was a big debate at the start of modern logic that boiled down to deciding if the statement, "All x are y" implies that "Some x exists" by definition. The modern convention is that it does not.

If I were to walk into a bar and announce that I can beat any pink elephant in the bar, that would be a true statement. The fact that there are no pink elephants in the bar merely shows that the problem is reduced to the minimum case. If this seems unnatural, then convert the ALL and ANY predicates into EXISTS predicates and look at the way that this rule preserves the formal mathematical properties that:

1. $(\forall x)P(x) = (\exists x)P(x)$
2. $(\exists x)P(x) = (\forall x)P(x)$

The Table1.x <comp op> ALL (SELECT y FROM Table2 WHERE <search condition>) predicate converts to:

```
.. NOT EXISTS
    (SELECT *
      FROM Table1, Table2
     WHERE Table1.x <comp op> Table2.y
       AND NOT <search condition>)..
```

The Table1.x <comp op> ANY (SELECT y FROM Table2 WHERE <search condition>) predicate converts to:

```
.. EXISTS
    (SELECT *
      FROM Table1, Table2
     WHERE Table1.x <comp op> Table2.y
      AND <search condition>) ..
```

Of the two quantified predicates, the <comp op> ALL predicate is used more. The ANY predicate is more easily replaced and more naturally written with an EXISTS() predicate or an IN() predicate. In fact, the Standard defines the IN() predicate as shorthand for = ANY and the NOT IN() predicate as shorthand for <> ANY, which is how most people would construct them in English.

The <comp op> ALL predicate is probably the more useful of the two, since it cannot be written in terms of an IN() predicate. The trick with it is to make sure that its subquery defines the set of values in which you are interested. For example, to find the authors whose books all sell for $49.95 or more, you could write:

```
SELECT *
 FROM Authors AS A1
WHERE 49.95
```

```
<= ALL (SELECT book_price
         FROM Books AS B1
        WHERE A1.author_name = B1.author_name);
```

The best way to think of this is to reverse the usual English sentence, "Show me all x that are y" in your mind so that it says "y is the value of all x" instead.

## 23.3 The ALL Predicate and Extrema Functions

It is counter intuitive at first that these two predicates are *not* the same in SQL:

```
x >= (SELECT MAX(y) FROM Table1)
x >= ALL (SELECT y FROM Table1)
```

but you have to remember the rules for the extrema functions—they drop out all the NULLs before returning the greater or least values. The ALL predicate does not drop NULLs, so you can get them in the results.

However, if you know that there are no NULLs in a column or are willing to drop the NULLS yourself, then you can use the ALL predicate to construct single queries to do work that would otherwise be done by two queries. For example, given the table of products and store manager we used earlier in this chapter, to find which manager handles the largest number of products, you would first construct a CTE and use it twice:

```
WITH TotalProducts (manager_name, product_tally)
AS
(SELECT manager_name, COUNT(*)
    FROM Stores
   GROUP BY manager_name)
SELECT manager_name
 FROM TotalProducts
WHERE product_tally
      = (SELECT MAX(product_tally)
           FROM TotalProducts);
```

But Alex Dorfman found a single query solution instead:

```
SELECT manager_name, COUNT(*)
 FROM Stores
GROUP BY manager_name
HAVING COUNT(*) + 1
   > ALL (SELECT DISTINCT COUNT(*)
            FROM Stores
           GROUP BY manager_name);
```

The use of the SELECT DISTINCT in the subquery is to guarantee that we do not get duplicate rows when two managers handle the same number of products. You can also add a .. WHERE dept IS NOT NULL clause to the subquery to get the effect of a true MAX() aggregate function.

## 23.4 The UNIQUE Predicate

The UNIQUE predicate is a test for the absence of redundant duplicate rows in a subquery. The UNIQUE keyword is also used as a table or column constraint. This predicate is used to define the constraint. The syntax for this predicate is:

```
<unique predicate> ::= UNIQUE <table subquery>
```

If any two rows in the subquery are equal to each other, the predicate is FALSE. However, the definition in the standard is worded in the negative, so that NULLs get the benefit of the doubt. The query can be written as an EXISTS predicate that counts rows, thus:

```
EXISTS (SELECT <column list>
    FROM <subquery>
   WHERE (<column list>) IS NOT NULL
   GROUP BY <column list>
   HAVING COUNT(*) > 1);
```

An empty subquery is always TRUE, since you cannot find two rows, and therefore duplicates do not exist. This makes sense on the face of it.

NULLs are easier to explain with an example, say a table with only two rows, ('a', 'b') and ('a', NULL). The first columns of each row are non-NULL and are equal to each other, so we have a match so far. The second column in the second row is NULL and cannot compare to anything, so we skip the second column pair, and go with what we have, and the test is TRUE. This is giving the NULLs the benefit of the doubt, since the NULL in the second row could become 'b' some day and give us a duplicate row.

Now consider the case where the subquery has two rows, ('a', NULL) and ('a', NULL). The predicate is still TRUE, because the NULLs do not test equal or unequal to each other—not because we are making NULLs equal to each other.

As you can see, it is a good idea to avoid NULLs in UNIQUE constraints.

The UNIQUE column constraint is implemented in most SQL products with a CREATE UNIQUE INDEX <index name> ON <table>(<column list>) statement hidden under the covers.

Standard SQL does not have indexes or any physical data access methods defined, but a vendor consortium agreed on this basic syntax.

Another way to do check uniqueness is to use hashing. When you get a hash clash (also known as a hash collision), then you look to see if the values are identical or not. A lot of research work is being done with Perfect and Minimal Perfect Hashing for databases. This technique is much faster than indexing for large databases since it requires only one hash probe instead of several index tree traversals.

## 23.5 The DISTINCT Predicate

This is a test of whether two row values are distinct from each other. The simple expression was discussed with the simple comparison operators. This is a logical extension to rows, just as we need with the simple comparison operators. The BNF is defined as:

```
<distinct predicate> ::=
<row value predicand 1>
IS [NOT] DISTINCT FROM <row value predicand 2>
```

Following the usual pattern,

```
<row value predicand 1> IS NOT DISTINCT FROM <row value
   predicand 2>
```

means

```
NOT (<row value predicand 1> IS DISTINCT FROM <row value
   predicand 2>)
```

The two `<row value predicand>`s have to be of the same degree, and the columns in the same ordinal position have to match on data types so that equality testing is possible.

The distinct predicate is `TRUE` if all the columns are `DISTINCT FROM` the corresponding column in the other predicand; otherwise, it is `FALSE`. There is no `UNKNOWN` result.

If two `<row value predicand>`s are not distinct, then they are said to be duplicates. If a number of `<row value predicand>`s are all duplicates of each other, then all except one are said to be redundant duplicates.

# 24

# THE SIMPLE SELECT STATEMENT

The good news about SQL is that the programmer only needs to learn the SELECT statement to do almost all his work! The bad news is that the statement can have so many nested clauses that it looks like a Victorian novel! The SELECT statement is used to query the database. It combines one or more tables, can do some calculations, and finally puts the results into a result table that can be passed on to the host language.

I have not spent much time on simple one-table SELECT statements you see in introductory books. I am assuming that you are experienced SQL programmers and got enough of those queries when you were learning SQL.

But it is worth going back to those basics and thinking about the conceptual model used in SQL. The simple query is the foundation of more and more complex queries.

## 24.1 SELECT Statement Execution Order

There is an effective order to the execution of the clauses of an SQL SELECT statement that does not seem to be covered in most beginning SQL books. It explains why some things work in SQL and others do not.

## 24.2 One-Level SELECT Statement

The simplest possible SELECT statement is just SELECT * FROM Sometable;, which returns the entire table as it stands. You can actually write this as TABLE Sometable in Standard SQL, but nobody seems to use that syntax. Though the syntax rules say that all you need are the SELECT and FROM clauses, in practice there is almost always a WHERE clause.

**Joe Celko's SQL for Smarties. DOI: 10.1016/B978-0-12-382022-8.00024-7**

Let's look at the basic SELECT statement in detail. The syntax for the statement is:

```
[WITH <common table expression list>]
SELECT [ALL | DISTINCT] <scalar expression list>
  FROM <table expression>
[WHERE <search condition>]
[GROUP BY <grouping column list>]
[HAVING <group condition>];
```

The order of execution is effectively as follows. This does not mean that an SQL compiler must do things exactly in this order, just that the final results have to be the same.

1. Materialize the `[WITH <common table expression list>]` so that the body of the query can use it. The SQL engine does not have to actually do this, and more often than not, it will expand the text of the CTE as in-line code. The table expressions come into existence in the order they are written, so you can reference a prior expression in the current list member. I am going to ignore this feature for now and stick with the basics.
2. Execute the `FROM <table expression>` clause and construct the working result table defined in that clause. This working table will exist only in the scope of the SELECT statement. The FROM can have all sorts of other table expressions, but the point is that they eventually return a single working table as a result. We will get into the details of those expressions later, with particular attention to the JOIN operators, derived tables, CTEs, and correlated subqueries.

   The fiction is that a simple list of table names or expressions yield an implicit CROSS JOIN. No product actually uses a CROSS JOIN to construct the intermediate table—the working table would get too large, too fast. For example, a 1000-row table and another 1000-row table would CROSS JOIN to get a 1,000,000-row working table. This is just the conceptual model we use to describe behavior.
3. If there is a WHERE clause, the search condition in it is applied to each row of the FROM clause result table. The rows that test TRUE are retained; the rows that test FALSE or UNKNOWN are deleted from the working table.

   This table is different from other tables in that each column retains the table name from which it was derived. Thus if table A and table B both have a column named x, there will be a column A.x and a column B.x in the results of the FROM clause. This is why it is a good practice to use fully qualified column names. Or to rename columns with an AS operator.

   The WHERE clause is where the action is. The predicate can be simple search conditions or quite complex and have nested subqueries. The syntax of a subquery is a SELECT statement, which is inside parentheses—failure to use parentheses is a common error for new SQL programmers. Subqueries are where the original SQL got the name "Structured English Query Language"—the ability to nest SELECT statements was the "structured" part. We will deal with those in another section.

The simplest WHERE clauses are made up of two kinds of search conditions. There are search arguments, called SARGs in the literature, that filter out rows from one table in the working table. They usually have a simple comparison predicate, function call, or reference other columns in the same table. The second kind of search conditions are join predicates. These involve predicates with a reference to two or more tables.

4. If there is a GROUP BY clause, it is executed next. It uses the FROM and WHERE clause working table and breaks these rows into groups where the columns in the <grouping column list> all have the same value. Grouping is *not quite* like equality. NULLs are treated as if they were all equal to each other, and form their own group. Each group is then reduced to a single row in a new result table that replaces the old one.

   Only four things make sense as group characteristics: the columns that define the groups, the aggregate functions that summarize group characteristics, function calls and constants, and expressions built from those three things.

   Originally, each row in the grouped table represented information about its group; it was at one higher level of aggregation. Today, Standard SQL allows constructs that create rows that represent aggregation at multiple levels. There are ways to get the same result by using UNIONs and table expressions, which we will discuss later.

5. If there is a HAVING clause, it is applied to each of the grouped rows in the current working table. The rows that test TRUE are retained; the groups that test FALSE or UNKNOWN are deleted. If there is no GROUP BY clause, the HAVING clause treats the whole table as a single group. It is *not true* that there must be a GROUP BY clause.

   Aggregate functions used in the HAVING clause usually appear in the SELECT clause, but that is not part of the standard. Nor does the SELECT clause have to include all the grouping columns.

6. Finally, the SELECT clause is applied to the result table. If a column does not appear in the <expression list> of the SELECT clause, it is dropped from the final results. Expressions can be constants or column names, or they can be calculations made from constants, columns, functions, and scalar subqueries.

If the SELECT clause has the DISTINCT option, redundant duplicate rows are deleted from the final result table. The phrase "redundant duplicate" means that one copy of the row is retained. If the SELECT clause has the explicit ALL option or is missing the [ALL | DISTINCT] option, then all duplicate rows are preserved in the final results table. Frankly, although it is legal syntax, nobody really uses the SELECT ALL option. Finally, the results are returned.

This means that the scalar subqueries, function calls, and expressions in the SELECT are done after all the other clauses are done. The AS operator can give names to expressions in the SELECT list. These new data element names come into existence *all at once*, but *after* the WHERE clause, GROUP BY clause, and HAVING clause have been executed; you cannot use them in the SELECT list or the WHERE clause for that reason. SQL does not work "from left to right" as they would in a sequential file/procedural language model. In those languages, these two statements produce different results:

```
READ (a, b, c) FROM File_X;
READ (c, a, b) FROM File_X;
```

whereas these two statements return the same data, in different orders:

```
SELECT a, b, c FROM Table_X;
SELECT c, a, b FROM Table_X;
```

Think about what a confused mess this statement is in the SQL model.

```
SELECT f(c2) AS c1, f(c1) AS c2 FROM Foobar;
```

That is why such nonsense is illegal syntax.

Let us carry an example out in painful detail, with a two-table join.

```
SELECT S.sex_code, COUNT(*), AVG(S.age),
     (MAX(S.age) - MIN(S.age)) AS age_range
  FROM Students AS S, Gradebook AS G
WHERE grade = 'A'
    AND S.stud_nbr = G.stud_nbr
GROUP BY S.sex_code
HAVING COUNT(*) > 3;
```

The two starting tables look like this:

```
CREATE TABLE Students
(stud_nbr INTEGER NOT NULL PRIMARY KEY,
stud_name CHAR(50) NOT NULL,
sex_code INTEGER NOT NULL
   CHECK (sex_code IN (0, 1, 2)), --iso code
stud_age INTEGER NOT NULL); -- bad design; compute from
   birth date
```

```
Students
stud_nbr  stud_name  sex_code  stud_age
=======================================
1         'smith'    1         16
2         'smyth'    2         17
3         'smoot'    2         16
4         'Adams'    2         17
5         'Jones'    1         16
6         'Celko'    1         17
7         'Vennor'   2         16
8         'Murray'   1         18

CREATE TABLE Gradebook
(stud_nbr INTEGER NOT NULL PRIMARY KEY
   REFERENCES Students(stud_nbr)
    ON DELETE CASCADE
    ON UPDATE CASCADE,
grade CHAR(1) NOT NULL
   CHECK (grade IN ('A', 'B', 'C', 'D', 'F'));

Gradebook
stud_nbr  grade
===============
1         'A'
2         'B'
3         'C'
4         'D'
5         'A'
6         'A'
7         'A'
8         'A'
```

The `CROSS JOIN` in the `FROM` clause looks like this:

**CROSS JOIN Working Table**

| Students | | | | Gradebook | |
|---|---|---|---|---|---|
| stud_nbr | stud_name | sex_code | stud_age | stud_nbr | grade |
| 1 | 'smith' | 1 | 16 | 1 | 'A' |
| 1 | 'smith' | 1 | 16 | 2 | 'B' |
| 1 | 'smith' | 1 | 16 | 3 | 'C' |
| 1 | 'smith' | 1 | 16 | 4 | 'D' |
| 1 | 'smith' | 1 | 16 | 5 | 'A' |
| 1 | 'smith' | 1 | 16 | 6 | 'A' |
| 1 | 'smith' | 1 | 16 | 7 | 'A' |
| 1 | 'smith' | 1 | 16 | 8 | 'A' |

*(Continued)*

| Students | | | | Gradebook | |
|---|---|---|---|---|---|
| stud_nbr | stud_name | sex_code | stud_age | stud_nbr | grade |
| 2 | 'smyth' | 2 | 17 | 1 | 'A' |
| 2 | 'smyth' | 2 | 17 | 2 | 'B' |
| 2 | 'smyth' | 2 | 17 | 3 | 'C' |
| 2 | 'smyth' | 2 | 17 | 4 | 'D' |
| 2 | 'smyth' | 2 | 17 | 5 | 'A' |
| 2 | 'smyth' | 2 | 17 | 6 | 'A' |
| 2 | 'smyth' | 2 | 17 | 7 | 'A' |
| 2 | 'smyth' | 2 | 17 | 8 | 'A' |
| 3 | 'smoot' | 2 | 16 | 1 | 'A' |
| 3 | 'smoot' | 2 | 16 | 2 | 'B' |
| 3 | 'smoot' | 2 | 16 | 3 | 'C' |
| 3 | 'smoot' | 2 | 16 | 4 | 'D' |
| 3 | 'smoot' | 2 | 16 | 5 | 'A' |
| 3 | 'smoot' | 2 | 16 | 6 | 'A' |
| 3 | 'smoot' | 2 | 16 | 7 | 'A' |
| 3 | 'smoot' | 2 | 16 | 8 | 'A' |
| 4 | 'Adams' | 2 | 17 | 1 | 'A' |
| 4 | 'Adams' | 2 | 17 | 2 | 'B' |
| 4 | 'Adams' | 2 | 17 | 3 | 'C' |
| 4 | 'Adams' | 2 | 17 | 4 | 'D' |
| 4 | 'Adams' | 2 | 17 | 5 | 'A' |
| 4 | 'Adams' | 2 | 17 | 6 | 'A' |
| 4 | 'Adams' | 2 | 17 | 7 | 'A' |
| 4 | 'Adams' | 2 | 17 | 8 | 'A' |
| 5 | 'Jones' | 1 | 16 | 1 | 'A' |
| 5 | 'Jones' | 1 | 16 | 2 | 'B' |
| 5 | 'Jones' | 1 | 16 | 3 | 'C' |
| 5 | 'Jones' | 1 | 16 | 4 | 'D' |
| 5 | 'Jones' | 1 | 16 | 5 | 'A' |
| 5 | 'Jones' | 1 | 16 | 6 | 'A' |
| 5 | 'Jones' | 1 | 16 | 7 | 'A' |
| 5 | 'Jones' | 1 | 16 | 8 | 'A' |
| 6 | 'Celko' | 1 | 17 | 1 | 'A' |
| 6 | 'Celko' | 1 | 17 | 2 | 'B' |
| 6 | 'Celko' | 1 | 17 | 3 | 'C' |
| 6 | 'Celko' | 1 | 17 | 4 | 'D' |
| 6 | 'Celko' | 1 | 17 | 5 | 'A' |
| 6 | 'Celko' | 1 | 17 | 6 | 'A' |
| 6 | 'Celko' | 1 | 17 | 7 | 'A' |
| 6 | 'Celko' | 1 | 17 | 8 | 'A' |

*(Continued)*

| Students | | | | Gradebook | |
|---|---|---|---|---|---|
| stud_nbr | stud_name | sex_code | stud_age | stud_nbr | grade |
| 7 | 'Vennor' | 2 | 16 | 1 | 'A' |
| 7 | 'Vennor' | 2 | 16 | 2 | 'B' |
| 7 | 'Vennor' | 2 | 16 | 3 | 'C' |
| 7 | 'Vennor' | 2 | 16 | 4 | 'D' |
| 7 | 'Vennor' | 2 | 16 | 5 | 'A' |
| 7 | 'Vennor' | 2 | 16 | 6 | 'A' |
| 7 | 'Vennor' | 2 | 16 | 7 | 'A' |
| 7 | 'Vennor' | 2 | 16 | 8 | 'A' |
| 8 | 'Murray' | 1 | 18 | 1 | 'A' |
| 8 | 'Murray' | 1 | 18 | 2 | 'B' |
| 8 | 'Murray' | 1 | 18 | 3 | 'C' |
| 8 | 'Murray' | 1 | 18 | 4 | 'D' |
| 8 | 'Murray' | 1 | 18 | 5 | 'A' |
| 8 | 'Murray' | 1 | 18 | 6 | 'A' |
| 8 | 'Murray' | 1 | 18 | 7 | 'A' |
| 8 | 'Murray' | 1 | 18 | 8 | 'A' |

There are two search conditions in the `WHERE`. The first predicate grade = 'A' needs only the Students table, so it is a SARG. In fact, an optimizer in a real SQL engine would have removed those rows in the Students table that failed the test before doing the `CROSS JOIN`. The second predicate is `S.stud_nbr = G.stud_nbr`, which requires both tables and the constructed row from the two table; a join condition. Now remove the rows that do not meet the conditions. After the `WHERE` clause, the result table looks like this:

## Cross Join after WHERE Clause

| Students | | | | Gradebook | |
|---|---|---|---|---|---|
| stud_nbr | stud_name | sex_code | stud_age | stud_nbr | grade |
| 1 | 'smith' | 1 | 16 | 1 | 'A' |
| 5 | 'Jones' | 1 | 16 | 5 | 'A' |
| 6 | 'Celko' | 1 | 17 | 6 | 'A' |
| 7 | 'Vennor' | 2 | 16 | 7 | 'A' |
| 8 | 'Murray' | 1 | 18 | 8 | 'A' |

We have a GROUP BY clause that will group the working table by sex_code, thus:

GROUP BY sex_code

| Students | | | | Gradebook | | |
|---|---|---|---|---|---|---|
| stud_nbr | stud_name | sex_code | stud_age | stud_nbr | grade | |
| 1 | 'smith' | 1 | 16 | 1 | 'A' | sex_code = 1 |
| 5 | 'Jones' | 1 | 16 | 5 | 'A' | |
| 6 | 'Celko' | 1 | 17 | 6 | 'A' | |
| 8 | 'Murray' | 1 | 18 | 8 | 'A' | |
| 7 | 'Vennor' | 2 | 16 | 7 | 'A' | sex_code = 2 |

and the aggregate functions in the SELECT clause are computed for each group:

Aggregate Functions

| sex_code | COUNT(*) | AVG(stud_age) | (MAX(stud_age)–MIN(stud_age)) AS age_range |
|---|---|---|---|
| 2 | 1 | 16.00 | (16 - 16) = 0 |
| 1 | 4 | 16.75 | (18 - 16) = 2 |

The HAVING clause is applied to each group, the SELECT statement is applied last, and we get the final results:

HAVING Clause and SELECT Clause

| sex_code | COUNT(*) | AVG(stud_age) | age_range |
|---|---|---|---|
| 1 | 4 | 16.75 | 2 |

Obviously, no real implementation actually produces these intermediate tables; that would be insanely expensive. They are just a model of how a statement works. The `FROM` clause can have `JOIN`s and other operators that create working tables in more complex ways, but the same steps are followed in this order in a nested fashion. That means subqueries in the `WHERE` clause are parsed and expanded the same way as a simple query.

The simple `SELECT` is also the easiest to optimize. Simple `SELECT` statements should do most of the work in a well-designed, normalized schema.

# 25

# ADVANCED SELECT STATEMENTS

In the previous chapter, we took a look at the basic SELECT statement. Now we need to look at other ways to nest subqueries and build the working table in the FROM clause with other syntax.

## 25.1 Correlated Subqueries

One of the classics of software engineering is a short paper by the late Edsger Dijkstra entitled "Go To Statement Considered Harmful" (*Communications of the ACM*, Vol. 11, No. 3, March 1968, pp. 147–148). In this paper he argued for dropping the GOTO statement from programming languages in favor of what we now called Structured Programming.

One of his observations was that programs that used only BEGIN-END blocks, WHILE loops, and IF-THEN-ELSE statements were easier to read and maintain. Programs that jumped around via GOTO statements were harder to follow because the execution path could have arrived at a statement label from anywhere in the code. Algol, the first of the blocked structured programming languages, had all of those control structures but still kept the GOTO—it was considered a fundamental part of programming! Before Dijkstra, nobody had really understood the power of limiting the scope of variables and control structures in procedural code. The basic idea of a scope is that a block of code can reference only variables that are declared in the block. Failing to find a local variable, the containing blocks are then inspected from the inside out.

We have the same concept in SQL queries. A correlated subquery is a subquery that references columns in the tables of its containing query. The general structure might look like:

```
SELECT T1.x, T1.y, T1.z
 FROM TableOne AS T1
WHERE T1.x
   = (SELECT T2.x, T2.y, T2.z
      FROM TableTwo AS T2
```

Joe Celko's SQL for Smarties. DOI: 10.1016/B978-0-12-382022-8.00025-9

```
WHERE T2.y
 = (SELECT foobar
      FROM TableThree AS T3
     WHERE T3.x = T1.x
      AND T3.y = T2.y
      AND T3.z = 42));
```

Look at the innermost query. The predicate (T3.z = 42) is local to this query. The predicate (T3.y = T2.y) works because this query is in the scope of the query with T2 in the FROM clause. Likewise, The predicate (T3.x = T1.x) works because this query is in the scope of the query with T1 in the FROM clause. If I had not qualified the table names in the innermost WHERE clause, the predicate (T3.x = x) would refer to the most local x, which gives us (T3.x = T3.x), which is always TRUE or UNKNOWN. That is absurd.

But a predicate like (T3.z = floob) might reference table T1, T2, or T3, depending on which one has the nearest column floob; which table would be determined by working outward. This is why it is important to qualify column names.

The tables can reference the same table under a different correlation name. Consider a query to find all the students who are younger than the oldest student of their gender:

```
SELECT S1.stud_nbr, S1.stud_name, S1.sex_code, S1.stud_age
 FROM Students AS S1
WHERE stud_age
  < (SELECT MAX(stud_age)
       FROM Students AS S2
      WHERE S1.sex_code = S2.sex_code);
```

1. Let's work it out in detail. The fiction in SQL is that we create local tables S1 and S2, which happen to have the same data and structure as the Students table. A copy of the Students table is made for each correlation name, S1 and S2. Obviously, this is not how it is implemented in a real SQL compiler. Following the same steps we used in simple SELECT Statements, expand the outer query.

| stud_nbr | stud_name | sex_code | stud_age |
|---|---|---|---|
| 1 | 'Smith' | 1 | 16 |
| 2 | 'Smyth' | 2 | 17 |
| 3 | 'Smoot' | 2 | 16 |
| 4 | 'Adams' | 2 | 17 |
| 5 | 'Jones' | 1 | 16 |
| 6 | 'Celko' | 1 | 17 |
| 7 | 'Vennor' | 2 | 16 |
| 8 | 'Murray' | 1 | 18 |

2. When you get to the WHERE clause, and find the innermost query, you will see that you need to get data from the containing query. The model of execution says that each outer row has the subquery executed on it in parallel with the other rows. Assume we are working on student (1, 'Smith'), who is male. The query in effect becomes:

```
SELECT 1, 'Smith', 1, 16
 FROM Students AS S1
WHERE 16 < (SELECT MAX(stud_age)
      FROM Students AS S2
     WHERE 1 = S2.sex_code);
```

   As an aside, the search conditions (1 = S2.sex_code) and (S2.sex_code = 1) are equivalent. The choice is largely a matter of the programmer's culture; do you read from left to right or right to left?

3. The subquery can now be calculated for male students; the maximum stud_age is 18. When we expand this out for all the other rows, this will give us the effect of this set of parallel queries.

```
SELECT 1, 'Smith', 1, 16 FROM Students AS S1 WHERE 16 < 18;
SELECT 2, 'Smyth', 2, 17 FROM Students AS S1 WHERE 17 < 17;
SELECT 3, 'Smoot', 2, 16 FROM Students AS S1 WHERE 16 < 17;
SELECT 4, 'Adams', 2, 17 FROM Students AS S1 WHERE 17 < 17;
SELECT 5, 'Jones', 1, 16 FROM Students AS S1 WHERE 16 < 18;
SELECT 6, 'Celko', 1, 17 FROM Students AS S1 WHERE 17 < 18;
SELECT 7, 'Vennor', 2, 16 FROM Students AS S1 WHERE 16 < 17;
SELECT 8, 'Murray', 1, 18 FROM Students AS S1 WHERE 18 < 18;
```

4. These same steps have been done for each row in the containing query. The model is that all the subqueries are resolved at once. With cheaper and cheaper parallel hardware, this might be true some day, but no implementation really does it that way currently. The usual approach in real SQL compilers is to build procedural loops in the database engine that scan through both tables. What table is in what loop is decided by the optimizer. The final results are:

| stud_nbr | stud_name | sex_code | stud_age |
|---|---|---|---|
| 1 | 'Smith' | 1 | 16 |
| 3 | 'Smoot' | 2 | 16 |
| 5 | 'Jones' | 1 | 16 |
| 6 | 'Celko' | 1 | 17 |
| 7 | 'Vennor' | 2 | 16 |

Again, no real product works this way, but it has to produce the same results as this process.

There is no limit to the depth of nesting of correlated subqueries in theory. In practice, it is probably a good heuristic to keep the nesting under five levels. This is a number that shows up in human psychology as a limit on how many things we can handle mentally. The classic study is George Miller's "The Magical Number Five Plus or Minus Two: Some Limits on Our Capacity for Processing Information" (*The Psychological Review*, 1956).

These examples used scalar subqueries, but you can also use correlated subqueries that return a collection of tables. For example, to find all of Professor Celko's students, we might use this query:

```
SELECT S1.stud_nbr, S1.stud_name, S1.sex_code, S1.stud_age
 FROM Students AS S1
WHERE S1.stud_nbr
  IN (SELECT T.stud_nbr
       FROM Teachers AS T1
      WHERE S1.stud_nbr = T1.stud_nbr
       AND T1.teacher_name = 'Celko');
```

Another problem is that many SQL programmers do not fully understand the rules for scope of derived table names. If an infixed join is given a derived table name, then all the table names inside it are hidden from containing expressions. For example, this will fail:

```
SELECT a, b, c -- wrong!
FROM (Foo
  INNER JOIN
  Bar
  ON Foo.y >= Bar.x) AS Foobar (x, y)
   INNER JOIN
   Flub
   ON Foo.y <= Flub.z;
```

because the table name Foo is not available to the second `INNER JOIN`. However, the following will work because Foobar is exposed:

```
SELECT a, b, c
FROM (Foo
  INNER JOIN
  Bar
  ON Foo.y >= Bar.x) AS Foobar (x, y)
   INNER JOIN
   Flub
   ON Foobar.y <= Flub.z;
```

If you start nesting lots of derived table expressions you can force an order of execution in the query. It is not a generally a good idea to try to outguess the optimizer, so watch overscoping your nested queries.

So far I have shown fully qualified column names. It is a good programming practice, but it is not required. Assume that Foo and Bar both have a column named w. These statements will produce an ambiguous name error:

```
SELECT a, b, c
FROM Foo
  INNER JOIN
  Bar ON y >= x
  INNER JOIN
  Flub ON y <= w;

SELECT a, b, c
FROM Foo, Bar, Flub
WHERE y BETWEEN x AND w
```

But this statement will work from inside the parentheses first, and then does the outermost `INNER JOIN` last.

```
SELECT a, b, c
FROM Foo
  INNER JOIN
  (Bar
    INNER JOIN
    Flub ON y <= w)
  ON y >= x;
```

If Bar did not have a column named w, the parser would go to the next containing expression, find Foo.w, and use it.

## 25.2 Infixed `INNER JOIN`s

SQL-92 added new syntax for `JOIN`s using infixed operators in the `FROM` clause. The `JOIN` operators are quite general and flexible, allowing you to do things in a single statement that you could not do in the older notation. The basic syntax is

```
<joined table> ::=
 <cross join> | <qualified join> | (<joined table>)

<cross join> ::= <table reference> CROSS JOIN
   <table reference>

<qualified join> ::=
  <table reference> [NATURAL] [<join type>] JOIN
     <table reference> [<join specification>]

<join specification> ::= <join condition> | <named columns join>
```

```
<join condition> ::= ON <search condition>

<named columns join> ::= USING (<join column list>)

<join type> ::= INNER | <outer join type> [OUTER] | UNION

<outer join type> ::= LEFT | RIGHT | FULL

<join column list> ::= <column name list>

<table reference> ::=
  <table name> [[AS] <correlation name>[(<derived column
    list>)]]
      | <derived table>
         [AS] <correlation name> [(<derived
           column list>)]
      | <joined table>

<derived table> ::= <table subquery>

<column name list> ::=
  <column name> [{<comma> <column name>}..]
```

An INNER JOIN is done by forming the CROSS JOIN and then removing the rows that do not meet the JOIN search conditions given in the ON clause, just like we did with the original FROM.. WHERE syntax. The ON clause can be as elaborate as you want to make it, as long as it refers to tables and columns within its scope. If a <qualified join> is used without a <join type>, INNER is implicit. But it is good documentation to spell out all the JOIN operators.

However, in the real world, most INNER JOINs are done using equality tests on columns with the same names in different tables, rather than on elaborate search conditions. Equi-JOINs are so common that Standard SQL has two shorthand ways of specifying them. The USING (c1, c2, .., cn) clause takes the column names in the list and replaces them with the clause ON ((T1.c1, T1.c2, .., T1.cn) = (T2.c1, T2.c2, .., T2.cn)). Likewise, the NATURAL option is shorthand for a USING() clause that is a list of all the column names that are common to both tables. If NATURAL is specified, a JOIN specification cannot be given; it is already there.

A strong warning: Do *not* use NATURAL JOIN in production code. Any change to the column names or addition of new columns will change the join at runtime. This is also why you do not use SELECT * in production code. But the NATURAL JOIN is more dangerous. As Daniel Morgan pointed out, a NATURAL JOIN between two tables with a vague generic column name like "comments" for unrelated data elements can give you a meaningless join containing megabytes of text.

The same sort of warning applies to the USING clause. Neither of these options is widely implemented or used. If you find out that product_id, product_nbr and upc were all used for the same data element in your schema, you should do a global change to make sure that one data element has one and only one name.

There is a myth among ACCESS programmers that the ON clause can contain only JOIN conditions and the WHERE can contain only search conditions. This is not true, and the difference in the position of the search conditions is not important. The product generated code in that format because this was the execution plan used by the simple compiler.

Having said this, separating the conditions this way can have some advantages for documentation. It becomes easy to remove the WHERE clause and have a candidate for a VIEW. But there are trade-offs.

## 25.3 OUTER JOINs

OUTER JOINs used to be done with proprietary vendor syntax. Today, the use of the Standard OUTER JOIN is universal. An OUTER JOIN is a JOIN that preserves all the rows in one or both tables, even when they do not have matching rows in the second table. The unmatched columns in the unpreserved table are filled with NULLs to complete the join and return rows with the right structure.

Let's take a real-world situation. I have a table of orders and a table of suppliers that I wish to JOIN for a report to tell us how much business we did with each supplier. With a traditional inner join, the query would be this:

```
SELECT S.sup_id, S.sup_name, O.order_nbr, O.order_amt
 FROM Suppliers AS S, Orders AS O
WHERE S.sup_id = O.sup_id;
```

or with the infixed syntax:

```
SELECT S.sup_id, S.sup_name, O.order_nbr, O.order_amt
 FROM Suppliers AS S -- preserved table
      INNER JOIN
      Orders AS O
      ON S.sup_id = O.sup_id;
```

Some supplier totals include credits for returned merchandise, and our total business with them works out to zero dollars. Other suppliers never got an order from us at all, so we did zero dollars' worth of business with them, too. But the first case will show up in the query result and be passed on to the report, whereas the second case will disappear in the INNER JOIN. Having zero liters of beer in my glass and not having a glass at all are very different situations.

If we had used an OUTER JOIN, preserving the Suppliers table, we would have all the suppliers in the results. When a supplier with no orders was found in the Orders table, the order_nbr and order_amt columns would be given a NULL value in the result row.

```
SELECT S.sup_id, S.sup_name, O.order_nbr, O.order_amt
 FROM Suppliers AS S
   OUTER LEFT JOIN
   Orders AS O
   ON S.sup_id = O.sup_id;
```

### 25.3.1 A Bit of History

Before the SQL-99 Standard, there was no Standard OUTER JOIN syntax, so you had to construct it by hand with a messy UNION in products like very early versions of DB2 from IBM like this:

```
SELECT sup_id, sup_name, order_amt -- regular INNER JOIN
 FROM Suppliers, Orders
WHERE Suppliers.sup_id = Orders.sup_id
UNION ALL
SELECT sup_id, sup_name, CAST(NULL AS INTEGER) --
   preserved rows
 FROM Suppliers
WHERE NOT EXISTS
  (SELECT *
    FROM Orders
   WHERE Suppliers.sup_id = Orders.sup_id);
```

You have to use a NULL with the correct data type to make the UNION work, hence the CAST() functions. Some products are smart enough that just NULL by itself will be given the correct data type, but this is portable and safer.

The other alternative is to insert a constant of some sort to give a more meaningful result. This is easy in the case of a CHARACTER column, where a message like '{{NONE}}' can be quickly understood. It is much harder in the case of a numeric column, where we could have a balance with a supplier that is positive, zero, or negative because of returns and credits. There really is a difference between a vendor that we did not use and a vendor whose returns and credits canceled out its orders.

In the second edition of this book, I described the proprietary OUTER JOIN extensions in detail. Today, they are gone and replaced by the Standard syntax. The vendor extensions were all different in syntax or semantics or both. Since they are mercifully gone, I am not going to tell you about them in this edition.

The name LEFT OUTER JOIN comes from the fact that the preserved table is on the left side of the operator. Likewise, a RIGHT OUTER JOIN would have the preserved table on the right-hand side, and the FULL OUTER JOIN preserves both tables.

Here is how OUTER JOINs work in Standard SQL. Assume you are given:

| Table1 | | Table2 | |
|---|---|---|---|
| a | b | a | c |
| 1 | w | 1 | r |
| 2 | x | 2 | s |
| 3 | y | 3 | t |
| 4 | z | | |

and the OUTER JOIN expression:

```
Table1
LEFT OUTER JOIN
Table2
ON Table1.a = Table2.a      ◄ JOIN condition
 AND Table2.c = 't';     ◄ single table condition
```

We call Table1 the "preserved table" and Table2 the "unpreserved table" in the query. What I am going to give you is a little different, but equivalent to the ANSI/ISO standards.

1. We build the CROSS JOIN of the two tables. Scan each row in the result set.
2. If the predicate tests TRUE for that row, then you keep it. You also remove all rows derived from it from the CROSS JOIN.
3. If the predicate tests FALSE or UNKNOWN for that row, then keep the columns from the preserved table, convert all the columns from the unpreserved table to NULLs, and remove the duplicates.

So let us execute this by hand:

```
Let ◄ = passed the first predicate
Let ● = passed the second predicate
```

```
         Table1 CROSS JOIN Table2
          a      b      a       c

          1      w      1       r ◄
          1      w      2       s
          1      w      3       t ●
          2      x      1       r
          2      x      2       s ◄
          2      x      3       t ●
          3      y      1       r
          3      y      2       s
          3      y      3       t ◄ ● the TRUE set
          4      z      1       r
          4      z      2       s
          4      z      3       t ●
```

```
   Table1 LEFT OUTER JOIN Table2
 a      b      a       c

 3      y      3       t ◄ only TRUE row

 1      w     NULL    NULL Sets of duplicates
 1      w     NULL    NULL
 1      w     NULL    NULL

 2      x     NULL    NULL
 2      x     NULL    NULL
 2      x     NULL    NULL

 3      y     NULL    NULL ◄ derived from the TRUE set - Remove
 3      y     NULL    NULL

 4      z     NULL    NULL
 4      z     NULL    NULL
 4      z     NULL    NULL
```

The final results:

```
         Table1 LEFT OUTER JOIN Table2
         a         b         a        c

         1         w         NULL     NULL
         2         x         NULL     NULL
         3         y         3        t
         4         z         NULL     NULL
```

The basic rule is that every row in the preserved table is represented in the results in at least one result row.

Consider the two famous Chris Date tables from his "Suppliers and Parts" database used in his textbooks.

| Suppliers | SupParts | | |
|---|---|---|---|
| sup_id | sup_id | part_nbr | part_qty |
| S1 | S1 | P1 | 100 |
| S2 | S1 | P2 | 250 |
| S3 | S2 | P1 | 100 |
| | S2 | P2 | 250 |

If you write the `OUTER JOIN` with only the join predicate in the `ON` clause, like this:

```
SELECT Suppliers.sup_id, SupParts.part_nbr, SupParts.
   part_qty
 FROM Suppliers
   LEFT OUTER JOIN
   SupParts
   ON Suppliers.sup_id = SupParts.sup_id
WHERE part_qty < 200;
```

you get:

| sup_id | part_nbr | part_qty |
|---|---|---|
| 'S1' | 'P1' | 100 |
| 'S2' | 'P1' | 100 |

But if we put the search predicate in the `ON` clause, we get this result.

```
SELECT Suppliers.sup_id, SupParts.part_nbr, SupParts.
   part_qty
 FROM Suppliers
   LEFT OUTER JOIN
   SupParts
   ON Suppliers.sup_id = SupParts.sup_id
    AND part_qty < 200;
```

You get:

| sup_id | part_nbr | part_qty |
|---|---|---|
| 'S1' | 'P1' | 100 |
| 'S2' | 'P1' | 100 |
| 'S3' | NULL | NULL |

Another problem was that you could not show the same table as preserved and unpreserved in the proprietary syntax options, but it is easy in Standard SQL. For example to find the students who have taken Math 101 and might have taken Math 102:

```
SELECT C1.stud_nbr, C1.math_course, C2.math_course
 FROM (SELECT stud_nbr, math_course, math_course
     FROM Courses
    WHERE math_course = 'Math 101') AS C1
   LEFT OUTER JOIN
   (SELECT stud_nbr, math_course, math_course
     FROM Courses
    WHERE math_course = 'Math 102') AS C2
   ON C1.stud_nbr = C2.stud_nbr;
```

A third problem is that the order of execution matters with a chain of `OUTER JOIN`s. That is to say, `((T1 OUTER JOIN T2) OUTER JOIN T3)` does not produce the same results as `(T1 OUTER JOIN (T2 OUTER JOIN T3))`.

## 25.3.2 NULLs and OUTER JOINs

The `NULL`s that are generated by the `OUTER JOIN` can occur in columns derived from source table columns that have been declared to be `NOT NULL`. Even if you tried to avoid all the problems with `NULL`s by making every column in every table of your schema `NOT NULL`, they could still occur in `OUTER JOIN` and OLAP

| T1 | | T2 | |
|---|---|---|---|
| a | x | b | x |
| 1 | 'r' | 7 | 'r' |
| 2 | 'v' | 8 | 's' |
| 3 | NULL | 9 | NULL |

function results. However, a table can have NULLs and still be used in an OUTER JOIN. Consider different JOINs on the following two tables, which have NULLs in the common column.

A natural INNER JOIN on column x can only match those values that are equal to each other. But NULLs do not match to anything, even to other NULLs. Thus, there is one row in the result, on the value 'r' in column x in both tables.

```
T1 INNER JOIN T2 ON T1.x = T2.x
a    T1.x    b    T2.x
========================
1    'r'     7    'r'
```

Now do a LEFT OUTER JOIN on the tables, which will preserve table T1, and you get

```
T1 LEFT OUTER JOIN T2 ON T1.x = T2.x
a    T1.x    b       T2.x
=============================
1    'r'     7       'r'
2    'v'     NULL    NULL
3    NULL    NULL    NULL
```

Again, there are no surprises. The original INNER JOIN row is still in the results. The other two rows of T1 that were not in the equi-JOIN do show up in the results, and the columns derived from table T2 are filled with NULLs. The RIGHT OUTER JOIN would also behave the same way. The problems start with the FULL OUTER JOIN, which looks like this:

```
T1 FULL OUTER JOIN T2 ON (T1.x = T2.x)
a       T1.x    b       T2.x
============================
1       'r'     7       'r'
2       'v'     NULL    NULL
3       NULL    NULL    NULL
NULL    NULL    8       's'
NULL    NULL    9       NULL
```

The way this result is constructed is worth explaining in detail.

First do an INNER JOIN on T1 and T2, using the ON clause condition, and put those rows (if any) in the results. Then all rows in T1 that could not be joined are padded out with NULLs in the columns derived from T2 and inserted into the results. Finally, take the rows in T2 that could not be joined, pad them out with NULLs, and insert them into the results. The bad news is that the original tables cannot be reconstructed from an OUTER JOIN. Look at the results of the FULL OUTER JOIN, which we will call R1, and SELECT the first columns from it:

```
SELECT T1.a, T1.x FROM R1

a       x
===========
1       'r'
2       'v'
3       NULL
NULL    NULL
NULL    NULL
```

The created NULLs remain and could not be differentiated from the original NULLs. But you cannot throw out those duplicate rows, because they may be in the original table T1. There is now a function, GROUPING (<column name>), used with the CUBE, ROLLUP, and GROUPING SET() options, that returns a 1 for original NULLs or data and 0 for created NULLs. Your vendor may allow this function to be used with the OUTER JOINs.

### 25.3.3 NATURAL versus Searched OUTER JOINs

It is worth mentioning in passing that Standard SQL has a NATURAL LEFT OUTER JOIN, but it is not implemented in most versions of SQL.

A NATURAL JOIN has only one copy of the common column pairs in its result. The searched OUTER JOIN has both of the original columns, with their table-qualified names. The NATURAL JOIN has to have a correlation name for the result table to identify the shared columns. We can build a NATURAL LEFT OUTER JOIN by using the COALESCE() function to combine the common column pairs into a single column and put the results into a VIEW where the columns can be properly named, thus:

```
CREATE VIEW NLOJ12 (x, a, b)
AS SELECT COALESCE(T1.x, T2.x), T1.a, T2.b
 FROM T1 LEFT OUTER JOIN T2
   ON T1.x = T2.x;

NLOJ12

x         a    b
=================
'r'       1    7
'v'       2    NULL
NULL      3    NULL
```

Unlike the NATURAL JOINs, the searched OUTER JOIN does not have to use a simple one-column equality as the JOIN search condition. The search condition can have several search conditions, use other comparisons, and so forth. For example,

```
T1 LEFT OUTER JOIN T2 ON (T1.x < T2.x)
a    T1.x     b       T2.x
==========================
1    'r'      8       's'
2    'v'      NULL    NULL
3    NULL     NULL    NULL
```

as compared to:

```
T1 LEFT OUTER JOIN T2 ON (T1.x > T2.x)
a    T1.x     b       T2.x
==========================
1    'r'      NULL    NULL
2    'v'      7       'r'
2    'v'      8       's'
3    NULL     NULL    NULL
```

## 25.3.4 Self OUTER JOINs

There is no rule that forbids an OUTER JOIN on the same table. In fact, this kind of self-join is a good trick for "flattening" a normalized table into a horizontal report. To illustrate the method, start with a skeleton table defined as:

```
CREATE TABLE Credits
(student_nbr INTEGER NOT NULL,
course_name CHAR(8) NOT NULL,
PRIMARY KEY (student_nbr, course_name));
```

This table represents student ids and a course name for each class they have taken. However, our rules say that students cannot get credit for 'CS-102' until they have taken the prerequisite 'CS-101' course; they cannot get credit for 'CS-103' until they have taken the prerequisite 'CS-102' course; and so forth. Let's first load the table with some sample values.

Notice that student #1 has both courses, student #2 has only the first of the series, and student #3 jumped ahead of sequence

| Credits | |
|---|---|
| student_nbr | course_name |
| 1 | 'CS-101' |
| 1 | 'CS-102' |
| 2 | 'CS-101' |
| 3 | 'CS-102' |

and therefore cannot get credit for his 'CS-102' course until he goes back and takes 'CS-101' as a prerequisite.

What we want is basically a histogram (bar chart) for each student, showing how far he or she has gone in his or her degree program. Assume that we are only looking at two courses; the result of the desired query might look like this (NULL is used to represent a missing value):

```
(1, 'CS-101', 'CS-102')
(2, 'CS-101', NULL)
```

Clearly, this will need a self-JOIN, since the last two columns come from the same table, Credits. You have to give correlation names to both uses of the Credits table in the OUTER JOIN operator when you construct a self OUTER JOIN, just as you would with any other SELF-JOIN, thus:

```
SELECT student_nbr, C1.course_name, C2.course_name
 FROM Credits AS C1
   LEFT OUTER JOIN
   Credits AS C2
   ON C1.stud_nbr_nbr = C2.stud_nbr_nbr
    AND C1.course_name = 'CS-101'
    AND C2.course_name = 'CS-102';
```

### 25.3.5 Two or More OUTER JOINs

Some relational purists feel that every operator should have an inverse, and therefore they do not like the OUTER JOIN. Others feel that the created NULLs are fundamentally different from the explicit NULLs in a base table and should have a special token. SQL uses its general-purpose NULLs and leaves things at that. Getting away from theory, you will also find that vendors have often done strange things with the ways their products work.

A major problem is that OUTER JOIN operators do not have the same properties as INNER JOIN operators. The order in which FULL OUTER JOINs are executed will change the results (a mathematician would say that they are not associative). To show some of the problems that can come up when you have more than two tables, let us use three very simple two-column tables. Notice that some of the column values match and some do not match, but the three tables have all possible pairs of column names in them.

```
CREATE TABLE T1 (a INTEGER NOT NULL, b INTEGER NOT NULL);
INSERT INTO T1 VALUES (1, 2);
```

```
CREATE TABLE T2 (a INTEGER NOT NULL, c INTEGER NOT NULL);
INSERT INTO T2 VALUES (1, 3);

CREATE TABLE T3 (b INTEGER NOT NULL, c INTEGER NOT NULL);
INSERT INTO T3 VALUES (2, 100);
```

Now let's try some of the possible orderings of the three tables in a chain of LEFT OUTER JOINS. The problem is that a table can be preserved or unpreserved in the immediate JOIN and in the opposite state in the containing JOIN.

```
SELECT T1.a, T1.b, T3.c
 FROM ((T1 NATURAL LEFT OUTER JOIN T2)
   NATURAL LEFT OUTER JOIN T3);

Result
a  b  c
==========
1  2  NULL

SELECT T1.a, T1.b, T3.c
 FROM ((T1 NATURAL LEFT OUTER JOIN T3)
   NATURAL LEFT OUTER JOIN T2);

Result
a  b  c
=========
1  2  100

SELECT T1.a, T1.b, T3.c
 FROM ((T1 NATURAL LEFT OUTER JOIN T3)
   NATURAL LEFT OUTER JOIN T2);

Result
a     b     c
==================
NULL  NULL  NULL
```

Even worse, the choice of column in the SELECT list can change the output. Instead of displaying T3.c, use T2.c and you will get:

```
SELECT T1.a, T1.b, T2.c
 FROM ((T2 NATURAL LEFT OUTER JOIN T3)
   NATURAL LEFT OUTER JOIN T1);

Result
a     b     c
==============
NULL  NULL  3
```

The compiler should give you error messages about ambiguous column names.

## 25.3.6 OUTER JOINs and Aggregate Functions

At the start of this chapter, we had a table of orders and a table of suppliers, which were to be used to build a report to tell us how much business we did with each supplier. The query that will do this is:

```
SELECT Suppliers.sup_id, sup_name, SUM(order_amt)
 FROM Suppliers
   LEFT OUTER JOIN
   Orders
   ON Suppliers.sup_id = Orders.sup_id
GROUP BY sup_id, sup_name;
```

Some suppliers' totals include credits for returned merchandise, such that our total business with them worked out to zero dollars. Each supplier with which we did no business will have a NULL in its order_amt column in the OUTER JOIN. The usual rules for aggregate functions with NULL arguments apply, so these suppliers will also show a zero total amount. It is also possible to use a function inside an aggregate function, so you could write SUM(COALESCE(T1.x, T2.x)) for the common column pairs.

If you need to tell the difference between a true sum of zero and the result of a NULL in an OUTER JOIN, use the MIN() or MAX() function on the questionable column. These functions both return a NULL result for a NULL input, so an expression inside the MAX() function could be used to print the message MAX(COALESCE(order_amt, 'No Orders')), for example.

Likewise, these functions could be used in a HAVING clause, but that would defeat the purpose of an OUTER JOIN.

## 25.3.7 FULL OUTER JOIN

The FULL OUTER JOIN is a mix of the LEFT and RIGHT OUTER JOINs, with preserved rows constructed from both tables. The statement takes two tables and puts them in one result table. Again, this is easier to explain with an example than with a formal definition.

```
  T1        T2
a  x      b  x
================
1  'r'    7  'r'
2  'v'    8  's'
3  NULL   9  NULL
```

```
T1 FULL OUTER JOIN T2 ON (T1.x = T2.x)
a       T1.x    b       T2.x
================================================
1       'r'     7       'r' ◀ T1 INNER JOIN T2
2       'v'     NULL    NULL ◀preserved from T1
3       NULL    NULL    NULL ◀preserved from T1
NULL    NULL    8       's' ◀ preserved from T2
NULL    NULL    9       NULL ◀ preserved from T2
```

## 25.4 UNION JOIN Operators

There is also a `UNION JOIN` in Standard SQL that returns the results of a `FULL OUTER JOIN` without the rows that were in the `INNER JOIN` of the two tables. No SQL product has implemented it as of 2009 and nobody seems to want it. But it is part of the SAS statistical system (www.sas.com) in their the PROC SQL options.

```
T1 UNION JOIN T2 ON (T1.x = T2.x)
a         T1.x      b         T2.x
=====================================================
2         'v'       NULL      NULL ◀preserved from T1
3         NULL      NULL      NULL ◀preserved from T1
NULL      NULL      8         's' ◀ preserved from T2
NULL      NULL      9         NULL ◀ preserved from T2
```

As an example of this, you might want to combine the medical records of male and female patients into one table with this query.

```
SELECT *
 FROM (SELECT 'male', prostate FROM Males)
   OUTER UNION
  (SELECT 'female', pregnancy FROM Females);
```

to get a result table like this:

| Result | | | |
|---|---|---|---|
| male | prostate | female | pregnancy |
| 'male' | 'no' | NULL | NULL |
| 'male' | 'no' | NULL | NULL |
| 'male' | 'yes' | NULL | NULL |
| 'male' | 'yes' | NULL | NULL |
| NULL | NULL | 'female' | 'no' |
| NULL | NULL | 'female' | 'no' |
| NULL | NULL | 'female' | 'yes' |
| NULL | NULL | 'female' | 'yes' |

Frédéric Brouard came up with a nice trick for writing a similar join. That is, a join on one table, say a basic table of student data, with either a table of data particular to domestic students or another table of data particular to foreign students, based on the value of a parameter. This differs from a true UNION JOIN in that it has to have a "root" table to use for the outer JOINs.

```
CREATE TABLE Students
(student_nbr INTEGER NOT NULL PRIMARY KEY,
student_type CHAR(1) NOT NULL DEFAULT 'D'
   CHECK (student_type IN ('D', 2, ..))
..);

CREATE TABLE DomesticStudents
(student_nbr INTEGER NOT NULL PRIMARY KEY,
   REFERENCES Students(student_nbr),
..);

CREATE TABLE ForeignStudents
(student_nbr INTEGER NOT NULL PRIMARY KEY,
   REFERENCES Students(student_nbr),
..);

SELECT Students.*, DomesticStudents.*, ForeignStudents.*
 FROM Students
   LEFT OUTER JOIN
   DomesticStudents
   ON CASE Students.stud_type
      WHEN 'D' THEN 1 ELSE NULL END
      = 1
    LEFT OUTER JOIN
    ForeignStudents
    ON CASE Student.stud_type WHEN 2 THEN 1 ELSE NULL END
       = 1;
```

## 25.5 Scalar SELECT Expressions

A SELECT expression that returns a single row with a single value can be used where a scalar expression can be used. If the result of the scalar query is empty, it is converted to a NULL. This will sometimes, but not always, let you write an OUTER JOIN as a query within the SELECT clause; thus, this query will work only if each supplier has one or zero orders:

```
SELECT sup_id, sup_name, order_nbr,
   (SELECT order_amt
     FROM Orders
```

```
        WHERE Suppliers.sup_id = Orders.sup_id)
       AS order_amt
    FROM Suppliers;
```

However, I could write:

```
SELECT sup_id, sup_name,
   (SELECT COUNT(*)
     FROM Orders
    WHERE Suppliers.sup_id = Orders.sup_id)
 FROM Suppliers;
```

instead of writing:

```
SELECT sup_id, sup_name, COUNT(*)
 FROM Suppliers
   LEFT OUTER JOIN
   Orders
   ON Suppliers.sup_id = Orders.sup_id
GROUP BY sup_id, sup_name;
```

## 25.6 Old versus New JOIN Syntax

The infixed OUTER JOIN syntax was meant to replace several different vendor options that all had different syntax and semantics. It was absolutely needed. The INNER JOIN and OUTER JOIN operators are universal now. They are binary operators, and programmers are used to binary operators—add, subtract, multiply, and divide are all binary operators. E-R diagrams use lines between tables to show a relational schema.

But this leads to a linear approach to problem solving that might not be such a good thing in SQL. Consider this statement, which would have been written in the traditional syntax as:

```
SELECT a, b, c
FROM Foo, Bar, Flub
WHERE Foo.y BETWEEN Bar.x AND Flub.z;
```

With the infixed syntax, I can write this same statement in any of several ways. For example:

```
SELECT a, b, c
FROM (Foo
  INNER JOIN
  Bar
  ON Foo.y >= Bar.x)
    INNER JOIN
    Flub
    ON Foo.y <= Flub.z;
```

or:

```
SELECT a, b, c
FROM Foo
  INNER JOIN
    (Bar
    INNER JOIN
    Flub
    ON Foo.y <= Flub.z)
  ON Foo.y >= Bar.x;
```

I leave it to you to find all the permutations, with or without the parentheses. None of them will show you the 3-ary relationship.

Humans tend to see things that are close together as a unit or as having a relationship. It is a law of visual psychology and typesetting called the Law of Proximity. The extra reserved words in the infixed notation tend to work against proximity; you have to look in many places to find the parts of a.

The infixed notation invites a programmer to add one table at a time to the chain of JOINs. First I built and tested the Foo-Bar join and when I was happy with the results, I added Flub. Step-wise program refinement was one of the mantras of structured programming. But this is a procedural approach to programing and we want to use a declarative approach. Instead of having a sequence of steps, we want to see a description of the final result as a whole.

But look at the code; can you see that there is a BETWEEN relationship among the three tables? It is not easy, is it? In effect, you see only pairs of tables and not the whole problem. SQL is an "all-at-once" set-oriented language, not a "step-wise" language. This is much like the conceptual difference between addition with a simple binary + operator and the generalized n-ary summation operator with a Σ.

Am I against infixed JOINs? No, but it is a bit more complicated than it first appears, and if there are some OUTER JOINs in the mix, things can be very complicated. Just be careful with the new toys, kids.

## 25.7 Constrained JOINs

We can relate two tables together based on quantities in each of them. These problems take the form of pairing items in one set with items in another. The extra restriction is that the set of pairs has constraints at the level of the result that a row-by-row join does not. Here the values are identifiers and cannot be repeated in the results.

Let us assume we have two tables, X and Y. Some possible situations are:

1. A row in X matches one and only one row in Y. There can be one matching function that applies to one set, or each set can have its own matching function

   An example of one matching function is an optimization with constraints. For example, you are filling an egg carton with a set of colored eggs given rules about how the colors can be arranged. A lot of logic puzzles use this model.

   The classic example of two matching functions is the Stable Marriages problem, where the men rank the women they want to marry and the women rank the men they want to marry.
2. A row in X matches one or more rows in Y: knapsack or bin packing problems, where one bin holds one or more items and we try to optimize the arrangement.

   In all cases, there can be a unique answer or several answers or no valid answer at all. Let's give some examples and code for them.

## 25.7.1 Inventory and Orders

The simplest example is filling customer orders from the inventories that we have at various stores. To make life easier, assume that we have only one product, process orders in increasing customer_id order (this could be temporal order as well), and draw from store inventory by increasing store_id (this could be nearest store).

```
CREATE TABLE Inventory
(store_id INTEGER NOT NULL PRIMARY KEY,
item_qty INTEGER NOT NULL CHECK (item_qty >= 0));

INSERT INTO Inventory (store_id, item_qty)
VALUES (10, 2), (20, 3), (30, 2);

CREATE TABLE Orders
(customer_id CHAR(5) NOT NULL PRIMARY KEY,
item_qty INTEGER NOT NULL CHECK (item_qty > 0));

INSERT INTO Orders (customer_id, item_qty)
VALUES ('Bill', 4), ('Fred', 2);
```

What we want to do is fill Bill's order for four units by taking two units from store #1, and two units from store #2. Next we process Fred's order with the one unit left in store #1 and one unit from store #3.

```
SELECT I.store_id, O.customer_id,
  (CASE WHEN O.end_running_qty <= I.end_running_qty
```

```
    THEN O.end_running_qty
    ELSE I.end_running_qty END
  - CASE WHEN O.start_running_qty >= I.start_running_qty
      THEN O.start_running_qty
      ELSE I.start_running_qty END)
  AS items_consumed_tally
FROM (SELECT I1.store_id,
      SUM(I2.item_qty) - I1.item_qty,
      SUM(I2.item_qty)
    FROM Inventory AS I1, Inventory AS I2
    WHERE I2.store_id <= I1.store_id
    GROUP BY I1.store_id, I1.item_qty)
  AS I (store_id, start_running_qty, end_running_qty)
  INNER JOIN
   (SELECT O1.customer_id,
       SUM(O2.item_qty) - O1.item_qty,
       SUM(O2.item_qty) AS end_running_qty
     FROM Orders AS O1, Orders AS O2
     WHERE O2.customer_id <= O1.customer_id
    GROUP BY O1.customer_id, O1.item_qty)
    AS O (store_id, start_running_qty, end_running_qty)
    ON O.start_running_qty < I.end_running_qty
     AND O.end_running_qty > I.start_running_qty;
```

This can also be done with ordinal functions.

## 25.7.2 Stable Marriages

This is a classic programming problem from procedural language classes. The set up is fairly simple; you have a set of potential husbands and an equal-sized set of potential wives. We want to pair them up into stable marriages.

What is a stable marriage? In 25 words or less, it is a marriage in which neither partner can do better. You have a set of $n$ men and a set of $n$ women. All the men have a preference scale for all the women, which ranks them from 1 to $n$ without gaps or ties. The women have the same ranking system for the men. The goal is to pair off the men and women into $n$ marriages such that there is no pair in your final arrangement where Mr. X and Ms. Y are matched to each other when they both would rather be matched to someone else.

For example, let's assume the husbands are ('Joe Celko', 'Brad Pitt') and the wives are ('Jackie Celko', 'Angelina Jolie"). If Jackie got matched to Mr. Pitt, she would be quite happy. And I would enjoy Ms. Jolie's company. However, Mr. Pitt and Ms. Jolie can both do better than us. Once they are paired up they will stay that way, leaving Jackie and I still wed.

The classic Stable Marriage algorithms usually are based on backtracking. These algorithms try a combination of couples, and then attempt to fix any unhappy matches. When the algorithm hits on a situation where nobody can improve their situation, they stop and give an answer.

Two important things to know about this problem: (1) there is always a solution and (2) there is often more than one solution. Remember that a stable marriage is not always a happy marriage. In fact, in this problem, although there is always at least one arrangement of stable marriages in any set, you most often find many different pairings that produce a set of stable marriages. Each set of marriages will tend to maximize either the happiness of the men or the women.

```
CREATE TABLE Husbands
(man CHAR(2) NOT NULL,
woman CHAR(2) NOT NULL,
PRIMARY KEY (man, woman),
ranking INTEGER NOT NULL);

CREATE TABLE Wives
(woman CHAR(2) NOT NULL,
man CHAR(2) NOT NULL,
PRIMARY KEY (woman, man),
ranking INTEGER NOT NULL);

CREATE TABLE Wife_Perms
(perm INTEGER NOT NULL PRIMARY KEY,
wife_name CHAR(2) NOT NULL);
```

—The men's preferences

```
INSERT INTO Husbands -- husband #1
VALUES ('h1', 'w1', 5), ('h1', 'w2', 2),
('h1', 'w3', 6), ('h1', 'w4', 8),
('h1', 'w5', 4), ('h1', 'w6', 3),
('h1', 'w7', 1), ('h1', 'w8', 7);

INSERT INTO Husbands -- husband #2
VALUES ('h2', 'w1', 6), ('h2', 'w2', 3),
('h2', 'w3', 2), ('h2', 'w4', 1),
('h2', 'w5', 8), ('h2', 'w6', 4),
('h2', 'w7', 7), ('h2', 'w8', 5);

INSERT INTO Husbands -- husband #3
VALUES ('h3', 'w1', 4), ('h3', 'w2', 2),
('h3', 'w3', 1), ('h3', 'w4', 3),
('h3', 'w5', 6), ('h3', 'w6', 8),
('h3', 'w7', 7), ('h3', 'w8', 5);
```

```
INSERT INTO Husbands -- husband #4
VALUES ('h4', 'w1', 8), ('h4', 'w2', 4),
('h4', 'w3', 1), ('h4', 'w4', 3),
('h4', 'w5', 5), ('h4', 'w6', 6),
('h4', 'w7', 7), ('h4', 'w8', 2);

INSERT INTO Husbands -- husband #5
VALUES ('h5', 'w1', 6), ('h5', 'w2', 8),
('h5', 'w3', 2), ('h5', 'w4', 3),
('h5', 'w5', 4), ('h5', 'w6', 5),
('h5', 'w7', 7), ('h5', 'w8', 1);

INSERT INTO Husbands -- husband #6
VALUES ('h6', 'w1', 7), ('h6', 'w2', 4),
('h6', 'w3', 6), ('h6', 'w4', 5),
('h6', 'w5', 3), ('h6', 'w6', 8),
('h6', 'w7', 2), ('h6', 'w8', 1);

INSERT INTO Husbands -- husband #7
VALUES ('h7', 'w1', 5), ('h7', 'w2', 1),
('h7', 'w3', 4), ('h7', 'w4', 2),
('h7', 'w5', 7), ('h7', 'w6', 3),
('h7', 'w7', 6), ('h7', 'w8', 8);

INSERT INTO Husbands -- husband #8
VALUES ('h8', 'w1', 2), ('h8', 'w2', 4),
('h8', 'w3', 7), ('h8', 'w4', 3),
('h8', 'w5', 6), ('h8', 'w6', 1),
('h8', 'w7', 5), ('h8', 'w8', 8);
```

—The women's preferences

```
INSERT INTO Wives -- wife #1
VALUES ('w1', 'h1', 6), ('w1', 'h2', 3),
('w1', 'h3', 7), ('w1', 'h4', 1),
('w1', 'h5', 4), ('w1', 'h6', 2),
('w1', 'h7', 8), ('w1', 'h8', 5);

INSERT INTO Wives -- wife #2
VALUES ('w2', 'h1', 4), ('w2', 'h2', 8),
('w2', 'h3', 3), ('w2', 'h4', 7),
('w2', 'h5', 2), ('w2', 'h6', 5),
('w2', 'h7', 6), ('w2', 'h8', 1);

INSERT INTO Wives -- wife #3
VALUES ('w3', 'h1', 3), ('w3', 'h2', 4),
('w3', 'h3', 5), ('w3', 'h4', 6),
('w3', 'h5', 8), ('w3', 'h6', 1),
('w3', 'h7', 7), ('w3', 'h8', 2);

INSERT INTO Wives -- wife #4
VALUES ('w4', 'h1', 8), ('w4', 'h2', 2),
('w4', 'h3', 1), ('w4', 'h4', 3),
```

```
('w4', 'h5', 7), ('w4', 'h6', 5),
('w4', 'h7', 4), ('w4', 'h8', 6);

INSERT INTO Wives -- wife #5
VALUES ('w5', 'h1', 3), ('w5', 'h2', 7),
('w5', 'h3', 2), ('w5', 'h4', 4),
('w5', 'h5', 5), ('w5', 'h6', 1),
('w5', 'h7', 6), ('w5', 'h8', 8);

INSERT INTO Wives -- wife #6
VALUES ('w6', 'h1', 2), ('w6', 'h2', 1),
('w6', 'h3', 3), ('w6', 'h4', 6),
('w6', 'h5', 8), ('w6', 'h6', 7),
('w6', 'h7', 5), ('w6', 'h8', 4);

INSERT INTO Wives -- wife #7
VALUES ('w7', 'h1', 6), ('w7', 'h2', 4),
('w7', 'h3', 1), ('w7', 'h4', 5),
('w7', 'h5', 2), ('w7', 'h6', 8),
('w7', 'h7', 3), ('w7', 'h8', 7);

INSERT INTO Wives -- wife #8
VALUES ('w8', 'h1', 8), ('w8', 'h2', 2),
('w8', 'h3', 7), ('w8', 'h4', 4),
('w8', 'h5', 5), ('w8', 'h6', 6),
('w8', 'h7', 1), ('w8', 'h8', 3);
```

—This auxiliary table helps us create all permutations of the wives.

```
INSERT INTO Wife_Perms
VALUES (1, 'w1'), (2, 'w2'), (4, 'w3'), (8, 'w4'),
      (16, 'w5'), (32, 'w6'), (64, 'w7'), (128, 'w8');
```

The query builds all permutation of wives and then filters them for blocking pairs in an elaborate `NOT EXISTS()` predicate.

```
SELECT A.wife_name AS h1, B.wife_name AS h2,
   C.wife_name AS h3, D.wife_name AS h4,
   E.wife_name AS h5, F.wife_name AS h6,
   G.wife_name AS h7, H.wife_name AS h8
 FROM Wife_Perms AS A, Wife_Perms AS B,
   Wife_Perms AS C, Wife_Perms AS D,
   Wife_Perms AS E, Wife_Perms AS F,
   Wife_Perms AS G, Wife_Perms AS H
WHERE A.perm + B.perm + C.perm + D.perm
   + E.perm + F.perm + G.perm + H.perm = 255
 AND NOT EXISTS
  (SELECT *
    FROM Husbands AS W, Husbands AS X, Wives AS Y,
      Wives AS Z
    WHERE W.man = X.man
```

```
AND W.ranking > X.ranking
AND X.woman = Y.woman
AND Y.woman = Z.woman
AND Y.ranking > Z.ranking
AND Z.man = W.man
AND W.man||W.woman
 IN ('h1'||A.wife_name, 'h2'||B.wife_name,
   'h3'||C.wife_name, 'h4'||D.wife_name,
   'h5'||E.wife_name, 'h6'||F.wife_name,
    h7'||G.wife_name, 'h8'||H.wife_name)
AND Y.man||Y.woman
 IN ('h1'||A.wife_name, 'h2'||B.wife_name,
   'h3'||C.wife_name, 'h4'||D.wife_name,
   'h5'||E.wife_name, 'h6'||F.wife_name,
   'h7'||G.wife_name, 'h8'|| H.wife_name))
```

The results look like this:

| h1 | h2 | h3 | h4 | h5 | h6 | h7 | h8 |
|---|---|---|---|---|---|---|---|
| w3 | w6 | w4 | w8 | w1 | w5 | w7 | w2 |
| w3 | w6 | w4 | w1 | w7 | w5 | w8 | w2 |
| w6 | w4 | w3 | w8 | w1 | w5 | w7 | w2 |
| w6 | w3 | w4 | w8 | w1 | w5 | w7 | w2 |
| w6 | w4 | w3 | w1 | w7 | w5 | w8 | w2 |
| w6 | w3 | w4 | w1 | w7 | w5 | w8 | w2 |
| w2 | w4 | w3 | w8 | w1 | w5 | w7 | w6 |
| w2 | w4 | w3 | w1 | w7 | w5 | w8 | w6 |
| w7 | w4 | w3 | w8 | w1 | w5 | w2 | w6 |

## 25.7.3 Ball and Box Packing

This example was taken from the BeyondRelational web site SQL Challenge #22 in January 2010. We have some boxes and balls; our job is to put the balls into those boxes. But wait a second! The balls should be filled into the boxes based on some rules and preferences configured by the user. Here are the rules.

1. A box can have only one ball.
2. A ball can be placed only in one box.
3. The number of balls and number of boxes will always be the same.
4. All boxes should be filled and all balls should be used.

5. There will be a configuration table where the preferences of the user will be stored. The preference setting should be followed when putting a ball into a box.
6. In addition to this, there will be a configuration table where the preferences of the user will be stored. The preference setting should be followed when putting a ball into a box.

```
CREATE TABLE Boxes
(box_nbr INTEGER NOT NULL PRIMARY KEY,
box_name VARCHAR(20) NOT NULL);

INSERT INTO Boxes (box_nbr, box_name)
VALUES (1, 'Box 1'), (2, 'Box 2'), (3, 'Box 3'),
  (4, 'Box 4'), (5, 'Box 5'), (6, 'Box 6');

CREATE TABLE Balls
(ball_nbr INTEGER NOT NULL PRIMARY KEY,
ball_name VARCHAR(20) NOT NULL);

INSERT INTO Balls (ball_name)
VALUES (1, 'Ball 1'), (2, 'Ball 2'), (3, 'Ball 3'),
  (4, 'Ball 4'), (5, 'Ball 5'), (6, 'Ball 6');

CREATE TABLE Preferences
(box_nbr INTEGER NOT NULL
   REFERENCES Boxes (box_nbr),
ball_nbr INTEGER NOT NULL
   REFERENCES Balls (ball_nbr),
PRIMARY KEY (box_nbr, ball_nbr));

INSERT INTO Preferences (box_nbr, ball_nbr)
VALUES (1, 1),
  (2, 1), (2, 3),
  (3, 2), (3, 3),
  (4, 1), (4, 2), (4, 3), (4, 4), (4, 5), (4, 6),
  (5, 4), (5, 5),
  (6, 5);
```

## Results

| box_name | ball_name |
|---|---|
| 'Box 1' | 'Ball 1' |
| 'Box 2' | 'Ball 3' |
| 'Box 3' | 'Ball 2' |
| 'Box 4' | 'Ball 6' |
| 'Box 5' | 'Ball 4' |
| 'Box 6' | 'Ball 5' |

This answer is done in parts to expose the logic via CTEs. The BallsInBoxes CTE gives us *all* the possible arrangements of six balls in six boxes. This is passed to the PreferredBallsInBoxes CTE to apply the preference rules, but allow duplicate balls if two or more boxes want them. Finally, the main query makes sure that we keep only the rows with unique balls.

The use of the `IN()` predicates to assure that the row has no duplicate columns is easy to extend to any number of items, but a bit bulky to read. But it is remarkably fast in the SQL engines where we tested it.

```
WITH
BallsInBoxes (bx1, bx2, bx3, bx4, bx5, bx6)
AS
(SELECT B1.ball_nbr, B2.ball_nbr, B3.ball_nbr,
   B4.ball_nbr, B5.ball_nbr, B6.ball_nbr
  FROM Balls AS B1, Balls AS B2, Balls AS B3,
   Balls AS B4, Balls AS B5, Balls AS B6
 WHERE B1.ball_nbr NOT IN (B2.ball_nbr, B3.ball_nbr,
    B4.ball_nbr, B5.ball_nbr, B6.ball_nbr)
   AND B2.ball_nbr NOT IN (B3.ball_nbr, B4.ball_nbr,
    B5.ball_nbr, B6.ball_nbr)
   AND B3.ball_nbr NOT IN (B4.ball_nbr, B5.ball_nbr,
    B6.ball_nbr)
   AND B4.ball_nbr NOT IN (B5.ball_nbr, B6.ball_nbr)
   AND B5.ball_nbr NOT IN (B6.ball_nbr)),

PreferredBallsInBoxes (bx1, bx2, bx3, bx4, bx5, bx6)
AS
(SELECT bx1, bx2, bx3, bx4, bx5, bx6
  FROM BallsInBoxes AS BB
 WHERE BB.bx1
   IN (SELECT ball_nbr
        FROM Preferences AS P
       WHERE box_nbr = 1)
  AND BB.bx2
   IN (SELECT ball_nbr
        FROM Preferences AS P
       WHERE box_nbr = 2)
  AND BB.bx3
   IN (SELECT ball_nbr
        FROM Preferences AS P
       WHERE box_nbr = 3)
  AND BB.bx4
   IN (SELECT ball_nbr
        FROM Preferences AS P
       WHERE box_nbr = 4)
  AND BB.bx5
   IN (SELECT ball_nbr
        FROM Preferences AS P
       WHERE box_nbr = 5)
```

```
   AND BB.bx6
    IN (SELECT ball_nbr
        FROM Preferences AS P
       WHERE box_nbr = 6))

SELECT bx1, bx2, bx3, bx4, bx5, bx6
 FROM PreferredBallsInBoxes AS PBB1
WHERE PBB1.bx NOT IN (PBB2.bx, PBB3.bx, PBB4.bx, PBB5.bx,
    PBB6.bx)
  AND PBB2.bx NOT IN (PBB3.bx, PBB4.bx, PBB5.bx, PBB6.bx)
  AND PBB3.bx NOT IN (PBB4.bx, PBB5.bx, PBB6.bx)
  AND PBB4.bx NOT IN (PBB5.bx, PBB6.bx)
  AND PBB5.bx NOT IN (PBB6.bx);
```

## 25.8 Dr. Codd's T-Join

In the *Second Version of the Relational Model* (1990), Dr. E. F. Codd introduced a set of new theta operators, called T-operators, which were based on the idea of a best-fit or approximate equality. The algorithm for the operators is easier to understand with an example modified from Dr. Codd.

The problem is to assign the classes to the available classrooms. We want `(class_size < room_size)` to be true after the assignments are made. This will allow us a few empty seats in each room for late students. We can do this in one of two ways. The first way is to sort the tables in ascending order by classroom size and the number of students in a class. We start with the following tables:

```
CREATE TABLE Rooms
(room_nbr CHAR(2) PRIMARY KEY,
room_size INTEGER NOT NULL);

CREATE TABLE Classes
(class_nbr CHAR(2) PRIMARY KEY,
class_size INTEGER NOT NULL);
```

These tables have the following rows in them:

Classes

| class_nbr | class_size |
|---|---|
| 'c1' | 80 |
| 'c2' | 70 |
| 'c3' | 65 |
| 'c4' | 55 |

(*Continued*)

Classes

| class_nbr | class_size |
|---|---|
| 'c5' | 50 |
| 'c6' | 40 |

Rooms

| room_nbr | room_size |
|---|---|
| 'r1' | 70 |
| 'r2' | 40 |
| 'r3' | 50 |
| 'r4' | 85 |
| 'r5' | 30 |
| 'r6' | 65 |
| 'r7' | 55 |

The goal of the T-JOIN problem is to assign a class that is smaller than the classroom given it (class_size < room_size). Dr. Codd gives two approaches to the problem, ascending order algorithm and descending order algorithm.

1. **Ascending Order Algorithm**

   Sort both tables into ascending order. Reading from the top of the Rooms table, match each class with the first room that will fit.

| Classes | | Rooms | |
|---|---|---|---|
| class_nbr | class_size | room_nbr | room_size |
| 'c6' | 40 | 'r5' | 30 |
| 'c5' | 50 | 'r2' | 40 |
| 'c4' | 55 | 'r3' | 50 |
| 'c3' | 65 | 'r7' | 55 |
| 'c2' | 70 | 'r6' | 65 |
| 'c1' | 80 | 'r1' | 70 |
| | | 'r4' | 85 |

This gives us:

Results

| class_nbr | class_size | room_nbr | room_size |
|---|---|---|---|
| 'c2' | 70 | 'r4' | 85 |
| 'c3' | 65 | 'r1' | 70 |
| 'c4' | 55 | 'r6' | 65 |
| 'c5' | 50 | 'r7' | 55 |
| 'c6' | 40 | 'r3' | 50 |

2. **Descending Order Algorithm**
   Sort both tables into descending order. Reading from the top of the Classes table, match each class with the first room that will fit.

| Classes | | Rooms | |
|---|---|---|---|
| class_nbr | class_size | room_nbr | room_size |
| 'c1' | 80 | 'r4' | 85 |
| 'c2' | 70 | 'r1' | 70 |
| 'c3' | 65 | 'r6' | 65 |
| 'c4' | 55 | 'r7' | 55 |
| 'c5' | 50 | 'r3' | 50 |
| 'c6' | 40 | 'r2' | 40 |
| | | 'r5' | 30 |

Results

| class_nbr | class_size | room_nbr | room_size |
|---|---|---|---|
| 'c1' | 80 | 'r4' | 85 |
| 'c3' | 65 | 'r1' | 70 |
| 'c4' | 55 | 'r6' | 65 |
| 'c5' | 50 | 'r7' | 55 |
| 'c6' | 40 | 'r3' | 50 |

Notice that the answers are different! Dr. Codd has never given a definition in relational algebra of the T-Join, so I proposed that we need one. Informally, for each class, we want the smallest room that will hold it, while maintaining the T-JOIN condition. Or for each room, we want the largest class that will fill it, while maintaining the T-JOIN condition. These can be two different things, so you must decide which table is the driver. But either way, I am advocating a "best fit" over Codd's "first fit" approach.

Other theta conditions can be used in place of the "less than" shown here. If "less than or equal" is used, all the classes are assigned to a room in this case, but not in all cases. This is left to you as an exercise.

The first attempts in Standard SQL are versions grouped by queries. They can, however, produce some rows that would be left out of the answers Dr. Codd was expecting. The first JOIN can be written as:

```
SELECT class_nbr, class_size, MIN(room_size)
 FROM Rooms, Classes
WHERE Classes.class_size < Rooms.room_size
GROUP BY class_nbr, class_size;
```

This will give a result table with the desired room sizes, but not the room numbers. You cannot put the other columns in the SELECT list, since it would conflict with the GROUP BY clause. But also note that the classroom with 85 seats ('r4') is used twice, once by class 'c1' and then by class 'c2':

**Results**

| class_nbr | class_size | MIN(room_size) |
|---|---|---|
| c1 | 80 | 85 ◂room r4 |
| c2 | 70 | 85 ◂ room r4 |
| c3 | 65 | 70 |
| c4 | 55 | 65 |
| c5 | 50 | 55 |
| c6 | 40 | 50 |

Your best bet after this is to use the query in an EXISTS clause:

```
SELECT *
 FROM Rooms, Classes
WHERE EXISTS (SELECT class_nbr, class_size, MIN(room_size)
      FROM Rooms, Classes
      WHERE Classes.class_size < Rooms.room_size
      GROUP BY class_nbr, class_size);
```

However, some versions of SQL will not allow a grouped subquery and others will balk at an aggregate function in an EXISTS predicate. The only way I have found to rectify this was to save the results to a temporary table, then JOIN it back to the Cartesian product of Rooms and Classes. Putting the columns for Rooms into the SELECT list of the same query schema can do the second T-JOIN:

```
SELECT room_nbr, room_size, MAX(class_size)
 FROM Rooms, Classes
WHERE Classes.class_size < Rooms.room_size
GROUP BY room_nbr, room_size;
```

This time, the results are the same as those Dr. Codd got with his procedural algorithm:

Results

| room_nbr | room_size | MAX(class_size) |
|---|---|---|
| 'r4' | 85 | 80 |
| 'r1' | 70 | 65 |
| 'r6' | 65 | 55 |
| 'r7' | 55 | 50 |
| 'r3' | 50 | 40 |

If you do a little arithmetic on the data, you find that we have 360 students and 395 seats, six classes and seven rooms. This solution uses the fewest rooms, but note that the 70 students in class 'c2' are left out completely. Room 'r2' is left over, but it has only 40 seats.

As it works out, the best fit of rooms to classes is given by changing the matching rule to "less than or equal." This will leave the smallest room empty and pack the other rooms to capacity, thus:

```
SELECT class_nbr, class_size, MIN(room_size)
 FROM Rooms, Classes
WHERE Classes.class_size <= Rooms.room_size
GROUP BY class_nbr, class_size;
```

## 25.8.1 Stobbs Solution

Christopher Stobbs came up with this query when I posted this problem as a puzzle at the SQL Server Central web site in 2010. Starting from the innermost query, rank each class according to size with each room where the class can fit, keeping only the best fit. Go out one level and rank the position of the room's size for each class (removes duplicate class allocation), and include only the top ranked for each class. We now have a result when we outer join back to the classes.

```
SELECT C1.class_nbr, C1.class_size, Subset.room_nbr,
   Subset.room_size
 FROM Classes AS C1
  LEFT OUTER JOIN
  (SELECT *
   FROM (SELECT C.*, R.*,
         ROW_NUMBER()
         OVER (PARTITION BY Class_Size
              ORDER BY first_rank) AS second_rank
     FROM (SELECT C.*, R.*,
           ROW_NUMBER()
           OVER (PARTITION BY room_nbr
               ORDER BY class_size DESC) AS first_rank
        FROM Classes AS C2, Rooms AS R
        WHERE R.room_size >= C2.class_size
        )AS Class_Ranks
      WHERE first_rank = 1
     )AS Room_Ranks
    WHERE second_rank = 1) AS Subset
   ON C1.class_nbr = Subset.class_nbr;
```

## 25.8.2 Pierre's Solution

Another answer came from pierre-702284, who posted a similar answer that can handle duplicate values by using the `DENSE_RANK()` function and some math to get a fit for classes and rooms.

```
SELECT C.class_nbr, C.class_size, room_nbr, room_size
 FROM Classes AS C
  LEFT OUTER JOIN
  (SELECT class_nbr, room_nbr, room_size,
     ROW_NUMBER()
     OVER (PARTITION BY class_nbr
          ORDER BY room_alloc_pref)
     AS class_alloc_pref
   FROM (SELECT class_nbr, room_nbr, room_size,
        ROW_NUMBER()
        OVER (PARTITION BY room_alloc_order
            ORDER BY class_alloc_order)
        AS room_alloc_pref
     FROM (SELECT class_nbr, room_nbr, room_size,
          DENSE_RANK()
          OVER (ORDER BY class_size DESC)
```

```
  AS class_size_order,
  DENSE_RANK()
  OVER (ORDER BY class_size DESC, class_nbr)
  AS class_alloc_order,
  DENSE_RANK() OVER (ORDER BY room_size DESC)
  AS room_size_order,
  DENSE_RANK() OVER (ORDER BY room_size DESC,
    room_nbr)
  AS room_alloc_order
FROM Rooms, Classes
WHERE room_size >= class_size;
```

# References

Gusfierld, Dan and Irving, Robert W. *The Stable Marriage Problem: Structure & Algorithms*. ISBN 0-262-07118-5.

Knuth, Donald E. CRM Proceedings & Lecture Notes, Vol #10, “Stable Marriage and Its Relation to Other Combinatorial Problems.” ISBN 0-8218-0603-3.

This booklet, which reproduces seven expository lectures given by the author in November 1975, is a gentle introduction to the analysis of algorithms using the beautiful theory of stable marriages as a vehicle to explain the basic paradigms of that subject.

Wirth, Nicklaus. Algorithms + Data Structures = Programs. Section 3.6. ISBN 0-13-022418-9.

This section gives an answer in Pascal and a short analysis of the algorithm. In particular, I used his data for my example. He gives several answers, which give varying “degrees of happiness” for husbands and wives.

# 26

# VIRTUAL TABLES: VIEWs, DERIVED TABLES, CTEs, AND MQTs

VIEWs, derived tables, and CTEs (Common Table Expression) are ways of putting a query into a named schema object. By that, I mean these things hold the query text rather than the results of the query. They are executed as needed and then we see the results.

A VIEW is also called a virtual table, to distinguish it from temporary and base tables. The definition of a VIEW in Standard SQL requires that it act as if an actual physical table is created when its name is invoked. Whether or not the database system actually materializes the results or uses other mechanisms to get the same effect is implementation defined. The definition of a VIEW is kept in the schema tables to be invoked by name wherever a table could be used. If the VIEW is updatable, then additional rules apply.

The SQL Standard separates administrative (ADMIN) privileges from user (USER) privileges. Table creation is administrative and query execution is a user privilege, so users cannot create their own VIEWs or TEMPORARY TABLEs without having Administrative privileges granted to them. However, a user can create a CTE, which is a local, temporary virtual table.

## 26.1 VIEWs in Queries

The Standard SQL syntax for the VIEW definition is:

```
CREATE VIEW <table name> [(<view column list>)]
AS <query expression>
[WITH [<levels clause>] CHECK OPTION]

<levels clause>::= CASCADED | LOCAL
```

Joe Celko's SQL for Smarties. DOI: 10.1016/B978-0-12-382022-8.00026-0

The `<levels clause>` option in the `WITH CHECK OPTION` did not exist in SQL-89 and it is still not widely implemented. Section 26.5 will discuss this clause in detail. This clause has no effect on queries, but only on `UPDATE`, `INSERT INTO`, and `DELETE FROM` statements.

A `VIEW` is different from a `TEMPORARY TABLE`, derived table, and base table. You cannot put constraints on a `VIEW`, as you can with base and `TEMPORARY` tables. A `VIEW` has no existence in the database until it is invoked, whereas a `TEMPORARY TABLE` is persistent. A derived table exists only in the query in which it is created.

The name of the `VIEW` must be unique within the database schema, like a table name. The `VIEW` definition cannot reference itself, since it does not exist yet. Nor can the definition reference only other `VIEW`s; the nesting of `VIEW`s must eventually resolve to underlying base tables. This only makes sense; if no base tables were involved, what would you be viewing?

## 26.2 Updatable and Read-Only VIEWs

Unlike base tables, `VIEW`s are either updatable or read-only, but not both. `INSERT`, `UPDATE`, and `DELETE` operations are allowed on updatable `VIEW`s and base tables, subject to any other constraints. `INSERT`, `UPDATE`, and `DELETE` are not allowed on read-only `VIEW`s, but you can change their base tables, as you would expect.

An updatable `VIEW` is one that can have each of its rows associated with exactly one row in an underlying base table. When the `VIEW` is changed, the changes pass through the `VIEW` to that underlying base table unambiguously. Updatable `VIEW`s in Standard SQL are defined only for queries that meet these criteria:

1. They are built on only one table
2. They have no `GROUP BY` clause
3. They have no `HAVING` clause
4. They have no aggregate functions
5. They have no calculated columns
6. They have no `UNION`, `INTERSECT`, or `EXCEPT`
7. They have no `SELECT DISTINCT` clause
8. Any columns excluded from the `VIEW` must be `NULL`-able or have a `DEFAULT` in the base table, so that a whole row can be constructed for insertion.

By implication, the `VIEW` must also contain a key of the table. In short, we are absolutely sure that each row in the `VIEW` maps back to one and only one row in the base table.

Some updating is handled by the `CASCADE` option in the referential integrity constraints on the base tables, not by the `VIEW` declaration.

The definition of updatability in Standard SQL is actually pretty limited, but very safe. The database system could look at information it has in the referential integrity constraints to widen the set of allowed updatable VIEWs. You will find that some implementations are now doing just that, but it is not common yet. The SQL standard definition of an updatable VIEW is actually a subset of the possible updatable VIEWs, and a very small subset at that. The major advantage of this definition is that it is based on syntax and not semantics. For example, these VIEWs are logically identical:

```
CREATE VIEW Foo1 -- updatable, has a key!
AS SELECT *
    FROM Foobar
  WHERE x IN (1,2);

CREATE VIEW Foo2 -- not updateable!
AS SELECT *
    FROM Foobar
  WHERE x = 1
 UNION ALL
 SELECT *
    FROM Foobar
  WHERE x = 2;
```

But Foo1 is updateable and Foo2 is not. Although I know of no formal proof, I suspect that determining if a complex query resolves to an updatable query for allowed sets of data values possible in the table is an NP-complete problem.

Without going into details, here is a list of types of queries that can yield updatable VIEWs, as taken from "VIEW Update Is Practical" (Goodman, 1990):

1. Projection from a single table (Standard SQL)
2. Restriction/projection from a single table (Standard SQL)
3. UNION VIEWs
4. Set Difference Views
5. One-to-One Joins
6. One-to-One Outer Joins
7. One-to-Many Joins
8. One-to-Many Outer Joins
9. Many-to-Many Joins
10. Translated and Coded columns

The CREATE TRIGGER mechanism for tables specifies an action to be performed BEFORE, AFTER, or INSTEAD OF a regular INSERT, UPDATE, or DELETE to that table. It is possible for a user to write INSTEAD OF triggers on VIEWs, which catch the changes and route them to the base tables that make up the VIEW. The database designer has complete control over the way VIEWs are handled.

## 26.3 Types of VIEWs

The type of SELECT statement and its purpose can classify VIEWs. The strong advantage of a VIEW is that it will produce the correct results when it is invoked, based on the current data. Trying to do the same sort of things with temporary tables or computed columns within a table can be subject to errors and slower to read from disk.

### 26.3.1 Single-Table Projection and Restriction

In practice, many VIEWs are projections or restrictions on a single base table. This is a common method for obtaining security control by removing rows or columns that a particular group of users is not allowed to see. These VIEWs are usually implemented as in-line macro expansion, since the optimizer can easily fold their code into the final query plan.

### 26.3.2 Calculated Columns

One common use for a VIEW is to provide summary data across a row. For example, given a table with measurements in metric units, we can construct a VIEW that hides the calculations to convert them into English units.

It is important to be sure that you have no problems with NULL values when constructing a calculated column. For example, given a Personnel table with columns for both salary and commission, you might construct this VIEW:

```
CREATE VIEW Payroll (emp_nbr, paycheck_amt)
AS
SELECT emp_nbr, (salary + COALESCE(commission), 0.00)
 FROM Personnel;
```

Office workers do not get commissions, so the value of their commission column will be NULL, so we use the COALESCE() function to change the NULLs to zeros.

### 26.3.3 Translated Columns

Another common use of a VIEW is to translate codes into text or other codes by doing table lookups. This is a special case of a joined VIEW based on a FOREIGN KEY relationship between two tables. For example, an order table might use a part number that we wish to display with a part name on an order entry screen. This is done with a JOIN between the order table and the inventory table, thus:

```
CREATE VIEW Screen (part_nbr, part_name, ...)
AS SELECT Orders.part_nbr, Inventory.part_name, ...
    FROM Inventory, Orders
  WHERE Inventory.part_nbr = Orders.part_nbr;
```

Sometimes the original code is kept and sometimes it is dropped from the VIEW. As a general rule, it is a better idea to keep both values even though they are redundant. The redundancy can be used as a check for users, as well as a hook for nested joins in either of the codes.

The idea of JOIN VIEWs to translate codes can be expanded to show more than just one translated column. The result is often a "star" query with one table in the center, joined by FOREIGN KEY relations to many other tables to produce a result that is more readable than the original central table.

Missing values are a problem. If there is no translation for a given code, no row appears in the VIEW, or if an OUTER JOIN was used, a NULL will appear. The programmer should establish a referential integrity constraint to CASCADE changes between the tables to prevent loss of data.

### 26.3.4 Grouped VIEWs

A grouped VIEW is based on a query with a GROUP BY clause. Since each of the groups may have more than one row in the base from which it was built, these are necessarily read-only VIEWs. Such VIEWs usually have one or more aggregate functions and they are used for reporting purposes. They are also handy for working around weaknesses in SQL. Consider a VIEW that shows the largest sale in each state. The query is straightforward:

```
CREATE VIEW BigSales (state, sales_amt_total)
AS SELECT state_code, MAX(sales_amt)
    FROM Sales
  GROUP BY state_code;
```

SQL does not require that the grouping column(s) appear in the select clause, but it is a good idea in this case.

These VIEWs are also useful for "flattening out" one-to-many relationships. For example, consider a Personnel table, keyed on the employee number (emp_nbr), and a table of dependents, keyed on a combination of the employee number for each dependent's parent (emp_nbr) and the dependent's own serial number (dep_id). The goal is to produce a report of the employees by name with the number of dependents each has.

```
CREATE VIEW DepTally1 (emp_nbr, dependent_cnt)
AS SELECT emp_nbr, COUNT(*)
```

```
  FROM Dependents
 GROUP BY emp_nbr;
```

The report is then simply an `OUTER JOIN` between this `VIEW` and the Personnel table.

The `OUTER JOIN` is needed to account for employees without dependents with a `NULL` value, like this:

```
SELECT emp_name, dependent_cnt
FROM Personnel AS P1
  LEFT OUTER JOIN
  DepTally1 AS D1
  ON P1.emp_nbr = D1.emp_nbr;
```

### 26.3.5 UNION-ed VIEWs

Until recently, a `VIEW` based on a `UNION` or `UNION ALL` operation was read-only because there is no way to map a change onto just one row in one of the base tables. The `UNION` operator will remove duplicate rows from the results. Both the `UNION` and `UNION ALL` operators hide which table the rows came from. Such `VIEW`s must use a `<view column list>`, because the columns in a `UNION [ALL]` have no names of their own. In theory, a `UNION` of two disjoint tables, neither of which has duplicate rows in itself, should be updatable.

Using the problem given in Section 26.3.4 on grouped `VIEW`s, this could also be done with a `UNION` query that would assign a count of zero to employees without dependents, thus:

```
CREATE VIEW DepTally2 (emp_nbr, dependent_cnt)
AS (SELECT emp_nbr, COUNT(*)
    FROM Dependents
  GROUP BY emp_nbr)
 UNION
(SELECT emp_nbr, 0
    FROM Personnel AS P2
  WHERE NOT EXISTS (SELECT *
        FROM Dependents AS D2
        WHERE D2.emp_nbr = P2.emp_nbr));
```

The report is now a simple `INNER JOIN` between this `VIEW` and the Personnel table. The zero value, instead of a `NULL` value, will account for employees without dependents. The report query looks like this:

```
SELECT empart_name, dependent_cnt
 FROM Personnel, DepTally2
WHERE DepTally2.emp_nbr = Personnel.emp_nbr;
```

Recent releases of some of the major databases, such as Oracle and DB2, support inserts, updates, and deletes from such views. Under the covers, each partition is a separate table, with a rule for its contents. One of the most common partitioning is temporal, so each partition might be based on a date range. The goal is to improve query performance by allowing parallel access to each partition member.

The trade-off is a heavy overhead under the covers with the UNION-ed VIEW partitioning, however. For example, DB2 attempts to insert any given row into each of the tables underlying the UNION ALL view. It then counts how many tables accepted the row. It has to process the entire view, one table at a time, and collect the results.

1. If exactly one table accepts the row, the insert is accepted.
2. If no table accepts the row, a "no target" error is raised.
3. If more than one table accepts the row, then an "ambiguous target" error is raised.

The use of INSTEAD OF triggers gives the user the effect of a single table, but there can still be surprises. Think about three tables; A, B, and C. Table C is disjoint from the other two. Tables A and B overlap. So I can always insert into C and may or may not be able to insert into A and B if I hit overlapping rows.

Going back to my Y2K consulting days, I ran into a version of such a partition by calendar periods. Their Table C was set up on Fiscal quarters and got leap year wrong because one of the fiscal quarters ended on the last day of February.

Another approach somewhat like this is to declare explicit partitioning rules in the DDL with a proprietary syntax. The system will handle the housekeeping and the user sees only one table. In the Oracle model, the goal is to put parts of the logical table to different physical tablespaces. Using standard data types, the Oracle syntax looks like this:

```
CREATE TABLE Sales
(invoice_nbr INTEGER NOT NULL PRIMARY KEY,
sale_year INTEGER NOT NULL,
sale_month INTEGER NOT NULL,
sale_day INTEGER NOT NULL)
PARTITION BY RANGE (sale_year, sale_month, sale_day)
(PARTITION  sales_q1  VALUES  LESS  THAN  (1994,  04,  01)
   TABLESPACE tsa,
PARTITION  sales_q2  VALUES  LESS  THAN  (1994,  07,  01)
   TABLESPACE tsb,
PARTITION  sales_q3  VALUES  LESS  THAN  (1994,  10,  01)
   TABLESPACE tsc,
PARTITION  sales  q4  VALUES  LESS  THAN  (1995,  01,  01)
   TABLESPACE tsd);
```

Again, this will depend on your product, since this has to do with the physical database and not the logical model.

### 26.3.6 JOINs in VIEWs

A VIEW whose query expression is a joined table is not usually updatable even in theory.

One of the major purposes of a joined view is to "flatten out" a one-to-many or many-to-many relationship. Such relationships cannot map one row in the VIEW back to one row in the underlying tables on the "many" side of the JOIN. Anything said about a JOIN query could be said about a joined view, so they will not be dealt with here, but in a chapter devoted to a full discussion of joins.

### 26.3.7 Nested VIEWs

A point that is often missed, even by experienced SQL programmers, is that a VIEW can be built on other VIEWs. The only restrictions are that circular references within the query expressions of the VIEWs are illegal and that a VIEW must ultimately be built on base tables. One problem with nested VIEWs is that different updatable VIEWs can reference the same base table at the same time. If these VIEWs then appear in another VIEW, it becomes hard to determine what has happened when the highest-level VIEW is changed. As an example, consider a table with two keys:

```
CREATE TABLE Canada
(english INTEGER NOT NULL UNIQUE,
french INTEGER NOT NULL UNIQUE,
eng_word CHAR(30),
fren_word CHAR(30));

INSERT INTO Canada
VALUES (1, 2, 'muffins', 'croissants'),
   (2, 1, 'bait', 'escargots');

CREATE VIEW EnglishWords
AS SELECT english, eng_word
   FROM Canada
 WHERE eng_word IS NOT NULL;

CREATE VIEW FrenchWords
AS SELECT french, fren_word
   FROM Canada
 WHERE fren_word IS NOT NULL);
```

We have now tried the escargots and decided that we wish to change our opinion of them:

```
UPDATE EnglishWords
 SET eng_word = 'appetizer'
WHERE english = 2;
```

Our French user has just tried haggis and decided to insert a new row for his experience:

```
UPDATE FrenchWords
  SET fren_word = 'Le swill'
WHERE french = 3;
```

The row that is created is (NULL, 3, NULL, 'Le swill'), since there is no way for VIEW FrenchWords to get to the VIEW EnglishWords columns. Likewise, the English VIEW user can construct a row to record his translation, (3, NULL, 'Haggis', NULL). But neither of them can consolidate the two rows into a meaningful piece of data.

To delete a row is also to destroy data; the French-speaker who drops 'croissants' from the table also drops 'muffins' from VIEW EnglishWords.

## 26.4 How VIEWs Are Handled in the Database Engine

Standard SQL requires a system schema table with the text of the VIEW declarations in it. What would be handy, but is not easily done in all SQL implementations, is to trace the VIEWs down to their base tables by printing out a tree diagram of the nested structure. You should check your user library and see if it has such a utility program (for example, FINDVIEW in the old SPARC library for SQL/DS). There are several ways to handle VIEWs, and systems will often use a mixture of them. The major categories of algorithms are materialization and in-line text expansion.

### 26.4.1 View Column List

The <view column list> is optional; when it is not given, the VIEW will inherit the column names from the query. The number of column names in the <view column list> has to be the same as the degree of the query expression. If any two columns in the query have the same column name, you must have a <view column list> to resolve the ambiguity. The same column name cannot be specified more than once in the <view column list>.

### 26.4.2 VIEW Materialization

Materialization means that whenever you use the name of the VIEW, the database engine finds its definition in the schema information tables and creates a working table with the name that has the appropriate column names with the appropriate data types. Finally, this new table is filled with the results of the SELECT statement in the body of the VIEW definition.

The decision to materialize a VIEW as an actual physical table is implementation-defined in Standard SQL, but the VIEW must act as if it were a table when accessed for a query. If the VIEW is not updatable, this approach automatically protects the base tables from any improper changes and is guaranteed to be correct. It uses existing internal procedures in the database engine (create table, insert from query), so this is easy for the database to do.

The downside of this approach is that it is not very fast for large VIEWs, uses extra storage space, cannot take advantage of indexes already existing on the base tables, usually cannot create indexes on the new table, and cannot be optimized as easily as other approaches. However, materialization is the best approach for certain VIEWs. A VIEW whose construction has a hidden sort is usually materialized. Queries with SELECT DISTINCT, UNION, GROUP BY, and HAVING clauses are usually implemented by sorting to remove duplicate rows or to build groups. As each row of the VIEW is built, it has to be saved to compare it to the other rows, so it makes sense to materialize it.

Some products also give you the option of controlling the materializations yourself. The vendor terms vary. A "snapshot" means materializing a table that also includes a time stamp. A "result set" is a materialized table that is passed to a front-end application program for display. Check your particular product.

## 26.4.3 In-Line Text Expansion

Another approach is to store the text of the CREATE VIEW statement and work it into the parse tree of the SELECT, INSERT, UPDATE, or DELETE statements that use it. This allows the optimizer to blend the VIEW definition into the final query plan. For example, you can create a VIEW based on a particular department, thus:

```
CREATE VIEW SalesDept (dept_name, city_name, ...)
AS SELECT 'Sales', city_name, ...
  FROM Departments
 WHERE dept_name = 'Sales';
```

and then use it as a query, thus:

```
SELECT *
 FROM SalesDept
WHERE city_name = 'New York';
```

The parser expands the VIEW into text (or an intermediate tokenized form) within the FROM clause. The query would become, in effect,

```
SELECT *
 FROM (SELECT 'Sales', city_name, ...
    FROM Departments
    WHERE dept_name = 'Sales')
   AS SalesDept (dept_name, city_name, ...)
WHERE city_name = 'New York';
```

and the query optimizer would then "flatten it out" into

```
SELECT *
 FROM Departments
WHERE (dept_name = 'sales')
  AND (city_name = 'New York');
```

Though this sounds like a nice approach, it had problems in early systems where the in-line expansion does not result in proper SQL. An earlier version of DB2 was one such system. To illustrate the problem, imagine that you are given a DB2 table that has a long identification number and some figures in each row. The long identification number is like those 40-digit monsters they give you on a utility bill—they are unique only in the first few characters, but the utility company prints the whole thing out anyway. Your task is to create a report that is grouped according to the first six characters of the long identification number. The immediate naive query uses the substring operator:

```
SELECT SUBSTRING(long_id FROM 1 TO 6), SUM(amt1),
   SUM(amt2), ...
 FROM TableA
GROUP BY id;
```

This does not work; it is incorrect SQL, since the `SELECT` and `GROUP BY` lists do not agree. Other common attempts include `GROUP BY SUBSTRING(long_id FROM 1 TO 6)`, which will fail because you cannot use a function, and `GROUP BY 1`, which will fail because you can use a column position only in a `UNION` statement (column position is now deprecated in Standard SQL) and in the `ORDER BY` in some products.

The `GROUP BY` has to have a list of simple column names drawn from the tables of the `FROM` clause. The next attempt is to build a `VIEW`:

```
CREATE VIEW BadTry (short_id, amt1, amt2, ...)
AS SELECT SUBSTRING(long_id FROM 1 TO 6), amt1, amt2, ...
  FROM TableA;
```

and then do a grouped select on it. This is correct SQL, but it does not work in the old DB2. The compiler apparently tried to insert the `VIEW` into the `FROM` clause, as we have seen, but when it expands it out, the results are the same as those of the incorrect first query attempt with a function call in the GROUP BY clause. The trick was to force DB2 to materialize the VIEW so that you can name the column constructed with the SUBSTRING() function. Anything that causes a sort will do this—the SELECT DISTINCT, UNION, GROUP BY, and HAVING clauses, for example.

Since we know that the short identification number is a key, we can use this VIEW:

```
CREATE VIEW Shorty (short_id, amt1, amt2, ...)
AS SELECT DISTINCT SUBSTRING(long_id FROM 1 TO 6), amt1,
   amt2, ...
  FROM TableA;
```

Then the report query is:

```
SELECT short_id, SUM(amt1), SUM(amt2), ...
 FROM Shorty
GROUP BY short_id;
```

This works fine in DB2. I am indebted to Susan Vombrack of Loral Aerospace for this example. Incidentally, this can be written in Standard SQL as

```
SELECT *
FROM (SELECT SUBSTRING(long_id FROM 1 TO 6) AS short_id,
     SUM(amt1), SUM(amt2), ...
    FROM TableA
   GROUP BY long_id)
GROUP BY short_id;
```

The name on the substring result column in the subquery expression makes it recognizable to the parser.

## 26.4.4 Pointer Structures

Finally, the system can handle VIEWs with special data structures for the VIEW. This is usually an array of pointers into a base table constructed from the VIEW definition. This is a good way to handle updatable VIEWs in Standard SQL, since the target row in the base table is at the end of a pointer chain in the VIEW structure. Access will be as fast as possible.

The pointer structure approach cannot easily use existing indexes on the base tables. But the pointer structure can be implemented as an index with restrictions. Furthermore, multitable VIEWs can be constructed as pointer structures that allow direct access to the related rows in the table involved in the JOIN. This is very product-dependent, so you cannot make any general assumptions.

### 26.4.5 Indexing and Views

Note that VIEWs cannot have their own indexes. However, VIEWs can inherit the indexing on their base tables in some implementations. Like tables, VIEWs have no inherent ordering, but a programmer who knows his particular SQL implementation will often write code that takes advantage of the quirks of that product. In particular, some implementations allow you to use an ORDER BY clause in a VIEW (they are allowed only on cursors in standard SQL). This will force a sort and could materialize the VIEW as a working table. When the SQL engine has to do a sequential read of the entire table, the sort might help or hinder a particular query. There is no way to predict the results.

## 26.5 WITH CHECK OPTION Clause

If WITH CHECK OPTION is specified, the viewed table has to be updatable. This is actually a fast way to check how your particular SQL implementation handles updatable VIEWs. Try to create a version of the VIEW in question using the WITH CHECK OPTION and see if your product will allow you to create it. The WITH CHECK OPTION is part of the SQL-89 standard, which was extended in Standard SQL by adding an optional <levels clause>. CASCADED is implicit if an explicit LEVEL clause is not given. Consider a VIEW defined as

```
CREATE VIEW V1
AS SELECT *
  FROM Foobar
 WHERE col1 = 'A';
```

and now UPDATE it with

```
UPDATE V1 SET col1 = 'B';
```

The UPDATE will take place without any trouble, but the rows that were previously seen now disappear when we use V1 again. They no longer meet the WHERE clause condition! Likewise, an INSERT INTO statement with VALUES (col1 = 'B') would insert just fine, but its rows would never be seen again in this VIEW. VIEWs created this way will always have all the rows that meet the criteria and that can be handy. For example, you can set up a VIEW of rows with a status code of 'to be done', work on them, and change a status code to 'finished', and they will disappear from your view. The important point is that the WHERE clause condition was checked only at the time when the VIEW was invoked.

The WITH CHECK OPTION makes the system check the WHERE clause condition upon insertion or UPDATE. If the new or changed row fails the test, the change is rejected and the VIEW remains the same. Thus, the previous UPDATE statement would get an error message and you could not change certain columns in certain ways. For example, consider a VIEW of salaries under $30,000 defined with a WITH CHECK OPTION to prevent anyone from giving a raise above that ceiling.

The WITH CHECK OPTION clause does not work like a CHECK constraint.

```
CREATE TABLE Foobar (col_a INTEGER);

CREATE VIEW TestView (col_a)
AS
SELECT col_a FROM Foobar WHERE col_a > 0
WITH CHECK OPTION;

INSERT INTO TestView VALUES (NULL); -- This fails!

CREATE TABLE Foobar_2 (col_a INTEGER CHECK (col_a > 0));
INSERT INTO Foobar_2(col_a)
VALUES (NULL); -- This succeeds!
```

The WITH CHECK OPTION must be TRUE whereas the CHECK constraint can be either TRUE or UNKNOWN. Once more, you need to watch out for NULLs.

Standard SQL has introduced an optional <levels clause>, which can be either CASCADED or LOCAL. If no <levels clause> is given, a <levels clause> of CASCADED is implicit. The idea of a CASCADED check is that the system checks all the underlying levels that built the VIEW, as well as the WHERE clause condition in the VIEW itself. If anything causes a row to disappear from the VIEW, the UPDATE is rejected. The idea of a WITH LOCAL check option is that only the local WHERE clause is checked. The underlying VIEWs or tables from which this VIEW is built might also be affected, but we do not test for those effects. Consider two VIEWs built on each other from the salary table:

```
CREATE VIEW Lowpay
AS SELECT *
  FROM Personnel
 WHERE salary <= 250;

CREATE VIEW Mediumpay
AS SELECT *
  FROM Lowpay
 WHERE salary >= 100;
```

If neither VIEW has a WITH CHECK OPTION, the effect of updating Mediumpay by increasing every salary by $1000 will be passed without any check to Lowpay. Lowpay will pass the changes to the underlying Personnel table. The next time Mediumpay is used, Lowpay will be rebuilt in its own right and Mediumpay rebuilt from it, and all the employees will disappear from Mediumpay.

If only Mediumpay has a WITH CASCADED CHECK OPTION on it, the UPDATE will fail. Mediumpay has no problem with such a large salary, but it would cause a row in Lowpay to disappear, so Mediumpay will reject it. However, if only Mediumpay has a WITH LOCAL CHECK OPTION on it, the UPDATE will succeed. Mediumpay has no problem with such a large salary, so it passes the change along to Lowpay. Lowpay, in turn, passes the change to the Personnel table and the UPDATE occurs. If both VIEWs have a WITH CASCADED CHECK OPTION, the effect is a set of conditions, all of which have to be met. The Personnel table can accept UPDATEs or INSERTs only where the salary is between $100 and $250.

This can become very complex. Consider an example from an ANSI X3H2 paper by Nelson Mattos of IBM (Celko, 1993). Let us build a five-layer set of VIEWs, using xx and yy as place holders for CASCADED or LOCAL, on a base table T1 with columns c1, c2, c3, c4, and c5, all set to a value of 10, thus:

```
CREATE VIEW V1 AS SELECT * FROM T1 WHERE (c1 > 5);

CREATE VIEW V2 AS SELECT * FROM V1 WHERE (c2 > 5)
   WITH xx CHECK OPTION;

CREATE VIEW V3 AS SELECT * FROM V2 WHERE (c3 > 5);

CREATE VIEW V4 AS SELECT * FROM V3 WHERE (c4 > 5)
   WITH yy CHECK OPTION;

CREATE VIEW V5 AS SELECT * FROM V4 WHERE (c5 > 5);
```

When we set each one of the columns to zero, we get different results, which can be shown in this chart, where 'S' means success and 'F' means failure:

| xx/yy | c1 | c2 | c3 | c4 | c5 |
|---|---|---|---|---|---|
| cascade/cascade | F | F | F | F | S |
| local/cascade | F | F | F | F | S |
| local/local | S | F | S | F | S |
| cascade/local | F | F | S | F | S |

To understand the chart, look at the last line. If xx = CASCADED and yy = LOCAL, updating column c1 to zero via V5 will fail, whereas updating c5 will succeed. Remember that a successful UPDATE means the row(s) disappear from V5.

Follow the action for `UPDATE V5 SET c1 = 0;` `VIEW V5` has no with check options, so the changed rows are immediately sent to V4 without any testing. `VIEW` V4 does have a `WITH LOCAL CHECK OPTION`, but column c1 is not involved, so V4 passes the rows to V3. `VIEW` V3 has no with check options, so the changed rows are immediately sent to V2. `VIEW` V2 does have a `WITH CASCADED CHECK OPTION`, so V2 passes the rows to V1 and awaits results. `VIEW` V1 is built on the original base table and has the condition c1 > 5, which is violated by this `UPDATE`. VIEW V1 then rejects the `UPDATE` to the base table, so the rows remain in V5 when it is rebuilt. Now the action for

```
UPDATE V5 SET c3 = 0;
```

`VIEW` V5 has no with check options, so the changed rows are immediately sent to V4, as before. `VIEW` V4 does have a `WITH LOCAL CHECK OPTION`, but column c3 is not involved, so V4 passes the rows to V3 without awaiting the results. `VIEW` V3 is involved with column c3 and has no with check options, so the rows can be changed and passed down to V2 and V1, where they `UPDATE` the base table. The rows are not seen again when V5 is invoked, because they will fail to get past `VIEW` V3. The real problem comes with `UPDATE` statements that change more than one column at a time. For example,

```
UPDATE V5 SET c1 = 0, c2 = 0, c3 = 0, c4 = 0, c5 = 0;
```

will fail for all possible combinations of `<levels clause>`s in the example schema.

Standard SQL defines the idea of a set of conditions that are inherited by the levels of nesting. In our sample schema, these implied tests would be added to each `VIEW` definition:

```
local/local
V1 = none
V2 = (c2 > 5)
V3 = (c2 > 5)
V4 = (c2 > 5) AND (c4 > 5)
V5 = (c2 > 5) AND (c4 > 5)

cascade/cascade
V1 = none
V2 = (c1 > 5) AND (c2 > 5)
V3 = (c1 > 5) AND (c2 > 5)
V4 = (c1 > 5) AND (c2 > 5) AND (c3 > 5) AND (c4 > 5)
V5 = (c1 > 5) AND (c2 > 5) AND (c3 > 5) AND (c4 > 5)

local/cascade
V1 = none
V2 = (c2 > 5)
```

```
V3 = (c2 > 5)
V4 = (c1 > 5) AND (c2 > 5) AND (c4 > 5)
V5 = (c1 > 5) AND (c2 > 5) AND (c4 > 5)

cascade/local
V1 = none
V2 = (c1 > 5) AND (c2 > 5)
V3 = (c1 > 5) AND (c2 > 5)
V4 = (c1 > 5) AND (c2 > 5) AND (c4 > 5)
V5 = (c1 > 5) AND (c2 > 5) AND (c4 > 5)
```

### 26.5.1 WITH CHECK OPTION as CHECK( ) clause

Lothar Flatz, an instructor for Oracle Software Switzerland made the observation that although Oracle cannot put subqueries into CHECK() constraints, and triggers would not be possible because of the mutating table problem, you can use a VIEW that has a WITH CHECK OPTION to enforce subquery constraints.

For example, consider a hotel registry that needs to have a rule that you cannot add a guest to a room that another is or will be occupying. Instead of writing the constraint directly, like this:

```
CREATE TABLE Hotel
(room_nbr INTEGER NOT NULL,
arrival_date DATE NOT NULL,
departure_date DATE NOT NULL,
guest_name CHAR(30) NOT NULL,
CONSTRAINT schedule_right
CHECK (H1.arrival_date <= H1.departure_date),
CONSTRAINT no_overlaps
CHECK (NOT EXISTS
   (SELECT *
     FROM Hotel AS H1, Hotel AS H2
    WHERE H1.room_nbr = H2.room_nbr
     AND H2.arrival_date < H1.arrival_date
     AND H1.arrival_date < H2.departure_date)));
```

The schedule_right constraint is fine, since it has no subquery, but many products will choke on the no_overlaps constraint. Leaving the no_overlaps constraint off the table, we can construct a VIEW on all the rows and columns of the Hotel base table and add a WHERE clause that will be enforced by the WITH CHECK OPTION.

```
CREATE VIEW Hotel_V (room_nbr, arrival_date, departure_date,
   guest_name)
AS SELECT H1.room_nbr, H1.arrival_date, H1.departure_date,
   H1.guest_name
```

```
  FROM Hotel AS H1
 WHERE NOT EXISTS
  (SELECT *
     FROM Hotel AS H2
    WHERE H1.room_nbr = H2.room_nbr
    AND H2.arrival_date < H1.arrival_date
    AND H1.arrival_date < H2.departure_date)
  AND H1.arrival_date <= H1.departure_date
WITH CHECK OPTION;
```

For example,

```
INSERT INTO Hotel_V
VALUES (1, '2006-01-01', '2006-01-03', 'Ron Coe');
COMMIT;
INSERT INTO Hotel_V
VALUES (1, '2006-01-03', '2006-01-05', 'John Doe');
```

will give a `WITH CHECK OPTION` clause violation on the second `INSERT INTO` statement, as we wanted.

## 26.6 Dropping VIEWs

VIEWs, like tables, can be dropped from the schema. The Standard SQL syntax for the statement is:

```
DROP VIEW <table name> <drop behavior>

<drop behavior>:: = [CASCADE | RESTRICT]
```

The `<drop behavior>` clause did not exist in SQL-86, so vendors had different behaviors in their implementation. The usual way of storing VIEWs was in a schema-level table with the VIEW name, the text of the VIEW, and other information. When you dropped a VIEW, the engine usually removed the appropriate row from the schema tables. You found out about dependencies when you tried to use VIEWs built on other VIEWs that no longer existed. Likewise, dropping a base table could cause the same problem when the VIEW was accessed.

The CASCADE option will find all other VIEWs that use the dropped VIEW and remove them also. If RESTRICT is specified, the VIEW cannot be dropped if there is anything that is dependent on it. This implies a structure for the schema tables that is different from just a simple single table.

The bad news is that some older products will let you drop the table(s) from which the view is built, but not drop the view itself.

```
CREATE TABLE Foobar (col_a INTEGER);
CREATE VIEW TestView
AS SELECT col_a
```

```
  FROM Foobar;

DROP TABLE Foobar; -- drop the base table
```

Unless you also cascaded the DROP TABLE statement, the text of the view definition was still in the system. Thus, when you reuse the table and column names, they are resolved at runtime with the view definition.

```
CREATE TABLE Foobar
(foo_key CHAR(5) NOT NULL PRIMARY KEY,
col_a REAL NOT NULL);
INSERT INTO Foobar VALUES ('Celko', 3.14159);
```

This is a potential security flaw and a violation of the SQL Standard, but be aware that it exists. Notice that the data type of TestView.col_a changed from INTEGER to REAL along with the new version of the table.

## 26.7 Hints on Using VIEWs versus TEMPORARY TABLEs

Sometimes this decision is very easy for a programmer. In the Standard SQL model, the user cannot create either a VIEW or a TEMPORARY TABLE. The creation of any schema object belongs to the database administrator, so the user has to use what he or she is given. However, you should know how to use each structure and which one is best for which situation.

### 26.7.1 Using VIEWs

Do not nest VIEWs too deeply; the overhead of building several levels eats up execution time and the extra storage for materialized VIEWs can be expensive. Complex nesting is also hard to maintain. One way to figure out what VIEWs you should have is to inspect the existing queries for repeated subqueries or expressions. These are good candidates for VIEWs.

One of the major uses of VIEWs is security. The DBA can choose to hide certain columns from certain classes of users through a combination of security authorizations and VIEWs. Standard SQL has provisions for restricting access to tables at the column level, but most implementations do not have that feature yet.

Another security trick is to add a column to a table that has a special user or security-level identifier in it. The VIEW hides this column and gives the user only what he or she is supposed to see. One possible problem is that a user could try to change something in the VIEW that violates other table constraints; when his attempt returns an error message, he has gotten some information about the security system that we might like to have hidden from him.

The best way to approach VIEWs is to think of how a user wants to see the database and then give him a set of VIEWs that make it look as if the database had been designed just for his applications.

### 26.7.2 Using TEMPORARY TABLEs

The GLOBAL TEMPORARY TABLE can be used to pass data among users, which is something that a VIEW cannot do. The LOCAL TEMPORARY TABLE has two major advantages. The user can load it with the results of a complex, time-consuming query once and use that result set over and over in his session, greatly improving performance. This also prevents the system from locking out other users from the base tables from which the complex query was built.

Dr. Codd discussed the idea of a snapshot, which is an image of a table at a particular moment in time. But it is important to know just what that moment was. You can use a temporary table to hold such a snapshot by adding a column with the DEFAULT of the CURRENT TIMESTAMP.

The Standard SQL model of temporary tables I have just described is not yet common in most implementations. In fact, many SQL products do not have the concept of a temporary table at all, whereas other products allow the users to create temporary tables on the fly. Such tables might last only for their session and are visible only to their creator. These tables may or may not have indexes, constraints, VIEWs, referential integrity, or much of anything else declared on them; they are a pure "scratch table" for the user. Some products allow a user to create a global temporary table that can be accessed by other users. But, again, this is not the ANSI/ISO model.

### 26.7.3 Flattening a Table with a VIEW

Given a table with the monthly sales data shown as an attribute (the monthly amounts have to be NULL-able to hold missing values for the future) like this:

```
CREATE TABLE AnnualSales1
(salesman CHAR(15) NOT NULL PRIMARY KEY,
jan DECIMAL(5,2),
feb DECIMAL(5,2),
mar DECIMAL(5,2),
```

```
apr DECIMAL(5,2),
may DECIMAL(5,2),
jun DECIMAL(5,2),
jul DECIMAL(5,2),
aug DECIMAL(5,2),
sep DECIMAL(5,2),
oct DECIMAL(5,2),
nov DECIMAL(5,2),
"dec" DECIMAL(5,2) -- reserved word!
);
```

The goal is to "flatten" it out so that it looks like this:

```
CREATE TABLE AnnualSales2
(salesman CHAR(15) NOT NULL PRIMARY KEY,
month_name CHAR(3) NOT NULL
   CONSTRAINT valid_month_abbrev
   CHECK (month_name IN ('Jan', 'Feb', 'Mar', 'Apr',
        'May', 'Jun', 'Jul', 'Aug',
        'Sep', 'Oct', 'Nov', 'Dec')),
sales_amount DECIMAL(5,2) NOT NULL,
PRIMARY KEY(salesman, month_name));
```

The trick is to build a VIEW of the original table with a number beside each month:

```
CREATE VIEW NumberedSales
AS SELECT salesman,
    1 AS M01, jan,
    2 AS M02, feb,
    3 AS M03, mar,
    4 AS M04, apr,
    5 AS M05, may,
    6 AS M06, jun,
    7 AS M07, jul,
    8 AS M08, aug,
    9 AS M09, sep,
   10 AS M10, oct,
   11 AS M11, nov,
   12 AS M12, "dec"
 FROM AnnualSales1;
```

Now you can use the auxiliary table of sequential numbers or you can use a VALUES table constructor to build one. The flattened VIEW is:

```
CREATE VIEW AnnualSales2 (salesman, month, sales_amt)
AS SELECT S1.salesman,
  (CASE WHEN A.nbr = M01 THEN 'Jan'
     WHEN A.nbr = M02 THEN 'Feb'
     WHEN A.nbr = M03 THEN 'Mar'
```

```
        WHEN A.nbr = M04 THEN 'Apr'
        WHEN A.nbr = M05 THEN 'May'
        WHEN A.nbr = M06 THEN 'Jun'
        WHEN A.nbr = M07 THEN 'Jul'
        WHEN A.nbr = M08 THEN 'Aug'
        WHEN A.nbr = M09 THEN 'Sep'
        WHEN A.nbr = M10 THEN 'Oct'
        WHEN A.nbr = M11 THEN 'Nov'
        WHEN A.nbr = M12 THEN 'Dec'
        ELSE NULL END),
      (CASE WHEN A.nbr = M01 THEN jan
        WHEN A.nbr = M02 THEN feb
        WHEN A.nbr = M03 THEN mar
        WHEN A.nbr = M04 THEN apr
        WHEN A.nbr = M05 THEN may
        WHEN A.nbr = M06 THEN jun
        WHEN A.nbr = M07 THEN jul
        WHEN A.nbr = M08 THEN aug
        WHEN A.nbr = M09 THEN sep
        WHEN A.nbr = M10 THEN oct
        WHEN A.nbr = M11 THEN nov
        WHEN A.nbr = M12 THEN "dec"
        ELSE NULL END)
  FROM AnnualSales AS S1
      CROSS JOIN
      (VALUES (1), (2), (3), (4), (5), (6),
         (7), (8), (9), (10), (11), (12)) AS A(nbr);
```

If your SQL product has derived tables, this can be written as a single VIEW query.

This technique lets you convert an attribute into a value, which is highly nonrelational, but very handy for a report. The advantage of using a VIEW over using a temporary table to hold the crosstabs query given in another chapter is that the VIEW will change automatically when the underlying base table is changed.

## 26.8 Using Derived Tables

A user can build a derived table inside a query. It exists only in the scope of the statement that creates it. The AS operator allows us to give names to the derived table and its columns. The syntax is very simple, but the scoping rules often confuse new users.

```
(<query expression>) [[AS] <table name> [(<column list>)]]
```

### 26.8.1 Derived Tables in the FROM Clause

Most of the parts of the syntax are optional as you see, but it is a very good idea to use them. Treat it the same way you would a base table; give it and its columns meaningful names, so you can reference the derived table without ambiguity.

The tricky part is in the scoping rules for the subquery expressions. Consider this set of expressions:

```
SELECT * -- wrong
 FROM (Foo
   LEFT OUTER JOIN
   Bar
   ON Foo.x = Bar.x)
     INNER JOIN
     Floob
     ON Floob.y = x;
```

Foo, Bar, and Floob are exposed to the outermost query, so x is an ambiguous column name that might belong to Foo or Bar. Change this slightly.

```
SELECT * -- still wrong
 FROM (Foo AS F1
   LEFT OUTER JOIN
   Bar AS B1
   ON F1.x = B1.x)
     INNER JOIN Floob
     ON Floob.y = Foo.x;
```

The aliases F1 and B1 hide the base tables from the outermost query, so Foo.x is not an exposed column name. One solution is to create an alias for the whole query expression and rename the ambiguous columns.

```
SELECT *
 FROM ((SELECT x FROM Foo)
  LEFT OUTER JOIN
  (SELECT x FROM Bar)
  ON Foo.x = Bar.x)
  AS Foobar(x1, x2)
   INNER JOIN Floob
   ON Floob.y = x1;
```

The outermost query sees only Foobar and cannot reference either Foo or Bar.

The order of execution of the infixed JOIN operators is from left to right. It does not make any difference with INNER JOINs and CROSS JOINs, but it is very important when you have OUTER JOINs. I strongly recommend that you qualify all the column names.

### 26.8.2 Derived Tables with a VALUES Constructor

SQL-99 freed the VALUES constructor from the INSERT INTO statement and allows it to build tables. You can see an example of this in Section 26.7.3 for a single-column table. This construct is now generalized to construct rows in a table, such as

```
VALUES ('John', 7), ('Mark', 8), ('Fred', 10), ('Sam', 7)
```

However, such a table cannot have constraints, not does it have a name until you add an AS clause. Think of it as a "table constant" rather than as a proper table that can be modified, have constraints, and so forth. Obviously, all the rows must be union compatible, but the system will pick the default data types. One way around this is to explicitly cast the columns to the desired data types. Doing this for one row is usually enough to force the other rows to follow that pattern.

```
VALUES ('pi', CAST (3.14159265358979323846264338327950
        AS DOUBLE PRECISION))
```

The columns can contain any scalar expression:

```
(VALUES ((SELECT MAX(x) FROM Foo), 42),
        ((SELECT MAX(y) FROM Bar), (12+2)),
          (12, 3))
AS Weird (a, b)
```

To use this construct you need to add some other things around it to make it into a derived table, thus:

```
SELECT <local name>.*
 FROM (VALUES (..), (..), ..)
   AS <local_name>(<column name list>)
```

## 26.9 Common Table Expressions

The WITH clause was added in SQL-99 and the goal was to allow you to factor out common table expressions rather than repeating the same code over and over as derived tables.

### 26.9.1 Simple Common Table Expressions

The simple common table expressions are a list of one or more derived tables that appear in front of a SELECT statement. These derived tables are created in the order in which they are declared. This means that one CTE element can reference only prior CTE elements. The basic syntax is:

```
<cte element>::=
<table name> [(<column list>)]
AS <subquery expression>

<cte list>::= <cte element> |<cte list>, <cte element>

<cte select statement>::= WITH <cte list> <select statement>;
```

As a simple example, consider a report that tells us the item(s) that had the highest sales volume, measured in dollars. First, build a query in the `WITH` clause to total each item by its UPC code. Then using this, find which item has the highest total sales.

```
WITH ItemSummary (upc, item_price_tot)
AS
(SELECT upc, SUM(item_price)
  FROM OrderDetails
 GROUP BY upc)
-- main query
SELECT P1.upc, P1.item_price_tot
  FROM ItemSummary AS P1
WHERE P1.item_price_tot
  = (SELECT MAX(P1.item_price_tot)
      FROM ItemSummary AS P2);
```

Without this feature, the ItemSummary query either would have been repeated in two places or put into a `VIEW`. A programmer without `ADMIN` privileges cannot create a view, so this is his or her best option. Although not so bad in this case, imagine if we had a complex expression to replicate.

## 26.10 Recursive Common Table Expressions

There is also a recursive option. A recursive definition of a set has two parts. The fixed point or invariant is where things start. Then more elements are added to the set, step by step, by applying a rule to the previous step results. The syntax for this construct includes a `UNION [ALL]`:

```
<cte select statement>::=
WITH RECURSIVE <fixed point cte element>
UNION [ALL]
<step cte element>
<select statement>;
```

The classic example that procedural programmers get in their textbooks is the Factorial function, (n!) which is defined by:

```
CREATE FUNCTION Fact (IN n INTEGER)
RETURNS INTEGER
IF n IN (0,1)
THEN RETURN 1;
ELSE RETURN (n * Fact(n-1));
END IF;
```

This is a simple recursive function, which could have been done with iteration. This kind of recursion is called linear recursion in the SQL Standards and it is the easiest one. This is not the only kind of recursion. If you want to have some fun, write the Ackermann function in your favorite procedural language. It looks very simple, but it isn't.

```
CREATE FUNCTION Ack (IN m INTEGER, IN n INTEGER)
RETURNS INTEGER
BEGIN
IF m = 0
THEN RETURN (n+1);
END IF;
IF m > 0 AND n = 0
THEN RETURN Ack(m-1, 1);
END IF;
IF m > 0 AND n > 0
THEN RETURN Ack(m-1, Ack(m, n-1));
END IF;
END;
```

When (m = 0), it is a simple increment function. When (m = 1), it is addition done with recursive calls to incrementation. As m increases, it then becomes multiplication, exponentiation, hyper-exponentiation, and worse. Each level invokes the prior level until everything is done with an increment. The result and the depth of recursion both grow fast; Ack(4,2) is an integer of 19,729 decimal digits.

## 26.10.1 Simple Incrementation

The Recursive CTE is most often used to replace a loop. For example to build a look-up table of some function, f(i), will look like this:

```
WITH RECURSIVE Increment (i, function_value)
AS
(SELECT i, j
  FROM (VALUES (1, f(1))))
UNION
```

```
SELECT (i+1), f(i+1)
 FROM Increment
WHERE (i+1) <= 1000)
SELECT i, function_value FROM Increment;
```

This is not a good idea, but it is popular and you need to know the skeleton. You will be better off using `SEQUENCE`, or `ROW_NUMBER()` instead.

### 26.10.2 Simple Tree Traversal

Let's make a simple adjacency list model of a bill of materials and parse it recursively.

```
CREATE TABLE BillOfMaterials
(part_name VARCHAR(20) NOT NULL PRIMARY KEY,
assembly_nbr INTEGER, - null is the final assembly
subassembly_nbr INTEGER NOT NULL);
```

The assembly_nbr for the finished product row is set to `NULL` to show that it is not part of another assembly. The following recursive SQL using a common table expression will do the trick (note that we have named our common table expression "Explosion"):

```
WITH RECURSIVE Explosion (assembly_nbr, subassembly_nbr,
   part_name)
AS
(SELECT BOM.assembly_nbr, BOM.subassembly_nbr, BOM.part_
   name
  FROM BillOfMaterials AS BOM
 WHERE BOM.subassembly_nbr = 12 -- traversal starting point
UNION
SELECT Child.assembly_nbr, Child.subassembly_nbr, Child.
   part_name
 FROM Explosion AS Parent, BillOfMaterials AS Child
WHERE Parent.subassembly_nbr = Child.assembly_nbr)
-- main select statement
SELECT assembly_nbr, subassembly_nbr, part_name
FROM Explosion;
```

This will find all the parts that make up subassembly #12. It begins by pulling a starting set from the BillOfMaterials table, then doing a `UNION` with itself. The original BillOfMaterials table is now hidden inside the expression. Standard SQL requires the use of the keyword `RECURSION` to signal the compiler to keep running until no more rows are added to the Explosion table. The main `SELECT` statement can now use Explosion like any other table.

## 26.11 Materialized Query Tables

Materialized query tables (MQTs), which are known by the names snapshot tables, automatic summary tables, or materialized views, precompute the results of a query and keep them in the materialized query table. The database engine can use these results instead of recomputing them for user queries. The idea is that this is faster than recomputing the same query over and over.

There will be some product differences, but the table is created with a modified CREATE TABLE statement that includes the query that refreshes the data. Since these are base tables, they can usually be modified with INSERT, UPDATE, and DELETE statements.

However, there are some restrictions on the queries that can be used to build them. It is a good idea to use references to columns and simple functions.

Here is an example of DB2 syntax. The defining query finds payroll data about employees whose job title is 'Designer'.

```
CREATE TABLE Designers
AS
(SELECT D.dept_name, P.first_name, P.last_name,
    P.salary_amt, P.commission_amt, P.bonus_amt, P.job_title
 FROM Departments AS D, Personnel AS PE
WHERE D.dept_nbr = P.emp_dept_nbr)
DATA INITIALLY IMMEDIATE
REFRESH DEFERRED
ENABLE QUERY OPTIMIZATION
MAINTAINED BY USER;
```

I can now use this table:

```
SELECT D.dept_name, D.location, D.first_name, D.last_name,
  (D.salary_amt  +  D.commission_amt  +  D.bonus_amt)  AS
   compensation_tot
 FROM Designers AD D
WHERE D.job_title = 'Designer';
```

The extra clauses tell us the following.

1. DATA INITIALLY IMMEDIATE: We load that table when it is initially invoked.
2. REFRESH DEFERRED: The table is not refreshed automatically. Other vendors may refresh data using a clock or database event.
3. ENABLE QUERY OPTIMIZATION: Signal the optimizer to use it when it will help. This is very proprietary.
4. MAINTAINED BY USER: The user will refresh the data with the command "REFRESH TABLE <table name>;".

27

# PARTITIONING DATA IN QUERIES

This section is concerned with how to break the data in SQL into meaningful subsets that can then be presented to the user or passed along for further reduction.

## 27.1 Coverings and Partitions

We need to define some basic set operations. A covering is a collection of subsets, drawn from a set, whose union is the original set. A partition is a covering whose subsets do not intersect each other. Cutting up a pizza is a partitioning; smothering it in two layers of pepperoni slices is a covering.

Partitions are the basis for most reports. The property that makes partitions useful for reports is aggregation: the whole is the sum of its parts. For example, a company budget is broken into divisions, divisions are broken into departments, and so forth. Each division budget is the sum of its department's budgets, and the sum of the division budgets is the total for the whole company again. We would not be sure what to do if a department belonged to two different divisions because that would be a covering and not a partition.

### 27.1.1 Partitioning by Ranges

A common problem in data processing is classifying things by the way they fall into a range on a numeric or alphabetic scale. The best approach to translating a code into a value when ranges are involved is to set up a table with the high and the low values for each translated value in it. This was covered in the section on auxiliary tables in more detail, but here is a quick review.

Any missing values will easily be detected and the table can be validated for completeness. For example, we could create a table of ZIP code ranges and two-character state abbreviation codes like this:

```
CREATE TABLE ZipCodes
(state_code CHAR(2) NOT NULL PRIMARY KEY,
```

Joe Celko's SQL for Smarties. DOI: 10.1016/B978-0-12-382022-8.00027-2

```
low_zip CHAR(5) NOT NULL UNIQUE,
high_zip CHAR(5) NOT NULL UNIQUE,
CONSTRAINT zip_order_okay CHECK(low_zip < high_zip),
... );
```

Here is a query that looks up the city name and state code from the ZIP code in the AddressBook table to complete a mailing label with a simple JOIN that looks like this:

```
SELECT A1.name, A1.street, SZ.city, SZ.state_code, A1.zip
 FROM ZipCodes AS SZ, AddressBook AS A1
WHERE A1.zip BETWEEN SZ.low_zip AND SZ.high_zip;
```

You need to be careful with this predicate. If one of the three columns involved has a NULL in it, the BETWEEN predicate becomes UNKNOWN and will not be recognized by the WHERE clause. If you design the table of range values with the high value in one row equal to or greater than the low value in another row, both of those rows will be returned when the test value falls on the overlap.

## 27.1.2 Single-Column Range Tables

If you know that you have a partitioning in the range value tables, you can write a query in SQL that will let you use a table with only the high value and the translation code. The grading system table would have ((100, 'A'), (89, 'B'), (79, 'C'), (69, 'D'), and (59, 'F')) as its rows. Likewise, a table of the state code and the highest ZIP code in that state could do the same job as the BETWEEN predicate in the previous query.

```
CREATE TABLE StateZip2
(high_zip CHAR(5) NOT NULL,
state CHAR(2) NOT NULL,
PRIMARY KEY (high_zip, state));
```

We want to write a query to give us the greatest lower bound or least upper bound on those values. The greatest lower bound (glb) operator finds the largest number in one column that is less than or equal to the target value in the other column. The least upper bound (lub) operator finds the smallest number greater than or equal to the target number. Unfortunately, this is not a good trade-off, because the subquery is fairly complex and slow. The "high and low" columns are a better solution in most cases. Here is a second version of the AddressBook query, using only the high_zip column from the StateZip2 table:

```
SELECT name, street, city, state, zip
 FROM StateZip2, AddressBook
WHERE state =
```

```
(SELECT state
   FROM StateZip2
  WHERE high_zip =
   (SELECT MIN(high_zip)
      FROM StateZip2
     WHERE Address.zip <= StateZip2.high_zip));
```

If you want to allow for multiple-row matches by not requiring that the look-up table have unique values, the equality subquery predicate should be converted to an `IN()` predicate.

## 27.1.3 Partition by Functions

It is also possible to use a function that will partition the table into subsets that share a particular property. Consider the cases where you have to add a column with the function result to the table because the function is too complex to be reasonably written in SQL.

One common example of this technique is the Soundex function, where it is not a vendor extension; the Soundex family assigns codes to names that are phonetically alike. The complex calculations in engineering and scientific databases that involve functions that SQL does not have are another example of this technique.

SQL was never meant to be a computational language. However, many vendors allow a query to access functions in the libraries of other programming languages. You must know what the cost in execution time for your product is before doing this. One version of SQL uses a threaded-code approach to carry parameters over to the other language's libraries and return the results on each row—the execution time is horrible. Some versions of SQL can compile and link another language's library into the SQL.

Although this is a generalization, the safest technique is to unload the parameter values to a file in a standard format that can be read by the other language. Then use that file in a program to find the function results and create `INSERT INTO` statements that will load a table in the database with the parameters and the results. You can then use this working table to load the result column in the original table.

## 27.1.4 Partition by Sequences

We are looking for patterns over a history that has a sequential ordering to it. This ordering could be temporal or via a sequence numbering. For example, given a payment history we want to break it into groupings of behavior, say whether or not the payments were on time or late.

```
CREATE TABLE PaymentHistory
(payment_nbr INTEGER NOT NULL PRIMARY KEY,
paid_on_time CHAR(1) DEFAULT 'Y' NOT NULL
  CHECK(paid_on_time IN ('Y', 'N')));

INSERT INTO PaymentHistory
VALUES (1006, 'Y'),
   (1005, 'Y'),
   (1004, 'N'),
   (1003, 'Y'),
   (1002, 'Y'),
   (1001, 'Y'),
   (1000, 'N');
```

The results we want assign a grouping number to each run of on-time/late payments, thus:

| grp | payment_nbr | paid_on_time |
|---|---|---|
| 1 | 1006 | 'Y' |
| 1 | 1005 | 'Y' |
| 2 | 1004 | 'N' |
| 3 | 1003 | 'Y' |
| 3 | 1002 | 'Y' |
| 3 | 1001 | 'Y' |
| 4 | 1000 | 'N' |

Here is a solution from Hugo Kornelis that depends on the payments always being numbered consecutively.

```
SELECT (SELECT COUNT(*)
    FROM PaymentHistory AS H2,
      PaymentHistory AS H3
  WHERE H3.payment_nbr = H2.payment_nbr + 1
    AND H3.paid_on_time <> H2.paid_on_time
    AND H2.payment_nbr >= H1.payment_nbr) + 1 AS grp,
 payment_nbr, paid_on_time
FROM PaymentHistory AS H1;
```

This is very useful when looking for patterns in a history. A more complex version of the same problem would involve more than two categories. Consider a table with a sequential numbering and a list of products that have been received.

What we want is the average quality score value for a sequential grouping of the same Product. For example, I need an average of Entries 1, 2, and 3 because this is the first grouping of the same product type, but I do not want that average to include entry #8, which is also Product A, but in a different "group."

```
CREATE TABLE ProductTests
(batch_nbr INTEGER NOT NULL PRIMARY KEY,
prod_code CHAR(1) NOT NULL,
prod_quality DECIMAL(8.4) NOT NULL);

INSERT INTO ProductTests (batch_nbr, prod_code,
   prod_quality)
VALUES (1, 'A', 80),
  (2, 'A', 70),
  (3, 'A', 80),
  (4, 'B', 60),
  (5, 'B', 90),
  (6, 'C', 80),
  (7, 'D', 80),
  (8, 'A', 50),
  (9, 'C', 70);
```

The query then becomes:

```
SELECT X.prod_code, MIN(X.batch_nbr) AS start_batch_nbr,
   end_batch_nbr,
  AVG(B4.prod_quality) AS avg_prod_quality
 FROM (SELECT B1.prod_code, B1.batch_nbr,
      MAX(B2.batch_nbr) AS end_batch_nbr
  FROM ProductTests AS B1, ProductTests AS B2
  WHERE B1.batch_nbr <= B2.batch_nbr
   AND B1.prod_code = B2.prod_code
   AND B1.prod_code
    = ALL (SELECT prod_code
         FROM ProductTests AS B3
         WHERE B3.batch_nbr BETWEEN B1.batch_nbr
               AND B2.batch_nbr)
  GROUP BY B1.prod_code, B1.batch_nbr) AS X
  INNER JOIN
  ProductTests AS B4 -- join to get the quality measurements
  ON B4.batch_nbr BETWEEN X.batch_nbr AND X.end_batch_nbr
 GROUP BY X.prod_code, X.end_batch_nbr;

Results
prod_code start_batch_nbr end_batch_nbr avg_prod_quality
=========================================================
'A'        1              3             76.6666
'B'        4              5             75.0000
'C'        6              6             80.0000
'D'        7              7             80.0000
'A'        8              8             50.0000
'C'        9              9             70.0000
```

### 27.1.5 Partition with Windows

Tim Miller had a similar problem. Given a table of transactions, he wanted a single row to summarize each report period.

```
CREATE TABLE Transactions
(report_period INTEGER NOT NULL,
trans_nbr INTEGER NOT NULL PRIMARY KEY,
trans_qty INTEGER NOT NULL);
```

Plamen Ratchev gave this method:

```
SELECT report_period, SUM(trans_qty) AS trans_qty_tot,
  MAX(CASE WHEN rk1 = 1 THEN trans_nbr END) AS
     start_trans_nbr,
  MAX(CASE WHEN rk2 = 1 THEN trans_nbr END) AS
     end_trans_nbr,
 FROM (SELECT report_period, trans_qty, trans_nbr,
       ROW_NUMBER() OVER(ORDER BY trans_nbr ASC) AS rk1,
       ROW_NUMBER() OVER(ORDER BY trans_nbr DESC) AS rk2
    FROM Transactions) AS T
GROUP BY report_period;
```

But you can extend the idea of windowed functions and use them.

```
SELECT report_period,
  SUM(trans_qty) OVER (PARTITION BY report_period)
   AS trans_qty_tot,
  MAX(trans_nbr) OVER (PARTITION BY report_period)
   AS start_trans_nbr,
  MIN(trans_nbr) OVER (PARTITION BY report_period)
   AS end_trans_nbr
 FROM Transactions;
```

This should be easy to optimize because the `PARTITION BY` subclauses are identical in all three summary values.

## 27.2 Relational Division

Relational division is one of the eight basic operations in Codd's relational algebra. The idea is that a divisor table is used to partition a dividend table and produce a quotient or results table. The quotient table is made up of those values of one column for which a second column had all of the values in the divisor.

This is easier to explain with an example. We have a table of pilots and the planes they can fly (dividend); we have a table of planes in the hangar (divisor); we want the names of the pilots who can fly every plane (quotient) in the hangar. To get this result, we divide the PilotSkills table by the planes in the hangar.

```
CREATE TABLE PilotSkills
(pilot CHAR(15) NOT NULL,
plane CHAR(15) NOT NULL,
PRIMARY KEY (pilot, plane));

PilotSkills
pilot plane
=========================
'Celko' 'Piper Cub'
'Higgins' 'B-52 Bomber'
'Higgins' 'F-14 Fighter'
'Higgins' 'Piper Cub'
'Jones' 'B-52 Bomber'
'Jones' 'F-14 Fighter'
'smith' 'B-1 Bomber'
'smith' 'B-52 Bomber'
'smith' 'F-14 Fighter'
'Wilson' 'B-1 Bomber'
'Wilson' 'B-52 Bomber'
'Wilson' 'F-14 Fighter'
'Wilson' 'F-17 Fighter'

CREATE TABLE Hangar
(plane CHAR(15) NOT NULL PRIMARY KEY);

Hangar
plane
=============
'B-1 Bomber'
'B-52 Bomber'
'F-14 Fighter'

PilotSkills DIVIDED BY Hangar
pilot
=============================
'smith'
'Wilson'
```

In this example, Smith and Wilson are the two pilots who can fly everything in the hangar. Notice that Higgins and Celko know how to fly a Piper Cub, but we don't have one right now. In Codd's original definition of relational division, having more rows than are called for is not a problem.

The important characteristic of a relational division is that the `CROSS JOIN` of the divisor and the quotient produces a valid subset of rows from the dividend. This is where the name comes from, since the `CROSS JOIN` acts like a multiplication operator.

### 27.2.1 Division with a Remainder

There are two kinds of relational division. Division with a remainder allows the dividend table to have more values than the divisor, which was Dr. Codd's original definition. For example, if a pilot can fly more planes than just those we have in the hangar, this is fine with us. The query can be written as:

```
SELECT DISTINCT pilot
 FROM PilotSkills AS PS1
WHERE NOT EXISTS
   (SELECT *
     FROM Hangar
    WHERE NOT EXISTS
      (SELECT *
        FROM PilotSkills AS PS2
        WHERE (PS1.pilot = PS2.pilot)
         AND (PS2.plane = Hangar.plane)));
```

The quickest way to explain what is happening in this query is to imagine a World War II movie where a cocky pilot has just walked into the hangar, looked over the fleet, and announced, "There ain't no plane in this hangar that I can't fly!" We want to find the pilots for whom there does not exist a plane in the hangar for which they have no skills. The use of the `NOT EXISTS()` predicates is for speed. Most SQL implementations will look up a value in an index rather than scan the whole table.

This query for relational division was made popular by Chris Date in his textbooks, but it is neither the only method nor always the fastest. Another version of the division can be written so as to avoid three levels of nesting. Although it is not original with me, I have made it popular in my books.

```
SELECT PS1.pilot
  FROM PilotSkills AS PS1, Hangar AS H1
 WHERE PS1.plane = H1.plane
 GROUP BY PS1.pilot
HAVING COUNT(PS1.plane) = (SELECT COUNT(plane) FROM
   Hangar);
```

There is a serious difference in the two methods. Burn down the hangar, so that the divisor is empty. Because of the `NOT EXISTS()` predicates in Date's query, all pilots are returned from a division by an empty set. Because of the `COUNT()` functions in my query, no pilots are returned from a division by an empty set.

In the sixth edition of his book, *Introduction to Database Systems* (Addison-Wesley, 1995, ISBN 0-191-82458-2), Chris Date defined another operator (DIVIDEBY ... PER), which produces the same results as my query, but with more complexity.

### 27.2.2 Exact Division

The second kind of relational division is exact relational division. The dividend table must match exactly to the values of the divisor without any extra values.

```
SELECT PS1.pilot
 FROM PilotSkills AS PS1
    LEFT OUTER JOIN
    Hangar AS H1
    ON PS1.plane = H1.plane
GROUP BY PS1.pilot
HAVING COUNT(PS1.plane) = (SELECT COUNT(plane) FROM
   Hangar)
  AND COUNT(H1.plane) = (SELECT COUNT(plane) FROM Hangar);
```

This says that a pilot must have the same number of certificates as there are planes in the hangar, and these certificates all match to a plane in the hangar, not to something else. The "something else" is shown by a created NULL from the LEFT OUTER JOIN.

Please do not make the mistake of trying to reduce the HAVING clause with a little algebra to:

```
HAVING COUNT(PS1.plane) = COUNT(H1.plane)
```

because it does not work; it will tell you that the hangar has (n) planes in it and the pilot is certified for (n) planes, but not that those two sets of planes are equal to each other.

### 27.2.3 Note on Performance

The nested EXISTS() predicates version of relational division was made popular by Chris Date's textbooks, and the author is associated with popularizing the COUNT(*) version of relational division. The Winter 1996 edition of *DB2 On-Line Magazine* (http://www.db2mag.com/96011ar:htm) had an article entitled "Powerful SQL: Beyond the Basics," by Sheryl Larsen, which gave the results of testing both methods. Her conclusion for DB2 was that the nested EXISTS() version is better when the quotient has less than 25% of the dividend table's rows and the COUNT(*) version is better when the quotient is more than 25% of the dividend table.

On the other hand, Matthew W. Spaulding at SnapOn Tools reported his test on SQL Server 2000 with the opposite results.

He had a table with two million rows for the dividend and around 1000 rows in the divisor, yielding a quotient of around 1000 rows as well. The `COUNT` method completed in well under one second, where as the nested `NOT EXISTS` query took roughly five seconds to run.

The moral of the story is to test both methods on your particular product.

### 27.2.4 Todd's Division

A relational division operator proposed by Stephen Todd is defined on two tables with common columns that are joined together, dropping the `JOIN` column and retaining only those non-`JOIN` columns that meet a criterion.

We are given a table, JobParts(`job_nbr, part_nbr`), and another table, SupParts(`sup_nbr, part_nbr`), of suppliers and the parts that they provide. We want to get the supplier-and-job pairs such that supplier sn supplies all the parts needed for job jn. This is not quite the same thing as getting the supplier-and-job pairs such that job jn requires all the parts provided by supplier sn.

You want to divide the JobParts table by the SupParts table. A rule of thumb: The remainder comes from the dividend, but all values in the divisor are present.

| JobParts | | SupParts | | Result = JobSups | |
|---|---|---|---|---|---|
| job | pno | sno | pno | job | sno |
| 'j1' | 'p1' | 's1' | 'p1' | 'j1' | 's1' |
| 'j1' | 'p2' | 's1' | 'p2' | 'j1' | 's2' |
| 'j2' | 'p2' | 's1' | 'p3' | 'j2' | 's1' |
| 'j2' | 'p4' | 's1' | 'p4' | 'j2' | 's4' |
| 'j2' | 'p5' | 's1' | 'p5' | 'j3' | 's1' |
| 'j3' | 'p2' | 's1' | 'p6' | 'j3' | 's2' |
| | | 's2' | 'p1' | 'j3' | 's3' |
| | | 's2' | 'p2' | 'j3' | 's4' |
| | | 's3' | 'p2' | | |
| | | 's4' | 'p2' | | |
| | | 's4' | 'p4' | | |
| | | 's4' | 'p5' | | |

Pierre Mullin submitted the following query to carry out the Todd division:

```
SELECT DISTINCT JP1.job, SP1.supplier
 FROM JobParts AS JP1, SupParts AS SP1
WHERE NOT EXISTS
  (SELECT *
    FROM JobParts AS JP2
    WHERE JP2.job = JP1.job
    AND JP2.part
     NOT IN (SELECT SP2.part
         FROM SupParts AS SP2
        WHERE SP2.supplier = SP1.supplier));
```

This is really a modification of the query for Codd's division, extended to use a `JOIN` on both tables in the outermost `SELECT` statement. The `IN` predicate for the second subquery can be replaced with a `NOT EXISTS` predicate; it might run a bit faster, depending on the optimizer.

Another related query is finding the pairs of suppliers who sell the same parts. In this data, that would be the pairs (s1, p2), (s3, p1), (s4, p1), (s5, p1):

```
SELECT S1.sup, S2.sup
 FROM SupParts AS S1, SupParts AS S2
WHERE S1.sup < S2.sup -- different suppliers
  AND S1.part = S2.part -- same parts
GROUP BY S1.sup, S2.sup
HAVING COUNT(*) = (SELECT COUNT (*) -- same count of parts
       FROM SupParts AS S3
       WHERE S3.sup = S1.sup)
  AND COUNT(*) = (SELECT COUNT (*)
       FROM SupParts AS S4
       WHERE S4.sup = S2.sup);
```

This can be modified into Todd's division easily by adding the restriction that the parts must also belong to a common job.

Steve Kass came up with a specialized version that depends on using a numeric code. Assume we have a table that tells us which players are on which teams:

```
CREATE TABLE TeamAssignments
(player_id INTEGER NOT NULL
   REFERENCES Players(player_id)
   ON DELETE CASCADE
   ON UPDATE CASCADE,
team_id CHAR(5) NOT NULL
   REFERENCES Teams(team_id)
   ON DELETE CASCADE
   ON UPDATE CASCADE,
PRIMARY KEY (player_id, team_id));
```

To get pairs of Players on the same team:

```
SELECT P1.player_id, P2.player_id
 FROM Players AS P1, Players AS P2
WHERE P1.player_id < P2.player_id
GROUP BY P1.player_id, P2.player_id
HAVING P1.player_id + P2.player_id
   = ALL (SELECT SUM(P3.player_id)
          FROM TeamAssignments AS P3
          WHERE P3.player_id IN (P1.player_id, P2.player_id)
          GROUP BY P3.team_id);
```

### 27.2.5 Division with JOINs

Standard SQL has several JOIN operators that can be used to perform a relational division. To find the pilots who can fly the same planes as Higgins use this query:

```
SELECT SP1.Pilot
 FROM (((SELECT plane FROM Hangar) AS H1
    INNER JOIN
    (SELECT pilot, plane FROM PilotSkills) AS SP1
    ON H1.plane = SP1.plane)
   INNER JOIN (SELECT *
         FROM PilotSkills
         WHERE pilot = 'Higgins') AS H2
   ON H2.plane = H1.plane)
GROUP BY Pilot
HAVING COUNT(*) >= (SELECT COUNT(*)
         FROM PilotSkills
WHERE pilot = 'Higgins');
```

The first JOIN finds all the planes in the hangar for which we have a pilot. The next JOIN takes that set and finds which of those match up with (SELECT * FROM PilotSkills WHERE pilot = 'Higgins') skills. The GROUP BY clause will then see that the intersection we have formed with the joins has at least as many elements as Higgins has planes. The GROUP BY also means that the SELECT DISTINCT can be replaced with a simple SELECT. If the theta operator in the GROUP BY clause is changed from >= to =, the query finds an exact division. If the theta operator in the GROUP BY clause is changed from >= to <= or <, the query finds those pilots whose skills are a superset or a strict superset of the planes that Higgins flies.

It might be a good idea to put the divisor into a VIEW for readability in this query and as a clue to the optimizer to calculate it once. Some products will execute this form of the division query faster than the nested subquery version, because they will use the PRIMARY KEY information to precompute the joins between tables.

### 27.2.6 Division with Set Operators

The Standard SQL set difference operator, EXCEPT, can be used to write a very compact version of Dr. Codd's relational division. The EXCEPT operator removes the divisor set from the dividend set. If the result is empty, we have a match; if there is anything left over, it has failed. Using the pilots-and-hangar-tables example, we would write:

```
SELECT DISTINCT Pilot
 FROM PilotSkills AS P1
WHERE (SELECT plane FROM Hangar
   EXCEPT
   SELECT plane
   FROM PilotSkills AS P2
  WHERE P1.pilot = P2.pilot) IS NULL;
```

Again, informally, you can imagine that we got a skill list from each pilot, walked over to the hangar, and crossed off each plane he could fly. If we marked off all the planes in the hangar, we would keep this guy. Another trick is that an empty subquery expression returns a NULL, which is how we can test for an empty set. The WHERE clause could just as well have used a NOT EXISTS() predicate instead of the IS NULL predicate.

## 27.3 Romley's Division

This somewhat complicated relational division is due to Richard Romley at Salomon Smith Barney. The original problem deals with two tables. The first table has a list of managers and the projects they can manage. The second table has a list of Personnel, their departments, and the project to which they are assigned. Each employee is assigned to one and only one department and each employee works on one and only one project at a time. But a department can have several different projects at the same time, so a single project can span several departments.

```
CREATE TABLE MgrProjects
(mgr_name CHAR(10) NOT NULL,
project_id CHAR(2) NOT NULL,
PRIMARY KEY(mgr_name, project_id));

INSERT INTO Mgr_Project
VALUES ('M1', 'P1'), ('M1', 'P3'),
  ('M2', 'P2'), ('M2', 'P3'),
  ('M3', 'P2'),
  ('M4', 'P1'), ('M4', 'P2'), ('M4', 'P3');

CREATE TABLE Personnel
(emp_id CHAR(10) NOT NULL,
```

```
dept CHAR(2) NOT NULL,
project_id CHAR(2) NOT NULL,
UNIQUE (emp_id, project_id),
UNIQUE (emp_id, dept),
PRIMARY KEY (emp_id, dept, project_id));

-- load department #1 data
INSERT INTO Personnel
VALUES ('Al', 'D1', 'P1'),
  ('Bob', 'D1', 'P1'),
  ('Carl', 'D1', 'P1'),
  ('Don', 'D1', 'P2'),
  ('Ed', 'D1', 'P2'),
  ('Frank', 'D1', 'P2'),
  ('George', 'D1', 'P2');

-- load department #2 data
INSERT INTO Personnel
VALUES ('Harry', 'D2', 'P2'),
  ('Jack', 'D2', 'P2'),
  ('Larry', 'D2', 'P2'),
  ('Mike', 'D2', 'P2'),
  ('Nat', 'D2', 'P2');

-- load department #3 data
INSERT INTO Personnel
VALUES ('Oscar', 'D3', 'P2'),
  ('Pat', 'D3', 'P2'),
  ('Rich', 'D3', 'P3');
```

The problem is to generate a report showing for each manager of each department whether he or she is qualified to manage none, some, or all the projects being worked on within the department. To find who can manage some, but not all, of the projects, use a version of relational division.

```
SELECT M1.mgr_name, P1.dept_name
 FROM MgrProjects AS M1
    CROSS JOIN
    Personnel AS P1
WHERE M1.project_id = P1.project_id
GROUP BY M1.mgr_name, P1.dept_name
HAVING COUNT(*) <> (SELECT COUNT(emp_id)
          FROM Personnel AS P2
          WHERE P2.dept_name = P1.dept_name);
```

The query is simply a relational division with a <> instead of an = in the HAVING clause. Richard came back with a modification of my answer that uses a characteristic function inside a single aggregate function.

```
SELECT DISTINCT M1.mgr_name, P1.dept_name
 FROM (MgrProjects AS M1
    INNER JOIN
    Personnel AS P1
    ON M1.project_id = P1.project_id)
    INNER JOIN
    Personnel AS P2
    ON P1.dept_name = P2.dept_name
GROUP BY M1.mgr_name, P1.dept_name, P2.project_id
HAVING MAX (CASE WHEN M1.project_id = P2.project_id
      THEN 1 ELSE 0 END) = 0;
```

This query uses a characteristic function whereas my original version compares a count of Personnel under each manager to a count of Personnel under each project_id. The use of "`GROUP BY M1.mgr_name, P1.dept_name, P2.project_id`" with the "`SELECT DISTINCT M1.mgr_name, P1.dept_name`" is really the tricky part in this new query. What we have is a three-dimensional space with the (x, y, z) axis representing (`mgr_name, dept_name, project_id`), and then we reduce it to two dimensions (`mgr_name, dept`) by seeing if Personnel on shared `project_ids` cover the department or not.

That observation lead to the next changes. We can build a table that shows each combination of manager, department, and the level of authority they have over the projects they have in common. That is the derived table T1 in the following query; (authority = 1) means the manager is not on the project and (authority = 2) means that he or she is on the project_id:

```
SELECT T1.mgr_name, T1.dept_name,
  CASE SUM(T1.authority)
  WHEN 1 THEN 'None'
  WHEN 2 THEN 'All'
  WHEN 3 THEN 'some'
  ELSE NULL END AS power
 FROM (SELECT DISTINCT M1.mgr_name, P1.dept_name,
      MAX (CASE WHEN M1.project_id = P1.project_id
           THEN 2 ELSE 1 END) AS authority
    FROM MgrProjects AS M1
     CROSS JOIN
     Personnel AS P1
  GROUP BY m.mgr_name, P1.dept_name, P1.project_id) AS T1
GROUP BY T1.mgr_name, T1.dept_name;
```

Another version, using the airplane hangar example:

```
SELECT PS1.pilot,
  CASE WHEN COUNT(PS1.plane) > (SELECT COUNT(plane) FROM
     Hanger)
```

```
        AND COUNT(H1.plane) = (SELECT COUNT(plane)FROM
           Hanger)
     THEN 'more than all'
     WHEN COUNT(PS1.plane) = (SELECT COUNT(plane) FROM
        Hanger)
         AND COUNT(H1.plane) = (SELECT COUNT(plane) FROM
           Hanger)
     THEN 'exactly all '
     WHEN MIN(H1.plane) IS NULL
     THEN 'none '
     ELSE 'some ' END AS skill_level
   FROM PilotSkills AS PS1
     LEFT OUTER JOIN
     Hanger AS H1
     ON PS1.plane = H1.plane
   GROUP BY PS1.pilot;
```

We can now sum the authority numbers for all the projects within a department to determine the power this manager has over the department as a whole. If he or she had a total of one, the manager has no authority over personnel on any project in the department. If he or she had a total of two, the manager has power over all personnel on all projects in the department. If he or she had a total of three, the manager has both a 1 and a 2 authority total on some projects within the department. Here is the final answer.

## Results

| mgr_name | dept | power |
|---|---|---|
| M1 | D1 | Some |
| M1 | D2 | None |
| M1 | D3 | Some |
| M2 | D1 | Some |
| M2 | D2 | All |
| M2 | D3 | All |
| M3 | D1 | Some |
| M3 | D2 | All |
| M3 | D3 | Some |
| M4 | D1 | All |
| M4 | D2 | All |
| M4 | D3 | All |

## 27.4 Boolean Expressions in an RDBMS

Given the usual "hangar and pilots" schema, we want to create and store queries that involve Boolean expressions, such as "Find the pilots who can fly a Piper Cub and also an F-14 or F-17 Fighter." The trick is to put the expression into the disjunctive canonical form. In English that means a bunch of AND-ed predicates that are then OR-ed together, like this. Any Boolean function can be expressed this way. This form is canonical when each Boolean variable appears exactly once in each term. When all variables are not required to appear in every term, the form is called a disjunctive normal form. The algorithm to convert any Boolean expression into disjunctive canonical form is a bit complicated, but can be found in a good book on circuit design. Our simple example would convert to this predicate.

```
('Piper Cub' AND 'F-14 Fighter') OR ('Piper Cub' AND 'F-17
   Fighter')
```

which we load into this table:

```
CREATE TABLE BooleanExpressions
(and_grp INTEGER NOT NULL,
skill CHAR(10) NOT NULL,
PRIMARY KEY (and_grp, skill));

INSERT INTO BooleanExpressions
VALUES (1, 'Piper Cub'), (1, 'F-14 Fighter'),
   (2, 'Piper Cub'), (2, 'F-17 Fighter');
```

Assume we have a table of job candidates:

```
CREATE TABLE Candidates
(candidate_name CHAR(15) NOT NULL,
skill CHAR(10) NOT NULL,
PRIMARY KEY (candidate_name, skill));

INSERT INTO Candidates
VALUES ('John', 'Piper Cub'), --winner
  ('John', 'B-52 Bomber'),
  ('Mary', 'Piper Cub'), --winner
  ('Mary', 'F-17 Fighter'),
  ('Larry', 'F-14 Fighter'), --winner
  ('Larry', 'F-17 Fighter'),
  ('Moe', 'F-14 Fighter'), --winner
  ('Moe', 'F-17 Fighter'),
  ('Moe', 'Piper Cub'),
  ('Celko', 'Piper Cub'), -- loser
  ('Celko', 'Blimp'),
  ('smith', 'Kite'), -- loser
  ('smith', 'Blimp');
```

The query is simple now:

```
SELECT DISTINCT C1.candidate_name
 FROM Candidates AS C1, BooleanExpressions AS Q1
WHERE C1.skill = Q1.skill
GROUP BY Q1.and_grp, C1.candidate_name
HAVING COUNT(C1.skill)
   = (SELECT COUNT(*)
       FROM BooleanExpressions AS Q2
      WHERE Q1.and_grp = Q2.and_grp);
```

You can retain the COUNT() information to rank candidates. For example, Moe meets both qualifications, but other candidates meet only one of the two.

## 27.5 FIFO and LIFO Subsets

This will be easier to explain with an example for the readers who have not worked with an Inventory system before. Imagine that we have a warehouse of one product to which we add stock once a day with the following data:

```
CREATE TABLE InventoryReceipts
(receipt_nbr INTEGER PRIMARY KEY,
purchase_date DATETIME NOT NULL,
qty_on_hand INTEGER NOT NULL
  CHECK (qty_on_hand >= 0),
unit_price DECIMAL (12,4) NOT NULL);
```

The business now sells 100 units on 2006-01-05. How do you calculate the value of the stock sold? There is not one right answer, but here are some options:

1. Use the current replacement cost, which is $10.00 per unit as of January 5, 2006. That would mean the sale costs us $1000.00 because of a recent price break.

**InventoryReceipts**

| receipt_nbr | purchase_date | qty_on_hand | unit_price |
|---|---|---|---|
| 1 | '2015-01-01' | 15 | 10.00 |
| 2 | '2015-01-02' | 25 | 12.00 |
| 3 | '2015-01-03' | 40 | 13.00 |
| 4 | '2015-01-04' | 35 | 12.00 |
| 5 | '2015-01-05' | 45 | 10.00 |

2. Use the current average price per unit. We have a total of 160 units, for which we paid a total of $1840.00, and that gives us an average cost of $11.50 per unit, or $1150.00 in total inventory costs.
3. `LIFO`, stands for Last In, First Out. We start by looking at the most recent purchases and work backward through time.
   2006-01-05 45 * $10.00 = $450.00 and 45 units
   2006-01-04 35 * $12.00 = $420.00 and 80 units
   2006-01-03 20 * $13.00 = $260.00 and 100 with 20 units left over for a total of $1130.00 in inventory cost.
4. `FIFO`, stands for First In, First Out. We start by looking at the earliest purchases and work forward through time.
   2006-01-01 15 * $10.00 = $150.00 and 15 units
   2006-01-02 25 * $12.00 = $300.00 and 40 units
   2006-01-03 40 * $13.00 = $520.00 and 80 units
   2006-01-04 20 * $12.00 = $240.00 with 15 units left over for a total of $1210.00 in inventory costs.

The first two scenarios are trivial to program. The `LIFO` and `FIFO` are more interesting because they involve looking at matching the order against blocks of inventory in a particular order. Consider this view:

```
CREATE VIEW LIFO (stock_date, unit_price, tot_qty_on_hand,
   tot_cost)
AS
SELECT R1.purchase_date, R1.unit_price, SUM(R2.qty_
   on_hand), SUM(R2.qty_on_hand *
R2.unit_price)
FROM InventoryReceipts AS R1,
  InventoryReceipts AS R2
WHERE R2.purchase_date >= R1.purchase_date
GROUP BY R1.purchase_date, R1.unit_price;
```

A row in this view tells us the total quantity on hand, the total cost of the goods in inventory, and what we were paying for items on each date. The quantity on hand is a running total. We can get the `LIFO` cost with this query.

```
SELECT (tot_cost - ((tot_qty_on_hand -:order_qty_on_hand)
   * unit_price)) AS cost
 FROM LIFO AS L1
WHERE stock_date
  = (SELECT MAX(stock_date)
     FROM LIFO AS L2
     WHERE tot_qty_on_hand >=:order_qty_on_hand);
```

This is straight algebra and a little logic. Find the most recent date that we had enough (or more) quantity on hand to meet the order. If by dumb blind luck, there is a day when the quantity on hand exactly matched the order, return the total cost as the answer. If the order was for more than we have in stock, then return nothing. If we go back to a day when we had more in stock than the order was for, then look at the unit price on that day, multiply by the overage, and subtract it.

Alternatively, you can use a derived table and a CASE expression. The CASE expression computes the cost of units that have a running total quantity less than the:order_qty_on_hand and then does algebra on the final block of inventory that would put the running total over the limit. The outer query does a sum on these blocks.

```
SELECT SUM(R3.v) AS cost
 FROM (SELECT R1.unit_price
      * CASE WHEN SUM(R2.qty_on_hand) <=:order_qty_on_hand
        THEN R1.qty_on_hand
        ELSE:order_qty_on_hand
          - (SUM(R2.qty_on_hand) - R1.qty_on_hand) END
    FROM InventoryReceipts AS R1,
       InventoryReceipts AS R2
  WHERE R1.purchase_date <= R2.purchase_date
  GROUP BY R1.purchase_date, R1.qty_on_hand, R1.unit_price
  HAVING (SUM(R2.qty_on_hand) - R1.qty_on_hand)
     <=:order_qty_on_hand)
 AS R3(v);
```

FIFO can be done with a similar VIEW or derived table.

```
CREATE VIEW FIFO (stock_date, unit_price, tot_qty_on_hand,
   tot_cost)
AS
SELECT R1.purchase_date, R1.unit_price,
  SUM(R2.qty_on_hand), SUM(R2.qty_on_hand *
R2.unit_price)
FROM InventoryReceipts AS R1,
  InventoryReceipts AS R2
WHERE R2.purchase_date <= R1.purchase_date
GROUP BY R1.purchase_date, R1.unit_price;
```

with the corresponding query:

```
SELECT (tot_cost - ((tot_qty_on_hand -:order_qty_on_hand)
   * unit_price)) AS cost
 FROM FIFO AS F1
WHERE stock_date
   = (SELECT MIN (stock_date)
       FROM FIFO AS F2
      WHERE tot_qty_on_hand >= :order_qty_on_hand);
```

# 28

# GROUPING OPERATIONS

I am separating the partitions and grouping operations based on the idea that a group has *group* properties that we are trying to find, so we get a single row back for each group. A partition is simply a way of subsetting the original table, so we get a table back as a result.

## 28.1 GROUP BY Clause

The GROUP BY clause is based on simple partitions. A partition of a set divides the set into subsets such that (1) the union of the subsets returns the original set and (2) the intersection of the subsets is empty. Think of it as cutting up a pizza pie—each piece of pepperoni belongs to one and only one slice of pizza. When you get to the section on SQL-99 OLAP extensions, you will see "variation on a theme" in the ROLLUP and CUBE operators, but this is where it all starts.

The GROUP BY clause takes the result of the FROM and WHERE clauses, then puts the rows into groups defined as having the same values for the columns listed in the GROUP BY clause. Each group is reduced to a single row in the result table. This result table is called a grouped table, and all operations are now defined on groups rather than on the original rows.

By convention, the NULLs are treated as one group. The order of the grouping columns in the GROUP BY clause does not matter, but since all or some of the column names have to appear in the SELECT list, you should probably use the same order in both lists for readability.

Please note the SELECT column names might be a subset of the GROUP BY clause column names, but never the other way around. Let us construct a sample table called "Villes" to explain in detail how this works. The table is declared as:

```
CREATE TABLE Villes
(state_code CHAR(2) NOT NULL, -- usps codes
 city_name CHAR(25) NOT NULL,
 PRIMARY KEY (city_name, state_code));
```

Joe Celko's SQL for Smarties. DOI: 10.1016/B978-0-12-382022-8.00028-4

and we populate it with the names of cities that end in '-ville' in each state. The first problem is to find a count of the number of such cities by state_code. The immediate naive query might be:

```
SELECT state_code, city_name, COUNT(*)
  FROM Villes
GROUP BY state_code;
```

The groups for Tennessee would have the rows ('TN', 'Nashville') and ('TN', 'Knoxville'). The first position in the result is the grouping column, which has to be constant within the group. The third column in the SELECT clause is the COUNT(*) for the group, which is clearly two. The city_name column is a problem. Since the table is grouped by states, there can be at most 50 groups, one for each state_code. The COUNT(*) is clearly a single value and it applies to the group as a whole. But what possible single value could I output for a city_name in each group? Should I pick a typical city_name and use it? If all the cities have the same name, should I use that name, and otherwise output a NULL? The worst possible choice would be to output both rows with the COUNT(*) of 2, since each row would imply that there are two cities named Nashville and two cities named Knoxville in Tennessee.

Each row represents a single group, so anything in it must be a characteristic of the group, not of a single row in the group. This is why there is a rule that the SELECT list must be made up only of grouping columns with optional aggregate function expressions.

### 28.1.1 NULLs and Groups

SQL puts the NULLs into a single group, as if they were all equal. The other option, which was used in some of the first SQL implementations before the standard, was to put each NULL into a group by itself. That is not an unreasonable choice. But to make a meaningful choice between the two options, you would have to know the semantics of the data you are trying to model. SQL is a language based on syntax, not semantics.

For example, if a NULL is being used for a missing diagnosis in a medical record, you know that each patient will probably have a different disease when the NULLs are resolved. Putting the NULLs in one group would make sense if you wanted to consider unprocessed diagnosis reports as one group in a summary. Putting each NULL in its own group would make sense if you wanted to consider each unprocessed diagnosis report as an action item for treatment of the relevant class of diseases. Another example was a traffic ticket database that used NULL for a missing auto tag. Obviously, there is more than one car without a tag in the database. The general scheme for getting separate groups for each NULL is straightforward:

```
SELECT x, ..
 FROM Table1
WHERE x IS NOT NULL
GROUP BY x
UNION ALL
SELECT x, ..
 FROM Table1
WHERE x IS NULL;
```

There will also be cases, such as the traffic tickets, where you can use another GROUP BY clause to form groups where the principal grouping columns are NULL. For example, the VIN (Vehicle Identification Number) is taken when the car is missing a tag, and it would provide a grouping column.

## 28.2 GROUP BY and HAVING

One of the biggest problems in working with the GROUP BY clause is understanding how the WHERE and HAVING clauses work with it. Consider the query to find all departments with fewer than five programmers:

```
SELECT dept_nbr
 FROM Personnel
WHERE job_title = 'Programmer'
GROUP BY dept_nbr
HAVING COUNT(*) < 5;
```

The result of this query does not have a row for any departments with no programmers. The order of execution of the clauses does WHERE first, so those employees whose jobs are not equal to 'Programmer' are never passed to the GROUP BY clause. You have missed data that you might want to trap.

The next query will also pick up those departments that have no programmers, because the COUNT(DISTINCT x) function will return a zero for an empty set.

```
SELECT DISTINCT dept_nbr
 FROM Personnel AS P1
WHERE 5 > (SELECT COUNT(DISTINCT P2.emp_nbr)
     FROM Personnel AS P2
     WHERE P1.dept_nbr = P2. dept_nbr
     AND P2.job_title = 'Programmer');
```

If there is no GROUP BY clause, the HAVING clause will treat the entire table as a single group. Many early implementations of

SQL required that the HAVING clause belong to a GROUP BY clause, so you might see old code written under that assumption.

Since the HAVING clause applies only to the rows of a grouped table, it can reference only the grouping columns and aggregate functions that apply to the group. That is why this query would fail:

```
SELECT dept_nbr -- Invalid Query!
 FROM Personnel
GROUP BY dept_nbr
HAVING COUNT(*)< 5
  AND job_title = 'Programmer';
```

When the HAVING clause is executed, job is not in the grouped table as a column—it is a property of a row, not of a group. Likewise, this query would fail for much the same reason:

```
SELECT dept_nbr -- Invalid Query!
 FROM Personnel
WHERE COUNT(*)< 5
  AND job_title = 'Programmer'
GROUP BY dept_nbr;
```

The COUNT(*) does not exist until after the departmental groups are formed.

## 28.2.1 Group Characteristics and HAVING Clause

You can use the aggregate functions and the HAVING clause to determine certain characteristics of the groups formed by the GROUP BY clause. For example, given a simple grouped table with three columns like this:

```
SELECT col1, col2
 FROM Foobar
GROUP BY col1, col2
HAVING .. ;
```

you can determine the following properties of the groups with these HAVING clauses:

HAVING COUNT (DISTINCT col_x) = COUNT (col_x)—col_x has all distinct values

HAVING COUNT(*) = COUNT(col_x);—There are no NULLs in the column

HAVING MIN(col_x - <const>) = -MAX(col_x - <const>)—col_x deviates above and below const by the same amount

HAVING MIN(col_x) * MAX(col_x) < 0—Either MIN or MAX is negative, not both

HAVING MIN(col_x) * MAX(col_x) > 0—col_x is either all positive or all negative

HAVING MIN(SIGN(col_x)) = MAX(SIGN(col_x))—col_x is all positive, all negative, or all zero

HAVING MIN(ABS(col_x)) = 0;—col_x has at least one zero

HAVING MIN(ABS(col_x)) = MIN(col_x)—col_x >= 0 (although the where clause can handle this, too)

HAVING MIN(col_x) = -MAX(col_x)—col_x deviates above and below zero by the same amount

HAVING MIN(col_x) * MAX(col_x) = 0—Either one or both of MIN or MAX is zero

HAVING MIN(col_x) < MAX(col_x)—col_x has more than one value (may be faster than count (*) > 1)

HAVING MIN(col_x) = MAX(col_x)—col_x has one value or NULLs --

HAVING (MAX(seq) - MIN(seq)+1) = COUNT(seq)—The sequential numbers in seq have no gaps

Tom Moreau contributed most of these suggestions.

Let me remind you again, that if there is no GROUP BY clause, the HAVING clause will treat the entire table as a single group. This means that if you wish to apply one of the tests just given to the whole table, you will need to use a constant in the SELECT list.

This will be easier to see with an example. You are given a table with a column of unique sequential numbers that start at 1. When you go to insert a new row, you must use a sequence number that is not currently in the column—that is, fill the gaps. If there are no gaps, then and only then can you use the next highest integer in the sequence.

```
CREATE TABLE Batting_Lineup
(batting_seq INTEGER NOT NULL PRIMARY KEY
     CHECK (seq > 0),
player_name CHAR(5) NOT NULL);

INSERT INTO Batting_Lineup
VALUES (1, 'Tom'), (2, 'Dick'), (4, 'Harry'), (5, 'Moe');
```

How do I find if I have any gaps?

```
EXISTS (SELECT 'gap'
     FROM Batting_Lineup
   HAVING COUNT(*) = MAX(batting_seq))
```

You could not use SELECT batting_seq because the column values will not be identical within the single group made from the table, so the subquery fails with a cardinality violation. Likewise, SELECT * fails because the asterisk is converted into a column name picked by the SQL engine. Here is the insertion statement:

```
INSERT INTO Batting_Lineup (batting_seq, junk)
VALUES (CASE WHEN EXISTS -- no gaps
       (SELECT 'no gaps'
```

```
          FROM Batting_Lineup
        HAVING COUNT(*) = MAX(batting_seq))
     THEN (SELECT MAX(batting_seq) FROM Batting_Lineup) + 1
     ELSE (SELECT MIN(batting_seq) -- gaps
           FROM Batting_Lineup
          WHERE (batting_seq - 1)
            NOT IN (SELECT batting_seq FROM Batting_Lineup)
          AND batting_seq > 0) - 1 END,
'Celko');
```

The ELSE clause has to handle a special situation when 1 is in the batting_seq column, so that it does not return an illegal zero. The only tricky part is waiting for the entire scalar subquery expression to compute before subtracting one; writing `MIN(batting_seq -1)` or `MIN(batting_seq) -1` in the SELECT list could disable the use of indexes in many SQL products.

## 28.3 Multiple Aggregation Levels

The rule in SQL is that you cannot nest aggregate functions, such as:

```
SELECT depart_name, MIN(COUNT(stapler_nbr)) -- illegal
   syntax!
  FROM Companies
 GROUP BY depart_name;
```

The usual intent of this is to get multiple levels of aggregation; this example probably wanted the smallest count of staplers within each department. But this makes no sense because a department (i.e., group) can have only one count, one minimum, one maximum, one average, and so forth for any expression. The nature of descriptive statistics is that they reduce a group characteristic to a scalar value.

### 28.3.1 Grouped VIEWs for Multiple Aggregation Levels

Business reports usually are based on a hierarchy of nested levels of aggregation. This type of report is so common that there are tools that perform only this sort of task. For example, sales are grouped under the salesmen who made them, then salesman's departments are grouped into districts, districts are grouped into regions, and so on until we have summary information at the company level. Each level is a partition of the level above it. The summary information can be constructed from the level immediately beneath it in the hierarchy.

SQL now has CUBE and ROLLUP options we will discuss later which replace these coding tricks. Frankly, using a report writer will be faster and more powerful than writing SQL code to do the job.

One trick is to use VIEWs with GROUP BY clauses to build the reporting levels. Using a Sales report example, the following UNION-ed query will get a report for each level, from the lowest, most detailed level (salesman), through districts and regions, to the highest level (the company).

```
SELECT region_nbr, district_nbr, salesman, SUM(sales_amt)
 FROM Sales
GROUP BY region_nbr, district_nbr, salesman
UNION
SELECT region_nbr, district_nbr, '{SALESMEN}',
   SUM(sales_amt)
 FROM Sales
GROUP BY region_nbr, district_nbr
UNION
SELECT region_nbr, '{OFFICE}', '{SALESMEN}',
   SUM(sales_amt)
 FROM Sales
GROUP BY region_nbr
UNION
SELECT '{REGION}', '{OFFICE}', '{SALESMEN}',
   SUM(sales_amt)
 FROM Sales;
```

The constant strings inside the curly brackets will sort below any alphabetic strings in ASCII, and thus will appear on the end of each grouping in the hierarchy. After having shown you this trick, I need to point out its flaws.

### 28.3.2 Subquery Expressions for Multiple Aggregation Levels

The Standard SQL permits you to use a table subquery in a FROM clause and a scalar subquery anywhere that you would use an expression. This lets us do some multilevel aggregation in a single query. For example, to find how each salesman did in his sales district_nbr, you can write:

```
SELECT salesman, region_nbr, district_nbr, SUM(sales_amt)
   AS salesman_tot,
  (SELECT SUM(sales_amt)
    FROM Sales AS S1
    WHERE S1.region_nbr = S2.region_nbr
     AND S1.district_nbr = S2.district_nbr)
```

```
       AS district_nbr_tot
    FROM Sales AS S2
  GROUP BY salesman, region_nbr, district_nbr,
       district_nbr_tot;
```

This query will work because the subquery is a constant for each group. The subquery could also be used in an expression to give the percentage of the district_nbr total each salesman contributed.

A trickier query is to find aggregates of aggregates—something like the average of the total sales of the districts for each region_nbr. Beginning SQL programmers would try to write queries like this:

```
SELECT region_nbr, AVG(SUM(sales_amt)) AS region_nbr_average
   -- Invalid SQL
 FROM Sales
GROUP BY district_nbr, region_nbr;
```

and the parser would gag on `AVG(SUM(sales_amt))` and return an error message about nesting aggregate functions. Standard SQL will let you get the desired effect with a little more work. You need a subquery that will compute the sum of the sales for each district_nbr within a region_nbr.

This table then needs to be averaged for each region_nbr, thus:

```
SELECT T1.region_nbr, AVG(T1.district_nbr_total) AS
   region_nbr_average
  FROM (SELECT region_nbr, district_nbr, SUM(sales_amt)
      FROM Sales
    GROUP BY region_nbr, district_nbr) AS T1 (region_nbr,
       district_nbr, district_nbr_total)
GROUP BY T1.region_nbr;
```

The best guess would be that the subquery would be constructed once as a materialized table, then used by the `SELECT` statement in the usual way. Do not think that Standard SQL would let you write:

```
SELECT region_nbr,
   AVG(SELECT SUM(sales_amt) -- Invalid SQL
      FROM Sales AS S1
      WHERE S1.region_nbr = S2.region_nbr
      GROUP BY district_nbr) AS region_nbr_average
 FROM Sales AS S2
GROUP BY region_nbr;
```

The parameter for an aggregate function still cannot be another aggregate function or a subquery. The reason for this prohibition is that though this particular subquery is scalar, other subqueries might have multiple rows and/or multiple columns and not be able to return a single value.

### 28.3.3 CASE Expressions for Multiple Aggregation Levels

Another trick is to replace the nesting of aggregate functions with expressions that return a characteristic of a subset of the group. Given a table with movie names and a numeric rating assigned to them by our reviewers, for each movie we might want to know:

1. What was the worst rating and how many times did it occur?
2. What was the best rating and how many times did it occur?

This can be done with this query:

```
SELECT movie_name,
    MIN(rating) AS worst_rating,
    COUNT(CASE WHEN NOT EXISTS
         (SELECT *
          FROM Reviews AS R2
         WHERE R2.movie_name = R1.movie_name
          AND R2.rating < R1.rating)
     THEN 1 ELSE NULL END) AS worst_tally,
    MAX(rating) AS best_rating,
    COUNT(CASE WHEN NOT EXISTS
         (SELECT *
           FROM Reviews AS R3
         WHERE R3.movie_name = R1.movie_name
         AND R3.rating > R1.rating)
     THEN 1 ELSE NULL END) AS best_tally
 FROM Reviews AS R1
GROUP BY movie_name;
```

The subquery expression in each of the `NOT EXISTS()` predicates is building a subset within each movie's reviews such that they are the highest (or lowest). This subset of identical values is then counted in the outermost query. This avoids using a nested aggregate function.

## 28.4 Grouping on Computed Columns

SQL-99 allows queries that are grouped on the result of a computed column. For example, to do a report by months on sales, you can write:

```
SELECT EXTRACT(MONTH FROM sale_date) AS rpt_month,
   SUM(sales_amt)
 FROM Sales
GROUP BY rpt_month;
```

This is a departure from the SQL processing model in previous standards that allowed only column names. In the original model, the SELECT statement computes the expressions in the SELECT clause last, so the computed columns do not exist until after the grouping is done, so there should be no way to group on them.

However, you can fake it in older versions of SQL by using a subquery expression in the FROM clause to build a working table with the computation in it:

```
SELECT salesmonth, SUM(sales_amt)
 FROM (SELECT EXTRACT(MONTH FROM sale_date) AS salesmonth,
        sales_amt
     FROM Sales)
GROUP BY salesmonth;
```

or by using a correlated subquery expression in the SELECT clause:

```
SELECT DISTINCT EXTRACT(MONTH FROM S1.sale_date),
   (SELECT SUM(S2.sales_amt)
     FROM Sales AS S2
   WHERE EXTRACT(MONTH FROM S2.sale_date)
     = EXTRACT(MONTH FROM S1.sale_date))
FROM Sales AS S1;
```

The first version will probably run faster, since it does not have as many computations in it.

## 28.5 Grouping into Pairs

The idea is easier to show than to say. You are given a table of people and want to generate a list that has pairs of men and women for a dinner party.

```
CREATE TABLE People
(person_name VARCHAR(15) NOT NULL,
sex_code INTEGER DEFAULT 1 NOT NULL -- iso sex_code codes
   CHECK (sex_code IN (1, 2));

INSERT INTO People
VALUES ('Bob', 1), ('Ed', 1), ('Joe', 1), ('Dave', 1);

INSERT INTO People
VALUES ('Sue', 2), ('Joan', 2), ('Kate', 2),
  ('Mary', 2), ('Petra', 2), ('Nancy', 2);
```

Here's a solution from Steve Kass:

```
SELECT A.person_name, A.sex_code, COUNT(*) AS rank
 FROM People AS A, People AS B
WHERE B.person_name <= A.person_name
  AND B.sex_code = A.sex_code
GROUP BY A.person_name, A.sex_code;
```

For each name, COUNT(*) is the alphabetical "rank" of the name in the table, counting only names of the same sex_code. The join makes this happen, because COUNT(*) counts the number of rows in the table with the same sex_code as name and that comes before or equal to name in alphabetical order. Then the results are ordered by this "rank" value first, then by sex_code to order the names with matching rank.

Although on the right track, the single fact of a dinner couple is split across two rows. You cannot look at one row and answer the question, "Do you have a date?" with this query result. But the basic idea is good and you can get your pairs on one line:

```
SELECT M1.person_name AS male, F1.person_name AS female,
   COALESCE (M1.rank, F1.rank)
 FROM (SELECT P1.person_name, COUNT(P2.person_name)
     FROM People AS P1, People AS P2
    WHERE P2.person_name <= P1.person_name
     AND P1.sex_code = 1
     AND P2.sex_code = 1
   GROUP BY P1.person_name) AS M1(person_name, rank)
   FULL OUTER JOIN
   (SELECT P1.person_name, COUNT(P2.person_name)
     FROM People AS P1, People AS P2
    WHERE P2.person_name <= P1.person_name
     AND P1.sex_code = 2
     AND P2.sex_code = 2
   GROUP BY P1.person_name) AS F1(person_name, rank)
  ON M1.rank = F1.rank;
```

I assume that alphabetical ordering of the two subsets makes the pairs for matching. This query ought to handle the case where there is an unlike number of males and females by padding with NULLs. It also returns proper pairings without the use of an ORDER BY, thus avoiding an actual or hidden CURSOR.

A more modern version of this query is:

```
SELECT M1.person_name AS male, F1.person_name AS female,
   COALESCE (M1.rank, F1.rank)
 FROM (SELECT P1.person_name,
       ROW_NUMBER() OVER(ORDER BY P1.person_name) AS rank
    FROM People AS P1
   WHERE P1.sex_code = 1)
  FULL OUTER JOIN
  (SELECT P2.person_name,
       ROW_NUMBER() OVER(ORDER BY P2.person_name) AS rank
    FROM People AS P2
   WHERE P1.sex_code = 2)
  ON M1.rank = F1.rank;
```

## 28.6 Sorting and GROUP BY

Though it is not required by the standard, most implementations will automatically sort the results of a grouped query. Internally, the groups were built by first sorting the table on the grouping columns, then aggregating them. The NULL group can sort either high or low, depending on the vendor.

An ORDER BY clause whose columns are not in the same order as those in the GROUP BY clause can be expensive to execute if the optimizer does not ignore the extra sort request. It is also possible to sort a grouped table on an aggregate or calculated column. For example, to show the Sales regions in order of total sales, you would write:

```
SELECT region_nbr, district_nbr,
   SUM(sales_amt) AS district_sales_amt
 FROM Sales
GROUP BY region_nbr, district_nbr;
```

Since it is possible that two or more regions could have the same Sales volume, it is always a good idea to sort by the region_nbr column, then by the district_nbr column. The extra sorting is cheap to execute and requires no extra storage. It is very likely that your SQL implementation is using a nonstable sort.

A stable sort preserves the original order of the rows with equal valued sort keys. For example, I am given a deck of playing cards to sort by rank and suit. If I first sort by rank, assuming aces high, I would get a deck with all the deuces, followed by all the treys, and so forth until I got to the aces. Within each of these groups, the suits could be in any order.

If I then sorted the deck on the suits of the cards, I would get (assuming bridge sorting order) deuces of clubs, diamonds, hearts, and finally spades, as the highest rank, followed by treys of clubs, diamonds, hearts, and spades, and so forth up to the aces.

If the second sort were a nonstable sort, it could destroy the ordering of the suits. A second sort that was a stable sort would keep the ordering in the suits.

Stable sorts are almost always slower than nonstable sorts, so nonstable sorts are preferred by most database systems. However, a smart optimizer can see an existing order in the intermediate working table and replace the usual nonstable sort with a stable sort, thereby avoiding extra work. The optimizer can also use clustered indexes and other sources of preexisting ordering in the data.

However, you should never depend on the default ordering of a particular SQL product, since this will not be portable.

If ordering is important, use an ORDER BY clause with all the desired columns explicitly given in it. In Standard SQL, you will have to use an AS clause on each of the aggregate functions to give it a name that can be used in the ORDER BY clause.

A common vendor extension was to permit an integer specifying the ordinal position of the expression in the `SELECT` clause in an `ORDER BY`. The problem with this is that a change to the `SELECT` clause can trash the results. This has been dropped from most products today.

# 29

# SIMPLE AGGREGATE FUNCTIONS

The simple aggregate functions are the ones that came with SQL from the beginning. Every product will have them. They are usually fast because optimizers and index structures often store this data for their own use.

Simple aggregate functions first construct a column of values as defined by the parameter. The parameter is usually a single column name, but it can be an expression with scalar functions and calculations. Pretty much the only things that cannot be used as parameters are other aggregate functions (e.g., `SUM(AVG(x))` is illegal) and a subquery (e.g., `AVG(SELECT col1 FROM SomeTable WHERE ...)` is illegal). A subquery could return more than one value, so it would not fit into a column and an aggregate function would have to try to build a column within a column.

Once the working column is constructed, all the `NULL`s are removed and the function performs its operation. As you learn the definitions I am about to give, stress the words *known* values to remind yourself that the `NULL`s have been dropped.

There are two options, `ALL` and `DISTINCT`, that are shown as keywords inside the parameter list. The keyword `ALL` is optional and is never really used in practice. It says that all the rows in the working column are retained for the final calculation. The keyword `DISTINCT` is not optional in these functions. It removes all redundant duplicate values from the working column before the final calculation. Let's look at the particulars of each aggregate function. They fall into three categories:

1. Mathematical operations: The average (or arithmetic mean) and the sum (or arithmetic total). These work for all numeric data types.
2. The extrema functions: Minimum and maximum for all data types.
3. The counting functions: This is just the simple tally of the rows in the working table. The table cardinality is really a different animal that happens to look like the count function.

Let's go into details.

Joe Celko's SQL for Smarties. DOI: 10.1016/B978-0-12-382022-8.00029-6

## 29.1 COUNT( ) Functions

There are two forms of the COUNT() function, cardinality and expression counting.

COUNT(*) returns the number of rows in a table (called the cardinality of the table in relational terms); it is the only standard aggregate function that uses an asterisk as a parameter. This function is very useful and usually will run quite fast, since it can use system information about the table size. Remember that NULL values are also counted, because this function deals with entire rows and not column values. There is no such thing as a NULL row—a row exists or it does not without regard to contents.

An empty table has a COUNT(*) of zero, which makes sense. However, all the other aggregate functions we will discuss in this section will return an empty set as the result; they are given an empty set as input—*ab nilo, ex nilo* in Latin. Although it is too late to change SQL, we would have been better off with syntax that uses a table expression in a parameter for cardinality, much like the EXISTS() predicate.

You would think that using the COUNT(*) would be easy, but there are a lot of subtle tricks to it. Think of a database of the presidencies of the United States, with columns for the first name, middle initial(s), and last name of each US president who held that office, along with his political party and his term(s) in office. It might look like this:

```
CREATE TABLE Parties
(party_code CHAR(2) NOT NULL PRIMARY KEY,
party_name VARCHAR(25) NOT NULL);

INSERT INTO Parties
VALUES ('D', 'Democratic'),
  ('DR', 'Democratic Republican'),
  ('R', 'Republican'),
  ('F', 'Federalist'),
  ('W', 'Whig'),
  ('L', 'Libertarian');

CREATE TABLE Presidencies
(first_name CHAR(11) NOT NULL,
initial VARCHAR(4) DEFAULT ' ' NOT NULL, -- one space
last_name CHAR(11) NOT NULL,
party_code CHAR(2) NOT NULL
  REFERENCES Parties(party_code)
start_term_year INTEGER NOT NULL UNIQUE
   CHECK (start_term_year > 1789),
end_term_year INTEGER); -- null means current
```

Presidencies

| first_name | initial | last_name | party | start_term_year | end_term_year |
|---|---|---|---|---|---|
| 'George' | '' | 'Washington' | 'F' | 1789 | 1797 |
| 'John' | '' | 'Adams' | 'F' | 1797 | 1801 |
| 'Thomas' | '' | 'Jefferson' | 'DR' | 1801 | 1809 |
| 'James' | '' | 'Madison' | 'DR' | 1809 | 1817 |
| 'James' | '' | 'Monroe' | 'DR' | 1817 | 1825 |
| 'John' | '' | 'Adams' | 'DR' | 1825 | 1829 |
| 'Andrew' | '' | 'Jackson' | 'D' | 1829 | 1837 |
| 'Martin' | '' | 'Van Buren' | 'D' | 1837 | 1841 |
| 'William' | 'H.' | 'Harrison' | 'W' | 1841 | 1841 |
| 'John' | '' | 'Tyler' | 'W' | 1841 | 1845 |
| 'James' | 'K.' | 'Polk' | 'D' | 1845 | 1849 |
| 'Zachary' | '' | 'Taylor' | 'W' | 1849 | 1850 |
| 'Millard' | '' | 'Fillmore' | 'W' | 1850 | 1853 |
| 'Franklin' | '' | 'Pierce' | 'D' | 1853 | 1857 |
| 'James' | '' | 'Buchanan' | 'D' | 1857 | 1861 |
| 'Abraham' | '' | 'Lincoln' | 'R' | 1861 | 1865 |
| 'Andrew' | '' | 'Johnson' | 'R' | 1865 | 1869 |
| 'Ulysses' | 'S.' | 'Grant' | 'R' | 1869 | 1877 |
| 'Rutherford' | 'B.' | 'Hayes' | 'R' | 1877 | 1881 |
| 'James' | 'A.' | 'Garfield' | 'R' | 1881 | 1881 |
| 'Chester' | 'A.' | 'Arthur' | 'R' | 1881 | 1885 |
| 'Grover' | '' | 'Cleveland' | 'D' | 1885 | 1889 |
| 'Benjamin' | '' | 'Harrison' | 'R' | 1889 | 1893 |
| 'Grover' | '' | 'Cleveland' | 'D' | 1893 | 1897 |
| 'William' | '' | 'McKinley' | 'R' | 1897 | 1901 |
| 'Theodore' | '' | 'Roosevelt' | 'R' | 1901 | 1909 |
| 'William' | 'H.' | 'Taft' | 'R' | 1909 | 1913 |
| 'Woodrow' | '' | 'Wilson' | 'D' | 1913 | 1921 |
| 'Warren' | 'G.' | 'Harding' | 'R' | 1921 | 1923 |
| 'Calvin' | '' | 'Coolidge' | 'R' | 1923 | 1929 |
| 'Herbert' | 'C.' | 'Hoover' | 'R' | 1929 | 1933 |
| 'Franklin' | 'D.' | 'Roosevelt' | 'D' | 1933 | 1945 |
| 'Harry' | 'S.' | 'Truman' | 'D' | 1945 | 1953 |
| 'Dwight' | 'D.' | 'Eisenhower' | 'R' | 1953 | 1961 |
| 'John' | 'F.' | 'Kennedy' | 'D' | 1961 | 1963 |
| 'Lyndon' | 'B.' | 'Johnson' | 'D' | 1963 | 1969 |
| 'Richard' | 'M.' | 'Nixon' | 'R' | 1969 | 1974 |
| 'Gerald' | 'R.' | 'Ford' | 'R' | 1974 | 1977 |
| 'James' | 'E.' | 'Carter' | 'D' | 1977 | 1981 |
| 'Ronald' | 'W.' | 'Reagan' | 'R' | 1981 | 1989 |
| 'George' | 'H.W.' | 'Bush' | 'R' | 1989 | 1993 |
| 'William' | 'J.' | 'Clinton' | 'D' | 1993 | 2001 |
| 'George' | 'W.' | 'Bush' | 'R' | 2001 | 2009 |
| 'Obama' | 'H.' | 'Barack' | 'D' | 2009 | NULL |

Your Civics teacher has just asked you to tell her how many people have been President of the United States. So you write the query as `SELECT COUNT(*) FROM Presidencies;` and get the wrong answer. For those of you who have been out of high school too long, more than one Adams, more than one John, more than one Bush, and more than one Roosevelt have served as president. Many people have had more than one term in office, and Grover Cleveland served two discontinuous terms. In short, this database is not a simple one-row, one-person system. What you really wanted was not `COUNT(*)`, but something that is able to look at unique combinations of multiple columns. You cannot do this in one column, so you need to construct an expression that is unique. The point is that you need to be very sure that the expression you are using as a parameter is really what you wanted to count.

The `COUNT([ALL] <value expression>)` returns the number of members in the `<value expression>` set. The `NULL`s have been thrown away before the counting took place and an empty set returns zero. The best way to read this is "Count the number of known values in this expression," with stress on the word known. In this example you might use `COUNT(first_name || ' ' || initial || ' ' || last_name);` if this was for display, you might also want to clean out the extra spaces.

The `COUNT(DISTINCT <value expression>)` returns the number of unique members in the `<value expression>` set. The `NULL`s have been thrown away before the counting took place and then all redundant duplicates are removed (i.e., we keep one copy). Again, an empty set returns a zero, just as with the other counting functions. Applying this function to a key or a unique column is the same as using the `COUNT(*)` function and the optimizer should be smart enough to spot it.

Notice that the use of the keywords `ALL` and `DISTINCT` follows the same pattern here as they did in the `[ALL | DISTINCT]` options in the `SELECT` clause of the query expressions. This is a common pattern in SQL.

### 29.1.1 Optimizing Aggregates with DISTINCT

This trick is due to Itzik Ben-Gan, and it may or may not help you depending on your optimizer. Assume you have to optimize queries that use both regular aggregates and ones with `DISTINCT`.

```
SELECT cust_id, COUNT(*) AS order_cnt,
   COUNT(DISTINCT order_date) AS order_day_cnt,
   SUM(order_amt) AS order_amt_tot
FROM Sales
GROUP BY cust_id;
```

The query groups the data by cust_id, and returns for each customer the total count of orders, distinct count of order dates (number of days with order activity), and total amount due from the customer. Some optimizers will do separate scans for the nondistinct aggregates and the distinct aggregates.

You can achieve the same task with a query that requires only one scan of the data. We use a CTE that groups the data by both customer id and order date, and then use it at a higher level of aggregation. Here's the complete solution:

```
WITH CustomerDailySales (cust_id, order_date, daily_order_
   cnt, order_amt_tot)
AS
(SELECT cust_id, order_date, COUNT(*), SUM(order_amt)
 FROM Sales
 GROUP BY cust_id, order_date)

SELECT cust_id,
   SUM(daily_order_cnt) AS daily_order_cnt,
   COUNT(order_date) AS order_day_distinct_cnt,
   SUM(order_amt) AS order_amt_tot
 FROM CustomerDailySales
GROUP BY cust_id;
```

This time, the optimizer scans the base table once, groups the data first to calculate aggregates based on (cust_id, order_date), and then aggregates on just the cust_id.

## 29.2 SUM( ) Function

This function works only with numeric values. You should also consult your particular product's manuals to find out the precision of the results for exact and approximate numeric data types. This is implementation-defined in the SQL Standards.

`SUM([ALL] <value expression>)` returns the numeric total of all known values. The `NULL`s are removed before the summation took place. An empty set returns an empty result set and not a zero. If there are other columns in the `SELECT` list, then that empty set will be converted into a `NULL`.

`SUM(DISTINCT <value expression>)` returns the numeric total of all known, unique values. The `NULL`s and all redundant duplicates have been removed before the summation took place. An empty set returns an empty result set and not a zero.

That last rule is hard for people to see. If there are other columns in the `SELECT` list, then that empty result set will be converted into a `NULL`. This is true for the rest of the Standard aggregate functions.

```
-- no rows
SELECT SUM(x)
FROM EmptyTable;

--one row with (0, NULL) in it
SELECT COUNT(*), SUM(x)
FROM EmptyTable;
```

The summation of a set of numbers looks as if it should be easy, but it is not. Make two tables with the same set of positive and negative approximate numeric values, but put one in random order and have the other sorted by absolute value. The sorted table will give more accurate results. The reason is simple; positive and negative values of the same magnitude will be added together and will get a chance to cancel each other out. There is also less chance of an overflow or underflow error during calculations. Most PC SQL implementations and a lot of mainframe implementations do not bother with this trick, because it would require a sort for every `SUM()` statement and would take a long time.

Whenever an exact or approximate numeric value is assigned to exact numeric, it may not fit into the storage allowed for it. SQL says that the database engine will use an approximation that preserves leading significant digits of the original number after rounding or truncating. The choice of whether to truncate or round is implementation-defined, however. This can lead to some surprises when you have to shift data among SQL implementations, or storage values from a host language program into an SQL table. It is probably a good idea to create the columns with one more decimal place than you think you need.

Truncation is defined as truncation toward zero; this means that 1.5 would truncate to 1, and −1.5 would truncate to −1. This is not true for all programming languages; everyone agrees on truncation toward zero for the positive numbers, but you will find that negative numbers may truncate away from zero (e.g., −1.5 would truncate to −2). SQL is also wishy-washy on rounding, leaving the implementation free to determine its method. There are two major types of rounding, the scientific method and the commercial method, which are discussed in Section 3.2.1 of Chapter 3.

## 29.3 AVG( ) Function

`AVG([ALL] <value expression>)` returns the average of the values in the value expression set. An empty set returns an empty result set. A set of all `NULL`s will become an empty set. Remember that in general AVG(x) is not the same as (SUM(x)/COUNT(*)); the SUM(x) function has thrown away the NULLs, but the COUNT(*) has not.

Likewise, AVG(DISTINCT <value expression>) returns the average of the distinct known values in the <value expression> set. Applying this function to a key or a unique column is the same as the using AVG(<value expression>) function.

Remember that in general AVG(DISTINCT x) is not the same as AVG(x) or (SUM(DISTINCT x)/COUNT(*)). The SUM(DISTINCT x) function has thrown away the duplicate values and NULLs, but the COUNT(*) has not. An empty set returns an empty result set.

The SQL engine is probably using the same code for the totaling in the AVG() that it used in the SUM() function. This leads to the same problems with rounding and truncation, so you should experiment a little with your particular product to find out what happens.

But even more troublesome than those problems is the problem with the average itself, because it does not really measure central tendency and can be very misleading. Consider the following chart, from Darrell Huff's superlative little book, *How to Lie with Statistics* (Huff, 1954; ISBN 978-0393310726). The Sample Company has 25 employees, earning the following salaries:

| Number of Employees | Salary | Statistic |
|---|---|---|
| 12 | $2,000 | Mode, Minimum |
| 1 | $3,000 | Median |
| 4 | $3,700 | |
| 3 | $5,000 | |
| 1 | $5,700 | Average |
| 2 | $10,000 | |
| 1 | $15,000 | |
| 1 | $45,000 | Maximum |

The average salary_amt (or, more properly, the arithmetic mean) is $5700. When the boss is trying to look good to the unions, he uses this figure. When the unions are trying to look impoverished, they use the mode, which is the most frequently occurring value, to show that the exploited workers are making $2000 (which is also the minimum salary_amt in this case).

A better measure in this case is the median, which will be discussed later; that is, the employee with just as many cases above him as below him. That gives us $3000. The rule for calculating the median is that if there is no actual entity with that value, you fake it.

Most people take an average of the two values on either side of where the median would be; others jump to the higher or lower value. The mode also has a problem because not every distribution of values has one mode. Imagine a country in which there are as many very poor people as there are very rich people and nobody in between. This would be a bimodal distribution. If there were sharp classes of incomes, that would be a multimodal distribution.

Some SQL products have median and mode aggregate functions as extensions, but they are not part of the SQL Standard. We will discuss how to write them in pure SQL in detail.

## 29.3.1 Averages with Empty Groups

Sometimes you need to count an empty set as part of the population when computing an average. This is easier to explain with an example that was posted on CompuServe. A fish and game warden is sampling different bodies of water for fish populations. Each sample falls into one or more groups (muddy bottoms, clear water, still water, and so on) and she is trying to find the average of something that is not there. This is neither quite as strange as it first sounds, nor quite as simple, either. She is collecting sample data on fish in a table like this:

```
CREATE TABLE Samples
(sample_id INTEGER NOT NULL,
fish_name CHAR(20) NOT NULL,
found_cnt INTEGER NOT NULL,
PRIMARY KEY (sample_id, fish_name));
```

The samples are then aggregated into sample groups. A single sample might fall into more than one group.

```
CREATE TABLE SampleGroups
(group_id INTEGER NOT NULL,
sample_id INTEGER NOT NULL,
PRIMARY KEY (group_id, sample_id);
```

Assume some of the data looks like this:

Samples

| sample_id | fish_name | found_cnt |
|---|---|---|
| 1 | 'Seabass' | 14 |
| 1 | 'Minnow' | 18 |
| 2 | 'Seabass' | 19 |

Sample Groups

| group_id | sample_id |
|---|---|
| 1 | 1 |
| 1 | 2 |
| 2 | 2 |

She needs to get the average number of each species of fish in the sample groups. For example, using sample group 1 as shown, which has samples 1 and 2, we could use the parameters : my_fish_name ='Minnow' and :my_group = 1 to find the average number of minnows in sample group 1, thus:

```
SELECT fish_name, AVG(found_cnt)
 FROM Samples
WHERE sample_id
  IN (SELECT sample_id
      FROM SampleGroups
     WHERE group_id = :my_group)
 AND fish_name = :my_fish_name
GROUP BY fish_name;
```

But this query will give us an average of 18 minnows, which is wrong. There were no minnows for sample_id = 2, so the average is ((18 + 0)/2) = 9. The other way is to do several steps to get the correct answer—first use a `SELECT` statement to get the number of samples involved, then another `SELECT` to get the sum, and then manually calculate the average.

The obvious answer is to enter a count of zero for each animal under each sample_id, instead of letting it be missing, so you can use the original query. You can create the missing rows with:

```
INSERT INTO Samples
SELECT M1.sample_id, M2.fish_name, 0
 FROM Samples AS M1, Samples AS M2
WHERE NOT EXISTS
  (SELECT *
    FROM Samples AS M3
   WHERE M1.sample_id = M3.sample_id
    AND M2.fish_name = M3.fish_name);
```

Unfortunately, it turns out that we have over 10,000 different species of fish and thousands of samples. This trick will fill up more disk space than we have on the machine. The best trick is to use this statement:

```
SELECT fish_name, SUM(found_cnt)/
   (SELECT COUNT(sample_id)
     FROM SampleGroups
    WHERE group_id = :my_group)
 FROM Samples
WHERE fish_name = :my_fish_name
GROUP BY fish_name;
```

This query is using the rule that the average is the sum of values divided by the count of the set. Another way to do this would be to use an OUTER JOIN and preserve all the group ids, but that would create NULLs for the fish that are not in some of the sample groups and you would have to handle the NULLs as zero.

## 29.3.2 Averages across Columns

The sum of several columns can be done with the COALESCE() function to effectively remove the NULLs by replacing them with zeroes like this:

```
SELECT (COALESCE(c1, 0.0)
   + COALESCE(c2, 0.0)
   + COALESCE(c3, 0.0)) AS c_total
 FROM Foobar;
```

Likewise, the minimum and maximum values of several columns can be done with a CASE expression, or the GREATEST() and LEAST() functions if you have that vendor extension.

Taking an average across several columns is easy if none of the columns are NULL. You simply add the values and divide by the number of columns. However, getting rid of NULLs is a bit harder. The first trick is to count the NULLs:

```
SELECT (COALESCE(c1-c1, 1)
   + COALESCE(c2-c2, 1)
   + COALESCE(c3-c3, 1)) AS null_cnt
 FROM Foobar;
```

The trick is to watch out for a row with all NULLs in it. This could lead to a division by zero error.

```
SELECT CASE WHEN COALESCE(c1, c2, c3) IS NULL
   THEN NULL
   ELSE (COALESCE(c1, 0.0)
     + COALESCE(c2, 0.0)
     + COALESCE(c3, 0.0))
     / (3 - (COALESCE(c1-c1, 1)
```

```
           + COALESCE(c2-c2, 1)
           + COALESCE(c3-c3, 1))
   END AS horizontal_avg
  FROM Foobar;
```

## 29.4 Extrema Functions

The `MIN()` and `MAX()` functions are known as extrema functions in mathematics. They assume that the elements of the set have an ordering, so that it makes sense to select a first or last element based on its value. SQL provides two simple extrema functions, and you can write queries to generalize these to (n) elements.

### 29.4.1 Simple Extrema Functions

`MAX([ALL | DISTINCT] <value expression>)` returns the greatest known value in the `<value expression>` set. This function will also work on character and temporal values, as well as numeric values. An empty set returns an empty result set. Technically, you can write `MAX(DISTINCT <value expression>)`, but it is the same as `MAX(ALL <value expression>)` or `MAX(<value expression>)`; this form exists only for completeness and nobody ever uses it.

`MIN([ALL | DISTINCT] <value expression>)` returns the smallest known value in the `<value expression>` set. This function will also work on character and temporal values, as well as numeric values. An empty set returns a `NULL`. Likewise, `MIN(DISTINCT <value expression>)` and `MIN (ALL <value expression>)` exist, but are defined only for completeness and nobody ever uses them.

The `MAX()` for a set of numeric values is the largest. The `MAX()` for a set of temporal data types is the one closest to '9999-12-31', which is the final data in the ISO 8601 Standard. The `MAX()` for a set of character strings is the last one in the ascending sort order. Likewise, the `MIN()` for a set of numeric values is the smallest. The `MIN()` for a set of temporal data types is furthest from '9999-12-31', which is the final data in the ISO 8601 Standard. The `MIN()` for a set of character strings is the first one in the ascending sort order, but you have to know the collation used.

People have a hard time understanding the `MAX()` and `MIN()` aggregate functions when they are applied to temporal data types. They seem to expect the `MAX()` to return the date closest to the current date. Likewise, if the set has no dates before the current date, they seem to expect the MIN() function to return the date closest to the current date. Human psychology wants to use the current time as an origin point for temporal reasoning.

Consider the predicate billing_date < (CURRENT_DATE - INTERVAL '90' DAY) as an example. Most people have to stop and figure out that this is looking for billings that are over 90 days past due. This same thing happens with MIN() and MAX() functions.

SQL also has funny rules about comparing VARCHAR strings, which can cause problems. When two strings are compared for equality, the shortest one is right-padded with blanks; then they are compared position for position. Thus, the strings 'John' and 'John' are equal. You will have to check your implementation of SQL to see which string is returned as the MAX() and which as the MIN(), or whether there is any pattern to it at all.

Another consideration is the collation used on columns. A column is sorted in an order defined by its collation; the same data element in different tables can have different local collations and therefore different extremas. Mixed collations like this are a sign of bad schema design.

There are some tricks with extrema functions in subqueries that differ from product to product. For example, to find the current employee status in a table of Salary Histories, the obvious query is:

```
SELECT emp_status, ..
 FROM SalaryHistory AS S0
WHERE S0.change_date
  = (SELECT MAX(S1.change_date)
      FROM SalaryHistory AS S1
     WHERE S0.emp_id = S1.emp_id);
```

But you can also write the query as:

```
SELECT emp_status, ..
 FROM SalaryHistory AS S0
WHERE NOT EXISTS
  (SELECT *
    FROM SalaryHistory AS S1
   WHERE S0.emp_id = S1.emp_id
    AND S0.change_date < S1.change_date);
```

The correlated subquery with a MAX() will be implemented by going to the subquery and building a working table, which is grouped by emp_id. Then for each group, you will keep track of the maximum and save it for the final result.

However, the NOT EXISTS version will find the first row that meets the criteria and when found, it will return TRUE. Therefore, the NOT EXISTS () predicate might run faster.

## 29.4.2 Generalized Extrema Functions

This is known as the Top (or Bottom) (n) values problems and it originally appeared in *EXPLAIN* magazine; it was submitted by Jim Wankowski of Hawthorne, CA (Wankowski). You are given a table of Personnel and their salaries. Write a single SQL query that will display the three highest salaries from that table. It is easy to find the maximum salary_amt with the simple query `SELECT MAX(salary_amt) FROM Personnel;`, but SQL does not have a maximum function that will return a group of high values from a column. The trouble with this query is that the specification is bad for several reasons.

1. How do we define best salary_amt in terms of an ordering? Is it base pay or does it include commissions? For the rest of this section, assume that we are using a simple table with a column that has the salary_amt for each employee.
2. What if we have three or fewer Personnel in the company? Do we report all the Personnel we do have? Or do we return a `NULL`, empty result set, or error message? This is the equivalent of calling the contest for lack of entries.
3. How do we handle two employees who tied? Include them all and allow the result set to be bigger than three? Pick an arbitrary subset and exclude someone? Or do we return a `NULL`, empty result set or error message?

To make these problem more explicit, consider this table:

Personnel

| emp_id | salary_amt |
|---|---|
| 'Able' | 1000.00 |
| 'Bill' | 900.00 |
| 'Charles' | 900.00 |
| 'Delta' | 800.00 |
| 'Eddy' | 700.00 |
| 'Fred' | 700.00 |
| 'George' | 700.00 |

Able, Bill, and Charles are the three highest paid Personnel, but \$1000.00, \$900.00, and \$800.00 are the three highest salaries. The highest salaries belong to Able, Bill, Charles, and Delta—a set with four elements.

The way that most new SQL programmers do this in other SQL products is produce a result with an ORDER BY clause, then read the first so many rows from that cursor result. In Standard SQL, cursors have an ORDER BY clause but no way to return a fixed number of rows. However, most SQL products have propriety syntax to clip the result set at exactly some number of rows. Oh, yes, did I mention that the whole table has to be sorted and that this can take some time if the table is large?

The best algorithm for this problem is the Partition algorithm by C. A. R. Hoare. This is the procedure in QuickSort that splits a set of values into three partitions—those greater than a pivot value, those less than the pivot, and those values equal to the pivot. The expected runtime is only (2*n) operations.

In practice, it is a good idea to start with a pivot at or near the k-th position you seek, because real data tends to have some ordering already in it. If the file is already in sorted order, this trick will return an answer in one pass. Here is the algorithm in Pascal.

```
CONST
 list_length = { some large number };
 ...
TYPE
 LIST = ARRAY [1..list_length] OF REAL;
 ...
PROCEDURE FindTopK (Kth INTEGER, records : LIST);
VAR pivot, left, right, start, finish: INTEGER;
BEGIN
start := 1;
finish := list_length;
WHILE start < finish
DO BEGIN
 pivot := records[Kth];
 left := start;
 right := finish;
 REPEAT
   WHILE (records[left] > pivot) DO left := left + 1;
   WHILE (records[right] < pivot) DO right := right - 1;
   IF (left >= right)
   THEN BEGIN { swap right and left elements }
     Swap (records[left], records[right]);
     left := left + 1;
     right := right - 1;
     END;
  UNTIL (left < right);
  IF (right < Kth) THEN start := left;
  IF (left > Kth) THEN finish := right;
  END;
```

```
{ the first k numbers are in positions 1 through kth, in no
   particular order except that the kth highest number is
   in position kth }
END.
```

The original articles in *EXPLAIN* magazine gave several solutions (Murchison; Wankowski).

One solution involved UNION operations on nested subqueries. The first result table was the maximum for the whole table, the second result table was the maximum for the table entries less than the first maximum, and so forth. The pattern is extensible. It looked like this:

```
SELECT MAX(salary_amt)
FROM Personnel
UNION
SELECT MAX(salary_amt)
FROM Personnel
WHERE salary_amt < (SELECT MAX(salary_amt)
        FROM Personnel)
UNION
SELECT MAX(salary_amt)
FROM Personnel
WHERE salary_amt < (SELECT MAX(salary_amt)
        FROM Personnel
       WHERE salary_amt
        < (SELECT MAX(salary_amt) FROM Personnel));
```

This answer can give you a pretty serious performance problem because of the subquery nesting and the UNION operations. Every UNION will trigger a sort to remove duplicate rows from the results, since salary_amt is not a UNIQUE column.

A special case of the use of the scalar subquery with the MAX() function is finding the last two values in a set to look for a change. This is most often done with date values for time series work. For example, to get the last two reviews for an employee:

```
SELECT :search_name, MAX(P1.review_date), P2.review_date
FROM Personnel AS P1, Personnel AS P2
WHERE P1.review_date < P2.review_date
 AND P1.emp_id = :search_name
 AND P2.review_date
  = (SELECT MAX(review_date) FROM Personnel)
GROUP BY P2.review_date;
```

The scalar subquery is not correlated, so it should run pretty fast and be executed only once.

An improvement on the UNION approach is to find the third highest salary_amt with a subquery, then return all the records with salaries that were equal or higher. This will handle ties; it looked like this:

```
SELECT DISTINCT salary_amt
 FROM Personnel
WHERE salary_amt
  >= (SELECT MAX(salary_amt)
      FROM Personnel
     WHERE salary_amt
       < (SELECT MAX(salary_amt)
           FROM Personnel
          WHERE salary_amt
            < (SELECT MAX(salary_amt)
                FROM Personnel)));
```

I am getting ahead of myself, but these days we have windowed queries that might perform better than any of these answers. But they might not; as usual, test alternate queries for yourself.

```
SELECT DISTINCT X.salary_amt
 FROM (SELECT salary_amt,
      DENSE_RANK()
      OVER (ORDER BY salary_amt DESC)
   FROM Personnel) AS X(salary_amt, sal_rank)
WHERE X.sal_rank <= 3;
```

Another answer is to use correlation names and return a single-row result table. This pattern is more easily extensible to larger groups; it will also present the results in sorted order without requiring the use of an `ORDER BY` clause. The disadvantage of this answer is that it will return a single row and not a column result. That might make it unusable for joining to other queries. It looked like this:

```
SELECT  MAX(P1.salary_amt),  MAX(P2.salary_amt),  MAX(P3.
   salary_amt)
 FROM Personnel AS P1, Personnel AS P2, Personnel AS P3
WHERE P1.salary_amt > P2.salary_amt
 AND P2.salary_amt > P3.salary_amt;
```

This approach will return the three highest salaries, assuming that you have at least three candidates. If not, you will be safer with this:

```
SELECT  MAX(P1.salary_amt),  MAX(P2.salary_amt),  MAX(P3.
   salary_amt)
 FROM Personnel AS P1
   LEFT OUTER JOIN
   Personnel AS P2
```

```
ON P1.salary_amt > P2.salary_amt
 LEFT OUTER JOIN
 Personnel AS P3
 ON P2.salary_amt > P3.salary_amt;
```

This will give NULLs if there are fewer than three salary amounts that qualify. This will run in Standard SQL-2003.

The worst way to do this is with scalar subquery expressions in the SELECT list. The query becomes:

```
SELECT (SELECT MAX (salary_amt)
     FROM Personnel) AS s1,
    (SELECT MAX (salary_amt)
      FROM Personnel
     WHERE salary_amt NOT IN (s1)) AS s2,
   (SELECT MAX (salary_amt)
     FROM Personnel
    WHERE salary_amt NOT IN (s1, s2)) AS s3,
   ...
   (SELECT MAX (salary_amt)
     FROM Personnel
    WHERE salary_amt NOT IN (s1, s2, ... s[n-1])) AS sn,
FROM Dummy;
```

where the table Dummy is anything, even an empty table.

Here is another version that will produce the ties on separate lines with the names of the personnel who made the cut. This answer is due to Pierre Boutquin.

```
SELECT P1.emp_id, P1.salary_amt
 FROM Personnel AS P1, Personnel AS P2
WHERE P1.salary_amt >= P2.salary_amt
GROUP BY P1.emp_id, P1.salary_amt
HAVING (SELECT COUNT(*) FROM Personnel) - COUNT(*) + 1 <= :n;
```

The idea is to use a little algebra. If we want to find (n of k) things, then the rejected subset of the set is of size (k-n). Using the sample data we would get this result.

Results

| emp_id | salary_amt |
|---|---|
| 'Able' | 1000.00 |
| 'Bill' | 900.00 |
| 'Charles' | 900.00 |

If we add a new employee at $900, we would also get him, but not a new employee at $800 or less. In many ways this is the most satisfying answer.

Here are two more versions of the solution:

```
SELECT P1.emp_id, P1.salary_amt
 FROM Personnel AS P1, Personnel AS P2
 GROUP BY P1.emp_id, P1.salary_amt
HAVING COUNT(CASE WHEN P1.salary_amt < P2.salary_amt
       THEN 1
       ELSE NULL END) + 1 <= :n;

SELECT P1.emp_id, P1.salary_amt
 FROM Personnel AS P1
   LEFT OUTER JOIN
   Personnel AS P2
   ON P1.salary_amt < P2.salary_amt
 GROUP BY P1.emp_id, P1.salary_amt
HAVING COUNT(P2.salary_amt) + 1 <= :n;
```

The subquery is unnecessary and can be eliminated with either of the previous solutions.

As an aside, if you were awake during your college set theory course, you will remember that John von Neumann's definition of ordinal numbers is based on nested sets. You can get a lot of ideas for self-joins from set theory theorems. John von Neumann was one of the greatest mathematicians of the last century and the inventor of the modern stored program computer and Game Theory. Know your nerd heritage!

It should be obvious that any number can replace three in the query. A subtle point is that the predicate `P1.salary_amt <= P2.salary_amt` will include the boundary value and so implies that if we have three or fewer Personnel, then we still have a result. If you want to call off the competition for lack of a quorum, then change the predicate to `P1.salary_amt < P2.salary_amt` instead.

Another way to express the query would be:

```
SELECT Elements.emp_id, Elements.salary_amt
 FROM Personnel AS Elements
 WHERE (SELECT COUNT(*)
     FROM Personnel AS Boundary
    WHERE Elements.salary_amt < Boundary.salary_amt) < 3;
```

Likewise, the `COUNT(*)` and comparisons in the scalar subquery expression can be changed to give slightly different results. You might want to test each version to see which one runs faster on your particular SQL product.

What if I want to allow ties? Then just change COUNT() to a COUNT(DISTINCT) function the HAVING clause, thus:

```
SELECT Elements.name, Elements.salary_amt
 FROM Personnel AS Elements, Personnel AS Boundary
WHERE Elements.salary_amt <= Boundary.salary_amt
GROUP BY Elements.name, Elements.salary_amt
HAVING COUNT(DISTINCT Boundary.salary_amt) <= 3;
```

This says that I want to count the values of salary_amt, not the salespersons, so that if two or more of the crew hit the same total, I will include them in the report as tied for a particular position. This also means that the results can be more than three rows because I can have ties. As you can see, it is easy to get a subtle change in the results with just a few simple changes to the predicates.

Notice that you can change the comparisons from <= to < and the COUNT(*) to COUNT(DISTINCT P2.salary_amt) to change the specification.

Ken Henderson came up with another version that uses derived tables and scalar subquery expressions in SQL.

```
SELECT P2.salary_amt
 FROM (SELECT (SELECT COUNT(DISTINCT P1.salary_amt)
          FROM Personnel AS P1
         WHERE P3.salary_amt >= P1.salary_amt) AS ranking,
       P3.salary_amt
    FROM Personnel AS P3) AS P2
WHERE P2.ranking <= 3;
```

You can get other aggregate functions by using this query with the IN predicate. Assume that I have SalaryHistory table from which I wish to determine the average pay for the three most recent pay changes of each employee. I am going to further assume that if you had three or fewer old salaries, you would still want to average the 1, 2, or 3 values you have on record.

```
SELECT S0.emp_id, AVG(S0.last_salary_amt)
 FROM SalaryHistory AS S0
WHERE S0.change_date
  IN (SELECT P1.change_date
      FROM SalaryHistory AS P1, SalaryHistory AS P2
     WHERE P1.change_date <= P2.change_date
     GROUP BY P1.change_date
     HAVING COUNT(*) <= 3)
 GROUP BY S0.emp_id;
```

### 29.4.3 Multiple Criteria Extrema Functions

Since the generalized extrema functions are based on sorting the data, it stands to reason that you could further generalize them to use multiple columns in a table. This can be done by changing the WHERE search condition. For example, to locate the top (n) tall and heavy employees for the basketball team, we could write:

```
SELECT P1.emp_id
 FROM Personnel AS P1, Personnel AS P2
WHERE P2.height >= P1.height -- major sort term
 OR (P2.height = P1.height -- next sort term
   AND P2.weight >= P1.weight)
GROUP BY P1.emp_id
HAVING COUNT(*) <= :n;
```

Procedural programmers will recognize this predicate because it is what they used to write to do a sort on more than one field in a file system. Now it becomes very important to look at the predicates at each level of nesting to be sure that you have the right theta operator. The ordering of the predicates is also critical—there is a difference in ordering by height within weight or by weight within height.

One improvement would be to use row comparisons:

```
SELECT P1.emp_id
 FROM Personnel AS P1, Personnel AS P2
WHERE (P2.height, P2.weight) <= (P1.height, P1.weight)
GROUP BY P1.emp_id
HAVING COUNT(*) <= 4;
```

The down side of this approach is that you cannot easily mix ascending and descending comparisons in the same comparison predicate. The trick is to make numeric columns negative to reverse the sense of the theta operator.

Before you attempt it, here is the scalar subquery version of the multiple extrema problems:

```
SELECT
(SELECT MAX(P0.height)
  FROM Personnel AS P0
  WHERE P0.weight = (SELECT MAX(weight)
           FROM Personnel AS P1)) AS s1,
(SELECT MAX(P0.height)
  FROM Personnel AS P0
  WHERE height NOT IN (s1)
    AND P0.weight = (SELECT MAX(weight)
            FROM Personnel AS P1
            WHERE height NOT IN (s1))) AS s2,
```

```
(SELECT MAX(P0.height)
  FROM Personnel AS P0
  WHERE height NOT IN (s1, s2)
    AND P0.weight = (SELECT MAX(weight)
              FROM Personnel AS P1
             WHERE height NOT IN (s1, s2))) AS s3
FROM Dummy;
```

Again, multiple criteria and their ordering would be expressed as multiple levels of subquery nesting. This picks the tallest people and decides ties with the greatest weight within that subset of personnel. Even though this looks awful and is hard to read, it does run fairly fast because the predicates are repeated and can be factored out by the optimizer.

Another form of multiple criteria is finding the generalized extrema functions within groupings; for example, find the top three salaries in each department. Adding the grouping constraints to the subquery expressions gives us an answer.

```
SELECT dept_nbr, salary_amt
 FROM Personnel AS P1
WHERE (SELECT COUNT(*)
   FROM Personnel AS P2
   WHERE P2.dept_nbr = P1.dept_nbr
    AND P2.salary_amt < P1.salary_amt) < :n;
```

or

```
SELECT P2.dept_nbr, MIN(P1.salary_amt)
 FROM Personnel AS P1, Personnel AS P2
WHERE P1.dept_nbr = P2.dept_nbr
 AND P1.salary_amt >= P2.salary_amt
GROUP BY P2.dept_nbr, P2.salary_amt
HAVING COUNT(DISTINCT P1.salary_amt) <= 3;
```

## 29.4.4 GREATEST( ) and LEAST( ) Functions

Oracle has a proprietary pair of functions that return greatest and least values, respectively—a sort of "horizontal" `MAX()` and `MIN()`. The syntax is `GREATEST (<list of values>)` and `LEAST (<list of values>)`. Awkwardly enough, DB2 allows `MIN` and `MAX` as synonyms for `LEAST` and `GREATEST`

If you have `NULL`s, then you have to decide if they sort high or low, if they are excluded, or if you propagate the `NULL`; you can define this function several ways.

If you don't have `NULL`s in the data:

```
CASE WHEN col1 > col2
THEN col1 ELSE col2 END
```

If you want the highest non-NULL value:

```
CASE WHEN col1 > col2
 THEN col1 ELSE COALESCE(col2, col1) END
```

If you want to return NULL where one of the cols is NULL:

```
CASE WHEN col1 > col2 OR col1 IS NULL
 THEN col1 ELSE col2 END
```

But for the rest of this section, let's assume (a < b) and `NULL` is high:

```
GREATEST (a, b) = b
GREATEST (a, NULL) = NULL
GREATEST (NULL, b) = NULL
GREATEST (NULL, NULL) = NULL
```

which we can write as:

```
GREATEST(x, y) ::= CASE WHEN (COALESCE (x, y) > COALESCE
   (y, x))
        THEN x
        ELSE y END
```

The rules for `LEAST()` are:

```
LEAST (a, b) = a
LEAST (a, NULL) = a
LEAST (NULL, b) = b
LEAST (NULL, NULL) = NULL
```

which is written:

```
LEAST(x, y) ::= CASE WHEN (COALESCE (x, y) <= COALESCE
   (y, x))
         THEN COALESCE (x, y)
         ELSE COALESCE (y, x) END
```

This can be done in Standard SQL, but takes a little bit of work. Let's assume that we have a table that holds the scores for each player in a series of five games, and we want to get his best score from all five games.

```
CREATE TABLE Games
(player CHAR(10) NOT NULL PRIMARY KEY,
score_1 INTEGER NOT NULL DEFAULT 0,
score_2 INTEGER NOT NULL DEFAULT 0,
score_3 INTEGER NOT NULL DEFAULT 0,
score_4 INTEGER NOT NULL DEFAULT 0,
score_5 INTEGER NOT NULL DEFAULT 0);
```

We want to find the `GREATEST (score_1, score_2, score_3, score_4, score_5)`.

```
SELECT player, MAX(CASE X.seq_nbr
         WHEN 1 THEN score_1
         WHEN 2 THEN score_2
         WHEN 3 THEN score_3
         WHEN 4 THEN score_4
         WHEN 5 THEN score_5
         ELSE NULL END) AS best_score
FROM Games
  CROSS JOIN
  (VALUES (1), (2), (3), (4), (5)) AS X(seq_nbr)
GROUP BY player;
```

Another approach is to use a pure CASE expression:

```
CASE
WHEN score_1 <= score_2 AND score_1 <= score_3
  AND score_1 <= score_4 AND score_1 <= score_5
THEN score_1
WHEN score_2 <= score_3 AND score_2 <= score_4
  AND score_2 <= score_5
THEN score_2
WHEN score_3 <= score_4 AND score_3 <= score_5
THEN score_3
WHEN score_4 <= score_5
THEN score_4
ELSE score_5
END
```

A final trick is to use a bit of algebra. You can define

```
GREATEST(a, b) ::= (a + b + ABS(a - b)) / 2
LEAST(a, b) ::= (a + b - ABS(a - b)) / 2
```

Then iterate on it as a recurrence relation on numeric values. For example, for three items, you can use GREATEST (a, GREATEST(b, c)), which expands out to:

```
((a + b) + ABS(a - b)
 + 2 * c + ABS((a + b) + ABS(a - b)
 - 2 * c))/4
```

You need to watch for possible overflow errors if the numbers are large and NULLs propagate in the math functions. Here is the answer for five scores.

```
(score_1 + score_2 + 2*score_3 + 4*score_4 + 8*score_5
+ ABS(score_1 - score_2) + ABS((score_1 + score_2)
  + ABS(score_1 - score_2) - 2*score_3)
+ ABS(score_1 + score_2 + 2*score_3 - 4*score_4 + ABS(score_1
  - score_2) + ABS((score_1 + score_2 - 2*score_3) +
  ABS(score_1 - score_2)))
```

```
+ ABS(score_1 + score_2 + 2*score_3 + 4*score_4 - 8*score_5
+ ABS(score_1 - score_2) + ABS((score_1 + score_2) +
  ABS(score_1 - score_2) - 2*score_3)
+ ABS(score_1 + score_2 + 2*score_3 - 4*score_4 + ABS(score_1
  - score_2) + ABS((score_1 + score_2 - 2*score_3) +
  ABS(score_1 - score_2))) )) / 16
```

## 29.5 The LIST( ) Aggregate Function

The LIST([DISTINCT] <string expression>) is part of Sybase's SQL Anywhere (formerly WATCOM SQL). It is the only aggregate function to work on character strings. It takes a column of strings, removes the NULLs, and merges them into a single result string having commas between each of the original strings. The DISTINCT option removes duplicates as well as NULLs before concatenating the strings together. This function is a generalized version of concatenation, just as SUM() is a generalized version of addition.

MySQL 4.1 extended this function into the GROUP_CONCAT() function, which does the same thing, but adds options for ORDER BY and SEPARATOR

This is handy when you use SQL to write SQL queries. As one simple example, you can apply it against the schema tables and obtain the names of all the columns in a table, then use that list to expand a SELECT * into the current column list.

### 29.5.1 LIST Aggregate with Recursive CTE

The first thing you will need to do is to add a column to give a sequence number to order each item to be put in the list. This can be done with a ROW_NUMBER()function, but let's assume the table already has such a column:

```
CREATE TABLE Make_String
(list_seq INTEGER NOT NULL PRIMARY KEY,
cat_string VARCHAR(10) NOT NULL);

INSERT INTO Make_String
VALUES (1, 'abc'), (2, 'bcd'), (3, 'cde'), (4, 'def'),
  (5, 'efg'), (6, 'fgh'), (7, 'ghi');
```

The desired result is:

```
'abc, bcd, cde, def, efg, fgh, ghi'
```

This can be done with a recursive CTE:

```
WITH RECURSIVE
String_Tail(list_seq, cat_string)
AS
```

```
(SELECT list_seq, cat_string
 FROM Make_String
 WHERE list_seq > 1),

String_Head(list, max_list_seq)
AS
(SELECT cat_string, 1
 FROM String_Head
UNION ALL
SELECT String_Head.cat_string || ', ' || String_Tail.
   cat_string,
   String_Head.max_list_seq + 1
 FROM String_Tail, String_Head
WHERE String_Tail.list_seq = String_Head.max_list_seq + 1)

SELECT cat_list
 FROM String_Head
WHERE max_list_seq
   = (SELECT MAX(list_seq)
     FROM Make_String);
```

The interesting side effect is that you get all the left-to-right concatenations.

## 29.5.2 The LIST( ) Function by Crosstabs

Carl Federl used this to get a similar result:

```
CREATE TABLE Crosstabs
(seq_nbr INTEGER NOT NULL PRIMARY KEY,
seq_nbr_1 INTEGER NOT NULL,
seq_nbr_2 INTEGER NOT NULL,
seq_nbr_3 INTEGER NOT NULL,
seq_nbr_4 INTEGER NOT NULL,
seq_nbr_5 INTEGER NOT NULL);

INSERT INTO Crosstabs
VALUES (1, 1, 0, 0, 0, 0),
   (2, 0, 1, 0, 0, 0),
   (3, 0, 0, 1, 0, 0),
   (4, 0, 0, 0, 1, 0),
   (5, 0, 0, 0, 0, 1);

SELECT Clothes.id,
   TRIM (MAX(SUBSTRING(item_name FROM 1 FOR seq_nbr_1 * 10))
|| ' ' || MAX(SUBSTRING(item_name FROM 1 FOR
   seq_nbr_2 * 10))
|| ' ' || MAX(SUBSTRING(item_name FROM 1 FOR
   seq_nbr_3 * 10))
|| ' ' || MAX(SUBSTRING(item_name FROM 1 FOR
   seq_nbr_4 * 10))
```

```
|| ' ' || MAX(SUBSTRING(item_name FROM 1 FOR
   seq_nbr_5 * 10)))
 FROM Clothes, Crosstabs
WHERE Clothes.seq_nbr = Crosstabs.seq_nbr
 AND Clothes.worn_flag = 'Y'
GROUP BY Clothes.id;
```

## 29.6 The PRD( ) Aggregate Function

Bob McGowan sent me a message on CompuServe asking for help with a problem. His client, a financial institution, tracks investment performance with a table something like this:

```
CREATE TABLE Performance
(portfolio_id CHAR(7) NOT NULL,
execute_date DATE NOT NULL,
rate_of_return DECIMAL(13,7) NOT NULL);
```

In order to calculate a rate of return over a date range, you use the formula:

```
(1 + rate_of_return [day_1])
* (1 + rate_of_return [day_2])
* (1 + rate_of_return [day_3])
* (1 + rate_of_return [day_4])
...
* (1 + rate_of_return [day_N])
```

How would you construct a query that would return one row for each portfolio's return over the date range? What Mr. McGowan really wants is an aggregate function in the SELECT clause to return a columnar product, like the SUM() returns a columnar total.

If you were a math major, you would write these functions as capital Sigma (<uppercase sigma>) for summation and capital Pi for product (<uppercase pi>). If such an aggregate function existed in SQL, the syntax for it would look something like:

```
PRD ([DISTINCT] <expression>)
```

Although I am not sure that there is any use for the DISTINCT option, the new aggregate function would let us write his problem simply as:

```
SELECT portfolio_id, PRD(1.00 + rate_of_return)
 FROM Performance
WHERE execute_date BETWEEN start_date AND end_date
GROUP BY portfolio_id;
```

### 29.6.1 PRD( ) Function by Expressions

There is a trick for doing this, but you need a second table that looks like this for a period of five days:

```
CREATE TABLE BigPi
(execute_date DATE NOT NULL,
day_1 INTEGER NOT NULL,
day_2 INTEGER NOT NULL,
day_3 INTEGER NOT NULL,
day_4 INTEGER NOT NULL,
day_5 INTEGER NOT NULL);
```

Let's assume we wanted to look at January 6 to 10, so we need to update the execute_date column to that range, thus:

```
INSERT INTO BigPi
VALUES ('2006-01-06', 1, 0, 0, 0, 0),
   ('2006-01-07', 0, 1, 0, 0, 0),
   ('2006-01-08', 0, 0, 1, 0, 0),
   ('2006-01-09', 0, 0, 0, 1, 0),
   ('2006-01-10', 0, 0, 0, 0, 1);
```

The idea is that there is a one in the column when BigPi.execute_date is equal to the n-th date in the range and zero otherwise. The query for this problem is:

```
SELECT portfolio_id,
   (SUM((1.00 + P1.rate_of_return) * M1.day_1) *
   SUM((1.00 + P1.rate_of_return) * M1.day_2) *
   SUM((1.00 + P1.rate_of_return) * M1.day_3) *
   SUM((1.00 + P1.rate_of_return) * M1.day_4) *
   SUM((1.00 + P1.rate_of_return) * M1.day_5)) AS product
FROM Performance AS P1, BigPi AS M1
WHERE M1.execute_date = P1.execute_date
AND P1.execute_date BETWEEN '2006-01-06' AND '2006-01-10'
GROUP BY portfolio_id;
```

If anyone is missing a rate_of_return entry on a date in that range, their product will be zero. That might be fine, but if you needed to get a NULL when you have missing data, then replace each SUM() expression with a CASE expression like this:

```
CASE WHEN SUM((1.00 + P1.rate_of_return) * M1.day_N) = 0.00
 THEN CAST (NULL AS DECIMAL(6, 4))
 ELSE SUM((1.00 + P1.rate_of_return) * M1.day_N)
END
```

or if your SQL has the full SQL set of expressions, with this version:

```
COALESCE (SUM((1.00 + P1.rate_of_return) * M1.day_N), 0.00)
```

### 29.6.2 The PRD( ) Aggregate Function by Logarithms

Roy Harvey, another SQL guru who answered questions on CompuServe, found a different solution. If you are old enough to have used a slide rule or if you had a good high school math class, you know that you can multiply numbers by adding their logarithms and then taking the exponential of the sum. The nice part of this solution is that you can also use the DISTINCT option in the SUM() function.

But there are a lot of warnings about this approach. The Standard allows only natural logarithms shown as LN(), but you will see LOG10() for the logarithm base 10 and perhaps LOG(<parameter>, <base>) for a general logarithm function. Since the logarithm of zero or less is undefined, the Standard requires an exception to be raised. But some older SQL might return a zero or a NULL. Likewise, the Standard also defines the exponential function as EXP() as its inverse.

The expression for the product of a column from logarithm and exponential functions is:

```
SELECT ((EXP (SUM (LN (CASE WHEN nbr = 0.00
                  THEN CAST (NULL AS FLOAT)
                  ELSE ABS(nbr) END))))
  * (CASE WHEN MIN (ABS (nbr)) = 0.00
      THEN 0.00
      ELSE 1.00 END)
  * (CASE WHEN MOD (SUM (CASE WHEN SIGN(nbr) = -1
                  THEN 1
                  ELSE 0 END), 2) = 1
      THEN -1.00
      ELSE 1.00 END) AS big_pi
FROM NumberTable;
```

The nice part of this is that you can also use the SUM (DISTINCT <expression>) option to get the equivalent of PRD (DISTINCT <expression>).

You should watch the data type of the column involved and use either integer 0 and 1 or decimal 0.00 and 1.00 as is appropriate in the CASE statements. It is worth studying the three CASE expressions that make up the terms of the Prod calculation.

The first CASE expression is to insure that all zeros and negative numbers are converted to a nonnegative or NULL for the SUM() function, just in case your SQL raises an exception.

The second CASE expression will return zero as the answer if there was a zero in the nbr column of any selected row. The MIN(ABS(nbr)) is a handy trick for detecting the existence of a zero in a list of both positive and negative numbers with an aggregate function.

The third CASE expression will return minus one if there was an odd number of negative numbers in the nbr column. The innermost CASE expression uses a SIGN() function, which returns +1 for a positive number, −1 for a negative number, and 0 for a zero. The SUM() counts the −1 results then the MOD() functions determines if the count was odd or even.

I present this version of the query first, because this is how I developed the answer. We can do a much better job with a little algebra and logic:

```
SELECT CASE MIN (SIGN (nbr))
   WHEN 1 THEN EXP (SUM (LN (nbr))) -- all positive numbers
   WHEN 0 THEN 0.00 -- some zeros
   WHEN -1 -- some negative numbers
   THEN (EXP (SUM (LN (ABS(nbr))))
     * (CASE WHEN
         MOD (SUM (ABS (SIGN(nbr)-1/ 2)), 2) = 1
         THEN -1.00 ELSE 1.00 END))
   ELSE CAST (NULL AS FLOAT) END AS big_pi
FROM NumberTable;
```

The idea is that there are three special cases—all positive numbers, one or more zeros, and some negative numbers in the set. You can find out what your situation is with a quick test on the SIGN() of the minimum value in the set.

Within the case where you have negative numbers, there are two subcases: (1) an even number of negatives or (2) an odd number of negatives. You then need to apply some high school algebra to determine the sign of the final result.

Itzak Ben-Gan had problems implementing this in an older version of SQL Server, which are worth passing along in case your SQL product also has them. The query as written returns a domain error in SQL Server, even though it should not had the result expressions in the CASE expression been evaluated *after* the conditional flow had performed a short circuit evaluation. Examining the execution plan of the previous query, it looks like the optimizer evaluates all the possible result expressions in a step prior to handling the flow of the CASE expression.

This means that in the expression after WHEN 1 ... the LN() function is also invoked in an intermediate phase for zeros and negative numbers, and in the expression after WHEN −1 ... the LN(ABS()) is also invoked in an intermediate phase for zeroes. This explains the domain error.

To handle this, I had to use the ABS() and NULLIF() functions in the positive numbers when CLAUSE, and the NULLIF() function in the negative numbers when CLAUSE:

```
 . . .
 WHEN 1 THEN EXP(SUM(LN(ABS(NULLIF(result, 0.00)))))
and
 . . .
 WHEN -1
 THEN EXP(SUM(LN(ABS(NULLIF(result, 0.00)))))
   * CASE . . .
```

If you are sure that you will have only positive values in the column being computed, then you can use

```
PRD(<exp>) = EXP(SUM(LN (<exp>)))
```

As an aside, the book *Bypasses: A Simple Approach to Complexity* (Z. A. Melzak, Wiley-Interscience, 1983, ISBN 0-471-86854-X), is a short mathematical book on the general principle of conjugacy. This is the method of using a transform and its inverse to reduce the complexity of a calculation.

## 29.7 Bitwise Aggregate Functions

This is not a recommended practice, since it will destroy First Normal Form (1NF) by overloading a column with a vector whose components have individual meanings. But it is common enough that I have to mention it. Instead of giving each attribute in the data model its own column, bad programmers will assign a meaning to each bit in the binary representation of an INTEGER or SMALLINT.

This leads to a huge problem with the hardware being ones-complement or twos-complement math, and how NULLs are handled. Microsoft SQL Server at one time implemented a BIT data type that was a true bit type that took only the values {0, 1} just like assembly languages. Later, it was made into a numeric data type that was NULL-able.

Some products will actually expose the physical model for the data types and have proprietary bit-wise BIT_AND and BIT_OR operators. Most products do not implement bit-wise aggregate Boolean operators, however. But I feel like a furniture maker who is telling you what are the best rocks with which to drive screws into wood.

To reiterate, an aggregate function must:

1. Drop all the NULLs.
2. Drop all redundant duplicates if DISTINCT is in the parameter list.

3. Retain all redundant duplicates if ALL or no other keyword is in the parameter list.
4. Perform the required calculation on the remaining values in the expression.
5. Return a NULL result for an empty set or for a set of all NULLs (which would be empty after application of (1)).

Notice that rules (2) and (3) do not matter with bitwise operators, since (a BIT_OR a) = a and (a BIT_AND a) = a.

### 29.7.1 Bitwise OR Aggregate Functions

Let's create a simple table that holds the columns of bits as an integer. The CHECK() constraint prevents negative numbers and bit strings of different lengths.

```
CREATE Table Foobar
(bits INTEGER -- nullable for testing
   CHECK(bits BETWEEN 0 AND 15));
```

What we want is a bit-wise OR on the bits column.

```
SELECT MAX (CASE WHEN MOD (bits/1, 2) = 1
         AND bits IS NOT NULL
       THEN 1 ELSE 0 END)
   + MAX (CASE WHEN MOD (bits/2, 2) = 1
           AND bits IS NOT NULL
        THEN 2 ELSE 0 END)
   + MAX (CASE WHEN MOD (bits/4, 2) = 1
           AND bits IS NOT NULL
       THEN 4 ELSE 0 END)
   + MAX (CASE WHEN MOD (bits/8, 2) = 1
           AND bits IS NOT NULL
       THEN 8 ELSE 0 END)
FROM Foobar;
```

The bits/1 is redundant, but I used it to show the pattern for the construction of this expression. The hope is that a good optimizer will use a CASE expression inside the MAX() function. This immediately tells the optimizer that the set of possible answers is limited (in these expressions, limited to {0, 2^n}) so that once any row has returned the highest possible value, the evaluation can stop. The bad news with this expression is that a NULL in the bits column will return 0000. This can be corrected by adding

```
SIGN(MAX(bits)) * (<bitwise OR expression>)
```

If Foobar is all zeros, then the SIGN() function will return a zero and an optimizer can spot this short-cut evaluation. If the table is empty or the bits column is all NULLs, the SIGN() will get a NULL from MAX(bits) and propagate it. If bits are declared NOT NULL, then do not use this factor.

### 29.7.2 Bitwise AND Aggregate Function

This code is obvious from the previous discussion. The MAX() now becomes a MIN(), since a single zero can set a bit in the aggregate to zero. The trick with the SIGN() function stays the same as before.

```
SELECT SIGN(MAX(bits)) *
   MIN (CASE WHEN MOD (bits/1, 2) = 1
          AND bits IS NOT NULL
      THEN 1 ELSE 0 END)
   + MIN (CASE WHEN MOD (bits/2, 2) = 1
           AND bits IS NOT NULL
      THEN 2 ELSE 0 END)
   + MIN (CASE WHEN MOD (bits/4, 2) = 1
           AND bits IS NOT NULL
      THEN 4 ELSE 0 END)
   + MIN (CASE WHEN MOD (bits/8, 2) = 1
          AND bits IS NOT NULL
      THEN 8 ELSE 0 END)
FROM Foobar;
```

30

# ADVANCED GROUPING, WINDOWED AGGREGATION, AND OLAP IN SQL

Most SQL programmers work with OLTP (Online Transaction Processing) databases and have had no exposure to Online Analytic Processing (OLAP) and data warehousing. OLAP is concerned with summarizing and reporting data, so the schema designs and common operations are very different from the usual SQL queries.

As a gross generalization, everything you knew in OLTP is reversed in a data warehouse.

1. OLTP changes data in short, frequent transactions. A data warehouse is bulk loaded with static data on a schedule. The data remains constant once it is in place.
2. OLTP databases want to store only the data needed to do its current work. A data warehouse wants all the historical data it can hold. In 2008, Teradata Corporation announced it had five customers running data warehouses larger than a petabyte. The "Petabyte Power Players" club included eBay, with 5 petabytes of data; Wal-Mart Stores, which has 2.5 petabytes; Bank of America, which is storing 1.5 petabytes; Dell, which has a 1 petabyte data warehouse; and an unnamed bank. The definition of a petabyte is 2^50 = 1,125,899,906,842,624 bytes = 1024 terabytes, or roughly 10^15 bytes.
3. OLTP queries tend to be for simple facts. Data warehouse queries tend to be aggregate relationships that are more complex. For example, an OLTP query might ask, "How much chocolate did Joe Celko buy?" whereas a data warehouse might ask, "What is the correlation between chocolate purchases, geographic location, and wearing tweed?"
4. OLTP wants to run as fast as possible. A data warehouse is more concerned with the accuracy of computations and it is willing to wait to get an answer to a complex query.

**Joe Celko's SQL for Smarties. DOI: 10.1016/B978-0-12-382022-8.00030-2**

5. Properly designed OLTP databases are normalized. A data warehouse is usually a Star or Snowflake Schema, which is highly denormalized. The Star Schema is due to Ralph Kimball; you can get more details about it in his books and articles.

## 30.1 Star Schema

The Star Schema is a violation of basic normalization rules. There is a large central fact table. This table contains all the facts about an event that you wish to report on, such as sales, in one place. In an OLTP, the inventory would be in one table, the sales in another table, customers in a third table, and so forth. In the data warehouse, they are all in one huge table.

The dimensions of the values in the fact table are in smaller tables that allow you to pick a scale or unit of measurement on that dimension in the fact table. For example, the time dimension for the Sales fact table might be grouped by year, month within year, week within month. Then a weight dimension could give you pounds, kilograms, or stock packaging sizes. A category dimension might classify the stock by department. And so forth. This lets me ask for my fact aggregated in any granularity of units I wish, and perhaps dropping some of the dimensions.

Until recent changes in SQL, OLAP queries had to be done with special OLAP-centric languages, such as Microsoft's Multidimensional Expressions (MDX). Be assured that the power of OLAP is not found in the wizards or GUIs presented in the vendor demos. The wizards and GUI are often the glitter that lures the uninformed.

Many aspects of OLAP are already integrated with the relational database engine itself. This blending of technology blurs the distinction between an RDBMS and OLAP data management technology, effectively challenging the passive role often relegated to relational databases with regard to dimensional data. The more your RDBMS can address the needs of both traditional relational data and dimensional data, then you can reduce the cost of OLAP-only technology and get more out of your investment in RDBMS technology, skills, and resources. But don't confuse what SQL can do for you with reporting tools or the power of a statistical package, either.

## 30.2 `GROUPING` Operators

OLAP functions add the `ROLLUP` and `CUBE` extensions to the `GROUP BY` clause. The `ROLLUP` and `CUBE` are often referred to as super-groups. They can be written in older Standard SQL using `GROUP BY` and `UNION` operators.

As expected, NULLs form their own group just as before. However, we now have a GROUPING(<column reference>) function, which checks for NULLs that are the results of aggregation over that <column reference> during the execution of a grouped query containing CUBE, ROLLUP, or GROUPING SET, returns one if they were created by the query, and returns a zero otherwise.

SQL:2003 added a multicolumn version that constructs a binary number from the ones and zeros of the columns in the list in an implementation-defined exact numeric data type. Here is a recursive definition:

```
GROUPING (<column ref 1>, ..., <column ref n-1>, <column
   ref n>)
```

is equivalent to:

```
(2 *(<column ref 1>, ..., <column ref n-1>) + GROUPING
   (<column ref n>))
```

### 30.2.1 GROUP BY GROUPING SET

The GROUPING SET(<column list>) is shorthand in SQL-99 for a series of UNION-ed queries that are common in reports. For example, to find the total:

```
SELECT dept_name, CAST(NULL AS CHAR(10)) AS job_title,
   COUNT(*)
 FROM Personnel
GROUP BY dept_name
UNION ALL
SELECT CAST(NULL AS CHAR(8)) AS dept_name, job_title,
   COUNT(*)
 FROM Personnel
GROUP BY job_title;
```

It can be rewritten like this:

```
SELECT dept_name, job_title, COUNT(*)
 FROM Personnel
GROUP BY GROUPING SET (dept_name, job_title);
```

There is a problem with all the OLAP grouping functions. They will generate NULLs for each dimension at the subtotal levels. How do you tell the difference between a real NULL and a generated NULL? This is a job for the GROUPING() function, which returns 0 for NULLs in the original data and 1 for generated NULLs that indicate a subtotal.

```
SELECT CASE GROUPING(dept_name)
   WHEN 1 THEN 'department total'
   ELSE dept_name END AS dept_name,
   CASE GROUPING(job_title)
   WHEN 1 THEN 'job total'
```

```
    ELSE job_title_name END AS job_title
  FROM Personnel
  GROUP BY GROUPING SETS (dept_name, job_title);
```

The grouping set concept can be used to define other OLAP groupings.

### 30.2.2 ROLLUP

A ROLLUP group is an extension to the GROUP BY clause in SQL-99 that produces a result set that contains subtotal rows in addition to the 'regular' grouped rows. Subtotal rows are super-aggregate rows that contain further aggregates whose values are derived by applying the same column functions that were used to obtain the grouped rows. A ROLLUP grouping is a series of grouping-sets.

```
GROUP BY ROLLUP (a, b, c)
```

is equivalent to:

```
GROUP BY GROUPING SETS
(a, b, c)
(a, b)
(a)
()
```

Notice that the (n) elements of the ROLLUP translates to (n + 1) grouping set. Another point to remember is that the order in which the grouping-expression is specified is significant for ROLLUP.

The ROLLUP is basically the classic totals and subtotals report presented as an SQL table.

### 30.2.3 CUBES

The CUBE super-group is the other SQL-99 extension to the GROUP BY clause that produces a result set that contains all the subtotal rows of a ROLLUP aggregation and, in addition, contains 'cross-tabulation' rows. Cross-tabulation rows are additional 'super-aggregate' rows. They are, as the name implies, summaries across columns if the data were represented as a spreadsheet. Like ROLLUP, a CUBE group can also be thought of as a series of grouping-sets. In the case of a CUBE, all permutations of the cubed grouping-expression are computed along with the grand total. Therefore, the n elements of a CUBE translate to 2n grouping-sets.

```
GROUP BY CUBE (a, b, c)
```

is equivalent to:

```
GROUP BY GROUPING SETS
(a, b, c) (a, b) (a, c) (b, c) (a) (b) (c) ()
```

Notice that the three elements of the CUBE translate to eight grouping sets. Unlike ROLLUP, the order of specification of elements doesn't matter for CUBE:

CUBE (julian_day, sales_person) is the same as CUBE (sales_person, julian_day).

CUBE is an extension of the ROLLUP function. The CUBE function not only provides the column summaries we saw in ROLLUP but also calculates the row summaries and grand totals for the various dimensions.

## 30.2.4 OLAP Examples of SQL

The following example illustrates advanced OLAP function used in combination with traditional SQL. In this example, we want to perform a ROLLUP function of sales by region and city.

```
SELECT B.region_nbr, S.city_id, SUM(S.sales_amt) AS
   total_sales
 FROM SalesFacts AS S, MarketLookup AS M
WHERE EXTRACT (YEAR FROM trans_date) = 2011
 AND S.city_id = B.city_id
 AND B.region_nbr = 6
GROUP BY ROLLUP(B.region_nbr, S.city_id);
```

The resultant set is reduced by explicitly querying region 6 and the year 1999. A sample result of the SQL follows. The result shows ROLLUP of two groupings (region, city) returning three totals, including region, city, and grand total.

**Yearly Sales by City and Region**

| region_nbr | city_id | total_sales |
|---|---|---|
| 6 | 1 | 81655 ◄ city within region total |
| 6 | 2 | 131512 |
| 6 | 3 | 58384 |
| ... | ... | ... |
| 6 | 30 | 1733 |
| 6 | 31 | 5058 |
| 6 | NULL | 1190902 ◄ region six total |
| NULL | NULL | 1190902 ◄ grand total |

## 30.3 The Window Clause

The window clause is also called the OVER() clause informally. The idea is that the table is first broken into partitions with the PARTITION BY subclause. The partitions are then sorted by the ORDER BY clause. An imaginary cursor sits on the current row where the windowed function is invoked. A subset of the rows in the current partition is defined by the number of rows before and after the current row; if there is a <window frame exclusion> option then certain rows are removed from the subset. Finally, the subset is passed to an aggregate or ordinal function to return a scalar value. The window functions are functions and follow the rules of any function, but with a different syntax. The window part can be either a <window name> or a <window specification>. The <window specification> gives the details of the window in the OVER() clause and this is how most programmers use it. However, you can define a window and give it a name, then use the name in the OVER() clauses of several statements.

The window works the same way, regardless of the syntax used. The BNF is:

```
<window function>::= <window function type> OVER <window
   name or specification>

<window function type>::=
 <rank function type> | ROW_NUMBER ()| <aggregate
   function>

<rank function type>::= RANK() | DENSE_RANK() | PERCENT_
   RANK() | CUME_DIST()

<window name or specification>::= <window name> | <in-line
   window specification>

<in-line window specification>::= <window specification>
```

The window clause has three subclauses: partitioning, ordering, and aggregation grouping or window frame.

### 30.3.1 PARTITION BY Subclause

A set of column names specifies the partitioning, which is applied to the rows that the preceding FROM, WHERE, GROUP BY, and HAVING clauses produced. If no partitioning is specified, the entire set of rows composes a single partition and the aggregate function applies to the whole set each time. Though the partitioning looks a bit like a GROUP BY, it is not the same thing. A GROUP BY collapses the rows in a partition into a single row. The partitioning within a window, though, simply organizes the rows into groups without collapsing them.

### 30.3.2 ORDER BY Subclause

The ordering within the window clause is like the ORDER BY clause in a CURSOR. It includes a list of sort keys and indicates whether they should be sorted ascending or descending. The important thing to understand is that ordering is applied within each partition. The other subclauses are optional, but don't make any sense without an ORDER BY and/or PARTITION BY in the function.

```
<sort specification list>::= <sort specification> [{,<sort
   specification>}...]

<sort specification>::= <sort key> [<ordering specification>]
   [<null ordering>]

<sort key>::= <value expression>

<ordering specification>::= ASC | DESC

<null ordering>::= NULLS FIRST | NULLS LAST
```

It is worth mentioning that the rules for an ORDER BY subclause have changed to be more general than they were in earlier SQL Standards.

1. A sort can now be a <value expression> and is not limited to a simple column in the select list. However, it is still a good idea to use only column names so that you can see the sorting order in the result set
2. <sort specification> specifies the sort direction for the corresponding sort key. If DESC is not specified in the i-th <sort specification>, then the sort direction for Ki is ascending and the applicable <comp op> is the <less than operator>. Otherwise, the sort direction for Ki is descending and the applicable <comp op> is the <greater than operator>.
3. If <null ordering> is not specified, then an implementation-defined <null ordering> is implicit. This was a big issue in earlier SQL Standards because vendors handled NULLs differently. NULLs are considered equal to each other.
4. If one value is NULL and the second value is not NULL, then
   - If NULLS FIRST is specified or implied, then first value <comp op> second value is considered to be TRUE.
   - If NULLS LAST is specified or implied, then first value <comp op> second value is considered to be FALSE.
   - If first value and second value are not NULL and the result of "first value <comp op> second value" is UNKNOWN, then the relative ordering of first value and second value is implementation dependent.
5. Two rows that are not distinct with respect to the <sort specification>s are said to be peers of each other. The relative ordering of peers is implementation dependent.

### 30.3.3 Window Frame Subclause

The tricky one is the window frame. Here is the BNF, but you really need to see code for it to make sense.

```
<window frame clause>::= <window frame units> <window
   frame extent>
[<window frame exclusion>]

<window frame units>::= ROWS | RANGE
```

RANGE works with a single sort key of numeric, datetime, or interval data type. It is for data that is a little fuzzy on the edges, if you will. If ROWS is specified, then sort list is made of exact numeric with scale zero.

```
<window frame extent>::= <window frame start> | <window
   frame between>

<window frame start>::=
UNBOUNDED PRECEDING | <window frame preceding> | CURRENT ROW

<window frame preceding>::= <unsigned value specification>
   PRECEDING
```

If the window starts at UNBOUNDED PRECEDING, then the lower bound is always the first row of the partition; likewise, CURRENT ROW explains itself. The <window frame preceding> is an actual count of preceding rows.

```
<window frame bound>::= <window frame start> | UNBOUNDED
   FOLLOWING | <window frame following>

<window frame following>::= <unsigned value specification>
   FOLLOWING
```

If the window starts at UNBOUNDED FOLLOWING, then the lower bound is always the last row of the partition; likewise, CURRENT ROW explains itself. The <window frame following> is an actual count of following rows.

```
<window frame between>::=
BETWEEN <window frame bound 1> AND <window frame bound 2>

<window frame bound 1>::= <window frame bound>

<window frame bound 2>::= <window frame bound>
```

The current row and its window frame have to stay inside the partition, so the following and preceding limits can effectively change at either end of the frame.

```
<window frame exclusion>::= EXCLUDE CURRENT ROW | EXCLUDE
   GROUP
| EXCLUDE TIES | EXCLUDE NO OTHERS
```

The `<window frame exclusion>` is not used much or widely implemented. It is also hard to explain. The term "peer" refers to duplicate values.

1. `EXCLUDE CURRENT ROW` removes the current row from the window.
2. `EXCLUDE GROUP` removes the current row and any peers of the current row.
3. `EXCLUDE TIES` removed any rows other than the current row that are peers of the current row.
4. `EXCLUDE NO OTHERS` makes sure that no additional rows are removed.

## 30.4 Windowed Aggregate Functions

The regular aggregate functions can take a window clause.

```
<aggregate function>
OVER([PARTITION BY <column list>]
   [ORDER BY <sort column list>]
  [<window frame>])

<aggregate function>::=
  MIN([DISTINCT | ALL] <value exp>) | MAX([DISTINCT |
     ALL] <value exp>)
 |SUM([DISTINCT | ALL] <value exp>) | AVG([DISTINCT | ALL]
   <value exp>)
 |COUNT([DISTINCT | ALL] [<value exp> | *])
```

There are no great surprises here. The window that is constructed acts as if it were a group to which the aggregate function is applied.

## 30.5 Ordinal Functions

The ordinal functions use the window clause but must have an `ORDER BY` subclause to make sense. They return an ordering of the row within its partition or window frame relative to the rest of the rows in the partition. They have no parameters.

### 30.5.1 Row Numbering

`ROW_NUMBER()` uniquely identifies rows with a sequential number based on the position of the row within the window defined by an ordering clause (if one is specified), starting with 1 for the first row and continuing sequentially to the last row in the window. If an ordering clause, `ORDER BY`, isn't specified in the window, the row numbers are assigned to the rows in arbitrary order.

### 30.5.2 RANK( ) and DENSE_RANK( )

RANK() assigns a sequential rank of a row within a window. The RANK() of a row is defined as one plus the number of rows that strictly precede the row. Rows that are not distinct within the ordering of the window are assigned equal ranks. If two or more rows are not distinct with respect to the ordering, then there will be one or more gaps in the sequential rank numbering. That is, the results of RANK() may have gaps in the numbers resulting from duplicate values.

DENSE_RANK() also assigns a sequential rank to a row in a window. However, a row's DENSE_RANK() is one plus the number of rows preceding it that are distinct with respect to the ordering. Therefore, there will be no gaps in the sequential rank numbering, with ties being assigned the same rank.

### 30.5.3 PERCENT_RANK( ) and CUME_DIST

These were added in the SQL:2003 Standard and are defined in terms of earlier constructs. Let <approximate numeric type>1 be an approximate numeric type with implementation-defined precision. PERCENT_RANK() OVER <window specification> is equivalent to:

```
CASE
WHEN COUNT(*)
 OVER(<window specification>
   RANGE BETWEEN UNBOUNDED PRECEDING
       AND UNBOUNDED FOLLOWING) = 1
THEN CAST (0 AS <approximate numeric type>)
ELSE (CAST (RANK ()
      OVER(<window specification>) AS <approximate numeric
         type>1) - 1)
   / (COUNT (*)
      OVER(<window specification>1
        RANGE BETWEEN UNBOUNDED PRECEDING
            AND UNBOUNDED FOLLOWING) - 1)
END
```

Likewise, the cumulative distribution is defined with an <approximate numeric type> with implementation-defined precision. CUME_DIST() OVER <window specification> is equivalent to:

```
(CAST (COUNT (*)
   OVER(<window specification>
     RANGE UNBOUNDED PRECEDING) AS <approximate numeric type>)
   / COUNT(*)
     OVER(<window specification>1
       RANGE BETWEEN UNBOUNDED PRECEDING
           AND UNBOUNDED FOLLOWING))
```

You can also go back and define the other windows in terms of each other, but it is only a curiosity and has no practical value.

`RANK() OVER <window specification>` is equivalent to:

```
(COUNT (*) OVER(<window specification> RANGE UNBOUNDED
   PRECEDING)
 -COUNT (*) OVER(<window specification> RANGE CURRENT ROW) + 1)
```

`DENSE_RANK() OVER(<window specification>)` is equivalent to:

```
COUNT (DISTINCT ROW (<value exp 1>, ...,<value exp n>))
OVER(<window specification> RANGE UNBOUNDED PRECEDING)
```

where `<value exp i>` is a sort key in the table.

`ROW_NUMBER() OVER WNS` is equivalent to:

```
COUNT (*)
OVER(<window specification> ROWS UNBOUNDED PRECEDING)
```

## 30.5.4 Some Examples

The `<aggregation grouping>` defines a set of rows upon which the aggregate function operates for each row in the partition. Thus, in our example, for each month, you specify the set including it and the two preceding rows.

```
SELECT SH.region_nbr, SH.sales_month, SH.sales_amt,
   AVG(SH.sales_amt)
   OVER(PARTITION BY SH.region_nbr
     ORDER BY SH.sales_month ASC
     ROWS 2 PRECEDING)
   AS moving_average,
   SUM(SH.sales_amt)
   OVER(PARTITION BY SH.region_nbr
     ORDER BY SH.sales_month ASC
     ROWS BETWEEN UNBOUNDED PRECEDING AND CURRENT ROW)
   AS moving_total
FROM SalesHistory AS SH;
```

Here, `AVG(SH.sales_amt) OVER(PARTITION BY...)` is the first OLAP function. The construct inside the `OVER()` clause defines the window of data to which the aggregate function, `AVG()` in this example, is applied.

The window clause defines a partitioned set of rows to which the aggregate function is applied. The window clause says to take SalesHistory table and then apply the following operations to it:

1. Partition SalesHistory by region
2. Order the data by month within each region.
3. Group each row with the two preceding rows in the same region.
4. Compute the windowed average on each grouping.

The database engine is not required to perform the steps in the order described here, but has to produce the same result set as if they had been carried out.

The second windowed function is a cumulative total to date for each region. It is a very column q = query pattern.

There are two main types of aggregation groups: physical and logical. In physical grouping, you count a specified number of rows that are before or after the current row. The SalesHistory example used physical grouping. In logical grouping, you include all the data in a certain interval, defined in terms of a quantity that can be added to, or subtracted from, the current sort key. For instance, you create the same group whether you define it as the current month's row plus:

1. The two preceding rows as defined by the `ORDER` clause.
2. Any row containing a month no less than two months earlier.

Physical grouping works well for contiguous data and programmers who think in terms of sequential files. Physical grouping works for a larger variety of data types than logical grouping, because it does not require operations on values.

Logical grouping works better for data that has gaps or irregularities in the ordering and for programmers who think in SQL predicates. Logical grouping works only if you can do arithmetic on the values (such as numeric quantities and dates).

You will find another query pattern used with these functions. The function invocations need to get names to be referenced, so they are put into a derived table, which is encased in a containing query

```
SELECT X.*
 FROM (SELECT <window function 1> AS W1,
      <window function 2> AS W2,
      ..
      <window function n> AS Wn
   FROM ..
  [WHERE ..]
 )ASX
[WHERE..]
[GROUP BY ..];
```

Using the `SELECT *` in the containing query is a handy way to save repeating a select clause list over and over.

## 30.6 Vendor Extensions

You will find that vendors have added their own proprietary windowed functions to their products. Although there is no good way to predict what they will do, there are two sets of common extensions. As a programming exercise, I suggest you try to write them in Standard SQL windowed functions so you can translate dialect SQL if you need to do so.

### 30.6.1 LEAD and LAG Functions

LEAD and LAG functions are nonstandard shorthands you will find in Oracle and other SQL products. Rather than compute an aggregate value, they jump ahead or behind the current row and use that value in an expression. They take three arguments and an OVER() clause. The general syntax is:

```
[LEAD | LAG] (<expr>, <offset>, <default>) OVER(<window
   specification>)
```

1. <expr> is the expression to compute from the leading or lagging row. <offset> is the position of the leading or lagging row relative to the current row; it has to be a positive integer that defaults to one.
2. <default> is the value to return if the <offset> points to a row outside the partition range.
   Here is a simple example:

```
SELECT dept_nbr, emp_id, sal_amt,
  LEAD(sal, 1, 0)
   OVER(PARTITION BY dept_nbr
       ORDER BY sal DESC NULLS LAST)AS lead_sal_amt,
  LAG (sal, 1, 0)
   OVER(PARTITION BY dept_nbr
       ORDER BY sal DESC NULLS LAST) AS lag_sal_amt
FROM Personnel
```

| dept_nbr | emp_id | sal_amt | lead_sal_amt | lag_sal_amt |
|---|---|---|---|---|
| 10 | 7839 | 5000.00 | 2450.00 | 0.00 |
| 10 | 7782 | 2450.00 | 1300.00 | 5000.00 ◄ example emp_id in dept 10 |
| 10 | 7934 | 1300.00 | 0.00 | 2450.00 |
| 20 | 7788 | 3000.00 | 3000.00 | 0.00 |
| 20 | 7902 | 3000.00 | 2975.00 | 3000.00 |
| 20 | 7566 | 2975.00 | 1100.00 | 3000.00 |
| 20 | 7876 | 1100.00 | 800.00 | 2975.00 |
| 20 | 7369 | 800.00 | 0.00 | 1100.00 |

Look at employee 7782, whose current salary is $2450.00. Looking at the salaries, we see that the first salary greater than his is $5000.00 and the first salary less than his is $1300.00. Look at employee 7934, whose current salary of $1300.00 puts him at the bottom of the company pay scale; his lead_salary_amt is defaulted to zero.

### 30.6.2 FIRST and LAST Functions

FIRST and LAST functions are nonstandard shorthands you will find in SQL products in various forms. Rather than compute an aggregate value, they sort a partition on one set of columns, then return an expression from the first or last row of that sort. The expression usually has nothing to do with the sorting columns. This is a bit like the joke about the British Sargent-Major ordering the troops to line up alphabetically by height. The general syntax is:

```
[FIRST | LAST](<expr>) OVER(<window specification>)
```

Using the imaginary Personnel table again:

```
SELECT emp_id, dept_nbr, hire_date,
  FIRST(hire_date)
  OVER(PARTITION BY dept_nbr
      ORDER BY emp_id)
  AS first_hire_by_dept
 FROM Personnel;
```

The results get the hire date for the employee who has the lowest employee id in each department.

| emp_id | dept_nbr | hire_date | first_hire_by_dept |
|---|---|---|---|
| 7369 | 20 | '2011-01-01' | '2011-01-01' ◄ first emp_id in dept 20 |
| 7566 | 20 | '2011-01-02' | '2011-01-01' |
| 7902 | 20 | '2011-01-02' | '2011-01-01' |
| 7788 | 20 | '2011-01-04' | '2011-01-01' |
| 7876 | 20 | '2011-01-07' | '2011-01-01' ◄ last emp_id in dept 20 |
| 7499 | 30 | '2011-01-27' | '2011-01-27' ◄ first emp_id in dept 30 |
| 7521 | 30 | '2011-01-09' | '2011-01-27' |
| 7844 | 30 | '2011-01-17' | '2011-01-27' |
| 7654 | 30 | '2011-01-18' | '2011-01-27' |
| 7900 | 30 | '2011-01-20' | '2011-01-27' ◄ last emp_id in dept 30 |

If we had used `LAST()` instead, the two chosen rows would have been:
(7876, 20, '2011-01-07', '2011-01-01')
(7900, 30, '2011-01-20', '2011-01-27')

The Oracle extensions `FIRST_VALUE` and `LAST_VALUE` are even stranger. They allow other ordinal and aggregate functions to be applied to the retrieved values. If you want to use them, I suggest that you look at product-specific references and examples.

You can do these with Standard SQL and a little work. The skeleton follows.

```
WITH FirstLastQuery
AS
(SELECT emp_id, dept_nbr,  ROW_NUMBER()
     OVER(PARTITION BY dept_nbr
         ORDER BY emp_id ASC) AS asc_order,
    ROW_NUMBER()
     OVER(PARTITION BY dept_nbr
         ORDER BY emp_id DESC) AS desc_order
 FROM Personnel)

SELECT A.emp_id, A.dept_nbr, OA.hire_date AS first_value,
   OD.hire_date AS last_value
 FROM FirstLastQuery AS A, FirstLastQuery AS OA,
   FirstLastQuery AS OD
WHERE OD.desc_order = 1
 AND OA.asc_order = 1;
```

## 30.7 A Bit of History

IBM and Oracle jointly proposed these extensions in early 1999 and thanks to ANSI's uncommonly rapid (and praiseworthy) actions, they are part of the SQL-99 Standard. IBM implemented portions of the specifications in DB2 UDB 6.2, which was commercially available in some forms as early as mid-1999. Oracle 8i version 2 and DB2 UDB 7.1, both released in late 1999, contain beefed-up implementations.

Other vendors contributed, including database tool vendors Brio, MicroStrategy, and Cognos and database vendor Informix, among others. A team lead by Dr. Hamid Pirahesh of IBM's Almaden Research Laboratory played a particularly important role. After his team had researched the subject for about a year and had come up with an approach to extend SQL in this area, he called Oracle. The companies then learned that each had independently done some significant work. With

Andy Witkowski playing a pivotal role at Oracle, the two companies hammered out a joint standards proposal in about two months. Red Brick was actually the first product to implement this functionality before the standard, but in a less complete form. You can find details in the ANSI document, "Introduction to OLAP Functions," by Fred Zemke, Krishna Kulkarni, Andy Witkowski, and Bob Lyle.

# 31

# DESCRIPTIVE STATISTICS IN SQL

SQL is not a statistical programming language. However, there are some tricks that will let you do simple descriptive statistics. Many vendors also include other descriptive statistics besides the required ones. Other sections of this book give portable queries for computing some of the more common statistics. Before using any of these queries, you should check to see if they already exist in your SQL product. Built-in functions will run far faster than these queries, so you should use them if portability is not vital. The most common extensions are the median, the mode, the standard deviation, N-tiles, and the variance.

If you need to do a detailed statistical analysis, then you can extract data with SQL and pass it along to a statistical programming language, such as SAS or SPSS. However, you can build a lot of standard descriptive statistics using what you do have.

## 31.1 The Mode

The mode is the most frequently occurring value in a set. If there are two such values in a set, statisticians call it a bimodal distribution; three such values make it trimodal; and so forth.

Most SQL implementations do not have a mode function, since it is easy to calculate. This version is from Shepard Towindo and it will handle multiple modes.

```
SELECT salary_amt, COUNT(*) AS salary_mode
 FROM Personnel
GROUP BY salary_amt
HAVING COUNT(*)
  >= ALL (SELECT COUNT(*)
      FROM Personnel
      GROUP BY salary_amt);
```

Here is a version that uses the window clause:

```
WITH
Freq (salary_amt, salary_amt_cnt)
AS
```

Joe Celko's SQL for Smarties. DOI: 10.1016/B978-0-12-382022-8.00031-4

```
(SELECT salary_amt,
    COUNT(*) OVER(PARTITION BY salary_amt)
  FROM Personnel)
SELECT F1. salary_amt
 FROM Freq AS F1
WHERE F1.salary_amt_cnt
  = (SELECT MAX (salary_amt_cnt)
     FROM Freq AS F2);
```

The mode is a weak descriptive statistic, because it can be changed by small amounts of additional data. For example, if we have 100,000 cases where the value of the part_color variable is 'red' and 99,999 cases where the value is 'green', the mode is 'red'. But when two more 'green's are added to the set, the mode switches to 'green'. A better idea is to allow for some variation, (k), in the values. In general the best way to compute (k) is probably as a percentage of the total number of occurrences. Of course, knowledge of the actual situation could change this.

```
SELECT AVG(salary_amt) AS mode
 FROM Personnel
GROUP BY salary_amt
HAVING COUNT(*)
 >= ALL (SELECT COUNT(*) * 0.95 -- or other percentages
      FROM Personnel
      GROUP BY salary_amt);
```

## 31.2 The AVG( ) Function

The simple mean is built into SQL as the `AVG()` aggregate function. One problem is that SQL likes to maintain the data types, so if x is an `INTEGER`, you may get an integer result. But even if you get decimal places, each product will have a default that you might not like. You can avoid this by writing `AVG(1.0 * x)` or `AVG(CAST (x AS FLOAT))` or `AVG(CAST (x AS DECIMAL (s, p)))` to be safe. This is implementation-defined, so check your product first.

Newbies tend to forget that the built-in aggregate functions drop the rows with `NULL`s before doing the computations. This means that `(SUM(x)/COUNT(*))` is not the same as `AVG(x)`. Consider `(x * 1.0)/COUNT(*)` versus `AVG(COALESCE(x * 1.0, 0.0))` as versions of the mean that handle `NULL`s differently.

Sample and population means are slightly different. A sample needs to use frequencies to adjust the estimate of the mean. The formula `SUM(x * 1.0 * abs_perc/100.0) AS mean_p` needs the `VIEW` we had at the start of this section.

The name `mean_p` is to remind us that it is a population mean and not the simple `AVG()` of the sample data in the table.

## 31.3 The Median

The median is defined as the value for which there are just as many cases with a value below it as above it. If such a value exists in the data set, this value is called the statistical median by some authors. If no such value exists in the data set, the usual method is to divide the data set into two halves of equal size such that all values in one half are lower than any value in the other half. The median is then the average of the highest value in the lower half and the lowest value in the upper half, and is called the financial median by some authors. The financial median is the most common term used for this median, so we will stick to it. Let us use Date's famous Parts table, from several of his textbooks (Date, 1983, 1995a), which has a column for the weight of parts in it, like this:

Parts

| part_nbr | part_name | part_color | part_wgt | city_name |
|---|---|---|---|---|
| 'p1' | 'Nut' | 'Red' | '12' | 'London' |
| 'p2' | 'Bolt' | 'Green' | '17' | 'Paris' |
| 'p3' | 'Cam' | 'Blue' | '12' | 'Paris' |
| 'p4' | 'Screw' | 'Red' | '14' | 'London' |
| 'p5' | 'Cam' | 'Blue' | '12' | 'Paris' |
| 'p6' | 'Cog' | 'Red' | '19' | 'London' |

First sort the table by weights and find the three rows in the lower half of the table. The greatest value in the lower half is 12; this is called the lower or left median value. The smallest value in the upper half is 14; this is called the upper or right median. Their average, and therefore the median, is 13. If the table had an odd number of rows, we would have looked at only one row after the sorting.

The median is a better measure of central tendency than the average, but it is also harder to calculate without sorting. This is a disadvantage of SQL as compared with procedural languages. This might be the reason that the median is not a common vendor extension in SQL implementations. However, the variance and standard deviation are quite common, probably because they are much easier to calculate since they require no sorting, but they are less useful to commercial users.

### 31.3.1 The Median as a Programming Problem

In the early 1990s, there were two popular database magazines, *DBMS* and *Database Programming & Design*. I wrote a regular column in *Database Programming & Design* and then moved over to *DBMS*. Chris Date got my old slot and then both magazines were bought out by the same publisher and eventually merged into *Intelligent Enterprise* magazine. During that period, Chris Date and I did "dueling banjoes" with RDBMS and SQL topics. One of the topics that suddenly became hot was writing a query for the median, with the then-current SQL Standard.

Date proposed two different solutions for the median (Date, 1992a; Celko and Date, 1993). His first solution was based on the fact that if you duplicate every row in a table, the median will stay the same. The duplication will guarantee that you always work with a table that has an even number of rows. The first version that appeared in his column was wrong and drew some mail from me and from others who had different solutions. Here is a corrected version of his first solution:

```
CREATE VIEW Temp1
AS SELECT part_wgt FROM Parts
 UNION ALL
 SELECT part_wgt FROM Parts;

CREATE VIEW Temp2
AS SELECT part_wgt
 FROM Temp1
 WHERE (SELECT COUNT(*) FROM Parts)
  <= (SELECT COUNT(*)
   FROM Temp1 AS T1
   WHERE T1.part_wgt >= Temp1.part_wgt)
 AND (SELECT COUNT(*) FROM Parts)
  <= (SELECT COUNT(*)
   FROM Temp1 AS T2
   WHERE T2.part_wgt <= Temp1.part_wgt);

SELECT AVG(DISTINCT part_wgt) AS median
FROM Temp2;
```

Today, you would use `CTE`s and not `VIEW`s.

This involves the construction of a doubled table of values, which can be expensive in terms of both time and storage space. The use of `AVG(DISTINCT x)` is important because leaving it out would return the simple average instead of the median. Consider the set of weights (12, 17, 17, 14, 12, 19). The doubled table, Temp1, is then (12, 12, 12, 12, 14, 14, 17, 17, 17, 17, 19, 19). But because of the duplicated values, Temp2 becomes (14, 14, 17, 17,

17, 17), not just (14, 17). The simple average is (96 / 6.0) = 16; it should be (31/2.0) = 15.5 instead.

## 31.3.2 Celko's First Median

A slight modification of Date's solution will avoid the use of a doubled table, but it depends on a CEILING() function, which was common but not yet standard in the 1990s.

```
SELECT MIN(part_wgt) -- smallest value in upper half
FROM Parts
WHERE part_wgt
 IN (SELECT P1.part_wgt
     FROM Parts AS P1, Parts AS P2
     WHERE P2.part_wgt >= P1.part_wgt
     GROUP BY P1.part_wgt
    HAVING COUNT(*)
     <= (SELECT CEILING(COUNT(*) / 2.0)
         FROM Parts))
UNION
SELECT MAX(part_wgt) -- largest value in lower half
FROM Parts
WHERE part_wgt
  IN (SELECT P1.part_wgt
      FROM Parts AS P1, Parts AS P2
      WHERE P2.part_wgt <= P1.part_wgt
     HAVING COUNT(*)
       <= SELECT CEILING(COUNT(*) / 2.0)
          FROM Parts));
```

or using the same idea and a CASE expression:

```
SELECT AVG(DISTINCT CAST(part_wgt AS FLOAT)) AS median
 FROM (SELECT MAX(part_wgt)
    FROM Parts AS B1
    WHERE (SELECT COUNT(*) + 1
       FROM Parts
       WHERE part_wgt < B1.part_wgt)
      <= (SELECT CEILING (COUNT(*)/2.0)
          FROM Parts)
    UNION ALL
    SELECT MAX(part_wgt)
     FROM Parts AS B
     WHERE (SELECT COUNT(*) + 1
        FROM Parts
        WHERE part_wgt < B.part_wgt)
       <= CASE (SELECT MOD (COUNT(*), 2)
           FROM Parts)
        WHEN 0
```

```
        THEN (SELECT CEILING (COUNT(*)/2.0) + 1
           FROM Parts)
        ELSE (SELECT CEILING (COUNT(*)/2.0)
           FROM Parts)
        END) AS Medians(part_wgt);
```

The CEILING() function is to be sure that if there is an odd number of rows in Parts, the two halves will overlap on that value. Again, truncation and rounding in division are implementation-defined, so you will need to experiment with your product.

## 31.3.3 Date's Second Median

Date's second solution (Date, 1995b) was based on Celko's median, folded into one query:

```
SELECT AVG(DISTINCT Parts.part_wgt) AS median
 FROM Parts
WHERE Parts.part_wgt
   IN (SELECT MIN(part_wgt)
        FROM Parts
       WHERE Parts.part_wgt
         IN (SELECT P2.part_wgt
              FROM Parts AS P1, Parts AS P2
             WHERE P2.part_wgt <= P1.part_wgt
             GROUP BY P2.part_wgt
            HAVING COUNT(*)
               <= (SELECT CEILING(COUNT(*) / 2.0)
                    FROM Parts))
      UNION
      SELECT MAX(part_wgt)
        FROM Parts
       WHERE Parts.part_wgt
         IN (SELECT P2.part_wgt
              FROM Parts AS P1, Parts AS P2
             WHERE P2.part_wgt >= P1.part_wgt
             GROUP BY P2.part_wgt
            HAVING COUNT(*)
               <= (SELECT CEILING(COUNT(*) / 2.0)
                    FROM Parts)));
```

Date mentions that this solution will return a NULL for an empty table and that it assumes there are no NULLs in the column. If there are NULLs, the WHERE clauses should be modified to remove them.

## 31.3.4 Murchison's Median

Rory Murchison of the Ætna Institute had a solution that modifies Date's first method by concatenating the key to each value to make sure that every value is seen as a unique entity. Selecting the middle values is then a special case of finding the n-th item in the table.

```
SELECT AVG(part_wgt)
 FROM Parts AS P1
WHERE EXISTS
   (SELECT COUNT(*)
     FROM Parts AS P2
    WHERE CAST(part_wgt AS CHAR(5)) || P2.part_nbr
      >= CAST(part_wgt AS CHAR(5)) || P1.part_nbr
    HAVING COUNT(*) = (SELECT FLOOR(COUNT(*) / 2.0)
              FROM Parts)
      OR COUNT(*) = (SELECT CEILING((COUNT(*) / 2.0)
              FROM Parts));
```

This method depends on being able to have a HAVING clause without a GROUP BY, which is part of the ANSI/ISO Standard but often missed by new programmers.

Another handy trick if you do not have FLOOR() and CEILING() functions is to use (COUNT(*) + 1) / 2.0 and COUNT(*) / 2.0 + 1 to handle the odd-and-even-elements problem. Just to work it out, consider the case where the COUNT(*) returns 8 for an answer: (8 + 1) / 2.0 = (9 / 2.0) = 4.5 and (8 / 2.0) + 1 = 4 + 1 = 5.

The 4.5 will round to 4 in DB2 and other SQL implementations. The case where the COUNT(*) returns 9 would work like this: (9 + 1) / 2.0 = (10 / 2.0) = 5 and (9 / 2.0) + 1 = 4.5 + 1 = 5.5, which will likewise round to 5 in DB2.

## 31.3.5 Celko's Second Median

This is another method for finding the median that uses a working table with the values and a tally of their occurrences from the original table. This working table should be quite a bit smaller than the original table, and very fast to construct if there is an index on the target column. The Parts table will serve as an example, thus:

```
-- construct Working table of occurrences by part_wgt
CREATE TABLE Working
(part_wgt REAL NOT NULL,
occurence_cnt INTEGER NOT NULL);

INSERT INTO Working (part_wgt, occurrence_cnt)
SELECT part_wgt, COUNT(*)
 FROM Parts
GROUP BY part_wgt;
```

Now that we have this table, we want to use it to construct a summary table that has the number of occurrences of each part's weight and the total number of data elements before and after we add them to the working table.

```
-- construct table of cumulative tallies
CREATE TABLE Summary
(part_wgt REAL NOT NULL,
occurence_cnt INTEGER NOT NULL, -- number of occurrences
pre_tally INTEGER NOT NULL, -- cumulative tally before
 post_tally INTEGER NOT NULL);

-- Cumulative tally after
INSERT INTO Summary
SELECT S2.part_wgt, S2.occurence_cnt, SUM(S1.occurence_cnt)
   - S2.occurence_cnt,
  SUM(S1.occurence_cnt)
FROM Working AS S1, Working AS S2
WHERE S1.part_wgt <= S2.part_wgt
GROUP BY S2.part_wgt, S2.occurence_cnt;
```

Let (n / 2.0) be the middle position in the table. There are two mutually exclusive situations. In the first case, the median lies in a position between the pre_tally and post_tally of one part_wgt value. In the second case, the median lies on the pre_tally of one row and the post_tally of another. The middle position can be calculated by the scalar subquery `(SELECT MAX(post_tally) / 2.0 FROM Summary)`.

```
SELECT AVG(S3.part_wgt) AS median
 FROM Summary AS S3
WHERE (S3.post_tally > (SELECT MAX(post_tally) / 2.0 FROM
   Summary)
 AND S3.pre_tally < (SELECT MAX(post_tally) / 2.0 FROM
   Summary))
 OR S3.pre_tally = (SELECT MAX(post_tally) / 2.0 FROM
   Summary)
 OR S3.post_tally = (SELECT MAX(post_tally) / 2.0 FROM
   Summary);
```

The first predicate, with the `AND` operator, handles the case where the median falls inside one part_wgt value; the other two predicates handle the case where the median is between two weights. A `BETWEEN` predicate will not work in this query.

These tables can be used to compute percentiles, deciles, and quartiles simply by changing the scalar subquery. For example, to find the highest tenth (first dectile), the subquery would be `(SELECT 9 * MAX(post_tally) / 10 FROM Summary)`; to find the highest two-tenths, `(SELECT 8 * MAX(post_tally) / 10 FROM Summary)`; and in general to find the highest n-tenths, `(SELECT (10 - n) * MAX(post_tally) / 10 FROM Summary)`.

## 31.3.6 Vaughan's Median with VIEWs

Philip Vaughan of San Jose, CA, proposed a simple median technique based on all of these methods. It derives a VIEW with unique weights and number of occurrences and then a VIEW of the middle set of weights.

```
CREATE VIEW ValueSet(part_wgt, occurence_cnt)
AS SELECT part_wgt, COUNT(*)
  FROM Parts
 GROUP BY part_wgt;
```

The MiddleValues VIEW is used to get the median by taking an average. The clever part of this code is the way that it handles empty result sets in the outermost WHERE clause that result from having only one value for all weights in the table. Empty sets sum to NULL because there is no element to map the index

```
CREATE VIEW MiddleValues(part_wgt)
AS SELECT part_wgt
 FROM ValueSet AS VS1
 WHERE (SELECT SUM(VS2.occurence_cnt)/2.0 + 0.25
   FROM ValueSet AS VS2) >
  (SELECT SUM(VS2.occurence_cnt)
   FROM ValueSet AS VS2
   WHERE VS1.part_wgt <= VS2.part_wgt) - VS1.occurence_cnt
  AND (SELECT SUM(VS2.occurence_cnt)/2.0 + 0.25
   FROM ValueSet AS VS2) >
  (SELECT SUM(VS2.occurence_cnt)
   FROM ValueSet AS VS2
   WHERE VS1.part_wgt >= VS2.part_wgt) - VS1.occurence_cnt;

SELECT AVG(part_wgt) AS median FROM MiddleValues;
```

## 31.3.7 Median with Characteristic Function

Anatoly Abramovich, Yelena Alexandrova, and Eugene Birger presented a series of articles in *SQL Forum* magazine on computing the median (*SQL Forum*, 1993, 1994). They define a characteristic function, which they call delta, using the SIGN() function. The delta or characteristic function accepts a Boolean expression as an argument and returns one if it is TRUE and zero if it is FALSE or UNKNOWN. We can construct the delta function easily with a CASE expression.

The authors also distinguish between the statistical median, whose value must be a member of the set, and the financial median, whose value is the average of the middle two members of the set. A statistical median exists when there is an odd number of items in the set. If there is an even number of items, you must decide if you want to use the highest value in the lower half (the left or lower median) or the lowest value in the upper half (the right or upper median).

The left statistical median of a unique column can be found with this query, if you will assume that we have a column called bin that represents the storage location of a part.

```
SELECT P1.bin
 FROM Parts AS P1, Parts AS P2
GROUP BY P1.bin
HAVING SUM(CASE WHEN (P2.bin <= P1.bin) THEN 1 ELSE 0 END)
  = (COUNT(*) / 2.0);
```

Changing the direction of the comparison in the `HAVING` clause will allow you to pick the right statistical median if a central element does not exist in the set. You will also notice something else about the median of a set of unique values: It is usually meaningless. What does the median bin number mean, anyway? A good rule of thumb is that if it does not make sense as an average, it does not make sense as a median.

The statistical median of a column with duplicate values can be found with a query based on the same ideas, but you have to adjust the `HAVING` clause to allow for overlap; thus, the left statistical median is found by:

```
SELECT P1.part_wgt
 FROM Parts AS P1, Parts AS P2
GROUP BY P1.part_wgt
HAVING SUM(CASE WHEN P2.part_wgt <= P1.part_wgt
      THEN 1 ELSE 0 END)
    >= (COUNT(*) / 2.0)
 AND SUM(CASE WHEN P2.part_wgt >= P1.part_wgt
      THEN 1 ELSE 0 END)
    >= (COUNT(*) / 2.0);
```

If Parts contains an even number of entries with the `(COUNT(*)/ 2)` entry not repeated, this query may return `FLOOR (AVG(DISTINCT part_wgt))`, as happens when SQL Server computes an average of integers. This can be fixed by changing the inner `SELECT` to:

```
SELECT (P1.part_wgt * 1.0) AS part_wgt
```

Notice that here the left and right medians can be the same, so there is no need to pick one over the other in many of the situations where you have an even number of items. Switching the comparison operators in the two `CASE` expressions will give you the right statistical median.

I would recommend using a combination of the right and left statistical medians to return a set of values about the center of the data, and then averaging them. Using a derived table, we can write the query as:

```
SELECT AVG(DISTINCT 1.0 * part_wgt)
FROM (SELECT P1.part_wgt
   FROM Parts AS P1, Parts AS P2
   GROUP BY P1.part_wgt
  HAVING SUM(CASE WHEN P2.part_wgt <= P1.part_wgt
         THEN 1 ELSE 0 END)
    >= (COUNT(*) / 2.0)
   AND SUM(CASE WHEN P2.part_wgt >= P1.part_wgt
       THEN 1 ELSE 0 END)
    >= (COUNT(*)/2.0));
```

and we can gain some additional control over the calculations.

This version will use one copy of the left and right median to compute the statistical median. However, by simply changing the `AVG(DISTINCT part_wgt)` to `AVG(part_wgt)`, the median will favor the direction with the most occurrences. This might be easier to see with an example. Assume that we have weights (13, 13, 13, 14) in the Parts table. A pure statistical median would be (13 + 14) / 2.0 = 13.5; however, weighting it would give (13 + 13 + 13 + 14) / 4.0 = 13.25, a number that is more representative of central tendency.

Another version of the financial median, which uses the `CASE` expression in both of its forms, is:

```
SELECT CASE MOD(COUNT(*), 2)
  WHEN 0  -- even sized table
  THEN (P1.part_wgt + MIN(CASE WHEN P2.part_wgt > P1.part_wgt
                THEN P2.part_wgt
                ELSE NULL END)))/2.0
  ELSE P2.part_wgt -- odd sized table
  END AS median
 FROM Parts AS P1, Parts AS P2
GROUP BY P1.part_wgt
HAVING COUNT(CASE WHEN P1.part_wgt >= P2.part_wgt
      THEN 1 ELSE NULL END)
  = (COUNT(*) + 1) / 2;
```

This answer is due to the late Ken Henderson. The only instance in which this is correct is when Parts has an odd number of entries and the middle `(COUNT(*) / 2 + 1)` entry is not repeated in the data.

Another approach to avoid derived tables is:

```
SELECT CASE
  WHEN MOD (COUNT(*), 2) = 0
   AND SUM(CASE
      WHEN P2.part_wgt > P1.part_wgt
```

```
        THEN 1 ELSE 0 END)
      = (COUNT(*) / 2)
   THEN (P1.part_wgt
     + MIN(CASE
         WHEN P2.part_wgt > P1.part_wgt
         THEN P2.part_wgt
         ELSE NULL END)
     ) / 2.0
   ELSE P1.part_wgt
   END AS median
  FROM Parts AS P1, Parts AS P2
 GROUP BY P1.part_wgt
 HAVING SUM(CASE
      WHEN P2.part_wgt <= P1.part_wgt
      THEN 1 ELSE 0 END)
   >= ((COUNT(*) + 1) / 2)
  AND SUM(CASE
      WHEN P2.part_wgt >= P1.part_wgt
      THEN 1 ELSE 0 END)
     >= (COUNT(*)/2 + 1);
```

This is due to Michael Sheehan, who also made some corrections to other versions of the Median. He felt that this was not very pretty, but it explicitly captures the only scenario in which an average is actually necessary.

### 31.3.8 Celko's Third Median

Another approach involves looking at a picture of a line of sorted values and seeing where the median would fall. Every value in column part_wgt of the table partitions the table into three sections, the values that are less than part_wgt, equal to part_wgt, or greater than part_wgt. We can get a profile of each value with a tabular subquery expression.

Now the question is how to define a median in terms of the partitions. Clearly, the definition of a median means that if (lesser = greater) then part_wgt is the median.

If there are more greater values than half the size of the table, then part_wgt cannot be a median. Likewise, if there are more elements in the lesser values than half the size of the table, then part_wgt cannot be a median.

If (lesser + equal) = greater, then part_wgt is a left-hand median. Likewise, if (greater + equal) = lesser, then part_wgt is a right-hand median. However, if part_wgt is the median, then both lesser and greater have to have tallies less than half the size of the table. That translates into the following SQL.

```
SELECT AVG(DISTINCT part_wgt)
FROM (SELECT P1.part_nbr, P1.part_wgt,
```

```
      SUM(CASE WHEN P2.part_wgt < P1.part_wgt
        THEN 1 ELSE 0 END),
      SUM(CASE WHEN P2.part_wgt = P1.part_wgt
        THEN 1 ELSE 0 END),
      SUM(CASE WHEN P2.part_wgt > P1.part_wgt
        THEN 1 ELSE 0 END)
    FROM Parts AS P1, Parts AS P2
    GROUP BY P1.part_nbr, P1.part_wgt)
     AS Partitions (part_nbr, part_wgt, lesser, equal, greater)
 WHERE lesser = greater
  OR (lesser <= (SELECT COUNT(*) FROM Parts)/2.0
   AND greater <= (SELECT COUNT(*) FROM Parts)/2.0);
```

The reason for not expanding the VIEW in the FROM clause into a tabular subquery expression is that the table can be used for other partitions of the table, such as quintiles.

It is also worth noting that you can use either AVG(DISTINCT i) or AVG(i) in the SELECT clause. The AVG(DISTINCT i) will return the usual median when there are two values. This happens when you have an even number of rows and a partition in the middle, such as (1, 2, 2, 3, 3, 3), which has (2, 3) in the middle, which gives us 2.5 for the median. The AVG(i) will return the weighted median instead. This happens when you also factor in the number of times the two values are in the middle of a table with an even number of rows. The table with (1, 2, 2, 3, 3, 3) would return (2, 2, 3, 3, 3) in the middle, which gives us 2.6 for the weighted median. The weighted median is a more accurate description of the data.

I sent this first attempt to Richard Romley, who invented the method of first working with groups when designing a query. It made it quite a bit simpler, but let me take you through the steps so you can see the reasoning.

Look at the WHERE clause. It could use some algebra and since it deals only with aggregate functions and scalar subqueries, you could move it into a HAVING clause. Moving things from the WHERE clause into the HAVING clause in a grouped query is important for performance, but it is not always possible.

But first let's do some algebra on the expression in the WHERE clause.

```
lesser <= (SELECT COUNT(*) FROM Parts)/2.0
```

Since we already have lesser, equal, and greater for every row in the derived table Partitions, and since the sum of lesser, equal, and greater must always be exactly equal to the total number of rows in the Parts table, we can replace the scalar subquery with this expression:

```
lesser <= (lesser + equal + greater)/2.0
```

But this is the same as:

```
2.0 * lesser <= lesser + equal + greater
```

which becomes:

```
2.0 * lesser - lesser <= equal + greater
```

which becomes:

```
lesser <= equal + greater
```

So the query becomes:

```
SELECT AVG(DISTINCT part_wgt)
 FROM (SELECT P1.part_nbr, P1.part_wgt,
        SUM(CASE WHEN P2.part_wgt < P1.part_wgt
            THEN 1 ELSE 0 END),
        SUM(CASE WHEN P2.part_wgt = P1.part_wgt
            THEN 1 ELSE 0 END),
        SUM(CASE WHEN P2.part_wgt > P1.part_wgt
            THEN 1 ELSE 0 END)
     FROM Parts AS P1, Parts AS P2
     GROUP BY P1.part_nbr, P1.part_wgt)
    AS Partitions (part_nbr, part_wgt, lesser, equal, greater)
WHERE lesser = greater
 OR (lesser <= equal + greater
   AND greater <= equal + lesser);
```

Still looking at the WHERE clause, we can rewrite it with DeMorgan's law.

```
WHERE lesser = greater
 OR (equal >= lesser - greater
  AND equal >= greater - lesser)
```

which is the same as:

```
WHERE lesser = greater
 OR equal >= ABS(lesser - greater)
```

But if the first condition was true (lesser = greater), the second must necessarily also be true (i.e., equal >= 0), so the first clause is redundant and can be eliminated completely.

```
WHERE equal >= ABS(lesser - greater)
```

So much for algebra. Instead of a WHERE clause operating on the columns of the derived table, why not perform the same test as a HAVING clause on the inner query that derives Partitions? This eliminates all but one column from the derived table, it will run lots faster, and it simplifies the query down to this:

```
SELECT AVG(DISTINCT part_wgt)
 FROM (SELECT P1.part_wgt
```

```
    FROM Parts AS P1, Parts AS P2
    GROUP BY P1.part_nbr, P1.part_wgt
   HAVING SUM(CASE WHEN P2.part_wgt = P1.part_wgt
          THEN 1 ELSE 0 END)
      >= ABS(SUM(CASE WHEN P2.part_wgt < P1.part_wgt
              THEN 1
              WHEN P2.part_wgt > P1.part_wgt
              THEN -1
              ELSE 0 END)))
  AS Partitions;
```

If you prefer to use functions instead of a CASE expression, then use this version of the query:

```
SELECT AVG(DISTINCT part_wgt)
 FROM (SELECT P1.part_wgt
     FROM Parts AS P1, Parts AS P2
     GROUP BY P1.part_nbr, P1.part_wgt
    HAVING SUM(ABS(1 - SIGN(P1.part_wgt - P2.part_wgt))
      >= ABS(SUM(SIGN (P1.part_wgt - P2.part_wgt)))
  AS Partitions;
```

## 31.3.9 Ken Henderson's Median

In many SQL products, the fastest way to find the median is to use a cursor and just go to the middle of the sorted table. Ken Henderson published a version of this with a cursor that can be translated in SQL/PSM. Assume that table Foobar has a column named "x" for which we wish to find the median.

```
BEGIN
DECLARE idx INTEGER;
DECLARE median DECIMAL(20, 5);
DECLARE median2 DECIMAL(20, 5);

DECLARE Median_Cursor CURSOR FOR
SELECT x
 FROM Foobar
 ORDER BY x
FOR READ ONLY;

SET idx
 = CASE
   WHEN MOD((SELECT COUNT(*) FROM Foobar), 2) = 0
   THEN (SELECT COUNT(*) FROM Foobar)/2
   ELSE ((SELECT COUNT(*) FROM Foobar)/2) + 1 END;

OPEN Median_Cursor;
FETCH ABSOLUTE idx FROM Median_Cursor INTO median;
IF MOD(idx, 2) = 0
THEN FETCH Median_Cursor INTO median2;
```

```
  SET median = (median + median2)/2;
END IF;
CLOSE Median_Cursor;
END;
```

If the distribution is symmetrical and has only a single peek, then the mode, median, and mean are the same value. If not, then the distribution is somehow skewed. If `(mode < median < mean)` then the distribution is skewed to the right. If `(mode > median > mean)` then the distribution is skewed to the left.

## 31.3.10 OLAP Medians

The new OLAP functions allow you to replace `COUNT()` functions with row numberings.

```
WITH SortedData (x, hi, lo)

AS SELECT AVG(x) AS median FROM (SELECT x, ROW_NUMBER()
   OVER(ORDER BY x, key_col ASC), ROW_NUMBER() OVER(ORDER
   BY x, key_col DESC) FROM RawData) WHERE hi IN (lo, lo+1,
   lo-1);
```

or a slight modification:

```
SELECT AVG(x)
 FROM (SELECT x,
       ROW_NUMBER() OVER(ORDER BY x, key_col DESC) AS a,
       ROW_NUMBER() OVER(ORDER BY x, key_col) AS b
    FROM Foo) AS d
WHERE (b - a) BETWEEN -1 AND 1;, key_col
```

This might be slower than you would like, since the CTE might do two sorts to get the “hi” and “lo” values. At the time of this writing, these are new to SQL products, so not as much work has gone into them. A smarter optimizer would map the i-th element of a sorted list of (n) items in ASC order to the (n-i+1)-th element for DESC.

Another OLAP simple median by Peso uses a little more math.

```
SELECT AVG(x)
 FROM (SELECT x,
       2 * ROW_NUMBER() OVER(ORDER BY x)
         - COUNT(*) OVER() AS y
    FROM RawData)
WHERE y BETWEEN 0 AND 2;
```

This can be modified a bit to get the weighted median:

```
-- Weighted Median by Peso
SELECT SUM(y) / SUM(t)
```

```
  FROM (SELECT SUM(x) OVER(PARTITION BY x) AS y,
       2 * ROW_NUMBER() OVER(ORDER BY x)
        - COUNT(*) OVER() AS z,
       COUNT(*) OVER(PARTITION BY x) AS t
     FROM RawData)
 WHERE z BETWEEN 0 AND 2;
```

This is probably the best solution in this section, but I kept the older ones here to demonstrate the thought process when you have limited tools.

Adam Machanic pointed out a problem with my first attempt at using `ROW_NUMBER()` for the median. Let's set up a scratch table with repeated values:

```
DECLARE Foo TABLE (x INTEGER NOT NULL);
INSERT INTO Foo
VALUES (1), (2), (2), (3), (3), (3);
```

The most common approach to calculate the median value I have seen is:

```
SELECT AVG(x)
 FROM (SELECT x,
        ROW_NUMBER() OVER(ORDER BY x DESC) AS a,
        ROW_NUMBER() OVER(ORDER BY x ASC) AS b
    FROM Foo) AS Med
WHERE (b - a) BETWEEN -1 AND 1;
```

Too bad this does not work. Let's look at the rows in derived table Med:

| X | a | b | (a - b) |
|---|---|---|---|
| 1 | 6 | 1 | 5 |
| 2 | 4 | 2 | 2 |
| 2 | 5 | 3 | 2 |
| 3 | 1 | 4 | -3 |
| 3 | 2 | 5 | -3 |
| 3 | 3 | 6 | -3 |

As you can see, the difference calculated by (a – b) suddenly doesn't match! The problem is that the two called to `ROW_NUMBER()`

are *separate* function calls. The duplicate rows can be in any order. There is an assumption that we would get:

| X | a | b | (a - b) |
|---|---|---|---|
| 1 | 6 | 1 | 5 |
| 2 | 5 | 2 | 3 |
| 2 | 4 | 3 | 1◄candidate row x=2 |
| 3 | 3 | 4 | -1◄candidate row x=3 |
| 3 | 2 | 5 | -3 |
| 3 | 1 | 6 | -3 |

The assumption comes from the idea that the ascending and descending ROW_NUMBER() values could be computed at the same time using the formula:

```
ROW_NUMBER() OVER(ORDER BY x ASC)
= (COUNT(*) - ROW_NUMBER() OVER(ORDER BY x DESC) + 1)
```

This is a nice optimizer trick, but it is not required. This is why we need to add a key to the ORDER BY list to assure that the ascending list is the physical reverse order of the descending list.

## 31.4 Variance and Standard Deviation

The standard deviation is a measure of how far away from the average the values in a normally distributed population are. It is hard to calculate in SQL, because it involves a square root and standard SQL has only the basic four arithmetic operators.

Many vendors will allow you to use other math functions, but in all fairness, most SQL databases are in commercial applications and have little or no need for engineering or statistical calculations. The usual trick is to load the raw data into an appropriate host language, such as FORTRAN, and do the work there.

The variance is defined as the standard deviation squared, so we can avoid taking a square root and keep the calculations in pure SQL. The queries look like this:

```
CREATE TABLE Samples (x REAL NOT NULL);
INSERT INTO Samples (x)
VALUES (64.0), (48.0), (55.0), (68.0), (72.0),
   (59.0), (57.0), (61.0), (63.0), (60.0),
   (60.0), (43.0), (67.0), (70.0), (65.0),
   (55.0), (56.0), (64.0), (61.0), (60.0);
```

```
SELECT ((COUNT(*) * SUM(x * x)) - (SUM(x) * SUM(x)))
   /(COUNT(*) * (COUNT(*)-1)) AS variance
FROM Samples;
```

If you want to check this on your own SQL product, the correct answer is 48.9894 ... or just 49 depending how you handle rounding. If your SQL product has a standard deviation operator, use it instead.

## 31.5 Average Deviation

If you have a version of SQL with an absolute value function, `ABS()`, you can also compute the average deviation following this pattern, thus:

```
BEGIN
SELECT AVG(x) INTO :in_average FROM Samples;
SELECT SUM(ABS(x - :in_average)) / COUNT(x) AS AverDeviation
 FROM Samples;
END;
```

This is a measure of how much data values drift away from the average, without any consideration of the direction of the drift.

## 31.6 Cumulative Statistics

A cumulative or running statistic looks at each data value and how it is related to the whole data set. The most common examples involve changes in an aggregate value over time or on some other well-ordered dimension. A bank balance, which changes with each deposit or withdrawal, is a running total over time.

In earlier versions of SQL, you needed to use temporary tables and self-joins. They are complicated and ugly, so I will jump right to the modern syntax. The most natural example for most people is a bank statement with a running balance.

```
SELECT acct_nbr, trans_date,
   SUM(B1.trans_amt)
    OVER(PARTITION BY acct_nbr
        ORDER BY trans_date, trans_type,
      ROWS BETWEEN UNBOUNDED PRECEDING AND CURRENT ROW)
  AS acct_balance
FROM BankAccounts;
```

If we showed the withdrawals before the deposits on that day, the balance could fall below zero, which might trigger some actions we do not want. The rule in banking is that deposits are credited before withdrawals on the same day. We could replace the transaction date with a timestamp to show all deposits with a time before all withdrawals to fool the query. This is a really bad design decision. You are combining a transaction type into a temporal value and you are destroying a true fact or creating a false one in the database. Use another column, such as:

```
trans_type CHAR(1) DEFAULT 'W' NOT NULL
    CHECK (trans_type IN ('D', 'W'))
```

But remember that not all situations have a clearly defined policy like this.

### 31.6.1 Running Differences

Another kind of statistic, related to running totals, is running differences. In this case, we have the actual amount of something at various points in time and we want to compute the change since the last reading. Here is a quick scenario: We have a clipboard and a paper form on which we record the quantities of a chemical in a tank at different points in time from a gauge. We need to report the time, the gauge reading, and the difference between each reading and the preceding one. Here is some sample result data, showing the calculation we need:

| tank_nbr | reading_time | tank_qty | tank_diff |
|---|---|---|---|
| '50A' | '2015-02-01 07:30' | 300 | NULL ◀ starting data |
| '50A' | '2015-02-01 07:35' | 500 | 200 |
| '50A' | '2015-02-01 07:45' | 1200 | 700 |
| '50A' | '2015-02-01 07:50' | 800 | -400 |
| '50A' | '2015-02-01 08:00' | NULL | NULL |
| '50A' | '2015-02-01 09:00' | 1300 | 500 |
| '51A' | '2015-02-01 07:20' | 6000 | NULL ◀ starting data |
| '51A' | '2015-02-01 07:22' | 8000 | 2000 |
| '51A' | '2015-02-01 09:30' | NULL | NULL |
| '51A' | '2015-02-01 00:45' | 5000 | -3000 |
| '51A' | '2015-02-01 01:00' | 2500 | -2500 |

The NULL values mean that we missed taking a reading. The trick is a correlated subquery expression that computes the difference between the quantity in the current row and the quantity in the row with the largest known time value that is less than the time in the current row on the same date and on the same tank.

```
SELECT tank_nbr, reading_time,
   (tank_qty
    - (SELECT tank_qty
        FROM Deliveries AS D1
        WHERE D1.tank_nbr = D0.tank_nbr -- same tank
         AND D1.reading_time
          = (SELECT MAX (D2.reading_time) -- most recent
              FROM Deliveries AS D2
              WHERE D2.tank_nbr = D0.tank_nbr -- same tank
               AND D2.reading_time < D0.reading_time)))
          AS tank_diff
FROM Deliveries AS D0;
```

or with the window clause:

```
SELECT tank_nbr, reading_time, tank_qty,
   (tank_qty
    - MAX(tank_qty)
      OVER(PARTITION BY tank_nbr
          ORDER BY reading_time DESC
        ROWS 1 PRECEDING))
   AS tank_diff
FROM Deliveries;
```

### 31.6.2 Cumulative Percentages

Cumulative percentages are a bit more complex than running totals or differences. They show what percentage of the whole set of data values the current subset of data values is. Again, this is easier to show with an example than to say in words. You are given a table of the sales made by your sales force, which looks like this:

```
CREATE TABLE Sales
(salesman_id CHAR(10)NOT NULL,
client_name CHAR(10) NOT NULL,
sales_amt DECIMAL (9,2) NOT NULL,
PRIMARY KEY (salesman_id, client_name));
```

The problem is to show each salesman, his client, the amount of that sale, what percentage of his total sales volume that one sale represents, and the cumulative percentage of his total sales we have reached at that point. We will sort the clients from the largest amount to the smallest. This problem is based on a salesman's report originally written for a small commercial printing company. The idea was to show the salesmen where their business was coming from and to persuade them to give up their smaller accounts (defined as the lower 20%) to new salesmen. The report let the salesman run his finger down the page and see which customers represented the top 80% of his income.

We can use derived tables to build layers of aggregation in the same query.

```
SELECT S0.salesman_id, S0.client_name, S0.sales_amt,
   ((S0.sales_amt * 100)/ ST.salesman_id_total)
   AS percent_of_total,
   (SUM(S1.sales_amt)
    /((S0.sales_amt * 100)/ ST.salesman_id_total))
   AS cum_percent
FROM Sales AS S0
   INNER JOIN
   Sales AS S1
   ON (S0.salesman_id, S0.client_name)
    <= (S1.salesman_id, S1.client_name)
   INNER JOIN
   (SELECT S2.salesman_id, SUM(S1.sales_amt)
     FROM Sales AS S2
    GROUP BY S2.salesman_id)
   AS ST(salesman_id, salesman_id_total)
   ON S0.salesman_id = ST.salesman_id
GROUP BY S0.salesman_id, S0.client_name, S0.sales_amt;
```

However, if your SQL allows subqueries in the `SELECT` clause but not in the `FROM` clause, you can fake it with this query:

```
SELECT S0.salesman_id, S0.client_name, S0.sales_amt
 (S0.sales_amt * 100.00/ (SELECT SUM(S1.sales_amt)
         FROM Sales AS S1
         WHERE S0.salesman_id = S1.salesman_id))
 AS percentage_of_total,
 (SELECT SUM(S3.sales_amt)
   FROM Sales AS S3
   WHERE S0.salesman_id = S3.salesman_id
    AND (S3.sales_amt > S0.sales_amt
     OR (S3.sales_amt = S0.sales_amt
      AND S3.client_name >= S0.client_name))) * 100.00
 / (SELECT SUM(S2.sales_amt)
    FROM Sales AS S2
    WHERE S0.salesman_id = S2.salesman_id) AS cum_percent
FROM Sales AS S0;
```

These queries will probably run like glue. However, we have some new window functions in the SQL:2003 Standard. They are called the distribution functions and they compute a relative rank of a row R within its window partition as an approximate numeric ratio between zero and one. There are two variants, `PERCENT_RANK` and `CUME_DIST`.

PERCENT_RANK is defined as (<rank of current row> -1)/ (<count of rows in the partition>- 1). It is defined as:

```
CASE
WHEN COUNT(*)
 OVER(<partition and order clauses>
   RANGE BETWEEN UNBOUNDED PRECEDING
       AND UNBOUNDED FOLLOWING) = 1
THEN CAST (0 AS <approximate numeric type>)
ELSE (CAST (RANK ()
      OVER(<partition and order clauses>)
    AS <approximate numeric type>) - 1)
   /(COUNT (*)
     OVER(<partition and order clauses>
       RANGE BETWEEN UNBOUNDED PRECEDING
           AND UNBOUNDED FOLLOWING) - 1)
END
```

The choice for <approximate numeric type> and its precision are implementation-defined.

CUME_DIST is defined as (<count of preceding rows> / <count of rows in the partition>). Again, it can be written:

```
(CAST (COUNT (*)
   OVER(<partition and order clauses>
     RANGE UNBOUNDED PRECEDING)
  AS <approximate numeric type>)
/ COUNT(*)
  OVER(<partition and order clauses>
    RANGE BETWEEN UNBOUNDED PRECEDING
        AND UNBOUNDED FOLLOWING))
```

The <approximate numeric type> and <partition and order clauses> are the same actual text in each case when you expand them.

## 31.6.3 Ordinal Functions

How do you rank your salesmen given a SalesReport table that looks like this?

```
CREATE TABLE SalesReport
(salesman_id CHAR(20) NOT NULL PRIMARY KEY
 REFERENCES Salesforce(salesman_id),
sales_tot DECIMAL (8,2) NOT NULL);
```

This statistic is called a ranking. A ranking is shown as integers that represent the ordinal values (first, second, third, and so on) of the elements of a set based on one of the values. In this case, sales personnel are ranked by their total sales within a territory_nbr. The one with the highest total sales is in first place, the next highest is in second place, and so forth.

The hard question is how to handle ties. The rule is that if two salespersons have the same value, they have the same ranking and there are no gaps in the rankings. This is the nature of ordinal numbers—there cannot be a third place without a first and a second place.

Today we have RANK() and DENSE_RANK() ordinal functions, but this was not always the case. A query that will do this for us is:

```
SELECT S1.salesman_id, S1.sales_tot,
   (SELECT COUNT(DISTINCT sales_tot)
     FROM SalesReport AS S2
     WHERE S2.sales_tot >= S1.sales_tot) AS rank
FROM SalesReport AS S1;
```

You might also remember that is really a version of the generalized extrema functions we already discussed. Another way to write this query is thus:

```
SELECT S1.salesman_id, MAX(S1.sales_tot),
   SUM (CASE
     WHEN (S1.sales_tot || S1.name)
      <= (S2.sales_tot || S2.name)
     THEN 1 ELSE 0 END) AS rank
 FROM SalesReport AS S2, SalesReport AS S2
WHERE S1.salesman_id <> S2.salesman_id
GROUP BY S1.salesman_id, S1.territory_nbr;
```

This query uses the MAX() function on the nongrouping columns in the SalesReport to display them so that the aggregation will work. It is worth looking at the four possible variations on this basic query to see what each change does to the result set.

Version 1: COUNT(DISTINCT) and >= yields a ranking.

```
SELECT S1.salesman_id, S1.sales_tot,
 (SELECT COUNT(DISTINCT sales_tot)
    FROM SalesReport AS S2
   WHERE S2.sales_tot >= S1.sales_tot) AS rank
FROM SalesReport AS S1;
```

| salesman_id | sales_tot | rank |
|---|---|---|
| 'Wilson' | 990.00 | 1 |
| 'Smith' | 950.00 | 2 |
| 'Richards' | 800.00 | 3 |

| salesman_id | sales_tot | rank |
|---|---|---|
| 'Quinn' | 700.00 | 4 |
| 'Parker' | 345.00 | 5 |
| 'Jones' | 345.00 | 5 |
| 'Hubbard' | 345.00 | 5 |
| 'Date' | 200.00 | 6 |
| 'Codd' | 200.00 | 6 |
| 'Blake' | 100.00 | 7 |

Version 2: `COUNT(DISTINCT)` and > yields a ranking, but it starts at zero.

```
SELECT S1.salesman_id, S1.sales_tot,
  (SELECT COUNT(DISTINCT sales_tot)
    FROM SalesReport AS S2
    WHERE S2.sales_tot > S1.sales_tot) AS rank
 FROM SalesReport AS S1;
```

| salesman_id | sales_tot | rank |
|---|---|---|
| 'Wilson' | 990.00 | 0 |
| 'Smith' | 950.00 | 1 |
| 'Richard' | 800.00 | 2 |
| 'Quinn' | 700.00 | 3 |
| 'Parker' | 345.00 | 4 |
| 'Jones' | 345.00 | 4 |
| 'Hubbard' | 345.00 | 4 |
| 'Date' | 200.00 | 5 |
| 'Codd' | 200.00 | 5 |
| 'Blake' | 100.00 | 6 |

Version 3: `COUNT(ALL)` and >= yields a standing that starts at one.

```
SELECT S1.salesman_id, S1.sales_tot,
   (SELECT COUNT(sales_tot)
     FROM SalesReport AS S2
     WHERE S2.sales_tot >= S1.sales_tot) AS standing
 FROM SalesReport AS S1;
```

| salesman_id | sales_tot | standing |
|---|---|---|
| 'Wilson' | 990.00 | 1 |
| 'Smith' | 950.00 | 2 |
| 'Richard' | 800.00 | 3 |
| 'Quinn' | 700.00 | 4 |
| 'Parker' | 345.00 | 7 |
| 'Jones' | 345.00 | 7 |
| 'Hubbard' | 345.00 | 7 |
| 'Date' | 200.00 | 9 |
| 'Codd' | 200.00 | 9 |
| 'Blake' | 100.00 | 10 |

**Version 4:** `COUNT(ALL)` **and** > **yields a standing that starts at zero.**

```
SELECT S1.salesman_id, S1.sales_tot,
   (SELECT COUNT(sales_tot)
     FROM SalesReport AS S2
     WHERE S2.sales_tot > S1.sales_tot) AS standing
 FROM SalesReport AS S1;
```

| salesman_id | sales_tot | standing |
|---|---|---|
| 'Wilson' | 990.00 | 0 |
| 'Smith' | 950.00 | 1 |
| 'Richard' | 800.00 | 2 |
| 'Quinn' | 700.00 | 3 |
| 'Parker' | 345.00 | 4 |
| 'Jones' | 345.00 | 4 |
| 'Hubbard' | 345.00 | 4 |
| 'Date' | 200.00 | 7 |
| 'Codd' | 200.00 | 7 |
| 'Blake' | 100.00 | 9 |

Another system used in some British schools and horse racing will also leave gaps in the numbers, but in a different direction. For example given this set of marks:

| Marks | class_standing |
|---|---|
| 100 | 1 |
| 90 | 2 |
| 90 | 2 |
| 70 | 4 |

Both students with 90 were second because only one person had a higher mark. The student with 70 was fourth because there were three people ahead of him. With our data that would be:

```
SELECT S1.salesman_id, S1.sales_tot,
   (SELECT COUNT(S2. sales_tot)
     FROM SalesReport AS S2
    WHERE S2.sales_tot > S1.sales_tot) + 1
   AS british
 FROM SalesReport AS S1;
```

| salesman_id | sales_tot | british |
|---|---|---|
| 'Wilson' | 990.00 | 1 |
| 'Smith' | 950.00 | 2 |
| 'Richard' | 800.00 | 3 |
| 'Quinn' | 700.00 | 4 |
| 'Parker' | 345.00 | 5 |
| 'Jones' | 345.00 | 5 |
| 'Hubbard' | 345.00 | 5 |
| 'Date' | 200.00 | 8 |
| 'Codd' | 200.00 | 8 |
| 'Blake' | 100.00 | 10 |

As an aside for the mathematicians among the readers, I always use the heuristics that it helps solve an SQL problem to think in terms of sets. What we are looking for in these ranking queries is how to assign an ordinal number to a subset of the SalesReport table. This subset is the rows with an equal or higher sales volume than the salesman at whom we are looking. Or in other words, one copy of the SalesReport table provides the elements of the subsets and the other copy provides the boundary of the subsets. This count is really a sequence of nested subsets.

If you happen to have had a good set theory course, you would remember John von Neumann's definition of the n-th ordinal number; it is the set of all ordinal numbers less than the n-th number.

### 31.6.4 Quintiles and Related Statistics

Once you have the ranking, it is fairly easy to classify the data set into percentiles, quintiles, or deciles. These are courser versions of a ranking that use subsets of roughly equal size. A quintile is one fifth of the population, a decile is one tenth of the population, and a percentile is one one-hundredth of the population. I will present quintiles here, since whatever we do for them can be generalized to other partitionings. This statistic is popular with schools, so I will use the SAT scores for a mythical group of students for my example.

```
SELECT T1.student_id, T1.score, T1.rank,
  CASE WHEN T1.rank <= 0.2 * T2.population_size THEN 1
    WHEN T1.rank <= 0.4 * T2.population_size THEN 2
    WHEN T1.rank <= 0.6 * T2.population_size THEN 3
    WHEN T1.rank <= 0.8 * T2.population_size THEN 4
    ELSE 5 END AS quintile
FROM (SELECT S1.student_id, S1.score,
      (SELECT COUNT(*)
        FROM SAT_Scores AS S2
       WHERE S2.score >= S1.score)
    FROM SAT_Scores AS S1) AS T1(student_id, score, rank)
   CROSS JOIN
   SELECT COUNT(*) FROM SAT_Scores)
    AS T2(population_size);
```

The idea is straightforward; compute the rank for each element, then put it into a bucket whose size is determined by the population size. There are the same problems with ties that we had with rankings and what to do when the population is skewed.

You may or may not find vendor extensions for this, so be careful.

## 31.7 Cross Tabulations

A cross tabulation, or crosstabs for short, is a common statistical report. It can be done in IBM's QMF tool, using the ACROSS summary option, and in many other SQL-based reporting packages.

SPSS, SAS, and other statistical packages have library procedures or language constructs for crosstabs. Many spreadsheets can load the results of SQL queries and perform a crosstabs within the spreadsheet.

If you can use a reporting package on the server in a client/server system instead of the following method, do so. It will run faster and in less space than the method discussed here.

However, if you have to use the reporting package on the client side, the extra time required to transfer data will make these methods on the server side much faster.

Having said all this, Standard SQL has `CUBE` and `ROLLUP` options in the `GROUP BY`, which does all this for you. The following programming tricks are mostly of historical interest.

A one-way crosstabs "flattens out" a table to display it in a report format. Assume that we have a table of sales by product and the dates the sales were made. We want to print out a report of the sales of products by years for a full decade. The solution is to create a table and populate it to look like an identity matrix (all elements on the diagonal are 1, all others zero) with a rightmost column of all ones to give a row total, then `JOIN` the Sales table to it.

```
CREATE TABLE Sales
(product_name CHAR(15) NOT NULL,
product_price DECIMAL(5,2) NOT NULL,
order_qty INTEGER NOT NULL,
sales_year INTEGER NOT NULL);

CREATE TABLE Crosstabs
(sales_year INTEGER NOT NULL,
year1 INTEGER NOT NULL,
year2 INTEGER NOT NULL,
year3 INTEGER NOT NULL,
year4 INTEGER NOT NULL,
year5 INTEGER NOT NULL,
row_total INTEGER NOT NULL);
```

The table would be populated as follows:

| sales_year | year1 | year2 | year3 | year4 | year5 | row_total |
|---|---|---|---|---|---|---|
| 1990 | 1 | 0 | 0 | 0 | 0 | 1 |
| 1991 | 0 | 1 | 0 | 0 | 0 | 1 |
| 1992 | 0 | 0 | 1 | 0 | 0 | 1 |
| 1993 | 0 | 0 | 0 | 1 | 0 | 1 |
| 1994 | 0 | 0 | 0 | 0 | 1 | 1 |

The query to produce the report table is:

```
SELECT S1.product_name,
  SUM(S1.order_qty * S1.product_price * C1.year1),
  SUM(S1.order_qty * S1.product_price * C1.year2),
  SUM(S1.order_qty * S1.product_price * C1.year3),
  SUM(S1.order_qty * S1.product_price * C1.year4),
  SUM(S1.order_qty * S1.product_price * C1.year5),
  SUM(S1.order_qty * S1.product_price * C1.row_total)
 FROM Sales AS S1, Crosstabs AS C1
WHERE S1.year = C1.year
GROUP BY S1.product_name;
```

Obviously, `SUM(S1.product_price * S1.order_qty)` is the total dollar amount of each product in each year. The yearN column will be either a one or a zero. If it is a zero, the total dollar amount in the SUM() is zero; if it is a one, the total dollar amount in the SUM() is unchanged.

This solution lets you adjust the time frame being shown in the report by replacing the values in the year column to whatever consecutive years you wish. A two-way crosstabs takes two variables and produces a spreadsheet with all values of one variable on the rows and all values of the other represented by the columns. Each cell in the table holds the `COUNT` of entities that have those values for the two variables. `NULL`s will not fit into a crosstabs very well, unless you decide to make them a group of their own or to remove them.

There are also totals for each column and each row and a grand total. Crosstabs of (n) variables are defined by building an n-dimensional spreadsheet. But you cannot easily print (n) dimensions on two-dimensional paper. The usual trick is to display the results as a two-dimensional grid with one or both axes as a tree structure. The way the values are nested on the axis is usually under program control; thus, "race within sex" shows sex broken down by race, whereas "sex within race" shows race broken down by sex.

Assume that we have a table, Personnel (emp_nbr, sex, race, job_nbr, salary_amt_amt), keyed on employee number, with no `NULL`s in any columns. We wish to write a crosstabs of employees by sex and race, which would look like this:

| | asian | black | cauc | hisp | Other | totals |
|---|---|---|---|---|---|---|
| Male | 3 | 2 | 12 | 5 | 5 | 27 |
| Female | 1 | 10 | 20 | 2 | 9 | 42 |
| TOTAL | 4 | 12 | 32 | 7 | 14 | 69 |

The first thought is to use a GROUP BY and write a simple query, thus:

```
SELECT sex, race, COUNT(*)
 FROM Personnel
GROUP BY sex, race;
```

This approach works fine for two variables and would produce a table that could be sent to a report writer program to give a final version. But where are your column and row totals? This means you also need to write these two queries:

```
SELECT race, COUNT(*) FROM Personnel GROUP BY race;
SELECT sex, COUNT(*) FROM Personnel GROUP BY sex;
```

However, what I wanted was a table with a row for males and a row for females, with columns for each of the racial groups, just as I drew it.

But let us assume that we want to get this information broken down within a third variable, say job code. I want to see the job_nbr and the total by sex and race within each job code. Our query set starts to get bigger and bigger. A crosstabs can also include other summary data, such as total or average salary_amt within each cell of the table.

## 31.7.1 Crosstabs by Cross Join

A solution proposed by John M. Baird of Datapoint, in San Antonio, Texas, involves creating a matrix table for each variable in the crosstabs, thus:

SexMatrix

| Sex | Male | Female |
|---|---|---|
| 'M' | 1 | 0 |
| 'F' | 0 | 1 |

RaceMatrix

| Race | asian | black | cauc | hisp | other |
|---|---|---|---|---|---|
| Asian | 1 | 0 | 0 | 0 | 0 |
| Black | 0 | 1 | 0 | 0 | 0 |

*(Continued)*

| Race | asian | black | cauc | hisp | other |
|---|---|---|---|---|---|
| Cauc | 0 | 0 | 1 | 0 | 0 |
| Hisp | 0 | 0 | 0 | 1 | 0 |
| Other | 0 | 0 | 0 | 0 | 1 |

The query then constructs the cells by using a CROSS JOIN (Cartesian product) and summation for each one, thus:

```
SELECT job_nbr,
   SUM(asian * male) AS AsianMale,
   SUM(asian * female) AS AsianFemale,
   SUM(black * male) AS BlackMale,
   SUM(black * female) AS BlackFemale,
   SUM(cauc * male) AS CaucMale,
   SUM(cauc * female) AS CaucFemale,
   SUM(hisp * male) AS HispMale,
   SUM(hisp * female) AS HispFemale,
   SUM(other * male) AS OtherMale,
   SUM(other * female) AS OtherFemale
 FROM Personnel, SexMatrix, RaceMatrix
 WHERE RaceMatrix.race = Personnel.race
  AND SexMatrix.sex = Personnel.sex
 GROUP BY job_nbr;
```

Numeric summary data can be obtained from this table. For example, the total salary_amt for each cell can be computed by SUM(<race> * <sex> * salary_amt) AS <cell name> in place of what we have here.

## 31.7.2 Crosstabs by OUTER JOINs

Another method, due to Jim Panttaja, uses a series of temporary tables or VIEWs and then combines them with OUTER JOINs.

```
CREATE VIEW Guys (race, maletally)
AS SELECT race, COUNT(*)
  FROM Personnel
  WHERE sex = 'M'
  GROUP BY race;
```

Correspondingly, you could have written:

```
CREATE VIEW Dolls (race, femaletally)
AS
SELECT race, COUNT(*)
 FROM Personnel
```

```
 WHERE sex = 'F'
 GROUP BY race;
```

But they can be combined for a crosstabs, without column and row totals, like this:

```
SELECT Guys.race, maletally, femaletally
 FROM Guys
   LEFT OUTER JOIN
   Dolls
   ON Guys.race = Dolls.race;
```

The idea is to build a starting column in the crosstabs, then progressively add columns to it. You use the `LEFT OUTER JOIN` to avoid missing-data problems.

## 31.7.3 Crosstabs by Subquery

Another method takes advantage of the orthogonality of correlated subqueries in SQL-92. Think about what each row or column in the crosstabs wants.

```
SELECT DISTINCT race,
   (SELECT COUNT(*)
     FROM Personnel AS P1
    WHERE P0.race = P1.race
      AND sex = 'M') AS MaleTally,
   (SELECT COUNT(*)
     FROM Personnel AS P2
    WHERE P0.race = P2.race
     AND sex = 'F') AS FemaleTally
 FROM Personnel AS P0;
```

An advantage of this approach is that you can attach another column to get the row tally by adding:

```
(SELECT COUNT(*)
  FROM Personnel AS P3
 WHERE P0.race = P3.race) AS RaceTally
```

Likewise, to get the column tallies, union the previous query with:

```
SELECT 'Summary',
   (SELECT COUNT(*)
     FROM Personnel
    WHERE sex = 'M') AS GrandMaleTally,
   (SELECT COUNT(*)
     FROM Personnel
    WHERE sex = 'F') AS GrandFemaleTally,
   (SELECT COUNT(*)
     FROM Personnel) AS GrandTally
 FROM Personnel;
```

### 31.7.4 Crosstabs by CASE Expression

Probably the best method is to use the CASE expression. If you need to get the final row of the traditional crosstabs, you can add:

```
SELECT sex,
  SUM(CASE race WHEN 'cauc' THEN 1 ELSE 0 END) AS cauc,
  SUM(CASE race WHEN 'black' THEN 1 ELSE 0 END) AS black,
  SUM(CASE race WHEN 'asian' THEN 1 ELSE 0 END) AS asian,
  SUM(CASE race WHEN 'hisp' THEN 1 ELSE 0 END) AS latino,
  SUM(CASE race WHEN 'other' THEN 1 ELSE 0 END) AS other,
  COUNT(*) AS row_total
 FROM Personnel
GROUP BY sex
UNION ALL
SELECT ' ',
  SUM(CASE race WHEN 'cauc' THEN 1 ELSE 0 END),
  SUM(CASE race WHEN 'black' THEN 1 ELSE 0 END),
  SUM(CASE race WHEN 'asian' THEN 1 ELSE 0 END),
  SUM(CASE race WHEN 'hisp' THEN 1 ELSE 0 END),
  SUM(CASE race WHEN 'other' THEN 1 ELSE 0 END),
  COUNT(*) AS column_total
 FROM Personnel;
```

## 31.8 Harmonic Mean and Geometric Mean

The Harmonic mean is defined as the reciprocal of the arithmetic mean of the reciprocals of the values of a set. It is appropriate when dealing with rates and prices. Of limited use, it is found mostly in averaging rates.

```
SELECT COUNT(*)/SUM(1.0/x) AS harmonic_mean
 FROM Foobar;
```

The geometric mean is the exponential of the mean of the logs of the data items. You can also express it as the n-th root of the product of the (n) data items. This second form is more subject to rounding errors than the first. The geometric mean is sometimes a better measure of central tendency than the simple arithmetic mean when you are analyzing change-over-time.

```
SELECT EXP (AVG (LOG (nbr))) AS geometric_mean
 FROM NumberTable;
```

If you have negative numbers this will blow up because the logarithm is not defined for values less than or equal to zero.

## 31.9 Multivariable Descriptive Statistics in SQL

More and more SQL products are adding more complicated descriptive statistics to their aggregate function library. For example, Ingres comes with a very nice set of such tools.

Many of the single-column aggregate functions for which we just gave code are built-in functions. If you have that advantage, then use them. They will have corrections for floating point rounding errors and be more accurate.

Descriptive statistics are not all single-column computations. You often want to know relationships among several variables for prediction and description. Let's pick one of these statistics, which is representative of this class of functions, and see what problems we have writing our own aggregate function for it.

### 31.9.1 Covariance

The covariance is defined as a measure of the extent to which two variables move together. Financial analysts use it to determine the degree to which return on two securities is related over time. A high covariance indicates similar movements. This code is due to Steve Kass:

```
CREATE TABLE Samples
(sample_nbr INTEGER NOT NULL PRIMARY KEY,
x FLOAT NOT NULL,
y FLOAT NOT NULL);

INSERT INTO Samples
VALUES (1, 3, 9), (2, 2, 7), (3, 4, 12), (4, 5, 15),
   (5, 6, 17);

SELECT sample_nbr, x, y,
   ((1.0/n) * SUM((x - xbar) * (y - ybar))) AS covariance
 FROM Samples
   CROSS JOIN
   (SELECT COUNT(*), AVG(x), AVG(y) FROM Samples)
   AS A (n, xbar, ybar)
GROUP BY n;
```

### 31.9.2 Pearson's r

One of the most useful statistics is Pearson's r, or the linear correlation coefficient. It measures the strength of the linear association between two variables. In English, given a set of observations (x1, y1), (x2, y2), ..., (xn, yn), I want to know, when one variable goes up or down, how well does the other variable follow it?

The correlation coefficient always takes a value between +1 and –1. Positive one means that they match to each exactly. Negative one means that increasing values in one variable correspond to decreasing values in the other variable. A correlation value close to zero indicates no association between the variables. In the real world, you will not see positive or negative ones very often—this would mean that you are looking at a natural law and not a statistical relationship. The values in-between are much more realistic, with 0.70 or greater being a strong correlation.

The formula translates into SQL in a straightforward manner.

```
CREATE TABLE Samples
(sample_name CHAR(3) NOT NULL PRIMARY KEY,
x REAL, y REAL);
INSERT INTO Samples
VALUES ('a', 1.0, 2.0), ('b', 2.0, 5.0), ('c', 3.0, 6.0);

-- r= 0.9608

SELECT (SUM(x - AVG(x)) * (y - AVG(y)))
    / SQRT(SUM((x - AVG(x))^2) * SUM((y - AVG(y))^2))
    AS pearson_r
FROM Samples;
```

where `SQRT()` is the square root function, which is quite common in SQL today and ^2 is the square of the number. Some products use `POWER(x, n)` instead of the exponent notation, or you can use repeated multiplication.

### 31.9.3 NULLs in Multivariable Descriptive Statistics

If (x, y) = (NULL, NULL) then the query will drop the pair in the aggregate functions, as per the usual rules of SQL. But what is the correct (or reasonable) behavior if (x, y) has one and only one NULL in the pair? We can make several arguments.

1. Drop the pairs that contain any NULLs. That is quick and easy with a `WHERE x IS NOT NULL AND y IS NOT NULL` clause added to the query. The argument is that if you do not know one or both values, how can you know what their relationship is?
2. Convert `(x, NULL)` to `(x, AVG(y))` and `(NULL, y)` to `(AVG(x), y)`. The idea is to "smooth out" the missing values with a reasonable replacement that is based on the whole set from which known values were drawn. There might be better replacement values in a particular situation, but that idea would still hold.
3. I can argue for replacing `(NULL, NULL)` with `(a, a)` for some value to say that the NULLs are in the same grouping. This kind of "pseudo-equality" is the basis for putting NULLs into one group in a `GROUP BY` operation. I am not sure what the correct practice for the `(x, NULL)` and `(y, NULL)` pairs are.

4. First calculate a linear regression with the known pairs, say y = (a + b * x), and then fill in the expected values. If you forgot your high school algebra, that would be y[i] = a + b * x[i] for the pair (x[i], NULL), and x[i] = (y - a) / b.
5. In Standard SQL, you get an SQLSTATE warning code to show that an aggregate function has dropped NULLs before doing the computations. I could catch that message and use it to report to the user about the missing data.

I can also use COUNT(*) and COUNT(x + y) to determine how much data is missing. I think we would all agree that if I have a small subset of non-NULL pairs, then my correlation is less reliable than if I obtained it from a large subset of non-NULL pairs.

There is no right answer to this question. You will need to know the nature of your data to make a good decision.

## 31.10 Statistical Functions in SQL:2006

Although these exist in the SQL:2006 Standards, they are not widely implemented. Someone decided to implement most of the statistical functions from a freshman statistics course and got it approved. They have an "SQL twist" to them so they can handle NULLs and search conditions.

I am not going to try to teach a freshman "statistics in a SQL:2006" course; if you don't know these terms, get a book.

### 31.10.1 Variance, Standard Deviation, and Descriptive Stats

Frankly, I do not like these extensions and I hope they do not catch on. From a philosophical viewpoint, these are things that reduce data to information and SQL is a *data integrity and retrieval* language and is not supposed to do this. From a practical viewpoint, SQL is a *data integrity and retrieval* language that does not do math with the precision and accuracy that a statistical language does.

Given a table with an independent variable expression, X, and a dependent variable expression, Y, we have predefined calculations based on the usual definitions.

Let N be the cardinality of a target table, let SUMX be the sum of the column of values of <independent variable expression>, let SUMY be the sum of the column of values of <dependent variable expression>, let SUMX2 be the sum of the squares of values in the <independent variable expression> column, let SUMY2 be the sum of the squares of values in the <dependent variable expression> column, and let SUMXY be the sum of the row-wise products of the value in the `<independent variable expression>` column times the value in the `<dependent variable expression>` column.

`STDDEV_POP` = Population Standard Deviation. This is equivalent to `SQRT(VAR_POP(X))`.

`STDDEV_SAMP` = Sample Standard Deviation.

`VAR_POP` = Population Variance. This equivalent to SQRT(VAR_SAMP(X)).

`VAR_SAMP` = Sample Variance.

`COVAR_POP` = Covariance of the population.

`COVAR_SAMP` = Covariance of the sample. If `N` is one, then the result is the `NULL` value, otherwise, the result is `(SUMXY-SUMX * SUMY/N)/(N-1)`.

## 31.10.2 Correlation

`CORR` = Pearson's r correlation. If `N * SUMX2 = SUMX * SUMX`, then the result is the `NULL` value. If `N * SUMY2 = SUMY * SUMY`, then the result is the `NULL` value. Otherwise, the result is `SQRT(POWER(N * SUMXY-SUMX * SUMY,2) / ((N * SUMX2-SUMX * SUMX) * (N * SUMY2-SUMY * SUMY)))`.

`REGR_SLOPE` =

`REGR_INTERCEPT` =

`REGR_COUNT` = the result is `N`. If `N` is zero, then the result is the NULL value.

`REGR_R2` = If `N * SUMX2 = SUMX * SUMX`, then the result is the `NULL` value. If `N * SUMY2` equals `SUMY * SUMY`, then the result is one. Otherwise, the result is `POWER(N * SUMXY-SUMX * SUMY,2) / ((N * SUMX2-SUMX * SUMX) * (N * SUMY2-SUMY * SUMY))`. If the exponent of the approximate mathematical result of the operation is not within the implementation-defined exponent range for the result data type, then the result is the NULL value.

Here is a list of shorthands.

```
REGR_AVGX = SUMX/N
REGR_AVGY = SUMY/N
REGR_SXX = (SUMX2-SUMX * SUMX/N)
REGR_SYY = (SUMY2-SUMY * SUMY/N)
REGR_SXY = (SUMXY-SUMX * SUMY/N)
```

## 31.10.3 Distribution Functions

These are extensions to the usual ordinal functions, like `ROW_NUMBER()`, `RANK()`, and `DENSE_RANK()`. The distribution functions compute a relative rank of a row R within the window partition of R defined by a window, expressed as an approximate numeric ratio between 0.0 and 1.0. There are two variants, indicated by the keywords PERCENT_RANK and CUME_DIST.

If PERCENT_RANK() is specified, then the relative rank of a row R is defined as (RK-1)/(NR-1), where RK is defined to be the RANK of R and NR is defined to be the number of rows in the window partition of R.

If CUME_DIST() is specified, then the relative rank of a row R is defined as NP/NR, where NP is defined to be the number of rows preceding or peer with R in the window ordering of the window partition of R, and NR is defined to be the number of rows in the window partition of R.

# 32

# SUBSEQUENCES, REGIONS, RUNS, GAPS, AND ISLANDS

We have already talked about the GROUP BY clause in queries. The groups in a GROUP BY do not depend on any orderings. But you will often want to make other groupings that depend on an ordering of some kind. Examples of this sort of data would be ticket numbers, time series data taken at fixed intervals, and the like, which can have missing data or subsequences that are of interest. These things are easier to explain with examples. Consider a skeleton table with a sequential key and seven rows.

```
CREATE TABLE List
(list_seq INTEGER NOT NULL PRIMARY KEY,
list_val INTEGER NOT NULL UNIQUE);

INSERT INTO List
VALUES (1, 99), (2, 10), (3, 11), (4, 12), (5, 13),
   (6, 14), (7, 0);
```

A subsequence in the list_val column can be increasing, decreasing, monotonic, or not. Let's look at rows where the values are increasing uniformly by steps of one. You can find subsequences of size three that follow the rule—(10, 11, 12), (11, 12, 13), and (12, 13, 14)—but the longest subsequence is (10, 11, 12, 13, 14), and it is of size five.

A run is like a sequence, but the numbers do not have to be consecutive, just increasing (or decreasing) and in sequence. For example, given the run {(1, 1), (2, 2), (3, 12), (4, 15), (5, 23)}, you can find subruns of size three: (1, 2, 12), (2, 12, 15), and (12, 15, 23).

A region is contiguous and all the values are the same. For example, {(1, 1), (2, 0), (3, 0), (4, 0), (5, 25)} has a region of zeros that is three items long.

In procedural languages, you would simply sort the data and scan it. In SQL, you used to have to define everything in terms of sets and fancy joins to get an ordering if it was not in the data. Today, we have ROW_NUMBER() to get us a sequence number for ordering the data.

Joe Celko's SQL for Smarties. DOI: 10.1016/B978-0-12-382022-8.00032-6

## 32.1 Finding Subregions of Size (n)

This example is adapted from *SQL and Its Applications* (Lorie and Daudenarde, 1991). You are given a table of theater seats, defined by:

```
CREATE TABLE Theater
(seat_nbr INTEGER NOT NULL PRIMARY KEY,-- sequencing
   number
occupancy_status CHAR(1) DEFAULT 'A' NOT NULL-- values
    CONSTRAINT valid_occupancy_status
    CHECK (occupancy_status IN ('A', 'S'));
```

where an occupancy_status code of 'A' means available and 'S' means sold. Your problem is to write a query that will return the subregions of (n) consecutive seats still available. Assume that consecutive seat numbers means that the seats are also consecutive for a moment, ignoring rows of seating where seat_nbr(n) and seat_nbr((n) + 1) might be on different physical theater rows. For (n) = 3, we can write a self-JOIN query, thus:

```
SELECT T1.seat_nbr, T2.seat_nbr, T3.seat_nbr
 FROM Theater AT T1, Theater AT T2, Theater AT T3
WHERE T1.occupancy_status = 'A'
  AND T2.occupancy_status = 'A'
  AND T3.occupancy_status = 'A'
  AND T2.seat_nbr = T1.seat_nbr + 1
  AND T3.seat_nbr = T2.seat_nbr + 1;
```

The trouble with this answer is that it works only for (n = 3) and nothing else. This pattern can be extended for any (n), but what we really want is a generalized query where we can use (n) as a parameter to the query.

The solution given by Lorie and Daudenarde starts with a given seat_nbr and looks at all the available seats between it and ((n) − 1) seats further up. The real trick is switching from the English-language statement, "All seats between here and there are available," to the passive-voice version, "Available is the occupancy_status of all the seats between here and there," so that you can see the query.

```
SELECT seat_nbr, ' thru ', (seat_nbr + (:n - 1))
 FROM Theater AS T1
WHERE occupancy_status = 'A'
  AND 'A' = ALL (SELECT occupancy_status
           FROM Theater AS T2
          WHERE T2.seat_nbr > T1.seat_nbr
           AND T2.seat_nbr <= T1.seat_nbr + (:n - 1));
```

Please notice that this returns subregions. That is, if seats (1, 2, 3, 4, 5) are available, this query will return (1, 2, 3), (2, 3, 4), and (3, 4, 5) as its result set.

## 32.2 Numbering Regions

Instead of looking for a region, we want to number the regions in the order in which they appear. For example, given a view or table with a payment history we want to break it into groupings of behavior, say whether or not the payments were on time or late.

```
CREATE TABLE PaymentHistory
(payment_nbr INTEGER NOT NULL PRIMARY KEY,
paid_on_time_flg CHAR(1) DEFAULT 'Y' NOT NULL
   CHECK(paid_on_time_flg IN ('Y', 'N')));

INSERT INTO PaymentHistory
VALUES (1006, 'Y'), (1005, 'Y'),
(1004, 'N'),
(1003, 'Y'), (1002, 'Y'), (1001, 'Y'),
(1000, 'N');
```

In the results, we want to assign a grouping number to each run of on-time/late payments, thus.

Results

| grping | payment_nbr | paid_on_time_flg |
|---|---|---|
| 1 | 1006 | 'Y' |
| 1 | 1005 | 'Y' |
| 2 | 1004 | 'N' |
| 3 | 1003 | 'Y' |
| 3 | 1002 | 'Y' |
| 3 | 1001 | 'Y' |
| 4 | 1000 | 'N' |

A solution by Hugo Kornelis depends on the payments always being numbered consecutively.

```
SELECT (SELECT COUNT(*)
     FROM PaymentHistory AS H2,
       PaymentHistory AS H3
    WHERE H3.payment_nbr = H2.payment_nbr + 1
     AND H3.paid_on_time_flg <> H2.paid_on_time_flg
     AND H2.payment_nbr >= H1.payment_nbr) + 1 AS grping,
  payment_nbr, paid_on_time_flg
FROM PaymentHistory AS H1;
```

This can be modified for more types of behavior.

Here is another version using the ordinal functions. Let's assume we have a test that returns 'A' or 'B' and we want to see clusters where the score stayed the same:

```
CREATE TABLE Tests
(sample_time TIMESTAMP NOT NULL PRIMARY KEY,
sample_score CHAR(1) NOT NULL);

INSERT INTO Tests
VALUES ('2014-01-01 12:00:00', 'A'),
   ('2014-01-01 12:01:00', 'A'),
   ('2014-01-01 12:02:00', 'A'),
   ('2014-01-01 12:03:00', 'B'),
   ('2014-01-01 12:04:00', 'B'),
   ('2014-01-01 12:05:00', 'A'),
   ('2014-01-01 12:06:00', 'A'),
   ('2014-01-01 12:07:00', 'A'),
   ('2014-01-01 12:08:00', 'A'),
   ('2014-01-01 12:09:00', 'B'),
   ('2014-01-01 12:10:00', 'B'),
   ('2014-01-01 12:11:00', 'A'),
   ('2014-01-01 12:12:00', 'A'),
   ('2014-01-01 12:13:00', 'C'),
   ('2014-01-01 12:14:00', 'D'),
   ('2014-01-01 12:15:00', 'A');

SELECT MIN(X.sample_time) AS cluster_start,
   MAX(X.sample_time) AS cluster_end,
   MIN(X.sample_score) AS cluster_score
FROM (SELECT sample_time, sample_score,
     (ROW_NUMBER () OVER (ORDER BY sample_time)
            • ROW_NUMBER() OVER (PARTITION BY sample_score

         ORDER BY sample_time))
FROM Tests) AS X(sample_time, sample_score, cluster_nbr)
GROUP BY cluster_nbr;
```

These groupings are called clusters or islands, or "OLAP sorting" in the literature.

## 32.3 Finding Regions of Maximum Size

A query to find a region, rather than a subregion of a known size, of seats was presented in *SQL Forum* (Rozenshtein, Abramovich, and Birger, 1993).

```
SELECT T1.seat_nbr AS start_seat_nbr, T2.seat_nbr
   AS end_seat_nbr
 FROM Theater AS T1, Theater AS T2
```

```
WHERE T1.seat_nbr < T2.seat_nbr
  AND NOT EXISTS
      (SELECT *
        FROM Theater AS T3
       WHERE (T3.seat_nbr BETWEEN T1.seat_nbr AND
          T2.seat_nbr
        AND T3.occupancy_status <> 'A')
         OR (T3.seat_nbr = T2.seat_nbr + 1
            AND T3.occupancy_status = 'A')
         OR (T3.seat_nbr = T1.seat_nbr - 1
            AND T3.occupancy_status = 'A'));
```

The trick here is to look for the starting and ending seats in the region. The starting seat_nbr of a region is to the right of a sold seat_nbr and the ending seat_nbr is to the left of a sold seat_nbr. No seat_nbr between the start and the end has been sold.

If you only keep the available seat_nbrs in a table, the solution is a bit easier. It is also a more general problem that applies to any table of sequential, possibly noncontiguous, data:

```
CREATE TABLE AvailableSeating
(seat_nbr INTEGER NOT NULL
    CONSTRAINT valid_seat_nbr
    CHECK (seat_nbr BETWEEN 001 AND 999));

INSERT INTO Seatings
VALUES (199), (200), (201), (202), (204),
   (210), (211), (212), (214), (218);
```

where you need to create a result that will show the start and finish values of each sequence in the table, thus:

Results

| start_seat_nbr | end_seat_nbr |
|---|---|
| 199 | 202 |
| 204 | 204 |
| 210 | 212 |
| 214 | 214 |
| 218 | 218 |

This is a common way of finding the missing values in a sequence of tickets sold, unaccounted for invoices, and so forth. Imagine a number line with closed dots for the numbers that are in the table and open dots for the numbers that are not. What do you see about a sequence? Well, we can start with a fact that anyone who has done inventory knows. The number of elements in a sequence is equal to the ending sequence number minus the starting sequence number plus one. This is a basic property of ordinal numbers:

(finish − start + 1) = count of open seats

This tells us that we need to have a self-JOIN with two copies of the table, one for the starting value and one for the ending value of each sequence. Once we have those two items, we can compute the length with our formula and see if it is equal to the count of the items between the start and finish.

```
SELECT S1.seat_nbr, MAX(S2.seat_nbr)-- start and rightmost
   item
 FROM AvailableSeating AS S1
   INNER JOIN
   AvailableSeating AS S2-- self-join
   ON S1.seat_nbr <= S2.seat_nbr
    AND (S2.seat_nbr - S1.seat_nbr + 1)-- formula for length
     = (SELECT COUNT(*)-- items in the sequence
        FROM AvailableSeating AS S3
       WHERE S3.seat_nbr BETWEEN S1.seat_nbr
               AND S2.seat_nbr)
        AND NOT EXISTS (SELECT *
                FROM AvailableSeating AS S4
               WHERE S1.seat_nbr - 1
                 = S4.seat_nbr)
GROUP BY S1.seat_nbr;
```

Finally, we need to be sure that we have the furthest item to the right as the end item. Each sequence of (n) items has (n) subsequences that all start with the same item. So we finally do a GROUP BY on the starting item and use a MAX() to get the rightmost value.

However, there is a faster version with three tables. This solution is based on another property of the longest possible sequences. If you look to the right of the last item, you do not find anything. Likewise, if you look to the left of the first item, you do not find anything either. These missing items that are "just over the border" define a sequence by framing it. There also cannot be any "gaps"—missing items—inside those borders. That translates into SQL as:

```
SELECT S1.seat_nbr, MIN(S2.seat_nbr)-- start and leftmost
   border
 FROM AvailableSeating AS S1, AvailableSeating AS S2
WHERE S1.seat_nbr <= S2.seat_nbr
  AND NOT EXISTS-- border items of the sequence
   (SELECT *
      FROM AvailableSeating AS S3
```

```
    WHERE S3.seat_nbr NOT BETWEEN S1.seat_nbr AND
      S2.seat_nbr
     AND (S3.seat_nbr = S1.seat_nbr - 1
       OR S3.seat_nbr = S2.seat_nbr + 1))
GROUP BY S1.seat_nbr;
```

We do not have to worry about getting the rightmost item in the sequence, but we do have to worry about getting the leftmost border. Once we do a `GROUP BY`, but use a `MIN()` to get what we want.

Since the second approach uses only three copies of the original table, it should be a bit faster. Also, the `EXISTS()` predicates can often take advantage of indexing and thus run faster than subquery expressions, which require a table scan.

The new ordinal functions allow you to answer these queries without explicit self-joins or a sequencing column. Since self-joins are expensive, it is better to use ordinal functions that might be optimized. Consider a single column of integers:

```
CREATE TABLE Foobar (data_val INTEGER NOT NULL PRIMARY KEY);
INSERT INTO Foobar
VALUES (1), (2), (5), (6), (7), (8), (9), (11), (12), (22);
```

Here is a query to get the final results:

```
WITH X (data_val, data_seq, absent_data_grp)
AS
(SELECT data_val,
   ROW_NUMBER() OVER (ORDER BY data_val ASC) ,
   (data_val
    - ROW_NUMBER() OVER (ORDER BY data_val ASC))
  FROM Foobar)

SELECT absent_data_val, COUNT(*), MIN(data_val) AS
   start_data_val
 FROM X
GROUP BY absent_data_val;
```

The CTE produces this result. The absent_data_grp tells you how many values are missing from the data values, just not what they are.

| data_val | data_seq | absent_data_grp |
|---|---|---|
| 1 | 1 | 0 |
| 2 | 2 | 0 |
| 5 | 3 | 2 |
| 6 | 4 | 2 |

*(Continued)*

| data_val | data_seq | absent_data_grp |
|---|---|---|
| 7 | 5 | 2 |
| 8 | 6 | 2 |
| 9 | 7 | 2 |
| 11 | 8 | 3 |
| 12 | 9 | 3 |
| 22 | 10 | 12 |

The final query gives us:

| absent_data_grp | COUNT(*) | start_data_val |
|---|---|---|
| 0 | 2 | 1 |
| 2 | 5 | 5 |
| 3 | 2 | 11 |
| 12 | 1 | 22 |

so, the maximum contiguous sequence is five rows. Since it starts at 5, we know that the contiguous set is {5, 6, 7, 8, 9}.

## 32.4 Bound Queries

Another form of query asks if there was an overall trend between two points in time bounded by a low value and a high value in the sequence of data. This is easier to show with an example. Let us assume that we have data on the selling prices of a stock in a table. We want to find periods of time when the price was generally increasing.

Consider this data:

MyStock

| sale_date | stock_price |
|---|---|
| '2011-12-01' | 10.00 |
| '2011-12-02' | 15.00 |
| '2011-12-03' | 13.00 |
| '2011-12-04' | 12.00 |
| '2011-12-05' | 20.00 |

The stock was generally increasing in all the periods that began on December 1 or ended on December 5—that is, it finished higher at the ends of those periods, in spite of the slump in the middle. A query for this problem is:

```
SELECT S1.sale_date AS start_date, S2.sale_date AS
   finish_date
 FROM MyStock AS S1, MyStock AS S2
WHERE S1.sale_date < S2.sale_date
 AND NOT EXISTS
   (SELECT *
     FROM MyStock AS S3
     WHERE S3.sale_date BETWEEN S1.sale_date AND
        S2.sale_date
      AND S3.stock_price
       NOT BETWEEN S1.stock_price AND S2.stock_price);
```

## 32.5 Run and Sequence Queries

Runs are informally defined as sequences with gaps. That is, we have a set of unique numbers whose order has some meaning, but the numbers are not all consecutive. Time series information where the samples are taken at irregular intervals is an example of this sort of data. Runs can be constructed in the same manner as the sequences by making a minor change in the search condition. Let's do these queries with an abstract table made up of a sequence number and a value:

```
CREATE TABLE Runs
(list_seq INTEGER NOT NULL PRIMARY KEY,
list_val INTEGER NOT NULL);
```

Runs

| list_seq | list_val |
|---|---|
| 1 | 6 |
| 2 | 41 |
| 3 | 12 |
| 4 | 51 |
| 5 | 21 |
| 6 | 70 |
| 7 | 79 |

*(Continued)*

| list_seq | list_val |
|---|---|
| 8 | 62 |
| 9 | 30 |
| 10 | 31 |
| 11 | 32 |
| 12 | 34 |
| 13 | 35 |
| 14 | 57 |
| 15 | 19 |
| 16 | 84 |
| 17 | 80 |
| 18 | 90 |
| 19 | 63 |
| 20 | 53 |
| 21 | 3 |
| 22 | 59 |
| 23 | 69 |
| 24 | 27 |
| 25 | 33 |

One of the problems is that we do not want to get back all the runs and sequences of length one. Ideally, the length (n) of the run should be adjustable. This query will find runs of length (n) or greater; if you want runs of exactly (n), change the "greater than" to an equal sign.

```
SELECT R1.list_seq AS start_list_seq,
   R2.list_seq AS end_list_seq_nbr
 FROM Runs AS R1, Runs AS R2
WHERE R1.list_seq < R2.list_seq-- start and end points
 AND (R2.list_seq - R1.list_seq) > (:n - 1)-- length
    restrictions
 AND NOT EXISTS-- ordering within the end points
   (SELECT *
      FROM Runs AS R3, Runs AS R4
     WHERE R4.list_seq BETWEEN R1.list_seq AND R2.list_seq
      AND R3.list_seq BETWEEN R1.list_seq AND R2.list_seq
      AND R3.list_seq < R4.list_seq
      AND R3.list_val > R4.list_val);
```

What this query does is set up the S1 sequence number as the starting point and the S2 sequence number as the ending point of the run. The monster subquery in the `NOT EXISTS()` predicate is looking for a row in the middle of the run that violates the ordering of the run. If there is none, the run is valid. The best way to understand what is happening is to draw a linear diagram. This shows that as the ordering, list_seq, increases, so must the corresponding values, list_val.

A sequence has the additional restriction that every value increases by 1 as you scan the run from left to right. This means that in a sequence, the highest value minus the lowest value, plus one, is the length of the sequence.

```
SELECT R1.list_seq AS start_list_seq, R2.list_seq AS
   end_list_seq_nbr
 FROM Runs AS R1, Runs AS R2
WHERE R1.list_seq < R2.list_seq
  AND (R2.list_seq - R1.list_seq) = (R2.list_val -
     R1.list_val)-- order condition
  AND (R2.list_seq - R1.list_seq) > (:n - 1)-- length
     restrictions
  AND NOT EXISTS
    (SELECT *
      FROM Runs AS R3
      WHERE R3.list_seq BETWEEN R1.list_seq AND R2.list_seq
       AND((R3.list_seq - R1.list_seq)
         <> (R3.list_val - R1.list_val)
        OR (R2.list_seq - R3.list_seq)
          <> (R2.list_val - R3.list_val)));
```

The subquery in the `NOT EXISTS` predicate says that there is no point in between the start and the end of the sequence that violates the ordering condition.

Obviously, any of these queries can be changed from increasing to decreasing, from strictly increasing to simply increasing or simply decreasing, and so on, by changing the comparison predicates. You can also change the query for finding sequences in a table by altering the size of the step from 1 to k, by observing that the difference between the starting position and the ending position should be k times the difference between the starting value and the ending value.

### 32.5.1 Filling in Missing Numbers

A fair number of SQL programmers want to reuse a sequence of numbers for keys. Although I do not approve of the practice of generating a meaningless, unverifiable key after the creation of an entity, the problem of inserting missing numbers is interesting. The usual specifications are:

1. The sequence starts with 1, if it is missing or the table is empty.
2. We want to reuse the lowest missing number first.

3. Do not exceed some maximum value; if the sequence is full, then give us a warning or a NULL. Another option is to give us (MAX(list_seq) +1) so we can add to the high end of the list.

This answer is a good example of thinking in terms of sets rather than doing row-at-a-time processing.

```
SELECT MIN(new_list_seq)
 FROM (SELECT CASE
     WHEN list_seq + 1 NOT IN (SELECT list_seq FROM List)
     THEN list_seq + 1
     WHEN list_seq - 1 NOT IN (SELECT list_seq FROM List)
     THEN list_seq - 1
     WHEN 1 NOT IN (SELECT list_seq FROM List)
     THEN 1 ELSE NULL END
   FROM List
   WHERE list_seq BETWEEN 1
         AND (SELECT MAX(list_seq) FROM List)
  AS P(new_list_seq);
```

The idea is to build a table expression of some of the missing values, then pick the minimum one. The starting value, 1, is treated as an exception. Since an aggregate function cannot take a query expression as a parameter, we have to use a derived table.

Along the same lines, we can use aggregate functions in a CASE expression:

```
SELECT CASE WHEN MAX(list_seq) = COUNT(*)
     THEN CAST(NULL AS INTEGER)
    -- THEN MAX(list_seq) + 1 as other option
     WHEN MIN(list_seq) > 1
     THEN 1
     WHEN MAX(list_seq) <> COUNT(*)
     THEN (SELECT MIN(list_seq)+1
        FROM List
        WHERE (list_seq)+1
          NOT IN (SELECT list_seq FROM List))
    ELSE NULL END
 FROM List;
```

The first WHEN clause sees if the table is already full and returns a NULL; the NULL has to be cast as an INTEGER to become an expression that can then be used in the THEN clause. However, you might want to increment the list by the next value.

The second WHEN clause looks to see if the minimum sequence number is 1 or not. If so, it uses 1 as the next value.

The third WHEN clause handles the situation when there is a gap in the middle of the sequence. It picks the lowest missing number. The ELSE clause is in case of errors and should not be executed.

The order of execution in the CASE expression is important. It is a way of forcing an inspection from front to back of the table's values. Simpler methods based on group characteristics would be:

```
SELECT COALESCE(MIN(L1.list_seq) + 1, 1)
 FROM List AS L1
  LEFT OUTER JOIN
  List AS L2
  ON L1.list_seq = L2.list_seq - 1
WHERE L2.list_seq IS NULL;
```

or:

```
SELECT MIN(list_seq + 1)
 FROM (SELECT list_seq FROM List
  UNION ALL
  SELECT list_seq
   FROM (VALUES (0)))
  AS X(list_seq)
WHERE (list_seq +1)
  NOT IN (SELECT list_seq FROM List);
```

Finding entire gaps follows from this pattern and we get this short piece of code.

```
SELECT (s + 1) AS gap_start,
   (e - 1) AS gap_end
 FROM (SELECT L1.list_seq, MIN(L2.list_seq)
   FROM List AS L1, List AS L2
   WHERE L1.list_seq < L2.list_seq
   GROUP BY L1.list_seq)
  AS G(s, e)
WHERE (e - 1) > s;
```

or without the derived table:

```
SELECT (L1.list_seq + 1) AS gap_start,
   (MIN(L2.list_seq) - 1) AS gap_end
 FROM List AS L1, List AS L2
WHERE L1.list_seq < L2.list_seq
GROUP BY L1.list_seq
HAVING (MIN(L2.list_seq) - L1.list_seq) > 1;
```

## 32.6 Summation of a Series

Before we had the ordinal functions, building a running total of the values in a table was a difficult task. Let's build a simple table with a sequencing column and the values we wish to total.

```
CREATE TABLE Series
(list_seq INTEGER NOT NULL PRIMARY KEY,
list_val INTEGER NOT NULL);

SELECT list_seq, list_val,
   SUM (list_val)
    OVER (ORDER BY list_seq
      ROWS BETWEEN UNBOUNDED PRECEDING AND CURRENT ROW)
   AS running_tot
 FROM Series;
```

A sample result would look like this:

| list_seq | list_val | running_tot |
|---|---|---|
| 1 | 6 | 6 |
| 2 | 41 | 47 |
| 3 | 12 | 59 |
| 4 | 51 | 110 |
| 5 | 21 | 131 |
| 6 | 70 | 201 |
| 7 | 79 | 280 |
| 8 | 62 | 342 |
| ... | | |

This is the form we can use for most problems of this type with only one level of summation. It is easy to write an UPDATE statement to store the running total in the table, if it does not have to be recomputed each query. But things can be worse. This problem came from Francisco Moreno and on the surface it sounds easy. First, create the usual table and populate it:

```
CREATE TABLE Series
(list_seq INTEGER NOT NULL,
list_val REAL NOT NULL,
running_avg REAL);

INSERT INTO Series
VALUES (0, 6.0, NULL),
  (1, 6.0, NULL),
  (2, 10.0, NULL),
  (3, 12.0, NULL),
  (4, 14.0, NULL);
```

The goal is to compute the average of the first two terms, then add the third list_val to the result and average the two of them, and so forth. This is not the same thing as:

```
SELECT list_seq, list_val,
   AVG(list_val)
   OVER (ORDER BY list_seq
     ROWS BETWEEN UNBOUNDED PRECEDING AND CURRENT ROW)
   AS running_avg
FROM Series;
```

In this data, we want this answer:

| list_seq | list_val | running_avg |
|---|---|---|
| 0 | 6.0 | NULL |
| 1 | 6.0 | 6.0 |
| 2 | 10.0 | 8.0 |
| 3 | 12.0 | 10.0 |
| 4 | 14.0 | 12.0 |

| list_seq | list_val | running_avg |
|---|---|---|
| 1 | 12.0 | NULL |
| 2 | 10.0 | NULL |
| 3 | 12.0 | NULL |
| 4 | 14.0 | NULL |

The obvious approach is to do the calculations directly.

```
UPDATE Series
 SET running_tot = (Series.list_val
        + (SELECT S1.running_tot
           FROM Series AS S1
           WHERE S1.list_seq = Series.list_seq - 1))/2.0
WHERE running_tot IS NULL;
```

But there is a problem with this approach. It will only calculate one list_val at a time. The reason is that this series is much more complex than a simple running total.

What we have is actually a double summation, in which the terms are defined by a continued fraction. Let's work out the first four answers by brute force and see if we can find a pattern.

```
answer1 = (12)/2 = 6
answer2 = ((12)/2 + 10)/2 = 8
answer3 = (((12)/2 + 10)/2 + 12)/2 = 10
answer4 = (((((12)/2 + 10)/2 + 12)/2) + 14)/2 = 12
```

The real trick is to do some algebra and get rid of the nested parentheses.

```
answer1 = (12)/2 = 6
answer2 = (12/4) + (10/2) = 8
answer3 = (12/8) + (10/4) + (12/2) = 10
answer4 = (12/16) + (10/8) + (12/4) + (14/2) = 12
```

When we see powers of 2, we know we can do some algebra:

```
answer1 = (12)/2^1 = 6
answer2 = (12/(2^2)) + (10/(2^1)) = 8
answer3 = (12/(2^3)) + (10/(2^2)) + (12/(2^1)) = 10
answer4 = (12/2^4) + (10/(2^3)) + (12/(2^2)) +
   (14/(2^1)) = 12
```

The problem is that you need to "count backward" from the current list_val to compute higher powers for the previous terms of the summation. That is simply `(current_list_val - previous_list_val + 1)`. Putting it all together, we get this expression.

```
UPDATE Series
 SET running_avg
   = (SELECT SUM(list_val
        * POWER(2,
            CASE WHEN S1.list_seq > 0
              THEN Series.list_seq - S1.list_seq + 1
              ELSE NULL END))
        FROM Series AS S1
        WHERE S1.list_seq < = Series.list_seq);
```

The `POWER`(base, exponent) function is part of SQL:2003, but check your product for implementation-defined precision and rounding.

## 32.7 Swapping and Sliding Values in a List

You will often want to manipulate a list of values, changing their sequence position numbers. The simplest such operation is to swap two values in your table.

```
CREATE PROCEDURE SwapValues
(IN low_list_seq INTEGER, IN high_list_seq INTEGER)
LANGUAGE SQL
BEGIN-- put them in order
SET least_list_seq
 = CASE WHEN low_list_seq <= high_list_seq
     THEN low_list_seq ELSE high_list_seq;
SET greatest_list_seq
 = CASE WHEN low_list_seq <= high_list_seq
     THEN high_list_seq ELSE low_list_seq;
UPDATE Runs-- swap
 SET list_seq = least_list_seq + ABS(list_seq
   - greatest_list_seq)
WHERE list_seq IN (least_list_seq, greatest_list_seq);
END;
```

The CASE expressions could be folded into the UPDATE statement, but it makes the code harder to read.

Inserting a new value into the table is easy:

```
CREATE PROCEDURE InsertValue (IN new_value INTEGER)
LANGUAGE SQL
INSERT INTO Runs (list_seq, list_val)
VALUES ((SELECT MAX(list_seq) FROM Runs) + 1, new_value);
```

A bit trickier procedure is moving one value to a new position and sliding the remaining values either up or down. This mimics the way a physical queue would act. Here is a solution from Dave Portas.

```
CREATE PROCEDURE SlideValues
(IN old_list_seq INTEGER, IN new_list_seq INTEGER)
LANGUAGE SQL
UPDATE Runs
 SET list_seq
   = CASE
     WHEN list_seq = old_list_seq THEN new_list_seq
     WHEN list_seq BETWEEN old_list_seq AND new_list_seq
        THEN list_seq - 1
     WHEN list_seq BETWEEN new_list_seq AND old_list_seq
        THEN list_seq + 1
     ELSE list_seq END
WHERE list_seq BETWEEN old_list_seq AND new_list_seq
 OR list_seq BETWEEN new_list_seq AND old_list_seq;
```

This handles moving a value to a higher or lower position in the table. You can see how calls or slight changes to these procedures could do other related operations.

One of the most useful tricks is to have calendar table that has a Julianized date column. Instead of trying to manipulate temporal data, convert the dates to a sequence of integers and treat the queries as regions, runs, gaps, and so forth.

The sequence can be made up of calendar days or Julianized business days, which do not include holidays and weekend. There are a lot of possible methods.

## 32.8 Condensing a List of Numbers

The goal is to take a list of numbers and condense them into contiguous ranges. Show the high and low values for each range; if the range has one number, then the high and low values will be the same. This answer is due to Steve Kass.

```
SELECT MIN(i) AS low, MAX(i) AS high
FROM (SELECT N1.i, COUNT(N2.i) - N1.i
   FROM Numbers AS N1, Numbers AS N2
   WHERE N2.i <= N1.i
   GROUP BY N1.i)
  AS N(i, gp)
GROUP BY gp;
```

## 32.9 Folding a List of Numbers

It is possible to use the Series table to give columns in the same row, which are related to each other, values with a little math instead of self-joins.

For example, given the numbers 1 to (n), you might want to spread them out across (k) columns. Let (k = 3) so we can see the pattern.

```
SELECT list_seq,
   CASE WHEN MOD((list_seq + 1), 3) = 2
       AND list_seq + 1 <= :n
     THEN (list_seq + 1)
     ELSE NULL END AS second,
   CASE WHEN MOD((list_seq + 2), 3) = 0
       AND (list_seq + 2) <= :n
     THEN (list_seq + 2)
     ELSE NULL END AS third
 FROM Series
WHERE MOD((list_seq + 3), 3) = 1
 AND list_seq <= :n;
```

Columns that have no value assigned to them will get a `NULL`. That is, for (n = 8) the incomplete row will be (`7, 8, NULL`) and for (n = 7) it would be (`7, NULL, NULL`). We never get a row with (`NULL, NULL, NULL`).

The use of math can be fancier. In a golf tournament, the players with the lowest and highest scores are matched together for the next round. Then the players with the second lowest and second highest scores are matched together, and so forth. If there are an odd number of players, the player with the middle score sits out that round. These pairs can be built with a simple query.

```
SELECT list_seq AS low_score,
   CASE WHEN list_seq <= (:n - list_seq)
     THEN (:n - list_seq) + 1
     ELSE NULL END AS high_score
FROM Series AS S1
WHERE S1.list_seq
   <= CASE WHEN MOD(:n, 2) = 1
      THEN FLOOR(:n/2) + 1
      ELSE (:n/2) END;
```

If you play around with the basic math functions, you can do quite a bit.

## 32.10 Coverings

Vadim Tropashko proposed the problem of writing the shortest SQL query that would return a minimal cover of a set of intervals. For example, given this table, how do you find the contiguous numbers that are completely covered by the given intervals?

```
CREATE TABLE Intervals
(x INTEGER NOT NULL,
y INTEGER NOT NULL,
CHECK (x <= y),
PRIMARY KEY (x, y));

INSERT INTO Intervals
VALUES (1, 3),(2, 5),(4, 11),
  (10, 12), (20, 21),
  (120, 130), (120, 128), (120, 122),
  (121, 132), (121, 122), (121, 124), (121, 123),
  (126, 127);
```

The query should return:

Results

| min_x | MAX(y) |
|---|---|
| 1 | 12 |
| 20 | 21 |
| 120 | 132 |

Dieter Nöth found an answer with OLAP functions:

```
SELECT min_x, MAX(y)
 FROM (SELECT x, y,
      MAX(CASE WHEN x <= MAX_Y THEN NULL ELSE x END)
      OVER (ORDER BY x, y
        ROWS UNBOUNDED PRECEDING) AS min_x
    FROM (SELECT x, y,
          MAX(y)
          OVER(ORDER BY x, y
          ROWS BETWEEN UNBOUNDED PRECEDING
          AND 1 PRECEDING) AS max_y
        FROM Intervals)
       AS DT)
   AS DT
GROUP BY min_x;
```

Here is a query that uses a self-join and three levels of correlated subquery that uses the same approach.

```
SELECT I1.x, MAX(I2.y) AS y
 FROM Intervals AS I1
  INNER JOIN
  Intervals AS I2
  ON I2.y > I1.x
WHERE NOT EXISTS
  (SELECT *
    FROM Intervals AS I3
    WHERE I1.x - 1 BETWEEN I3.x AND I3.y)
      AND NOT EXISTS
       (SELECT *
         FROM Intervals AS I4
         WHERE I4.y > I1.x
          AND I4.y < I2.y
          AND NOT EXISTS
           (SELECT *
             FROM Intervals AS I5
             WHERE I4.y + 1 BETWEEN I5.x AND I5.y))
GROUP BY I1.x;
```

And this is essentially the same format, but converted to use left anti-semi-joins instead of subqueries. I do not think it is shorter, but it might execute better on some platforms and some people prefer this format to subqueries.

```
SELECT I1.x, MAX(I2.y) AS y
 FROM Intervals AS I1
  INNER JOIN
  Intervals AS I2
  ON I2.y > I1.x
```

```
    LEFT OUTER JOIN
    Intervals AS I3
    ON I1.x - 1 BETWEEN I3.x AND I3.y
     LEFT OUTER JOIN
     (Intervals AS I4
     LEFT OUTER JOIN
     Intervals AS I5
     ON I4.y + 1 BETWEEN I5.x AND I5.y)
    ON I4.y > I1.x
     AND I4.y < I2.y
     AND I5.x IS NULL
WHERE I3.x IS NULL
  AND I4.x IS NULL
GROUP BY I1.x;
```

If the table is large, the correlated subqueries (version 1) or the quintuple self-join (version 2) will probably make it slow. But we were asked for a short query, not for a quick one.

Tony Andrews came with this answer.

```
SELECT Starts.x, Ends.y
 FROM (SELECT x, ROW_NUMBER() OVER(ORDER BY x) AS rn
   FROM (SELECT x, y,
        LAG(y) OVER(ORDER BY x) AS prev_y
      FROM Intervals)
   WHERE prev_y IS NULL
    OR prev_y < x) AS Starts,
 (SELECT y, ROW_NUMBER() OVER(ORDER BY y) AS rn
   FROM (SELECT x, y,
        LEAD(x) OVER(ORDER BY y) AS next_x
      FROM Intervals)
      WHERE next_x IS NULL
       OR y < next_x) AS Ends
WHERE Starts.rn = Ends.rn;
```

John Gilson decided that using recursion is an interesting take on this and made this offering:

```
WITH RECURSIVE Cover (x, y, n)
AS (SELECT x, y, (SELECT COUNT(*) FROM Intervals)
  FROM Intervals
  UNION ALL
  SELECT CASE WHEN I3.x <= I.x THEN I3.x ELSE I.x END,
     CASE WHEN I3.y >= I.y THEN I3.y ELSE I.y END,
     I3.n - 1
   FROM Intervals AS I, Cover AS C
   WHERE I.x <= I3.y
    AND I.y >= I3.x
    AND (I.x <> I3.x OR I.y <> I3.y)
    AND I3.n > 1);
```

```
SELECT DISTINCT C1.x, C1.y
FROM Cover AS C1
WHERE NOT EXISTS
  (SELECT *
    FROM Cover AS C2
    WHERE C2.x <= C1.x
     AND C2.y >= C1.y
     AND (C1.x <> C2.x OR C1.y <> C2.y))
ORDER BY C1.x;
```

Finally, try this approach. Assume we have the usual Series auxiliary table. Now we find all the holes in the range of the intervals and put them in a VIEW or a WITH clause derived table.

```
CREATE VIEW Holes (hole)
AS
SELECT list_seq
 FROM Series
WHERE list_seq <= (SELECT MAX(y) FROM Intervals)
  AND NOT EXISTS
   (SELECT *
     FROM Intervals
     WHERE list_seq BETWEEN x AND y)
   UNION (SELECT list_seq FROM (VALUES (0))
      AS L(list_seq)
   UNION SELECT MAX(y) + 1 FROM Intervals
      AS R(list_seq)-- right sentinel value
   );
```

The query picks start and end pairs that are on the edge of a hole and counts the number of holes inside that range. Covering has no holes inside its range.

```
SELECT Starts.x, Ends.y
 FROM Intervals AS Starts,
  Intervals AS Ends,
  Series AS S-- usual auxiliary table
WHERE S.list_seq BETWEEN Starts.x AND Ends.y-- restrict
   list_seq numbers
  AND S.list_seq < (SELECT MAX(hole) FROM Holes)
  AND S.list_seq NOT IN (SELECT hole FROM Holes)-- not a
     hole
  AND Starts.x - 1 IN (SELECT hole FROM Holes)-- on a left
     cusp
  AND Ends.y + 1 IN (SELECT hole FROM Holes)-- on a right
     cusp
GROUP BY Starts.x, Ends.y
HAVING COUNT(DISTINCT list_seq) = Ends.y - Starts.x + 1;
   -- no holes
```

33

# MATRICES IN SQL

Arrays are not the same thing as matrices. An *array* is a data structure whose elements are accessed by a numeric value called an index. A *matrix* is an array with mathematical operations defined on it. A matrix can be one, two, three, or more dimensional structures. The most common mathematical convention has been to use the letters i, j, and k for the indexes.

SQL had neither arrays nor matrices because the only data structure in the Relational Model is a table. Arrays violate the rules of First Normal Form (1NF) required for a relational database, which say that all columns are scalars.

This was unfortunately changed in SQL:2003 with the addition of collection types. You can now declare a column to be an array of one of the SQL data types. The array is one-dimensional and has no mathematical operations on it. There is an array constructor and a comparison operation. The constructor can be a comma separated list or a query with an ORDER BY clause.

There is no obvious way to display or transmit a multidimensional array column as a result set. Different languages and different compilers for the same language store arrays in column-major or row-major order, so there is no standard. There is no obvious way to write constraints on nonscalar values.

The goal of SQL was to be a database language that would operate with a wide range of host languages. To meet that goal, the scalar data types are as varied as possible to match the host language data types, but as simple in structure as possible to make the transfer of data to the host language as easy as possible. The extensions after SQL-92 ruin all of these advantages.

## 33.1 Arrays via Named Columns

An array in other programming languages has a name and subscripts by which the array elements are referenced. The array elements are all of the same data type and the subscripts are all

Joe Celko's SQL for Smarties. DOI: 10.1016/B978-0-12-382022-8.00033-8

sequential integers. Some languages start numbering at zero, some start numbering at one, and some let the user set the upper and lower bounds. For example, a Pascal array declaration would look like this:

```
foobar : ARRAY [1..5] OF INTEGER;
```

Would have integer elements foobar[1], foobar[2], foobar[3], foobar[4], and foobar[5]. The same structure is most often mapped into an SQL declaration as:

```
CREATE TABLE Foobar1
(element1 INTEGER NOT NULL,
element2 INTEGER NOT NULL,
element3 INTEGER NOT NULL,
element4 INTEGER NOT NULL,
element5 INTEGER NOT NULL);
```

The elements cannot be accessed by the use of a subscript in this table as they can in a true array. That is, to set the array elements equal to zero in Pascal takes one statement with a FOR loop in it:

```
FOR i := 1 TO 5 DO foobar[i] := 0;
```

The same action in SQL would be performed with the statement:

```
UPDATE Foobar1
 SET element1 = 0,
   element2 = 0,
   element3 = 0,
   element4 = 0,
   element5 = 0;
```

because there is no subscript that can be iterated in a loop. Any access has to be based on column names and not on subscripts. These "pseudo-subscripts" lead to building column names on the fly in dynamic SQL, giving code that is both slow and dangerous. Even worse, some users will use the same approach in table names to destroy their logical data model.

Let's assume that we design an Employee table with separate columns for the names of four children, and we start with an empty table and then try to use it.

1. What happens if we hire a man with fewer than four children? We can fire him immediately or make him have more children. We can restructure the table to allow for fewer children. The usual, and less drastic, solution is to put NULLs in the columns for the nonexistent children. We then have all the problems associated with NULLs to handle.

2. What happens if we hire a man with five children?
   We can fire him immediately or order him to kill one of his children. We can restructure the table to allow five children. We can add a second row to hold the information on children 5 through 8; however, this destroys the uniqueness of the emp_id, so it cannot be used as a key. We can overcome that problem by adding a new column for record number, which will form a two-column key with the emp_id. This leads to needless duplication in the table.
3. What happens if the employee dies?
   We will delete all his children's data along with his, even if the company owes benefits to the survivors. You could have a status of 'dead' for the employee and a lot of logic in any statement about his family; this will not be pretty.
4. What happens if the child of an employee dies?
   We can fire him or order him to get another child immediately. We can restructure the table to allow only three children. We can overwrite the child's data with NULLs and get all of the problems associated with NULL values.
   This last one is the most common decision. But what if we had used the multiple-row trick and this employee had a fifth child—should that child be brought up into the vacant slot in the current row and the second row of the set deleted?
5. What happens if the employee replaces a dead child with a new one?
   Should the new child's data overwrite the NULLs in the dead child's data? Should the new child's data be put in the next available slot and overwrite the NULLs in those columns?

Some of these choices involve rebuilding the database. Others are simply absurd attempts to restructure reality to fit the database. The real point is that each insertion or deletion of a child involves a different procedure, depending on the size of the group to which he belongs. File systems had variant records that could change the size of their repeating groups.

Consider instead a table of employees and another table for the children:

```
CREATE TABLE Personnel
(emp_id INTEGER NOT NULL PRIMARY KEY,
emp_name CHAR(30) NOT NULL,
...);

CREATE TABLE Dependents
(emp_id INTEGER NOT NULL
  REFERENCES Personnel(emp_id)
  ON UPDATE CASCADE,
child_name CHAR(30) NOT NULL,
```

```
PRIMARY KEY (emp_id, child_name),
birth_date DATE NOT NULL,
sex_code CHAR(1) NOT NULL);
```

To add a child, you insert a row into Children. To remove a child, you delete a row from Children. There is nothing special about the fourth or fifth child that requires the database system to use special procedures. There are no NULLs in either table.

The trade-off is that the number of tables in the database schema increases, but the total amount of storage used will be smaller, because you will keep data only on children who exist rather than using NULLs to hold space. The goal is to have data in the simplest possible format so that any host program can use it.

Gabrielle Wiorkowski, in her excellent DB2 classes, used an example of a table for tracking the sales made by salespersons during the past year. That table could be defined as:

```
CREATE TABLE AnnualSales1
(salesman CHAR(15) NOT NULL PRIMARY KEY,
jan DECIMAL(5,2),
feb DECIMAL(5,2),
mar DECIMAL(5,2),
apr DECIMAL(5,2),
may DECIMAL(5,2),
jun DECIMAL(5,2),
jul DECIMAL(5,2),
aug DECIMAL(5,2),
sep DECIMAL(5,2),
oct DECIMAL(5,2),
nov DECIMAL(5,2),
"dec" DECIMAL(5,2) -- DEC[IMAL] is a reserved word
);
```

We have to allow for NULLs in the monthly sales_amts in the first version of the table, but the table is actually quite a bit smaller than it would be if we were to declare it as:

```
CREATE TABLE AnnualSales2
(salesman CHAR(15) NOT NULL PRIMARY KEY,
sale_month CHAR(3)
  CONSTRAINT valid_month_abbrev
  CHECK (sale_month IN ('Jan', 'Feb', 'Mar', 'Apr',
     'May', 'Jun', 'Jul', 'Aug',
     'Sep', 'Oct', 'Nov', 'Dec'),
sales_amt DECIMAL(5,2) NOT NULL,
PRIMARY KEY(salesman, sale_month));
```

In Wiorkowski's actual example in DB2, the break-even point for DASD storage was April; that is, the storage required for

AnnualSales1 and AnnualSales2 is about the same in April of the given year.

Queries that deal with individual salespersons will run much faster against the AnnualSales1 table than queries based on the AnnualSales2 table, because all the data is in one row in the AnnualSales1 table. They may be a bit messy and may have to have function calls to handle possible NULL values, but they are not very complex.

The only reason for using AnnualSales1 is that you have a data warehouse and all you want to see is summary information, grouped into years. This design is not acceptable in an OLTP system.

## 33.2 Arrays via Subscript Columns

Another approach to faking a multidimensional array is to map arrays into a table with an integer column for each subscript, thus:

```
CREATE TABLE Foobar2
(i INTEGER NOT NULL PRIMARY KEY
 CONSTRAINT valid_array_index
 CHECK(i BETWEEN 1 AND 5),
element_val REAL NOT NULL);
```

This looks more complex than the first approach, but it is closer to what the original Pascal declaration was doing behind the scenes. Subscripts resolve to unique physical addresses, so it is not possible to have two values for foobar[i]; hence, i is a key. The Pascal compiler will check to see that the subscripts are within the declared range; hence the CHECK() clause.

The first advantage of this approach is that multidimensional arrays are easily handled by adding another column for each subscript. The Pascal declaration,

```
ThreeD : ARRAY [1..3, 1..4, 1..5] OF REAL;
```

is mapped over to:

```
CREATE TABLE ThreeD
(i INTEGER NOT NULL
   CONSTRAINT valid_i
   CHECK(i BETWEEN 1 AND 3),
j INTEGER NOT NULL
   CONSTRAINT valid_j
   CHECK(j BETWEEN 1 AND 4),
k INTEGER NOT NULL
   CONSTRAINT valid_k
   CHECK(k BETWEEN 1 AND 5),
```

```
element_val REAL NOT NULL,
PRIMARY KEY (i, j, k));
```

Obviously, SELECT statements with GROUP BY clauses on the subscript columns will produce row and column totals, thus:

```
SELECT i, j, SUM(element_val) -- sum across the k columns
FROM ThreeD
GROUP BY i, j;

SELECT i, SUM(element_val) -- sum across the j and k columns
FROM ThreeD
GROUP BY i;

SELECT SUM(element_val) -- sum the entire array
FROM ThreeD;
```

If the original one element/one column approach were used, the table declaration would have 120 columns, named "element_val_111" through "element_val_345". This would be too many names to handle in any reasonable way; you would not be able to use the GROUP BY clauses for array projection, either.

Another advantage of this approach is that the subscripts can be data types other than integers. DATE and TIME data types are often useful, but CHARACTER and approximate numeric data types can have their uses too.

## 33.3 Matrix Operations in SQL

A matrix is not quite the same thing as an array. Matrices are mathematical structures with particular properties that we cannot take the time to discuss here. You can find that information in a college freshman algebra book. Though it is possible to do many matrix operations in SQL, it is not a good idea, because such queries and operations will eat up resources and run much too long. SQL was never meant to be a language for calculations.

Let us assume that we have two-dimensional arrays that are declared as tables, using two columns for subscripts, and that all columns are declared with a NOT NULL constraint.

The presence of NULLs is not defined in linear algebra and I have no desire to invent a three-valued linear algebra of my own. Another problem is that a matrix has rows and columns that are not the same as the rows and columns of an SQL table; as you read the rest of this section, be careful not to confuse the two.

```
CREATE TABLE MyMatrix
(element_val INTEGER NOT NULL, -- could be any numeric data
   type
```

```
i INTEGER NOT NULL CHECK (i > 0),
j INTEGER NOT NULL CHECK (j > 0),
CHECK ((SELECT MAX(i) FROM MyMatrix)
  = (SELECT COUNT(i) FROM MyMatrix)),
CHECK ((SELECT MAX(j) FROM MyMatrix)
  = (SELECT COUNT(j) FROM MyMatrix)));
```

The constraints see that the subscripts of each element are within proper range. I am starting my subscripts at one, but a little change in the logic would allow any value.

## 33.3.1 Matrix Equality

This test for matrix equality is from the article "SQL Matrix Processing" by Mrdalj, Vujovic, and Jovanovic in the July 1996 issue of *Database Programming & Design*. Two matrices are equal if their cardinalities and the cardinality of the their intersection are all equal.

```
SELECT COUNT(*) FROM MatrixA
UNION
SELECT COUNT(*) FROM MatrixB
UNION
SELECT COUNT(*)
 FROM MatrixA AS A, MatrixB AS B
WHERE A.i = B.i
  AND A.j = B.j
  AND A.element_val = B.element_val;
```

If this query returns one number, then MartixA and MatrixB are equal. Another way to do this uses set difference.

```
NOT EXISTS
 (SELECT * FROM MatrixA
  EXCEPT
  SELECT * FROM MatrixB)
AND NOT EXISTS
 (SELECT * FROM MatrixB
  EXCEPT
  SELECT * FROM MatrixA)
```

## 33.3.2 Matrix Addition

Matrix addition and subtraction are possible only between matrices of the same dimensions. The obvious way to do the addition is simply:

```
SELECT A.i, A.j, (A.element_val + B.element_val) AS total
 FROM MatrixA AS A, MatrixB AS B
WHERE A.i = B.i
  AND A.j = B.j;
```

But properly, you ought to add some checking to be sure the matrices match. We can assume that both start numbering subscripts with either one or zero.

```
SELECT A.i, A.j, (A.element_val + B.element_val) AS total
 FROM MatrixA AS A, MatrixB AS B
WHERE A.i = B.i
 AND A.j = B.j
 AND (SELECT COUNT(*) FROM MatrixA)
   = (SELECT COUNT(*) FROM MatrixB)
 AND (SELECT MAX(i) FROM MatrixA)
   = (SELECT MAX(i) FROM MatrixB)
 AND (SELECT MAX(j) FROM MatrixA)
   = (SELECT MAX(j) FROM MatrixB));
```

Likewise, to make the addition permanent, you can use the same basic query in an `UPDATE` statement:

```
UPDATE MatrixA
 SET element_val = element_val
        + (SELECT element_val
            FROM MatrixB
           WHERE MatrixB.i = MatrixA.i
            AND MatrixB.j = MatrixA.j)
WHERE (SELECT COUNT(*) FROM MatrixA)
  = (SELECT COUNT(*) FROM MatrixB)
 AND (SELECT MAX(i) FROM MatrixA)
  = (SELECT MAX(i) FROM MatrixB)
 AND (SELECT MAX(j) FROM MatrixA)
  = (SELECT MAX(j) FROM MatrixB));
```

## 33.3.3 Matrix Multiplication

Multiplication by a scalar constant is direct and easy:

```
UPDATE MyMatrix
 SET element_val = element_val * :constant;
```

Matrix multiplication is not as big a mess as might be expected.

Remember that the first matrix must have the same number of rows as the second matrix has columns. That means A[i, k] * B[k, j] = C[i, j], which we can show with an example:

```
CREATE TABLE MatrixA
(i INTEGER NOT NULL
 CHECK (i BETWEEN 1 AND 10), -- pick your own bounds
k INTEGER NOT NULL
 CHECK (k BETWEEN 1 AND 10), -- must match MatrixB.k range
```

```
element_val INTEGER NOT NULL,
PRIMARY KEY (i, k));

MatrixA
i  k  element_val
=================
1  1   2
1  2  -3
1  3   4
2  1  -1
2  2   0
2  3   2

CREATE TABLE MatrixB
(k INTEGER NOT NULL
 CHECK (k BETWEEN 1 AND 10), -- must match MatrixA.k range
j INTEGER NOT NULL
 CHECK (j BETWEEN 1 AND 4), -- pick your own bounds
element_val INTEGER NOT NULL,
PRIMARY KEY (k, j));

MatrixB
k  j  element_val
=================
1  1  -1
1  2   2
1  3   3
2  1   0
2  2   1
2  3   7
3  1   1
3  2   1
3  3  -2

CREATE VIEW MatrixC(i, j, element_val)
AS
SELECT i, j, SUM(MatrixA.element_val * MatrixB.element_val)
 FROM MatrixA, MatrixB
WHERE MatrixA.k = MatrixB.k
GROUP BY i, j;
```

This is taken directly from the definition of matrix multiplication.

### 33.3.4 Matrix Transpose

The transpose of a matrix is easy to do:

```
CREATE VIEW TransA (i, j, element_val)
AS SELECT j, i, element_val FROM MatrixA;
```

Again, you can make the change permanent with an UPDATE statement:

```
UPDATE MatrixA
 SET i = j, j = i;
```

Multiplication by a column or row vector is just a special case of matrix multiplication, but a bit easier. Given the vector V and MatrixA:

```
SELECT i, SUM(A.element_val * V.element_val)
FROM MatrixA AS A, VectorV AS V
WHERE V.j = A.i
GROUP BY A.i;
```

Cross tabulations and other statistical functions traditionally use an array to hold data. But you do not need a matrix for them in SQL.

It is possible to do other matrix operations in SQL, but the code becomes so complex, and the execution time so long, that it is simply not worth the effort. If a reader would like to submit queries for eigenvalues and determinants, I will be happy to put them in future editions of this book.

### 33.3.5 Row and Column Sorting

You can sort a row or a column with the ROW_NUMBER() function in Standard SQL:

```
UPDATE MatrixA
 SET i = ROW_NUMBER() OVER (ORDER BY element_val)
WHERE j = :my_column;
```

and likewise:

```
UPDATE MatrixA
 SET j = ROW_NUMBER() OVER (ORDER BY element_val)
WHERE i = :my_column;
```

### 33.3.6 Other Matrix Operations

If you had a good math course at some point in your education, you might remember the terms "Determinant," "Inverse," and "Eigenvalue," which have to do with using matrices to solve simultaneous equations. It is probably possible to write general queries for them with recursive CTEs and other functions. Do not do it. SQL is not a computational language and it will not run very well for a matrix of any size. Use Mathematica, MathLab, or some other product meant for this kind of thing.

## 33.4 Flattening a Table into an Array

Reports and data warehouse summary tables often want to see an array laid horizontally across a line. The original one element_val/ one column approach to mapping arrays was based on seeing such reports and duplicating that structure in a table. A subscript is often an enumeration, denoting a month or another time period, rather than an integer.

For example, a row in a "Salesmen" table might have a dozen columns, one for each month of the year, each of which holds the total commission earned in a particular month. The year is really an array, subscripted by the month. The subscripts-and-value approach requires more work to produce the same results. It is often easier to explain a technique with an example. Let us imagine a company that collects time cards from its truck drivers, each with the driver's name, the week within the year (numbered 0 to 51 or 52, depending on the year), and his total hours. We want to produce a report with one line for each driver and 6 weeks of his time across the page. The Timecards table looks like this:

```
CREATE TABLE Timecards
(driver_name CHAR(25) NOT NULL,
week_nbr INTEGER NOT NULL
 CONSTRAINT valid_week_nbr
 CHECK(week BETWEEN 0 AND 52)
work_hrs INTEGER
  CONSTRAINT zero_or_more_hours
  CHECK(work_hrs >= 0),
PRIMARY KEY (driver_name, week_nbr));
```

We need to "flatten out" this table to get the desired rows for the report. First create a working storage table from which the report can be built.

```
CREATE TEMPORARY TABLE TimeReportWork -- working storage
(driver_name CHAR(25) NOT NULL,
wk1 INTEGER, -- important that these columns are NULL-able
wk2 INTEGER,
wk3 INTEGER,
wk4 INTEGER,
wk5 INTEGER,
wk6 INTEGER);
```

Notice two important points about this table. First, there is no primary key; second, the weekly data columns are `NULL`-able. This table is then filled with time card values, thus:

```
INSERT INTO TimeReportWork (driver_name, wk1, wk2, wk3,
   wk4, wk5, wk6)
```

```
SELECT driver_name,
 SUM(CASE (week_nbr = :rpt_week_nbr)
  THEN work_hrs ELSE 0 END) AS wk1,
 SUM(CASE (week_nbr = :rpt_week_nbr - 1)
  THEN work_hrs ELSE 0 END) AS wk2,
 SUM(CASE (week_nbr = :rpt_week_nbr - 2)
  THEN work_hrs ELSE 0 END) AS wk3,
 SUM(CASE (week_nbr = :rpt_week_nbr - 3)
  THEN work_hrs ELSE 0 END) AS wk4,
 SUM(CASE (week_nbr = :rpt_week_nbr - 4)
  THEN work_hrs ELSE 0 END) AS wk5,
 SUM(CASE (week_nbr = :rpt_week_nbr - 5)
  THEN work_hrs ELSE 0 END) AS wk6
 FROM Timecards
WHERE week_nbr BETWEEN :rpt_week_nbr AND (:rpt_week_nbr - 5);
```

The number of the weeks in the `WHERE` clauses will vary with the period covered by the report. The parameter `:rpt_week_nbr` is week of the report and it computes backwards for the prior five weeks. If a driver did not work in a particular week, the corresponding weekly column gets a zero hours total. However, if the driver has not worked at all in the last six weeks, we could lose him completely (no time cards, no summary). Depending on the nature of the report, you might consider using an `OUTER JOIN` to a Personnel table to be sure you have all the driver's names.

The `NULL`s are coalesced to zero in this example, but if you drop the ..`ELSE 0` clauses, the `SUM()` will have to deal with a week of all `NULL`s and return a `NULL`. This lets you tell the difference between a driver who was missing for the reporting period and a driver who worked zero hours and turned in a time card for that during the period. That difference could be important for computing the payroll.

## 33.5 Comparing Arrays in Table Format

It is often necessary to compare one array or set of values with another when the data is represented in a table. Remember that comparing a set with a set does not involve ordering the elements, whereas an array does. For this discussion, let us create two tables, one for employees and one for their dependents. The children are subscripted in the order of their births; that is, 1 is the oldest living child, and so forth.

```
CREATE TABLE Personnel
(emp_id INTEGER PRIMARY KEY,
emp_name CHAR(15) NOT NULL,
... );
```

```
CREATE TABLE Dependents
(emp_id INTEGER NOT NULL -- the parent
dependent_name CHAR(15) NOT NULL, -- the array element
birth_seq INTEGER NOT NULL, -- the array subscript
PRIMARY KEY (emp_id, dependent_name));
```

The query, "Find pairs of employees whose children have the same set of names," is very restrictive, but we can make it more so by requiring that the children be named in the same birth order. Both Mr. X and Mr. Y must have exactly the same number of dependents; both sets of names must match. We can assume that no parent has two children with the same name (George Foreman does not work here) or born at the same time (we will order twins). Let us begin by inserting test data into the Dependents table, thus:

Dependents

| emp_id | dependent_name_name | birth_seq |
|---|---|---|
| 1 | 'Dick' | 2 |
| 1 | 'Harry' | 3 |
| 1 | 'Tom' | 1 |
| 2 | 'Dick' | 3 |
| 2 | 'Harry' | 1 |
| 2 | 'Tom' | 2 |
| 3 | 'Dick' | 2 |
| 3 | 'Harry' | 3 |
| 3 | 'Tom' | 1 |
| 4 | 'Harry' | 1 |
| 4 | 'Tom' | 2 |
| 5 | 'Curly' | 2 |
| 5 | 'Harry' | 3 |
| 5 | 'Moe' | 1 |

In this test data, employees 1, 2, and 3 all have dependents named 'Tom', 'Dick', and 'Harry'.

The birth order is the same for the children of employees 1 and 3, but not for employee 2.

For testing purposes, you might consider adding an extra child to the family of employee 3, and so forth, to play with this data.

Though there are many ways to solve this query, this approach will give us some flexibility that others would not. Construct a VIEW that gives us the number of dependents for each employee:

```
CREATE VIEW FamilySize (emp_id, tally)
AS
SELECT emp_id, COUNT(*)
FROM Dependents
GROUP BY emp_id;
```

Create a second VIEW that holds pairs of employees who have families of the same size.

This VIEW is also useful for other statistical work, but that is another topic.

```
CREATE VIEW Samesize (emp_id1, emp_id2, tally)
AS SELECT F1.emp_id, F2.emp_id, F1.tally
 FROM Familysize AS F1, Familysize AS F2
 WHERE F1.tally = F2.tally
  AND F1.emp_id < F2.emp_id;
```

We will test for set equality by doing a self-JOIN on the dependents of employees with families of the same size. If one set can be mapped onto another with no children left over, and in the same birth order, then the two sets are equal.

```
SELECT D1.emp_id, ' named his ',
   S1.tally, ' kids just like ',
   D2.emp_id
 FROM Dependents AS D1, Dependents AS D2, Samesize AS S1
WHERE S1.emp_id1 = D1.emp_id
 AND S1.emp_id2 = D2.emp_id
 AND D1.dependent_name = D2.dependent_name
 AND D1.birth_seq = D2.birth_seq
GROUP BY D1.emp_id, D2.emp_id, S1.tally
HAVING COUNT(*) = S1.tally;
```

If birth order is not important, then drop the predicate D1.birth_seq = D2.birth_seq from the query.

This is a form of exact relational division with a second column equality test as part of the criteria.

34

# SET OPERATIONS

By set operations, I mean union, intersection, and set differences where the sets in SQL are tables. These are the basic operators used in elementary set theory, which has been taught in the US public school systems for decades. Since the relational model is based on sets, you would expect that SQL would have had a good variety of set operators from the start. But this was not the case. Standard SQL has added the basic set operators, but they are still not common in actual products.

There is another problem in SQL that you did not have in high school set theory. SQL tables are multisets (also called bags), which means that, unlike sets, they allow duplicate elements (rows or tuples). Dr. Codd's relational model is stricter and uses only true sets. SQL handles these duplicate rows with an `ALL` or `DISTINCT` modifier in different places in the language; `ALL` preserves duplicates and `DISTINCT` removes them.

So that we can discuss the result of each operator formally, let R be a row that is a duplicate of some row in TableA, or of some row in TableB, or of both. Let m be the number of duplicates of R in TableA and let n be the number of duplicates of R in TableB, where (m >= 0) and (n >= 0). Informally, the engines will pair off the two tables on a row-per-row basis in set operations. We will see how this works for each operator.

For the rest of this discussion, let us create two tables with the same structure, which we can use for examples.

```
CREATE TABLE S1 (a1 CHAR(1));
INSERT INTO S1
VALUES ('a'), ('a'), ('b'), ('b'), ('c');

CREATE TABLE S2 (a2 CHAR(1));
INSERT INTO S2
VALUES ('a'), ('b'), ('b'), ('b'), ('c'), ('d');
```

Joe Celko's SQL for Smarties. DOI: 10.1016/B978-0-12-382022-8.00034-X

## 34.1 UNION and UNION ALL

UNIONs have been supported since SQL-86, with this infixed syntax:

```
<table expression> UNION [ALL] <table expression>
```

The two versions of the UNION statement take two tables and build a result table from them. The two tables must be union compatible, which means that they have exactly the same number of columns, and that each column in the first table has the same data type (or automatically cast to it) as the column in the same position in the second table. That is, their rows have the same structure, so they can be put in the same final result table. Most implementations will do some data type conversions to create the result table, but this can be implementation-dependent and you should check it out for yourself.

There are two forms of the UNION statement: the UNION and the UNION ALL. The simple UNION is the same operator you had in high school set theory; it returns the rows that appear in either or both tables and removes redundant duplicates from the result table. The phrase "redundant duplicates" sounds funny; but it means that you leave one copy of the row in the table. The sample tables will yield:

```
(SELECT a1 FROM S1
UNION
SELECT a2 FROM S2)
==================
a
b
c
d
```

In many early SQL implementations, merge-sorting the two tables, discarding duplicates during the sorting, did this removal. This had the side effect that the result table is sorted, but you cannot depend on that. Later implementations use hashing, indexing, and parallel processing to find the duplicates.

The UNION ALL preserves the duplicates from both tables in the result table. Most early implementations simply appended one table to the other in physical storage. They used file systems based on physically contiguous storage, so this was easy and used the file system code. But, again, you cannot depend on any ordering in the results of either version of the UNION statement. Again, the sample tables will yield:

```
(SELECT a1 FROM S1
UNION ALL
```

```
SELECT a2 FROM S2)
==================
'a'
'a'
'a'
'b'
'b'
'b'
'b'
'b'
'c'
'c'
'd'
```

You can assign names to the columns by using the AS operator to make the result set into a derived table, thus:

```
SELECT rent, utilities, phone
 FROM
(SELECT a, b, c FROM OldLocations WHERE city = 'Boston'
UNION
SELECT x, y, z FROM NewLocations WHERE city = 'New York')
AS Cities (rent, utilities, phone);
```

A few SQL products will attempt to optimize UNIONs if they are made on the same table. Those UNIONs can often be replaced with OR-ed predicates. For example:

```
SELECT city_name, 'Western'
 FROM Cities
WHERE market_code = 't'
UNION ALL
SELECT city_name, 'Eastern'
 FROM Cities
WHERE market_code = 'v';
```

could be rewritten (probably more efficiently) as:

```
SELECT city_name,
   CASE market_code
   WHEN 't' THEN 'Western'
   WHEN 'v' THEN 'Eastern' END
FROM Cities
WHERE market_code IN ('v', 't');
```

It takes system architecture based on domains rather than tables to optimize UNIONs if they are made on different tables.

Doing a UNION to the same table is the same as a SELECT DISTINCT, but the SELECT DISTINCT will probably run faster and preserve the column names too.

### 34.1.1 Order of Execution

UNION and UNION ALL operators are executed from left to right unless parentheses change the order of execution. Since the UNION operator is associative and commutative, the order of a chain of UNIONs will not affect the results. However, order and grouping can affect performance. Consider two small tables that have many duplicates between them. If the optimizer does not consider table sizes, this query:

```
(SELECT * FROM SmallTable1)
UNION
(SELECT * FROM BigTable)
UNION
(SELECT * FROM SmallTable2);
```

will merge SmallTable1 into BigTable, then merge SmallTable2 into that first result. If the rows of SmallTable1 are spread out in the first result table, locating duplicates from SmallTable2 will take longer than if we had written the query, thus:

```
(SELECT * FROM SmallTable1)
UNION
(SELECT * FROM SmallTable2)
 UNION
(SELECT * FROM BigTable);
```

Again, optimization of UNIONs is highly product-dependent, so you should experiment with it.

### 34.1.2 Mixed UNION and UNION ALL Operators

If you know that there are no duplicates, or that duplicates are not a problem in your situation, use UNION ALL instead of UNION for speed. For example, if we are sure that BigTable has no duplicates in common with SmallTable1 and SmallTable2, this query will produce the same results as before but should run much faster:

```
((SELECT * FROM SmallTable1)
 UNION
(SELECT * FROM SmallTable2))
 UNION ALL
(SELECT * FROM BigTable);
```

But be careful when mixing UNION and UNION ALL operators. The left-to-right order of execution will cause the last operator in the chain to have an effect on the results.

### 34.1.3 UNION of Columns from the Same Table

A useful trick for building the union of columns from the same table is to use a CROSS JOIN and a CASE expression, thus:

```
SELECT CASE WHEN S1.seq_nbr = 1 THEN F1.col1
            WHEN S1.seq_nbr = 2 THEN F1.col2
            ELSE NULL END
  FROM Foobar AS F1
    CROSS JOIN
    Series AS S1(seq_nbr)
 WHERE S1.seq_nbr IN (1, 2)
```

This acts like the UNION ALL statement, but change the SELECT to SELECT DISTINCT and you have a UNION. The advantage of this statement over the more obvious UNION is that it makes one pass through the table. Given a large table, that can be important for good performance.

## 34.2 INTERSECT and EXCEPT

The INTERSECT and EXCEPT set operators take two tables and build a new table from them. The two tables must be "union compatible," which means that they have the same number of columns, and that each column in the first table has the same data type (or automatically cast to it) as the column in the same position in the second table.

That is, their rows have the same structure, so they can be put in the same final result table. Most implementations will do some data type conversions to create the result table, but this is very implementation-dependent and you should check it out for yourself. Like the UNION, the result of an INTERSECT or EXCEPT should use an AS operator if you want to have names for the result table and its columns.

Oracle was the first major vendor to have the EXCEPT operator with the keyword MINUS. The set difference is the rows in the first table, except for those that also appear in the second table. It answers questions like, "Give me all the employees except the salesmen" in a natural manner.

Let's take our two multisets and use them to explain the basic model, by making a mapping between them:

```
S1 = {a, a, b, b,    c   }
  ↕   ↕   ↕      ↕
S2 = {a,    b, b, b, c, d}
```

The INTERSECT and EXCEPT operators remove all duplicates from both sets, so we would have:

```
S1 = {a, b, c   }
   ↕  ↕  ↕
S2 = {a, b, c, d}
```

and therefore,

```
S1 INTERSECT S2 = {a, b, c}
```

and,

```
S2 EXCEPT S1 = {d}
S1 EXCEPT S2 = {}
```

When you add the ALL option, things are trickier. The mapped pairs become the unit of work. The INTERSECT ALL keeps each pairing, so that

```
S1 INTERSECT ALL S2 = {a, b, b, c}
```

and the EXCEPT ALL throws them away, retaining what is left in the first set, thus:

```
S2 EXCEPT ALL S1 = {b, d}
```

Trying to write the INTERSECT and EXCEPT with other operators is trickier than it looks. It has to be general enough to handle situations where there is no key available and the number of columns is not known.

Standard SQL defines the actions for duplicates in terms of the count of duplicates of matching rows. Let (m) be the number of rows of one kind in S1 and (n) be the number in S2. The UNION ALL will have (m + n) copies of the row. The INTERSECT ALL will have LEAST(m, n) copies. EXCEPT ALL will have the greater of either the first table's count minus the second table's count or zero copies.

The immediate impulse of a programmer is to write the code with EXISTS() predicates. The bad news is that it does not work because of NULLs. This is easier to show with code. Let's redo our two sample tables.

```
CREATE TABLE S1 (a1 CHAR(1));
INSERT INTO S1
VALUES ('a'), ('a'), ('b'), ('b'), ('c'), (NULL), (NULL);

CREATE TABLE S2 (a2 CHAR(1));
INSERT INTO S2
VALUES ('a'), ('b'), ('b'), ('b'), ('c'), ('d'), (NULL);
```

Now build a view to hold the tally of each value in each table.

```
CREATE VIEW DupCounts (a, s1_dup, s2_dup)
AS
SELECT S.a, SUM(s1_dup), SUM(s2_dup)
 FROM (SELECT S1.a1, 1, 0
    FROM S1
   UNION ALL
  SELECT S2.a2, 0, 1
    FROM S2) AS S(a, s1_dup, s2_dup)
GROUP BY S.a, s1_dup, s2_dup;
```

The GROUP BY will put the NULLs into a separate group giving them the right tallies. Now code is a straightforward implementation of the definitions in Standard SQL.

```
-- S1 EXCEPT ALL S2
SELECT DISTINCT D1.a, (s1_dup - s2_dup) AS dups
  FROM DupCounts AS D1,
    Series AS S1
 WHERE S1.seq_nbr <= (s1_dup - s2_dup);
```

```
-- S1 INTERSECT ALL S2
SELECT DISTINCT D1.a,
       CASE WHEN s1_dup <= s2_dup
         THEN s1_dup ELSE s2_dup END
       AS tally
  FROM DupCounts AS D1,
    Series AS S1
 WHERE S1.seq_nbr <= CASE WHEN s1_dup <= s2_dup
       THEN s1_dup ELSE s2_dup END;
```

Notice that we had to use SELECT DISTINCT. Without it, the sample data will produce this table.

| A | tally |
|---|---|
| NULL | 1 |
| A | 1 |
| B | 2 |
| B | 2 ◀ redundant row |
| C | 1 |

The nonduplicated versions are easy to write from the definitions in the Standards. In effect their duplication tallies are set to one.

```
-- S1 INTERSECT S2
SELECT D1.a
  FROM DupCounts AS D1
```

```
 WHERE s1_dup > 0
   AND s2_dup > 0;

-- S1 EXCEPT S2
SELECT D1.a
  FROM DupCounts AS D1
 WHERE s1_dup > 0
   AND s2_dup = 0;

-- S2 EXCEPT S1
SELECT D1.a
  FROM DupCounts AS D1
 WHERE s2_dup > 0
   AND s1_dup = 0;
```

### 34.2.1 INTERSECT and EXCEPT without NULLs and Duplicates

INTERSECT and EXCEPT are much easier if each of the two tables does not have NULLs and duplicate values in them. Intersection is simply:

```
SELECT *
 FROM S1
WHERE EXISTS
   (SELECT *
     FROM S2
     WHERE S1.a1 = S2.a2);
```

or:

```
SELECT *
 FROM S2
WHERE EXISTS
   (SELECT *
     FROM S1
     WHERE S1.a1 = S2.a2);
```

You can also use:

```
SELECT DISTINCT S2.*
 FROM (S2 INNER JOIN S1 ON S1.a1 = S2.a2);
```

This is given as a motivation for the next piece of code, but you may find that some SQL engines do joins faster than EXISTS() predicates and vice versa, so it is a good idea to have more than one trick in your bag.

The set difference can be written with an OUTER JOIN operator. This code is due to Jim Panttaja.

```
SELECT DISTINCT S2.*
 FROM (S2 LEFT OUTER JOIN S1
```

```
  ON S1.a1 = S2.a2)
WHERE S1.a1 IS NULL;
```

### 34.2.2 INTERSECT and EXCEPT with NULLs and Duplicates

These versions of INTERSECT and EXCEPT are due to Itzak Ben-Gan. They make very good use of the UNION and DISTINCT operators to implement set theory definitions.

```
-- S1 INTERSECT S2
SELECT D.a
FROM (SELECT DISTINCT a1 FROM S1
   UNION ALL
   SELECT DISTINCT a2 FROM S2) AS D(a)
GROUP BY D.a
HAVING COUNT(*) > 1;

-- S1 INTERSECT ALL S2
SELECT D2.a
FROM (SELECT D1.a, MIN(cnt) AS mincnt
   FROM (SELECT a1, COUNT(*)
      FROM S1
     GROUP BY a1
    UNION ALL
    SELECT a2, COUNT(*)
      FROM S2
     GROUP BY a2) AS D1(a, cnt)
   GROUP BY D1.a
   HAVING COUNT(*) > 1) AS D2
 INNER JOIN
 Series
ON seq_nbr <= min_cnt;

-- S1 EXCEPT ALL S2
SELECT D2.a
 FROM (SELECT D1.a, SUM(cnt)
     FROM (SELECT a1, COUNT(*)
        FROM S1
       GROUP BY a1
      UNION ALL
      SELECT a2, -COUNT(*)
        FROM S2
       GROUP BY a2)
     AS D1(a, cnt)
   GROUP BY D1.a
   HAVING SUM(cnt) > 0)
  AS D2(a, dups)
  INNER JOIN
  Series ON seq_nbr <= D2.dups;
```

The Series table is discussed in other places in this book. It is a table of integers from 1 to (n) that is used to replace iteration and counting in SQL. Obviously, (n) has to be large enough for these statements to work.

## 34.3 A Note on ALL and SELECT DISTINCT

Here is a series of observations about the relationship between the ALL option in set operations and the SELECT DISTINCT options in a query from Beught Gunne.

Given two tables with duplicate values:

```
CREATE TABLE A (i INTEGER NOT NULL);
INSERT INTO A VALUES (1), (1), (2), (2), (4), (4);

CREATE TABLE B (i INTEGER NOT NULL);
INSERT INTO B VALUES (2), (2), (3), (3);
```

The UNION and INTERSECT operations have regular behavior in that:

```
(A UNION B) = SELECT DISTINCT (A UNION ALL B) =
   ((1), (2), (3))
```

and:

```
(A INTERSECT B) = SELECT DISTINCT (A INTERSECT ALL B) = (2)
```

However,

```
(A EXCEPT B) <> SELECT DISTINCT (A EXCEPT ALL B)
```

or more literally, `(1) <> ((1), (2))` for the tables given in the example. And likewise, we have:

```
(B EXCEPT A) = SELECT DISTINCT (B EXCEPT ALL A) = (3)
```

by a coincidence of the particular values used in these tables.

## 34.4 Equality and Proper Subsets

At one point, when SQL was still in the laboratory at IBM, there was a CONTAINS operator that would tell you if one table was a subset of another. It disappeared in later versions of the language and no vendor picked it up. Set equality was never part of SQL as an operator, so you would have to have used the two expressions ((A CONTAINS B) AND (B CONTAINS A)) to find out.

Today, you can use the methods shown in the section on Relational Division to determine containment or equality. Or you can use set theory expressions, such as NOT EXISTS ((A EXCEPT B)

UNION (B EXCEPT A)). Which method is fastest is going to depend on the SQL product and the access method used.

However, Itzak Ben-Gan came up with a novel approach for finding containment and equality that is worth a mention.

```
SELECT SUM(DISTINCT match_col)
 FROM (SELECT CASE
       WHEN S1.col
         IN (SELECT S2.col FROM S2)
       THEN 1 ELSE -1 END
   FROM S1) AS X(match_col)
HAVING SUM(DISTINCT match_col) = :n;
```

You can set (:n) to 1, 0, or –1 for each particular test.

When I find a matching row in S1, I get a one; when I find a mismatched row in S1, I get a –1, and they sum together to give me a zero. Therefore, S1 is a proper subset of S2. If they sum to one, then they are equal. If they sum to –1, they are disjoint.

# 35

# SUBSETS

I am defining subset operations as queries, which extract a particular subset from a given set, as opposed to set operations, which work among sets. The obvious way to extract a subset from a table is just to use a WHERE clause, which will pull out the rows that meet that criterion. But not all the subsets we want are easily defined by such a simple predicate. This chapter is a collection of tricks for constructing useful, but not obvious, subsets from a table.

## 35.1 Every N-th Item in a Table

SQL is a set-oriented language, which cannot identify individual rows by their physical positions in a disk file that holds a table. Instead, a unique logical key is detected by logical expressions and a row is retrieved. If you are given a file of employees and you want to pick out every n-th employee for a survey where the ordering of that file is based on their employee identification numbers, the job is easy. You write a procedure that loops through the file and writes every n-th one to a second file.

The immediate thought of how to do this in SQL is that you can simply compute `MOD(emp_nbr, :n)` and save those employee rows where this function is zero. The trouble is that employees are not issued consecutive identification numbers. The identification numbers are unique, however.

In the old days, you had to use vendor extensions that exposed a physical row locator that gives a sequential numbering to the physical records. Such things are highly proprietary, but because these features are so low-level they will run very fast on that one particular product. Today we have the ordinal functions, so we can use:

```
SELECT P1.emp_nbr
 FROM (SELECT P.emp_nbr,
        ROW_NUMBER()
        OVER(ORDER BY emp_nbr)
    FROM Personnel) AS P1(emp_nbr, emp_seq)
WHERE MOD (emp_seq, :n) = 0;
```

Joe Celko's SQL for Smarties. DOI: 10.1016/B978-0-12-382022-8.00035-1

A nonordinal function version of the same query looks like this:

```
SELECT P1.emp_nbr
 FROM Personnel AS P1, Personnel AS P2
WHERE P1.emp_nbr >= P2.emp_nbr
GROUP BY P1.emp_nbr
HAVING MOD (COUNT(*), :n) = 0;
```

This query will count the number of P2 rows with a value less than the P1 row. This older trick should be slower than the `ROW_NUMBER()` version, but you might see this in older code.

## 35.2 Random Rows from a Table

The answer is that, basically, you cannot directly pick a set of random rows from a table in SQL. There is no randomize operator in Standard SQL and you do not often find the same pseudorandom number generator function in various vendor extensions either.

Picking random rows from a table for a statistical sample is a handy thing and you do it in other languages with a pseudorandom number generator. There are two kinds of random drawings from a set, with or without replacement. If SQL had a random number function, I suppose these would be shown as `RANDOM(x)` and `RANDOM(DISTINCT x)`, where x is a seed or dummy value. As examples in the real world, dealing a Poker hand is a random with no replacement situation, whereas shooting craps is a random with replacement situation. If two players in a Poker game get identical cards, you are using a Pinochle deck. In a Crap game, each roll of the dice is independent of the previous one and can repeat (that is how you win).

The problem is that SQL is a set-oriented language and wants to do an operation "all at once" on a well-defined set of rows. Random sets are defined by a nondeterministic procedure by definition, instead of a deterministic logic expression.

The SQL/PSM language does have an option to declare or create a procedure that is `DETERMINISTIC` or `NOT DETERMINISTIC`. The `DETERMINISTIC` option means that the optimizer can compute this function once for a set of input parameter values and then use that result everywhere in the current SQL statement where a call to the procedure with those parameters appears. The `NOT DETERMINISTIC` option means given the same parameters, you might not get the same results for each call to the procedure within the same SQL statement.

Unfortunately, SQL products can have proprietary extensions that vary: the random number function in Oracle is nondeterministic and the one in SQL Server is deterministic (i.e., pseudo-random number generator procedures). For example, using RANDOM() as the random number function:

```
CREATE TABLE RandomNbrs
(seq_nbr INTEGER NOT NULL PRIMARY KEY,
random_nbr FLOAT NOT NULL);

INSERT INTO RandomNbrs
VALUES (1, RANDOM()),
  (2, RANDOM()),
  (3, RANDOM());
```

will result in the three rows all getting the same value in the random_nbr column in versions of SQL Server, but three potentially different numbers in versions of Oracle.

Although subqueries are not allowed in DEFAULT clauses, system-related functions like CURRENT_TIMESTAMP, CURRENT_USER are allowed. In some SQL implementations, this includes the RANDOM() function.

```
CREATE TABLE RandomNbrs2
(seq_nbr INTEGER PRIMARY KEY,
random_nbr FLOAT -- warning! not Standard SQL
     DEFAULT (
(CASE (CAST(RANDOM() + 0.5 AS INTEGER) * -1)
WHEN 0.0 THEN 1.0 ELSE -1.0 END)
* MOD (CAST(RANDOM() * 100000 AS INTEGER), 10000)
* RANDOM())
NOT NULL);

INSERT INTO RandomNbrs2
VALUES (1, DEFAULT);
 (2, DEFAULT),
 (3, DEFAULT),
 (4, DEFAULT),
 (5, DEFAULT),
 (6, DEFAULT),
 (7, DEFAULT),
 (8, DEFAULT),
 (9, DEFAULT),
 (10, DEFAULT);
```

Here is a sample output from an SQL Server 7.0 implementation.

| seq_nbr | random_nbr |
|---|---|
| 1 | -121.89758452446999 |
| 2 | -425.61113508053933 |
| 3 | 3918.1554683876675 |
| 4 | 9335.2668286173412 |
| 5 | 54.463890640027664 |
| 6 | -5.0169085346410522 |
| 7 | -5435.63417246276 |
| 8 | 915.9835973796487 |
| 9 | 28.109161998753301 |
| 10 | 741.79452047043048 |

The best way to do this is to add a column to the table to hold a random number, then use an external language with a good pseudo-random number generator in its function library to load the new column with random values with a cursor in a host language. You have to do it this way because random number generators work differently from other function calls. They start with an initial value called a "seed" (shown as Random[0] in the rest of this discussion) provided by the user or the system clock. The seed is used to create the first number in the sequence, Random[1]. Then each call, Random[n], to the function uses the previous number to generate the next one, Random[n + 1].

The term "pseudo-random number generator" often is referred to as a just "random number generator," but this is technically wrong. You can get true random numbers from things like radioactive decay or other physical phenomena in chaotic systems. All the generators will eventually return a value that appeared in the sequence earlier and the procedure will hang in a cycle. Procedures are deterministic and we are living in a mathematical heresy when we try to use them to produce truly random results. However, if the sequence has a very long cycle and meets some other tests for randomness over the range of the cycle, then we can use it.

There are many kinds of generators. The linear congruence pseudo-random number generator family has generator formulas of the form:

```
Random[n + 1]:= MOD ((x * Random[n] + y), m);
```

There are restrictions on the relationships among x, y, and m that deal with their relative primality. Knuth gives a proof that if

```
Random[0] is not a multiple of 2 or 5
m = 10^e where (e >= 5)
y = 0
MOD (x, 200) is in the set (3, 11, 13, 19, 21, 27, 29, 37, 53,
59, 61, 67, 77, 83, 91, 109, 117, 123, 131, 133, 139, 141, 147,
163, 171, 173, 179, 181, 187, 189, 197)
```

then the period will be 5 * 10^(e-2).

There are old favorites that many C programmers use from this family, such as:

```
Random(n + 1) := (Random(n) * 1103515245) + 12345;
Random(n + 1) := MOD ((16807 * Random(n)), ((2^31) - 1));
```

The first formula has the advantage of not requiring a `MOD` function, so it can be written in Standard SQL. However, the simplest generator that can be recommended (Park and Miller) uses:

```
Random(n + 1) := MOD ((48271 * Random(n)), ((2^31) - 1));
```

Notice that the modulus is a prime number; this is important.

The period of this generator is ((2^31) – 2), which is 2, 147, 483, 646, or over two billion numbers before this generator repeats. You must determine if this is long enough for your application.

If you have an `XOR` function in your SQL, then you can also use shift register algorithms. The `XOR` is the bitwise exclusive `OR` that works on an integer as it is stored in the hardware; I would assume 32 bits on most small computers. Some usable shift register algorithms are:

```
Random(n + 1) := Random(n - 103) XOR Random(n - 250);
Random(n + 1) := Random(n - 1063) XOR Random(n - 1279);
```

One method for writing a random number generator on the fly when the vendor's library does not have one is to pick a seed using one or more key columns and a call to the system clock's fractional seconds, such as `RANDOM(keycol + EXTRACT (SECOND FROM CURRENT_TIME)) * 1000`. This avoids problems with patterns in the keys, while the key column values assure uniqueness of the seed values.

Another method is to use a `PRIMARY KEY` or `UNIQUE` column(s) and apply a hashing algorithm. You can pick one of the random number generator functions already discussed and use the unique values as if it were the seed as a quick way to get a hashing function. Hashing algorithms try to be uniformly distributed, so if you can find a good one, you will approach nearly unique random selection. The trick is that the hashing algorithm has to be simple enough to be written in the limited math available in SQL.

Once you have a column of random numbers you can convert the random numbers into a randomly ordered sequence with this statement.

```
UPDATE RandomNbrs
 SET random_nbr = (SELECT COUNT(*)
          FROM Series AS S1
          WHERE S1.random_nbr <= Series.seq_nbr);
```

To get one random row from a table, you can use this approach:

```
CREATE VIEW LotteryDrawing (keycol, ..., spin)
AS SELECT LotteryTickets.*,
    (RANDOM(<keycol> + <fractional seconds from clock>))
  FROM LotteryTickets
  GROUP BY spin
 HAVING COUNT(*) = 1;
```

then simply use this query:

```
SELECT *
 FROM LotteryDrawing
WHERE spin = (SELECT MAX(spin)
       FROM LotteryDrawing)
```

The pseudo-random number function is not Standard SQL, but it is common enough. Using the keycol as the seed *probably* means that you will get a different value for each row, but we can avoid duplicates with the `GROUP BY. HAVING`. Adding the fractional seconds will change the result every time, but it might be illegal in some SQL products, which disallow variable elements in `VIEW` definitions.

Let's assume you have a function called `RANDOM()` that returns a random number between 0.00 and 1.00. If you just want one random row out of the table, and you have a numeric key column, Tom Moreau proposed that you could find the `MAX()` and `MIN()`, then calculate a random number between them.

```
SELECT L1.*
 FROM LotteryDrawing AS L1
WHERE col_1
  = (SELECT MIN(keycol)
      + (MAX (keycol) – MIN (keycol) * RANDOM()))
     FROM LotteryDrawing AS L2);
```

Here is a version that uses the `COUNT(*)` functions and a self-join instead.

```
SELECT L1.*
 FROM LotteryDrawing AS L1
 WHERE CEILING ((SELECT COUNT(*) FROM LotteryDrawing)
        * RANDOM())
     = (SELECT COUNT(*)
         FROM LotteryDrawing AS L2
         WHERE L1.keycol <= L2.keycol);
```

The rounding away from zero is important, since we are in effect numbering the rows from one. The idea is to use the decimal fraction to hit the row that is far into the table when the rows are ordered by the key.

Having shown you this code, I have to warn you that the pure SQL has a good number of self-joins, and they will be expensive to run.

## 35.3 The CONTAINS Operators

Set theory has two symbols for subsets. One, $A \subset B$, means that set A is contained within set B; this is sometimes said to denote a proper subset. The other, $A \subseteq B$, means that A is contained in or equal to B, and is sometimes called just a subset or containment operator.

Standard SQL has never had an operator to compare tables against each other for equality or containment. Several college textbooks on relational databases mention a CONTAINS predicate, which does not exist in Standard SQL. This predicate existed in the original System R, IBM's first experimental SQL system, but it was dropped from later SQL implementations because of the expense of running it.

### 35.3.1 Proper Subset Operators

The IN() predicate is a test for membership. For those of you who remember your high school set theory, membership is shown with a stylized epsilon with the containing set on the right side: $a \in A$. Membership is for one element, whereas a subset is itself a set, not just an element. As an example of a subset predicate, consider a query to tell you the names of each employee who works on all the projects in department five. Using the System R syntax,

```
SELECT emp_name -- Not valid SQL!
 FROM Personnel
WHERE (SELECT project_nbr
    FROM JobAssignments
    WHERE Personnel.emp_nbr = JobAssignments.emp_nbr)
  CONTAINS
```

```
(SELECT project_nbr
  FROM Projects
  WHERE dept_nbr = 5);
```

In the second SELECT statement of the CONTAINS predicate, we build a table of all the projects in department five. In the first SELECT statement of the CONTAINS predicate, we have a correlated subquery that will build a table of all the projects each employee works on. If the table of the employee's projects is equal to or a superset of the department five table, the predicate is TRUE.

You must first decide what you are going to do about duplicate rows in either or both tables. That is, does the set {a, b, c} contain the multiset {a, b, b} or not? Some SQL set operations, such as SELECT and UNION, have options to remove or keep duplicates from the results, as in UNION ALL and SELECT DISTINCT.

I would argue that duplicates should be ignored and the multiset is a subset of the other. For our example, let us use a table of employees and another table with the names of the company bowling team members, which should be a proper subset of the Personnel table. For the bowling team to be contained in the set of employees, each bowler must be an employee, or, to put it another way, there must be no bowler who is not an employee.

```
NOT EXISTS
(SELECT *
  FROM Bowling AS B1
 WHERE B1.emp_nbr NOT IN (SELECT emp_nbr FROM Personnel))
```

## 35.3.2 Table Equality

How can I find out if two tables are equal to each other? This is a common programming problem and the specification sounds obvious.

When two sets, A and B, are equal then we know that:

1. Both have the same number of elements.
2. No elements in A are not in B.
3. No elements in B are not in A.
4. Set A is equal to the intersection of A and B.
5. Set B is equal to the intersection of A and B.
6. Set B is a subset of A.
7. Set A is a subset of B.

and probably a few other things vaguely remembered from an old math class. But equality is not as easy as it sounds in SQL because the language is based on multisets or bags, which allow duplicate elements, and the language has NULLs. Given this list of multisets, which pairs are equal to each other?

```
S0 = {a, b, c}
S1 = {a, b, NULL}
S2 = {a, b, b, c, c}
S3 = {a, b, NULL}
S4 = {a, b, c}
S5 = {x, y, z}
```

Everyone will agree that S0 = S4, because they are identical.

Everyone will agree that S5 is not equal to any other set because it has no elements in common with any of them. How do you handle redundant duplicates? If you ignore them, then S0 = S2. Should NULLs be given the benefit of the doubt and matched to any known value or not? Thus S0 = S1 and S0 = S3. But then do you want to say that S1 = S3 because we can pair up the NULLs with each other?

To make matters even worse, are two rows equal if they match on just their keys, on a particular subset of their columns, or on all their columns? The reason this question comes up in practice is that you often have to match up data from two sources that are slightly different versions of the same information (i.e., "Joe Celko" and "Joe F. Celko" are probably the same person, but you are not quite so sure about "Joseph Frank Celko").

The good part about matching things on the keys is that you do have a true set—keys are unique and cannot have NULLs. If you go back to the list of set equality tests that I gave at the start of this chapter, you can see some possible ways to code a solution.

If you use facts (2) and (3) in the list, then you might use NOT EXISTS() predicates.

```
..
WHERE NOT EXISTS (SELECT *
        FROM A
       WHERE A.keycol
        NOT IN (SELECT keycol
              FROM B
             WHERE A.keycol = B.keycol))
 AND NOT EXISTS (SELECT *
        FROM B
       WHERE B.keycol
        NOT IN (SELECT keycol
              FROM A
              WHERE A.keycol = B.keycol))
```

which can also be written as:

```
..
WHERE NOT EXISTS
   (SELECT *
     FROM A
```

```
      EXCEPT [ALL]
      SELECT *
       FROM B
       WHERE A.keycol = B.keycol)
    UNION
    SELECT *
     FROM B
       EXCEPT [ALL]
       SELECT *
        FROM A
        WHERE A.keycol = B.keycol))
```

The use of the optional EXCEPT ALL operators will determine how duplicates are handled. However, if you look at (1), (4), and (5) you might come with this answer:

```
..
WHERE (SELECT COUNT(*) FROM A)
  = (SELECT COUNT(*
     FROM A INNER JOIN B
       ON A.keycol = B.keycol)
 AND (SELECT COUNT(*) FROM B)
  = (SELECT COUNT(*)
     FROM A INNER JOIN B
       ON A.keycol = B.keycol)
```

This query will produce a list of the unmatched values; you might want to keep them in two columns instead of coalescing them as I have shown here.

```
SELECT DISTINCT COALESCE(A.keycol, B.keycol) AS non_matched_key
 FROM A
   FULL OUTER JOIN
   B
   ON A.keycol = B.keycol
 WHERE A.keycol IS NULL
   OR B.keycol IS NULL;
```

Eventually, you will be able to handle this with the INTERSECT [ALL] and UNION [ALL] operators in Standard SQL and tune the query to whatever definition of equality you wish to use.

Unfortunately, these examples are for just comparing the keys. What do we do if we have tables without keys or if we want to compare all the columns?

The GROUP BY, the DISTINCT, and a few other things in SQL treat NULLs as if they were equal to each other. This is probably the definition of equality we would like to use.

Remember that if one table has more columns or more rows than the other, we can stop right there since they cannot possibly be equal under that definition. We have to assume that the tables have the same number of columns, of the same type, and in the same positions. But row counts look useful. Imagine that there are two children, each with a bag of candy. To determine that both bags are identical, the first children can start by pulling a piece of candy out and asking the other, "How many red ones do you have?" If the two counts disagree, we know that the bags are different. Now ask about the green pieces, if we matched on reds. We do not have to match each particular piece of candy in one bag with a particular piece of candy in the other bag. The counts are enough information only if they differ. If the counts are the same more work needs to be done. We could each have one brown piece of candy but mine could be an M&M and yours could be a malted milk ball.

Now, generalize that idea. Let's combine the two tables into one big table, with an extra column, x0, to show from where each row originally came.

Now form groups based on all the original columns. Within each group, count the number of rows from one table and the number of rows from the second table. If the counts are different, there are unmatched rows.

This will handle redundant duplicate rows within one table. This query does not require that the tables have keys. The assumption in a GROUP BY clause is that all NULLs are treated as if they were equals. Here is the final query.

```
SELECT x1, x2, ..., xn,
   COUNT(CASE WHEN x0 = 'A'
       THEN 1 ELSE 0 END) AS a_tally,
   COUNT(CASE WHEN x0 = 'B'
       THEN 1 ELSE 0 END) AS b_tally
 FROM (SELECT 'A', A.* FROM A
   UNION ALL
   SELECT 'B', B.* FROM B) AS X (x0, x1, x2, ..., xn)
 GROUP BY x1, x2, x3, x4, .. xn
HAVING COUNT(CASE WHEN x0 = 'A' THEN 1 ELSE 0 END)
  <> COUNT(CASE WHEN x0 = 'B' THEN 1 ELSE 0 END);
```

You might want to think about the differences that changing the expression for the derived table X can make. If you use a UNION instead of a UNION ALL, then the row count for each group in both tables will be one. If you use a SELECT DISTINCT instead of a SELECT, then the row count in just that table will be one for each group.

### *Subset Equality*

A surprisingly usable version of set equality is finding identical subsets within the same table. These identical subsets can build partitions that are known as equivalence classes in set theory.

Let's use Chris Date's suppliers-and-parts table to find pairs of suppliers who provide exactly the same parts. That is, the set of parts from one supplier is equal to the set of parts from the other supplier.

```
CREATE TABLE SupParts
(sup_nbr CHAR(2) NOT NULL,
part_nbr CHAR(2) NOT NULL,
PRIMARY KEY (sup_nbr, part_nbr));
```

The usual way of proving that two sets are equal is to show that set A contains set B and set B contains set A.

Any of the methods given can be modified to handle two copies of the same table under aliases. Instead, consider another approach. First, JOIN one supplier to another on their common parts, eliminating the situation where the first supplier is also the second supplier, so that you have the intersection of the two subsets. If the intersection has the same number of pairs as each of the two subsets has elements, the two subsets are equal.

```
SELECT SP1.sup_nbr, SP2.sup_nbr, COUNT(*) AS part_count
 FROM SupParts AS SP1
   INNER JOIN
   SupParts AS SP2
    ON SP1.part_nbr = SP2.part_nbr
     AND SP1.sup_nbr < SP2.sup_nbr
GROUP BY SP1.sup_nbr, SP2.sup_nbr
HAVING COUNT(*) = (SELECT COUNT(*)
        FROM SupParts AS SP3
        WHERE SP3.sup_nbr = SP1.sup_nbr)
 AND COUNT(*) = (SELECT COUNT(*)
        FROM SupParts AS SP4
        WHERE SP4.sup_nbr = SP2.sup_nbr);
```

If there is an index on the supplier number in the SupParts table, it can provide the counts directly as well as helping with the JOIN operation. The only problem with this answer is that it is hard to see the groups of suppliers among the pairs. The part_count column helps a bit, but it does not assign a grouping identifier to the rows.

## 35.4 Gaps in a Series

Gaps can exist in a sequence of numbers or dates. For example, the set {1, 6, 7, 8, 9} has missing elements {2, 3, 4, 5}. Unless told otherwise, do not look for endpoints and just assume that the maximum value in the given set is the upper limit; that is, {10, 11, 12} is not a gap in this example.

Let's assume we have a table of people who bought tickets that are supposed to be in sequential order and we want to make a list of what is missing in each buyer_id's set of tickets.

```
CREATE TABLE Tickets
(buyer_id CHAR(5) NOT NULL,
ticket_nbr INTEGER DEFAULT 1 NOT NULL
      CHECK (ticket_nbr > 0),
PRIMARY KEY (buyer_id, ticket_nbr));

INSERT INTO Tickets
VALUES ('a', 2), ('a', 3), ('a', 4),
  ('b', 4),
  ('c', 1), ('c', 2), ('c', 3), ('c', 4), ('c', 5),
  ('d', 1), ('d', 6), ('d', 7), ('d', 9),
  ('e', 10);
```

If we can assume that there is a relatively small number of tickets, then you could use a table of sequential numbers from 1 to (n) and write:

```
SELECT DISTINCT T1.buyer_id, S1.seq_nbr
 FROM Tickets AS T1, Series AS S1
WHERE seq_nbr <= (SELECT MAX(ticket_nbr) -- set the range
      FROM Tickets AS T2
      WHERE T1.buyer_id = T2.buyer_id)
 AND seq_nbr NOT IN (SELECT ticket_nbr -- get missing
   numbers
        FROM Tickets AS T3
        WHERE T1.buyer_id = T3.buyer_id);
```

In effect, we are saying that a gap is a "sequence that is not in the table," but we also know something about each contiguous gap. The starting value of the gap − 1 and the ending value of the gap + 1 are both in the table. Furthermore, no value between the start and the end are in the table. This gives us some boundaries to look for.

```
SELECT T1.buyer_id,
   (T1.ticket_nbr + 1) AS gap_start,
   (MIN(T2.ticket_nbr) - 1) AS gap_end
 FROM (TABLE Tickets
   UNION ALL
   SELECT DISTINCT buyer_id, 0
    FROM Tickets) AS T1(buyer_id, ticket_nbr),
   Tickets AS T2
 WHERE T1.ticket_nbr < T2.ticket_nbr
  AND T1.buyer_id = T2.buyer_id
 GROUP BY T1.buyer_id, T1.ticket_nbr
HAVING MIN(T2.ticket_nbr) - T1.ticket_nbr > 1;
```

The trick here is realizing that the numbering starts with 1, so if 1 is missing from the set, there is no zero to form a boundary for it. Hence, a little UNION ALL trick to add a zero to the table.

Intuitively, the "inverse" problem—list the ranges of all numbers that are present—would be easier than the solution for missing numbers. Turns out it is not!

```
SELECT X.buyer_id, MIN(X.initial), X.final
FROM (SELECT T1.buyer_id, T1.ticket_nbr AS initial,
      MAX(T2.ticket_nbr) AS final
   FROM Tickets AS T1, Tickets AS T2
   WHERE T1.ticket_nbr <= T2.ticket_nbr
    AND (SELECT COUNT(DISTINCT T3.ticket_nbr)
       FROM Tickets AS T3
       WHERE T1.buyer_id = T3.buyer_id
        AND T3.ticket_nbr
          BETWEEN T1.ticket_nbr AND T2.ticket_nbr)
     = (T2.ticket_nbr - T1.ticket_nbr +1)
   GROUP BY T1.buyer_id, T1.ticket_nbr)
  AS X(buyer_id, initial, final)
GROUP BY buyer_id, final;
```

## 35.5 Covering for Overlapping Intervals

A related problem is finding a minimal covering for a set of overlapping intervals. This usually shows up in temporal queries where the intervals are durations of time, but the problem is easier to see with ranges of integers. For example, given:

```
Intervals = {(1, 2, 3), (2, 3, 4, 5), (4, 5, 6, 7, 8, 9,
   10, 11), (10, 11, 12), (20, 21)}
```

we want to get this set back: {(1, 12), (20, 21)}.

First, let's create and load a table of intervals.

```
CREATE TABLE Intervals
(x INTEGER NOT NULL,
y INTEGER NOT NULL,
CHECK (x <= y),
PRIMARY KEY (x, y));

INSERT INTO Intervals
VALUES (1, 3), (2, 5), (4, 11), (10, 12);
  (20, 21), (120, 130), (120, 128), (120, 122), (121, 132),
  (121, 122), (121, 124), (121, 123), (126, 127);
```

There are a lot of approaches to a solution. Let's start with older solutions and then move to more exotic SQL-99 solutions.

First, here is a query from Hugo Cornelius that uses a self-join and three nested correlated subqueries:

```
SELECT I1.x, MAX(I2.y) AS y
 FROM Intervals AS I1
   INNER JOIN
   Intervals AS I2
   ON I2.y > I1.x
WHERE NOT EXISTS
   (SELECT *
 FROM Intervals AS I3
WHERE I1.x - 1 BETWEEN I3.x AND I3.y)
 AND NOT EXISTS
   (SELECT *
     FROM Intervals AS I4
    WHERE I4.y > I1.x
     AND I4.y < I2.y
     AND NOT EXISTS
      (SELECT *
        FROM Intervals AS I5
       WHERE I4.y + 1 BETWEEN I5.x AND I5.y))
GROUP BY I1.x;
```

And here is another version of that approach, but converted to use left anti-semi-joins instead of subqueries. It might execute better on some platforms, and some people prefer this format to subqueries.

```
SELECT I1.x, MAX(I2.y) AS y
 FROM Intervals AS I1
   INNER JOIN
   Intervals AS I2
   ON I2.y > I1.x
    LEFT OUTER JOIN
    Intervals AS I3
    ON I1.x - 1 BETWEEN I3.x AND I3.y
     LEFT OUTER JOIN
     (Intervals AS I4
      LEFT OUTER JOIN
      Intervals AS I5
      ON I4.y + 1 BETWEEN I5.x AND I5.y)
     ON I4.y > I1.x
      AND I4.y < I2.y
      AND I5.x IS NULL
WHERE I3.x IS NULL
 AND I4.x IS NULL
GROUP BY I1.x;
```

If the table is large, the correlated subqueries (version 1) or the quintuple self-join (version 2) will probably make it slow.

A second approach in Standard SQL assumes we have the usual Series auxiliary table. Now we find all the holes in the range of the intervals and put them in a `VIEW`; later we could use a `WITH` clause derived table in SQL-99.

```
CREATE VIEW Holes(hole_nbr)
AS
SELECT seq_nbr
 FROM Series
WHERE seq_nbr <= (SELECT MAX(y) FROM Intervals)
 AND NOT EXISTS
  (SELECT *
    FROM Intervals
   WHERE seq_nbr BETWEEN x AND y)
UNION VALUES (0) -- get the edge of the universe
UNION (SELECT MAX(y) + 1 FROM Intervals);
```

The query picks start and end pairs that are on the edge of a hole and counts the number of holes inside that range. Covering has no holes inside its range.

```
SELECT Starts.x, Ends.y
 FROM Intervals AS Starts,
   Intervals AS Ends,
   Series AS S -- usual auxiliary table
WHERE S.seq_nbr BETWEEN Starts.x AND Ends.y -- restrict
   seq_nbr numbers
 AND S.seq_nbr < (SELECT MAX(hole) FROM Holes)
 AND S.seq_nbr NOT IN (SELECT hole FROM Holes) -- not a hole
 AND Starts.x - 1 IN (SELECT hole FROM Holes) -- on a left
   cusp
 AND Ends.y + 1 IN (SELECT hole FROM Holes) -- on a right
   cusp
GROUP BY Starts.x, Ends.y
HAVING COUNT(DISTINCT seq_nbr)
   = Ends.y - Starts.x + 1; -- no holes in range
```

Now that you have ordinal functions in your SQL, there are ways to use them to solve the problem. John Gilson came up with a recursive solution using DB2. Notice the use of a count in the `WITH` clause.

```
WITH RECURSIVE
IntervalTally (n) AS (SELECT COUNT(*) FROM Intervals),
Cover (x, y, n)
AS
(SELECT I1.x, I1.y, T.n
 FROM Intervals AS I1, IntervalTally AS T
 WHERE NOT EXISTS
  (SELECT *
```

```
    FROM Intervals AS I2
    WHERE I2.x <= I1.x
     AND I2.y >= I1.y
     AND (I2.x <> I1.x OR I2.y <> I1.y))
UNION ALL
SELECT CASE WHEN C.x <= I.x THEN C.x ELSE I.x END,
   CASE WHEN C.y >= I.y THEN C.y ELSE I.y END,
   C.n - 1
 FROM Intervals AS I, Cover AS C
WHERE I.x <= C.y
 AND I.y >= C.x
 AND (I.x < C.x OR I.y > C.y)
 AND C.n > 1)
-- main body of query
SELECT DISTINCT C1.x, C1.y
 FROM Cover AS C1
 WHERE NOT EXISTS
   (SELECT *
    FROM Cover AS C2
   WHERE C2.x <= C1.x
    AND C2.y >= C1.y
    AND (C1.x <> C2.x OR C1.y <> C2.y));
```

Dieter Nöth came up with this OLAP solution.

```
SELECT min_x, MAX(y)
 FROM (SELECT x, y,
        MAX(CASE WHEN x <= max_y THEN NULL ELSE x END)
        OVER(ORDER BY x, y ROWS UNBOUNDED PRECEDING)
       AS min_x
     FROM (SELECT x, y,
             MAX(y)
             OVER(ORDER BY x, y
               ROWS BETWEEN UNBOUNDED PRECEDING
                  AND 1 PRECEDING)
             AS max_y
          FROM Intervals) AS D1
   ) AS D2
GROUP BY min_x;
```

## 35.6 Picking a Representative Subset

This problem and solution for it are due to Ross Presser. The problem is to find a subset of rows such that each value in each of two columns appears in at least one row. The purpose is to produce a set of samples from a large table. The table has a club_name column and an ifc column; I want a set of samples that contains at least one of each club_name and at least one of each ifc, but no more than necessary.

```
CREATE TABLE Memberships
(member_id INTEGER NOT NULL PRIMARY KEY,
club_name CHAR(7) NOT NULL,
ifc CHAR(4) NOT NULL);

CREATE TABLE Samples
(member_id INTEGER NOT NULL PRIMARY KEY,
club_name CHAR(7) NOT NULL,
ifc CHAR(4) NOT NULL);

INSERT INTO Memberships
VALUES (6401715, 'aarprat', 'ic17'),
  (1058337, 'aarprat', 'ic17'),
  (0459443, 'aarpprt', 'ic25'),
  (4018210, 'aarpbas', 'ig21'),
  (2430656, 'aarpbas', 'ig21'),
  (6802081, 'aarpprd', 'ig29'),
  (4236511, 'aarpprd', 'ig29'),
  (2162104, 'aarpbas', 'ig21'),
  (2073679, 'aarpprd', 'ig29'),
  (8148891, 'aarpbas', 'ig21'),
  (1868445, 'aarpbas', 'ig21'),
  (6749213, 'aarpbas', 'ig21'),
  (8363621, 'aarppup', 'ig29'),
  (9999, 'aarppup', 'ic17'); -- redundant
```

To help frame the problem better, consider this subset, which has a row with both a redundant club_name value and ifc value.

**Nonminimal subset**

| member_id | club_name | ifc |
|---|---|---|
| 9999 | aarppup | ic17 ◄ redundant row |
| 1058337 | aarprat | ic17 ◄ ifc |
| 459443 | aarpprt | ic25 |
| 1868445 | aarpbas | ig21 |
| 2073679 | aarpprd | ig29 |
| 8363621 | aarppup | ig29 ◄ club_name |

There can be more than one minimal solution. But we would be happy to simply find a near-minimal solution.

David Portas came up with a query that gives a near-minimal solution. This will produce a sample containing at least one row of each value in the two columns. It is not guaranteed to give the *minimum* subset but it should contain at most (c + i − 1) rows, where (c) is the number of distinct clubs and (i) the number of distinct ifcs.

```
SELECT member_id, club_name, ifc
 FROM Memberships AS M
WHERE member_id
  IN
  (SELECT MIN(member_id)
    FROM Memberships
    GROUP BY club_name
   UNION ALL
   SELECT MIN(member_id)
    FROM Memberships AS M2
   GROUP BY ifc
   HAVING NOT EXISTS
     (SELECT *
       FROM Memberships
      WHERE member_id
       IN (SELECT MIN(member_id)
           FROM Memberships
          GROUP BY club_name)
      AND ifc = M2.ifc));
```

I am not sure it's possible to find the minimum subset every time unless you use an iterative solution. The results are very dependent on the exact data involved.

Ross Presser's iterative solution used a six-step system (following), and found that the number of rows resulting depended on both the order of the insert queries and on whether we used `MAX()` or `MIN()`. That said, the resulting row count varied only from 403 to 410 rows on a real run of 52,776 invoices for a set where (c = 325) and (i = 117). Portas's query gave a result of 405 rows, which is worse but not fatally worse.

```
-- first step: unique clubs
INSERT INTO Samples (member_id, club_name, ifc)
SELECT MIN(Randommid), club_name, MIN(ifc)
FROM Memberships
GROUP BY club_name
HAVING COUNT(*) = 1;

-- second step: unique ifcs where club_name not already
   there
INSERT INTO Samples (member_id, club_name, ifc)
SELECT MIN(Memberships.Member_id), MIN(Memberships.club_
   name), Memberships.ifc
```

```
FROM Memberships
GROUP BY Memberships.ifc
HAVING MIN(Memberships.club_name)
  NOT IN (SELECT club_name FROM Samples)
  AND COUNT(*) = 1;

-- intermezzo: views for missing ifcs, missing clubs
CREATE VIEW MissingClubs (club_name)
AS
SELECT Memberships.club_name
 FROM Memberships
   LEFT OUTER JOIN
   Samples
   ON Memberships.club_name = Samples.club_name
WHERE Samples.club_name IS NULL
GROUP BY Memberships.club_name;

CREATE VIEW MissingIfcs (ifc)
AS
SELECT Memberships.ifc
 FROM Memberships
   LEFT OUTER JOIN
   Samples
   ON Memberships.ifc = Samples.ifc
WHERE Samples.ifc IS NULL
GROUP BY Memberships.ifc;

-- third step: distinct missing clubs that are also
   missing ifcs
INSERT INTO Samples (member_id, club_name, ifc)
SELECT MIN(Memberships.Member_id),
   Memberships.club_name,
   MIN(Memberships.ifc)
 FROM Memberships, MissingClubs, MissingIfcs
WHERE Memberships.club_name = MissingClubs.club_name
 AND Memberships.ifc = MissingIfcs.ifc
GROUP BY Memberships.club_name;

-- fourth step: distinct missing ifcs that are also
   missing clubs
INSERT INTO Samples (member_id, club_name, ifc)
SELECT MIN(Memberships.member_id),
   MIN(Memberships.club_name),
   Memberships.ifc
 FROM Memberships, MissingClubs, MissingIfcs
WHERE Memberships.club_name = MissingClubs.club_name)
 AND Memberships.ifc = MissingIfcs.ifc
GROUP BY Memberships.ifc;

-- fifth step: remaining missing ifcs
INSERT INTO Samples (member_id, club_name, ifc)
```

```
SELECT MIN(Memberships.member_id),
   MIN(memberships.club_name),
   memberships.ifc
 FROM Memberships, MissingIfcs
WHERE Memberships.ifc = MissingIfcs.ifc
GROUP BY Memberships.ifc;

-- sixth step: remaining missing clubs
INSERT INTO Samples (Member_id, club_name, ifc)
SELECT MIN(Memberships.Member_id),
   Memberships.club_name,
   MIN(Memberships.ifc)
 FROM Memberships, MissingClubs
WHERE Memberships.club_name = MissingClubs.club_name
GROUP BY Memberships.club_name;
```

We can check the candidate rows for redundancy removal with the two views that were created earlier to be sure.

# 36

# TREES AND HIERARCHIES IN SQL

I have a separate book (*Trees and Hierarchies in SQL*, ISBN 978-1558609204) devoted to this topic in great detail, so this will be a very quick discussion of the three major approaches to modeling trees and hierarchies in SQL.

A tree is a special kind of directed graph. Graphs are data structures that are made up of nodes (usually shown as boxes or circles) connected by edges (usually shown as lines with arrowheads). Each edge represents a one-way relationship between the two nodes it connects. In an organizational chart, the nodes are positions that can be filled by employees and each edge is the "reports to" relationship. In a parts explosion (also called a bill of materials), the nodes are assembly units that eventually resolve down to individual parts from inventory, and each edge is the "is made of" relationship.

The top of the tree is called the root. In an organizational chart, it is the highest authority; in a parts explosion, it is the final assembly. The number of edges coming out of the node is its outdegree, and the number of edges entering it is its indegree. A binary tree is one in which a parent_node can have at most two children; more generally, an n-ary tree is one in which a node can have at most outdegree n.

The nodes of the tree that have no subtrees beneath them are called the leaf nodes. In a parts explosion, they are the individual parts, which cannot be broken down any further. The descendants, or children, of a node (the parent_node) are every node in the subtree that has the parent_node node as its root.

There are several ways to define a tree: It is a graph with no cycles; it is a graph where all nodes except the root have indegree 1 and the root has indegree zero. Another defining property is that a path can be found from the root to any other node in the tree by following the edges in their natural direction.

The tree structure and the nodes are very different things and therefore should be modeled in separate tables. But I am going to violate that design rule in this chapter and use an abstract tree in this chapter that looks like Figure 36.1.

**Joe Celko's SQL for Smarties. DOI: 10.1016/B978-0-12-382022-8.00036-3**

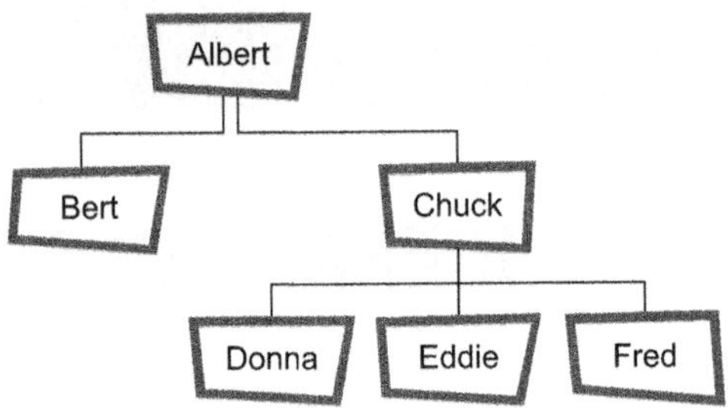


**Figure 36.1** Abstract Tree.

This little tree is small enough that you can remember what it looks like as you read the rest of this chapter, and it will illustrate the various techniques discussed here. I will use the terms child_node, parent_node, and node; you will see other terms used in various books on graphs.

## 36.1 Adjacency List Model

Most SQL databases have used the adjacency list model for two reasons. The first reason is that Dr. Codd came up with it in the early days of the relational model and nobody thought about it after that. The second reason is that the adjacency list is a way of "faking" pointer chains, the traditional programming method in procedural languages for handling trees. It is a recording of the edges in a "boxes and arrows" diagram, something like this simple table:

```
CREATE TABLE AdjTree
(child_node CHAR(2) NOT NULL,
parent_node CHAR(2), -- null is root
PRIMARY KEY (child_node, parent_node));
```

AdjTree

| child_node | parent_node |
|---|---|
| 'A' | NULL |
| 'B' | 'A' |
| 'C' | 'A' |
| 'D' | 'C' |
| 'E' | 'C' |
| 'F' | 'C' |

The queries for the leaf nodes and root are obvious. The root has a NULL parent_node and the leaf nodes have no subordinates. Each row models two nodes that share an adjacent edge in a directed. The Adjacency List Model is both the most common and the worst possible tree model. On the other hand, it is the best way to model any general graph.

## 36.1.1 Complex Constraints

The first problem is that the Adjacency List Model requires complex constraints to maintain any data integrity. In practice, the usual solution is to ignore the problems and hope that nothing bad happens to the structure. But if you care about data integrity, you need to be sure that:

1. There is only one root node. You may find that this is hard to write in many SQL products because they do not support CHECK() constraints that allow subquery expressions or aggregate functions.

```
CREATE TABLE AdjTree
(child_node CHAR(2) NOT NULL,
parent_node CHAR(2), -- null is root
PRIMARY KEY (child_node, parent_node),
CONSTRAINT one_root
CHECK((SELECT COUNT(*)
   FROM AdjTree
   WHERE parent_node IS NULL) = 1)
..);
```

2. There are no cycles. Unfortunately, this cannot be done without a trigger. The trigger code has to trace all the paths looking for a cycle. The most obvious constraint, to prohibit a single node cycle in the graph, would be:

```
CHECK (child_node <> parent_node) -- cannot be your own father!
```

But that does not detect (n > 2) node cycles. We know that the number of edges in a tree is the number of nodes minus one, so this is a connected graph. That constraint looks like this:

```
CHECK ((SELECT COUNT(*) FROM AdjTree) -1 -- edges
   = (SELECT COUNT(parent_node) FROM AdjTree)) -- nodes
```

The COUNT(parent_node) will drop the NULL in the root row. That gives us the effect of having a constraint to check for one NULL:

```
CHECK((SELECT COUNT(*) FROM Tree WHERE parent_node IS
   NULL) = 1)
```

This is a necessary condition, but it is not a sufficient condition. Consider this data, in which 'D' and 'E' are both in a cycle and that cycle is not in the tree structure.

Cycle

| child_node | parent_node |
|---|---|
| 'A' | NULL |
| 'B' | 'A' |
| 'C' | 'A' |
| 'D' | 'E' |
| 'E' | 'D' |

One approach would be to remove all the leaf nodes and repeat this procedure until the tree is reduced to an empty set. If the tree does not reduce to an empty set, then there is a disconnected cycle.

```
CREATE FUNCTION TreeTest() RETURNS CHAR(6)
LANGUAGE SQL
BEGIN ATOMIC
DECLARE row_count INTEGER;
SET row_count
  = (SELECT COUNT(DISTINCT parent_node) + 1
     FROM AdjTree);
-- put a copy in a temporary table
INSERT INTO WorkTree
SELECT emp, parent_node FROM AdjTree;

WHILE row_count > 0
DO DELETE FROM WorkTree -- prune leaf nodes
 WHERE Tree.child_node
   NOT IN (SELECT T2.parent_node
        FROM Tree AS T2
        WHERE T2.parent_node IS NOT NULL);
 SET row_count = row_count -1;
END WHILE;
IF NOT EXISTS (SELECT * FROM WorkTree)
THEN RETURN ('Tree '); --pruned everything
ELSE RETURN ('Cycles'); --cycles were left
END IF;
END;
```

## 36.1.2 Procedural Traversal for Queries

The second problem is that the Adjacency List Model requires that you traverse from node to node to answer any interesting questions such as, "Does Mr. King have any authority over Mr. Jones?" or any aggregations up and down the tree.

```
SELECT P1.child_node, ' parent_node to ', C1.child_node
 FROM AdjTree AS P1, AdjTree AS C1
WHERE P1.child_node = C1.parent_node;
```

But something is missing here. This gives only the immediate parent_node of the node. Your parent_node's parent_node also has authority over you, and so forth up the tree until we find someone who has no subordinates. To go two levels deep in the tree, we need to do a more complex self-JOIN, thus:

```
SELECT B1.child_node, ' parent_node to ', E2.child_node
 FROM AdjTree AS B1, AdjTree AS E1, AdjTree AS E2
WHERE B1.child_node = E1.parent_node
 AND E1.child_node = E2.parent_node;
```

Unfortunately, you have no idea just how deep the tree is, so you must keep extending this query until you get an empty set back as a result. The practical problem is that most SQL compilers will start having serious problems optimizing queries with a large number of tables.

The other methods are to declare a CURSOR and traverse the tree with procedural code. This is usually painfully slow, but it will work for any depth of tree. It also defeats the purpose of using a nonprocedural language like SQL.

With recursive Common Table Expressions in SQL-99, you can also write a query that recursively constructs the transitive closure of the table by hiding the traversal. This feature is still slow compared to the nested sets model. Here is a simple recursive traversal that computes the level in the organizational chart.

```
WITH RECURSIVE PersonnelTraversal
AS -- start at the root
(SELECT emp_id,
    1 AS hierarchy_level
 FROM Personnel
WHERE mgr_emp_id IS NULL
UNION ALL
SELECT E.emp_id, -- add each level
   (X.hierarchy_level + 1) AS hierarchy_level
 FROM Personnel AS E,
   PersonnelTraversal AS X
WHERE X.emp_id = E.mgr_emp_id)
```

```
SELECT emp_id, hierarchy_level
 FROM PersonnelTraversal;
```

This is the basic skeleton for computations in an adjacency list model.

### 36.1.3 Altering the Table

Insertion of a new node is the only easy operation in the Adjacency list model. You simply do an `INSERT INTO` statement and check to see that the parent_node already exists in the table.

Deleting an edge in the middle of a tree will cause the table to become a forest of separate trees. You need some rules for rearranging the structure. The two usual methods are:

1. Promote a subordinate to the vacancy (and cascade the vacancy downward).
2. Assign all the subordinates to their parent_node's parent_node (the orphans go to live with grandparents).

Consider what has to happen when a middle level node is changed. The change must occur in both the child_node and parent_node columns.

```
UPDATE AdjTree
 SET child_node
   = CASE WHEN child_node = 'C'
      THEN 'C1',
      ELSE child_node END,
   parent_node
   = CASE WHEN parent_node= 'C'
      THEN 'C1',
      ELSE parent_node END
WHERE 'C' IN (parent_node, child_node);
```

## 36.2 The Path Enumeration Model

The next method for representing hierarchies in SQL was first discussed in detail by Stefan Gustafsson on an Internet site for SQL Server users. Later Tom Moreau and Itzak Ben-Gan developed it in more detail in their book, *Advanced Transact-SQL for SQL Server 2000* (ISBN 978-1-893115-82-8 ). This model stores the path from the root to each node as a string at that node.

Of course we purists might object that this is a denormalized table, since the path is not a scalar value. The worst case operation you can do in this representation is to alter the root of the tree. We then have to recalculate all the paths in the entire tree. But if the assumption is that structural modifications high in the tree are relatively uncommon, then this might not be a problem. The table for a simple tree we will use for this chapter looks like this:

```
CREATE TABLE PathTree
(node CHAR(2) NOT NULL PRIMARY KEY,
path VARCHAR (900) NOT NULL);
```

The example tree would get the following representation:

| node | path |
|---|---|
| 'A' | 'a/' |
| 'B' | 'a/b/' |
| 'C' | 'a/c/' |
| 'D' | 'a/c/d/' |
| 'E' | 'a/c/e/' |
| 'F' | 'a/c/f/' |

What we have done is concatenate the node names and separated them with a slash. All the operations will depend on string manipulations, so we'd like to have short node identifiers, so the paths will be short. We would prefer, but not require, identifiers of one length to make substrings easier.

You have probably recognized this because I used a slash separator; this is a version of the directory paths used in several operating systems such as the UNIX family and Windows.

### 36.2.1 Finding Subtrees and Nodes

The major trick in this model is the LIKE predicate. The subtree rooted at :mynode is found with this query.

```
SELECT node
 FROM PathTree
WHERE path LIKE '%' || :my_node || '%';
```

Finding the root node is easy, since that is the substring of any node up to the first slash. However, the leaf nodes are harder.

```
SELECT T1.node
 FROM PathTree AS T1
 WHERE NOT EXISTS
   (SELECT *
     FROM PathTree AS T2
    WHERE T2.path LIKE T1.path || '/_');
```

## 36.2.2 Finding Levels and Subordinates

The depth of a node is shown by the number of '/' in the path string. If you have a REPLACE(), which can remove the '/' characters, the difference between the length of the part with and without those characters gives you the level.

```
CREATE VIEW DetailedTree (node, path, level)
AS SELECT node, path,
     CHARLENGTH (path)
      - CHARLENGTH (REPLACE (path, '/', ''))
   FROM PathTree;
```

The immediate descendents of a given node can be found with this query, if you know the length of the node identifiers. In this sample data, that length is one character:

```
SELECT :mynode, T2.node
 FROM PathTree AS T1, PathTree AS T2
WHERE T1.node = :mynode
 AND T2.path LIKE T1.path || '_/';
```

This can be expanded with OR-ed like predicates that cover the possible lengths of the node identifiers.

## 36.2.3 Deleting Nodes and Subtrees

This is a bit weird at first, because the removal of a node requires that you first update all the paths. Let us delete node 'B' in the sample tree:

```
BEGIN ATOMIC
UPDATE PathTree
 SET path
   = REPLACE (path, 'b/', '')
WHERE POSITION ('b/' IN path) > 0;
DELETE FROM PathTree
WHERE node = 'B';
END;
```

Deleting a subtree rooted at :mynode is actually simpler:

```
DELETE FROM PathTree
WHERE path LIKE (SELECT path
        FROM PathTree
       WHERE node = :my_node ||'%';
```

## 36.2.4 Integrity Constraints

If a path has the same node in it twice, then there is a cycle in the graph. We can use a VIEW with just the node names in it to some advantage here.

```
CHECK (NOT EXISTS
   (SELECT *
     FROM NodeList AS D1, PathTree AS P1
     WHERE CHAR_LENGTH (REPLACE (D1.node, P1.path, ''))
       < (CHAR_LENGTH(P1.path) - CHAR_LENGTH(D1.node))
  ))
```

Unfortunately, a subquery in a constraint is not widely implemented yet.

## 36.3 Nested Set Model of Hierarchies

Since SQL is a set-oriented language, this is a better model for the approach discussed here. If you have used HTML, XML, or a language with a block structure, then you understand the basic idea of this model. The lft and rgt columns (their names are abbreviations for "left" and "right," which are reserved words in Standard SQL) are the count of the "tags" in an XML representation of a tree.

Imagine circles inside circles without any of them overlapping, the way you would draw a markup language structure. This has some predictable results that we can use for building queries.

If that mental model does not work for you, to convert the "boxes and arrows" graph into a Nested Set Model, think of a little worm crawling along the tree. The worm starts at the top, the root, and makes a complete trip around the tree. When he comes to a node, he puts a number in the cell on the side that he is visiting and increments his counter. Each node will get two

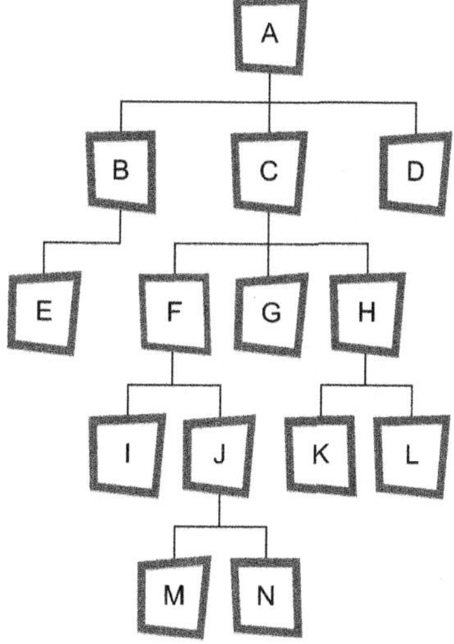


**Figure 36.2** Traditional "boxes & arrows" tree diagram.

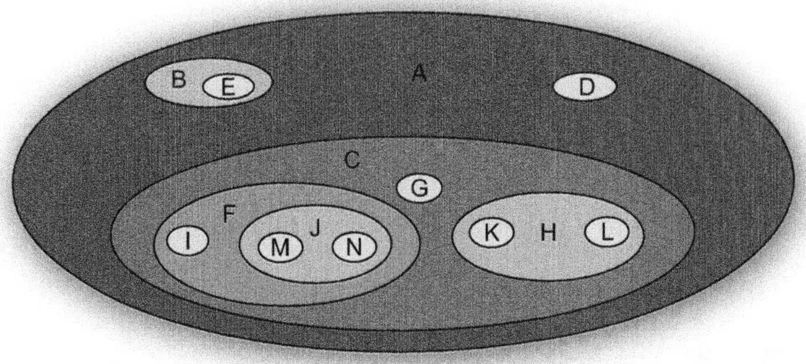


Figure 36.3 Nested sets tree diagram.

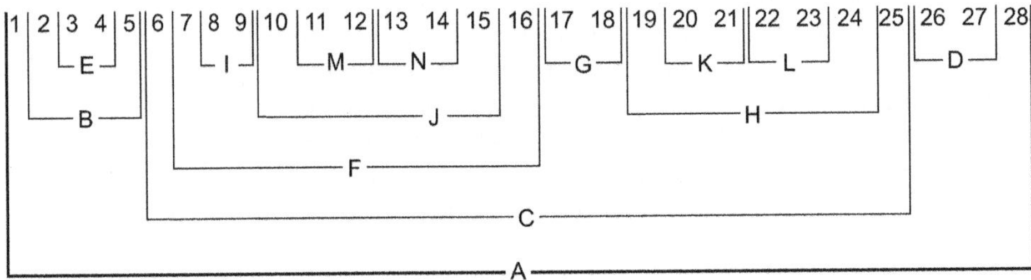


Figure 36.4 Linear nested sets tree diagram.

numbers, one for the right side and one for the left. Computer science majors will recognize this as a modified preorder tree traversal algorithm.

```
CREATE TABLE NestTree
(node CHAR(2) NOT NULL PRIMARY KEY,
lft INTEGER NOT NULL UNIQUE CHECK (lft > 0),
rgt INTEGER NOT NULL UNIQUE CHECK (rgt > 1),
CONSTRAINT order_okay CHECK (lft < rgt));
```

NestTree

| Node | lft | rgt |
|---|---|---|
| 'A' | 1 | 12 |
| 'B' | 2 | 3 |
| 'C' | 4 | 11 |
| 'D' | 5 | 6 |
| 'E' | 7 | 8 |
| 'F' | 9 | 10 |

Another nice thing is that the name of each node appears once and only once in the table. The path enumeration and adjacency list models used lots of self-references to nodes, which made updating more complex.

## 36.3.1 The Counting Property

The lft and rgt numbers have a definite meaning and carry information about the location and nature of each subtree. The root is always `(lft, rgt) = (1, 2 * (SELECT COUNT(*) FROM TreeTable))` and leaf nodes always have `(lft + 1 = rgt)`.

```
SELECT node AS root
 FROM NestTree
WHERE lft = 1;
SELECT node AS leaf
 FROM NestTree
WHERE lft = (rgt - 1);
```

Another very useful result of the counting property is that any node in the tree is the root of a subtree (the leaf nodes are a degenerate case) of size `(rgt - lft +1)/2`.

## 36.3.2 The Containment Property

In the Nested Set Model table, all the descendants of a node can be found by looking for the nodes with a rgt and lft number between the lft and rgt values of their parent_node node. For example, to find out all the subordinates of each boss in the corporate hierarchy, you would write:

```
SELECT Superiors.node, ' is a boss of ', Subordinates.node
 FROM NestTree AS Superiors, NestTree AS Subordinates
WHERE Subordinates.lft BETWEEN Superiors.lft AND Superiors
   .rgt;
```

This would tell you that everyone is also his own boss, so in some situations you would also add the predicate,

```
.. AND Subordinates.lft <> Superiors.lft
```

This simple self-`JOIN` query is the basis for almost everything that follows in the Nested Set Model. The containment property does not depend on the values of lft and rgt having no gaps, but the counting property does.

The level of a node in a tree is the number of edges between the node and the root, where the larger the depth number, the farther away the node is from the root. A path is a set of edges that directly connect two nodes.

The Nested Set Model uses the fact that each containing set is "wider" (where width = (rgt – lft)) than the sets it contains.

Obviously, the root will always be the widest row in the table. The level function is the number of edges between two given nodes; it is fairly easy to calculate. For example, to find the level of each subordinate node, you would use:

```
SELECT T2.node, (COUNT(T1.node) - 1) AS level
 FROM NestTree AS T1, NestTree AS T2
WHERE T2.lft BETWEEN T1.lft AND T1.rgt
GROUP BY T2.node;
```

The reason for using the expression `(COUNT(*) - 1)` is to remove the duplicate count of the node itself because a tree starts at level zero. If you prefer to start at one, then drop the extra arithmetic.

### 36.3.3 Subordinates

The Nested Set Model usually assumes that the subordinates are ranked by age, seniority, or in some way from left to right among the immediate subordinates of a node. The adjacency model does not have a concept of such rankings, so the following queries are not possible without extra columns to hold the rankings in the adjacency list model.

Most senior subordinate is found by this query:

```
SELECT Subordinates.node, ' is the oldest child_node of ',
   :my_node
 FROM NestTree AS Superiors, NestTree AS Subordinates
WHERE Superiors.node = :my_node
  AND Subordinates.lft - 1 = Superiors.lft; -- leftmost
    child_node
```

Most junior subordinate:

```
SELECT Subordinates.node, ' is the youngest child_node of ',
   :my_node
 FROM NestTree AS Superiors, NestTree AS Subordinates
WHERE Superiors.node = :my_node
  AND Subordinates.rgt = Superiors.rgt - 1; -- rightmost
    child_node
```

To convert a nested sets model into an adjacency list model with the immediate subordinates, use this query in a `VIEW`.

```
CREATE VIEW AdjTree (parent_node, child_node)
AS
SELECT B.node, E.node
 FROM NestTree AS E
```

```
LEFT OUTER JOIN
NestTree AS B
ON B.lft
 = (SELECT MAX(lft)
    FROM NestTree AS S
   WHERE E.lft > S.lft
    AND E.lft < S.rgt);
```

## 36.3.4 Hierarchical Aggregations

To find the level of each node, so you can print the tree as an indented listing. Technically, you should declare a cursor to go with the ORDER BY clause.

```
SELECT COUNT(T2.node) AS indentation, T1.node
  FROM NestTree AS T1, NestTree AS T2
 WHERE T1.lft BETWEEN T2.lft AND T2.rgt
 GROUP BY T1.lft, T1.emp
 ORDER BY T1.lft;
```

This same pattern of grouping will also work with other aggregate functions. Let's assume a second table contains the weight of each of the nodes in the NestTree. A simple hierarchical total of the weights by subtree is a two-table join.

```
SELECT   Superiors.node,   SUM   (Subordinates.weight)   AS
   subtree_weight
 FROM NestTree AS Superiors, NestTree AS Subordinates
   NodeWeights AS W
WHERE Subordinates.lft BETWEEN Superiors.lft AND Superiors.rgt
 AND W.node = Subordinates,node;
```

## 36.3.5 Deleting Nodes and Subtrees

Another interesting property of this representation is that the subtrees must fill from lft to rgt. In other tree representations, it is possible for a parent_node node to have a rgt child_node and no lft child_node. This lets you assign some significance to being the leftmost child_node of a parent_node. For example, the node in this position might be the next in line for promotion in a corporate hierarchy.

Deleting a single node in the middle of the tree is conceptually harder than removing whole subtrees. When you remove a node in the middle of the tree, you have to decide how to fill the hole.

There are two ways. The first method is to promote one of the children to the original node's position—Dad dies and the oldest son takes over the business. The second method is to connect the children to the parent_node of the original node—Mom dies and Grandma adopts the kids. This is the default action in a Nested Set Model because of the containment property; the deletion will destroy the counting property, however.

If you wish to close multiple gaps, you can do this by renumbering the nodes, thus.

```
UPDATE NestTree
 SET lft = (SELECT COUNT(*)
        FROM (SELECT lft FROM NestTree
           UNION ALL
          SELECT rgt FROM NestTree) AS LftRgt (seq_nbr)
        WHERE seq_nbr <= lft),
   rgt = (SELECT COUNT(*)
        FROM (SELECT lft FROM NestTree
           UNION ALL
          SELECT rgt FROM NestTree) AS LftRgt (seq_nbr)
WHERE seq_nbr <= rgt);
```

If the derived table LftRgt is a bit slow, you can use a temporary table and index it or use a `VIEW` that will be materialized.

```
CREATE VIEW LftRgt (seq_nbr)
AS SELECT lft FROM NestTree
 UNION
 SELECT rgt FROM NestTree;
```

This `VIEW` can also be used to check that the tree has all of the lft and rgt values it should with this query:

```
NOT EXISTS
(SELECT *
  FROM (SELECT seq_nbr, ROW_NUMBER() OVER (ORDER BY
     seq_nbr) AS rn
  FROM LftRgt) AS X
WHERE seq_nbr <> rn)
```

### 36.3.6 Converting Adjacency List to Nested Set Model

It would be fairly easy to load an adjacency list model table into a host language program, then use a recursive preorder tree traversal program from a college freshman data structures textbook to build the nested set model. Here is version with an explicit stack in SQL/PSM.

```
-- Tree holds the adjacency model
CREATE TABLE Tree
(node CHAR(10) NOT NULL,
parent_node CHAR(10));
```

```
-- Stack starts empty, will hold the nested set model
CREATE TABLE Stack
(stack_top INTEGER NOT NULL,
node CHAR(10) NOT NULL,
lft INTEGER,
rgt INTEGER);

BEGIN ATOMIC
DECLARE counter INTEGER;
DECLARE max_counter INTEGER;
DECLARE current_top INTEGER;

SET counter = 2;
SET max_counter = 2 * (SELECT COUNT(*) FROM Tree);
SET current_top = 1;

--clear the stack
DELETE FROM Stack;

-- push the root
INSERT INTO Stack
SELECT 1, node, 1, max_counter
 FROM Tree
WHERE parent_node IS NULL;

-- delete rows from tree as they are used
DELETE FROM Tree WHERE parent_node IS NULL;

WHILE counter <= max_counter- 1
 DO IF EXISTS (SELECT *
       FROM Stack AS S1, Tree AS T1
       WHERE S1.node = T1.parent_node
        AND S1.stack_top = current_top)
  THEN -- push when top has subordinates and set lft value
   INSERT INTO Stack
   SELECT  (current_top  +  1),  MIN(T1.node),  counter,
      CAST(NULL AS INTEGER)
    FROM Stack AS S1, Tree AS T1
    WHERE S1.node = T1.parent_node
     AND S1.stack_top = current_top;

    -- delete rows from tree as they are used
    DELETE FROM Tree
    WHERE node = (SELECT node
          FROM Stack
          WHERE stack_top = current_top + 1);
    -- housekeeping of stack pointers and counter
    SET counter = counter + 1;
    SET current_top = current_top + 1;
   ELSE -- pop the stack and set rgt value
    UPDATE Stack
     SET rgt = counter,
       stack_top = -stack_top -- pops the stack
```

```
      WHERE stack_top = current_top;
     SET counter = counter + 1;
     SET current_top = current_top - 1;
    END IF;
  END WHILE;
END;

-- the top column is not needed in the final answer
SELECT node, lft, rgt FROM Stack;
```

This is not the fastest way to do a conversion, but since conversions are probably not going to be frequent tasks, it might be good enough when translated into your SQL product's procedural language.

## 36.4 Other Models for Trees and Hierarchies

Other models for trees are discussed in a separate book (*Trees & Hierarchies in SQL,* ISBN 978-1558609204), but these three methods represent the major families of models. You can also use specialized models for specialized trees, such as binary trees. The real point is that you can use SQL for hierarchical structures, but you have to pick the right one for your task. I would classify the choices as:

1. Frequent node changes and infrequent structure changes. Example: organizational charts where personnel come and go, but the organization stays much the same.
2. Infrequent node changes with frequent structure changes. Example: a message board where the e-mails are the nodes that never change and the structure is simply extended with each new e-mail.
3. Infrequent node changes and infrequent structure changes. Example: historical data in a data warehouse that has a categorical hierarchy in place as a dimension.
4. Both frequent node changes and frequent structure changes. Example: a mapping system that attempts to find the best path from a central dispatch to the currently most critical node through a tree that is also changing. Let's make that a bit clearer with the concrete example of getting a fire truck from the engine house to the worst fire in its service area based on the traffic at the time.

I am not going to pick any particular tree model for any of those situations. The answer is, "Well, it all depends ..." once again.

37

# GRAPHS IN SQL

The terminology in graph theory pretty much explains itself; the concept of a bunch of lines connecting dots seems simple enough. But graph theory is surprisingly powerful and rich in mathematical complexity. You might want to read some of the books suggested in the last section of this chapter, if you never had a course in it before.

Graphs are important because they are a general way to represent many different types of data and their relationships. A few examples among many are:

- Social networks
- Friend of a friend
- Degree of separation
- Traffic routing

Here is a quick review of terms, though you will find other authors have different ones for the same concepts.

A graph is a data structure made up of nodes connected by edges. Edges can be directed (permit travel in only one direction) or undirected (permit travel in both directions). The number of edges entering a node is its indegree; likewise, the number of edges leaving a node is its outdegree. A set of edges that allow you to travel from one node to another is called a path. A cycle is a path that comes back to the node from which it started without crossing itself (this means that a big 'O' is fine but a figure '8' is not).

A tree is a type of directed graph that is important enough to have its own terminology. Its special properties and frequent use have made it important enough to be covered in a separate chapter. The following section will stress other useful kinds of generalized directed graphs. Generalized directed graphs are classified into nonreconvergent and reconvergent graphs. In a reconvergent graph there are multiple paths between at least one pair of nodes. Reconvergent graphs are either cyclic or acyclic.

**Joe Celko's SQL for Smarties. DOI: 10.1016/B978-0-12-382022-8.00037-5**

## 37.1 Adjacency List Model Graphs

The most common way to model a graph in SQL is with an adjacency list model. Each edge of the graph is shown as a pair of nodes in which the ordering matters, and then any values associated with that edge is shown in another column.

Here is the skeleton of the basic adjacency list model of a graph, with nodes in a separate table. This is the most common method for modeling graphs in SQL. Before we had recursive CTEs, you had to use cursors and procedural code for the interesting algorithms.

```
CREATE TABLE Nodes
(node_id INTEGER NOT NULL PRIMARY KEY,
« other attributes of the node »);

CREATE TABLE AdjacencyListGraph
(begin_node_id INTEGER NOT NULL
   REFERENCES Nodes (node_id)
   ON DELETE CASCADE,
end_node_id INTEGER NOT NULL
   REFERENCES Nodes (node_id)
   ON DELETE CASCADE,
« other attributes of the edge »,
PRIMARY KEY (begin_node_id, end_node_id));
```

Technically, the begin_node_id can be the same as the end_node_id and we can have a node without any edges. They are easy to diagram, as seen in Figure 37.1.

The "other attributes of the edge" are usually called weights. These attributes model distance or travel time for maps, electrical resistance for circuits, cost of a process in workflow networks,

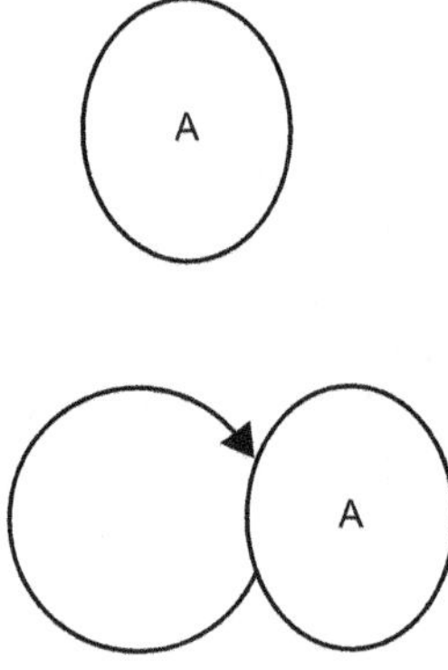


**Figure 37.1** Nodes.

and so on. They are usually expressed as a numeric value on some scale, and we want to do computations with them.

Likewise, the "other attributes of the node" are usually a name (say, "5 ohm resistor" in a circuit diagram) or where the weight (travel distance in a road map) is kept in the schema.

### 37.1.1 SQL and the Adjacency List Model

There are only two approaches with an adjacency list model of a graph. You can use procedural code, which has two more options—a procedure or a cursor. Or you can use a recursive CTE, but it is not recommended. Recursion is usually slow and most SQL products choke at a certain depth, usually some power of two.

The procedural approaches are usually direct translations of known algorithms from your favorite procedural programming languages into SQL/PSM. You replace the arrays with tables that mimic arrays.

Though still procedural under the covers, you can use recursive CTEs instead of loops and perhaps gain advantages from the query optimizer and parallelism. The *very* general skeleton of such queries is:

```
WITH RECURSIVE
SolutionGraph (source_node, dest_node, <wgt>, ..)
AS
(SELECT source_node, dest_node, <wgt>,
     <other attributes>, <possible counts>
  FROM AdjacencyListGraph
 UNION ALL
 SELECT G1.source_node, G2.dest_node,
     <computation on wgt>,
     <computation on other attributes>,
     <increment counts>
  FROM SolutionGraph AS G1, Graph AS G2
 WHERE G2.source_node = G1.dest_node
  AND G2.dest_node <> G1.source_node
  AND NOT EXISTS
   (SELECT *
     FROM Graph AS G3
    WHERE G3.source_node = G1.source_node
     AND G3.dest_node = G2.dest_node
     AND <special conditions>))

SELECT source_node, dest_node,
    <aggregate computation on wgt>,
    <aggregate computation on other attributes>,
    <final counts>
 FROM SoluitonGraph
WHERE <special conditions>
```

```
GROUP BY source_node, dest_node
HAVING <special conditions>;
```

In English, you start with an initial set of nodes and see if they are what you wanted; if not, then add more nodes recursively. This is not the only way to build graph algorithms, but it is a common design pattern. The bad news is that an iterative program can stop at the first right answer; recursive CTEs (and SQL in general) tend to find all the valid answers, no matter what the cost.

### 37.1.2 Paths with CTE

The following queries with CTEs is due to Frédéric Brouard of France. The sample data and the narrative are so delightful that I am using his material directly.

> *Perhaps you never go to France. So you may be interested by the fact that in Paris, there are beautiful girls, and in Toulouse a famous dish called Cassoulet, and a small plane constructor called Airbus. So the problem is to go by car from Paris to Toulouse using the speedway network. I just simplify for you (if you are lost and you do not know the pronunciation to ask people your way to Toulouse, it is simple. Just say "to loose" ...):*

```
CREATE TABLE Journeys
(depart_town VARCHAR(32) NOT NULL,
arrival_town VARCHAR(32) NOT NULL,
CHECK (depart_town <> arrival_town),
```

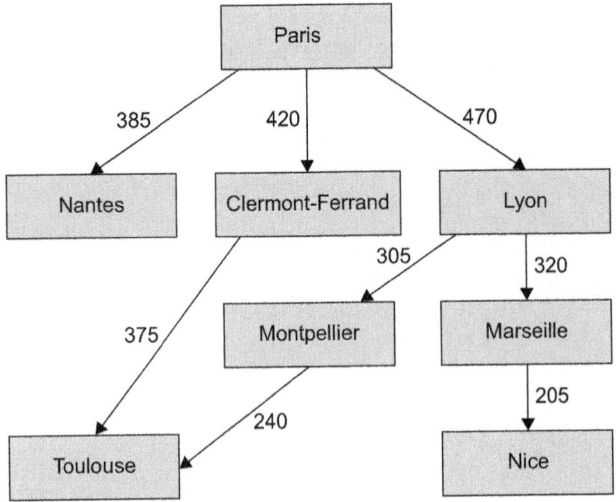


**Figure 37.2** The French road trip graph.

```
PRIMARY KEY (depart_town, arrival_town),
jny_distance INTEGER NOT NULL
   CHECK (jny_distance > 0));

INSERT INTO Journeys
VALUES ('Paris', 'Nantes', 385),
('Paris', 'Clermont-Ferrand', 420),
('Paris', 'Lyon', 470),
('Clermont-Ferrand', 'Montpellier', 335),
('Clermont-Ferrand', 'Toulouse ', 375),
('Lyon', 'Montpellier', 305),
385
420
470
375
335
305
320
205
240
('Lyon', 'Marseille', 320),
('Montpellier', 'Toulouse ', 240),
('Marseille', 'Nice', 205);
```

*Now we will try a very simple query, giving all the journeys between towns:*

```
WITH Trips (arrival_town)
 AS (SELECT DISTINCT depart_town
    FROM Journeys
   UNION ALL
   SELECT arrival_town
    FROM Journeys AS Arrivals,
      Journeys AS Departures
   WHERE Departures.arrival_town = Arrivals.depart_town)
SELECT DISTINCT arrival_town FROM Trips;
```

| arrival_town |
|---|
| Clermont-Ferrand |
| Lyon |
| Marseille |
| Montpellier |
| Paris |
| Nantes |
| Toulouse |
| Nice |

*This query is not very interesting because we do not know from which town we came. We just know the towns where we can go, and the fact that we have probably different ways to go to same place. Let us see if we can have some more information …*

*First, we want to start from Paris:*

```
WITH Trips (arrival_town)
 AS (SELECT DISTINCT depart_town
     FROM Journeys
    WHERE depart_town = 'Paris'
  UNION ALL
  SELECT arrival_town
   FROM Journeys AS Arrivals
     INNER Journeys AS Departures
        ON Departures.arrival_town = Arrivals.depart_town)
SELECT arrival_town FROM Journeys;
```

| arrival_town | |
|---|---|
| Paris | |
| Nantes | |
| Clermont-Ferrand | |
| Lyon | |
| Montpellier | |
| Marseille | |
| Nice | |
| Toulouse | ◀ goal |
| Montpellier | |
| Toulouse | ◀ goal |
| Toulouse | ◀ goal |

*We have probably three ways to go to Toulouse. Can we filter the destination? Sure!*

```
WITH Journeys (arrival_town)
 AS (SELECT DISTINCT depart_town
      FROM Journeys
    WHERE depart_town = 'Paris'
   UNION ALL
   SELECT arrival_town
    FROM Journeys AS Arrivals,
      Journeys AS Departures
   WHERE Departures.arrival_town = Arrivals.depart_town)
SELECT arrival_town
 FROM Journeys
WHERE arrival_town = 'Toulouse';
```

| arrival_town |
|---|
| Toulouse |
| Toulouse |
| Toulouse |

*We can refine this query by calculating the number of steps involved in the different ways:*

```
WITH Trips (arrival_town, steps)
 AS (SELECT DISTINCT depart_town, 0
      FROM Journeys
     WHERE depart_town = 'Paris'
    UNION ALL
    SELECT arrival_town, Departures.steps + 1
      FROM Journeys AS Arrivals,
        Journeys AS Departures
     WHERE Departures.arrival_town = Arrivals.depart_town)
SELECT arrival_town, steps
 FROM Trips
WHERE arrival_town = 'Toulouse';
```

| arrival_town | Steps |
|---|---|
| Toulouse | 3 |
| Toulouse | 2 |
| Toulouse | 3 |

*The cherry on the cake will be to know the distances of the different ways:*

```
WITH Trips (arrival_town, steps, total_distance)
AS
  (SELECT DISTINCT depart_town, 0, 0
   FROM Journeys
   WHERE depart_town = 'Paris'
   UNION ALL
   SELECT arrival_town, Departures.steps + 1,
      Departures.total_distance + Arrivals.jny_distance
    FROM Journeys AS Arrivals,
      Journeys AS Departures
    WHERE Departures.arrival_town = Arrivals.depart_town)
SELECT arrival_town, steps, total_distance
 FROM Trips
WHERE arrival_town = 'Toulouse';
```

| arrival_town | steps | total_distance |
|---|---|---|
| Toulouse | 3 | 1015 |
| Toulouse | 2 | 795 |
| Toulouse | 3 | 995 |

*The girl in the cake will be to know the different towns we visit by those different ways:*

```
WITH Trips (arrival_town, steps, total_distance, way)
 AS (SELECT DISTINCT depart_town, 0, 0,
         CAST('Paris' AS VARCHAR(MAX))
      FROM Journeys
     WHERE depart_town = 'Paris'
    UNION ALL
    SELECT arrival_town, Departures.steps + 1,
       Departures.total_distance + Arrivals.jny_distance,
       Departures.way ‖ ',' ‖Arrivals.arrival_town
     FROM Journeys AS Arrivals,
       Journeys AS Departures
     WHERE Departures.arrival_town = Arrivals.depart_town)
SELECT arrival_town, steps, total_distance, way
 FROM Trips
WHERE arrival_town = 'Toulouse ';
```

| arrival_town | steps | total_distance | way |
|---|---|---|---|
| Toulouse | 3 | 1015 | Paris, Lyon, Montpelier, Toulouse |
| Toulouse | 2 | 795 | Paris, Clermont-Ferrand, Toulouse |
| Toulouse | 3 | 995 | Paris, Clermont-Ferrand, Montpelier, Toulouse |

*And now, ladies and gentleman, the recursive query is proud to present to you how to solve a very complex problem, called the traveling salesman problem. This is one of the operational research problems for which Edsger Wybe Dijkstra found the first efficient algorithm and received the Turing Award in 1972.*

```
WITH Trips (arrival_town, steps, total_distance, way)
 AS (SELECT DISTINCT depart_town, 0, 0, CAST('Paris'
   AS VARCHAR(MAX))
     FROM Journeys
```

```
      WHERE depart_town = 'Paris'
      UNION ALL
      SELECT arrival_town, Departures.steps + 1,
         Departures.total_distance + Arrivals.jny_distance,
         Departures.way ||','||Arrivals.arrival_town
       FROM Journeys AS Arrivals,
         Journeys AS Departures
      WHERE Departures.arrival_town = Arrivals.depart_town),
 ShortestDistance (total_distance)
 AS (SELECT MIN(total_distance)
       FROM Journeys
      WHERE arrival_town = 'Toulouse')
SELECT arrival_town, steps, total_distance, way
 FROM Trips AS T
   ShortestDistance AS S
WHERE T.total_distance = S.total_distance
  AND arrival_town = 'Toulouse';
```

## 37.1.3 Nonacyclic Graphs

*In fact, one thing that is limiting the process in our network of speedways is that we have made routes with a single sense. I mean, we can go from Paris to Lyon, but we are not allowed to go from Lyon to Paris. For that, we need to add the reverse ways in the table, like:*

| depart_town | arrival_town | jny_distance |
|---|---|---|
| Lyon | Paris | 470 |

*This can be done by a very simple query:*

```
INSERT INTO Journeys
SELECT arrival_town, depart_town, jny_distance
FROM Journeys;
```

*The only problem is that previous queries will not work properly:*

```
WITH Journeys (arrival_town)
AS (SELECT DISTINCT depart_town
    FROM Journeys
    WHERE depart_town = 'Paris'
 UNION ALL
 SELECT arrival_town
  FROM Journeys AS Arrivals,
    Journeys AS Departures
```

```
 WHERE Departures.arrival_town = Arrivals.depart_town)
SELECT arrival_town
 FROM Journeys;
```

*This query will give you an error message about the maximum depth of recursion being violated. What happened? Simply, you are trying all ways including cycling ways like Paris, Lyon, Paris, Lyon, Paris … ad infinitum … Is there a way to avoid cycling routes? Maybe. In one of our previous queries, we have a column that gives the complete list of stepped towns. Why do we not use it to avoid cycling? The condition will be: do not pass through a town that is already in the way. This can be written as:*

```
WITH Trips (arrival_town, steps, total_distance, way)
 AS (SELECT DISTINCT depart_town, 0, 0, CAST('Paris' AS
   VARCHAR(255))
     FROM Journeys
     WHERE depart_town = 'Paris'
    UNION ALL
    SELECT arrival_town, Departures.steps + 1,
       Departures.total_distance + Arrivals.jny_distance,
       Departures.way ||','||Arrivals.arrival_town
    FROM Journeys AS Arrivals,
      Journeys AS Departures
    WHERE Departures.arrival_town = Arrivals.depart_town
     AND Departures.way NOT LIKE '%' || Arrivals.arrival_
       town || '%')
SELECT arrival_town, steps, total_distance, way
 FROM Trips
WHERE arrival_town = 'Toulouse';
```

| arrival_town | steps | total_distance | way |
|---|---|---|---|
| Toulouse | 3 | 1015 | Paris, Lyon, Montpellier, Toulouse |
| Toulouse | 4 | 1485 | Paris, Lyon, Montpellier, Clermont-Ferrand, Toulouse |
| Toulouse | 2 | 795 | Paris, Clermont-Ferrand, Toulouse |
| Toulouse | 3 | 995 | Paris, Clermont-Ferrand, Montpellier, Toulouse |

*As you see, a new route occurs. The worst in distance, but perhaps the most beautiful!*

*A* CTE *can simplify the expression of complex queries. Recursive queries must be employed where recursion is needed. Trust your*

*SQL product to terminate a bad query. There is usually an option to set the depth of recursion either in the SQL engine or as an* `OPTION` *clause at the end of the CTE clause.*

### 37.1.4 Adjacency Matrix Model

An adjacency matrix is a square array whose rows are out-nodes and columns are in-nodes of a graph. A 1 in a cell means that there is edge between the two nodes. Using the following graph, we would have an array like this:

| | A | B | C | D | E | F | G | H |
|---|---|---|---|---|---|---|---|---|
| A\| | 1 | 1 | 1 | 0 | 0 | 0 | 0 | 0 |
| B\| | 0 | 1 | 0 | 1 | 0 | 0 | 0 | 0 |
| C\| | 0 | 0 | 1 | 1 | 0 | 0 | 1 | 0 |
| D\| | 0 | 0 | 0 | 1 | 1 | 1 | 0 | 0 |
| E\| | 0 | 0 | 0 | 0 | 1 | 0 | 0 | 1 |
| F\| | 0 | 0 | 0 | 0 | 0 | 1 | 0 | 0 |
| G\| | 0 | 0 | 0 | 0 | 0 | 0 | 1 | 1 |
| H\| | 0 | 0 | 0 | 0 | 0 | 0 | 0 | 1 |

Many graph algorithms are based on the adjacency matrix model and can be translated into SQL. Go the appropriate chapter for the details of modeling matrices in SQL and in particular, look at the section on matrix multiplication in SQL. For example, Dijkstra's algorithm for the shortest distances between each pair of nodes in a graph looks like this in this array pseudo-code.

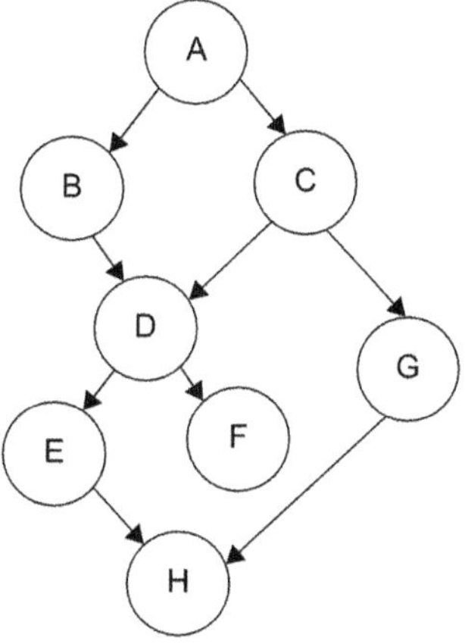


**Figure 37.3** Simple directed graph.

```
FOR k = 1 TO n
 DO FOR i = 1 TO n
  DO FOR j = 1 TO n
   IF a[i,k] + a[k,j] < a[i,j]
   THEN a[i,j] = a[i,k] + a[k,j]
   END IF;
  END FOR;
 END FOR;
END FOR;
```

You need to be warned that for a graph of (n) nodes, the table will be of size (n^2). The algorithms often run in (n^3) time. The advantage it has is that once you have completed a table, it can be used for look-ups rather than recomputing distances over and over.

Running the query against the data set:

```
INSERT INTO AdjacencyListGraph
VALUES ('a', 'd', 1),
  ('d', 'e', 1),
  ('e', 'c', 1),
  ('c', 'b', 1),
  ('b', 'd', 1),
  ('a', 'e', 5);
```

gives the result SET:

| source_node | dest_node | min_wgt |
|---|---|---|
| a | b | 4 |
| a | c | 3 |
| a | d | 1 |
| a | e | 2 |
| b | c | 3 |
| b | d | 1 |
| b | e | 2 |
| c | b | 1 |
| c | d | 2 |
| c | e | 3 |
| d | b | 3 |
| d | c | 2 |
| d | e | 1 |
| e | b | 2 |
| e | c | 1 |
| e | d | 3 |

Doing the Dijkstra algorithm would probably execute significantly faster in a language with arrays than in SQL.

## 37.2 Split Node Nested Set Models for Graphs

It is also possible to load an acyclic directed graph into a nested set model by splitting the nodes. It is a specialized trick for a certain class of graphs, not a general method like the adjacency list model graphs. Here is a skeleton table with minimal constrains for a Nested Sets Model of a tree.

```
CREATE TABLE NestedSetsGraph
(node_id INTEGER NOT NULL REFERENCES Nodes (node_id),
lft INTEGER NOT NULL CHECK (lft >= 1) PRIMARY KEY,
rgt INTEGER NOT NULL UNIQUE,
CHECK (rgt > lft),
UNIQUE (node_id, lft));
```

You split nodes by starting at the sink nodes and move up the tree. When you come to a node of (indegree > 1) replace it with that many copies of the node under each of its superiors. Continue to do this until you get to the root. The acyclic graph will become a tree, but with duplicated node values. There are advantages to this model when you want to avoid recursion. You are trading speed for storage space, however.

### 37.2.1 All Nodes in the Graph

The nodes in the Nodes table might not all be used in the graph, and those that are used can be repeated. It is safer to find the nodes in the graph with a simple view instead.

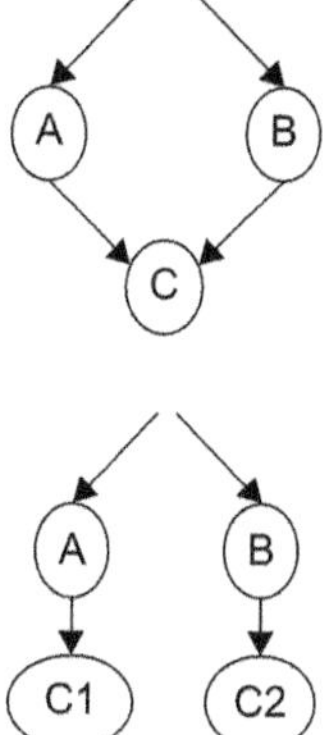


**Figure 37.4** Node splitting to avoid a cyclic graph.

```
CREATE VIEW GraphNodes (node_id)
AS
SELECT DISTINCT node_id FROM NestedSetsGraph;
```

This is worth its own subsection because of double counting problems in this model.

### 37.2.2 Path Endpoints

A path through a graph is a traversal of consecutive nodes along a sequence of edges. Clearly, the node at the end of one edge in the sequence must also be the node at the beginning of the next edge in the sequence. The length of the path is the number of edges that are traversed along the path.

Path endpoints are the first and last nodes of each path in the graph. For a path of length zero, the path endpoints are the same node. Yes, it is legal to have an edge that loops back around to the same node. And it is legal to have a node without any edges, but you cannot model that with adjacency list; thank goodness nobody usually cares about those isolated nodes.

If there is more than one path between two nodes, then each path will be distinguished by its own distinct set of number pairs for the nested-set representation.

If there is only one path (p) between two nodes but this path is a subpath of more than one distinct path then the endpoints of (p) will have number pairs for each of these greater paths. As a canonical form, the least numbered pairs are returned for these endpoints.

```
CREATE VIEW PathEndpoints
(begin_node_id, end_node_id,
begin_lft, begin_rgt,
end_lft, end_rgt)
AS
SELECT G1.node_id, G2.node_id,
   G1.lft, G1.rgt, G2.lft, G2.rgt
 FROM (SELECT node_id, MIN(lft), MIN(rgt)
     FROM NestedSetsGraph
    GROUP BY node_id) AS G1 (node_id, lft, rgt)
  INNER JOIN
  NestedSetsGraph AS G2
  ON G2.lft >= G1.lft
    AND G2.lft < G1.rgt;
```

### 37.2.3 Reachable Nodes

If a node is reachable from another node then a path exists from one node to the other. It is assumed that every node is reachable from itself.

```
CREATE VIEW ReachableNodes (begin_node_id, end_node_id)
AS
SELECT DISTINCT begin_node_id, end_node_id
 FROM PathEndpoints;
```

## 37.2.4 Edges

Edges are pairs of adjacent connected nodes in the graph. If edge E is represented by the pair of nodes (n0, n1) then (n1) is reachable from (n0) in a single traversal.

```
CREATE VIEW Edges (begin_node_id, end_node_id)
AS
SELECT begin_node_id, end_node_id
 FROM PathEndpoints AS PE
WHERE begin_node_id <> end_node_id
  AND NOT EXISTS
    (SELECT *
      FROM NestedSetsGraph AS G
     WHERE G.lft > PE.begin_lft
      AND G.lft < PE.end_lft
      AND G.rgt > PE.end_rgt);
```

## 37.2.5 Indegree and Outdegree

The indegree of a node (n) is the number of distinct edges ending at (n). Nodes that have zero indegree are not returned. Indegree of all nodes in the graph:

```
CREATE VIEW Indegree (node_id, node_indegree)
AS
SELECT N.node_id, COUNT(E.begin_node_id)
 FROM GraphNodes AS N
   LEFT OUTER JOIN
   Edges AS E
   ON N.node_id = E.end_node_id
GROUP BY N.node_id;
```

Outdegree of a node (n) is the number of distinct edges beginning at (n). Nodes that have zero outdegree are not returned. Outdegree of all nodes in the graph:

```
CREATE VIEW Outdegree (node_id, node_outdegree)
AS
SELECT N.node_id, COUNT(E.end_node_id)
 FROM GraphNodes AS N
   LEFT OUTER JOIN
   Edges AS E
   ON N.node_id = E.begin_node_id
GROUP BY N.node_id;
```

### 37.2.6 Source, Sink, Isolated, and Internal Nodes

A source node of a graph has a positive outdegree but zero indegree; that is, it has edges leading from, but not to, the node. This assumes there are no isolated nodes (nodes belonging to no edges).

```
CREATE VIEW SourceNodes (node_id, lft, rgt)
AS
SELECT node_id, lft, rgt
 FROM NestedSetsGraph AS G1
WHERE NOT EXISTS
  (SELECT *
    FROM NestedSetsGraph AS G
   WHERE G1.lft > G2.lft
     AND G1.lft < G2.rgt);
```

Likewise, a sink node of a graph has positive indegree but zero outdegree. It has edges leading to, but not from, the node. This assumes there are no isolated nodes.

```
CREATE VIEW SinkNodes (node_id)
AS
SELECT node_id
 FROM NestedSetsGraph AS G1
WHERE lft = rgt - 1
  AND NOT EXISTS
   (SELECT *
     FROM NestedSetsGraph AS G2
    WHERE G1.node_id = G2.node_id
      AND G2.lft < G1.lft);
```

An isolated node belongs to no edges; that is, it has zero indegree and zero outdegree. But we have agreed to leave them out of the model.

```
CREATE VIEW IsolatedNodes (node_id, lft, rgt)
AS
SELECT node_id, lft, rgt
 FROM NestedSetsGraph AS G1
WHERE lft = rgt - 1
  AND NOT EXISTS
    (SELECT *
      FROM NestedSetsGraph AS G2
     WHERE G1.lft > G2.lft
       AND G1.lft < G2.rgt);
```

An internal node of a graph has an (indegree > 0) and an (outdegree > 0); that is, it acts as both a source and a sink.

```
CREATE VIEW InternalNodes (node_id)
AS
SELECT node_id
```

```
 FROM (SELECT node_id, MIN(lft) AS lft, MIN(rgt) AS rgt
    FROM NestedSetsGraph
   WHERE lft < rgt - 1
  GROUP BY node_id) AS G1
WHERE EXISTS
  (SELECT *
    FROM NestedSetsGraph AS G2
   WHERE G1.lft > G2.lft
     AND G1.lft < G2.rgt)
```

### 37.2.7 Converting Acyclic Graphs to Nested Sets

Let's start with a simple graph in an adjacency list model.

```
INSERT INTO Nodes (node_id)
VALUES ('a'), ('b'), ('c'), ('d'),
   ('e'), ('f'), ('g'), ('h');

INSERT INTO AdjacencyListGraph (begin_node_id,
   end_node_id)
VALUES ('a', 'b'), ('a', 'c'), ('b', 'd'), ('c', 'd'),
   ('c', 'g'), ('d', 'e'), ('d', 'f'), ('e', 'h'),
   ('g', 'h');
```

We can convert this adjacency list model to the nested sets model with a simple stack algorithm. You might want to try to rewrite this with a recursive CTE.

```
-- Stack to keep track of nodes being traversed in depth-
   first fashion
CREATE TABLE NodeStack
(node_id INTEGER NOT NULL PRIMARY KEY
  REFERENCES Nodes (node_id),
distance INTEGER NOT NULL CHECK (distance >= 0),
lft INTEGER CHECK (lft >= 1),
rgt INTEGER,
CHECK (rgt > lft));

CREATE PROCEDURE AdjacencyListsToNestedSetsGraph ()
LANGUAGE SQL
READS SQL DATA
BEGIN
DECLARE path_length INTEGER;
DECLARE current_number INTEGER;
SET path_length = 0;
SET current_number = 0;
-- Clear the table that will hold the result
DELETE FROM NestedSetsGraph;
-- Initialize stack by inserting all source nodes of graph
INSERT INTO NodeStack (node_id, distance)
SELECT DISTINCT G1.begin_node_id, path_length
 FROM AdjacencyListGraph AS G1
```

```
WHERE NOT EXISTS
   (SELECT *
     FROM AdjacencyListGraph AS G2
    WHERE G2.end_node_id = G1.begin_node_id);

WHILE EXISTS (SELECT * FROM NodeStack)
DO
 SET current_number = current_number + 1;
 IF EXISTS (SELECT * FROM NodeStack WHERE distance
    = path_length)
 THEN UPDATE NodeStack
     SET lft = current_number
   WHERE distance = path_length
     AND NOT EXISTS
       (SELECT *
         FROM NodeStack AS S2
        WHERE distance = path_length
         AND S2.node_id < NodeStack.node_id);
    INSERT INTO NodeStack (node_id, distance)
    SELECT G.end_node_id, (S.distance + 1)
     FROM NodeStack AS S,
       AdjacencyListGraph AS G
    WHERE S.distance = path_length
     AND S.lft IS NOT NULL
     AND G.begin_node_id = S.node_id;

     SET path_length = (path_length + 1);
 ELSE SET path_length = (path_length - 1);
     UPDATE NodeStack
       SET rgt = current_number
      WHERE lft IS NOT NULL
       AND distance = path_length;

     INSERT INTO NestedSetsGraph (node_id, lft, rgt)
     SELECT node_id, lft, rgt
      FROM NodeStack
     WHERE lft IS NOT NULL
      AND distance = path_length;
   DELETE FROM NodeStack
    WHERE lft IS NOT NULL
     AND distance = path_length;
 END IF;
END WHILE;
END;
```

## 37.3 Points inside Polygons

Although not actually part of graph theory, this seemed to be the reasonable place to put this section since it is also related to spatial queries. A polygon can be described as a set of corner points in an (x, y) coordinate system. The usual query is to tell if a given point is inside or outside of the polygon.

This algorithm is due to Darel R. Finley. The main advantage it has is that it can be done in Standard SQL without trigonometry functions. The disadvantage is that it does not work for concave polygons. The work-around is to dissect the convex polygons into concave polygons, then add column for the name of the original area. The math behind the working code can be found here: http://local.wasp.uwa.edu.au/~pbourke/geometry/insidepoly/.

```
-- set up polygon, with any ordering of the corners
CREATE TABLE Polygon
(x FLOAT NOT NULL,
y FLOAT NOT NULL,
PRIMARY KEY (x, y));

INSERT INTO Polygon
VALUES (2.00, 2.00), (1.00, 4.00),
   (3.00, 6.00), (6.00, 4.00), (5.00, 2.00);

--set up some sample points
CREATE TABLE Points
(xx FLOAT NOT NULL,
yy FLOAT NOT NULL,
location VARCHAR(10) NOT NULL, -- answer the question in
   advance!
PRIMARY KEY (xx, yy));
INSERT INTO Points
VALUES (2.00, 2.00, 'corner'),
   (1.00, 5.00, 'outside'),
   (3.00, 3.00, 'inside'),
   (3.00, 4.00, 'inside'),
   (5.00, 1.00, 'outside'),
   (3.00, 2.00, 'side');

-- do the query
SELECT P1.xx, P1.yy, p1.location, SIGN(
SUM
(CASE WHEN (polyY.y < P1.yy AND polyY.x >= P1.yy
    OR polyY.x < P1.yy AND polyY.y >= P1.yy)
   THEN CASE WHEN polyX.y + (P1.yy - polyY.y)
        /(polyY.x - polyY.y) * (polyX.x - polyX.y)
             < P1.xx
       THEN 1 ELSE 0 END
   ELSE 0 END))AS flag
 FROM Polygon AS polyY, Polygon AS polyX, Points AS P1
GROUP BY P1.xx, P1.yy, p1.location;
```

When flag = 1, the point is inside, when flag = 0, it is outside.

| xx | yy | location | flag |
|---|---|---|---|
| 1.0 | 5.0 | outside | 0 |
| 2.0 | 2.0 | corner | 0 |
| 3.0 | 3.0 | inside | 1 |
| 3.0 | 4.0 | inside | 1 |
| 5.0 | 1.0 | outside | 0 |
| 3.0 | 2.0 | side | 1 |

Sides are counted as inside, but if you want to count the corner points as outside you should start the CASE expression with:

```
CASE WHEN EXISTS
   (SELECT * FROM Polygon
    WHERE x = P1.xx AND y = P1.yy)
  THEN 1 ..".
2,2
1,5
3,3
3,4
5,1
3,2
```

## 37.4 Graph Theory References


Berge, Claude. 2001. *The Theory of Graphs.* New York: Dover. ISBN 10: 0-486-41975-4.

Chartrand, Gary. 1984. *Introductory Graph Theory.* New York: Dover. ISBN 10: 0-486-24775-9. Fun and easy Dover reprint.

Cormen, Thomas H., Leiserson, Charles E., and Rivest, Ronald L. 1990. *Introduction to Algorithms.* McGraw-Hill Companies. ISBN 0-262-03141-8.

Even, Shimon. 1979. *Graph Algorithms.* Rockville, MD: Computer Science Press. ISBN 0-914894-21-8.

Fulkerson, D. R. (ed.). 1975. *Studies in Graph Theory, Vol. I.* American Mathematical Association. ISBN 0-88358-111-3.

———. 1975. *Studies in Graph Theory, Vol. II.* American Mathematical Association. ISBN 0-88358-112-3.

Harary, Frank. 1972. *Graph Theory.* Boston: Addison-Wesley. ISBN 0201-02787-9. Look for this author since he is a big name in the field.

Hartsfield, Nora and Ringel, Gerhard. 2003. *Pearls in Graph Theory: A Comprehensive Introduction.* New York: Dover. ISBN 10: 0-486-43232-7.

McHugh, James A. 1990. *Algorithmic Graph Theory.* Englewood Cliffs, NJ: Prentice-Hall. ISBN 0-13-023615-2.

Ore, Oystein (revised by Robin J. Wilson). 1990. *Graphs and Their Uses.* American Mathematical Association. ISBN 0-88358-635-2. This is a classic book written at the high school level.

Trudeau, Richard J. 1994. *Introduction to Graph Theory, Second Edition.* New York: Dover. ISBN 10: 0-486-67870-9.

# 38

# TEMPORAL QUERIES

Temporal data is the hardest type of data for people to handle conceptually. Perhaps time is difficult because it is dynamic and all other data types are static or perhaps because time allows multiple parallel events. This is an old puzzle that still catches people.

If a hen and a half lays an egg and a half in a day and a half, how many eggs will five hens lay in six days? Do not look at the rest of the page—try to answer the question in your head.

Suppose two hens lay four eggs in three days. That means that each hen laid two eggs during those three days, so each hen lays 2/3 of an egg per day. Now if you had five hens and six days, they would lay five times as many eggs per day, totaling 10/3 per day; multiply that by 6 days, and there would be 20 eggs.

The algebra in this problem looks like this, where we want to solve for the rate in terms of "eggs per day," a strange but convenient unit of measurement for summarizing the hen house output:

1½ hens * 1½ days * rate = 1½ eggs

The first urge is to multiple both sides by ⅔ in an attempt to turn ALL of the 1½'s into 1's. But what you actually get is:

1 hens * 1½ days * rate = 1 egg; multiple by eggs per hen

1½ days * rate = 1 egg per hen; divide by the number of hens

rate = ⅔ egg per hen per day;

## 38.1 Temporal Math

Almost every SQL implementation has a DATE data type, but the functions available for them vary quite a bit. The most common ones are a constructor that builds a date from integers or strings; extractors to pull out the month, day, or year; and some display options to format output. Since display should not be done in the database, I am not going to bother with the display options.

**Joe Celko's SQL for Smarties. DOI: 10.1016/B978-0-12-382022-8.00038-7**

In Standard SQL, the constructor is `CAST (<string expression> AS [DATE | TIME | TIMESTAMP])` for a string expression, or you can use literal constructors:

```
<date literal> ::= DATE <date string>
<time literal> ::= TIME <time string>
<timestamp literal> ::= TIMESTAMP <timestamp string>
```

In Standard SQL, the *only* ISO 8601 format allowed for datetime values are "yyyy-mm-dd" for dates, "hh:mm:ss.sssss" for times, and "yyyy-mm-dd hh:mm:ss.sssss" for timestamps, with the number of decimal places being implementation-defined. However, the FIPS-127 Standards want at least five decimal places in the seconds. This avoids problems like confusing the British (dd/mm/yy), American (mm/dd/yy), and other traditional national shorthands.

The ISO 8601 Standard has many other date and time formats that are not ambiguous, and could be added to the strings recognized by SQL. For example, a date without punctuation is legal (yyyymmdd) and so are strings with embedded letters. SQL does not have these options to keep things simple.

The extractor is the function `EXTRACT(<extract field> FROM <extract source>)` defined by:

```
<extract field> ::= <primary datetime field> | <time zone field>
<time zone field> ::= TIMEZONE_HOUR | TIMEZONE_MINUTE
<extract source> ::= <datetime value expression> | <inter-
   val value expression>
```

The extract field options are a little easier to see in a table (Table 38.1).

The obvious ordering is from most significant to least significant: `YEAR, MONTH, DAY, HOUR, MINUTE,` and `SECOND`.

The primary datetime fields other than `SECOND` contain non-negative integer values, constrained by the natural rules for dates

## Table 38.1 Extract Field Options

| Meaning of <primary datetime field> | Keyword |
|---|---|
| Year in Common Era Calendar (0001–9999) | YEAR |
| Month within year (01–12) | MONTH |
| Day within month (01–31) | DAY |
| Minute within hour (00–59) | MINUTE |
| Second within minute with decimal fractions (00–59.99 ...) | SECOND |
| Hour value of time zone displacement; can be positive or negative (–12 to +14) | TIMEZONE_HOUR |
| Minute value of time zone displacement; can be positive or negative (–12:59 to +14:00) | TIMEZONE_MINUTE |

using the Common Era calendar. SECOND, however, can be defined to have a <time fractional seconds precision> that indicates the number of decimal digits maintained following the decimal point in the seconds value, a nonnegative exact numeric value.

There are three classes of datetime data types defined within this part of ISO/IEC 9075 that are defined from the primary datetime fields:

DATE: contains YEAR, MONTH, and DAY
TIME: contains HOUR, MINUTE, and SECOND
TIMESTAMP: contains YEAR, MONTH, DAY, HOUR, MINUTE, and SECOND

Items of type datetime are comparable only if they have the same primary datetime fields.

You can assume that your SQL implementation at least has simple date arithmetic functions, although with different syntax from product to product. The basic functions you need are just those that work with dates:

A date plus or minus an interval of days yields a new date.
A date minus a second date yields an interval of days.

Here is a table of the valid combinations of <datetime> and <interval> data types in Standard SQL:

```
<datetime> - <datetime> = <interval>
<datetime> + <interval> = <datetime>
<interval> (* or /) <numeric> = <interval>
<interval> + <datetime> = <datetime>
<interval> + <interval> = <interval>
<numeric> * <interval> = <interval>
```

There are other rules, which deal with time zones and the relative precision of the two operands, that are intuitively obvious.

There should also be a function that returns the current date from the system clock. This function has a different name with each vendor: TODAY, SYSDATE, NOW(), CURRENT DATE, and getdate() are some examples. There may also be a function to return the day of the week from a date, which is sometimes called DOW() or WEEKDAY(). Standard SQL provides for CURRENT_DATE, CURRENT_TIME [(<time precision>)] and CURRENT_TIMESTAMP [(<timestamp precision>)] functions, which are self-explanatory.

You will also find ISO Standards for time in the BCE range, but only museums have any needs for this. Oracle supports dates well outside the ISO range, but almost nobody else does.

## 38.2 Personal Calendars

One of the most common applications of dates is to build calendars that list upcoming events or actions to be taken by their user. People have no trouble with using a paper calendar to trigger their own actions, but the idea of having an internal enterprise level calendar as a table in their database is somehow strange. Procedural programmers seem to prefer to write a function that calculates the date and matches it to events.

It is easier to make a table for cyclic data than people first think. The cycle has to repeat itself every 400 years, so today is on the same day of the week that it was on 400 years ago. This gives us 20,871 weeks or 146,097 days to model in a table. This is not a large table in modern computers.

Another trick that might apply to your SQL product is to use a sorted index that is in descending order. The idea is that most of your work will be done with recent dates, so if the physical ordering of the table lets you find those orders first, statements will run faster.

As an example, business days are defined as excluding Saturdays, Sundays, and certain holidays in Western countries, but the weekend is usually just Friday in Muslim countries.

Here is a classification system of holidays:

1. Fixed date every year.
2. Days relative to Easter.
3. Fixed date but will slide to make a three-day weekend. The 4th of July in the US, the day Columbus discovered America in Argentina, are examples.
4. Fixed date but slides to Monday if Saturday, or Tuesday if Sunday (UK Boxing Day is the only one).
5. Specific day of week after a given date (usually first/last Monday in a month but can be other days, like the first Thursday after November 22 = Thanksgiving).
6. Days relative to Greek Orthodox Easter (not always the same as Western Easter).
7. Fixed date in Hijri (Muslim) Calendar. This turns out to be only approximate due to the way the calendar works. An Imam has to see a full moon to begin the cycle and declare the holiday.
8. Days relative to previous Winter Solstice (Chinese holiday of Qing Ming Jie).
9. Civil holidays set by decree, such as a National Day of Mourning.

As you can see, some of these are getting a bit esoteric and a bit fuzzy. A calendar table for US secular holidays can be built from the data at this web site, so you will get the three-day weekends: http://www.smart.net/~mmontes/ushols.html.

## 38.3 Time Series

One of the major problems in the real world is how to handle a series of events that occur in the same time period or in some particular order. The best way to do this is in the DDL so that unwanted gaps and overlaps never get into the database in the first place. Alexander Kuznetsov came up with this DDL to prevent durations from overlapping with the DDL.

```
CREATE TABLE Events
(event_id INTEGER NOT NULL PRIMARY KEY,
some_value INTEGER NOT NULL,
start_date DATE NOT NULL,
end_date DATE NOT NULL,
prev_end_date DATE,
PRIMARY KEY(event_id, end_date),
UNIQUE(event_id, prev_end_date),
FOREIGN KEY(event_id, prev_end_date)
 REFERENCES Events(event_id, end_date),
CONSTRAINT no_overlaps
 CHECK (prev_end_date <= start_date),
CONSTRAINT starts_before_endding
 CHECK (start_date < end_date));
```

You can prohibit gaps altogether; just replace the following constraint:

```
CHECK (prev_end_date <= start_date),
```

with a stricter one, as follows:

```
CHECK (prev_end_date = start_date),
```

But if you allow gaps, the query to retrieve them is:

```
SELECT prev_end_date AS gap_start_date, start_date AS
   gap_end_date
 FROM Events
WHERE start_date > prev_end_date;
```

If you need to update column `end_date`, you have to also update `prev_end_date` for the next duration to match, as follows:

```
CREATE PROCEDURE UpdateEvent
DETERMINISTIC
SQL DATA
(IN in_event_id INTEGER,
IN in_old_end_date DATE.
IN in_new_end_date)
UPDATE Events
SET end_date
  = CASE
   WHEN end_date = in_old_end_date
   THEN in_new_end_date
   ELSE end_date END,
  prev_end_date
  = CASE
   WHEN prev_end_date = in_old_end_date
   THEN in_new_end_date
```

```
    ELSE prev_end_date END
  WHERE event_id = in_event_id
  AND in_old_end_date IN (end_date, prev_end_date);
```

You might think that an ON UPDATE CASCADE clause would do the work, but not all SQL products can use CASCADE for self-referencing constraints. Deferred constraints would allow for easier modifications, but this is not portable.

You probably did not use this skeleton schema, so let's talk about cleaning up tables with only (start_time, end_time) pairs.

### 38.3.1 Gaps in a Time Series

The time line can be partitioned into intervals and a set of intervals can be drawn from that partition for reporting. One of the stock questions on an employment form asks the prospective employee to explain any gaps in his record of employment. Most of the time this gap means that you were unemployed. If you are in data processing, you answer that you were consulting, which is a synonym for unemployed.

Given this table, how would you write an SQL query to display the time periods and their durations for each of the candidates?

```
CREATE TABLE JobApps
(candidate_name CHAR(25) NOT NULL,
job_title CHAR(15) NOT NULL,
start_date DATE NOT NULL,
end_date DATE, -- null means still employed
CONSTRAINT started_before_ended
CHECK(start_date <= end_date)
..);
```

Notice that the end date of the current job_code is set to NULL because SQL does not support an 'eternity' or 'end of time' value for temporal data types. Using '9999-12-31 23:59:59.999999', which is the highest possible date value that SQL can represent, is not a correct model and can cause problems when you do temporal arithmetic. The NULL can be handled with a COALESCE() function in the code, as I will show later.

It is obvious that this has to be a self-JOIN query, so you have to do some date arithmetic. The first day of each gap is the last day of an employment period plus 1 day, and that the last day of each gap is the first day of the next job_code minus 1 day. This start-point and end-point problem is the reason that SQL defined the OVERLAPS predicate this way.

All versions of SQL support temporal data types and arithmetic. But unfortunately, no two implementations look alike and few look like the ANSI standard. The first attempt at this query is usually something like the following, which will produce the right results, but with a lot of extra rows that are just plain wrong. Assume that if I add a number of days to a date, or subtract a number of days from it, I get a new date.

```
SELECT J1.candidate_name,
  (J1.end_date + INTERVAL '1' DAY) AS gap_start,
  (J2.start_date - INTERVAL '1' DAY) AS gap_end,
  (J2.start_date - J1.end_date) AS gap_length
FROM JobApps AS J1, JobApps AS J2
WHERE J1.candidate_name = J2.candidate_name
 AND (J1.end_date + INTERVAL '1' DAY) < J2.start_date;
```

Here is why this does not work. Imagine that we have a table that includes candidate_name 'Bill Jones' with the following work history:

Result

| candidate_name | job_title | start_date | end_date |
|---|---|---|---|
| 'John Smith' | 'Vice Pres' | '2010-01-10' | '2010-12-31' |
| 'John Smith' | 'President' | '2011-01-12' | '2012-12-31' |
| 'Bill Jones' | 'Scut Worker' | '2011-02-24' | '2011-04-21' |
| 'Bill Jones' | 'Manager' | '2012-01-01' | '2012-01-05' |
| 'Bill Jones' | 'Grand Poobah' | '2012-04-04' | '2012-05-15' |

We would get this as a result:

Result

| candidate_name | gap_start | gap_end | gap_length |
|---|---|---|---|
| 'John Smith' | '2011-01-01' | '2011-01-11' | 12 |
| 'Bill Jones' | '2011-04-22' | '2011-12-31' | 255 |
| 'Bill Jones' | '2012-01-06' | '2012-04-03' | 89 |
| 'Bill Jones' | '2011-04-22' | '2012-04-03' | 348 ◄ false data |

The problem is that the 'John Smith' row looks just fine and can fool you into thinking that you are doing fine. He had two jobs; therefore, there was one gap in between. However, 'Bill Jones' cannot be right because only two gaps can separate three jobs, yet the query shows three gaps.

The query does its JOIN on all possible combinations of start and end dates in the original table. This gives false data in the results by counting the end of one job_code, 'Scut Worker' and the start of another, 'Grand Poobah', as a gap. The idea is to use only the most recently ended job_code for the gap. This can be done with a MIN() function and a correlated subquery. The final result is this:

```
SELECT J1.candidate_name, (J1.end_date + INTERVAL '1' DAY)
   AS gap_start,
  (J2.start_date - INTERVAL '1' DAY) AS gap_end
 FROM JobApps AS J1, JobApps AS J2
WHERE J1.candidate_name = J2.candidate_name
 AND J2.start_date
  = (SELECT MIN(J3.start_date)
     FROM JobApps AS J3
     WHERE J3.candidate_name = J1.candidate_name
      AND J3.start_date > J1.end_date)
 AND (J1.end_date + INTERVAL '1' DAY)
   < (J2.start_date - INTERVAL '1' DAY)
UNION ALL
SELECT J1.candidate_name, MAX(J1.end_date) + INTERVAL '1' DAY,
   CURRENT_TIMESTAMP
 FROM JobApps AS J1
GROUP BY J1.candidate_name
HAVING COUNT(*) = COUNT(DISTINCT J1.end_date);
```

The length of the gap can be determined with simple temporal arithmetic. The purpose of the UNION ALL is to add the current period of unemployment, if any, to the final answer.

## 38.3.2 Continuous Time Periods

Given a series of jobs that can start and stop at any time, how can you be sure that an employee doing all these jobs was really working without any gaps? Let's build a table of timesheets for one employee.

```
TABLE Timesheets
(job_code CHAR(5) NOT NULL PRIMARY KEY,
start_date DATE NOT NULL,
 end_date DATE NOT NULL,
CONSTRAINT started_before_ended
 CHECK (start_date <= end_date));

INSERT INTO Timesheets (job_code, start_date, end_date)
VALUES ('j01', '2018-01-01', '2018-01-03');
  ('j02', '2018-01-06', '2018-01-10'),
  ('j03', '2018-01-05', '2018-01-08'),
  ('j04', '2018-01-20', '2018-01-25'),
  ('j05', '2018-01-18', '2018-01-23'),
  ('j06', '2018-02-01', '2018-02-05'),
```

```
('j07', '2018-02-03', '2018-02-08'),
('j08', '2018-02-07', '2018-02-11'),
('j09', '2018-02-09', '2018-02-10'),
('j10', '2018-02-01', '2018-02-11'),
('j11', '2018-03-01', '2018-03-05'),
('j12', '2018-03-04', '2018-03-09'),
('j13', '2018-03-08', '2018-03-14'),
('j14', '2018-03-13', '2018-03-20');
```

The most immediate answer is to build a search condition for all the characteristics of a continuous time period.

This algorithm is due to Mike Arney, a DBA at BORN Consulting. It uses derived tables to get the extreme start and ending dates of a contiguous run of durations.

```
SELECT Early.start_date, MIN(Latest.end_date)
 FROM (SELECT DISTINCT start_date
     FROM Timesheets AS T1
    WHERE NOT EXISTS
      (SELECT *
         FROM Timesheets AS T2
        WHERE T2.start_date < T1.start_date
         AND T2.end_date >= T1.start_date)
   ) AS Early (start_date)
   INNER JOIN
   (SELECT DISTINCT end_date
     FROM Timesheets AS T3
     WHERE NOT EXISTS
       (SELECT *
         FROM Timesheets AS T4
        WHERE T4.end_date > T3.end_date
         AND T4.start_date <= T3.end_date)
   ) AS Latest (end_date)
   ON Early.start_date <= Latest.end_dae
GROUP BY Early.start_date;
```

## Result

| start_date | end_date |
|---|---|
| '2018-01-01' | '2018-01-03' |
| '2018-01-05' | '2018-01-10' |
| '2018-01-18' | '2018-01-25' |
| '2018-02-01' | '2018-02-11' |
| '2018-03-01' | '2018-03-20' |

However, another way of doing this is a query, which will also tell you which jobs bound the continuous periods.

```
SELECT T2.start_date,
  MAX(T1.end_date) AS finish_date,
  MAX(T1.job_code || ' to ' || T2.job_code) AS
   job_code_pair
FROM Timesheets AS T1, Timesheets AS T2
WHERE T2.job_code <> T1.job_code
 AND T1.start_date BETWEEN T2.start_date AND T2.end_date
 AND T2.end_date BETWEEN T1.start_date AND T1.end_date
GROUP BY T2.start_date;
```

Result

| start_date | finish_date | job_code_pair |
|---|---|---|
| '2018-01-05' | '2018-01-10' | 'j02 to j03' |
| '2018-01-18' | '2018-01-25' | 'j04 to j05' |
| '2018-02-01' | '2018-02-08' | 'j07 to j06' |
| '2018-02-03' | '2018-02-11' | 'j08 to j07' |

```
DELETE FROM Results
WHERE EXISTS
 (SELECT R1.job_code_list
    FROM Results AS R1
   WHERE POSITION (Results.job_code_list
         IN R1.job_code_list) > 0);
```

A third solution will handle an isolated job_code like 'j01', as well as three or more overlapping jobs, like 'j06', 'j07' and 'j08'.

```
SELECT T1.start_date,
  MIN(T2.end_date) AS finish_date,
  MIN(T2.end_date + INTERVAL '1' DAY) -
  - MIN(T1.start_date) AS duration -- find any (T1.
   start_date)
FROM Timesheets AS T1, Timesheets AS T2
WHERE T2.start_date >= T1.start_date
AND T2.end_date >= T1.end_date
 AND NOT EXISTS
  (SELECT *
   FROM Timesheets AS T3
   WHERE (T3.start_date <= T2.end_date
     AND T3.end_date > T2.end_date)
   OR (T3.end_date >= T1.start_date
     AND T3.start_date < T1.start_date))
GROUP BY T1.start_date;
```

You will also want to look at how to consolidate overlapping intervals of integers.

A fourth solution uses the auxiliary Calendar table (see Section 38.8 for details) to find the dates that are and are not covered by any of the durations. The coverage flag and calendar date can then be used directly by other queries that need to look at the status of single days instead of date ranges.

```
SELECT C1.cal_date,
  SUM(DISTINCT
   CASE
   WHEN C1.cal_date BETWEEN T1.start_date AND T1.end_date
   THEN 1 ELSE 0 END) AS covered_date_flag
FROM Calendar AS C1, Timesheets AS T1
WHERE C1.cal_date BETWEEN (SELECT MIN(start_date FROM
   Timesheets)
          AND (SELECT MAX(end_date FROM Timesheets)
GROUP BY C1.cal_date;
```

This is reasonably fast because the `WHERE` clause uses static scalar queries to set the bounds and the Calendar table uses cal_date as a primary key, so it will have an index.

A slightly different version of the problem is to group contiguous measurements into durations that have the value on that measurement.

I have the following table:

```
CREATE TABLE Calibrations
(start_time TIMESTAMP DEFAULT CURRENT_TIMESTAMP
       NOT NULL PRIMARY KEY
end_time TIMESTAMP NOT NULL,
CONSTRAINT started_before_ended
CHECK (end_time = start_time + INTERVAL '1' MINUTE,
cal_value INTEGER NOT NULL);
```

with this data:

Calibrations

| start_time | end_time | cal_value |
|---|---|---|
| '2014-05-11 02:52:00.000' | '2014-05-11 02:53:00.000' | 8 |
| '2014-05-11 02:53:00.000' | '2014-05-11 02:54:00.000' | 8 |
| '2014-05-11 02:54:00.000' | '2014-05-11 02:55:00.000' | 8 |
| '2014-05-11 02:55:00.000' | '2014-05-11 02:56:00.000' | 8 |

*(Continued)*

Calibrations

| start_time | end_time | cal_value |
|---|---|---|
| '2014-05-11 02:56:00.000' | '2014-05-11 02:57:00.000' | 8 |
| '2014-05-11 02:57:00.000' | '2014-05-11 02:58:00.000' | 9 |
| '2014-05-11 02:58:00.000' | '2014-05-11 02:59:00.000' | 9 |
| '2014-05-11 02:59:00.000' | '2014-05-11 03:00:00.000' | 9 |
| '2014-05-11 03:00:00.000' | '2014-05-11 03:01:00.000' | 9 |
| '2014-05-11 03:01:00.000' | '2014-05-11 03:02:00.000' | 9 |
| '2014-05-11 03:02:00.000' | '2014-05-11 03:03:00.000' | 8 |
| '2014-05-11 03:03:00.000' | '2014-05-11 03:04:00.000' | 8 |
| '2014-05-11 03:04:00.000' | '2014-05-11 03:05:00.000' | 8 |

I want to be able to group this up so that it looks like this:

| start_time | end_time | cal_value |
|---|---|---|
| '2014-05-11 02:52:00.000' | '2014-05-11 02:57:00.000' | 8 |
| '2014-05-11 02:57:00.000' | '2014-05-11 03:02:00.000' | 9 |
| '2014-05-11 03:02:00.000' | '2014-05-11 03:05:00.000' | 8 |

The table being selected from is updated every minute with a new calibration value. The calibration value can change from minute to minute. I want a select statement that will sum up the start of the cal_value and the end of the calibration value before it changes.

```
SELECT MIN(start_time) AS start_time,
  MAX(end_time) AS end_time,
  cal_value
FROM (SELECT C1.start_time, C1.end_time, C1.cal_value,
      MIN(C2.start_time)
    FROM Calibrations AS C1
      LEFT OUTER JOIN
      Calibrations AS C2
      ON C1.start_time < C2.start_time
       AND C1.cal_value <> C2.cal_value
    GROUP BY C1.start_time, C1.end_time, C1.cal_value)
  AS T (start_time, end_time, cal_value, x_time))
GROUP BY cal_value, x_time;
```

## 38.3.3 Missing Times in Contiguous Events

Consider the following simple table, which we will use to illustrate how to handle missing times in events.

```
CREATE TABLE Events
(event_id CHAR(2) NOT NULL PRIMARY KEY,
start_date DATE NOT NULL,
end_date DATE,
CONSTRAINT proper_date_ordering
 CONSTRAINT started_before_ended (start_date < end_date));

INSERT INTO Events
VALUES
('A', '2014-01-01', '2014-12-31'),
('B', '2015-01-01', '2015-01-31'),
('C', '2015-02-01', '2015-02-29'),
('D', '2015-02-01', '2015-02-29');
```

Due to circumstances beyond our control the end_date column may contain a `NULL` instead of a valid date. Imagine that we had ('B', '2015-01-01', `NULL`) as a row in the table.

One reasonable solution is to populate the missing end_date with the (start_date -1 day) of the next period. This is easy enough.

```
UPDATE Events
 SET end_date
  = (SELECT MIN(E1.start_date) - INTERVAL '1' DAY)
     FROM Events AS E1
    WHERE E1.start_date > Events.start_date)
WHERE end_date IS NULL;
```

Likewise, if due to circumstances beyond our control, the start_date column may contain a `NULL` instead of a valid date. Imagine that we had ('B', `NULL`, '2015-01-31') as a row in the table. Using the same logic, we could take the last known ending date and add one to it to give us a guess at the missing starting value.

```
UPDATE Events
 SET start_date
  = (SELECT MIN(E1.end_date) + INTERVAL '1' DAY)
     FROM Events AS E1
    WHERE E1.end_date < Events.end_date)
WHERE start_date IS NULL;
```

This has a nice symmetry to it, but it does not cover all possible cases. Consider an event where we know nothing about the times:

```
INSERT INTO Events
VALUES
('A', '2014-01-01', '2014-12-31'),
```

```
('B', NULL, NULL),
('C', '2015-02-01', '2015-02-29'),
('D', '2015-02-01', '2015-02-29');
```

You can run each of the previous UPDATE statements and get the NULLs filled in with values. However, you can combine them into one update:

```
UPDATE Events
 SET end_date
  = CASE WHEN end_date IS NULL
   THEN (SELECT MIN(E1.start_date) - INTERVAL '1' DAY
      FROM Events AS E1
     WHERE E1.start_date > Events.start_date)
   ELSE end_date END,
  start_date
  = CASE WHEN start_date IS NULL
   THEN (SELECT MIN(E1.end_date) + INTERVAL '1' DAY
      FROM Events AS E1
     WHERE E1.end_date < Events.end_date)
   ELSE start_date END
WHERE start_date IS NULL
 OR end_date IS NULL;
```

The real problem is having no boundary dates on contiguous events, like this:

```
INSERT INTO Events
VALUES
('A', '2014-01-01', '2014-12-31'),
('B', '2015-01-01', NULL),
('C', NULL, '2015-02-29'),
('D', '2015-02-01', '2015-02-29');
```

The result of applying the previous update is that we get an error because it will try to set the start_date equal to end_date in both rows.

Given the restrictions that each event lasts for at least one day, event 'B' could have finished on any day between '2015-01-02' and '2015-02-27' and likewise, event 'C' could have begun on any day between '2015-01-03' and '2015-02-28'; note the two different durations.

Any rules we make for resolving the NULLs is going to be arbitrary. For example, we could give event 'B' the benefit of the doubt and assume that it lasted until '2015-02-27' or just as well given event 'C' the same benefit. I might make a random choice of a pair of dates (d, d+1) in the gap between 'B' and 'C' dates. I might pick a middle point.

However, this pairwise approach does not solve the problem of all the possible combinations of NULL dates.

Let me propose these rules and apply them in order:

1. If the start_date is `NOT NULL` and the end_date is `NOT NULL`, leave the row alone.
2. If the table has too many `NULL`s in a series, give up. Report too much missing data.
3. If the start_date `IS NULL` and the end_date `IS NOT NULL`, set the start_date to the day before the end_date.

```
UPDATE Events
 SET start_date
  = (SELECT MIN(E1.end_date) + INTERVAL '1' DAY)
      FROM Events AS E1
     WHERE E1.end_date < Events.end_date)
WHERE start_date IS NULL
 AND end_date IS NOT NULL;
```

4. If the start_date is `NOT NULL` and the end_date is `NULL`, set the end_date to the day before the next known start_date.

```
UPDATE Events
 SET end_date
  = (SELECT MIN(E1.start_date) - INTERVAL '1' DAY)
      FROM Events AS E1
     WHERE E1.start_date > Events.start_date)
WHERE start_date IS NOT NULL
 AND end_date IS NULL;
```

5. If the start_date and end_date are both `NULL`, look at the prior and following events to get the minimal start_date and/or end_date. This will leave a gap in the dates that has to be handled later.
For example:

```
('A', '2014-01-01', '2014-12-31'),
('B', '2015-01-01', NULL),
('C', NULL, '2015-02-29'),
('D', '2015-02-01', '2015-02-29');
```

becomes:

```
('A', '2014-01-01', '2014-12-31'),
('B', '2015-01-01', NULL),
('C', '2015-02-28', '2015-02-29'), ◄ rule #2
('D', '2015-02-01', '2015-02-29');
```

which becomes:

```
('A', '2014-01-01', '2014-12-31'),
('B', '2015-01-01', '2015-02-27'), ◄ rule #3
('C', '2015-02-28', '2015-02-29'),
('D', '2015-02-01', '2015-02-29');
```

Now consider this data:

```
('A', '2014-01-01', '2014-12-31'),
('B', NULL, NULL),
('C', '2015-02-01', '2015-02-29'),
('D', '2015-02-01', '2015-02-29');
```

which becomes:

```
('A', '2014-01-01', '2014-12-31'),
('B', '2015-01-01', '2015-01-31'), ◄ rule #4
('C', '2015-02-01', '2015-02-29'),
('D', '2015-02-01', '2015-02-29');
```

Consider this example:

```
('A', '2014-01-01', '2014-12-31'),
('B', NULL, NULL),
('C', NULL, '2015-02-29'),
('D', '2015-02-01', '2015-02-29');
```

## 38.3.4 Locating Dates

This little problem is sneakier than it sounds. I first saw it in *Explain* magazine, then met the author, Rudy Limeback, at the Database World conference in Boston years ago. The problem is to print a list of the employees whose birthdays will occur in the next 45 days. The employee files have each date of birth. The answer will depend on what date functions you have in your implementation of SQL, but Rudy was working with DB2.

What makes this problem interesting is the number of possible false starts. Most versions of SQL also have a library function `MAKEDATE`(year, month, day) or an equivalent, which will construct a date from three numbers representing a year, month, and day, and extraction functions to disassemble a date into integers representing the month, day, and year. The SQL standard would do this with the general function `CAST (<string> AS DATE)`, but there is no provision in the standard for using integers without first converting them to strings, either explicitly or implicitly. For example,

- Direct use of strings to build a date:

```
CAST ('2014-01-01' AS DATE)
```

- Concatenation causes integer to cast to strings:

```
CAST (2014 || '-'|| 01 ||'-' || 01 AS DATE)
```

The first "gotcha" in this problem is trying to use the component pieces of the dates in a search condition. If you were looking for birthdays all within the same month, it would be easy:

```
SELECT emp_name, emp_dob, CURRENT_DATE
FROM Personnel
WHERE EXTRACT(MONTH FROM CURRENT_DATE) = EXTRACT(MONTH
   FROM dob);
```

Attempts to extend this approach fall apart, however, since a 45-day period could extend across three months and possibly into the following year and might fall in a leap year. Very soon, the number of function calls is too high and the logic is too complex.

The second "gotcha" is trying to write a simple search condition with these functions to construct the birthday in the current year from the date of birth (dob) in the Employee table:

```
SELECT emp_name, emp_dob, CURRENT_DATE
 FROM Personnel
WHERE MAKEDATE(EXTRACT (YEAR FROM CURRENT_DATE), --
   birthday this year
      EXTRACT (MONTH FROM dob),
      EXTRACT (DAY FROM dob))
  BETWEEN CURRENT_DATE
   AND (CURRENT_DATE + INTERVAL 45 DAYS);
```

But a leap-year date of birth will cause an exception to be raised on an invalid date if this is not also a leap year. There is also another problem. The third "gotcha" comes when the 45-day period wraps into the next year. For example, if the current month is December 1992, we should include January 1993 birthdays, but they are not constructed by the `MAKEDATE()` function. At this point, you can build a messy search condition that also goes into the next year when constructing birthdays.

Rory Murchison of the Aetna Institute pointed out that if you are working with DB2 or some other SQL implementations, you will have an `AGE(date1 [, date2])` function. This returns the difference in years between date1 and date2. If date2 is missing, it defaults to `CURRENT_DATE`. The `AGE()` function can be constructed from other functions in implementations that do not support it. In Standard SQL, the expression would be (date2 – date1) `YEAR`, which would construct an `INTERVAL` value. That makes the answer quite simple:

```
SELECT emp_name, emp_dob, CURRENT_DATE
 FROM Personnel
WHERE INTERVAL (CURRENT_DATE - birthday) YEAR
  <INTERVAL (CURRENT_DATE - birthday + INTERVAL 45 DAYS) YEAR;
```

In English, this says that if the employee is a year older 45 days from now, he must have had a birthday in the meantime.

### 38.3.5 Starting and Ending Dates

Dates can be stored in several different ways in a database. The result is that there is no best way to calculate either the first day of the month or the last day of the month from a given date, nor it there a standard function for it.

To return the last day of the previous month, use this expression: `CURRENT_TIMESTAMP - INTERVAL (EXTRACT(DAY FROM CURRENT_TIMESTAMP) DAYS).`

Obviously, you can get the first day of this month with:

```
CURRENT_TIMESTAMP
- (EXTRACT (DAY FROM CURRENT_TIMESTAMP)
  + INTERVAL '1' DAY);
```

Another way is with a user-defined function.

```
CREATE FUNCTION LastDayOfMonth (IN my_date DATE)
RETURNS INTEGER
LANGUAGE SQL
DETERMINISTIC
RETURN
CAST(CASE
  WHEN EXTRACT(MONTH FROM my_date) IN (1, 3, 5, 7, 8, 10,
     12) THEN 31
  WHEN EXTRACT(MONTH FROM my_date) IN (4, 6, 9, 11)
     THEN 30
  ELSE CASE WHEN MOD(EXTRACT (YEAR FROM my_date)/100, 4) <> 0
     THEN 28
    WHEN MOD(EXTRACT (YEAR FROM my_date)/100, 400) = 0
       THEN 29
    WHEN MOD(EXTRACT (YEAR FROM my_date)/100, 100) = 0
       THEN 28
   ELSE 29 END
END AS INTEGER);
```

You can prevent overlaps in the DDL with this skeleton:

```
CREATE TABLE Events
(event_id INTEGER NOT NULL,
start_date DATE NOT NULL,
finish_date DATE NOT NULL,
prev_finish_date DATE,

--constraints
PRIMARY KEY (event_id, start_date),
UNIQUE (event_id, prev_finish_date),
FOREIGN KEY (event_id, prev_finish_date)
 REFERENCES Events(event_id, finish_date),
CHECK (prev_finish_date <= start_date),
CHECK (start_date < finish_date),
--other data);
```

### 38.3.6 Starting and Ending Times

Another problem that you will find in the real world is that people never read the ISO 8601 standards for temporal data and they insist upon writing midnight as '24:00:00' and letting it "leak" into the next day. That is, '2014-01-01 24:01:00' probably should have been '2014-01-02 00:01:00' instead. DB2 allows both 00 and 24 for the hour component of its TIMESTAMP data type, which exacerbates the problem. The EXTRACT() function is now more complicated than it needs to be.

The best bet, if you cannot teach people to use the ISO 8601 Standards, is to correct the string at input time. This can be done with a simple auxiliary time that looks like this:

```
TABLE FixTheClock
(input_date_string CHAR(6) NOT NULL,
input_time_pattern CHAR(25) NOT NULL PRIMARY KEY,
correct_time_string CHAR(25) NOT NULL);

INSERT INTO FixTheClock
VALUES ('2014-01-01', '2014-01-01 24:__:__.______', '2014-
   01-02 00:');
...
```

Then use a LIKE predicate to replace the pattern with the corrected time.

```
SELECT CASE WHEN R1.raw_input_timestamp LIKE
   F1.input_time_pattern
    THEN F1.correct_time_string
     || CAST (EXTRACT(TIMEZONE_MINUTE FROM R1.raw_input_
        timestamp) AS VARCHAR(10))
    ELSE raw_input_timestamp END, ...
FROM RawData AS R1, FixTheClock AS F1
WHERE F1.input_date_string = SUBSTRING (raw_input_time-
   stamp FROM 1 FOR 6);
```

Notice that this is strictly a string function and that the results will have to be cast to a temporal data type before being stored in the database.

## 38.4 Julian Dates

All SQL implementations support a DATE data type, but there is no standard defining how they should implement it internally. Some products represent the year, month, and day as parts of a double-word integer, others use Julianized dates, some use ISO ordinal dates, and some store dates as character strings. The programmer does not care as long as the dates work correctly.

There is a technical difference between a *Julian* date and a *Julianized* date. A Julian date is an astronomer's term that counts the number of days since 4713 January 1 BCE. This count is now well over 2 billion; nobody but astronomers use it. However, computer companies have corrupted the term to mean a count from some point in time from which they can build a date or time. The fixed point is usually the year 1, or 1900, or the start of the Gregorian calendar.

An ordinal date is an ISO Standard that gives the position of the date within its year, so it falls between 1 and 365 or 366. You will see this number printed on the bottom edges of desk calendar pages. The usual way to find the Julianized day within the current year is to use a simple program that stores the number of days in each month as an array and sums them with the day of the month for the date in question. The only difficult part is remembering to add 1 if the year is a leap year and the month is after February.

Here is a very fast and compact algorithm that computes the Julian date from a Gregorian date and vice versa. These algorithms appeared as Algorithm 199 (ACM, 1980) and were first written in ALGOL by Robert Tantzen. Here are SQL translations of the code:

```
CREATE FUNCTION Julianize1
(greg_day INTEGER, greg_month INTEGER, greg_year INTEGER)
RETURNS INTEGER
LANGUAGE SQL
DETERMINISTIC
BEGIN
DECLARE century INTEGER;
DECLARE yearincentury INTEGER;
IF (greg_month > 2)
THEN SET greg_month = greg_month - 3;
ELSE SET greg_month = greg_month + 9;
 SET greg_year = greg_year - 1;
END IF;
SET century = greg_year/100;
SET yearincentury = greg_year - 100 * century;
RETURN ((146097 * century)/4
  + (1461 * yearincentury)/4
  + (153 * greg_month + 2)/5 + greg_day + 1721119);
END;
```

Remember that the division will be integer division because the variables involved are all integers. Here is a Pascal procedure taken from *Numerical Recipes in Pascal* (William Press et al.; Cambridge University Press; Revised edition, 1990; ISBN 0-52138766-3) for converting a Georgian date to a Julian date. First, you need to know the difference between `TRUNCATE()` and

FLOOR(). The FLOOR() function is also called the greatest integer function; it returns the greatest integer less than its argument. The TRUNCATE() function returns the integer part of a number. Thus, they behave differently with negative decimals.

```
FLOOR(-2.5) = -3
FLOOR(-2) = -2
FLOOR(2.5) = 2
FLOOR(2) = 2
TRUNCATE(-2.5) = -2
TRUNCATE(-2) = -2
TRUNCATE(2.5) = 2
TRUNCATE(2) = 2
```

Here is an SQL/PSM version of the algorithm.

```
CREATE FUNCTION Julianize (IN greg_year INTEGER, IN greg_
   month INTEGER, IN greg_day INTEGER)
RETURNS INTEGER
LANGUAGE SQL
DETERMINISTIC
BEGIN
DECLARE gregorian INTEGER;
DECLARE greg_year INTEGER;
DECLARE jul_leap INTEGER;
DECLARE greg_month INTEGER;
SET gregorian = 588829;
IF greg_year = 0 -- error: no greg_year zero
THEN SIGNAL SQLSTATE 'no year zero'; -- not actual SQL
   state code!
END IF;
IF greg_year < 0
THEN SET greg_year = greg_year + 1;
END IF;
IF greg_month > 2
THEN SET greg_year = greg_year;
  SET greg_month = greg_month + 1;
ELSE SET greg_year = greg_year - 1;
  SET greg_month = greg_month + 13;
  END IF;
SET greg_day = TRUNCATE(365.2522 * greg_year)
  + TRUNCATE(30.6001 * greg_month)
  + greg_day + 1720995;
IF (greg_day + 31 * (greg_month + 12 * greg_year) >=
   gregorian)
THEN SET jul_leap = TRUNCATE(greg_year * 0.01);
 SET greg_day = greg_day + 2 - jul_leap + TRUNCATE(0.25 *
    jul_leap);
END IF;
END;
```

This algorithm to convert a Julian day number into a Gregorian calendar date is due to Peter Meyer. You need to assume that you have FLOOR() and TRUNCATE() functions.

```
CREATE PROCEDURE JulDate (IN julian INTEGER,
       OUT greg_year INTEGER,
       OUT greg_month INTEGER,
       OUT greg_day INTEGER)
LANGUAGE SQL
DETERMINISTIC
BEGIN
DECLARE z INTEGER;
DECLARE r INTEGER;
DECLARE g INTEGER;
DECLARE a INTEGER;
DECLARE b INTEGER;

SET z = FLOOR(julian - 1721118.5);
SET r = julian - 1721118.5 - z;
SET g = z - 0.25;
SET a = FLOOR(g/36524.25);
SET b = a - FLOOR(a/4.0);
SET greg_year = FLOOR((b + g)/365.25);
SET c = b + z - FLOOR(365.25 * greg_year);
SET greg_month = TRUNCATE((5 * c + 456)/153);
SET greg_day = c - TRUNCATE((153 * greg_month - 457)/5) +
   r;
IF greg_month > 12
THEN SET greg_year = greg_year + 1;
  SET greg_month = greg_month - 12;
END IF;
END;
```

There are two problems with these algorithms. First, the Julian day the astronomers use starts at noon. If you think about it, it makes sense because they are doing their work at night. The second problem is that the integers involved get large and you cannot use floating-point numbers to replace them because the rounding errors are too great. You need long integers that can go to 2.5 million.

## 38.5 Other Temporal Functions

Another common set of functions, which are not represented in standard SQL, deal with weeks. For example, Sybase's SQL Anywhere (nee WATCOM SQL) has a DOW(<date>) that returns a number between 1 and 7 to represent the day of the week (1 = Sunday, 2 = Monday, .., 7 = Saturday, following an ISO standard convention). You can also find functions that add or subtract weeks from a date given the number of the date within the year and so on. The function for finding the day of the week for a date is called Zeller's algorithm:

```
CREATE FUNCTION Zeller (IN z_year INTEGER, IN z_month
   INTEGER, IN z_day INTEGER)
RETURNS INTEGER
LANGUAGE SQL
DETERMINISTIC
BEGIN
DECLARE m INTEGER;
DECLARE d INTEGER;
DECLARE y INTEGER;
SET y = z_year;
SET m = z_month - 2;
IF (m <= 0)
THEN SET m = m + 12;
 SET y = y - 1;
END IF;
RETURN (MOD((z_day + (13 * m - 1)/5
 + 5 * MOD(y, 100)/4 - 7 * y/400), 7) + 1);
END;
```

DB2 and other SQLs have an `AGE(<date1>, <date2>)` function, which returns the difference in years between `<date1>` and `<date2>`.

The `OVERLAPS` predicate determines whether two chronological periods overlap in time (see Section 13.2 for details). A chronological period is specified either as a pair of `<datetimes>` (starting and ending) or as a starting `<datetime>` and an `<interval>`.

## 38.6 Weeks

Weeks are not part of the SQL temporal functions, but they are part of ISO 8601 Standards. Although not as common in the United States as it is in the Nordic countries and Europe, many commercial and industrial applications use the week within a year as a unit of time.

Week 01 of a year is defined as the first week that has the Thursday in that year, which is equivalent to the week that contains the fourth day of January. In other words, the first week of a New Year is the week that has the majority of its days in the New Year. Week 01 might also contain days from the previous year, so it does not align with the years. As an aside, American calendars put Sunday in the leftmost column and split the Friday-Saturday-Sunday weekend. European and other calendars put Sunday in the rightmost column. But Sunday is the last day of the week in ISO Standards.

The standard notation uses the letter 'W' to announce that the following two digits are a week number. The week number component of the vector can be separated with a hyphen or not, as required by space.

'1999-W01' or '1999W01'

A single digit between 1 and 7 can extend this notation for the day of the week. For example, the day 2010-01-05, which is the Tuesday (day 2) of the first week of 2010, can be shown as

'2010-W01-2' or '2010W012'

The ISO standard avoids explicitly stating the possible range of week numbers, but a little thought will show that the range is between 01 and 52 or between 01 and 53, depending on the particular year. There is one exception to the rule that a year has at least 52 weeks; 1753 when the Gregorian calendar was introduced had less than 365 days and therefore less than 52 weeks.

SQL Server programmers have to be very careful because their product has not followed ISO Standards for numbering the weeks in its function library. As of the SQL Sever 2008 release, they have a `ISOWEEK()` function as a kludge. Furthermore, it is not easy to see how to calculate the weeks between two different dates.

Here is an example from Rudy Limeback (SQL Consultant, r938.com) taken from http://searchdatabase.techtarget.com/ateQuestionNResponse/0,289625,sid13_cid517627_tax285649,00.html.

Suppose we have a beginning date of '2010-05-06' and an end date of '2010-05-19'. I would like to see the weeks as two because the 17th is not a Tuesday. There are a number of ways to approach this problem, and the solution depends on what the meaning of the word "week" is. Here is the calendar for that month, just in case you cannot figure it out in your head.

| Su | Mo | Tu | We | Th | Fr | Sa |
|---|---|---|---|---|---|---|
| | | | | | | 1 |
| 2 | 3 | 4 | 5 | 6 | 7 | 8 |
| 9 | 10 | 11 | 12 | 13 | 14 | 15 |
| 16 | 17 | 18 | 19 | 20 | 21 | 22 |
| 23 | 24 | 25 | 26 | 27 | 28 | 29 |
| 30 | 31 | | | | | |

In this example, we want the number of weeks between May 6 and 19.

**First method**: One. One week after the 6th is the 13th. Another week is the 20th. Since we are only as far as the 19th, it is not two weeks yet.

**Second method**: Two. The number of days is 14 if we count both the 6th and the 19th at the beginning and end of the specified range. Since there are seven days in a week, 14/7 = 2.

**Third method**: One. We should not count both the beginning and end days. We do not do it for years, for example. How many years are between 1999 and 2007? Most people would say 8, not 9, and they do this by subtracting the earlier from the later. So using days, 19 − 6 = 13. Then 13/7 = 1.857142 …,which truncates to one.

**Fourth method**: Two. We want a whole number of weeks, so it is okay to round 1.857142 up to 2.

**Fifth method**: One. Did you mean whole weeks? There's only one whole week in that date range, and it is the week from the 9th to the 15th. In fact, if the starting date were the 3rd and the ending date the 21st, that would be 18 (or 19) days, and there's still only one whole week in there.

**Sixth method**: Three. February 6th is in week 6 of 2003. February 19th is in week 8. Between them are several days from each of three different weeks.

**Seventh method**: Two. February 6th is in week 6 of 2003. February 19th is in week 8. Subtract the week numbers to get 2.

This is why Standard SQL prefers to deal with days, a nice unit of time that does not have fractional parts.

## 38.6.1 Sorting by Weekday Names

This trick is due to Craig S. Mullins. Given a table with a column containing the name of the day of the week, on which an event happened like this:

```
CREATE TABLE Foobar
(..
day_name CHAR(3) NOT NULL
  CHECK day_name
    IN ('SUN', 'MON', 'TUE', 'WED', 'THU', 'FRI', 'SAT'),
..);
```

how do we sort it properly? We'd want Sunday first, followed by Monday, Tuesday, Wednesday, and so on. Well, if we write the first query that comes to mind, the results will obviously be sorted improperly:

```
SELECT day_name, col1, col2, ..
 FROM Foobar
ORDER BY day_name;
```

The results from this query would be ordered alphabetically; in other words:

```
FRI
MON
SAT
SUN
THU
TUE
WED
```

Of course, one solution would be to design the table with a numeric column that uses Zeller's number. There is another solution that is both elegant and does not require any change to the database.

```
SELECT day_name, col1, c12, ...,
  POSITION (day_name IN 'SUNMONTUEWEDTHUFRISAT') AS day_nbr
 FROM Foobar
ORDER BY day_nbr;
```

Of course, you can go one step further if you'd like. Some queries may need to actually return the day of week. You can use the same technique with a twist to return the day of week value, given only the day's name.

```
CAST (POSITION (day_name IN 'SUNMONTUEWEDTHUFRISAT')/3 AS
   INTEGER) + 1;
```

Obviously the same trick can be used with the three-letter month abbreviations. This was very handy in the first release of ACCESS that did sort dates alphabetically.

## 38.7 Modeling Time in Tables

Since the nature of time is a continuum and the ISO model is half-open intervals, the best approach is to have (start_time, end_time) pairs for each event in a history. This is a state transition model of data, where the fact represented by the columns in that row were true for the time period given. For this to work, we need the constraint that the (start_time, end_time) pairs do not overlap.

A NULL ending time is the flag for an "unfinished fact," such as a hotel room stay that is still in progress. A history for an entity can clearly have at most one NULL at a time.

```
CREATE TABLE FoobarHistory
(foo_key INTEGER NOT NULL,
start_date DATE DEFAULT CURRENT_DATE NOT NULL,
```

```
PRIMARY KEY (foo_key, start_date),
end_date TIMESTAMP, -- null means current
foo_status INTEGER NOT NULL,
..
CONSTRAINT started_before_ended
 CHECK(start_date < end_date),

CONSTRAINT end_time_open_interval
 CHECK (end_date = CAST(end_date AS DATE)
       + INTERVAL '23:59:59.999' HOUR TO SECOND),

CONSTRAINT no_date_overlaps
 CHECK (NOT EXISTS
   (SELECT *
     FROM FoobarHistory AS H1, Calendar AS C1
    WHERE C1.cal_date BETWEEN H1.start_date
     AND H1.end_date
    GROUP BY foo_key
   HAVING COUNT(*) > 1)),

CONSTRAINT only_one_current_status
CHECK (NOT EXISTS
  (SELECT *
    FROM FoobarHistory AS H1
   WHERE H1.end_date IS NULL
   GROUP BY foo_key
  HAVING COUNT(*) > 1))
);
```

The Calendar table is explained in a following section. Table level CHECK() constraints are still not common in SQL implementations, so you might have to use a TRIGGER to enforce integrity.

The real trick here is that the start_date is a DATE data type, so it will set to 00:00:00.00000 when it is converted to a TIMESTAMP. The end_time is a TIMESTAMP, so we can place it almost, but not quite, to the next day. This will let us use BETWEEN predicates, as we will see in the next section. You could also do this in a VIEW, make both columns DATE data types and add the extra hours to end_time.

In practice this is going to be highly proprietary code and you might consider using triggers to keep the (start_time, end_time) pairs correct.

## 38.7.1 Using Duration Pairs

If the table does not have the (start_time, end_time) pairs, then they have to be built with a self-join of the queries, or we have to assume that the status changes are ordered properly. For example, how would you write a SELECT query for returning all

Projects whose current project status is 10, given the following schema?

```
CREATE TABLE Projects
(project_id INTEGER NOT NULL PRIMARY KEY,
project_name CHAR(15) NOT NULL);

CREATE TABLE ProjectStatusHistory
(project_id INTEGER NOT NULL
  REFERENCES Projects(project_id),

project_date DATE DEFAULT CURRENT_DATE NOT NULL,
project_status INTEGER NOT NULL,
PRIMARY KEY (project_id, project_date));
```

A solution from David Portas, which assumes that the project is still active, is:

```
SELECT P.project_id, P.project_name
 FROM Projects AS P
WHERE EXISTS
  (SELECT *
   FROM ProjectStatusHistory AS H
  WHERE H.project_id = P.project_id
 HAVING MAX(CASE WHEN H.project_status = 10
        THEN project_date END) = MAX(project_date));
```

But now try to answer the question, which projects had a status of 10 on a prior date?

```
SELECT X.project_id
 FROM (SELECT P1.project_id, P1.project_date AS start_date,
      MIN(P2.project_date) AS end_date
    FROM Projects AS P1
      LEFT OUTER JOIN
      Projects AS P2
      ON P1.project_id = P2.project_id
       AND P1.project_date < P2.project_date
   WHERE project_status = 10
   GROUP BY P1.project_id, P1.project_date)
  AS X(project_id, start_date, end_date)
WHERE :my_date BETWEEN X.start_date
       AND COALESCE (X.end_date, CURRENT_DATE);
```

The X derived table is what Projects would have looked like with (start_time, end_time) pairs.

The `COALESCE()` handles the use of `NULL` for an eternity marker. Depending on the circumstances, you might also use this form of the predicate.

```
WHERE :my_date BETWEEN X.start_date
       AND COALESCE (X.end_date, :my_date)
```

## 38.8 Calendar Auxiliary Table

Auxiliary tables are a way of building functions that would be difficult if not impossible to do with the limited computational power of SQL. They should not appear on the E-R diagrams for the database because they are not really a part of the model, but serve as adjuncts to all the tables and queries in the database that could use them.

This is very true with the calendar because it is so irregular that trying to figure out dates via computations is insanely complex. Look up the algorithm for finding Easter, Ramadan, and other lunar or lunar/solar holidays, for example.

Consider the Security and Exchange Commission (SEC) rule that a brokerage transaction must close within three business days as we mentioned earlier. A business day does not include Saturdays, Sundays, or holidays declared by the New York Stock Exchange. You can compute the occurrences of Saturdays and Sundays with a library function in many SQL products, but not the holidays. In fact, the New York Stock Exchange can be closed by a declared national emergency.

This calendar tables has two general forms. The first form maps single dates into some value and has the general declaration:

```
CREATE TABLE Calendar
(cal_date DATE NOT NULL PRIMARY KEY,
julian_day INTEGER NOT NULL
       CONSTRAINT valid_julian_day
       CHECK (julian_day BETWEEN 1 AND 366),
business_day INTEGER NOT NULL CHECK (business_day
   IN (0, 1)),
three_business_days DATE NOT NULL,
fiscal_month INTEGER NOT NULL
       CONSTRAINT valid_month_nbr
       CHECK (fiscal_month BETWEEN 1 AND 12),
fiscal_year INTEGER NOT NULL,
...);
```

Since this is probably going to be a static table that you fill with 10 or 20 years' worth of data at once (20 years is about 7000 rows—a very small table), you might consider dropping the constraints and keeping only the primary key.

The second form maps an `<interval>` into some value and has the general declaration, with the same constraints as we used in the last section:

```
CREATE TABLE EventCalendar
(event VARCHAR(30) NOT NULL PRIMARY KEY,
start_date DATE NOT NULL,
```

```
end_date TIMESTAMP NOT NULL,
...,
CONSTRAINT started_before_ended
 CHECK(start_date < end_date),

CONSTRAINT end_time_open_interval
CHECK (end_date = CAST(end_date AS DATE)
       + INTERVAL '23:59:59.99999' HOUR),

CONSTRAINT no_date_overlaps
 CHECK (..),

CONSTRAINT only_one_current_status
 CHECK (..));
```

The data for the calendar table can be built with the help of a good spreadsheet, since spreadsheets usually have more temporal functions than databases. Events tend to be volatile, so the constraints are a good idea.

## 38.8.1 Events and Dates

The Calendar table allows you to use a simple query to find which events were concurrent. The diagram in Figure 38.1 explains the solution.

```
SELECT event_id
 FROM Events
WHERE :my_date BETWEEN start_date AND end_date;
```

Or, if you have arranged the times so that you do not want the ends, then use:

```
SELECT event_id
 FROM Events
WHERE :my_time >=start_time
  AND :my_time < end_time;
```

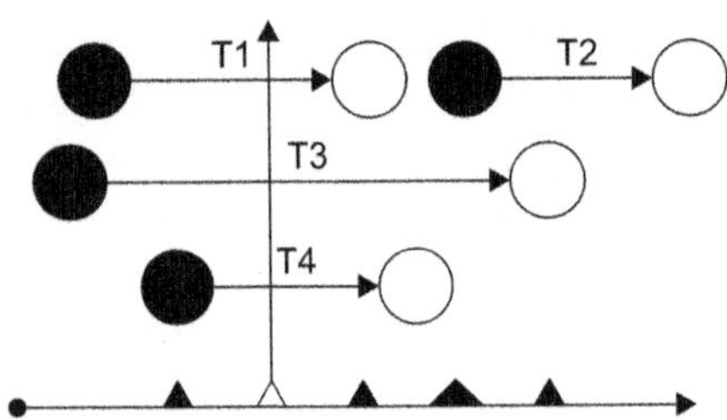


**Figure 38.1**

## 38.9 Problems with the Year 2000

The special problems with the year 2000 took on a life of their own in the computer community, so they rate a separate section in this book. Yes, I know you thought that the "Y2K Crisis" or "Millennium Bug" was over by now, but it still shows up and you need to think about it. The three major problems with representations of the year 2000 in computer systems are:

1. The year 2000 has a lot of zeros in it.
2. The year 2000 is a leap year.
3. The year 2000 is the last year of the old millennium
4. Many date fields are not really dates.

### 38.9.1 The Zeros

I like to call problem 1—the zeros in 2000—the "odometer problem" because it is in the hardware or system level. This is not the same as the millennium problem, where date arithmetic is invalid. If you are using a year-in-century format, the year 2000 is going to "roll over" like a car odometer that has reached its limit and leave a year that is assumed to be 1900 (or something else other than 2000) by the application program.

This problem lives where you cannot see it, in hardware and operating systems related to the system clock. Information on such problems is very incomplete, so you will need to keep yourself posted as new releases of your particular products come out.

Another subtle form of "the zero problem" is that some hashing and random number generators use parts of the system date as a parameter. Zero is a perfectly good number until you try to divide by it and your program aborts.

The problem is in mainframes. For example, the Unisys 2200 system was set to fail on the first day of 1996 because the 8th bit of the year field—which is a signed integer—would go to 1. Fortunately, the vendor had some solutions ready. Do you know what other hardware uses this convention? You might want to look.

The real killer will be with older Intel-based PCs. When the odometer wraps around, DOS jumps to 1980 most of the time and sometimes to 1984, depending on your BIOS chip. Windows 3.1 jumps to 1900 most of the time. Since PCs are now common as stand-alone units and as workstations, you can test this for yourself. Set the date and time to 2005-12-31 at 23:59:30 Hrs and let the clock run. What happens next depends on your BIOS chip and version of DOS.

The results can be that the clock display shows 12:00 AM and a date display of 01/01/00, so you think you have no problems. However, you will find that you have newly created files dated 1984 or 1980. Surprise!

This problem is passed along to application programs, but not always the way that you would think. Quicken Version 3 for the IBM PC running on MS-DOS 6 is one example. As you expect, directly inputting the date 2000-01-01 results in the year resetting to 1980 or 1984 off the system clock. But strangely enough, if you let the date wrap from 2005-12-31 into the year 2000, Quicken Version 3 interprets the change as 1901-01-01 and not as 1900.

It is worth doing a Google search for information on older software when you have to work with it.

### 38.9.2 Leap Year

Problem 2 always seems to shock people. You might remember being told in grade school that there are 365¼ days per year and that the accumulation of the fractional day creates a leap year every four years. Once more, your teachers lied to you; there are really 365.2422 days per year. Every four years, the extra 0.2400 days accumulate and create an additional day; this gives us a leap year. Every 400 years the extra 0.0022 days accumulate enough to create an additional day and give us this special leap year. Since most of us are not over 400 years old, we did not have to worry about this until the year 2000. However, every 100 years the missing 0.01 days (i.e., 365.25 – 365.2422 rounded up) balances out and we do not have a leap year.

The correct test for leap years in SQL/PSM is:

```
CREATE FUNCTION Test_Leapyear (IN my_year INTEGER)
RETURNS CHAR(3)
LANGUAGE SQL
DETERMINISTIC
RETURN (CASE WHEN MOD(my_year, 400) = 0
   THEN 'Yes'
   WHEN MOD(my_year, 100) = 0
   THEN 'No'
   ELSE CASE WHEN MOD(my_year, 4) = 0
        THEN 'Yes' ELSE 'No'
      END
   END);
```

Or if you would like a more compact form, you can use this solution from Phil Alexander, which will fit into in-line code as a search expression:

```
(MOD(my_year, 400) = 0
OR (MOD(my_year, 4) = 0 AND NOT (MOD(my_year, 100) = 0)))
```

People who did not know this algorithm wrote lots of programs. I do not mean COBOL legacy programs in your organization; I mean packaged programs for which you paid good money. The date functions in the first releases of Lotus, Excel, and Quattro Pro did not handle the day 2000-02-29 correctly. Lotus simply made an error and the others followed suit to maintain "Lotus compatibility" in their products. Microsoft Excel for Windows Version 4 shows correctly that the next day after 2000-02-28 is 2000-03-01. However, it thought that the next day after 1900-02-28 was also February 29 instead of March 01. Microsoft Excel for Macintosh did not handle the years 1900 through 1903.

Have you checked all of your word processors, spreadsheets, desktop databases, appointment calendars, and other off-the-shelf packages for this problem yet? Just key in the date 2000-02-29, then do some calculations with date arithmetic and see what happens.

With networked systems, this is a real nightmare. All you needed was one program on one node in the network to reject leap year day 2000 and the whole network was useless for that day; transactions might not reconcile for some time afterward. How many nodes do you think there are in the ATM banking networks in North America and Europe?

## 38.9.3 The Millennium

I saved problem 3 for last because it is the one best known in the popular and computer trade press. We programmers have not been keeping TRUE dates in fields for a few decades. Instead, we have been using one of several year-in-century formats. These will not work in the last year of the previous millennium. The first millennium of the Common Era calendar ends in the year 2000 and the second millennium begins with the year 2001—that is why Arthur C. Clarke used it for the title of his book.

If only we had been good programmers and not tried to save storage space at the expense of accuracy, we would have used ISO standard formats and would not have to deal with these problems today. Since we did not, programs have been doing arithmetic and comparisons based on the year-in-century and not on the year. A 30-year mortgage taken out in 1992 will be over in the year 2022, but when you subtract the two year-in-centuries, you get:

$(22 - 92) = -70$ years

This is a very early payoff of a mortgage!

It might be worth mentioning the old COBOL programmer trick of checking to see if the two-digit year is less than 30 (or some other magical number): if it is, we add 2000 to it, if it isn't then add 1900 to it and come up with a four-digit year. A lot of old COBOL programs will be exploding 20, 30, or 40 years from when they were written if they are still chugging along. If you consider how long COBOL has stayed in use, this is a real problem. Gary Barnett, Research Director of Ovum, reported in 2005 that COBOL accounted for 90% of all financial transactions estimates and 75% of transactions generally. You can find information on COBOL at http://www.infogoal.com/cbd/.

Inventory retention programs were throwing away good stock, thinking it is outdated—look at the 10-year retention required in the automobile industry. Lifetime product warranties were dishonored because the services schedule dates and manufacturing dates could not be resolved correctly. One hospital sent a geriatrics patient to the pediatrics ward because it keeps only two digits of the birth year. You can imagine your own horror stories or do a web search for books and articles from that period.

According to Benny Popek, of Coopers & Lybrand LLP (Xenakis, 1995), "This problem is so big that we will consider these bugs to be out of the scope of our normal software maintenance contracts. For those clients who insist that we should take responsibility, we'll exercise the cancellation clause and terminate the outsourcing contract."

Popek commented, "We've found that a lot of our clients are in denial. We spoke to one CIO who just refused to deal with the problem, since he's going to retire next year."

But the problem is subtler than just looking for date data fields. Timestamps often are buried inside encoding schemes. If the year-in-century is used for the high-order digits of a serial numbering system, then any program that depends on increasing serial numbers will fail. Those of you with magnetic tape libraries might want to look at your tape labels now. The five-digit code is used in many mainframe shops for archives and tape management software also has the convention that if programmers want a tape to be kept indefinitely, they code the label with a retention date of 99365. This method failed at the start of the year 2000 when the retention label had 00001 in it.

### 38.9.4 Weird Dates in Legacy Data

Some of the problems with dates in legacy data have been discussed in an article by Randall L. Hitchens (Hitchens, 1991) and in one by me on the same subject (Celko, 1981). The problem is subtler than Hitchens implied in his article, which dealt with nonstandard date formats. Dates hide in other places, not just in date fields. The most common places are serial numbers and computer-generated identifiers.

In the early 1960s, a small insurance company in Atlanta bought out an even smaller company that sold burial insurance policies to poor people in the Deep South. These policies guaranteed the subscriber a funeral in exchange for a weekly or monthly premium of a few dollars, and were often sold by local funeral homes; they are now illegal.

The burial insurance company used a policy number format identical to that of the larger company. The numbers began with the two digits of the year-in-century, followed by a dash, followed by an eight-digit sequential number.

The systems analysts decided that the easiest way to do this was to add 20 years to the first two digits. Their logic was that no customer would keep these cheap policies for 20 years—and the analyst who did this would not be working there in 20 years, so who cared? As the years passed, the company moved from a simple file system to a hierarchical database and was using the policy numbers for unique record keys. The system simply generated new policy numbers on demand, using a global counter in a policy library routine, and no problems occurred for decades.

There were about 100 burial policies left in the database after 20 years. Nobody had written programs to protect against duplicate keys, since the problem had never occurred. Then, one day, they created their first duplicate number. Sometimes the database would crash, but sometimes the child records would get attached to the wrong parent. This second situation was worse, since the company started paying and billing the wrong people.

The company was lucky enough to have someone who recognized the old burial insurance policies when he saw them. It took months to clean up the problem, because they had to search a warehouse to find the original policy documents. If the policies were still valid, there were insurance regulation problems because those policies had been made illegal in the intervening years.

In this case, the date was being used to generate a unique identifier. But consider a situation in which this same scheme is used, starting in the year 1999, for a serial number. Once the company goes into the year 2000, you can no longer select the largest serial number in the database and increment it to get the next one.

## 38.9.5 The Aftermath

The Y2K crisis is over now and we have some idea of the cost of this conversion. By various estimates, the total expenditure on remediation by governments and businesses ranged from a low of $200 billion to well over half a trillion dollars. As a result of Y2K, many ISO Standards—not just SQL—require that dates be in ISO 8601 format.

The other good side effect was that people actually looked at their data and became aware of their data quality levels. Most companies would not have done such a data audit without the "Y2K Crisis" looming over their heads.

This was also a major reason that the SQL Standards spent so much time on, well, time.

39

# OPTIMIZING SQL

There is no set of rules for writing code that will take the best advantage of every query optimizer on every SQL product every time. The query optimizers depend on the underlying architecture and are simply too different for many universal rules; however, we can make a few general statements. Just remember that you have to test code. What would improve performance in one SQL implementation might not do anything at all in another or make the performance worse. Even worse, the next release of the *same* SQL can perform differently.

There are two kinds of optimizers: cost-based and rule-based. A rule-based optimizer (such as Oracle before Version 7.0) will parse a query and execute it in the order in which it was written, perhaps doing some reorganization of the query into an equivalent form using some syntax rules. *Basically, it is no optimizer at all.* The only reason I mention them is that small in-memory databases will use a rule-based optimizer because it cannot afford the overhead of statistics and extra code. If the entire database is in primary storage, there is not much need for traditional optimizations that deal with reducing disk access.

A cost-based optimizer looks at both the query and the statistical data about secondary storage, the current data in cache shared by sessions, and decides on the best way to execute the query. These decisions involve deciding on the access methods to use, which data to bring into main storage, what sorting technique to use, and so forth. Most of the time (but not all), it will make better decisions than a human programmer would have simply because it has more information.

An old heuristic was to order the tables in the `FROM` clause in ascending or descending order by size. This was helpful in the old days because as the number of tables increases, many optimizers do not try all the combinations of possible `JOIN` orderings; the number of combinations is factorial. So the optimizer fell back on the order in the `FROM` clause. This kicked in when the number

Joe Celko's SQL for Smarties. DOI: 10.1016/B978-0-12-382022-8.00039-9

of tables got over 5 (5! = 120 permutations to test, but 6! = 720 and 10! = 3,628,800). Do not worry about it today. Most modern optimizers keep descriptive statistics of the data and make decisions based on the actual data distributions.

Ingres has had one of the best optimizers, which extensively reorders a query before executing it. It is one of the few products that can find most semantically identical queries and reduce them to the same internal form.

Rdb, a DEC product that now belongs to Oracle, uses a searching method taken from an AI (Artificial Intelligence) game-playing program to inspect the costs of several different approaches before making a decision. DB2 has a system table with a statistical profile of the base tables. In short, no two products use exactly the same optimization techniques.

## 39.1 Access Methods

For this discussion, let us assume that we have a disk storage system of some kind. In a few years, this might not be true when we make some more breakthroughs in Solid State Disk (SSD).

In disk systems, there are four basic methods of getting to data: table scans or sequential reads of all the rows in the table, access via some kind of tree index, hashing, and bit vector indexes.

### 39.1.1 Sequential Access

The table scan is a sequential read of all the data in the order in which it appears in physical storage, grabbing one page of memory at a time. Most databases do not physically remove deleted rows, so a table can use a lot of physical space and yet hold little data. Depending on just how dynamic the database is, you may want to run a utility program to reclaim storage and compress the database. The performance can suddenly improve drastically after database reorganization.

Today, many SQL products can partition a table and distribute the data so that it can be accessed in parallel. This is not part of the ANSI/ISO Standards, but you have to know your product. If the table is partitioned sometimes the optimizer is smart enough to be able to skip partitions, or to scan only the relevant partitions based on the partitioning key and the query.

This does not apply to columnar databases; they store each column of a table in its own structure and have to assemble the rows from those structures. SQL does not guarantee that a query will return the rows in the same order each time it is executed.

## 39.1.2 Indexed Access

Indexed access returns one row or data page at a time. The index is probably going to be a B-tree, B+ tree, T-Tree or trie (popular with in-memory databases), or some other flavor. Obviously, if you do not have an index on a table, then you cannot use indexed access on it. Even if you do have an index on the table, the formulation of your predicates and the particular DBMS optimizer you are using may preclude you from being able to use the index.

An index can be sequential or nonsequential. A sequential index has a table that is in sorted order in the physical storage. Obviously, there can be only one sequential index on a table. Sequential indexes keep the table in sorted order, so a table scan will often produce results in that order. A sequential index will also tend to put duplicates of the indexed column values on the same page of physical memory, which may speed up aggregate functions.

Sequential in this sense is the Sybase/SQL Server term "clustered"; Oracle uses "clustered" to mean a single data page that contains matching rows from multiple tables. The first version of this was IBM's old ISAM (Indexed Sequential Access Method) file system, and it is still in use on mainframes. If you aggregate your data, then a sequential index on those columns can be a huge improvement; the read/write head jumps immediately to the physically contiguous storage where the data resides.

As tables get bigger, the deeper the tree structure becomes, and it requires more and more probes to locate the physical records with the data.

## 39.1.3 Hashed Indexes

Writing hashing functions is not easy. The idea is that given input values, the hashing function will return a physical storage address. If two or more values have the same hash value ("hash clash" or "collision"), then they are put into the same "bucket" in the hash table, or they are run through a second hashing function.

Let me give a *very* simplified example. Given a key that can be expressed as a binary integer, divide it by 5 and use the remainder as the hash, which will be {0, 1, 2, 3, 4}. If I have the keys 42, 35, and 120 they will hash to 2, 0, and 0, respectively. I use the value 2 to go to a hash table, usually an array of pointer chains in main storage, and I find the physical address of the record that holds the row with a key of 2. But when I am asked to find the row with a key of 35, I also hash to the one with a key 120.

I can resolve the collision by chaining the hash table elements together by pointers and follow it until I find what I wanted. Alternatively, I can apply another hash function and look in another location. Hashing is fast, simple math so doing several of these function calls is cheap and you seldom need more than five attempts. In this super-simple case, I might divide by 7 and get 6.

If the index is on a unique column, the ideal situation is what is called a minimal perfect hashing function—each value hashes to a unique physical storage address and there are no empty spaces in the hash table. The next best situation for a unique column is what is called a perfect hashing function—every value hashes to one physical storage address without collisions, but there are some empty spaces in the physical hash table storage.

A hashing function for a nonunique column should hash to a bucket small enough to fit into main storage. In the Teradata SQL engine, which is based on hashing, any row can be found in at most two probes, and 90% or more of the accesses require only one probe.

### 39.1.4 Bit Vector Indexes

The fact that a particular occurrence of an entity has a particular value for a particular attribute is represented as a single bit in a vector or array. Predicates are handled by doing Boolean bit operations on the arrays. These techniques are very fast for large amounts of data and are used by the SAND database engine from Sand Technology and Foxpro's Rushmore indexes.

## 39.2 How to Index

There are two kinds of indexes; primary and secondary. Primary indexes are those that are required to preserve primary keys, uniqueness constraints, and in products with multiple table indexes, those that enforce `FOREIGN KEY` relationships. Secondary indexes are added for performance.

Without giving you a computer science lecture, a computer problem is called NP-complete if it gets so big, so fast, that it is not practical to solve it for a reasonable-sized set of input values.

Usually this means that you have to try all possible combinations to find the answer. Finding the optimal indexing arrangement is known to be NP-complete. If you want the details refer to the following:

Comer, D. 1978. "The Difficulty of Optimum Index Selection." *ACM Transactions on Database Systems* 3(4):440–445.

Paitetsky-Shapiro, G. 1983. "The Optimal Selection of Secondary Indexes in NP-Complete." *SIGMOD Record* 13(2):72–75.

This does not mean that you cannot optimize indexing for a particular database schema and set of input queries, but it does mean that you cannot write a program that will do it for all possible relational databases and query sets.

Over-indexing can slow inserts, updates, and deletes because the extra indexes have to be changed when the base table is changed. But it can also confuse the optimizer and slow down queries.

Here are some tips for faster DML statements. Like all heuristics, these tips will not be valid for all products in all situations, but they are how the smart money bets. In fairness, most optimizers are smart enough to do many of these things internally today.

## 39.2.1 Use Simple Search Conditions

Where possible, write simple search conditions. Optimizers have trouble using an index with complicated expressions or function calls. SQL is not built for algebra, so you are not going to get a search condition reduced to a simpler expression if it requires any serious effort.

Functions have to be evaluated each time they are invoked, so it can be impossible to use an index. The exception is with SQLs that allow a function to be used in creating an index. You will need to know your product and its particular syntax, but here is an example with a nonstandard trig function. First consider a simple index on a single column:

```
CREATE INDEX Foobar_idx ON Foobar (x);
```

and the query:

```
SELECT x, sin(x), a, b, c
 FROM Foobar
WHERE sin(x) = 0.08715; -- x = 5
```

Since SQL is not a computational language most implementations have simple algebraic simplifications at best. There is no way the optimizer can use Foobar_idx. However, if we had:

```
CREATE INDEX Foobar_Sin_idx ON Foobar (sin(x));
```

this index could be used. But it would be useless for the query:

```
SELECT x, sin(x), a, b, c
 FROM Foobar
WHERE x = 5;
```

If a column appears in a mathematical or string expression, then the optimizer cannot use its indexes.

The not-equal <> comparison has some unique problems. Some optimizers assume that this comparison will return more rows than it rejects, so they will prefer a sequential scan and will not use an index on a column involved in such a comparison. This is not always true, however. For example, to find someone in Ireland who is not a Catholic, you would normally write:

```
SELECT last_name, first_name, religion_name
 FROM Ireland
WHERE religion_name <> 'Catholic';
```

The way around this is to break up the inequality like this:

```
SELECT *
 FROM Ireland
WHERE religion_name < 'Catholic'
   OR religion_name > 'Catholic';
```

and force the use of an index. However, without an index on religion_name, the OR-ed version of the predicate could take longer to run.

Another trick is to avoid the x IS NOT NULL predicate and use x >= <minimal constant> instead. The NULLs are kept in different ways in different implementations, not always in the same physical storage area as their columns. As a result, the SQL engine has to do extra searching. For example, if we have a CHAR(3) column that holds a NULL or three letters, we could look for missing data with:

```
SELECT sale_nbr, alpha_code
 FROM Sales
WHERE alpha_code IS NOT NULL;
```

but it might be better written as:

```
SELECT sale_nbr, alpha_code
 FROM Sales
WHERE alpha_code >= 'AAA';
```

because it avoids the extra reads.

## 39.2.2 Simple String Expressions

Likewise, string expressions can be expensive. In particular, favor a LIKE over a SIMILAR TO predicate. The regular expression is more complex to compute each time. I would recommend getting a book on regular expressions to learn how to write them in an optimal fashion; it is not something I can cover here.

But with the LIKE predicate, avoid '%' in favor of '_' in the pattern string.

For example, consider this table with a fixed length CHAR(5) column:

```
SELECT student_first_name, student_last_name,
   homeroom_nbr
 FROM Students
WHERE homeroom_nbr LIKE 'A-1__'; -- two underscores in
   pattern
```

may or may not use an index on the homeroom_nbr column. However, if we know that the last two positions are always numerals, then we can replace this query with:

```
SELECT student_first_name, student_last_name,
   homeroom_nbr
 FROM Students
WHERE homeroom_nbr BETWEEN 'A-100' AND 'A-199';
```

This query can use an index on the homeroom_nbr column. Notice that this trick assumes that the homeroom_nbr column is CHAR(5), and not a VARCHAR(5) column. If it were VARCHAR(5), then the second query would pick 'A-1' but the original LIKE predicate would not. String equality and BETWEEN predicates pad the shorter string with blanks on the right before comparing them; the LIKE predicate does not pad either the string or the pattern.

## 39.2.3 Simple Temporal Expressions

Avoid temporal math whenever possible for the same reasons we avoided complex string and numeric expressions. Internally the irregular nature of the Common Era calendar and the base-60 Babylonian temporal model makes the math pretty ugly.

Temporal data can be stored at the DATE or TIMESTAMP level of granularity; use the coarsest level that does the job. Carrying work out to nanoseconds when a date will do saves complicated programming. As an example of this, look at MS SQL Server code before the SQL Server 2008 added a subset of the ANSI Standard DATE data type. The product only had a version of TIMESTAMP and programmers spent huge amounts of computer time setting the TIME portion to '00:00:00' to kludge a DATE data type.

For example, given a table of tasks and their start and finish dates, to find the tasks that took three days to complete, we could write:

```
SELECT task_nbr
 FROM Tasks
WHERE (finish_date - start_date) = INTERVAL '3' DAY
  AND start_date >= DATE '2015-01-01';
```

But since most of the reports deal with the finish dates, we have an index on that column. This means that the query will run faster if it is rewritten as:

```
SELECT task_nbr
 FROM Tasks
WHERE finish_date = (start_date + INTERVAL '3' DAY)
  AND start_date >= DATE '2015-01-01';
```

## 39.3 Give Extra Information

Optimizers are not always able to draw conclusions that a human being can draw. The more information contained in the query, the better the chance that the optimizer will be able to find an improved execution plan. The best to do this is with constraints in the DDL. These constraints will be picked up by the optimizer for all queries, inserts, updates, and deletions without writing any extra code.

However, if you do not have the constraints, you can provide them in your code. For example, given this query:

```
SELECT sale_nbr, alpha_code
 FROM Sales
WHERE sale_amt >= 500.00;
```

If the DDL has a column constraint on the alpha_code like this:

```
CREATE TABLE Sales
(..
alpha_code CHAR(3) NOT NULL
  CHECK (alpha_code SIMILAR TO 'A[:UPPER:]C'),
..);
```

The query effectively becomes:

```
SELECT sale_nbr, alpha_code
 FROM Sales
WHERE sale_amt >= 500.00;
  AND alpha_code SIMILAR TO 'A[:UPPER:]C';
```

Do not confuse this extra data with redundant logical expressions that might be recalculated and can be expensive. For example:

```
SELECT sale_nbr, alpha_code
 FROM Sales
WHERE sale_amt >= 500.00
  AND alpha_code SIMILAR TO 'A[:UPPER:]C'
  AND alpha_code BETWEEN 'AAA' AND 'ZZZ';
```

might redo the BETWEEN predicate for every row. It does not provide any information that can be used for a JOIN, and, very clearly, if the LIKE predicate is TRUE, then the BETWEEN predicate also has to be TRUE.

Do not confuse this extra data with hints, pragmas, or other vendor terms for interventions into the execution plan. Optimizer hints can be either suggestions or commands, depending on your SQL. The problem with mandatory hints is that they stay there forever. When the statistics, table structures, indexes, or other things change, the hints do not. Nobody dares to remove them because they are just not sure why they are there. This is the SQL version of the old programming maxim that there is nothing more permanent than a "temporary" code patch.

## 39.4 Index Multiple Columns Carefully

For obvious physical reasons, you can create only one sequential index on a table. The decision as to which columns to use in the index can be important to performance. There is a "superstition" among older DBAs who have worked with ISAM files and network and hierarchical databases that the PRIMARY KEY must be done with a sequential index. This stems from the fact that in the older file systems, files had to be sorted on their keys. All searching and navigation was based on this.

This is not true in SQL systems. The PRIMARY KEY's uniqueness will probably be preserved by a unique index, but it does not have to be a *sequential* unique index. Consider a table of employees keyed by a unique employee identification number. Updates are done with the employee ID number, of course, but very few queries use it for ordering reports. Updating individual rows in a table will actually be about as fast with a sequential or a nonsequential index. Both tree structures will be the same, except for the final physical position to which they point.

However, it might be that the most important corporate unit for reporting purposes is the department, not the employee. A sequential index on the employee ID number would sort the table in employee ID order. There is no inherent meaning in that ordering; in fact, I would be more likely to sort a list of employees by their last names than by their ID numbers.

However, a sequential index on the (nonunique) department code would sort the table in department order and put employees in the same department on the same physical page of storage. The result would be that fewer pages would be read to answer queries.

Modern SQL products can use multiple indexes for AND and OR search criteria. If the index has all the columns needed for a query, it is possible that the SQL engine will never read the base tables.

## 39.5 Watch the IN Predicate

The IN predicate is really shorthand for a series of OR-ed equality tests. There are two forms: either an explicit list of values is given or a subquery is used to make such a list of values.

The database engine has no statistics about the relative frequency of the values in a list of constants, so it will assume that the list is in the order in which they are to be used. People like to order lists alphabetically or by magnitude, but it would be better to order the list from most frequently occurring values to least frequent. It is also pointless to have duplicate values in the constant list, since the predicate will return TRUE if it matches the first duplicate it finds and will never get to the second occurrence. Likewise, if the predicate is FALSE for that value, the program wastes computer time traversing a needlessly long list.

Many SQL engines perform an IN predicate with a subquery by building the result set of the subquery first as a temporary working table, then scanning that result table from left to right. This can be expensive in many cases. For example,

```
SELECT P1.first_name, P1.last_name
 FROM Personnel AS P1, BowlingTeam AS B1
WHERE P1.last_name
  IN (SELECT last_name
      FROM BowlingTeam AS B1
     WHERE P1.emp_nbr = B1.emp_nbr)
       AND P1.last_name
        IN (SELECT last_name
             FROM BowlingTeam AS B2
            WHERE P1.emp_nbr = B2.emp_nbr);
```

will not run as fast as:

```
SELECT P1.first_name, P1.last_name
 FROM Personnel AS P1
WHERE first_name || last_name
  IN (SELECT first_name || last_name
      FROM BowlingTeam AS B1
     WHERE P1.emp_nbr = B1.emp_nbr);
```

which can be further simplified to:

```
SELECT P1.first_name, P1.last_name
 FROM Personnel AS P1
WHERE first_name || last_name
  IN (SELECT first_name || last_name
      FROM BowlingTeam);
```

or using Standard SQL row constructors to:

```
SELECT P1.first_name, P1.last_name
 FROM Personnel AS P1
WHERE (first_name, last_name)
  IN (SELECT first_name, last_name
      FROM BowlingTeam);
```

since there can be only one row with a complete name in it.

The first version of the query may make two passes through the Bowling Team table to construct two separate result tables. The second version makes only one pass to construct the concatenation of the names in its result table. Likewise, the row constructor version should make only one pass.

The optimizer is supposed to figure out when two queries are the same and will not be fooled by two queries with the same meaning and different syntax. For example, the SQL standard defines:

```
SELECT *
 FROM Warehouse AS W1
WHERE onhand_qty IN (SELECT order_qty FROM Sales);
```

as identical to:

```
SELECT *
 FROM Warehouse
WHERE onhand_qty = ANY (SELECT order_qty FROM Sales);
```

but you will find that some older SQL engines prefer the first version to the second because they do not convert the expressions into a common internal form. Very often, things like the choice of operators and their order make a large performance difference.

The first query can be converted to this "flattened" `JOIN` query:

```
SELECT W1.*
 FROM Warehouse AS W1, Sales AS S1
WHERE W1.onhand_qty = S1.order_qty;
```

This form will often be faster if there are indexes to help with the `JOIN`.

## 39.6 Avoid UNIONs

A UNION is often implemented by constructing the two result sets, then merging them together usually with a sort to get rid of redundant duplicates. The optimizer works only within a single SELECT statement or subquery. For example,

```
SELECT *
 FROM Personnel
WHERE work_city_name = 'New York'
UNION
SELECT *
 FROM Personnel
WHERE home_city_name = 'Chicago';
```

is the same as:

```
SELECT DISTINCT *
 FROM Personnel
WHERE work_city_name = 'New York'
   OR home_city_name = 'Chicago';
```

which will usually run faster.

Another trick is to use the UNION ALL in place of the UNION whenever duplicates are not a problem. The UNION ALL is implemented as an append operation, without the need for a sort to aid duplicate removal.

## 39.7 Prefer Joins over Nested Queries

A nested query is hard to optimize. Optimizers try to "flatten" nested queries so that they can be expressed as JOINs and the best order of execution can be determined. Consider the database:

```
CREATE TABLE Authors
(author_nbr INTEGER NOT NULL PRIMARY KEY,
author_name CHAR(50) NOT NULL);

CREATE TABLE Titles
(isbn CHAR(10)NOT NULL PRIMARY KEY,
book_title CHAR(50) NOT NULL
advance_amt DECIMAL(8,2) NOT NULL);

CREATE TABLE Authorship
(author_nbr INTEGER NOT NULL REFERENCES
   Authors(author_nbr),
isbn CHAR(10)NOT NULL REFERENCES Titles(isbn),
royalty_rate DECIMAL(5,4) NOT NULL,
PRIMARY KEY (author_nbr, isbn));
```

This query finds authors who are getting less than 50% royalties:

```
SELECT author_nbr
 FROM Authors
WHERE author_nbr
  IN (SELECT author_nbr
       FROM Authorship
      WHERE royalty < 0.50)
```

which could also be expressed as:

```
SELECT DISTINCT Authors.author_nbr
 FROM Authors, Authorship
WHERE Authors.author_nbr = Authorship.author_nbr
  AND royalty_rate < 0.50;
```

The `SELECT DISTINCT` is important. Each author's name will occur only once in the Authors table. Therefore, the `IN` predicate query should return one occurrence of O'Leary. Assume that O'Leary wrote two books; with just a `SELECT`, the second query would return two O'Leary rows, one for each book.

## 39.8 Use Fewer Statements

The more work you can do with one statement, the fewer times the SQL engine will have to access the database. Fewer statements also mean less code to maintain.

The `MERGE` statement is the most powerful example of this heuristic. I strongly suggest that you look at old code and try to find updates and inserts to the same table in stored procedures and see what can be done with a single `MERGE` statement.

A better example of the power of this heuristic is found in a contest sponsored by Advanced DataTools (http://www.advancedatatools.com/), an `INFORMIX` consultancy. Cleaning up their sample code you were given a schema with the following tables and sample data:

```
CREATE TABLE State_Taxes -- 52 rows
(state_code CHAR(2) NOT NULL PRIMARY KEY,
state_name CHAR(15) NOT NULL,
sales_tax_rate DECIMAL(16,2) NOT NULL);

CREATE TABLE Customers -- 101,000 rows
(customer_nbr INTEGER NOT NULL PRIMARY KEY,
cust_last_name CHAR(30) NOT NULL,
cust_first_name CHAR(30) NOT NULL,
customer_address CHAR(50) NOT NULL,
city_name CHAR(20) NOT NULL,
state_code CHAR(2) NOT NULL
-- REFERENCES State_Codes(state_code),
zip_code CHAR(5) NOT NULL,
```

```
start_date DATE DEFAULT CURRENT_DATE NOT NULL,
balance_due_amt DECIMAL(16,2) NOT NULL,
billing_notes CHAR(2000) NOT NULL,
product_nbr CHAR(4) NOT NULL
-- REFERENCES Products (product_nbr));

CREATE TABLE Products -- 10 rows
(product_nbr NOT NULL PRIMARY KEY,
product_name CHAR(50) NOT NULL,
product_type CHAR(4) NOT NULL,
product_price DECIMAL(16,2) NOT NULL);
```

The contestants were not allowed to change these tables and were to create a Bills table that gets dropped and recreated with each run. At the end of the process there will be 605,280 bills. They could change the system configuration and add other things.

The process steps were simple and had these business rules:

1. Bills are generated in batches for two products (limited to two to avoid a long transaction).
2. Next, Bills are generated for two more products. A final batch of Bills are generated for two products.
3. The best customers are given a $10 discount.
4. The bill total is calculated for each row (product_price – product_discount) + sales_tax = total_bill decimal.
5. The customer balance is updated. Totals are displayed to check row and dollar counts.
6. A checkpoint is performed; this is the last step and must be performed. We want everything safely written to disk.

The benchmark, which had three inserts to Bills and two updates to Customers, took about 40 hours to run; add one index and it will run in 30 minutes. With a few changes to the configuration, it can run in 5 to 6 minutes, and with some more changes it can run in under 2 minutes.

The tricks that were used were to add an index on Bills so it could be joined to the Customers via the customer_nbr (you can get the same effect with a `REFERENCES` clause). This dropped the time from 40 hours to 30 minutes. Several entries created too many indexes and slowed the process.

The winning answer from Eric Rowell was under 1 minute. His answer put all the work into one `INSERT` statement and a `TRIGGER` on `EACH ROW` so that as each bill was inserted, it would update the corresponding Customers row.

## 39.9 Avoid Sorting

The `SELECT DISTINCT`, `GROUP BY`, and `ORDER BY` clauses usually cause a sort in most SQL products, so avoid them unless you really need them. Use them if you need to remove duplicates or if you need to guarantee a particular result set order explicitly. In the case of a small result set, the time to sort it can be longer than the time to process redundant duplicates.

The UNION, INTERSECT, and EXCEPT clauses can do sorts to remove duplicates; the exception is when an index exists that can be used to eliminate the duplicates without sorting. In particular, the UNION ALL will tend to be faster than the plain UNION, so if you have no duplicates or do not mind having them, then use it instead. There are not enough implementations of INTERSECT ALL and EXCEPT ALL to make a generalization yet.

The GROUP BY often uses a sort to cluster groups together, does the aggregate functions and then reduces each group to a single row based on duplicates in the grouping columns. Each sort will cost you (n*log2(n)) operations, which is a lot of extra computer time that you can save if you do not need to use these clauses.

If a SELECT DISTINCT clause includes a set of key columns in it, then all the rows are already known to be unique. Since you can declare a set of columns to be a PRIMARY KEY in the table declaration, an optimizer can spot such a query and automatically change SELECT DISTINCT to just SELECT.

You can often replace a SELECT DISTINCT clause with an EXISTS() subquery, in violation of another rule of thumb that says to prefer unnested queries to nested queries.

For example, a query to find the students who are majoring in the sciences would be:

```
SELECT DISTINCT S1.name
FROM Students AS S1, ScienceDepts AS D1
WHERE S1.dept = D1.dept;
```

This can be better replaced with:

```
SELECT S1.name
 FROM Students AS S1
WHERE EXISTS
  (SELECT *
    FROM ScienceDepts AS D1
    WHERE S1.dept = D1.dept);
```

Another problem is that the DBA might not declare all candidate keys or might declare superkeys instead. Consider a table for a school schedule:

```
CREATE TABLE Schedule
(room_nbr INTEGER NOT NULL,
course_name CHAR(7) NOT NULL,
teacher_name CHAR(20) NOT NULL,
period_nbr INTEGER NOT NULL,
PRIMARY KEY (room_nbr, period_nbr));
```

This says that if I know the room and the period, I can find a unique teacher and course—"Third-period Freshman English in Room 101 is taught by Ms. Jones." However, I might have also added the constraint UNIQUE (teacher, period), since Ms. Jones can be in only one room and teach only one class during a given period. If the table was not declared with this extra constraint, the optimizer could not use it in parsing a query. Likewise, if the DBA decided to declare PRIMARY KEY (room_nbr, course_name, teacher_name, period_nbr), the optimizer could not break down this superkey into candidates keys.

Avoid using a HAVING or a GROUP BY clause if the SELECT or WHERE clause can do all the needed work. One way to avoid grouping is in situations where you know the group criterion in advance and then make it a constant. This example is a bit extreme, but you can convert:

```
SELECT project_type, AVG(cost)
 FROM Tasks
GROUP BY project_type
HAVING project_type = 'bricklaying';
```

to the simpler and faster:

```
SELECT 'bricklaying', AVG(cost)
 FROM Tasks
WHERE project_type = 'bricklaying';
```

Both queries have to scan the entire table to inspect values in the project column. The first query will simply throw each row into a bucket based on its project code, then look at the HAVING clause to throw away all but one of the buckets before computing the average.

The second query rejects those unneeded rows and arrives at one subset of projects when it scans.

Standard SQL has ways of removing GROUP BY clauses because it can use a subquery in a SELECT statement. This is easier to show with an example in which you are now in charge of the Widget-Only Company inventory. You get requisitions that tell how many widgets people are putting into or taking out of the warehouse on a given date. Sometimes that quantity is positive (returns); sometimes it is negative (withdrawals).

The table of requisitions looks like this:

```
CREATE TABLE Requisitions
(req_date DATE NOT NULL,
req_qty INTEGER NOT NULL
CONSTRAINT non_zero_qty
CHECK (req_qty <> 0));
```

Your job is to provide a running balance on the quantity on hand with a query. We want something like:

Result

| req_date | req_qty | onhand_qty |
|---|---|---|
| '2013-07-01' | 100 | 100 |
| '2013-07-02' | 120 | 220 |
| '2013-07-03' | -150 | 70 |
| '2013-07-04' | 501 | 20 |
| '2013-07-05' | -35 | 85 |

The classic SQL solution would be:

```
SELECT R1.req_date, R1.req_qty, SUM(R2.req_qty) AS
   onhand_qty
 FROM Requisitions AS R1, Requisitions AS R2
WHERE R2.req_date <= R1.req_date
GROUP BY R1.req_date, R1.req_qty;
```

Standard SQL can use a subquery in the SELECT list, even a correlated query. The rule is that the result must be a single value, hence the name scalar subquery; if the query results are an empty table, the result is a NULL.

In this problem, we need to do a summation of all the requisitions posted up to and including the date we are looking at. The query is a nested self-JOIN, thus:

```
SELECT R1.req_date, R1.req_qty,
   (SELECT SUM(R2.req_qty)
     FROM Requisitions AS R2
    WHERE R2.req_date <= R1.req_date) AS onhand_qty
FROM Requisitions AS R1;
```

Frankly, both solutions are going to run slowly compared to a procedural solution that could build the current quantity on hand from the previous quantity on hand from a sorted file of records. Both queries will have to build the subquery from the self-joined table based on dates. However, the first query will also probably sort rows for each group it has to build. The earliest date will have one row to sort, the second earliest date will have two rows, and so forth until the most recent date will sort all the rows. The second query has no grouping, so it just proceeds to the summation without the sorting.

## 39.10 Avoid CROSS JOINs

Consider a three-table JOIN like this.

```
SELECT P1.paint_color
 FROM Paints AS P1, Warehouse AS W1, Sales AS S1
WHERE W1.onhand_qty + S1.sold_qty = P1.gallons/2.5;
```

Because all the columns involved in the JOIN are in a single expression, their indexes cannot be used. The SQL engine will construct the CROSS JOIN of all three tables first, then prune that temporary working table to get the final answer. In Standard SQL, you can first do a subquery with a CROSS JOIN to get one side of the equation:

```
(SELECT (W1.onhand_qty + S1.sold_qty) AS stuff
 FROM Warehouse AS W1 CROSS JOIN Sales AS S1)
```

and push it into the WHERE clause, like this:

```
SELECT paint_color
 FROM Paints AS P1
WHERE EXISTS
   ((SELECT (W1.onhand_qty + S1.sold_qty)
      FROM Warehouse AS W1 CROSS JOIN Sales AS S1)
   = (P1.gallons/2.5));
```

The SQL engine, we hope, will do the two-table CROSS JOIN subquery and put the results into a temporary table. That temporary table will then be filtered using the Paints table, but without generating a three-table CROSS JOIN as the first form of the query did.

With a little algebra, the original equation can be changed around and different versions of this query built with other combinations of tables.

A good heuristic is that the FROM clause should only have those tables that provide columns to its matching SELECT clause.

## 39.11 Know Your Optimizer

One of the best tricks is to know what your optimizer favors. It is often the case that one query construction will have special code written for it that an equivalent query construction does not. Consider this simple adjacency list model of a tree.

```
CREATE TABLE Tree
(node_id CHAR(2) NOT NULL,
parent_node_id CHAR(2), -- null is root node
creation_date DATE DEFAULT CURRENT_TIMESTAMP NOT NULL);
```

Let's try to group all the parent_node_ids and display the creation_date of the most recent subordinate under that parent_node_id. This is a straightforward query that can be done with this statement.

```
SELECT node_id, T1.parent_node_id, T1.creation_date
 FROM Tree AS T1
WHERE NOT EXSTS
  (SELECT *
    FROM Tree AS T2
   WHERE T2.parent_node_id = T1.parent_node_id
     AND T2.creation_date > T1.creation_date);
```

The `EXISTS()` predicate says that there is no sibling younger than the one we picked, or, as an alternative, which uses an `OUTER JOIN` to do the same logic.

```
SELECT T1.node_id, T1.parent_node_id, T1.creation_date
 FROM Tree AS T1
   LEFT OUTER JOIN
   Tree AS T2
   ON T2.parent_node_id = T1.parent_node_id
    AND T2.creation_date > T1.creation_date
WHERE T2.node_id IS NULL;
```

However, this query was run in SQL Server 2000. Lee Tudor pointed out that SQL Server looks for a join to an aggregated self view on the group condition and aggregate. Performance is far superior to the alternates due to the query optimizer having a special way of dealing with it.

```
SELECT T1.node_id, T1.parent_node_id, T1.creation_date
 FROM Tree AS T1
   INNER JOIN
   (SELECT parent_node_id, MAX(creation_date)
     FROM Tree
    GROUP BY parent_node_id)
   AS T2 (parent_node_id, creation_date)
   ON T2.parent_node_id = T1.parent_node_id
    AND T2.creation_date = T1.creation_date;
```

The optimizer will change from release to release, but it is a good general statement that once a trick is coded into it, the trick will stay there until there is a major change in the product.

In 1988, Fabian Pascal published an article on the PC database systems available at the time in *Database Programming and Design* (vol. 1, #12, December 1998; "SQL Redundancy and DBMS Performance") in which he wrote seven logically equivalent queries as a test suite. These tests revealed vastly uneven performance for all the RDBMS products except Ingres. Ingres timings were approximately the same for all seven queries and Ingres had the best average time. The other products showed wide variations across the seven queries with the worst timing over an order of magnitude longer than its best. In the case of Oracle, the worst timing was over 600 times the best.

Although optimizers have gotten better over the years, there are still "hot spots" in specific optimizers that favor particular constructions.

## 39.12 Recompile Static SQL after Schema Changes

In most implementations, static SQL is compiled in a host program with a fixed execution plan. If a database schema object is altered, execution plans based on that object have to be changed.

In older SQL implementations, if a schema object was dropped, the programmer had to recompile the queries that referred to it. The SQL engine was not required to do any checking and most implementations did not. Instead, you could get a runtime error.

Even worse, you could have a scenario like this:

1. Create table A.
2. Create view VA on table A.
3. Use view VA.
4. Drop table A.
5. Create a new table A.
6. Use view VA.

What happens in step 6? That depended on your SQL product, but the results were not good. The worst result was that the entire schema could be hopelessly messed up. The best result was that VA in step 3 was not the VA in step 6, but was still usable.

Standard SQL added the option of specifying the behavior of any of the `DROP` statements as either `CASCADE` or `RESTRICT`. The `RESTRICT` option is the default in Standard SQL, and it will disallow the dropping of any schema object that is being used to define another object. For example, you cannot drop a base table that has `VIEW`s defined on it or is part of a referential integrity constraint if `RESTRICT` is used. The `CASCADE` option will drop any of the dependent objects from the schema when the original object is removed.

Be careful with this! The X/Open transaction model assumes a default action of `CASCADE` and some products may allow this to be set as a system parameter. The moral to the story is never use an implicit default on statements that can destroy your schema when an explicit clause is available.

Some products will automatically recompile static SQL when an index is dropped and some will not. However, few products automatically recompile static SQL when an index is added. Furthermore, few products automatically recompile static SQL when the statistical distribution within the data has changed. Oracle's Rdb is an exception to this, since it investigates possible execution paths when each query is invoked.

The DBA usually has to update the statistical information explicitly and ask for a recompilation. What usually happens is that one person adds an index and then compiles his program. The new index could either hinder or help other queries when they are recompiled, so it is hard to say whether the new index is a good or a bad thing for the overall performance of the system.

However, it is always bad is when two programmers build indexes that are identical in all but name and never tell each other. Most SQL implementations will not detect this. The duplication will waste both time and space. Whenever one index is updated, the other one will have to be updated also. This is one reason that only the DBA should be allowed to create schema objects.

## 39.13 Temporary Tables Are Sometimes Handy

Generally speaking temporary tables are a bad thing. It has to be materialized; if the intermediate result could have been put in main storage, then this is a waste. If the intermediate result is too big for main storage, then the optimizer will discover this and create secondary storage.

But sometimes temporary tables can hold intermediate results to avoid `CROSS JOIN`s and excessive recalculations. Remember that the ANSI/ISO temporary tables have every option a base table has, but they clean themselves. A materialized `VIEW` is also a form of temporary table, but you cannot index it. In this problem, we want to find the total amount of the latest balances in all our accounts.

Assume that the Payments table holds the details of each payment and that the payment numbers are increasing over time. The Accounts table shows the account identification number and the balance after each payment is made. The query might be done like this:

```
SELECT SUM(A1.acct_balance)
 FROM Accounts AS A1, Payments AS P1
WHERE P1.acct_nbr = A1.acct_nbr
  AND P1.payment_nbr
```

```
= (SELECT MAX(payment_nbr)
   FROM Payments AS P2
  WHERE P2.acct_nbr = A1.acct_nbr);
```

Since this uses a correlated subquery with an aggregate function, it will take a little time to run for each row in the answer. It might be faster to create a temporary working table or VIEW like this:

```
BEGIN
CREATE TABLE LastPayments
(act_nbr INTEGER NOT NULL,
last_payment_nbr INTEGER NOT NULL,
payment_amt DECIMAL(8,2) NOT NULL,
payment_date DATE NOT NULL,
. . . );

CREATE INDEX LPX ON LastPayment(act_nbr, payment_nbr);

INSERT INTO LastPayments
SELECT act_nbr, payment_nbr, MAX(payment_nbr)
FROM Payments
GROUP BY act_nbr, payment_nbr;

SELECT SUM(A1.balance) -- final answer
FROM Accounts AS A1, LastPayments AS LP1
WHERE LP1.acct_nbr = A1.acct_nbr
AND LP1.payment_nbr = A1.payment_nbr;

DROP TABLE LastPayments;

END;
```

Consider this three-table query that creates a list of combinations of items and all the different packages for which the selling price (price and box cost) is 10% of the warranty plan cost. Assume that any item can fit into any box we have and that any item can be put on any warranty plan.

```
SELECT I1.item
 FROM Inventory AS I1, Packages AS P1, Warranty AS W1
WHERE I1.price + P1.box = W1.plancost * 10;
```

Since all the columns appear in an expression, the engine cannot use indexes, so the query will become a large CROSS JOIN in most SQL implementations. This query can be broken down into a temporary table that has an index on the calculations, thus:

```
BEGIN
CREATE TABLE SellingPrices
(item_name CHAR (15) NOT NULL,
sell_price DECIMAL (8,2) NOT NULL);
```

```
-- optional index on the calculation
CREATE INDEX SPX ON SellingPrices (sell_price);

-- do algebra and get everything on one side of an
   equation
INSERT INTO SellingPrices (item_name, sell_price)
SELECT DISTINCT I1.item_name, (P1.box + I1.price) * 0.1
 FROM Inventory AS I1, packages AS P1;

-- do the last JOIN
SELECT DISTINCT SP1.item_name
 FROM SellingPrices AS SP1, Warranty AS W1
WHERE SP1.sell_price = W1.plancost;
END;
```

The Sybase/SQL Server family allows a programmer to create temporary tables on the fly. This is a totally different model of temporary table than the Standard SQL model. The standard model does not allow a `USER` to create any schema objects; that is `ADMIN`-only power.

Many lesser SQL products with such "ad hoc" creations have no indexes or constraints, therefore act like "scratch paper" with its own name, but do not give much help to the optimizer. This is a holdover from the days when we allocated scratch tapes in file systems to hold the results from one step to another in a procedural process.

You can often use derived tables in the query in place of these temporary tables. The derived table definition is put into the parse tree and the execution plan can take advantage of constraints, indexing, and self-joins.

## 39.14 Update Statistics

This is going to sound obvious, but the optimizer cannot work correctly without valid statistics. Some signs that your statistics need to be updated are:

1. Two queries with the same basic structure have different execution times.
2. This usually means that the statistical distribution has changed, so one of the queries is being executed under old assumptions.
3. You have just loaded a lot of new data. This is often a good time to do the update to the statistics because some products can get them as part of the loading operation.
4. You have just deleted a lot of old data. Unfortunately, deletion operations do not usually change statistics like insertions.
5. You have changed the query mix. For example, the end-of-the-month reports depend on shared views to aggregate data. In the

earlier SQL products, you could put these VIEWs into temporary tables and index those tables. This would allow the optimizer to gather statistics.

Today, the better SQL products will do the same job under the covers by materializing these VIEWs. You need to find out if you need to compute indexes and/or do the statistics.

## 39.15 Do Not Trust Newer Features

Newer features might look cool, but sometimes you will find that they have not been in your SQL long enough to be optimized. Experiment, and then put the better code into production while keeping the other code as a comment. When the new feature has settled in, swap the comment for the code.

For example, when SQL got the ordinal functions, they looked like a good way to replace self-joined queries. But the extra sorting in the early implementations sometimes was worse than a simple self-join. For example, I did a programming puzzle column for the Simple Talk web site run by Red Gate Software. (Celko's SQL Stumper: The Data Warehouse Problem; http://www.simple-talk.com/sql/t-sql-programming/celkos-sql-stumper-the-data-warehouse-problem-/). I took an old puzzle I had published decades ago and asked if the new ordinal functions and CTEs in SQL Server 2008 could beat the performance of a three-way self. The old version was much faster.

Consider a simple example, with the usual Personnel skeleton table. We want to know who the highest paid employee is in each department.

```
CREATE TABLE Personnel
(emp_name VARCHAR(20) NOT NULL PRIMARY KEY,
salary_amt DECIMAL (8,2) NOT NULL,
dept_name VARCHAR(20) NOT NULL)
```

1. The "traditional version" uses a self-join, which says to return this row if it has the greatest salary in the department. This is what most people will code.

```
SELECT P1.emp_name, P1.salary_amt, P1.dept_name
 FROM Personnel AS P1
WHERE P1.salary_amt
  = (SELECT MAX(salary_amt)
     FROM Personnel AS P2
     WHERE P2.dept_name = P1.dept_name)
```

2. The second "traditional version" uses a self-join that says to return this row if there is nobody with a greater salary.

```
SELECT P1.emp_name, P1.salary_amt, P1.dept_name
 FROM Personnel AS P1
WHERE NOT EXISTS
  (SELECT *
     FROM Personnel AS P2
    WHERE P2.salary_amt > P1.salary_amt
      AND P2.dept_name = P1.dept_name);
```

If the salary amounts referenced pay steps in another table or the department name was in a sequential index, then this can be quite fast. The `EXISTS()` uses the indexes rather than building the subquery we had in the first version.

But this is not very cool looking, so we will try some of the new features.

3. Use a `CTE` and a windowed `NAX()` to find the salary we want.

```
WITH P_Max (emp_name, salary_amt, dept_name, salary_amt_max)
AS
(SELECT emp_name, salary_amt, dept_name,
    MAX(salary_amt) OVER (PARTITION BY dept_name)
  FROM Personnel)
SELECT emp_name, salary_amt, dept_name
 FROM P_Max
WHERE salary_amt = salary_amt_max;
```

The maximum departmental salary is repeated over and over in the `CTE`, then filtered in the main query. A smart optimizer will use some of its `GROUP BY` tools to build the partitions and find a `MAX()`. In short, it will be very much like the first traditional solution.

4. But you can use the `GROUP BY` instead of partitions and find a `MAX()`. Versions #4 and #3 ought to be the same, but you need to check to be sure.

```
WITH P2 (dept_name, salary_amt_max)
AS
(SELECT dept_name, MAX(salary_amt)
  FROM Personnel
 GROUP BY dept_name)
SELECT P1.emp_name, P1.salary_amt, P1.dept_name
 FROM Personnel AS P1, P2
WHERE P1.dept_name = P2.dept_name
  AND P1.salary_amt = P2.salary_amt_max;
```

5. Does this mean that windowed functions are a waste? No, but neither are they magic. The following should be better than the other methods, if the optimizer has some smarts to it.

```
WITH P1 (emp_name, dept_name, salary_amt, rk)
AS
```

```
(SELECT emp_name, dept_name, salary_amt,
    DENSE_RANK()
     OVER(PARTITION BY dept_name
        ORDER BY salary_amt DESC)
 FROM Personnel)
SELECT emp_name, dept_name, salary_amt
 FROM P1
WHERE rk = 1;
```

The construct `(<ordinal function> OVER()..) AS x .. WHERE x = <constant>` is so common that better SQL products look for it and optimize it. `DENSE_RANK()` will handle ties for (rk = 1).

# REFERENCES

## General References

Adams, D. (2004). *The Hitchhiker's guide to the galaxy, 25th anniversary.* Crown.

## Logic

Bolc, L., & Borowik, P. (1992). *Many-valued logics.* New York: Springer-Verlag. [This book has a whole chapter devoted to three valued logic systems.]

Boole, G. (1854/1951). *An investigation of the laws of thought, on which are founded the mathematical theories of logic and probabilities.* New York: Macmillan and Co./New York: Dover Books. [The original is a rare collector's piece, but you can get a reprint of the original 1854 edition (Dover Books, 1951).]

Celko, J. (1992). SQL explorer: Voting systems. *DBMS Magazine, 11.*

## Mathematical Techniques

Gardner, M. (1983). *Wheels, life, and other mathematical amusements.* New York: W. H. Freeman.

Huff, D., & Geis, I. (illustrator). (1993, reissue). *How to lie with statistics.* New York: Norton.

Knuth, D. (1997). *The art of computer programming, volume 1: Fundamental algorithms* (3rd ed.). Reading, MA: Addison-Wesley.

Knuth, D. (1997). *The art of computer programming, volume 2: Semi-numeral algorithms* (3rd ed.). Reading, MA: Addison-Wesley.

Knuth, D. (1998). *The art of computer programming, volume 3: Sorting and searching* (3rd ed.). Reading, MA: Addison-Wesley.

Knuth, D. (2009). *The art of computer programming, volume 4, fascicles 0-4 (5 volume set).* Reading, MA: Addison-Wesley.

Melzak, Z. A. (1983). *Bypasses: A simple approach to complexity.* New York: Wiley InterScience.

Mrdalj, S., Vujovic, B., & Jovanovic, V. (1996, August). SQL matrix processing. *Database Programming and Design.*

## Random Numbers

Bays, C., & Sharp, W. E. (1992). Improved random numbers for your personal computer or workstation. *Geobyte, 7*(2), 25.

**Joe Celko's SQL for Smarties. DOI: 10.1016/B978-0-12-382022-8.00046-6**

Carta, D. G. (1990). Two fast implementations of the "minimal standard" random number generator. *Communications of the ACM, 33*(1), 87.

Chambers, W. G., & Dai, Z. D. (1991). Simple but effective modification to a multiplicative congruential random-number generator. *IEEE Proceedings: Computers and Digital Technology, 138*(3), 121.

Chassing, P. (1989). An optimal random number generator Zp. *Statistics and Probability Letters, 7*(4), 307.

Elkins, T. A. (1989). A highly random-number generator. *Computer Language, 6*(12), 59.

Hulquist, P. F. (1991). A good random number generator for microcomputers. *Simulation, 57*(4), 258.

Kao, C. (1989). A random number generator for microcomputers. *OR: The Journal of the Operational Research Society, 40*(7), 687.

Knuth, D. (1997). *The art of computer programming, volume 2: Semi-numeral Algorithms* (3rd ed.). Reading, MA: Addison-Wesley.

Komo, J. J. (1991). Decimal pseudo-random number generator. *Simulation, 57*(4), 228.

Leva, J. L. (1992a). Algorithm 712: A normal random number generator. *ACM Transactions on Mathematical Software, 18*(4), 454.

Leva, J. L. (1992b). A fast normal random number generator. *ACM Transactions on Mathematical Software, 18*(4), 449.

Macomber, J. H., & White, C. S. (1990). An n-dimensional uniform random number generator suitable for IBM-compatible microcomputers. *Interfaces, 20*(3), 49.

Maier, W. L. (1991). A fast pseudo random number generator. *Dr. Dobb's Journal, 17*(5), 152.

Marsaglia, G., Narasimhan, B., & Zaman, A. (1990). A random number generator for PCs. *Computer Physics Communications, 60*, 345–349.

Marsaglia, G., & Zaman, A. (1990). Toward a universal random number generator. *Statistics and Probability Letters, 8*, 35–39.

Morton, M. (1985). A digital dissolve for bit-mapped graphics screens. *Dr. Dobb's Journal, #48.*

Park, S. K., & Miller, K. W. (1988). Random number generators: Good ones are hard to find. *Communications of the ACM, 31*(10), 1201.

Press, W. H., et al. (1989). *Numerical recipes in Pascal: The art of scientific computing* (Rev. ed.). Cambridge, UK: Cambridge University Press.

Sezgin, F. (1990). On a fast and portable uniform quasi-random number generator. *Simulation Digest, 21*(2), 30.

## Scales and Measurements

Celko, J. (2009). *Joe Celko's data, measurements and standards in SQL (Morgan Kaufmann series in data management systems).*

Crocker, L., & Algina, J. (2006). *Introduction to classical and modern test theory.* Wadsworth Pub Co.

## Missing Values

Codd, E. F. (1975). Understanding relations. *FDT, 7,* 3–4.

Grahne, G. (1989). Horn tables—an efficient tool for handling incomplete information in databases. *ACM SIGACT/SIGMOD/SIGART Symposium on Principles of Database Systems,* 75–82.

Grant, J. (1977). Null values in relational databases. *Information Processing Letters, 6*(5).

Grant, J. (1979). Partial values in a tabular database model. *Information Processing Letters,* 6(5).

Honeyman, P. (1980). *Functional dependencies and the universal instance property in the relational model of database systems.* Doctoral Dissertation, Princeton University.

Lien, Y. E. (1979). Multivalued dependencies with null values in relational databases. *VLDB V,* Rio De Janeiro. ACM/IEEE.

Lipski, W. (1981a). On semantic issues connected with incomplete information. *ACM Transactions on Database Systems,* 262–296.

Lipski, W. (1981b). On databases with incomplete information. *Journal of the ACM, 28*(1), 41–47.

McGoveran, D. (1993). Nothing from nothing part I (or, what's logic got to do with it?). *Database Programming and Design, 6*(12), 32. [A four part series on missing values that argues against the SQL style NULL in favor of indicators.]

McGoveran, D. (1994a). Nothing from nothing part II: Classical logic: Nothing compares 2 U. *Database Programming and Design, 7*(1), 54.

McGoveran, D. (1994b). Nothing from nothing part III: Can't lose what you never had. *Database Programming and Design, 7*(2), 42.

McGoveran, D. (1994c). Nothing from nothing part IV: It's in the way that you use it. *Database Programming and Design, 7*(3), 54.

Rozenshtein, D. (1981). *Implementing null values in relations.* Unpublished.

Rozenshtein, D. (1995). *Optimizing transact SQL.* SQL Forum Press.

SPARC Study Group on Database Management Systems. (1975). Interim report 75-02-08 to the ANSI X3. *FDT-Bulletin ACM SIGMOD, 7*(2).

Vassiliou, Y. (1979). Null values in database management—a denotational semantics approach. *ACM SIGMOD Conference,* 162–169.

Vassiliou, Y. (1980). Functional dependencies and incomplete information. *VLDB VI,* Montreal. ACM/IEEE.

Walker, A. (1979). *A universal table relational database model with blank entries.* Unpublished manuscript.

Zaniolo. (1984). Database relations with null values. *Journal of Computer and System Sciences, 28*(1), 142–166.

## Regular Expressions

Friedl, J. E. F. (2006). *Mastering regular expressions* (3rd ed.). Cambridge, MA: O'Reilly Media.

Goyvaerts, J., & Levithan, S. (2009). *Regular expressions cookbook.* Cambridge, MA: O'Reilly Media.

Stubblebine, T. (2007). *Regular expression pocket reference: Regular expressions for Perl, Ruby, PHP, Python, C, Java and .NET* (2nd ed.). Sebastopol, CA: O'Reilly Media.

Forta, B. (2004). *Sams teach yourself regular expressions in 10 minutes.* Indianapolis, IN: Sams.

Good, N. A. (2005). *Regular expression recipes: A problem-solution approach.* Berkeley, CA: Apress.

## Graph Theory

Cormen, T. H., Leiserson, C. E., & Rivest, R. L. (1990). *Introduction to algorithms.* McGraw-Hill Companies.

Even, S. (1979). *Graph algorithms.* Rockville, MD: Computer Science Press [out of print].

Harary, F. (1992). *Graph theory.* Westview Press [on demand printing].

Ore, O. (1996). *Graphs and their uses* (revised by Robin J. Wilson). Providence, RI: American Mathematical Association.

Rozenshtein, D. (1997). *Tree and graph processing in SQL.* Peer to Peer Communications [out of print].

## Introductory SQL Books

Brouard, F. (2001). *SQL.* CampusPress. [Notebook is in French and covers the SQL-2003 Standard.]

Chappell, D., & Trimble, H., Jr. (2001). *A visual introduction to SQL* (2nd ed.). Wiley.

Date, C. J. (2003). *An introduction to database systems* (8th ed.). Reading, MA: Addison-Wesley.

Date, C. J., & Darwen, H. (1996). *A Guide to SQL standard* (4th ed.). Reading, MA: Addison-Wesley Professional.

Groff, J., & Weinberg, P. (2002). *SQL: The complete reference* (2nd ed.). McGraw-Hill Osborne Media.

Gulutzan, P., & Pelzer, T. (1999). *SQL-99 complete, really.* Gilroy, CA: CMP Books.

Gulutzan, P., & Pelzer, T. (2002). *SQL performance tuning.* Boston, MA: Addison-Wesley.

Hellerstein, J. M., & Stonebraker, M. (Eds.). (2005). *Readings in database systems* (4th ed.). Cambridge, MA: The MIT Press.

Limeback, R. (2008). *Simply SQL.* SitePoint at www.sitepoint.com.

Pascal, F. (1989). *SQL and relational basics.* Redwood City, CA: M&T Books [out of print].

Pascal, F. (1993). *Understanding relational databases.* John Wiley [out of print].

Takahashi, M., & Azuma, S. (2008). *The Manga guide to databases* (1st ed.). San Francisco: No Starch Press [English edition].

Tropashko, V. (2007). *SQL design patterns: Expert guide to SQL programming* (1st ed.). Rampant Techpress. [Note: This is *not* an intro book. You will need strong math.]

van der Lans, R. (2006). *Introduction to SQL: Mastering the relational database language* (4th ed.). Addison-Wesley Professional.
Viescas, J. L., & Hernandez, M. J. (2007). *SQL queries for mere mortals* (2nd ed.). Addison-Wesley Professional.

## Optimizing Queries

Gulutzan, P., & Pelzer, T. (1994). *Optimizing SQL: Embedded SQL in C.* R&D Technical Books.
Shasha, D. E., & Bonnet, P. (2002). *Database tuning.* San Francisco: Morgan Kaufmann.

## Temporal Data and the Year 2000 Problem

ANSI INCITS 30-1997. (R2008). Representation of calendar date and ordinal date for information interchange.
Arnold, R. S. (1995a, January). Millennium now: Solutions for century data change impact. *Application Development Trends.*
Arnold, R. S. (1995b). Resolving year 2000 problems in legacy software. *Presentation at Software Quality Week,* San Francisco.
Associated Press. (1995, May 25). Troubled time.
Celko, J., & McDonald, J. (1981, February). Father time software secrets allows updating of dates. *Information Systems News.* [This article was later quoted in *Vanity Fair* January 1999 (The Y2K Nightmare by Robert Sam Anson).]
Cini, A. (1995, January). System bug of the apocalypse. *Internetwork.*
Cohn, M. B. (1994, November 21). No need to fear the year 2000. *Computerworld,* 28(47), 35.
Fine, D. (1995, April 10). Companies brace for millennium. *Infoworld.*
Furman, J., Marotta, A., & Candiotti, C. (1995, April). Party when it's 1999. *Software Magazine.*
Hayes, B. (1995, January–February). Waiting for 01-01-00. *American Scientist, 83.*
Hitchens, R. L. (1991, January 28). Viewpoint. *Computerworld.*
ISO 8601. (1988). Data elements and interchange formats—information interchange—representation of dates and times.
ISO 8601:2004 (Revises ISO 8601:2000). Data elements and interchange formats—information interchange—representation of dates and times.
Murray, J. T., & Murray, M. J. (1984). *Computers in crisis.* Princeton, NJ: Petrocelli Books. [A solution, with code, for the Year 2000 problem.]
Ross, N. (1995, April). The end of the century is nearer than you think. *Application Development Trends.*
Rubin, H., & Woodward, J. *Millenium: A billion dollar software crisis* [videotape by The Computer Channel].
Sullivan, R. L. (1995, June 19). Ghosts in the machines. *Forbes.*

Tantzen, R. G. (1980). Algorithm 199: Conversion between calendar date and Julian day number. *Collected Algorithms from the ACM (Association for Computing Machinery).*

Xenakis, J. (1995, July). The millenium bug: The fine de Siécl computer virus. *CFO Magazine.*

Zerubavel, E. (1989). *The seven day circle.* Chicago: University of Chicago Press.

## SQL Programming Techniques

Celko, J. (1992, March). Implementing T-joins in SQL queries. *DBMS Magazine.*

Celko, J. (1993, September). Views: More than meets the eye. *Database Programming and Design.* [Letter citing Nelson Mattos, from an ANSI X3H2 paper.]

Celko, J., & Date, C. J. (1993, September). Access path: Lauds and lectures, kudos and critiques. *Database Programming and Design.* [Letter to the editor.]

## Classics

Bernstein, P. A. (1976). Synthesizing third normal form relations from functional dependencies. *ACM Transactions on Database Systems, 1*(4), 277–298.

Codd, E. F. (1970). A relational model of data for large shared data banks. *Communications of the ACM (Association for Computing Machinery), 13*(6), 377–387.

Codd, E. F. (1979). Extending the database relational model to capture more meaning. *ACM Transactions on Database Systems, 4*(4), 397–434.

Comer, D. (1978). The difficulty of optimum index selection. *ACM Transactions on Database Systems, 3*(4), 440–445.

Damerau, F. J. (1964). A technique for computer detection of correction of spelling errors. *Communications of the ACM, 7*(3).

Date, C. J. (1992, February). According to date: Shedding some light. *Database Programming and Design,* 15–17.

Dijkstra, E. (1968). Go to statement considered harmful. *Communications of the ACM, 11*(3), 147–148. [Addresses old versus new JOIN syntax.]

Goodman, N. (1990). VIEW update is practical. *InfoDB, 5*(2).

Information Systems Week (ISW). (1987, December). Code overload plagues NYC welfare system. *Information Systems Week.*

Limeback, R. (n.d.). SQL workshop challenge. *Explain,* (18).

Lorie, R. A., & Daudenarde, J.-J. (1991). *SQL and its applications.* Englewood Cliffs, NJ: Prentice-Hall.

Martinis, M. (1992, May). Letters column. *DBMS Magazine.*

Melton, J., & Simon, A. R. (1993). *Understanding the new SQL: Complete guide.* San Francisco: Morgan Kaufmann.

Murchison, R. (n.d.). SQL workshop challenge. *Explain,* (16).

Paitetsky-Shapiro, G. (1983). The optimal selection of secondary indexes in NP-complete. *SIGMOD Record, 13*(2), 72–75.
Palmer, R. (2007). *The bar code book* (5th ed.). Bloomington, IN: Trafford Publishing.
Philips, L. (1990). Hanging on the metaphone (a phonetic text-retrieval algorithm better than soundex). *Computer Language, 7*(12), 38.
Rozenshtein, D., Abramovich, A., & Birger, E. (1993). Loop-free SQL solutions for finding continuous regions. *SQL Forum, 2*(6).
Smithwick, T. (1991). Pascal version of Lawrence Philips' 1990 hanging on the metaphone (a phonetic text-retrieval algorithm better than soundex). *Computer Language, 7*(12), 38.
SQL Forum. (1993/1994). See articles by Anatoly Abramovich Yelena Alexandrova, and Eugene Birger (July/August 1993, March/April 1994).
Stevens, S. S. (1957). On the psychophysical law. *Psychological Review, 64*, 153–181.
Tillquist, J., & Kuo, F.-Y. (1989). An approach to the recursive retrieval problem in the relational database. *Communications of the ACM, 32*(2), 239.
van der Lans, R. (1990/1991). SQL portability. *The Relational Journal, 2*(6).
Verhoeff, J. (1969). Error detecting decimal codes. *Mathematical Centre Tract #29*. Amsterdam: The Mathematical Centre.
Vicik, R. (1993, July/August). Advanced transact SQL. *SQL*.

## Updatable Views

Codd, E. F. RV-6 view updating. *The relational model for database management, version 2.*
Date, C. J. (1986). Updating VIEWs. *Relational database: Selected writings*. Reading, MA: Addison-Wesley.
Date, C. J., & Darwen, H. (1991). Role of functional dependencies in query decomposition. *Relational database writings—1989–1991*. Reading, MA: Addison-Wesley.
Goodman, N. (1990). VIEW update is practical. *INFODB, 5*(2).
Umeshar, D., & Bernstein, P. A. (1982). On the correct translation of update operations on relational VIEWs. *ACM Transactions on Database Systems, 7*(3).

## Theory, Normalization, and Advanced Database Topics

Bernstein, P. A. (1976). Synthesizing third normal form relations from functional dependencies. *ACM Transactions on Database Systems, 1*(4), 277–298.
Codd, E. F. (1990). *The relational model for database management: Version 2*. Reading, MA: Addison Wesley.
Date, C. J. (1990). *Relational database writings—1985–1989*. Reading, MA: Addison-Wesley.

Date, C. J. (1992). *Relational database writings 1989–1991*. Reading, MA: Addison-Wesley.
Date, C. J. (1995). *Relational database writings 1991–1994*. Reading, MA: Addison-Wesley.
Date, C. J. (1998). *Relational database writings—1994–1997*. Reading, MA: Addison-Wesley.
Date, C. J. (2006). *Date on database: Writings 2000–2006*. New York: Apress.
Dutka, A., & Hanson, H. (1989). *Fundamentals of data normalization*. Reading, MA: Addison-Wesley.
Fagin, R. (1979). Normal forms and relational database operators. *Proceedings ACM SIGMOD International Conference on Management of Data*. [The definitive paper on the five normal forms.]
Fleming, C. C., & von Halle, B. (1989). *Handbook for relational database design*. Reading, MA: Addison-Wesley.
Kent, W. (1983). A simple guide to five normal forms in relational database theory. *Communications of the ACM, 26*(2).
Maier, D. (1983). *The theory of relational databases*. Redwood City, CA: Computer Science Press [out of print, but worth getting].
Teorey, T. J. (1994). *Database modeling and design* (2nd ed.). San Francisco: Morgan Kaufmann.

## Books on SQL-92 and SQL-99

Cannan, S., & Otten, G. (1992). *SQL: The standard handbook*. McGraw-Hill [out of print].
Gulutzan, P., & Pelzer, T. (1999). *SQL-99 complete, really*. Gilroy, CA: CMP Books.
Melton, J., & Simon, A. (1993). *Understanding the new SQL: A complete guide*. San Francisco: Morgan Kaufmann.

## Standards and Related Groups

On 2003-02-10, the old ANSI X3 Committee was merged into a new organization, the International Committee for Information Technology Standards (INCITS), which replaced the old X3H2 Database Standards Committee.

For ANSI and ISO Standards:
American National Standards Institute
5 West 43rd Street, 4 floor
New York, NY 10036
Tel: 1-212-642-4900
Fax: 1-212-398-0023
http://www.ansi.org/

The source for all kinds of Industry Standards:
IHS Headquarters
15 Inverness Way East
Englewood CO 80112

United States
Phone: 303-397-7956 or 800-854-7179
Fax: 303-397-2740
E-mail: http://www.ihs.com
Other Consortiums:
NIST (National Institute for Science & Technology)
Standards Information Center
100 Bureau Drive, Stop 2100,
Gaithersburg, MD 20899-2100
E-mail: ncsci@nist.gov
Phone: (301) 975-4040
TPC (Transaction Processing Council)
Presidio of San Francisco
572B Ruger St. (surface)
P.O. Box 29920 (mail)
San Francisco, CA 94129-0920
Voice: 415-561-6272
Fax: 415-561-6120
E-mail: webmaster@tpc.org

## Web Sites Related to SQL

The SQL home page is maintained by one of the X3H2 Committee members at www.jjc.com/sql_stnd.html.

Michael M. Gorman at Whitemarsh Information Systems has been the Secretary for the NCITS H2 Technical Committee since it was founded. His web site (www.wiscorp.com) has lots of information and draft standards.

You can also get query and technical help at www.inquiry.com/techtips/thesqlpro/index.html.

## Statistics

The American Statistical Association has their material online and you can find many articles on the computation of various statistics:
www.amstat.org/publications/tas/
www.amstat.org/publications/technometrics/

Chan, T. F., Golub, G. H., & LeVeque, R. J. (1983). Algorithms for computing the sample variance: Analysis and recommendations. *The American Statistician, 37*(3), 242–247.

Welford, B. P. (1962). Note on a method for calculating corrected sums of squares and products. *Technometrics, 4,* 419–420.

## Temporal Databases

Date, C., Darwen, H., & Lorentzos, N. A. (2002). *Temporal data and the relational model.* San Francisco: Morgan Kaufmann.

Jensen, C. S., Clifford, J., Elmasri, R., Gadia, S. K., Hayes P., & Jajodia, S. (Eds.). (1994). A glossary of temporal database concepts. *ACM SIGMOD Record, 23*(1), 52–64.

Johnston, T., & Weis, R. (2010). *Managing time in relational databases: How to design, update and query temporal data.* Morgan Kaufmann.

Ozsoyoglu, G., & Snodgrass, R. T. (1995). Temporal and real-time databases: A survey. *IEEE Transactions on Knowledge and Data Engineering, 7*(4), 513–532.

Snodgrass, R. T. (Ed.), Ahn, I., Ariav, G., Batory, D., Clifford, J., Dyreson, C. E.,Elmasri, R., Grandi F., Jensen C. S., Kaefer W., Kline, N., Kulkarni, K., Leung, T. Y. C., Lorentzos, N., Roddick, J. F., Segev, A., Soo, M. D., & Sripada, S. M. (1995). *The temporal query language TSQL2.* Norwell, MA: Kluwer Academic Publishers.

Snodgrass, R. T., Boehlen, M. H., Jensen, C. S., & Steiner, A. (1996a). Adding valid time to SQL/temporal. Change proposal, ANSI X3H2-96501r2, ISO/IEC JTC 1/SC 21/WG 3 DBL-MAD-146r2. Retrieved from ftp://ftp.cs.arizona.edu/tsql/tsql2/sql3/mad146.pdf.

Snodgrass, R. T., Boehlen, M. H., Jensen, C. S., & Steiner, A. (1996b). Adding transaction time to SQL/temporal. Change proposal, ANSI X3H2-96-502r2, ISO/IEC JTC1/SC21/WG3 DBL MAD147r2. Retrieved from ftp://ftp.cs.arizona.edu/tsql/tsql2/sql3/mad147.pdf.

Snodgrass, R. T., & Jensen, C. (1999). *Temporal databases.* San Francisco: Morgan Kaufmann. [The book is out of print, but the material is available on the University of Arizona web site, under the account of Dr. Snodgrass.]

Tansel, A., Clifford, J., Gadia, S. K., Jajodia, S., Segev, A., & Snodgrass, R. T. (Eds.). (1993). *Temporal databases: Theory, design, and implementation. Database systems and applications series.* Redwood City, CA: Benjamin/ Cummings Pub. Co.

Tsotras, V. J., & Kumar, A. (1996). Temporal database bibliography update. *ACM SIGMOD Record, 25*(1), 41–51.

Zaniolo, C., Ceri, S., Faloutsos, C., Snodgrass, R. T., Subrahmanian, V. S., & Zicari, R. (1997). *Advanced database systems.* San Francisco: Morgan Kaufmann.

## Miscellaneous Citations

Berenson, H., et al. (1995). *A critique of ANSI SQL isolation levels.* Microsoft Research Technical Report: MSR-TR-95-51.

Bose, R. C., & Nelson, R. J. A sorting problem. *Journal of the ACM, 9.*

Gonzales, M. L. (2003). *The IBM data warehouse.* New York: Wiley.

Gonzales, M. L. (2004, September 18). The SQL language of OLAP. *Intelligent Enterprise.*

Hegeman, F. (1993, February). Sorting networks. *The C/C++ User's Journal.*

Larsen, S. (1996, Winter). Powerful SQL: Beyond the basics. *DB2 Magazine.* [Article may be viewed online at www.db2mag.com/db_area/archives/1996/q4/9601lar.shtml.]

Melton, J. (1998). Understanding SQL's stored procedures. San Francisco: Morgan Kaufmann.
Moreau, T., & Ben-Gan, I. (2001). *Advanced transact-SQL for SQL server 2000.* Berkeley, CA: Apress.
Pascal, F. (1988/1998). SQL redundancy and DBMS performance. *Database Programming and Design, 1*(12).
The Unicode Consortium. (2003). *The unicode standard, version 4.0.* Reading, MA: Addison-Wesley.
Watson, E. J. (1962). Primitive polynomials (mod 2). *Mathematics of Computation, 16,* 368–369.
Zemke, F., Kulkami, K., Witkowski, A., & Lyle, B. Introduction to OLAP Functions. ANSI document.

# INDEX

Page numbers followed by *f* indicates a figure and *t* indicates a table.

## D

## O